GALLERIE D'ITALIA
PIAZZA SCALA
MILANO

BELLOTTO and CANALETTO
Wonder and Light

edited by
BOŻENA ANNA KOWALCZYK

SilvanaEditoriale   INTESA SANPAOLO

BELLOTTO and CANALETTO
Wonder and Light

With the patronage of

Ministero dei beni e delle attività culturali e del turismo

Milano

Gallerie d'Italia
Piazza Scala, 6 - Milano
25th November 2016 – 5th March 2017

Exhibition project promoted and conducted by

INTESA SANPAOLO

In collaboration with

Dresden, Gemäldegalerie Alte Meister, Staatliche Kunstsammlungen

Milan, Castello Sforzesco

Warszawa, Zamek Królewski

This exhibition is part of
Progetto Cultura of Intesa Sanpaolo

Curator
Bożena Anna Kowalczyk

General coordination
Gianfranco Brunelli

Layout design
Elena Brunello

Visual and graphic design project
Francesco Giordano

Condition reports for the works on display
Carlotta Beccaria & C. Studio Restauro sas

Footage and selected video clips
Fondazione Cineteca Italiana, Milan

Guided visits and educational workshops
Opera Laboratori Fiorentini

Audio-guide
S.T.A.R.T.

Project 'Il Bookshop delle Meraviglie'
TIWI for SkyArte HD

Multimedia partner
ETT Solutions

Digital reproduction from 'Quaderno di schizzi' by Canaletto
edited by Annalisa Perissa Torrini
design and concept Mauro Tarantino
photos Dino Zanella
Venice, Gallerie dell'Accademia

Diagnostics and restorations
Claudio Falcucci - M.I.D.A.; Filigrana di Margherita Errera; Luana Franceschet; Legatoria d'Arte e Restauro Niola Rosario; Santin Paola Conservazione e Restauro; Studio di Restauro Elena Allodi, Nexhibit Design srl; Julie Sutter, Sabine Bendfeldt, Gemäldegalerie Alte Meister, Galerie Neue Meister, Staatliche Kunstsammlungen Dresden

Organisation

Project management and coordination
Intesa Sanpaolo, Cultural Activities Sub Department

Head officer
Michele Coppola

Cultural initiatives, exhibition projects and artistic heritage office
Silvia Foschi *with* Alberto Mignani, Romina Paola Elia, Denise Baretta, Massimo Bianchi
in collaboration with Alessia Schiavi

Promotion, marketing and cultural partnership office
Marie-Evangéline Maillard *with* Simona Cantone, Gaia Dell'Orto, Andrea Rossetti

Museum complex coordination
Giovanni Morale

Layout coordination
Mariangela Taliento

Publishing and musical initiatives coordination
Rosanna Benedini *with* Roberto Rondena, Laura Tombola, Valeria Tortosa

Special thanks to the following divisions of the Intesa Sanpaolo Group for their collaboration

Procurement Head Office Department
Administration and Tax Head Office Department
Real Estate and Logistic Head Office Department
Legal Affairs Head Office Department – Group General Counsel
External Relations Head Office Department
Internal Communication Sub Department

Lenders

Alnwick Castle, The Duke of Northumberland Collection
Asolo, Museo Civico
Bassano del Grappa, Museo Civico
Bergamo, Fondazione Accademia Carrara
Budapest, Museum of Fine Arts
Cambridge, The Fitzwilliam Museum
Cleveland, Museum of Art
Darmstadt, Hessisches Landesmuseum
Dresda, Staatliche Kunstsammlungen, Gemäldegalerie Alte Meister
Dresda, Staatliche Kunstsammlungen, Kupferstich-Kabinett
Florence, Biblioteca Nazionale Centrale
Geneve, Musées d'art et d'histoire
Hannover, Niedersächsisches Landesmuseum, on permanent loan of Fritz Behrens-Foundation
Kingston, Agnes Etherington Art Centre, Queen's University
Leipzig, Museum der bildenden Künste
London, The National Gallery
London, Victoria and Albert Museum
Los Angeles, The J. Paul Getty Museum
Madrid, Museo Thyssen Bornemisza
Melbourne, National Gallery of Victoria
Milan, Archivio Storico Civico e Biblioteca Trivulziana
Milan, Biblioteca Centro Apice
Milan, Biblioteca Comunale Centrale, Palazzo Sormani
Milano, Civica Raccolta delle Stampe 'Achille Bertarelli'
Milan, Pinacoteca di Brera
Milan, Raccolte d'Arte Antica, Pinacoteca del Castello Sforzesco
Náměšť nad Oslavou, The National Heritage Institute, Regional Historic Sites Management in České Budějovice, Castle
Naples, Biblioteca Nazionale 'Vittorio Emanuele III'
Naples, Biblioteca della Società Napoletana di Storia Patria
Naples, Museo e Real Bosco di Capodimonte
New York, The Metropolitan Museum of Art
Paris, Institut de France, Musée Jacquemart-André
Parma, Galleria Nazionale
Rome, Accademia Nazionale di San Luca
Rome, Biblioteca Romana Sarti
Rome, Istituto Centrale per la Grafica
Saint Petersburg, The State Hermitage Museum
The Royal Collection / HM Queen Elizabeth II
Turin, Musei Reali, Biblioteca Nazionale Universitaria
Turin, Musei Reali, Galleria Sabauda
Turin, Pinacoteca Giovanni e Marella Agnelli
Warszawa, Muzeum Narodowe
Warszawa, Zamek Królewski Muzeum
Venice, Biblioteca Nazionale Marciana
Venice, Fondazione Musei Civici, Biblioteca del Museo Correr
Venice, Fondazione Musei Civici, Ca' Rezzonico, Museo del Settecento Veneziano
Venice, Fondazione Musei Civici, Museo Correr
Venice, Fondazione Musei Civici, Museo Correr, Gabinetto dei Disegni e delle Stampe
Venice, Fondazione Querini Stampalia
Venice, Istituto di Storia dell'Arte, Fondazione Giorgio Cini
Venice, Biblioteca di Storia dell'Arte, Fondazione Giorgio Cini
Verona, Fondazione Cariverona
Vilnius, The Wróblewski Library of the Lithuanian Academy of Sciences

Thanks also to
Doriana Marzocco Collection
London, Jean-Luc Baroni Ltd
London, Fabrizio Moretti Ltd
London, Pym's Gallery
Madrid, Abelló Collection
and other private collections

Special thanks for their collaboration to

Direzione Generale Archeologia, Belle Arti e Paesaggio
Direzione Generale Biblioteche e Istituti Culturali
Direzione Generale Musei
Polo Museale dell'Emilia Romagna
Soprintendenza Archeologia, Belle Arti e Paesaggio per Comune di Roma
Soprintendenza Archeologia, Belle Arti e Paesaggio per l'Area Metropolitana di Venezia e le Province di Belluno, Padova e Treviso
Soprintendenza Archeologia, Belle Arti e Paesaggio per la Città Metropolitana di Firenze e le Province di Pistoia e Prato
Soprintendenza Archeologia, Belle Arti e Paesaggio per la Città Metropolitana di Milano
Soprintendenza Archeologia, Belle Arti e Paesaggio per la Città Metropolitana di Torino
Soprintendenza Archeologia, Belle Arti e Paesaggio per le Province di Parma e Piacenza
Soprintendenza Archeologia, Belle Arti e Paesaggio per le Province di Verona, Rovigo e Vicenza
Soprintendenza Archivistica e Bibliografica della Campania
Soprintendenza Archivistica e Bibliografica del Lazio
Soprintendenza Archivistica e Bibliografica della Lombardia
Soprintendenza Archivistica e Bibliografica del Piemonte e della Valle d'Aosta
Soprintendenza Archivistica e Bibliografica della Toscana
Soprintendenza Archivistica e Bibliografica del Veneto e del Trentino Alto Adige

Arts Council England

Special thanks to

Juan Abelló Gallo, Antonello Accadia, Svetlana Adaksina, Ornella Agrillo, Mauro Alberti, Laura Maria Alegiani, Sergej Androsov, Maria Antonella Fusco, Marian Aparicio, Irina Artemieva, Adrienne Atkinson, Simon Atkinson, Sophie Aurand-Hovanessian, Laszlo Baan, Jean-Pierre Babelon, Carmen Bambach, Maria Lucia Baratti, Luca Massimo Barbero, Jean-Luc Baroni, Guglielmo Bartoletti, Katrin Bäsig, Laura Basso, Annamaria Bava, Clare Baxter, Hannah Belcher, Alex Bell, Sylvain Bellenger, Luca Bellingeri, Gabriella Belli, Andrea Bellieni, Sabine Bendfeldt, Claudia Benvestito, Elisabetta Bianchi, Maryline Billod, Annalisa Biondi, Daniela Bon, Orsola Bonifati, Katalin Borbély, Magdalena Borkowska, James Bradburne, Carla Brambilla, William Brown, Annalisa Bruni, Stephanie Buck, Katleen Burke, Simonetta Buttò, Lisa Cain, Gabriele Caioni, Marcellino Caloi, Thomas P. Campbell, Chiara Casarin, Daniela Cecchini, Cristina Celegon, Chiara Ceschi, Germana Chiodi, Keith Christiansen, Kateřina Cichrová, Hélène Couot Echiffre, Jacquelyn N. Coutré, Alberto Craievich, Hope Cullinan, Pierre Curie, Emanuela Daffra, Stefano Dalla Via, Lara Daly, Holger Dammhahn, Brigitte Daprà, Anna Maria De Gregorio, Renata De Lorenzo, Paolo De Tuoni, Orietta Dissegna, Zsuzsanna Dobos, Sabine Eisenbeiß, Alain Elkann, Ginevra Elkann, Tony Ellwood, Mark Evans, Gabriele Finaldi, Isabella Fiorentini, Matthias Fontaine, Paolo Fresco, David García-Ganuza de Mier, Davide Gasparotto, Natalia Gastelut, Marina Geneletti, Anja Gerdemann, Luciana Gerolami, Thea Giovannini, Cristina Gnoni, William M. Griswold, Anna Grochala, Marina Guerra, Mechthild Haas, Claire Hallinan, Francis Hampden, Amelia Harris, Andreas Henning, Alan Hobart, Piotr Kibort, Simone Isham, Silvia Iuorio, Linda Johnston, Theo Jülich, Andrea Jungmann, Ieva Kanepe, Hannah Kauffman, Antje-Fee Köllermann, Claudia Klugmann, Tim Knox, Stephan Koja, Cory Korkow, Anna Köves, Erika Kuliešienė, Natalia Ładyka, Silvia Lavazza, Marigusta Lazzari, Katja Lembke, Magdalena Lisowska, Carlo Lorenzetti, Aleksandra Łukasiewicz-Buczek, Isabella Marelli, Jean-Yves Marin, Paola Marini, Doriana e Claudio Marzocco, Giuliana Massetti, Alessandro Mazzucco, James McDonald, Kathleen McInerney, Maurizio Messina, Gudula Metze, Paola Milone, Sara Mittica, Cristina Mondin, Elisa Montali, Aldona Mordrzewska, Agnieszka Morawińska, Beatriz Moreno de Barreda, Fabrizio Moretti, Giovanna Mori, Francesco Moschini, Przemysław Mrozowski, Joanna Muirhead, Sigitas Narbutas, Jennifer Nicoll, Stefano Orsetti, Tova R. Ossad, David Packer, Gabriele Paetow, Enrica Pagella, Nuria Pareja Carneros, Stefano Parise, Rossella Patrizio, Peter Pavelec, Claudia Piergigli, Angela Pinto, Carla Pinzauti, Michail Piotrowsky, Patrizia Piscitello, Paolo Plebani, Emily Plunket, Valeria Poletto, Franca Porticelli, Timothy Potts, Marcella Pralormo, Charles H. Price, Jessie Price, Luciano Maria Provenzano, Silvia Pugliese, Antonella Ranaldi, Maria Antonietta Rascaglia, Katelyn Reeves, Vanessa Remington, Doris Elisabeth Richter, Sofia Rinaldi, Edmondo di Robilant, Emma Roccato, Cristiana Romalli, Conchita Romero, Martin Roth, Nancy Rosen, Andzrzej Rottermund, Christian Rümelin, Francis Russell, Elena Saggers, Claudio Salsi, Mario Scalini, Hans-Werner Schmidt, Sabine Schmidt, Annalisa Scotton, Maria Cristina Selloni, Betsy Severance, Desmond Shawe-Tylor, Gretchen Shie Miller, Guillermo Solana, Marcia Stele, Paola Strada, Dirk Syndram, Patrick Syz, Francesca Tasso, Tabitha Teuma, Letizia Treves, Roberto Trupiano, Barbara Tuzzolino, Michael Varcoe-Cocks, Carl Villis, Marco Voena, Joanna Watson, Baron Weidinger, Anna Pauline Weinke, Valentina Zanchin, Tomasz Zborowski, Antoni Ziemba

and for their generous support in granting loans from the private collection

Christie's, Old Master Paintings, London
Richard Green Ltd., London
Otto Naumann Ltd., New York
Robilant+Voena, London Milan St. Moritz
Sotheby's, Old Master Paintings and Old Master Drawings, London; Old Master Paintings, Milan and Vienna

Catalogue

Editor
Bożena Anna Kowalczyk

General coordination
Gianfranco Brunelli

Essays by
Bożena Anna Kowalczyk, Sergio Marinelli

Entries by
Sabine Bendfeldt, Andreas Henning,
Bożena Anna Kowalczyk, Andrzej Rottermund

Iconographic research
Alessia Schiavi

Italy is in the extraordinary position of having a cultural and artistic heritage of inestimable value, inherited from long centuries of flourishing civilisation. It is our moral duty to protect this richness, pass it down to future generations and valorise it in all of its beauty. For years, Intesa Sanpaolo has therefore prioritised social responsibility, making an active, concrete commitment to the field of art and culture. Our way of 'being a bank' is always partnered with, or better still, integrated with, 'creating culture'. A tangible example of this is the 'Progetto Cultura' (culture project), a multi-year plan for our activities geared towards the protection and promotion of Italian heritage (through the Restituzioni *programme) as well as the valorisation of the Group's architectural and artistic assets, which are today shared with the public. This inspired the development of a wide-ranging national project, strongly supported by Chairman Emeritus Giovanni Bazoli: the Gallerie d'Italia, Intesa Sanpaolo's art galleries, which display its art collections to the public in magnificent buildings. After the success of the project in Vicenza and Naples, a new gallery was added in 2011, hosted in a new, prestigious location in Piazza della Scala, in the centre of Milan. Places dedicated to finance have thus become a place of culture. We believe that the presence of the Gallerie d'Italia in Milan has made an important contribution to the city's cultural life, not only through its permanent displays of nineteenth- and twentieth-century art, but also through the major temporary exhibitions that have already been held in its spaces one after another in the span of just a few years. Instead of limiting itself to the role of sponsor, Intesa Sanpaolo organises and handles all of the phases involved in its exhibitions, from planning to realisation, working with public and private institutions in Italy and abroad, using an approach characterised by fruitful synergies and shared values. The decision to invest its energy, resources and funds in this way was motivated by the desire to not merely put the works on display but rather create real opportunities for the discovery of Italian history and art. Through their original narratives, the Piazza Scala exhibitions have invited reflection on Italian identity (as in the exhibition* La Grande Guerra*) and on the beauty and fragility of Italy's artistic heritage (as in the concluding exhibition for the* Restituzioni *programme) and have focused attention on some of the leading figures and decisive moments of the Italian tradition (as in* Hayez, Pittore del Romanticismo*). This new exhibition contributes to the valorisation of another great chapter in the history of Italian art: the view painting of the Venetian masters Bellotto and Canaletto, which was an extraordinary expression of Italian talent that conquered Europe. Their works stun for their vivid light, perfect perspectival organisation and infinitesimal detail: the perfect artistic interpretation of Enlightenment principles. Following on the heels of Hayez'and Milano dell'Ottocento, this exhibition celebrates the Age of Enlightenment, for which Milan was a major, originating centre. Looking to the future, the goal for the Gallerie d'Italia is to ensure the continued planning of major initiatives that promote knowledge of Italy's heritage and history, in the conviction that culture is an inescapable factor of growth, innovation and collective well-being.*

Gian Maria Gros-Pietro
President
Intesa Sanpaolo

Alongside the valorisation of the nineteenth- and twentieth-century collections of Fondazione Cariplo and Intesa Sanpaolo, the Gallerie d'Italia are continuing the series of major exhibitions begun in 2015 and developed for their prestigious venue in Piazza Scala. This series of exhibitions, which also includes the show dedicated to the Great War and the Francesco Hayez retrospective, link Milan to Italy in an international context and make an original contribution to the study of their respective themes, being curated by scholars who specialise almost exclusively in the treated subjects.

The new Piazza Scala exhibition – the first dedicated to Canaletto and Bellotto in Milan – goes to the heart of eighteenth-century painting, investigating the relationship between Bellotto and Canaletto, the two greatest exponents of the brilliant period of view painting. These were painters who not only had a deep tie to the city of their birth (Venice) as well as to Milan and other Italian cities but also and above all to Europe. The exhibition therefore has an international air, and should be read as an homage to the relationship between Italy and Europe.

The critical aim of the exhibition is two-fold. One the one hand, it endeavours to recognise Bernardo Bellotto, the nephew and student of Giovanni Antonio Canal (known as Canaletto), as a painter of equal talent. On the other hand, it seeks to overcome the commonplace that threatens to reduce the two Venetian artists' perspective virtuosity, landscape subjects and observational rigour to a kind of photographic topography of their time.

From the period of his apprenticeship in his uncle's workshop, in the second half of the 1730s, Bellotto aspired to freedom and independence. Canaletto was at the height of his fame and commercial success, and his student adopted his methods and techniques so seamlessly that their contemporaries were at pains to tell them apart. He thus won over the same English collectors, travelling on their Grand Tour, but also expressed the features of his own strong artistic personality right from the start: perspectival rigour, silvery, contrasting light and marked realism.

As he began to travel outside Venice – his trip to Milan in 1744 was decisive – Bellotto moved increasingly further away from Canaletto's example, developing his own interests, such as the analytic description of architecture and figures, which he characterised so clearly in terms of social milieu and variety of costume. The men and women who enliven Bellotto's view lend a touch of reality and vitality to the urban settings. The 'Enlightenment certainty of absolute verity' that Longhi saw in

Canaletto becomes, in Bellotto, subjective wonder for those looking at his works. The Saxon views are an example of this, for the way in which they confer an extraordinary breadth to the city through strong light and shadow effects.
The exhibition illustrates Bellotto's original contribution to eighteenth-century European painting, comparing his youthful work with that of Canaletto and highlighting their different interpretations of the views of Italian and European capitals. Bellotto is presented here for the first time as a passionate participant in the artistic and cultural trends of his time.
His interest in staying culturally up to date is highlighted as a key to interpreting his artistic choices, his personality and his intellectual independence.
Organised in partnership with the Gemäldegalerie in Dresden, the Royal Castle in Warsaw and Castello Sforzesco in Milan, the exhibition presents more than one hundred works by the two great view painters – including paintings, drawings and prints – many of which will be on view for the first time in Italy. The gathering together of this exceptional corpus *was made possible thanks to the generosity of Italian and international museums and collectors from all over the world – British Royal Collection, The National Gallery in London, Hermitage in St Petersburg, The Metropolitan Museum of Art in New York, J. Paul Getty Museum in Los Angeles, The Cleveland Museum of Art, National Gallery of Victoria in Melbourne, Pinacoteca di Brera in Milan, Museo di Capodimonte in Naples and Museo Correr in Venice, to cite just a few of the most prestigious lenders.*
In confirmation of its deep tie to Milan, Intesa Sanpaolo is committed to contributing to the valorisation of its historical centre – as demonstrated by the transformation of its offices in Piazza Scala into a museum space and site for cultural activities and its recent restoration of Casa Manzoni – and to creating initiatives that underline the fundamental role that Milan has always played in the artistic and cultural history of Italy.

Giovanni Bazoli
Chairman Emeritus
Intesa Sanpaolo

CONTENTS

CATALOGO

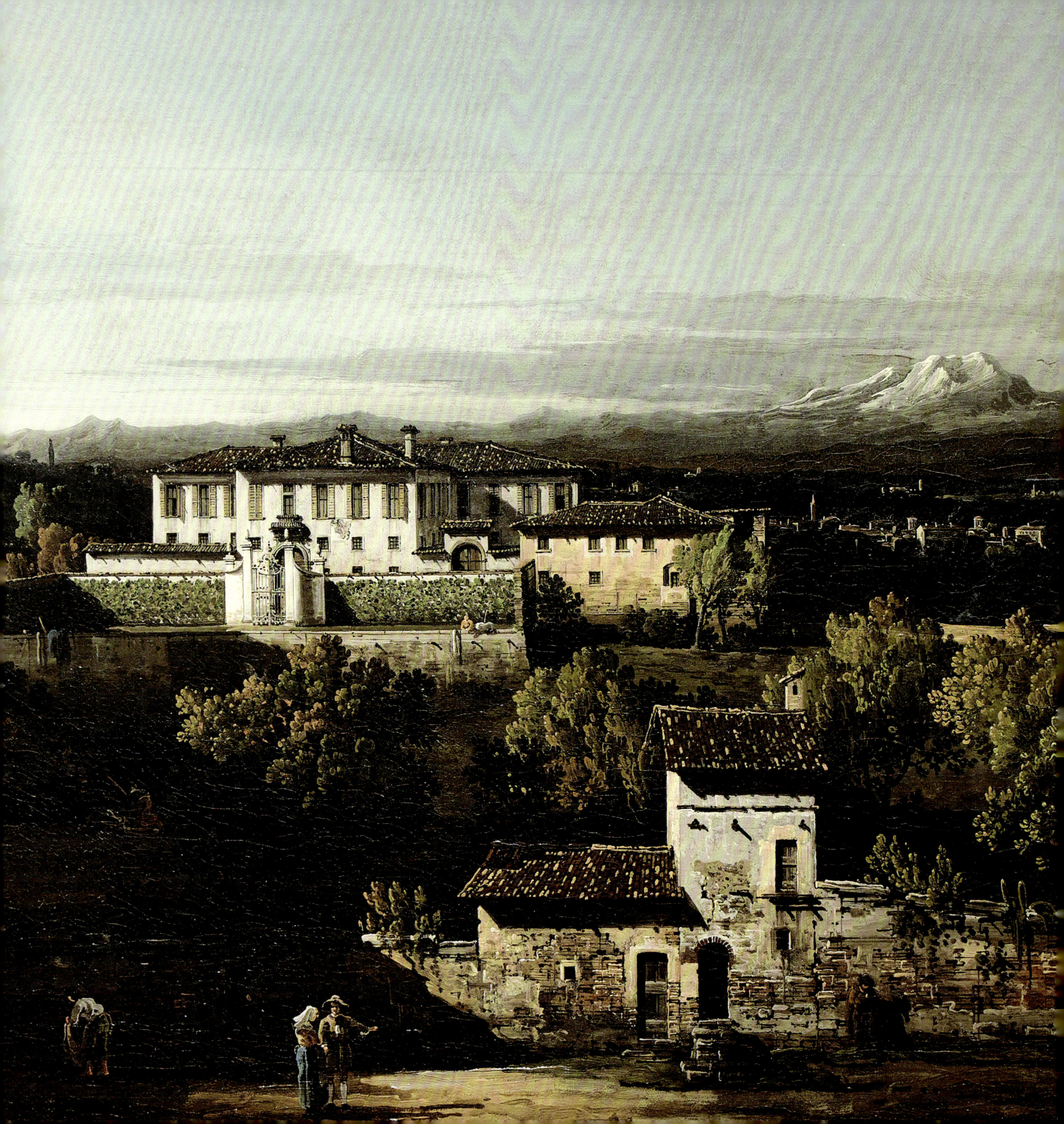

BELLOTTO AND CANALETTO: THE SUCCESS OF SEPARATION

BOŻENA ANNA KOWALCZYK

When his nephew Bernardo Francesco Paulo Ernesto Bellotto – the son of Fiorenza Domenica Canal and a junior notary, Lorenzo Bellotto – was born in the spring of 1722, Canaletto, known at the time by his family name, Antonio Canal, was already painting views of Venice.[1] The views in question were the early attempts of a set designer, work that he pursued for at least four years with his father Bernardo and older brother Cristoforo, creating sets for Teatro Sant'Angelo and Teatro San Cassiano in Venice and Teatro Capranica in Rome. In eighteenth-century Venice, which attracted the most famous singers and the six theatres of which were among the most active in Europe, theatre and music were passions shared by both aristocrats and foreign residents. And theatre served as a stepping stone for the young artist: it put him in contact with one of his first known patrons, Owen McSwiny (1676–1754), a theatre impresario of Irish origin who arrived in Venice in 1720–21 with the young Charles Lennox, Lord March (1701–1750), who later became the 2nd Duke of Richmond, and Joseph Smith (1674 ca.–1770), an English banker and merchant who lived in Venice. These were the figures who, in the span of just a few years, linked Canaletto's future to the British world of Grand Tour collectors. As early as 1722, and partly in 1723, he had passed the tests set by the latter two with flying colours: the architecture for *The Tomb of Lord Somers*[2] and *The Tomb of Archbishop Tillotson*[3] in collaboration with the figure and landscape painters Piazzetta, Pittoni and Cimaroli, for the series *Tombeaux des princes*, large commemorative paintings of the most famous figures in recent English history commissioned for Lord March's dining room at Goodwood House in Sussex,[4] and six views of San Marco for Smith.[5] In 1723, two additional figures of importance emerged for Canaletto, who were later also key for his nephew's future: Anton Maria Zanetti di Girolamo (1680–1767), who was also involved in the world of Venetian theatre, as we know from his numerous caricatures of actors and singers, and Prince Joseph Wenzel Liechtenstein (1696–1772), to whom he was probably introduced by Zanetti. The prince commissioned four large views from the artist, which were extraordinary interpretations of the genre introduced in Venice by Luca Carlevarijs.[6] Years later, in Vienna, in 1759–1760, Wenzel commissioned Bellotto to paint two views of his home in Rossau and its garden.[7] The most admired work in the Liechtenstein series, *Piazza San Marco, looking East*, now at the Thyssen-Bornemisza Museum in Madrid, documents the work being done at the time for a new pavement, which was meticulously recorded starting in February 1723 by Bellotto's godfather, Francesco Perabò, secretary of the Procuratia de Supra. But nothing is known of Canaletto's Venetian relationships or the people in his circle other than those connected to his patrons and buyers, confirmed in a series of letters.[8]
With the ever-growing quantity of information about Bellotto's education and training (an extraordinary source is the recently discovered inventory of his flat in Dresden[9]), bolstered by the substantial

Bernardo Bellotto, *Villa Perabò, Gazzada, Lombardy*, detail, 1744, oil on canvas, 65 x 100 cm. Milan, Pinacoteca di Brera (cat. 60) body of biographical information that was already known to the first scholars to the first scholars of the artist, Moritz Stübel and Hellmuth Allwill Fritzsche, the absence of secure information about Canaletto's personality and education seems all the more glaring.

His life was marked out by work and commissions, and the few known judgements of him are decidedly one-sided. McSwiny, who was Canaletto's most active agent in terms of placing his paintings in English collections during the second half of the 1720s, sent a letter to the Duke of Richmond in which he described Canaletto in what had by then become emblematic terms: 'The fellow is whimsical and vary's his prices every day and he that has a mind to have any of his work must not seem to be too fond of it, for he'll be the worse treated for it, both in the price, & in the painting too'.[10] On 30 December 1727, Zanetti wrote about Canaletto to his friend Arthur Pond in London in a more benevolent tone: since he had 'promoted' his work, he could count on the artist's 'utmost loyalty', ready to paint him views of his 'chosen locations' for '7 pounds', around 14 zecchini.[11] Whereas McSwiny was extremely critical of the artist: 'He's a covetous, greedy, fellow and because he's in reputation people are glad to get anything and at his own price';[12] in seven letters to Pond, and two to Francesco Gabburri in Florence, dated 24 July and 21 August 1728, Anton Maria Zanetti di Girolamo wrote about the artist with friendly indulgence.[13] We prefer to think of Canaletto in the same terms as Zanetti's cousin, Anton Maria Zanetti di Alessandro (1706–1778), Custodian of the Marciana and a distinguished art critic, who judged the artist by his work: 'effetti di mente serena e genio felice' (the fruit of a tranquil mind and prolific talent).[14]

It is not known which texts, acquaintances or debates led to the complete transformation of his taste from Baroque to Enlightenment-inspired at the end of the 1720s. The transition from Baroque chiaroscuro excitement to light, diffuse luminosity was common throughout the sphere of Venetian painting around 1730, led by Giambattista Tiepolo. The change in Canaletto's work, developed through experimentation over several years, but with more radical results than any other artist, involved and altered his technique and working methods. By around 1730, Canaletto's work fully satisfied the artistic ideals of the young Englishmen on their Grand Tour, who debated the new Enlightenment theories in the Venetian home of Smith, and it is difficult to imagine that he was not a convinced, passionate participant. The paintings he made – by then he was already a successful painter flooded with commissions: 'he has more work than he can do in any reasonable time…'[15] – were the works of a cultured artist familiar with the new scientific theories of Isaac Newton and George Berkeley – and he skilfully translated them into rational, convincing representations. Canaletto was a follower of the Enlightenment, it was his vocation, and he adhered to this position throughout his entire career. And yet, after his death on 20 April 1768 in his home in the Venetian parish of San Lio, in Corte Perina, where he had lived his entire life with the exception of a period in Rome in 1719-20 and his nine years in England, not a single book was listed in the inventory.

Bellotto was Canaletto's only assistant and student who understood his artistic credo, and he cultivated it through study and reading. His talent and creative intellect were matched by neither his older brother Pietro Bellotti (1725–ca. 1800), who was probably also apprenticed in their uncle's workshop, nor his granfather, Bernardo Canal (1673–1744), who had also transformed himself into a view painter. Bellotto must have received solid academic training, like his brother Michiel Bernardo Antonio Eugenio (1720–1778),[16] a 'printer and bookseller' who was documented as living with his wife 'Angiola' in Arezzo from 1749, 'in casa Fantini',[17] with whom Bellotto remained in contact even later, in Dresden. When Michiel left Venice in June 1736, Bernardo was already studying under their uncle.[18] The collaboration was interrupted in 1744, when Bellotto left Venice for Lombardy.

The young Bellotto learned Canaletto's elaborate working method, which is only simple and mechanical in appearance. The process involved making sketches with a *camera optica* in *plein-air* in a precise sequence, already having the idea of the perspective view of the location in mind, and then composed in the studio, according to the taste and inspiration of the moment. As early as 1946, Roberto Longhi understood the importance of the *camera optica* for the artist's freedom of poetic expression,[19] but debate over his use of this device – even though already affirmed by Anton Maria Zanetti di Alessandro[20] – nevertheless continued for a long while. If an optical camera lens had not been used to focus its subjects, view painting would have lacked the scientific basis that constitutes its foundation and is the source of its fascination. Bellotto learned to make technical, precisely constructed perspective drawings with the painting already in mind, using a straight edge and a compass, and extending the horizon line, a critical reference for every composition, from one edge to the other. Canaletto is recognised as having been one of the most brilliant draughtsmen of all time. And Joseph Smith's collection, a fundamental part of the Royal British Collections, contributed in no small part to this fame. At first he collected preparatory drawings and then, starting in 1734, began commissioning Canaletto to produce refined hatched or shaded with grey wash, some 'in memory of' paintings sold in England.[21] A good proportion of his collection comprises views and *capricci* of lagoon and mainland subjects, collected by Canaletto during his trip along the Brenta, up tu Padua in 1742, and the same places are depicted in the etchings. Bellotto contributed his own sketches to this repertoire, but few collector's drawings survive, just those commissioned by Smith (cat. 34, 48). Smith – whom the Canaletto scholars W.G. Constable and J.G. Links did not believe was also a patron of Bellotto – turns out to have commissioned, in 1742, the 'memories' of sold Canaletto paintings from him for his own collection (cat. 38, 39, 49) and, in 1745–46, the drawings with Verona subjects, after his appointment to the post of British Consul in Venice (cat. 34).

Bellotto was a prolific draughtsman, drawing in Venice and on his trips, especially for paintings. The volumes in his library in his flat in Dresden included two albums of drawings 'fatti da B. Bellotto de Canaletto', with 215 sheets of 'Lochi Obligati ed altri d'Inventione' (1077), 304 'Schizi di figure dal Naturale' (1078), and other loose drawings, 'Schizi di Figure sotto. 400. Carte' (1009) and 'Abozzi di Pitura, da 513 Carte' (1015), as well as a 'Cartela di Vari Studii miei ed altri Celebri Autori del Numero di 628 carte' (1012).[22] In terms of scholarship on the artist, this is the most terrible, inestimable loss out of all of the artist's possessions destroyed in the bombardment of Dresden in July 1760. The surviving drawings, composition and figure studies, number less than 200, some brought to Vienna at the end of 1758, a group of sketches executed in Dresden in 1762-1765, and some, the ones of figures, left behind in Venice in Canaletto's workshop (cat. 10). The few drawings that survive from his period of training in Canaletto's workshop are marked by a graphic style wholly different from that of the master and one can already see the difference between their two artistic personalities: Bellotto's is a nervous line, one that funnels all of its expression into the pure contour line; already in his early attempts, the young artist meticulously recorded even the most minute details. These were 'technical', experimental studies, stylistically elementary but with unerring perspective, confirming the strength of his training. The issue of the 'duplicates', a series of drawings strikingly similar in composition, the ones by Bellotto being basic sketches and the versions by Canaletto, commissioned by Smith, stunning works of art, should be seen as a natural procedure in the context of the busy atelier, where work was carried out at a frenetic rhythm, and the fruit of the skill and extraordinary inventiveness of the two artists.

Digital analysis of the two versions of the same hatched composition, *The Campo Santa Maria Formosa, Venice*, by Bellotto (cat. 3) and Canaletto (cat. 4), both from 1738–1740, which have a similar perspectival structure and the same figures in the same arrangment (one of the seven similar cases of apparently precise correspondence of drawings connected to the documentary sketches by Canaletto in the Cagnola album at the Gallerie dell'Accademia, Venice) has instead revealed significant differences in the positioning of the lines (fig. 1). Very few of them in fact actually coincide, the sure, decisive line of Canaletto overlaps the uncertain hand of Bellotto, 'adjusting' the shape of the dome of the church, its lantern, the bell tower, the heights of the roofs, the arrangement of the windows, balconies and chimneys and the silhouettes of the figures. This rigorous comparison makes the elementary character of Bellotto's sheet stand out all the more; it was the work of a beginner, which at sixteen years of age he of course was.

In the case of the *capricci*, the images were constructed following the same procedures as the topographic drawings, using precise measurements. The two versions of the *Capriccio with a Ruined Triumphal Arch on the Shores of the Lagoon*, identical in size, Bellotto's pure outline,[23] Canaletto's shaded with grey wash (cat. 30) turn out to have completely different aspects when compared through digital analysis, differences that can even be perceived by the naked eye: the outlines of the architecture coincide almost entirely with the exception of the different shape of the arch and the architrave of the temple, differences in the foliage and in the wavy lines that mark out the unevenness of the ground, which are fluid and confident in Canaletto's drawing, effective also in Bellotto's. In the figures, the only difference worthy of note is the tilt of the head of the soldier with his face towards the viewer (fig. 2). These were later drawings, from 1742–43, and made when Bellotto had already developed a sure hand. The subject was part of the intense formulation of motifs for the etchings, but was only once later repeated verbatim, by Bellotto, in one of his paintings of Asolo, while other drawings made for the pendant of this canvas were also translated into an etching (see cat. 29, 31-32).

Through the thirty-one highly complex engravings in the collection *Vedute Altre prese da i Luoghi altre inventate*, probably made between 1740 and 1744, Canaletto proved himself to also be an outstanding *peintre-graveur*.[24] Bellotto practised this technique, which was

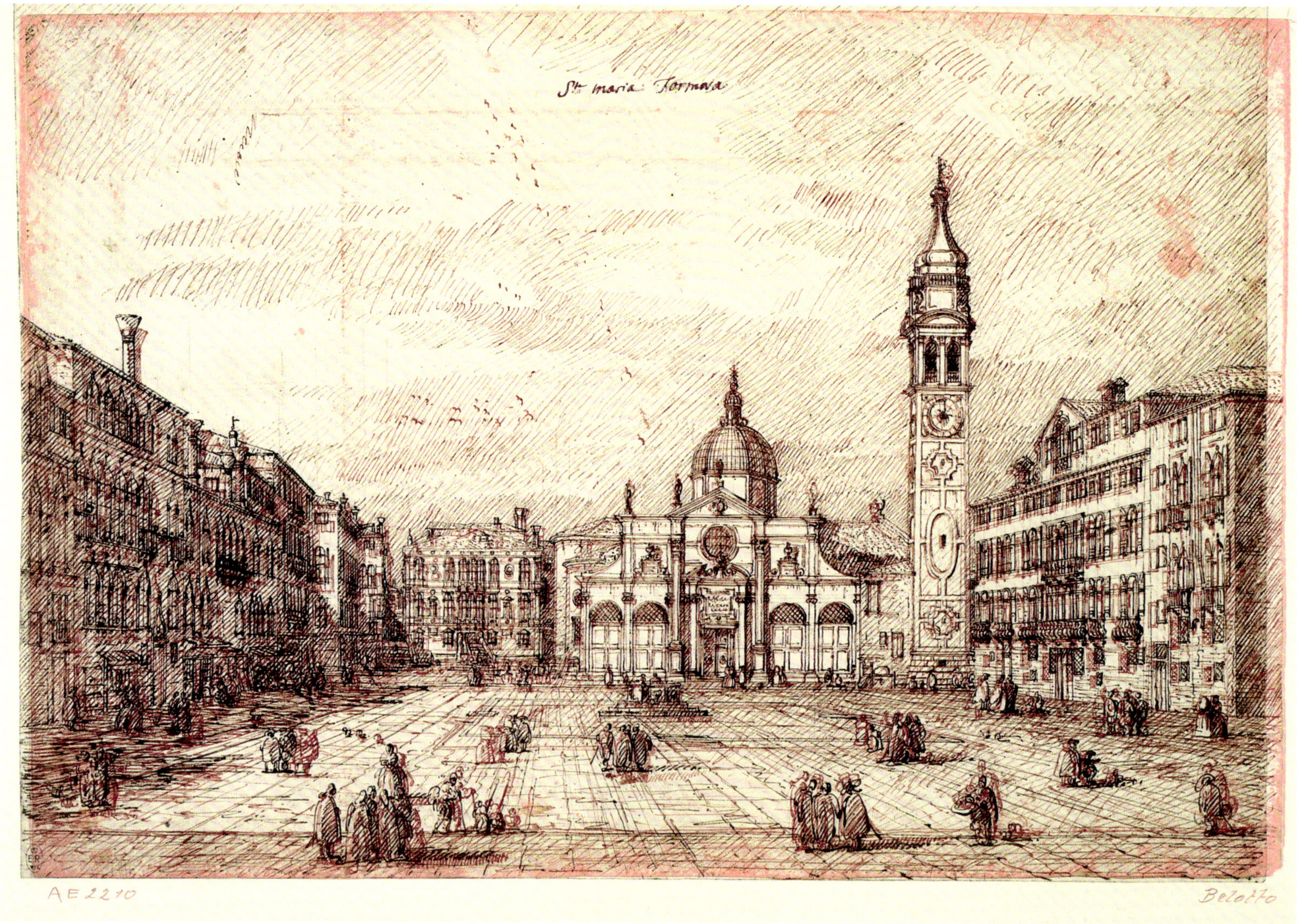

1. Superimposition of drawings: a. Bernardo Bellotto, *Campo Santa Maria Formosa, Venice*, 1738–39, pen and brown ink over pencil, 255 x 382–383 mm. Hessisches Landesmuseum, Darmstadt, AE 2210 (cat. 3), here reproduced in red; b. Canaletto, *Campo Santa Maria Formosa, Venice*, 1738–1740, pen and two shades of brown ink over pencil, 270 x 376 mm. The Royal Collection, RCIN 907478 (cat. 4). Digitally created image (FG/A, Francesco Giordano)

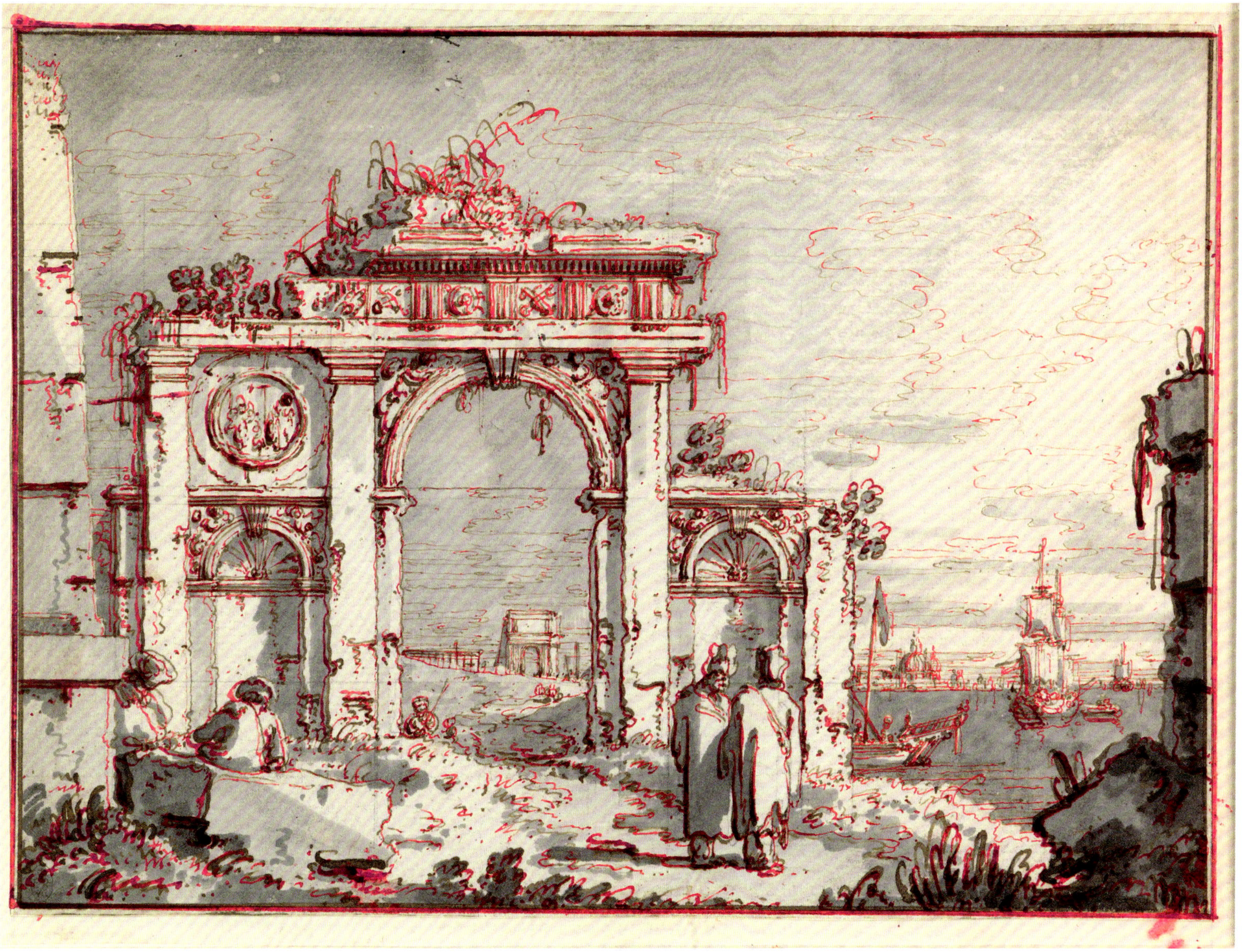

2. Superimposition of drawings. a. Canaletto, *Capriccio with a Ruined Triumphal Arch on the Shores of the Lagoon*, 1742–43, pen and brown ink, with blue-grey watercolour, on top of pencil 198 x 278 mm. The Royal Collection, RCIN 907533 (cat. 30); b. Bernardo Bellotto, *Capriccio with a Triumphal Arch on the Shores of the Lagoon*, 1742–43, pen and brown ink, 20.7 x 28.5 cm. Darmstadt, Hessisches Landesmuseum, AE 2221, here reproduced in red. Digitally created image (FG/A, Francesco Giordano)

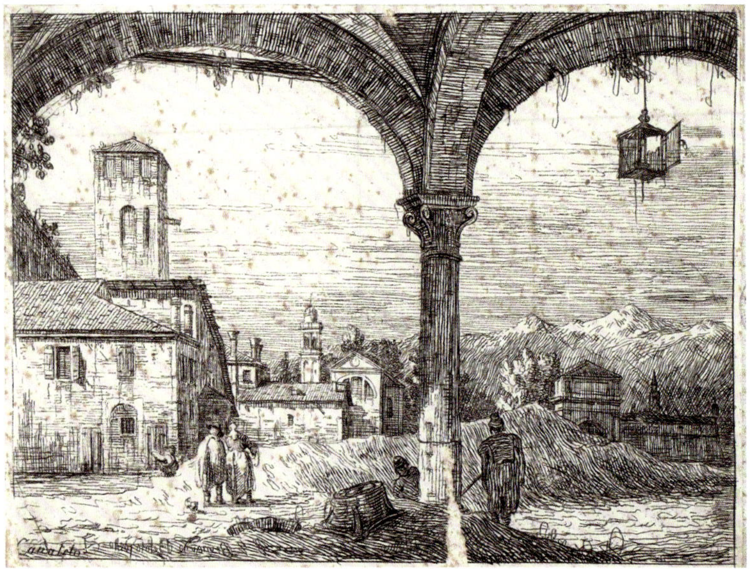

3. Bernardo Bellotto, *The Portico with a Lantern*, 1742–42, etching, 145 x 195 mm. Bassano del Grappa, Museo Civico, Coll. Rem. XIV 385 1800

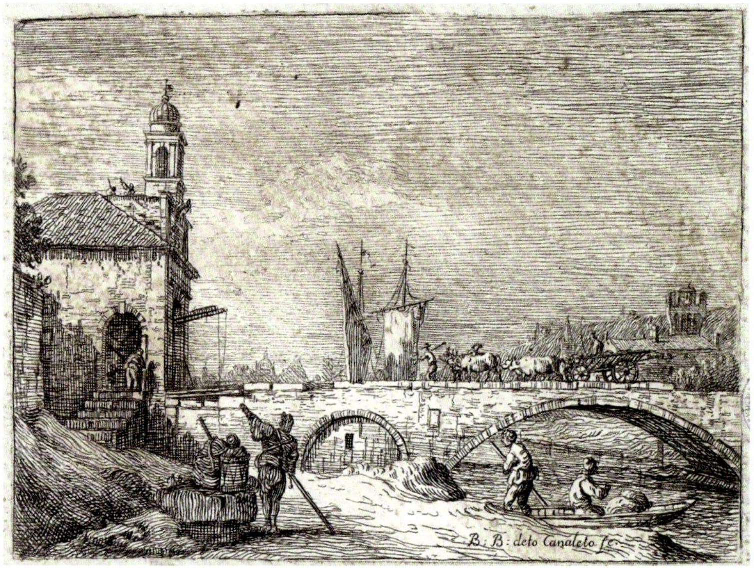

4. Bernardo Bellotto, *The Cart on the Bridge*, 1742–43, etching, 140 x 195 mm. Bassano del Grappa, Museo Civico, Coll. Rem. XIV 385 1799

extremely popular in Venice, in the early 1740s, making eight small prints with the same motifs. In his version of the *The Portico with a Lantern* (cat. 33a), one of Canaletto's large monumental plates and the most stunning for its imaginativeness and masterfully handled luminosity, with its dazzling areas of light left white, Bellotto repeated the overall idea of a fantasy city seen through a portic, but on a smaller scale, his portic, with two rather than three arches and its lantern moved to the right, frames a landscape of the mainland, with recognisable elements of Padua, with the hills on the horizon (fig. 3). While Canaletto's line is even and calm, dense in the shadowy foreground, where he used wavy lines to represent the irregularity of the ground, and thick and parallel in the sky, filled with white clouds, Bellotto's is scratchy and uneven. And in his version of Canaletto's small plate *The Cart on the Bridge* (cat. 33b), cut into three parts, Bellotto again picked up the general idea, here combining the motifs on the horizon and the ship backwards, showing that he knew the whole plate, of which no impression is known, leading us to imagine that the two worked together side by side, another study occasion (fig. 4). It is surprising that, starting in 1747 in Dresden, Bellotto was able to produce, based only on these early attempts, large plates with complicated compositions and complex lighting. In the first plates, his line is very close to that of Canaletto (cat. 70, 73) but then, after just a few years of experimentation, he had arrived at the point of being able to produce his masterpiece, *The Kreuzkirche, Dresden* (cat. 79). It appears as if there was a special agreement between the two painters during that period, with Canaletto signing his etchings under the name 'A. Canal' and Bellotto using Canaletto's ('B.B. detto Canaletto').[25]

Replicating the same compositions for multiple canvases was a way of handling commissions; they were not copies. Canaletto used his documentary sketches for various paintings, made at different times, increasing or reducing the foreground, expanding the view, adding different figures and boats. For Bellotto, the task was sizeable, since while still quite young he received commissions to replicate paintings that Canaletto had made in the 1720s, from the series of views of the Grand Canal made for Smith, which were the most frequently requested images of Venice and known through the album *Prospectus Magni Canalis Venetiarum* by Antonio Visentini (1688–1782), published in 1735. The young Bellotto worked from paintings by Canaletto that had been made using an already outdated technique that he 'translated' with talent, seriousness and diligence.

In *The Grand Canal Grande looking South, from Palazzi Foscari and Moro Lin to Santa Maria della Carità* (cat. 7), one of the first in the series of fifteen that Anton Maria Zanetti sent to Castle Howard in 1738–1740, Bellotto repeated the composition of one of those paintings, made in 1726–1727, now in the British Royal Collection (see the comparison illustration in cat. 7), with an already 'modern' perspectival layout and atmosphere (and use of a *camera optica*), but the outlines of the architecture and details, the painting of the water and the figures types were the work of an artist still at the beginning of his experimentation. Painted on a larger canvas, but not yet the size that later became his favourite, just over 60 x 90 cm, Bellotto showed in this youthful work his ability to select and mix colours like Canaletto and to use their viscosity in the layers of colour to indicate the faded colour of the walls, the folds of the sails and the edges of the clouds. Like Canaletto, he used black lines to mark out the details of buildings, but increased their descriptive incisiveness and intensity, cleverly and persistently using the new technique of creating incisions with the end of the brush at the last minute, with multiple layers of paint, insisting on the discolourations and effects of atmospheric fading. (figs. 5–8).

In the more mature *The Grand Canal looking East, from the Palazzo Loredan Cini in Campo San Vio, Venice* (cat. 13), from around 1742, Bellotto had already developed his own unique figure type, elongated, decisive, with which he completely replaced the one used by Canaletto in the works in Smith's house, from 1727-1728 (see the comparison illustration in cat. 13). He liked to insert solitary, melancholy figures in the foreground, with their backs turned to the viewer, and intensified his study of cracked walls. He developed his own approach to skies, making them an intense blue, and his own way of rendering the transparency of water. Like the young Canaletto, 'questo va sempre sul loco e forma tutto sul vero' (he always [went] in person to the location and make a form on the real),[26] in order to check, correct and update his subjects, with the result that the details of his paintings reveal elements and colours that he alone observed (figs. 9–10).

The level of attention increased when his model was Visentini's etchings, only one case of which is known, *The Molo looking West, the Column of Saint Theodore on the Right, Venice* (cat. 9). Here, Bellotto checked the accuracy of the distances, the light and the number of windows and chimneys, and added his own observations: the precision of the details of his description of the facades of the old granaries and the Zecca on the Molo exceeds that of both the print and the corresponding painting by Canaletto (figs. 11–12).

The date of his trip to Rome is unclear, the only certainty being that it took place before August 1743, when Canaletto's 'exceedingly famous' nephew displayed a view of Rome at the Festival of St Roche, identified as the *Santa Maria d'Aracoeli and the Campidoglio*, at Petworth House (The National Trust) (see the comparison illustration in cat. 44).[27] However, a topographical detail, together with archival sources that confirm that the artist was in Venice in February and July 1742, suggests a trip between late spring and early summer.[28] Bellotto would have returned to Venice just in time to bring Canaletto the drawings he had made in the presence of the monuments, needed for the five vertical views of Rome commissioned by Smith, which were signed and, importantly, dated 1742.[29] This traditional interpretation is not confirmed through analysis of the Roman works by the two artists. On the contrary, Bellotto travelled to Rome not only 'per consiglio del Zio' (upon his uncle's advice) [30] but also in his footsteps, using his early drawings mostly as a guide to ancient Rome and then admirably and completely independently developing an interest in the modern city (cat. 41, 49). His *Arch of Titus* (cat. 42) was in all probability made after the painting of the same subject in the series of five in Smith's collection, and not the other way around.[31]

Over the course of his career, Canaletto demonstrated time and time again his talent for using the most varied sources intelligently and with discretion. In the case of his Roman works, he had access to a vast collection of prints, if not in his own library, then in that of Smith.

It is not possible to date any of Bellotto's views of Rome to 1742, with the exception of two pendants, *The Roman Forum towards the Capitol with the Temple of Castor and Pollux, Rome* and *The Temple of Antoninus and Faustina in the Roman Forum, Rome*, which were replicas of paintings by Canaletto made after drawings from the trip he took in his youth (cat. 38, 39). The art of the replica became useful to Bellotto later during his Dresden period, when he painted two versions of the same view, for the king and the prime minister. A pure exercise and pure demonstration of skill, his second version was stunningly close to the original, even surpassing it in descriptive force and incisiveness (figs. 16–17). In his later version of *The Roman Forum towards the Capitol with the Temple of Castor and Pollux, Rome* (cat. 40), made after his trip to Rome, Bellotto not only corrected the architectural details but also transmitted a sense of melancholy that lends truth to the image of the place (fig. 18).

There was something prodigious in Bellotto's detachment from Canaletto's compositions and creation of his own, which were already brilliant, for their variation in light, architectural description and atmosphere. Rome must have enchanted him with its monuments, as

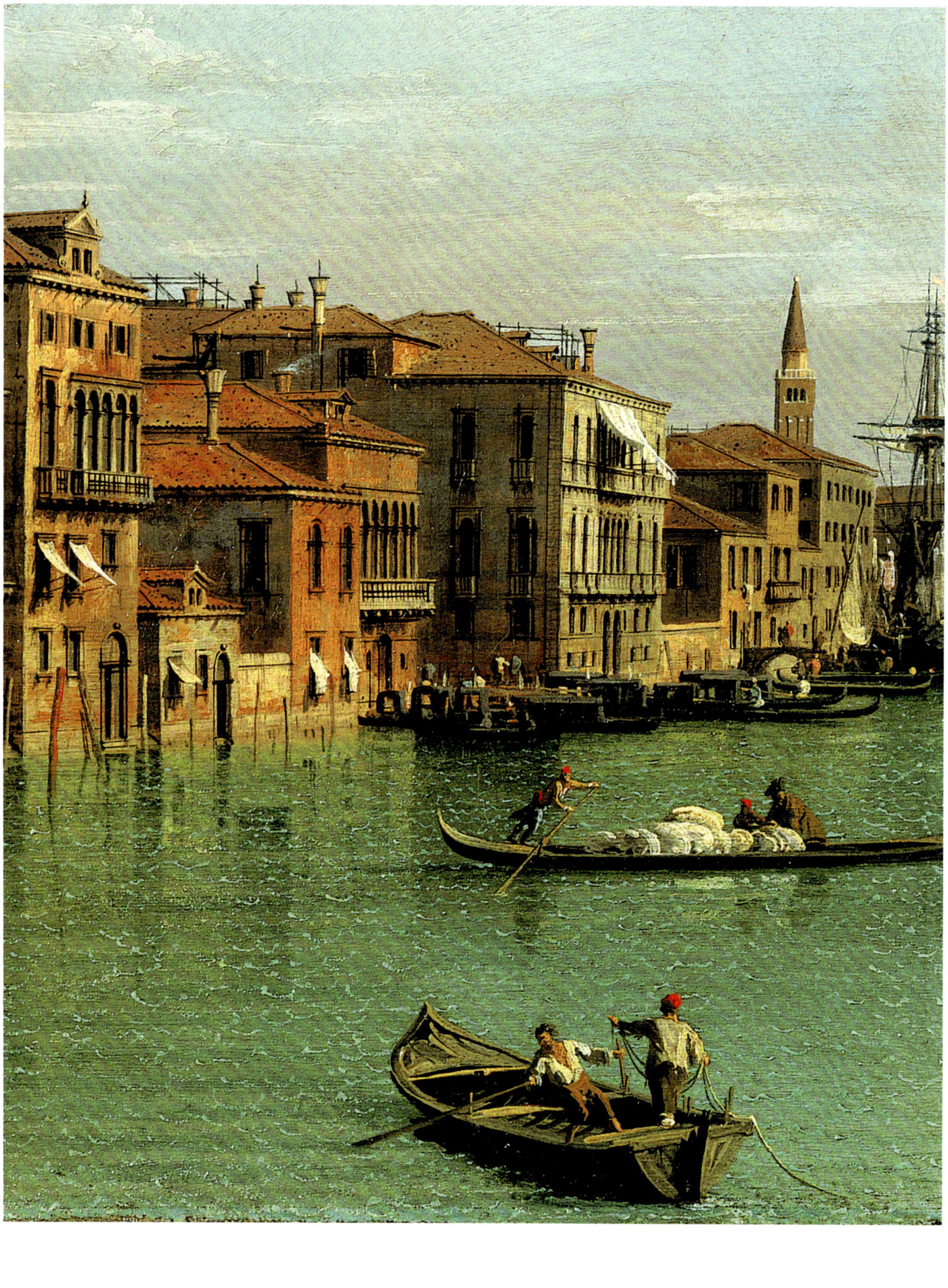

5. Canaletto, *The Grand Canal looking South from the Palazzi Foscari and Moro Lin to Santa Maria della Carità, Venice*, detail, 1726–27, oil on canvas, 49.9 x 80.3 cm. The Royal Collection, RCIN 401404

6. Bernardo Bellotto, *The Grand Canal looking South from the Palazzi Foscari and Moro Lin to Santa Maria della Carità, Venice*, detail, 1738–39, oil on canvas, 58.4 x 88.9 cm. Private Collection, courtesy of Fabrizio Moretti Ltd., London (cat. 7)

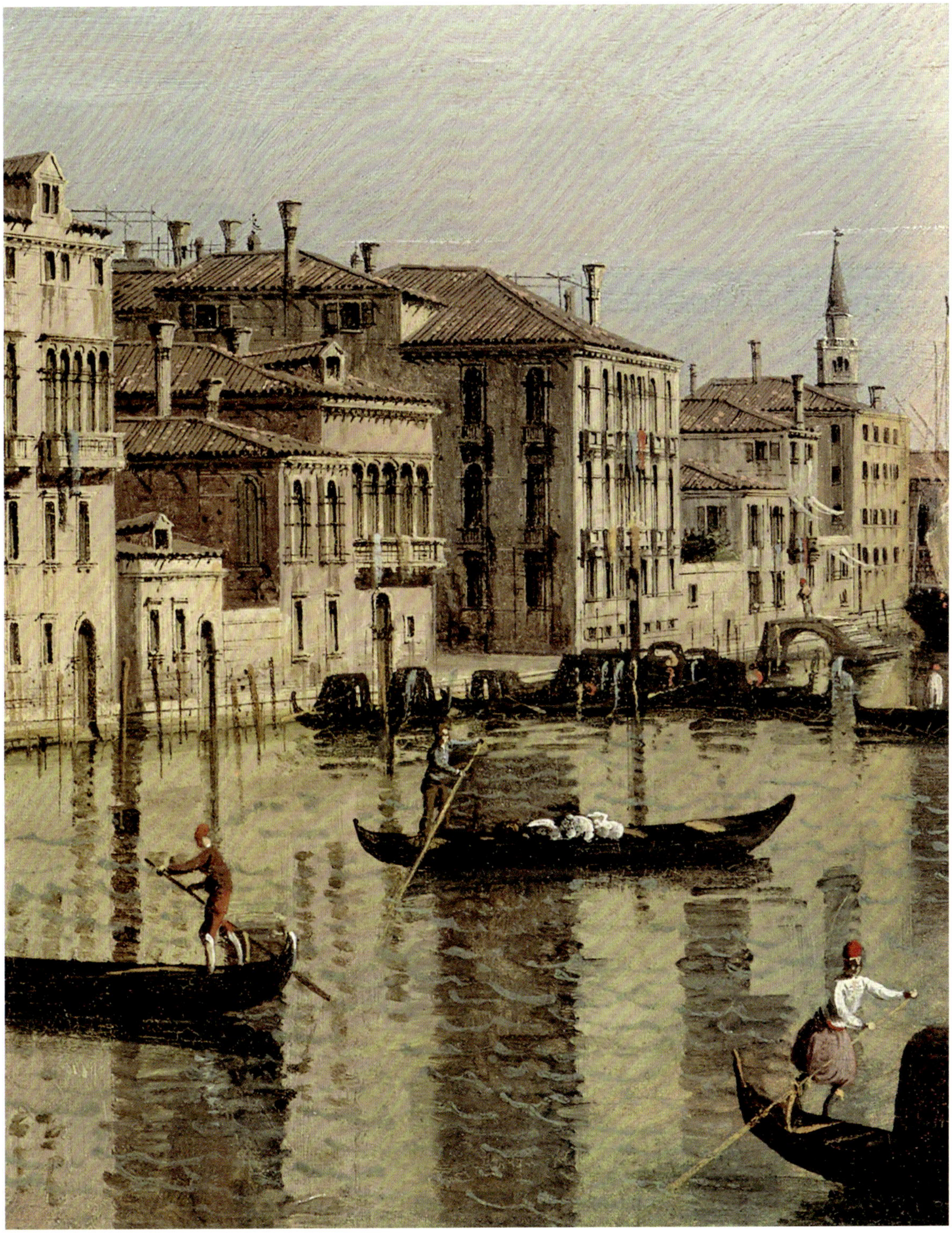

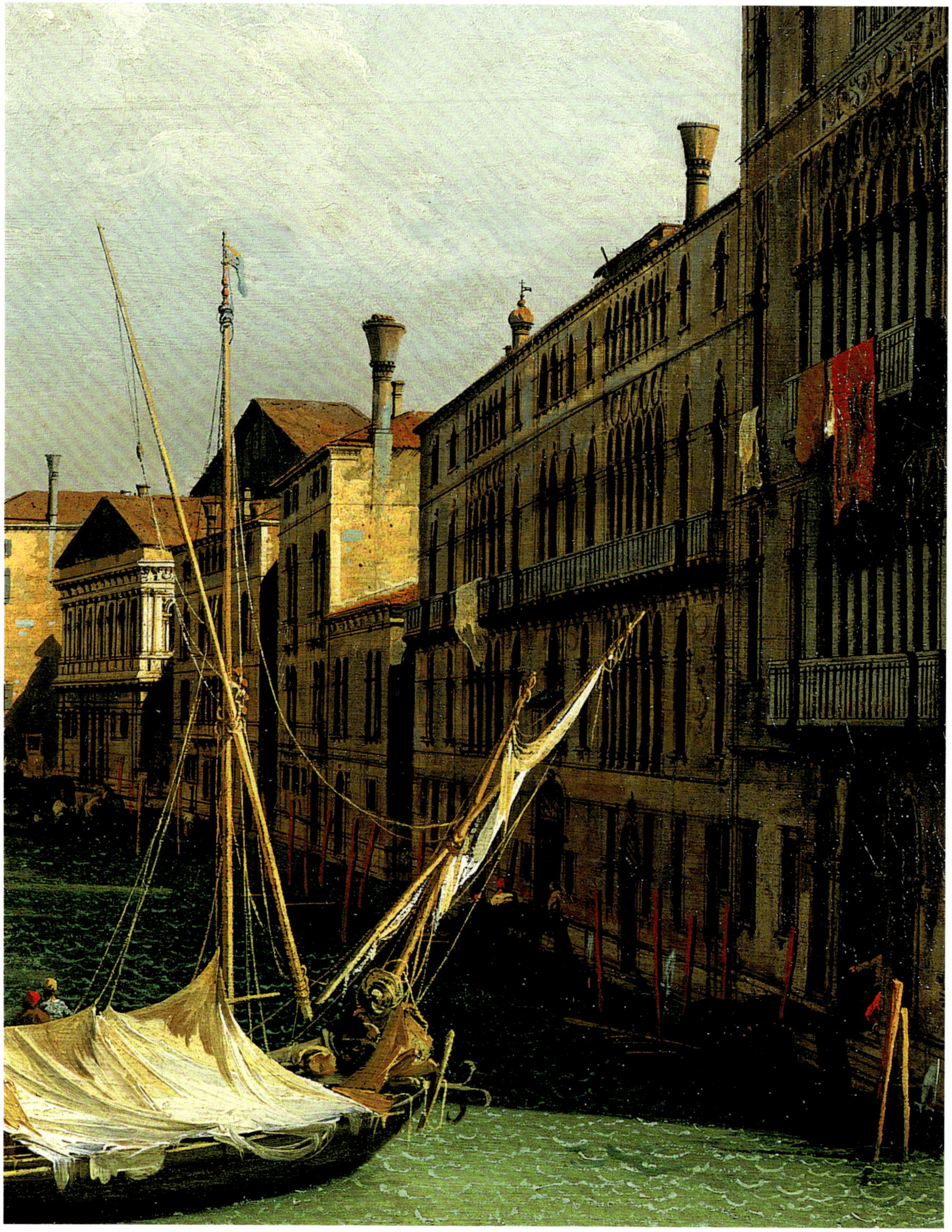

7. Canaletto, *The Grand Canal looking South from the Palazzi Foscari and Moro Lin to Santa Maria della Carità, Venice*, detail, 1726-27, oil on canvas, 49.9 x 80.3 cm. The Royal Collection, RCIN 401404

8. Bernardo Bellotto, *The Grand Canal looking South from the Palazzi Foscari and Moro Lin to Santa Maria della Carità, Venice*, detail, 1738–39,
oil on canvas; 58.4 x 88.9 cm.
Private Collection, courtesy of Fabrizio Moretti Ltd., London (cat. 7)

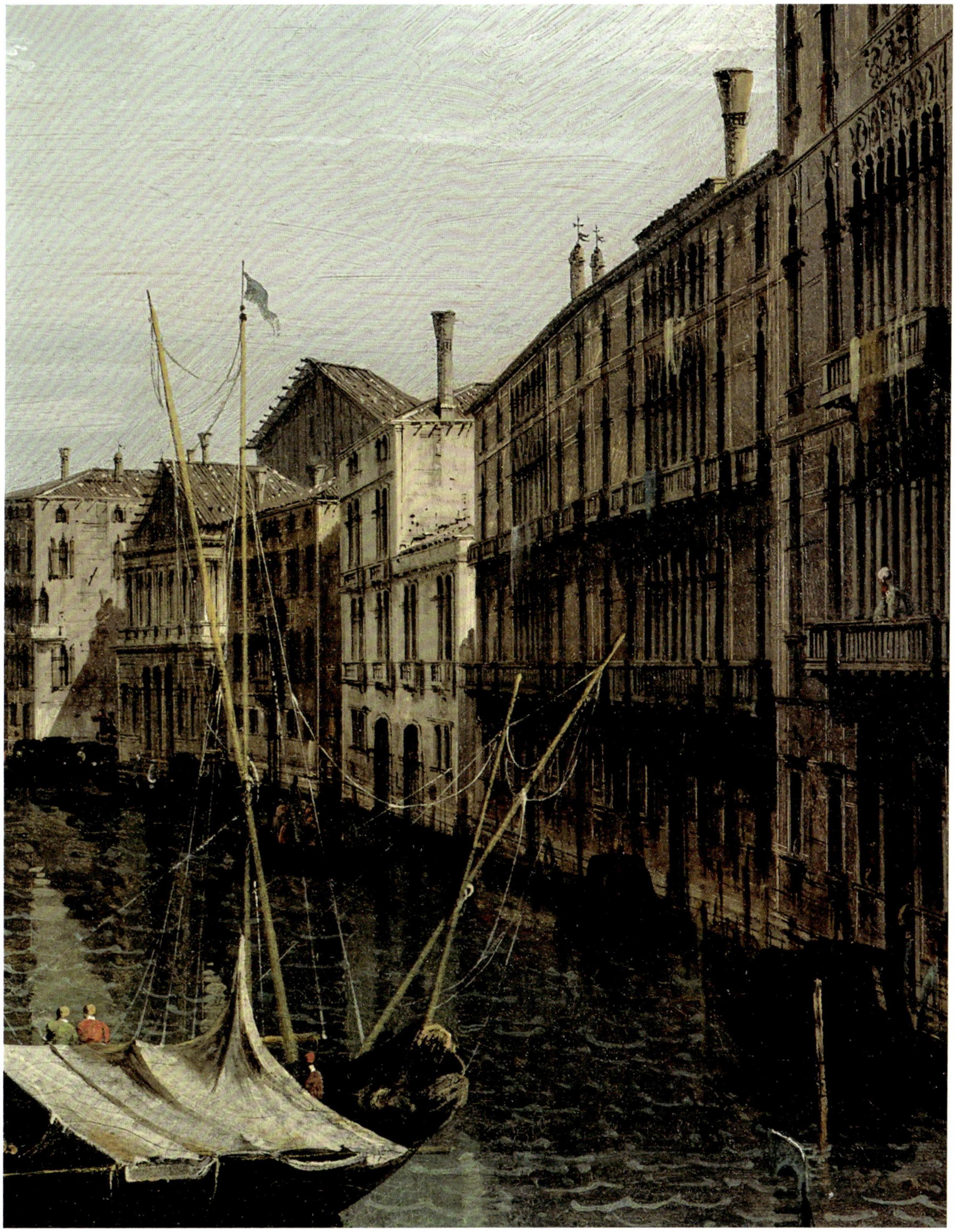

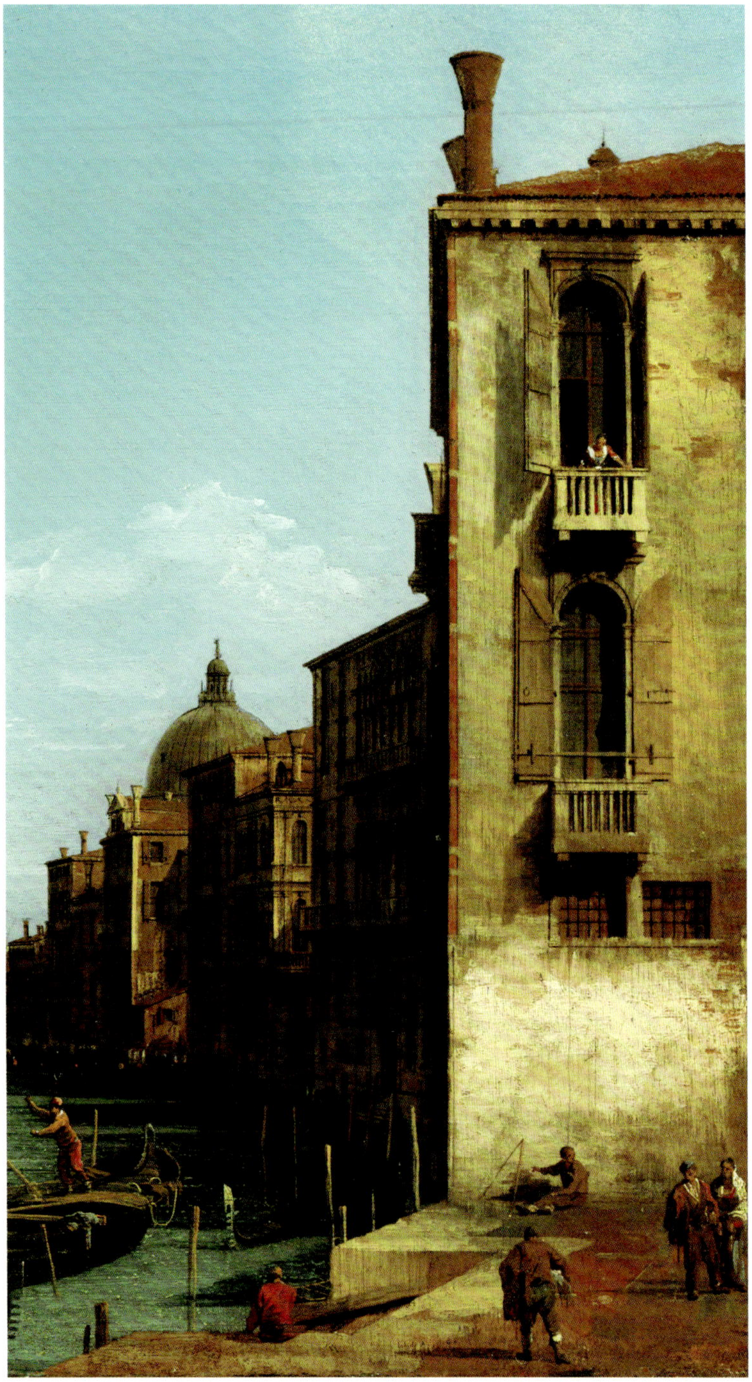

9. Canaletto, *The Grand Canal looking East, from the Palazzo Loredan Cini in Campo San Vio, Venice,* detail, 1728–29, oil on canvas, 49.9 x 80 cm. The Royal Collection, RCIN 400518

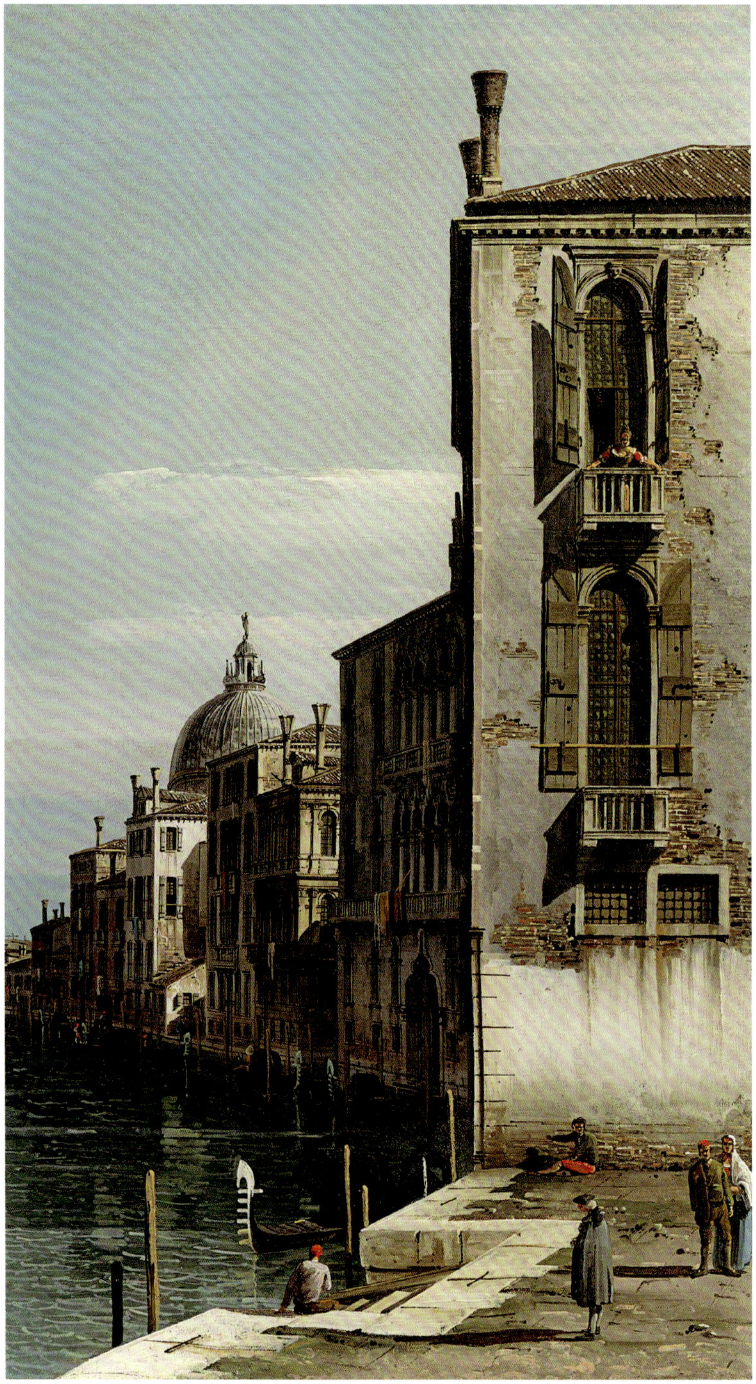

10. Bernardo Bellotto, *The Grand Canal looking East, from the Palazzo Loredan Cini in Campo San Vio, Venice,* detail, ca. 1742, oil on canvas, 61 x 97.5 cm. London, Private Collection (cat. 13)

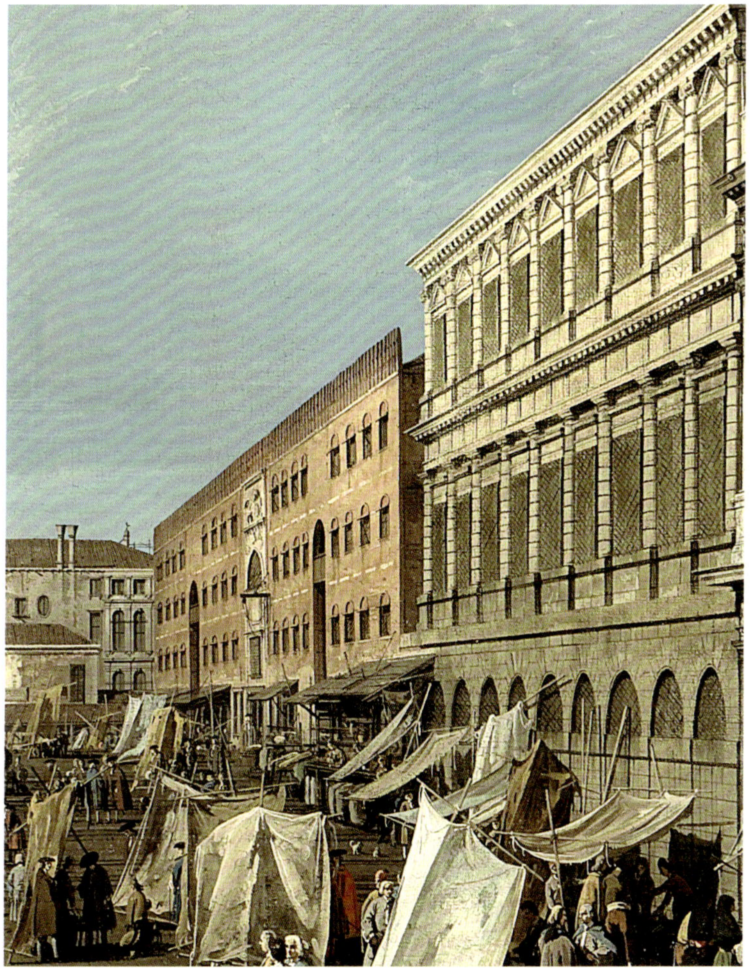

11. Canaletto, *The Molo looking West, the Column of Saint Theodore on the Right, Venice*, detail, ca. 1738, oil on canvas, 110.5 x 185.5 cm. Milan, Raccolta d'Arte Antica, Pinacoteca del Castello Sforzesco, 1474 (cat. 8)

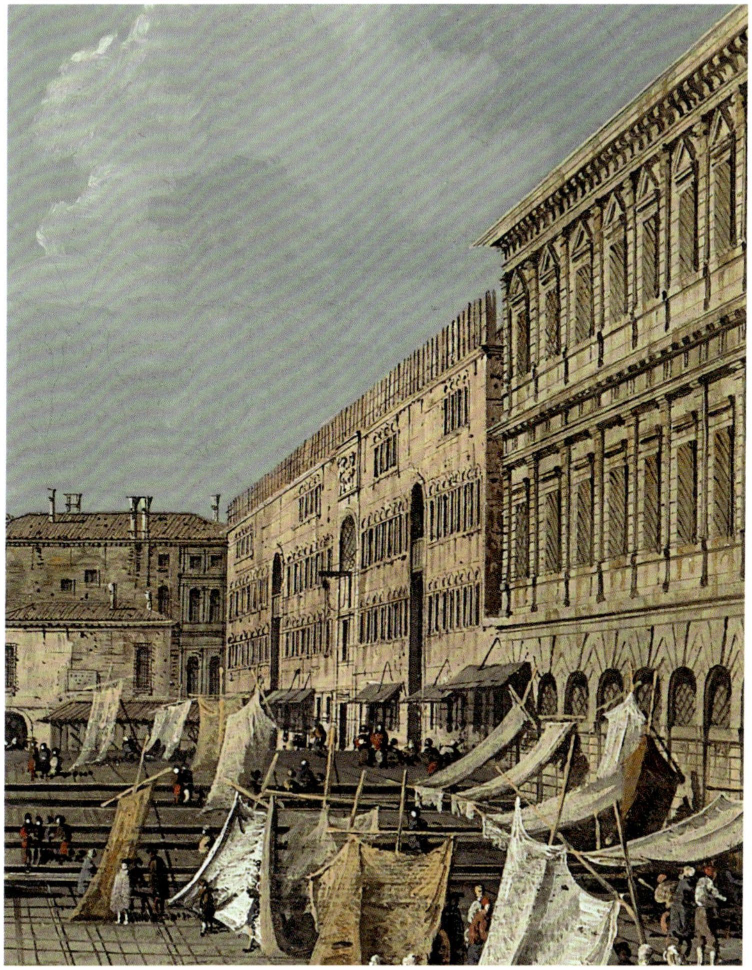

12. Bernardo Bellotto, *The Molo looking West, the Column of Saint Theodore on the Right, Venice*, detail, circa 1739, oil on canvas, 63.5 x 94.2 cm. Madrid, Abelló Collection (cat. 9)

had also happened to another Venetian artist, Giambattista Piranesi (1720–1778). The boldness with which he painted *The Piazza Navona, Rome* (cat. 49) surprises us today, demonstrating an innovative approach to painting for a view painter, namely painting the final part without reliance on a drawing, although his preparatory methods remained those of Canaletto.[32] On that trip, he seems to have purchased a great many books and volumes of prints for his library and documentation, by Etienne Du Pérac, Carlo Fontana, Giovanni Giacomo de Rossi and, above all, Francesco Borromini; he also read Vasari's biographies of Roman architects. He returned to Venice to paint the views of Rome and then departed immediately, in 1744, for Lombardy and then Turin and Verona. It was at this point that his relationship with Canaletto came to an end. George Vertue, an engraver and chronicler of the English art world, seems to have been well informed when, noting the doubts that had arisen as to the identity of the painter who had arrived in London, he reported:

> It seems his name and family was Canali – so he always was called – he had a sister who had a son who having some Genius was instructed by this his uncle Cannali. And this young stripling by

degrees came on forward in his profession being taken notice of for his improvements he was called Cannaleti – the young. But in time getting some degree of merrit. He being puffd up disobliged his Uncle who turned him adrift.[33]

Canaletto in London and then, from 1755, in Venice and Bellotto in Dresden, Vienna and Warsaw were two different painters and comparison of their works makes sense only if carried out in terms of taste. They were both active participants in the European culture of the time and it is not by chance that similar themes appear in their works: the *capriccio*, landscape,[34] theatre. Their training was so profoundly similar that it led them to devise similar perspective and lighting solutions and even – incredibly – the same figure types: elegant couples out on a stroll, soldiers, beggars (fig. 16–19). But in Canaletto's work everything stayed on the decorative, aesthetic plane; it was a sophisticated, sometimes witty, always serene game. Whereas Bellotto sought material and psychological truth. Canaletto reached the height of the refinement of his technique, the clarity of his colours and the sophisticated delicacy of his line between 1752 and 1754, a path begun in the last works that he produced in Venice before leaving for England. *Northumberland House, London* (cat. 67) is a masterpiece that speaks of English civilisation in a noble, aristocratic tone that must have bewitched his patron. During that same period, Bellotto produced lyric descriptions of the architecture, atmosphere and landscape of Dresden and Pirna, studying their actual forms, while his preparatory procedures remained essentially the same as those of Canaletto for his entire career.
The collection of drawings by Bellotto at the Muzeum Narodowe in Warsaw, the extraordinary value of which is not yet fully appreciated – one enthusiastic study, prepared by Juliusz Starzyński when the material was discovered, dates to 1933[35] –, are the most complete evidence of this aspect of his working method. At the same time, these sheets, with their complex perspective studies, which make up the fundamental part of the group, prepared for astounding architectural fantasies, represent Bellotto's more personal developments and the full expression of his interest in representing architecture from a perspectival and scientific point of view that was wholly distant from Canaletto.
This collection of around sixty sheets is dominated by drawings from Bellotto's second period in Dresden, from 1762 to 1765, and are the latest that survive. Forty-three in number, their brusque lines, marked out with a ruler for the architecture, and broken, scratchy lines for the figures show how the artist's drawing style had developed in a direction opposite to that of Canaletto, who in those same years was drawing in the most brilliant and fluid style of his career. Another smaller, but more valuable collection is formed by sketches for the portraits in the foregrounds of the paintings made for Prince Joseph Wenzel Liechtenstein, the *Liechtenstein Palace from the Garden Side*,[36] the *Liechtenstein Palace from the South-East* (Liechtenstein collection),[37] from 1759-60, and a series of small figures drawn with an efficient,

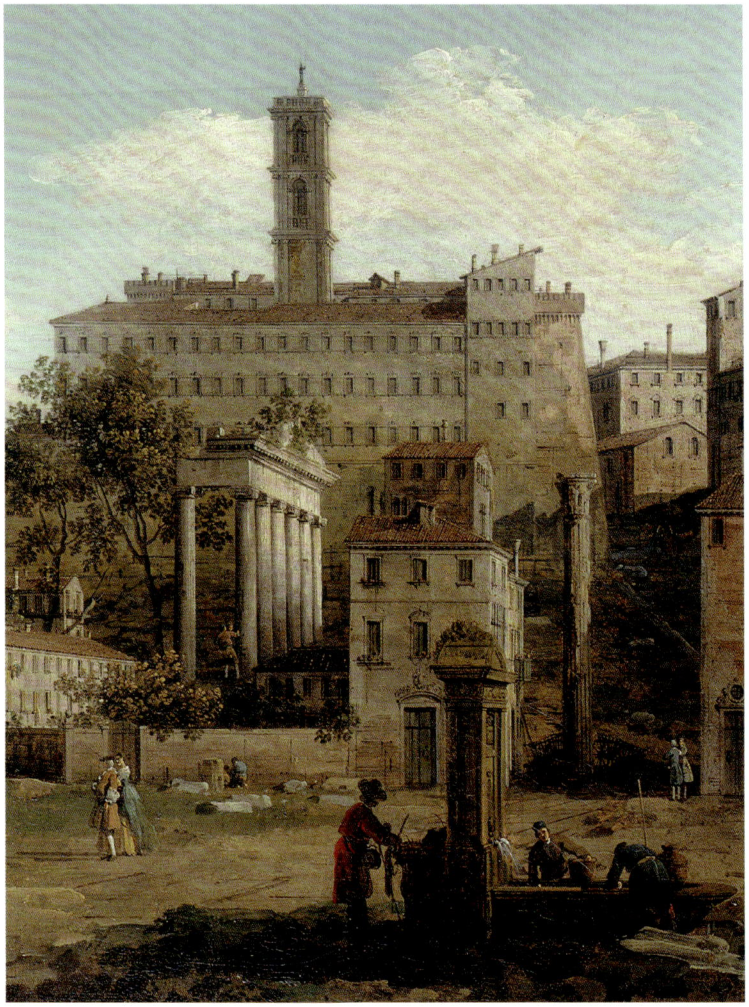

13. Canaletto, *The Roman Forum towards the Capitol with the Temple of Castor and Pollux, Rome*, detail, ca, 1742, oil on canvas, 61.9 x 95.3 cm.
The Royal Collection, RCIN 409047 (cat. 38)

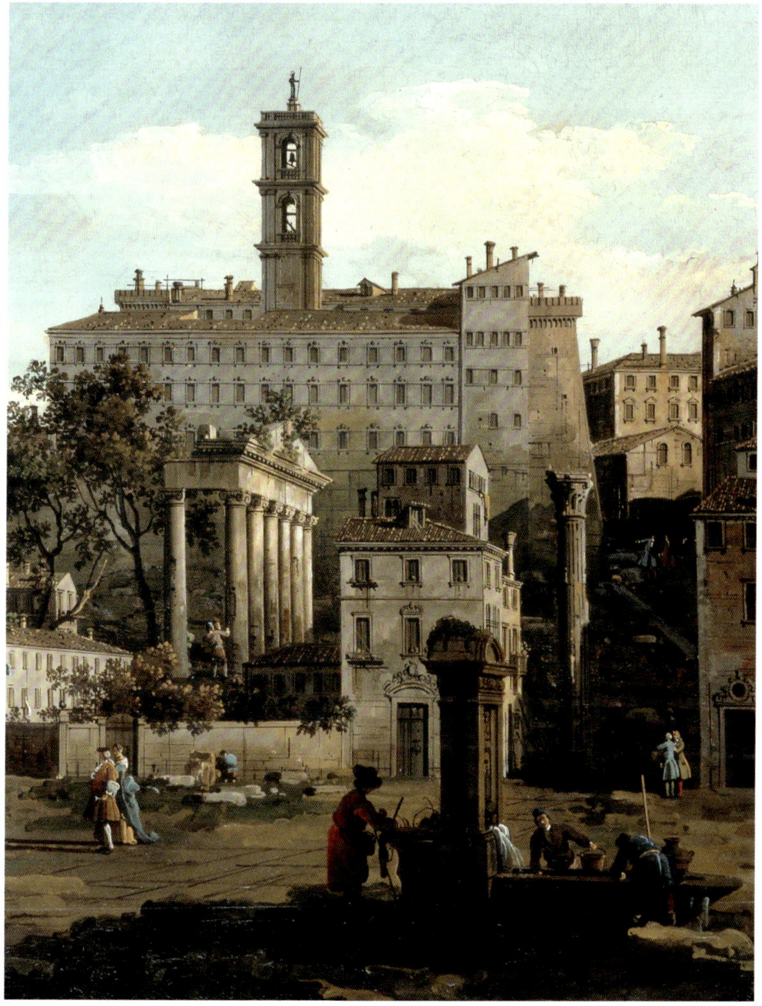

14. Bernardo Bellotto, *The Roman Forum towards the Capitol with the Temple of Castor and Pollux, Rome*, detail, ca. 1742, oil on canvas, 61.5 x 96.5 cm. Private Collection

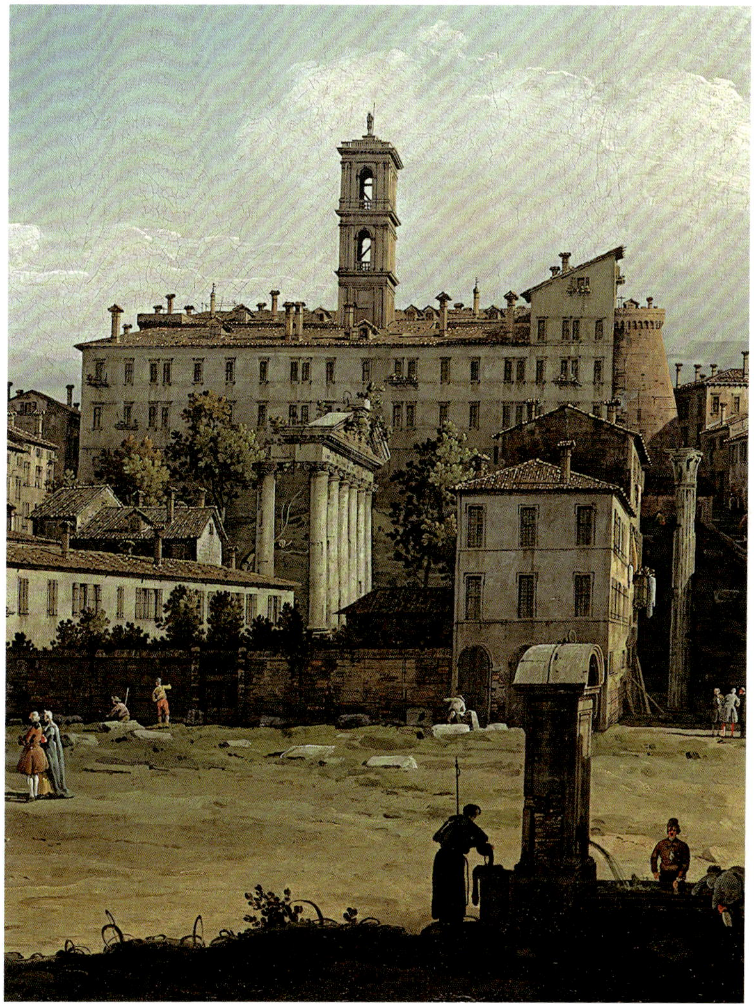

15. Bernardo Bellotto, *The Roman Forum towards the Capitol with the Temple of Castor and Pollux, Rome* detail, 1743, oil on canvas, 87 x 148 cm. Melbourne, National Gallery of Victoria, 964-3 (cat. 40)

light line that appears in the same size in *Vienna from the Belvedere*,[38] the poetry, grace and spirit of which has not yet been given its due. The three Italian sheets in the collection are extremely important compositional sketches, two of which are on view in this exhibition: *Santa Maria d'Aracoeli and the Capitol, Rome* (cat. 44) and *Vaprio and Canonica on the Adda, looking North-West, Lombardy* (cat. 58). Another group comprises figures studies drawn from paintings by Antoine Watteau and reproductive prints of his works.

The Warsaw drawings are the part of the artist's possessions that his relatives in Vilnius sold, together with the *Catalogo de Danni* (cat. 83), probably between 1822 and 1828, to Earl Konstanty Tyszkiewicz (1806–1868), who was a student at the university in the Lithuanian capital at the time. It seems that the Polish nobleman, who later became a distinguished archaeologist, ethnographer and historian, selected works according to his own interests, choosing mostly drawings with elements of classical architecture. Another part of

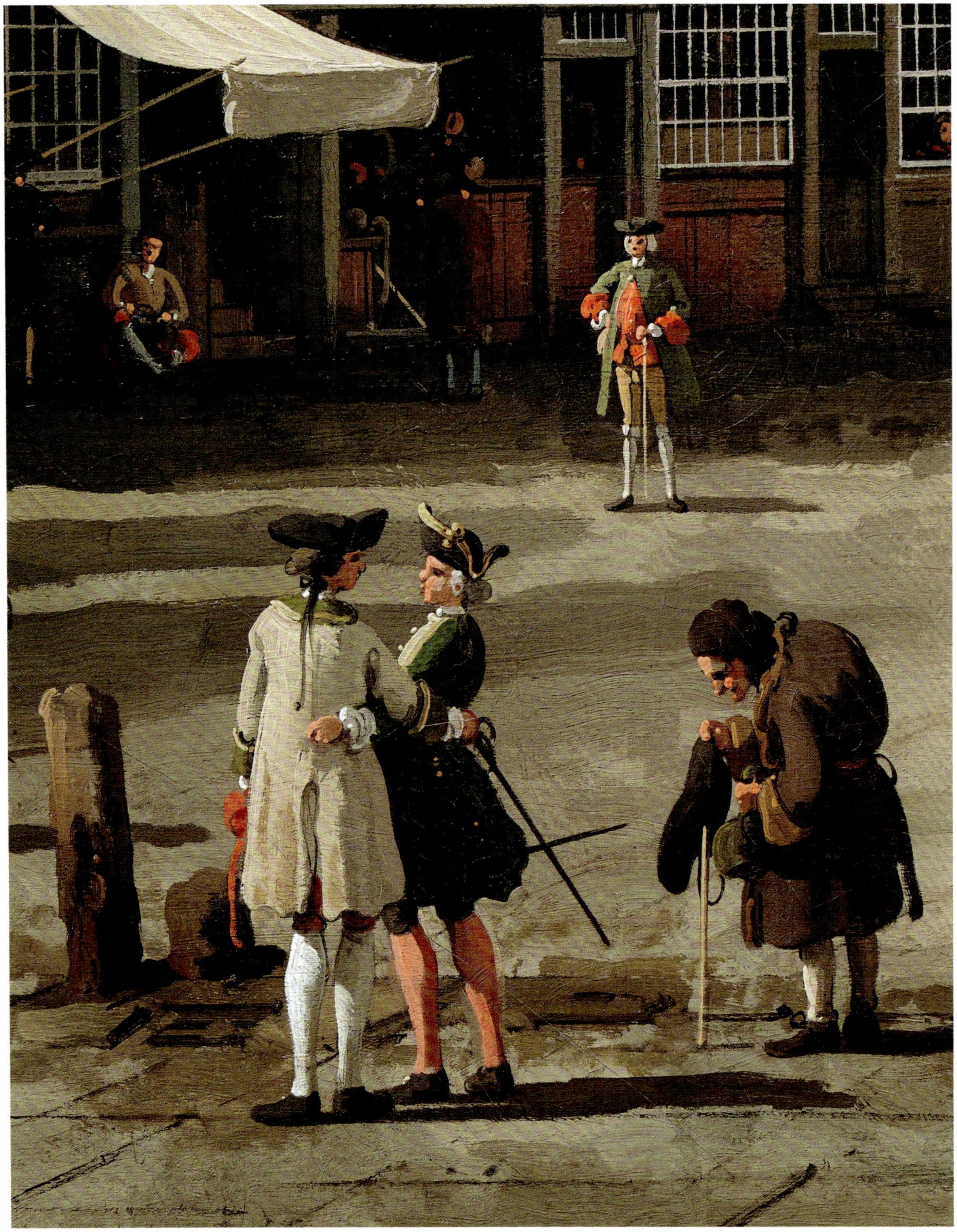

16. Canaletto, *Northumberland House, London*, detail, 1752–53, oil on canvas, 84 x 137 cm. Alnwick Castle, The Duke of Northumberland Collection, 03336 (cat. 67)

17. Canaletto, *Northumberland House, London*, detail, 1752–53, oil on canvas, 84 x 137 cm. Alnwick Castle, The Duke of Northumberland Collection, 03336 (cat. 67)

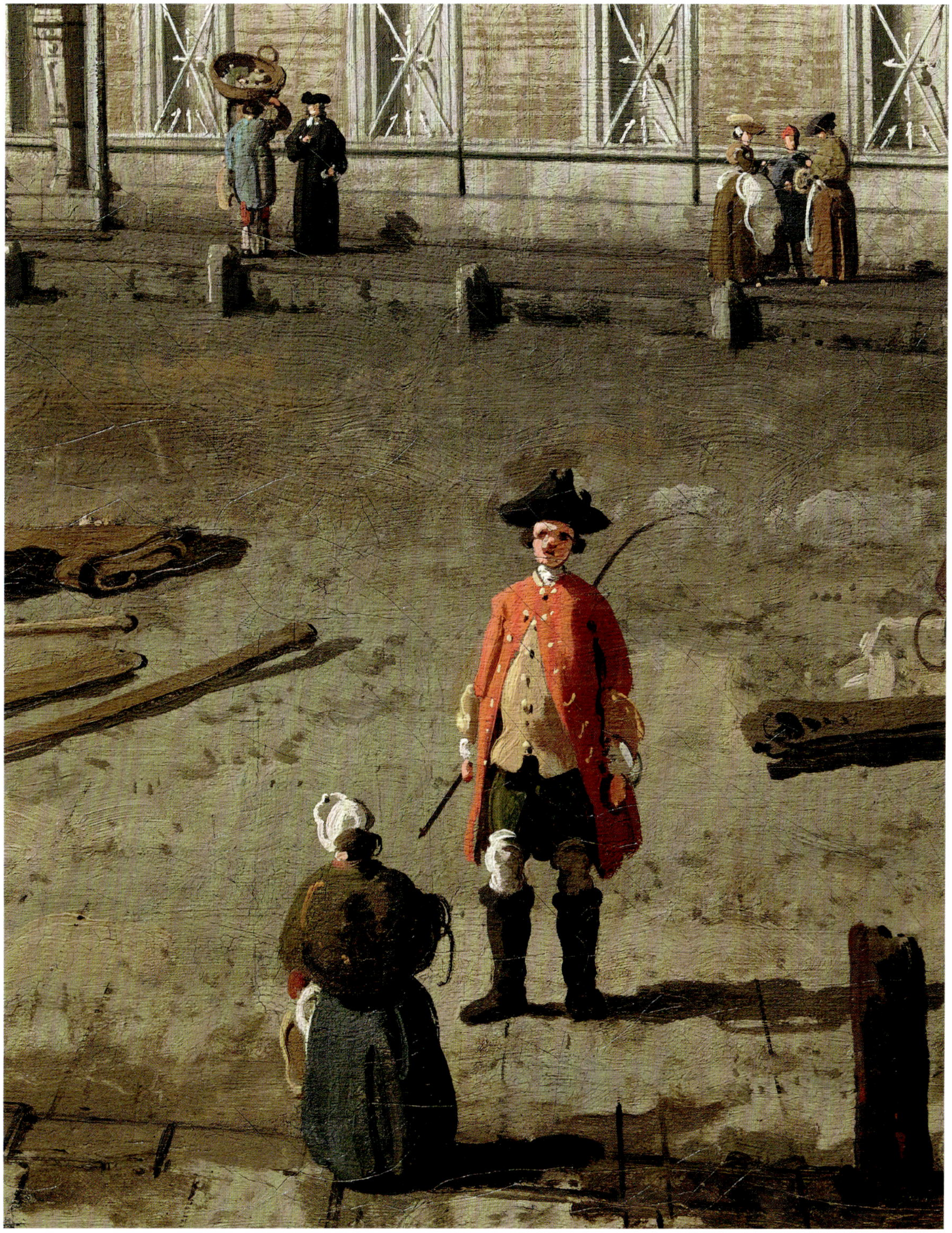

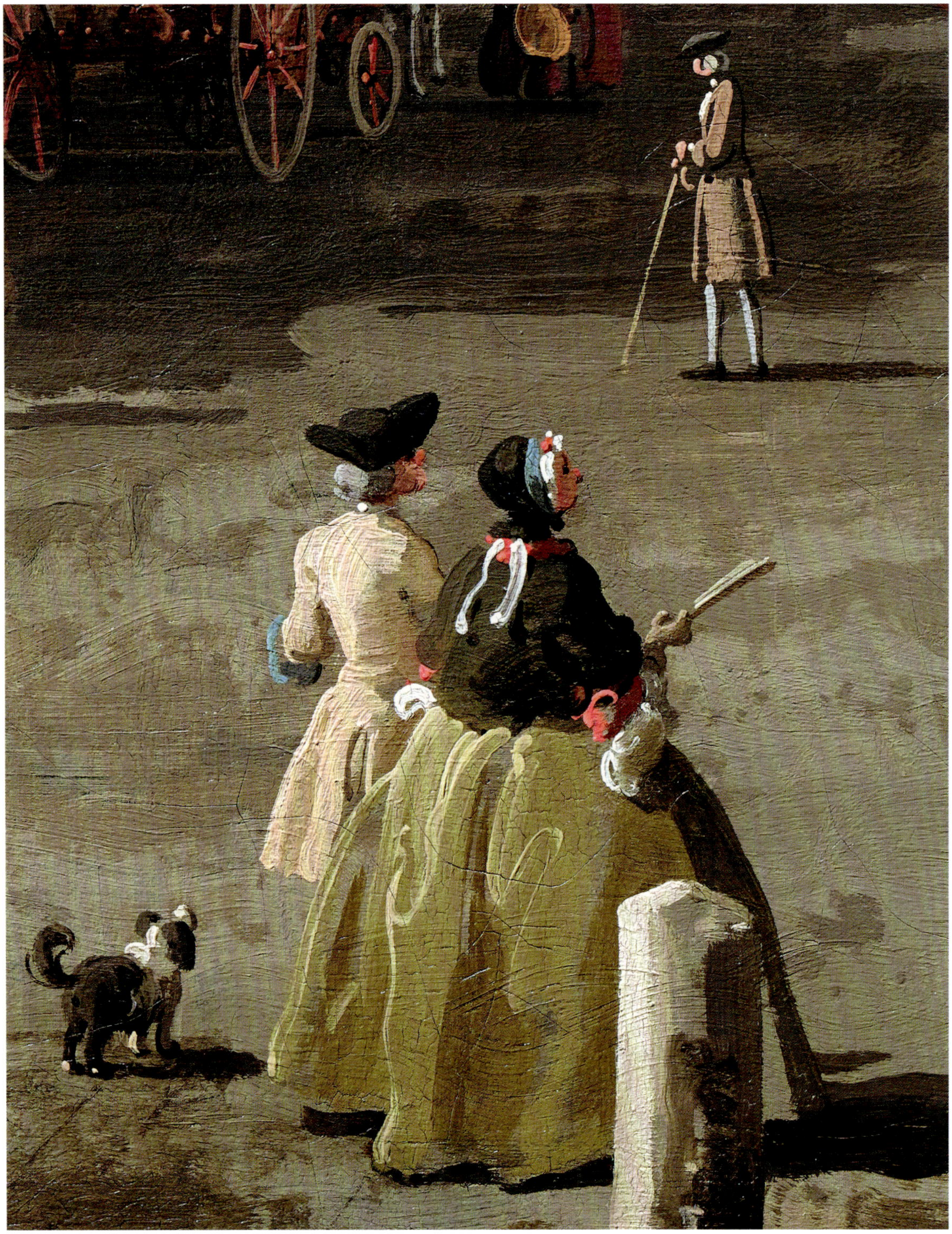

18. Canaletto, *Northumberland House, London*, detail, 1752–53, oil on canvas, 84 x 137 cm. Alnwick Castle, The Duke of Northumberland Collection, 03336 (cat. 67)

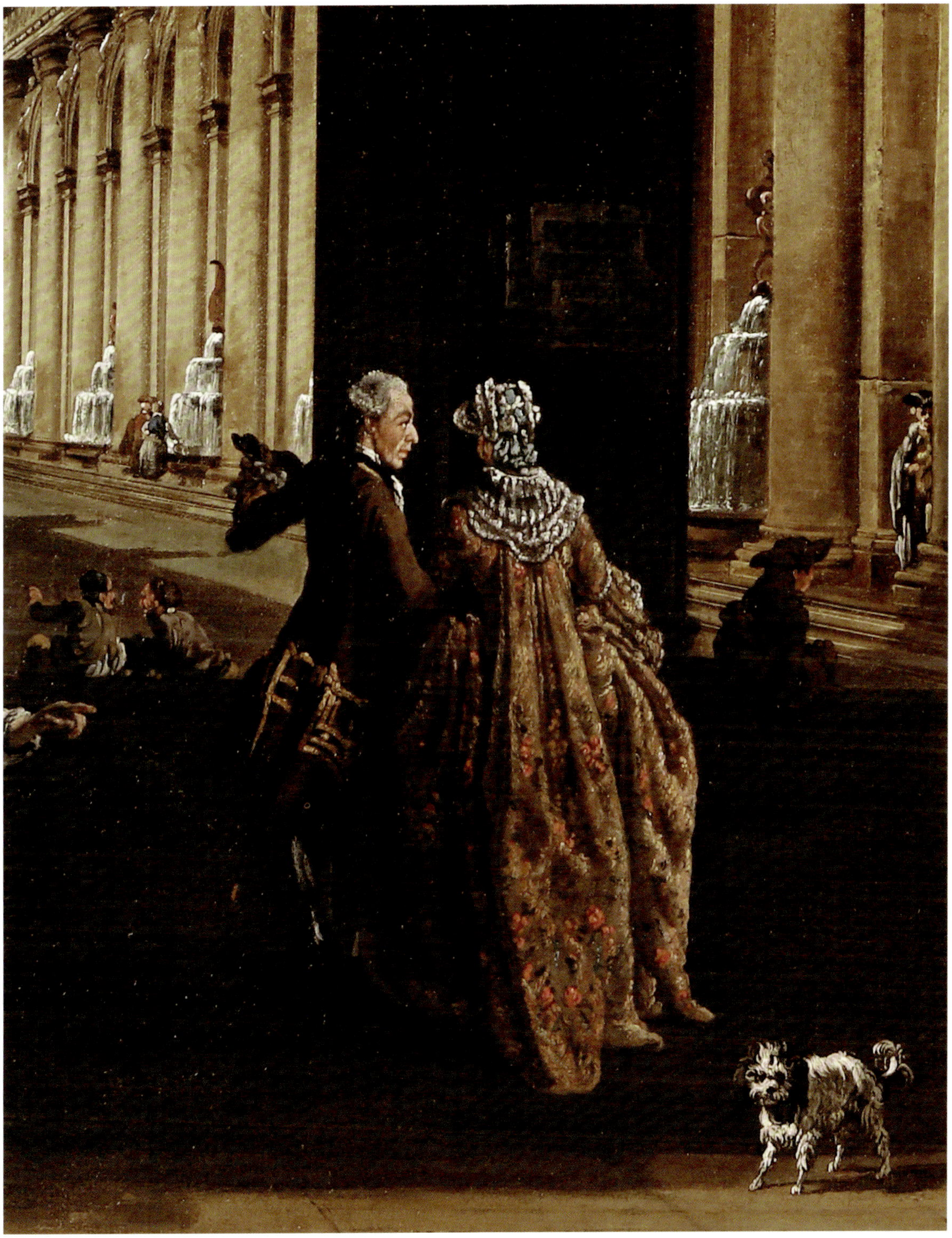

19. Bernardo Bellotto, *Architectural Capriccio with Self-Portrait*, detail, 1764–65, oil on canvas; 156.2 x 112.4 cm. Kingston (Ontario), Agnes Etherington Art Centre - Queen's University (cat. 82)

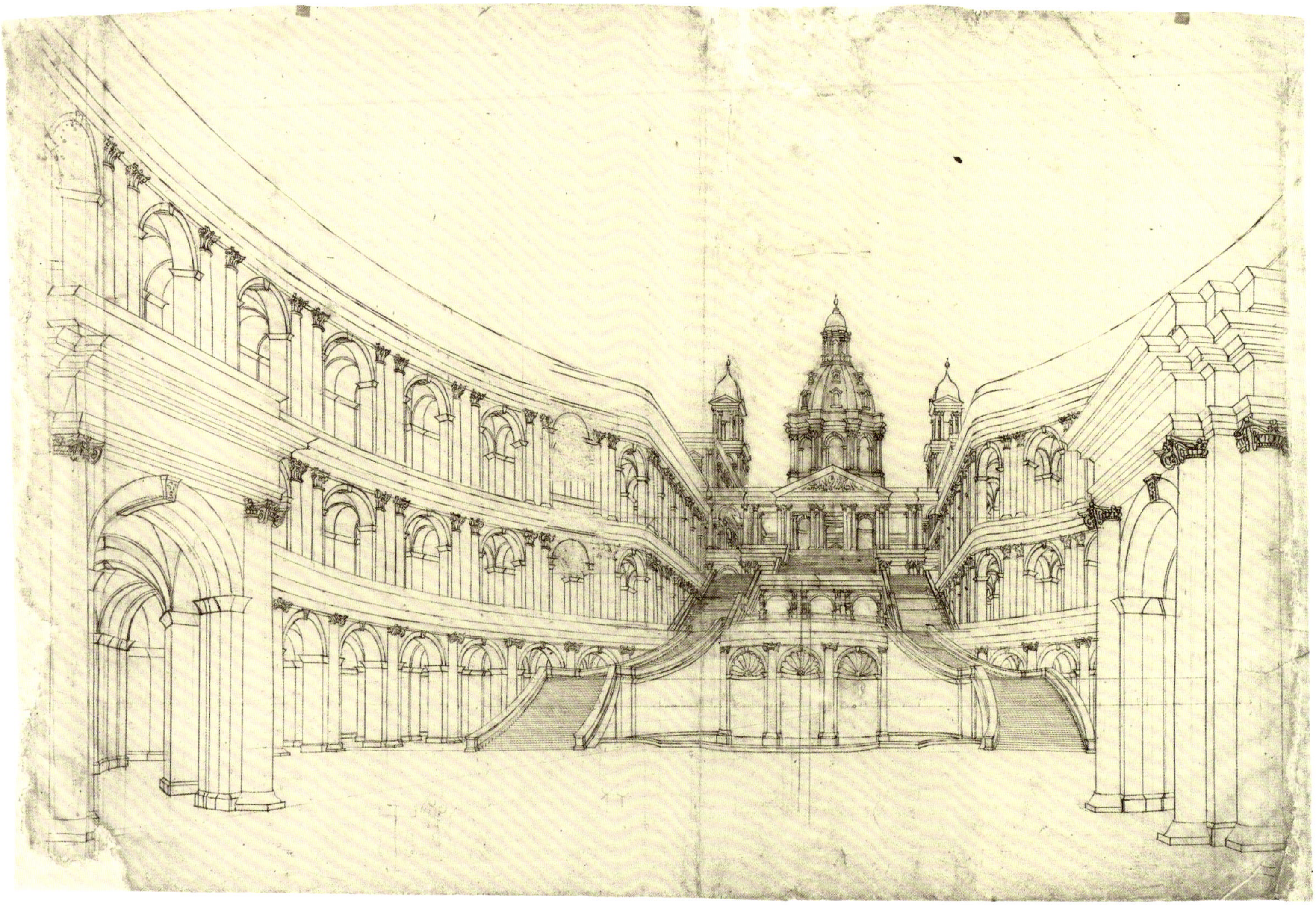

20. Bernardo Bellotto, *Fantasy View with a Domed Church and Porticoes (Temple of Love?)*, 1762–64, pen and brown ink, pen and brown ink over pencil line, freehand and with a ruler, marked with a compass, 437 x 630 mm. Warsaw, Muzeum Narodowe, Rys. Pol. 2070

Bellotto's personal collection, purchased by a professor at the same university, Ludwig Heinrich Bojanus, and added to the collection of the Hessisches Landesmuseum in Darmstadt in 1829, comprises Italian studies and *capricci*, none with figures, and a few architectural fantasies.

Bellotto organised his sketches by genre, and the drawings purchased by Earl Tyszkiewicz are grouped around a few specific paintings. This was done by someone who knew the artist's work, probably his son-in-law, Karol de Perthées (1740–1815), a great geographer and cartographer at the court of Stanisław II August Poniatowski. Made a noble by the king, after his death he moved with his family to Vilnius, where he taught at the university.

It is therefore possible to trace Bellotto's preparation of his complex compositions, which in that period were exclusively *capricci*, even though the surviving sketches never represent the complete work: highly detailed drawings of the whole, without figures; the

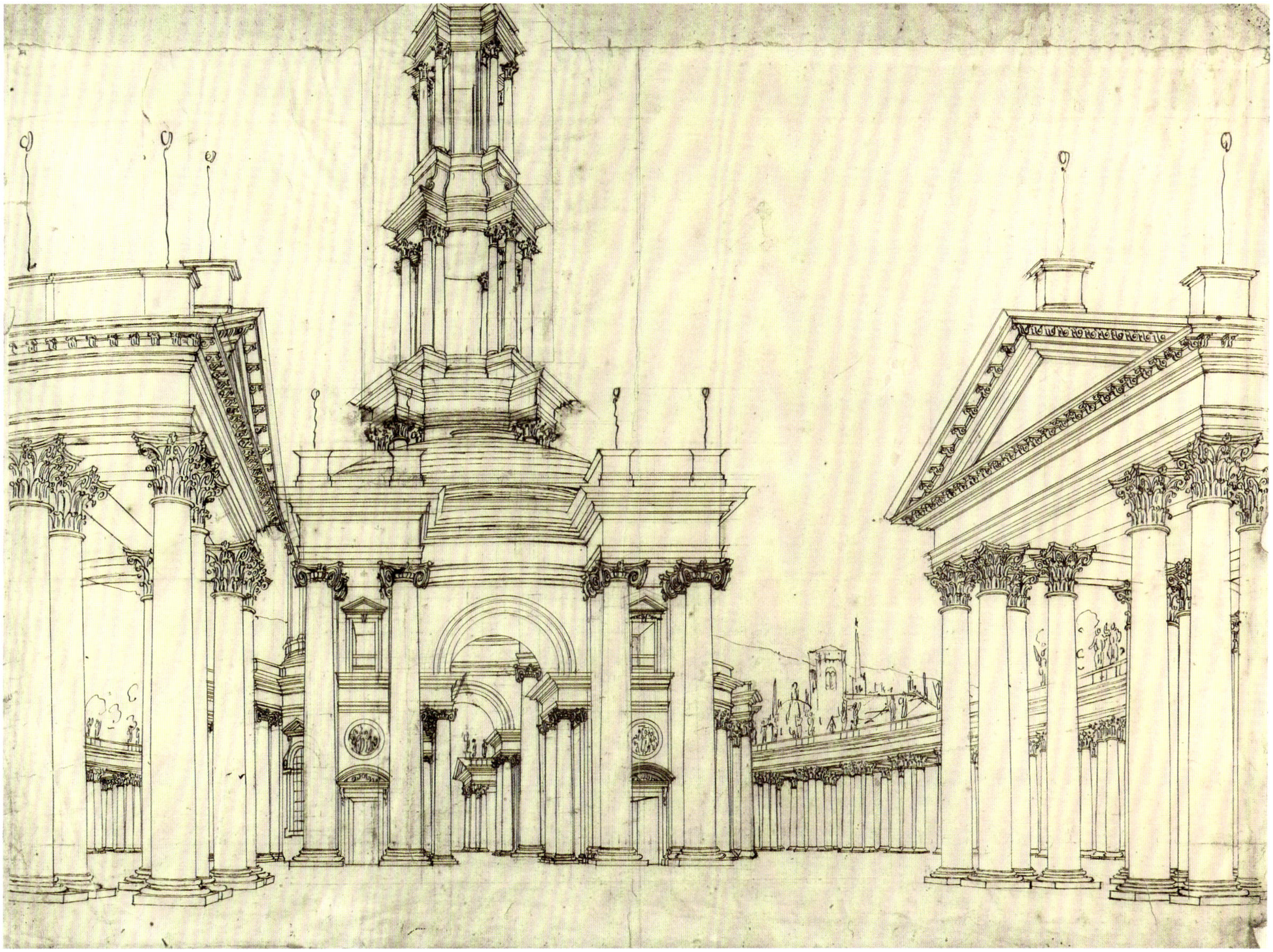

21. *Fantasy View with a Tower Structure and Porticoes (Temple of Venus?)*, 1762–ca. 1764, pen and brown ink, 468 x 649 mm. Darmstadt, Hessisches Landesmseum, AE 2178

same drawings but with small figures and statues already in places; separate figure studies that correspond with the ones planned but on a larger scale, the size they would be in the painting. The *Two Polish Hussars* (cat. 85) and the *Two Balkan Hajduks* (cat. 86) are, together with similar studies in the collection, examples of the meticulousness with which Bellotto included every detail of the costumes and hats, fixing the poses and facial expressions, noting the colours and all of the details which he then repeated faithfully in the paintings. He used the same figures in multiple canvases, but in different sizes, even reduced to half-size, as in the case of the *Two Balkan Hajduks*, who initially appeared in a *capriccio* of the Royal Gallery of Dresden from 1762 and were then

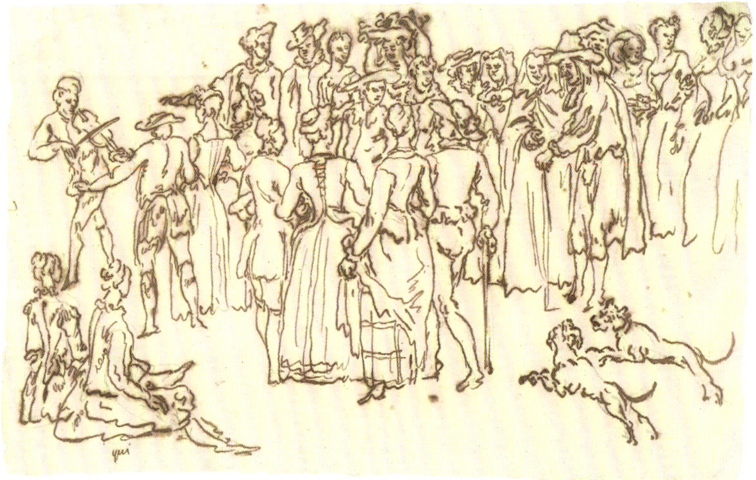

22. Bernardo Bellotto, *Figure Studies*, 1762–1764, pen and brown ink, 210 x 345 mm. Warsaw, Muzeum Narodowe, Rys. Pol. 2088

used in the *Architectural Capriccio* in the Kunsthalle of Hamburg from the same date (cf. cat. 85-86).

The collection includes a few remarkable large perspective studies, of the whole and projections of domes and colonnades, complete with precise written measurements that specify the various architectural elements.[39] Bellotto's library included the volume *Perspectiva Pictorum et Architettorum* by Andrea Pozzo, whose lesson he followed. These drawings were considered academic studies, without a precise aim, and perhaps useful for teaching at the Fine Arts Academy of Dresden, where the artist was appointed professor of perspective in 1764. Among the paintings by Bellotto that have not yet been found, every catalogue of the artist's work cites two in particular, with surprising titles far removed from the world of Canaletto, that were presented in March 1765, together with a version of the *Architectural Capriccio with Self-Portrait* (cat. 82) and *The Expulsion of the Money Changers from the Temple*, at an exhibition at the Academy of Fine Arts in Dresden.[40] One 'represented the Temple of Venus filled with statues of the various divinities. The pediment had a bas-relief of the Judgment of Paris. At the entrance of the temple were the priest welcoming the happy lovers, bringing with them a sacrificial victim'. The other was a 'Temple of Love, with a vast courtyard, surrounded by a colonnade, through the arch of which you could see the sacred pyre. This temple was also decorated with all of the figures of the gods. The bas-relief on the tympanum was of the chariot of Cupid, which was drawn by gods in chains. In the midst of allegories of the various nations were the self-portrait of the artist and portraits of a few quite well known personages'.[41] Both were quite large, 168 x 280 cm.

The drawings at the Museum of Warsaw include one of Bellotto's complex architectural studies (the two preparatory sheets for which include the precise measurements and projections for every structural element of the composition), *Fantasy View with a Domed Church and Porticoes* (fig. 20),[42] which matches the description of the setting for the *Temple of Love*; the structure of the temple recalls that of Sant'Agnese in Agone by Francesco Borromini, who seems to be the architect whom Bellotto admired above all others. A preparatory drawing for the pendant is at the Hessisches Landesmuseum in Darmstadt, an imposing, majestic composition with temples and colonnades.[43] I believe that the series of studies of Antoine Watteau must have been used for the figures of the large compositions (fig. 22). And yet, by signing himself during that period in Dresden 'Bernardo Bellotto de Canaletto' – perceiving the nobility added by his uncle's name – and citing a much earlier painting – *The Piazzetta, looking North, Venice*,[44] – in his *Architectural Capriccio with Self-Portrait* (cat. 82), Bellotto stressed his artistic link to Canaletto and a sense of nostalgia and memory.

Special thanks go to Piotr Kibort for his kind help in the vision and study of drawings from the Muzeum Narodowe in Warsaw, and for having put the images published in this essay at our disposal.

[1] For the archival documents pertinent to Bellotto and his family, beginning with his birth certificate, see several of my own publications: B.A. Kowalczyk, 'Il Bellotto veneziano nei documenti', *Arte Veneta*, 47, 1995, pp. 68–77; B.A. Kowalczyk, 'I primi sostenitori veneziani di Bernardo Bellotto', *Saggi e Memorie di Storia dell'Arte*, 23, 1999, pp. 198–218; B.A. Kowalczyk, '"Le origini veneziane di Pietro Bellotti", *Arte Veneta*', 59, 2002, pp. 268–269. Also see G. Marini, 'Con la propria industria e sua professione' Nuovi documenti sulla giovinezza di Bellotto, *Verona illustrata*, VI, 1993, pp. 125–140.

[2] W.G. Constable, *Canaletto. Giovanni Antonio Canal 1697-1768*, 2nd ed. revised by J.G. Links reissued with supplement and additional plates, Oxford 1989, vol. I, plate 94; vol. II, pp. 469–470, no. 516.

[3] Constable, *Canaletto*, op. cit., vol. I, plate 94; vol. II, p. 470, no. 517 .

[4] *Lettere artistiche del Settecento veneziano*, 4, *Owen McSwiny's letters 1720-1744*, edited by T.D. Llewellyn, Verona (Scripta), 2009, p. 67.

[5] For the more recent literature on Canaletto, see my exhibition catalogues, *Canaletto et Guardi. Les deux maîtres de Venise* (Paris, Musée Jacquemart-André), Brussels (Fonds Mercator), 2012; *Canaletto. Canaletto. Rome, Londres, Venise Le triomphe de la lumière* (Aix-en-Provence, Hôtel de Caumont), Brussels (Fonds Mercator), 2015.
[6] Constable, *Canaletto*, op. cit., no. 1, 182, 210, 290; B.A. Kowalczyk, in *Canaletto prima maniera*, exhibition catalogue, ed. B.A. Kowalczyk, with the collaboration of C. Ceschi and S. Guerriero (Venice, Fondazione Giorgio Cini), Milan (Electa), 2001, pp. 128–129.
[7] S. Kozakiewicz, *Bernardo Bellotto*, Milan (Görlich Editore), 1972, pp. 212 and 219, nos. 271 and 277.
[8] On the early Canaletto, see the collection of letters edited by M. Magrini in *Canaletto prima maniera*, op. cit., pp. 227–245.
[9] E. Manikowska, 'The rediscovery of Bernardo Bellotto's inventory', The Burlington Magazine, CLIV, 2012, January, pp. 32–36; E. Manikowska, *Bernardo Bellotto i jego drezdeński apartament. O tożsamości społecznej i artystycznej weneckiego wedutysty*, Warszawa, Instytut Sztuki Pan, 2014. See the essay in the present volume by S. Marinelli and cat. 83.
[10] M. Magrini, in *Canaletto prima maniera*, op. cit., p. 238, no. 34
[11] M. Magrini, in *Canaletto prima maniera*, op. cit., p. 239, no. 36.
[12] M. Magrini, in *Canaletto prima maniera*, op. cit., p. 244, no. 47; the letter was sent from Milan on 27 September 1730 to John Conduit.
[13] M. Magrini, in *Canaletto prima maniera*, op. cit., p. 239-243, nos. 35–40, 42–44.
[14] A.M. Zanetti, *Della pittura veneziana e delle opere pubbliche de' veneziani maestri*, Stamperia di Giambattista Albrizzi, Venezia 1771, Libro V, p. 462.
[15] M. Magrini, in *Canaletto prima maniera*, op. cit., p. 238, no. 34
[16] Regarding the date of birth of grandfather Bernardo Canal, unknown until present, Domenico Crivellari (to whom goes all my gratitude) has forwarded the following document to me: 'Bernardino Nicolò di Cesare Cristoforo Canal e della signora Elena sposi nato il 17 settembre 1673 al quale fu data l'acqua in casa, conforme agli esorcismi il N.H. Girolamo Querini fu de Francesco della nostra città, battezzò il Pievano' (Archivio Storico del Patriarcato di Venezia, Santa Maria Formosa Parish Church, *Registry of Baptisms*, 8, 2 March 1672–31 December 1693, dated 29 April 1675). For the date of birth of Michiel (Michele), see B.A. Kowalczyk, *Il Bellotto veneziano*, op. cit., pp. 68-69 and p. 76, *Appendice documentaria*, no. 2; for the date of his death, see E. Boffa, 'La stampa delle opere del Muratori (1767–1780) per Michele Bellotti stampatore vescovile', *Annali Aretini*, XXI (2013), Edizioni Fraternità dei Laici Arezzo, p. 143, note 6. The *Death Register* of the Arezzo Brotherhood of Laypersons gives the date of 21 November 1778: 'Michele fu Lorenzo Bellotti di Rovigo abitante in Arezzo sepolto in Pieve' (Michele, son of the late Lorenzo Bellotti of Rovigo, resident of Arezzo, buried in the parish church) (Reg. 897, c. 232v). The mention of Rovigo, misleading for Aretino historians who did not associate their printer with the Venetian painter, probably referred to their father Lorenzo, who had abandoned the family and Venice in around 1725.
[17] Archivio di Stato di Arezzo, *Tassa Macinato, 65, Trascrizioni Bocche*, Year 1749, c. 80.
[18] B.A. Kowalczyk, *Il Bellotto veneziano*, op. cit., p. 69.
[19] R. Longhi, *Viatico per cinque secoli della pittura veneziana*, Florence (Sansoni), 1946, p. 37.
[20] A.M. Zanetti, *Della pittura veneziana*, op. cit., p. 463.
[21] B.A. Kowalczyk, 'Canaletto e i disegni per Joseph Smith a Windsor Castle', in *Canaletto: il trionfo della veduta*, op. cit., pp. 31–39; also see, *Canaletto in Venice*, exhibition catalogue, ed. M. Clayton (London, Queen's Gallery; Edinburgh, Queen's Gallery, Palace of Holyroodhouse), London 2005.
[22] See cat. 83.
[23] S. Kozakiewicz, *Bernardo Bellotto*, op. cit., vol. I, pp. 23, 25; vol. II, p. 88, no. 117.
[24] The album of prints was published by Giambattista Pasquali at an unspecified date, but it was certainly after Smith's appointment to the post of British Consul on 6 June 1744, to whom it is dedicated. For the history of the dating of the edition of etchings up to 1950, see F. Montecuccoli degli Erri, *Canaletto incisore*, Venice 2002.
[25] The story of the nickname 'Canaletto' is complicated. In the 1720s, Canaletto signed with the name 'Canale' but in Zanetti and McSwiny's letters (see notes 8, 10–13) he is referred to as 'Canaletto', the name used to designate the artist in all subsequent documents. It is a typically Venetian diminutive, like 'Tiepoletto', perhaps used to distinguish him from his father. The artist continued to sign his works and invoices with the name 'Canal', then, towards the late 1740s he began to use 'de Canal' and add 'detto il Canaletto'. Very rarely, he signed his name 'Antonio Canaleto'. The fact that Bellotto, from very early on, used the same nickname – which today makes us think of usurpation – was completely natural in that family of painters.
[26] M. Magrini, in *Canaletto prima maniera*, op. cit., p. 230, no. 10 (letter by Alessandro Marchesin from Venice to Stefano Conti in Lucca, 6 October 1725)
[27] G. Zanetti, 'Memorie', *Archivio Veneto* XV, 1885, XXIX, p. 97.
[28] G. Marini, 'Il fiume e il castello. Precisazioni sul viaggio romano del Bellotto', *Artibus et Historiae*, 24, 1991, pp. 147-163.
[29] W.G. Constable, *Canaletto*, op. cit., vol. I, plates 70–72; vol. II, pp. 386, 389–392 and 394, no. 378, 382, 384, 386, 390.
[30] P. Orlandi and P. Guarienti, *Abecedario pittorico del M.R.P. Pellegrino Antonio Orlandi… corretto e notabilmente accresciuto da Pietro Guarienti*, Venice 1753, p. 101.
[31] See E. P. Bowron, in *Bernardo Bellotton 1722-1780*, exhibition catalogue, eds. B.A. Kowalczyk and M. Da Cortà Fumei (Venice, Museo Correr), Milan (Electa), 2001, p. 106.
[32] The technical investigation of the two artists' works is still at a preliminary stage and an overall vision is not yet available for comparison. See entry nos. 15, 40, 49, 53, 56-57, 59-61, 74, 94-95 in the present catalogue.
[33] G. Vertue, *Note Books*, Mss., London, British Library; published by Walpole Society, in six volumes. References to Canaletto can be found in Add. MSS. 23079 and 23074, The Walpole Society, XXII, *Vertue Note Books*, III, London-Oxford 1933-1934; the 1749 announcement is mentioned on p. 151.
[34] Canaletto's most notable achievement in the field of landscape painting should be noted here: the two paintings formerly in the Lovelace collection and now at the National Gallery of Art, Washington; W.G. Constable, *Canaletto*, op. cit., vol. I, plate 87; vol. II, pp. 445–446, nos. 473 and 474.
[35] J. Starzyński, Rysunki Canaletta w Warszawskiem Muzeum Narodowem', Biuletyn Historji Sztuki i Kultury, II, 1933-34, pp. 99–111.
[36] S. Kozakiewicz, *Bernardo Bellotto*, op. cit., vol. II, p. 212, no. 271.
[37] S. Kozakiewicz, *Bernardo Bellotto*, op. cit., vol. II, p. 219, no. 277.
[38] S. Kozakiewicz, *Bernardo Bellotto*, op. cit, vol. II, pp.193–194, no. 248.
[39] S. Kozakiewicz, *Bernardo Bellotto*, op. cit., pp. 275–276, nos. 342, 343 A-B, 344 and 345 A-B.
[40] H. Fritzsche, *Bernardo Belotto genannt Canaletto*, Burg bei Magdeburg 1936, pp. 126–127, nos. 200 and 201; S. Kozakiewicz, *Bernardo Bellotto*, op. cit, pp. 284, 287, nos. 360 and 361; A. Rizzi, *Bernardo Bellotto. Dresda, Vienna, Monaco*, Venice (Canal & Stamperia Editrice), p. 231, nos. P 4 and P 5.
[41] *Bibliothek der schönen Wissenschaften*, 1765, p. 369.
[42] S. Kozakiewicz, *Bernardo Bellotto*, op. cit., vol. II, p. 275, nos. 342 and 343 A and B.
[43] S. Kozakiewicz, *Bernardo Bellotto*, op. cit., vol. II, p. 276, no. 344.
[44] W.G. Constable, J.G. Links, *Canaletto*, op. cit., vol. I, plate 24; vol. II, pp. 216–217, no. 63.

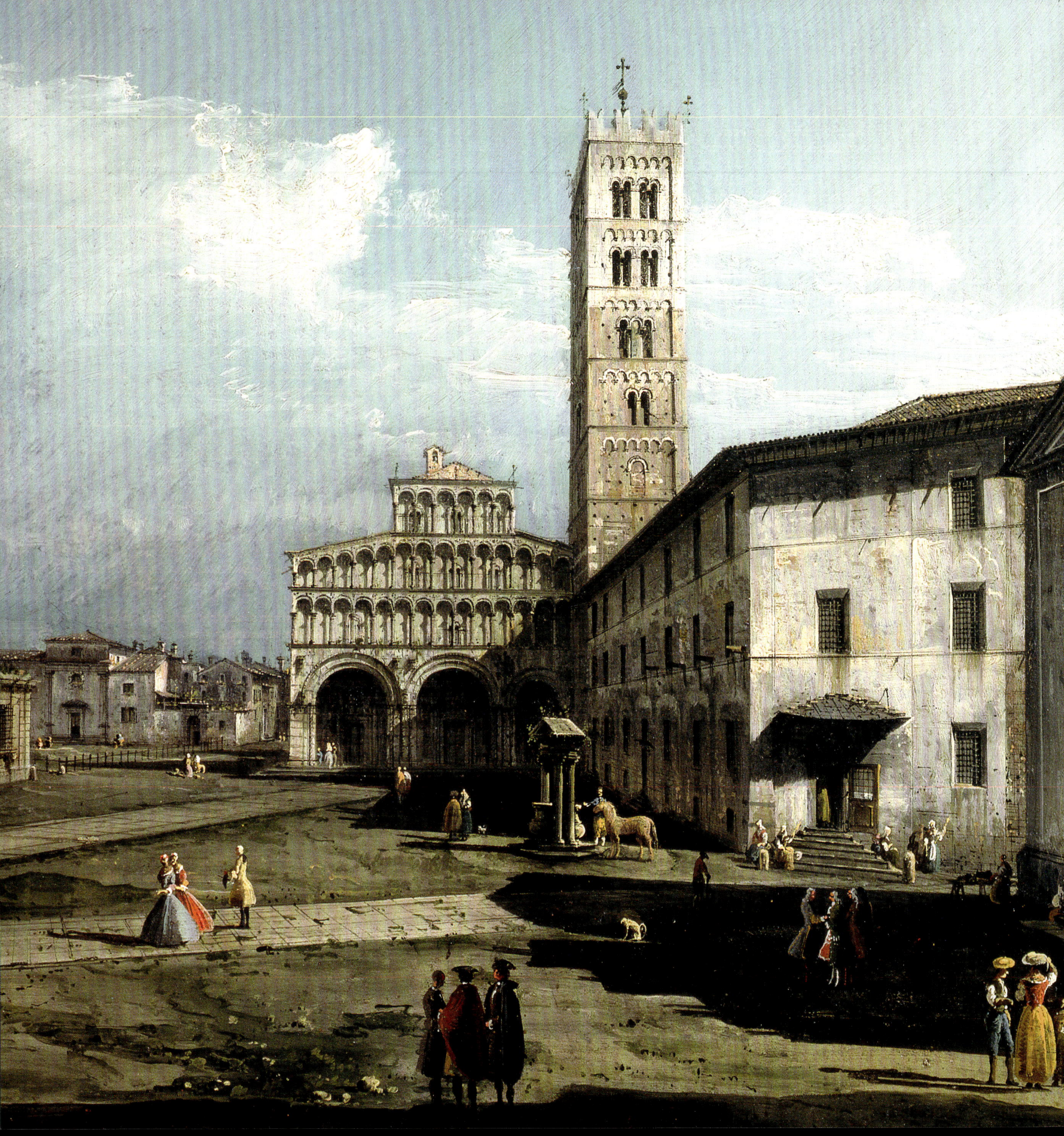

BLACK LIGHTS OF THE ENLIGHTENMENT'S PAINTER

SERGIO MARINELLI

A bizarre, unpredictable twist of fate revealed, more than two and a half centuries after its destruction, the astonishing substance of the library and painting collection of Bernardo Bellotto, left in boxes with his neighbours in Dresden and destroyed in 1760 when his home was levelled by the Prussians – the painter luckily already safe in Vienna. It has already been noted that his two paintings of the ruins after the bombing of Dresden are, in the context of view paintings, the first *Desastres de la guerra*, forty years before Goya's engravings, and even more moving and engaging for Bellotto, considering that they represented the destruction of his home and, as he well knew, his books, paintings, mirrors and more. The reason behind the inventory's release in 1762 was to recoup his losses, estimated to amount to the significant sum of 50,000 thalers.

Bernardo[1] always meant business. And his library was no exception.[2] He even had a copy of the *Conseils pour former une Bibliotheque peu Nombreuse mais Choisie*, 'par Formey' (Berlin 1755). But his library cannot be trivialised on the basis of how-to manuals: as far as we can tell, it was already nearly complete by that date, 1755. Looking through the astounding inventory of lost books, one might inevitably object that Bernardo was also a book dealer. But the publication dates for the volumes, almost always indicated, are always different and the titles create a cultural mosaic at first disconcerting but on final analysis quite coherent and consistent.

The coincidence that Bernardo's older brother was an episcopal printer in Arezzo, printing exclusively devotional works and religious content, would seem to have had a relative and possibly minimal impact.[3] The only text that we know with certainty had a provenance in his brother's printery is the complete works of abbot Giovanni Claudio Pasquini, the *Opere* (1751). The eighty copies that Michele sent to be sold in Dresden were clearly inventoried separately (unlike the single copy listed in the library) in the printery room, where they, too, perished in the flames. In reality, since Pasquini had been a poet at the Vienna court and so in Dresden, we can suppose that the complete edition of his works, which he himself very much desired, was printed by Michele on Bernardo's request, with a dedication to the minister Brühl, who was a great champion of the Venetian artist and was perhaps also asked to finance the endeavour. Bernardo was by that point especially involved in this dedication. Some of the texts in the library concerned, perhaps not coincidentally, authors connected to the abbot's theatrical reworkings (Cervantes, Molière) or with whom he had collaborated directly (Zeno, Metastasio).

Bernardo Bellotto, *The Piazza San Martino with the Cathedral, Lucca*, 1740, detail, oil on canvas, 50,8 x 72 cm. York, Museum Trust, York Art Gallery, YORAG: 771

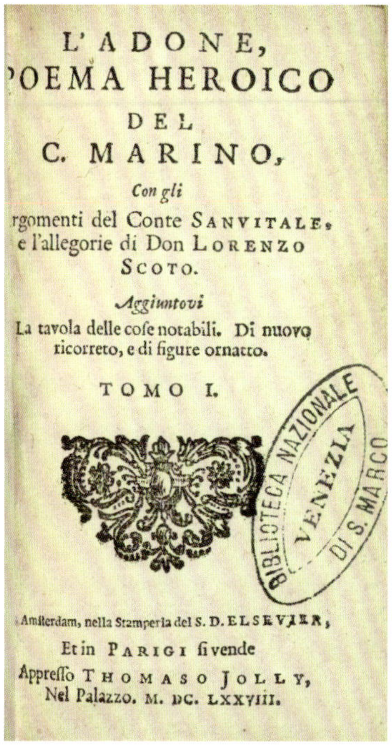
L'ADONE,
POEMA HEROICO
DEL
C. MARINO,
Con gli
argomenti del Conte SANVITALE,
e l'allegorie di Don LORENZO
SCOTO.
Aggiuntovi
La tavola delle cose notabili. Di nuovo
ricorreto, e di figure ornatto.
TOMO I.
Amsterdam, nella Stamperia del S. D. ELSEVIER;
Et in PARIGI si vende
Appresso THOMASO JOLLY,
Nel Palazzo. M. DC. LXXVIII.

1. Giambattista Marino, *L'Adone, poema heroico del C. Marino con gli argomenti del Conte [Fortuniano] Sanvitale, e l'allegorie di Don Lorenzo Scoto…*, Amsterdam 1678, tome I. Venice, Biblioteca Nazionale Marciana (221 C 203)

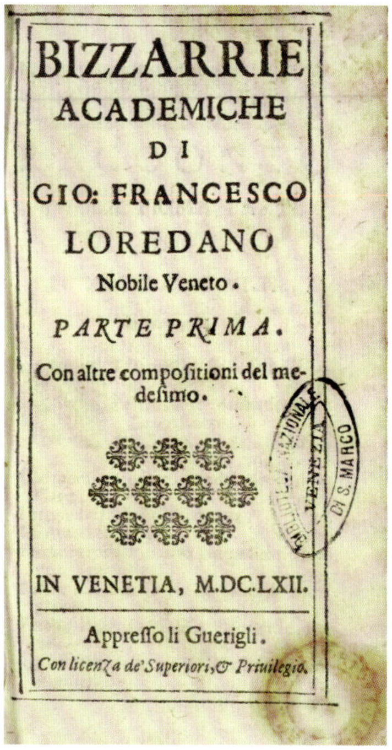
BIZZARRIE
ACADEMICHE
DI
GIO: FRANCESCO
LOREDANO
Nobile Veneto.
PARTE PRIMA.
Con altre compositioni del medesimo.
IN VENETIA, M.DC.LXII.
Appresso li Guerigli.
Con licenza de' Superiori, & Priuilegio.

2. Giovanni Francesco Loredan, *Bizzarrie academiche, Parte prima, con altre compositioni del medesimo*, Venice 1662. Venice, Biblioteca Nazionale Marciana (69 C 239)

The library's volume of caricatures by Ghezzi can be connected not only to Bellotto's sense of humour but also to Pasquini, who was himself the subject of one of them, dated 19 January 1725. In the Warsaw *Self-Portrait* (1765), the figure of an old man behind Bernardo, unmistakably dressed as an Italian abbot, with a large book in his hand, could plausibly be Pasquini. The abbot was already dead in 1763, but this very fact might support the concept of eternity underpinning the printing project promoted by Bernardo, who is represented in the magniloquent crimson of a Venetian senator, 'le Comte Canaletti', as Heinecken recalled, 'il prétendoit être Comte'. Unfortunately, the only image of Pasquini that we know, Ghezzi's caricature from thirty years before, is a fairly generic image of a poor man, and offers no support to the theory.
The books in the library, left in boxes in Dresden when he went to Vienna in 1759, are listed in minute detail, almost always with the publication date and location (noted here between parentheses), indicating that Bernardo knew to distinguish between the various editions. The account given here is a summary. It was, however, perhaps the most surprising artist's library in history, with more than one thousand titles – quite a lot for a thirty-six-year-old of modest origins – and ranged over fields that could never have been predicted, given our current knowledge of the painter.[4]
He, too, knew the classics: Dionysius of Halicarnassus (1723), Aelianus (1757), Pausanias (1733), Plautus, Terence (1722), Cesar (1558), Ciceron (1750), Horace (1756), Virgil (1575, 1751), Ovid (1524, 1737), Seneca (1643, 1749), Tacitus (1542, 1628, 1643), Pliny (1534, 1724), Philostratus (1737), Plutarch (1721). For Horace, our minds of course turn to the citation on the wall behind the self-portrait of Bellotto in Warsaw and in Kingston (1765), but this citation, 'Pictoribus/atque Poetis/quidlibet audendi/semper fuit/aequa potestas', written with mistakes in the first version of the picture, was not a generic *ut pictura poesis* attestation, as found in all of the other painters, but rather an unconditional claim of freedom of expression – as it was for literature, also for painting – in perfect tune with the books in the library. Giorgio Marini, in 1990, saw it addressed, perhaps rightly, not so much to tyrants as to the dogmatists of the Dresden Academy.
And then there were of course the moderns: Dante, Petrarch, the much beloved Boccaccio (1538, 1541, 1545, 1555, 1586, 1627, 1742), Ariosto (1614, 1617), Machiavelli (1551, 1689), Baldassar Castiglione (*Il cortigiano* 1532), Giovanni della Casa (1727), Castelvetro (1727), Berni (1726), Aretino (1660), Guicciardini (1738), Tasso (*Goffredo* 1652, *Aminta* 1619, 1655, 1745 'with prints by the celebrated Piazzetta', 1755, 1756), Guarini (1711, 1736), Anton Francesco Grazzini, called Il Lasca (1582), Marino (*Adone* 1680), Salvator Rosa (*Satire* 1719), Gianfrancesco Loredan (*Scherzi geniali* 1662), Ferrante Pallavicino (1651, 1658, 1671), Segneri, Apostolo Zeno (*Lettere* 1752), Metastasio (1750), Goldoni (1756). And rarities like Bernardo Morando (*Rosalinda* 1672), Luca Assarino (*Stratonica* 1639) and Forteguerri, Nicolò Carteromonaco (*Ricciardetto*, Paris 1738).
And foreign writers, who Bernardo, a true European citizen, did not seem to consider as such: Montaigne (1754, 1754), Corneille (1755), M.elle de Scudéry (*Artamene*, Venice 1651), La Fontaine (1747, 1756), Perrault (1698), Molière (1691), Madame de Lafayette (1678), Fenelon (1714, 1745, 1752), Beaumarchais (1722,

1729), Lesage (1744), l'abbé Prevost (1749), Milton (in a French imitation of *Paradise Lost* 1748), Joseph Addison and Richard Steele (*The Spectator* in French, 1754), Swift (*Gulliver* 1727), Defoe (*Robinson Crusoe* 1743), Fielding (*Tom Jones* 1750), Richardson (*Pamela* 1754), Baltasar Graciàn (1729, 1740), Cervantes. We also learn something about Molière's fame in Germanic countries from Rottmayr who, already in 1689, frescoing an *Allegory of Theatre* for the Salzburg Residenz, included only one book with the name of the French playwright on the spine.
But there were also the *Koran* (1746) (and a life of Muhammad) and, under the title *Novelle Persiane*, *One Thousand and One Nights* (1743). In any case, most of the authors in the library were foreign. The most common language was French.
A good proportion of the literary works were theatrical: Plautus, Terence, Tasso, Guarini, Grazzini, Corneille, Molière, Guidobaldo Bonarelli, Metastasio, Pasquini and Goldoni. And among the treatises were Giuseppe and Ferdinando Galli Bibiena, confirming Bernardo's activity, and greater aspirations, as a stage designer, evidently not wanting to stop at the engraved representation of *Le Turc Généreux* in Vienna, of 1759 (cat. 89). There were also histories of French and Italian theatre and (unspecified) collections of plays.
As for history, Bernardo seems to have been particularly interested in the lives of a few great figures (and not always the good ones): Timur (1723), Elizabeth I (1703, by Gregorio Leti), Richelieu (three biographies), Mazarin (two biographies), Cromwell, Peter I (1742). His contemporary heroes were evidently Maurice, Elector of Saxony (1752) and Frederick II of Prussia (1758), the very one responsible for the destruction of his house by cannon fire. But there is also Goudar's account of the earthquake in Lisbon, which shook the optimistic visions of the Enlightenment to their core (1756). Voltaire appears as the biographer of Louis XIV and Charles II, as well as of Molière, confirming the artist's interest in theatre. Among the historians, in addition to Machiavelli, Guicciardini and Sarpi, we find Platina (1608), Giovio (1558), Paolo Paruta (1605), Bentivoglio (1630, 1680) and, with his memoires, Montecuccoli (1752, 1756). And one of the most assiduously read politicians was Traiano Boccalini (1640, 1678, 1689). In any case, there were countless books on history, politics and geography, and many of which dealt with very current themes. There was even a *Racolta di varii scriti tutti in occasione della Guerra del*

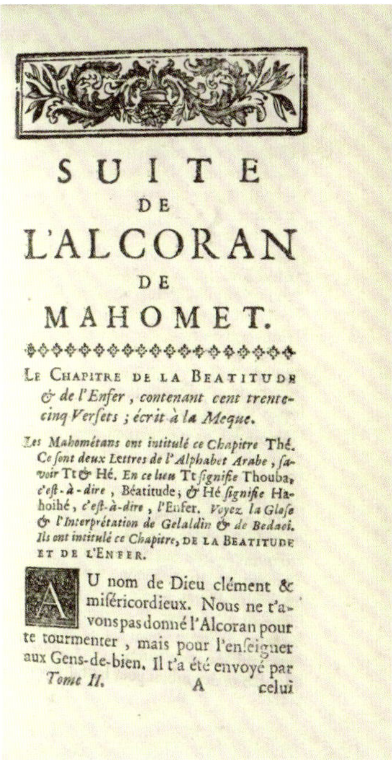
SUITE
DE
L'ALCORAN
DE
MAHOMET.

LE CHAPITRE DE LA BEATITUDE & de l'Enfer, contenant cent trente-cinq Verſets ; écrit à la Meque.

Les Mahométans ont intitulé ce Chapitre Thé. Ce ſont deux Lettres de l'Alphabet Arabe, ſavoir Tt & Hé. En ce lieu Tt ſignifie Thouba, c'eſt-à-dire, Béatitude ; & Hé ſignifie Hahoihé, c'eſt-à-dire, l'Enfer. Voyez la Gloſe & l'Interprétation de Geladdin & de Bedaoi. Ils ont intitulé ce Chapitre, DE LA BEATITUDE ET DE L'ENFER.

AU nom de Dieu clément & miſéricordieux. Nous ne t'avons pas donné l'Alcoran pour te tourmenter, mais pour l'enſeigner aux Gens-de-bien. Il t'a été envoyé par

Tome II. A celui

3. *L'Alcoran de Mohamet, traduit de l'arabe par André Du Ryer...* Nouvelle édition, Amsterdam, P. Martier, 1746, tome II. Venice, Biblioteca Nazionale Marciana (49 T 229)

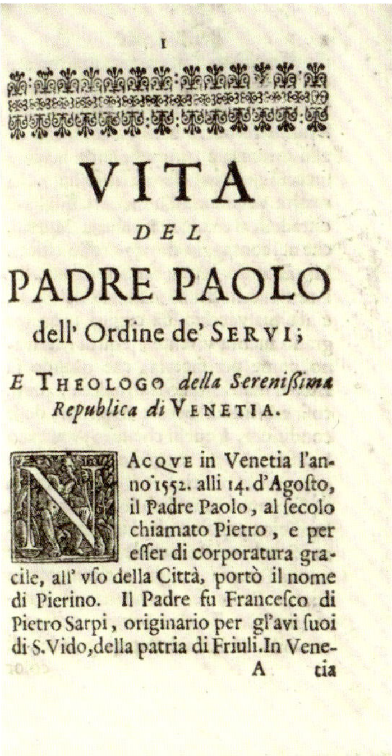
1

VITA
DEL
PADRE PAOLO
dell' Ordine de' SERVI;
E THEOLOGO della Sereniſſima Republica di VENETIA.

NACQVE in Venetia l'anno 1552. alli 14. d'Agoſto, il Padre Paolo, al ſecolo chiamato Pietro, e per eſſer di corporatura gracile, all' vſo della Città, portò il nome di Pierino. Il Padre fu Franceſco di Pietro Sarpi, originario per gl'avi ſuoi di S. Vido, della patria di Friuli. In Vene-

A tia

4. Paolo Sarpi, *Opere del padre Paolo Sarpi*, Venice 1687, tome I. Venice, Biblioteca Nazionale Marciana (146 D 257)

1756. Fino il 1758, about the earlier part of the war that destroyed his home in 1760. But, as evidence of his curiosity about history and deep Venetian identity, there was also *Histoire de la Legue Faite à Cambrai contre la Republique de Venise*, by Jean Baptiste Dubos (1710).
The more specifically philosophical texts included Agrippa von Nettesheim (1726), Erasmus (*Elogio*... 1715), Montaigne (1754, 1754), Tesauro (1672), Hume (1758), Newton (1744, 1749), Berkeley (1734), Montesquieu (*Consideration*... 1749), Voltaire (1748, 1756).
Noteworthy among the Italians were Sarpi (1629, 1687), Muratori and Maffei (*La scienza cavalleresca* 1710, as well as *Verona illustrata* in the first edition of 1731, almost certainly purchased when he was in Verona in 1745), Giannone (*Istoria civile*... 1753). A clear index of Bernardo's receptiveness to Enlightenment thought.

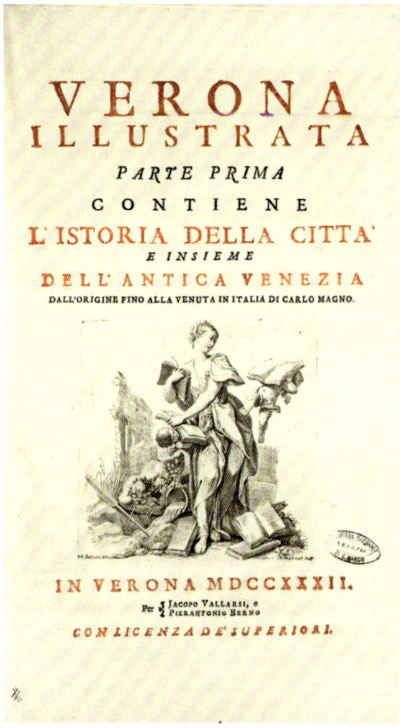
VERONA
ILLUSTRATA
PARTE PRIMA
CONTIENE
L'ISTORIA DELLA CITTA'
E INSIEME
DELL'ANTICA VENEZIA
DALL'ORIGINE FINO ALLA VENUTA IN ITALIA DI CARLO MAGNO.

IN VERONA MDCCXXXII.
Per Jacopo Vallarsi, e Pierantonio Berno
CON LICENZA DE' SUPERIORI.

5. Scipione Maffei, *Verona illustrata parte prima...*, in Verona, per Jacopo Vallarsi, e Pierantonio Berno, 1731–32. Venice, Biblioteca Nazionale Marciana (70 D 16)

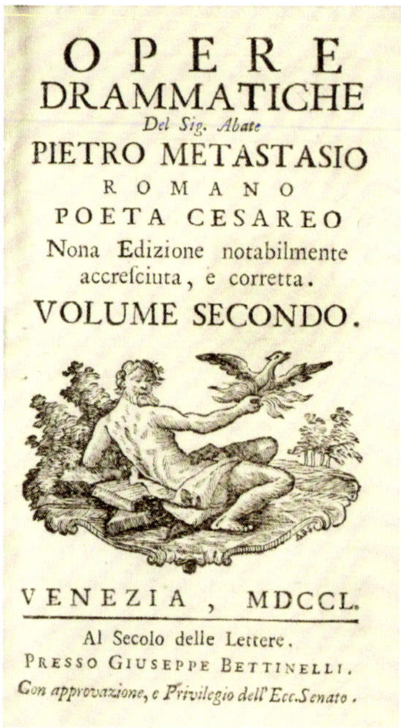
OPERE
DRAMMATICHE
Del Sig. Abate
PIETRO METASTASIO
ROMANO
POETA CESAREO
Nona Edizione notabilmente
accresciuta, e corretta.
VOLUME SECONDO.

VENEZIA, MDCCL.
Al Secolo delle Lettere.
Presso Giuseppe Bettinelli.
Con approvazione, e Privilegio dell'Ecc. Senato.

6. Pietro Metastasio, *Opere drammatiche del sig. abate Pietro Metastasio romano poeta cesareo. Nona edizione notabilmente accresciuta, e corretta*, Venezia, al Secolo delle lettere, presso Giuseppe Bettinelli, 1750–1752, tome II.
Milan, Archivio Storico Civico e Biblioteca Trivulziana (Triv. L 3588/II)

Perhaps only a reader of Muratori could have painted, for the first time, in 1740, the Romanesque facade of the church of San Martino in Lucca.

Paradoxically, the art-historical treatises seem less complete, although the library did include Philostratus, Dürer (1613), Benedetto Varchi (*Due lezioni*... 1549), Vignola (1726), Du Perac (*Antichità di Roma*... 1671), Francesco Sansovino (1581), Armenini, Cesare Vecellio (*Habiti antichi*), Cartari (1647), Borromini (1720), Andrea Pozzo (1700), Carlo Fontana (1725), Bianchini (1738), Orlandi (in the 1704 and 1753 editions), Ferdinando Galli Bibiena (1611 [*sic!*]), who was also the author of the first page of Pasquini's *Opere*, and Giuseppe, from the same family, Zanotti (1739), Descamps (*Vite dei pittori fiamminghi, olandesi e tedeschi* 1753), Cochin (1754) and Carli (*Le antichità di Capodistria*). There were even two works on anatomy. The volumes on technical drawing are more significant, particularly those of a military or ballistic nature, like *La science des ombres: par rapport au dessin avec Le Dessinateur au cabinet et à l'armée* (Paris 1750). These works, however, were published long after Bernardo's early period, and cannot have influenced his artistic formation. They seem to have been simply for deepening his knowledge.

The presence of the volume on Borromini is surprising and astonishing, but also illuminating with respect to Bernardo's artistic choices. Borromini, in step with Bellotto, had, for that matter, one of the largest artist's libraries of the seventeenth century, with more than 900 books, which are unfortunately only generically described.[5]

The illustrated volumes included the one by Rubens on the palaces of Genoa, one on Rubens in Luxemburg, Cignani di Parma drawn by his student Sebastiano Ricci and the *Officium Beatae Virginis* printed by Pasquali with engravings by Piazzetta. Bellotto, as a true bibliophile, seems to have purchased the works published by the most prestigious Venetian publishers, like Albrizzi and Pasquali, as soon as they were available.

The presence of the works by Sarpi and Loredan confirms a specific and deep awareness of historical Venetian identity, which one could have doubted in the exiled view painter. And it also leads us to believe that he supported a position of anti-papal distaste and the search for freedom from Church control that distinguished the Venetian 'libertines' of the seventeenth century. The two authors were obligatory in the libraries of eighteenth-centuries Venetian 'heretics'.

In his famous self-portrait, Bernardo stands in a fantastical monumental portico dressed in the crimson worn by Venetian senators, like a Procurator of St Mark. This must have been for him the most obvious symbol of the highest level of nobility and also his most secret, and mad, aspiration, with a vague hint, but only a hint, of self-irony, and looks to us, but perhaps only to us, like a Venetian Carnival costume. It must have been his dream, but in any case it is his only explicit identification. The architectural capriccios of his final period in Dresden also feature the figures of senators dressed in red, with long wigs and long trains, climbing up and down the steps of what would be an idealised version of the Ducal Palace of Venice. They recall not so much the affability of Alessandro Longhi's portraits, but rather the funerary wraiths of Tiepolo. It was a

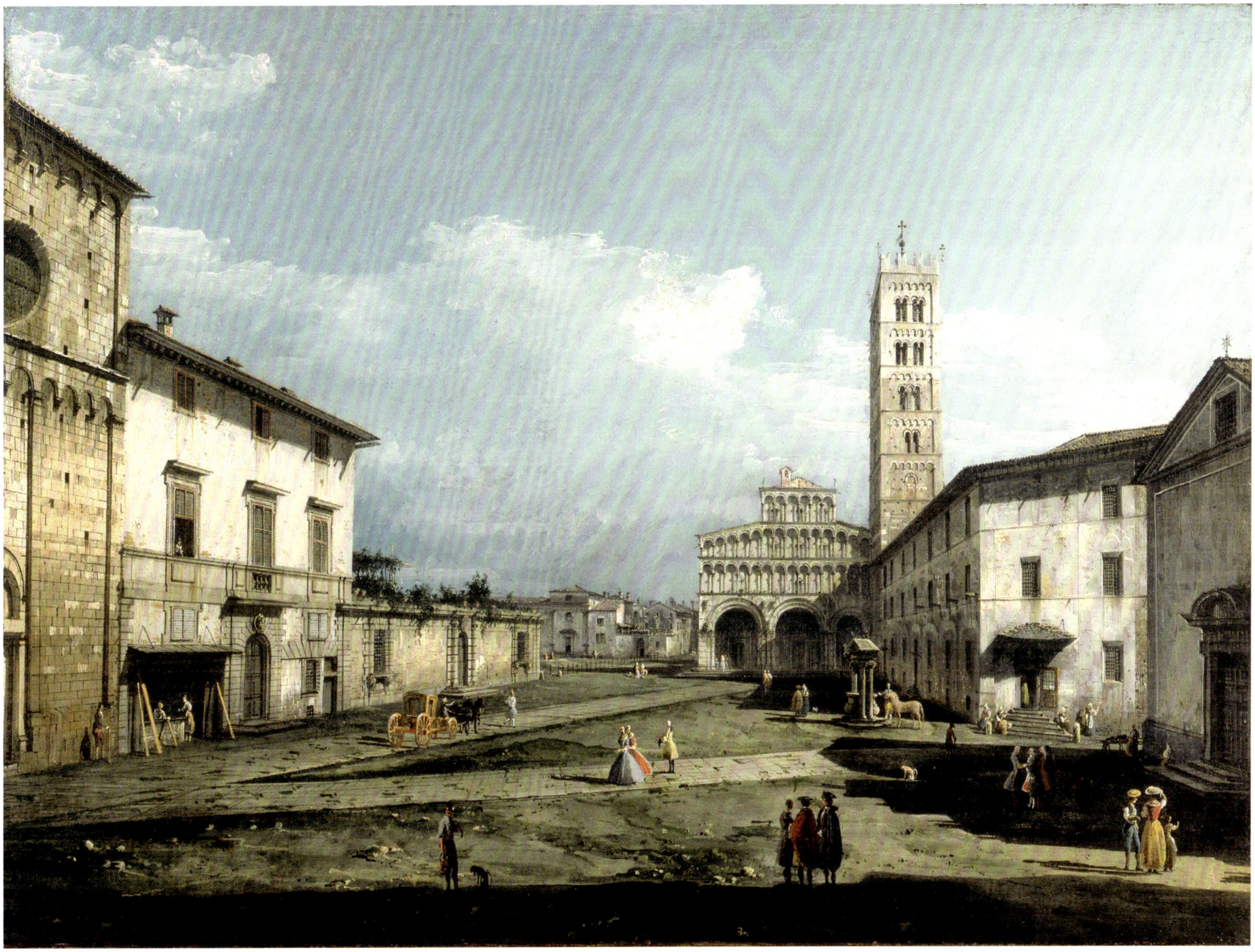
7. Bernardo Bellotto, *The Piazza San Martino with the Cathedral, Lucca.*, 1740, oil on canvas 50,8 x 72 cm. York, Museum Trust, York Art Gallery, 771

Venice that Bernardo could not have known personally, since he had never seen it again.
An essential key for interpreting Bernardo's political and ideological leanings is the surprising extent of works in the library by the collection's indisputably most represented author, the controversial Gregorio Leti, an intellectual adventurer in endless flight between Italy, Switzerland, France, England and the Netherlands, a convert from Catholicism to Calvinism. Among his most famous works were *L'inquisizione processata* (1681), *Il nipotismo di Roma* (1667), *Il puttanismo romano* (1668), *Il Cardinalismo di*

Santa Chiesa (1668), *Il Vaticano languente* (1677). Leti was also briefly in Venice, in contact with the Accademia degli Incogniti (Academy of the Unknowns), and he laboured for controversial editions of the works of Sarpi and Traiano Boccalini. He was, at least in publishing terms, one of the most ruthlessly anti-clerical and anti-papal writers of the seventeenth century, recently rediscovered after a period of near total oblivion and defined by Curzio Malaparte 'the greatest Italian pamphleteer'. The mere presence of these works leads us to hypothesise Bernardo's support for anti-clerical extremism, however never publicly displayed and unsuspected in the religious courts of Dresden, Vienna and Warsaw. Any doubt as to Bernardo's anti-clericalism is removed by the presence of the *Histoire de la Papesse Jeanne* 'de M:r. de Spanheim, av:[ec] Fig:[ures]'. And there was also Johann Lorenz Natter's *Apologie pour l'ordre des Francs-Maçons*. The counterpart of a few Christian theological texts, which in any case displays a balanced critical spirit, it does not even minimally counterbalance the cited titles in the library, which were almost all included in the *Index* of the Roman Church.

Bellotto's library was above all characterised by its astonishing variety. There are purely erotic novels, like *Les delices du cloitre ou la Nonne eclairée* (by an author who remains unknown), *Les spectacles nocturnes* by Jean-Baptiste Magny and *Le canapé couleur de feu* by Louis-Charles Fougeret de Monbron, as well as classics of magic and Satanism like *Demonomania* by Jean Bodin.[6]

In a certain way, it seems similar to the library of Giacomo Casanova, who was in Dresden in the middle of the 1760s and, probably, knew the painter, also being close to him in age (1725-1798), if they had not already met in Venice. And then Bernardo was a colleague, at the Dresden Academy, from 1764, of Giovan Battista Casanova, the writer's younger brother, an observant Mengsian and future director of the academy, but he never mentions this.

Bernardo had a strong liking for novels and yet was curious about an extremely varied range of themes. A trait highly consistent with the subtly narrative character of his paintings, as has already been noted by Roberto Longhi. In general, however, the library is characterised by important works, the ones still famous today.

But then there were the general, historical, political, geographical, naturalistic and anthropological works, which ranged from horseback riding and shells to the customs of the Native Americans, as well as writing manuals, grammar books, and dictionaries in various languages, Latin, Italian, French. There was also the *Nouvelle metode pour bien parler Italien*, by Veneroni, in French… (Paris 1688).[7] The wealth of geographical texts and interest can be seen, even if it was just unconsciously, as a predisposition to the future marriage of Bernardo's eldest daughter, Maria Josepha Friedrica, to Hermann Karl De Perthées, originally from Dresden (but the marriage took place in Warsaw, in 1769). When Maria died and left him a widow, he married the other daughter, Teresa. De Perthées was probably the most important geographer in north-eastern Europe at the time. And he was the one who told the king of Bernardo's death in 1780, diplomatically requesting immediate help for arranging '.. les affaires du defunt, qui ne sont que trop crittiques'.[8] The inventory was found among his papers in Vilnius, where he was a university professor.

The impression one gets is that Bernardo was a brilliant autodidact and that his library was his school, in the end also becoming his cultural portrait. With his precise choices: we know that he did not know a word of German, and held lectures at the Dresden Academy with his son Lorenzo, barely twenty, acting as interpreter. And by then he had been living in German territory for more than fifteen years. We learn this from Hagedorn, the director of the academy, who was a fanatical supporter of the superiority of the new German figurative culture and a subtle, but systematic, denigrator of Bernardo. Bernardo's library nevertheless also contained books and dictionaries in German, which cannot be attributed to the young Lorenzo, who was born in 1744 and not even fourteen when the inventory was prepared.

Certain holes in the collection are inexplicable: Vasari, Palladio, Ridolfi, Boschini, etc., but perhaps Bernardo brought some books with him, or kept some somewhere else. A reader, as we have discovered Bernardo was, could not have left all of his books in storage for years. Another inexplicable absence in the end is that of Francesco Algarotti, who might have handled the sale of some of his early paintings; his brother Bonomo was a witness at his wedding in 1741 and then a godfather at baptisms. The fatuous Algarotti was clearly disagreeable to Gerolamo Zanetti, the brother of the young Anton Maria, and it cannot be excluded that other 'serious' Venetians, like Bernardo, felt the same.

Nothing in the library seems to have been inherited. The recent publication dates of the books suggest in any case that the painter had purchased almost all of them at the start of his economic success, while travelling in Italy after 1742, or better, in Dresden, after 1746. Nevertheless, Apostolo Zeno, Marciana librarian and one of the authors in Bernardo's library, ensured that already in 1708, any new European book could be purchased on the Venetian market.[9]

It is inevitable to wonder what Bernardo's life was like after the total, simultaneous loss of his library and collection of paintings. We learn from Hagedorn that in Dresden in 1765, Bellotto, persecuted by creditors, who he thought wanted to take him to court, nearly went mad. He would of course have begun from scratch, but finding replacements, at least in Warsaw, would not have been easy or fast. A certain barbarism in Bernardo's work from the Warsaw period has always been unanimously noted, but not explicitly, between the lines by scholars, referring not to a qualitative decline but rather to a new, naturalistic immediacy that leaves behind the sophisticated, intellectual culture of Dresden. Perhaps the loss of the vast library, and the small gallery, was this, as well.

The picture gallery, which concludes the inventory, is also surprising, but seems to have been relatively more modest than the library, in part because Bernardo, wealthy though he was, did not have princely sums to spend and the list is no longer very eloquent, the works being lost. The 'Gabinetto di quadri' included paintings by Giambattista Pittoni and Francesco Fontebasso, two half-length figures by Piazzetta, two sketches for paintings by Sebastiano Ricci, five by Gaspare Diziani, and one by Giambattista Tiepolo,[10] a painting by Amigoni, one by *San Giuseppe* di Gianantonio Pellegrini and two half-length figures by Rubens. A more singular presence: 'Un ritrato d'una monarcha, meza figura, Fortunato Pasqueti' (a portrait of a monarch, half-length, Fortunato Pasqueti). Then, two heads by Van Dyck, two by Nogari, two by Nazzari and two by Giovanni Carboncino. As we see, Bernardo liked the symmetry of pairs, which must have served the display, or better the furnishings. Bernardo also often used the symmetry of pairs for his views.

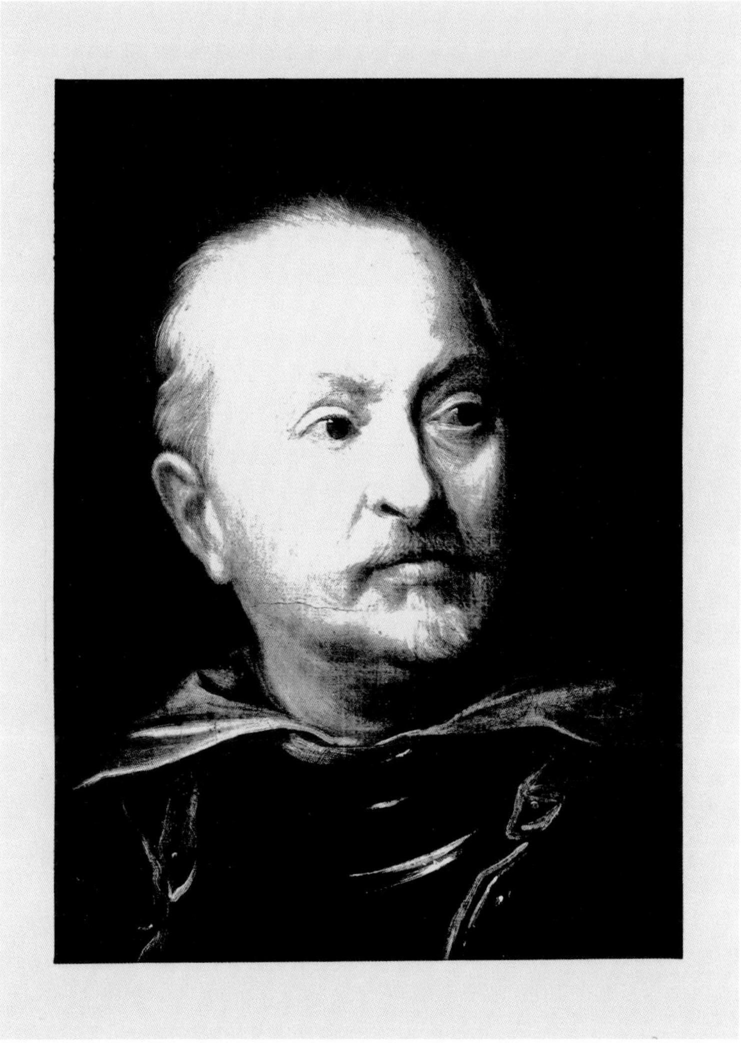

8. Giovanni Carboncino, *Male Haed.* Unknown location

The larger number of sketches by Diziani might be explained by the fact that Bellotto found them in Dresden, where Gaspare had lived for around four years, between 1717 and 1720, also working on stage sets.[11] Pellegrini was also in Dresden in 1725, painting inside buildings like the Hofkirche and the Zwinger, which were then depicted from the outside by Bellotto. Amigoni had been in Düsseldorf. The heads by Carboncino are surprising and one imagines, although it is not certain, that they were brought from Venice. At least the photo of a now-lost head of that kind, attributable to the artist, survives.[12] The paintings, for the most part heads, sketches and landscapes, must have all been more or less small format, to suit a home that was an apartment rather than an entire building. A home that was almost completely covered with Venetian mirrors, in the understandable taste of a 'capacious' view painter, and furnished with geographical and astronomical globes, musical instruments (a 'clavicembalo, con doppia tastadura intiero'), a 'bussola' and a 'grande canocchiale'. It was the house of an Enlightenment follower. But there were also 'pistole ed scioppo appesi alla muraglia' (pistols and a shotgun hung on the wall). So an Enlightenment follower who knew how to shoot.

Although he had a clear passion for genre heads, one notes the absence of the then-omnipresent figure of Denner, the most fashionable painter in Europe, together with all of the Germans and all of the French, as well as the pastels of Carriera (too expensive? not too close?), the greatest collector in the world of whom was the Dresden court, and of Francesco Pavona (the widow of whom was a co-tenant with Bernardo in the bombarded house and also the person with whom he left his boxes), in addition to the alleged Brescian forebear Pietro Bellotti. Bernardo must have been interested in having examples of the painting technique of his contemporaries and probably could not justify large canvases. They might also have been gifts, but they were certainly not explicit commissions. The sketches must have interested him as compositional paradigms, just as valid as such as large canvases, and not for the 'sketchy' painting, which was in itself extraneous to his work.

There were relatively few landscapes: two by Cimaroli, two by Zuccarelli, four by Marco Ricci. These were the landscape painters farthest distant from Bernardo. But the Flemish and French painters shine in their absence, possibly only of interest to him for their compositions, known through prints. And then there were twenty-two landscapes by Bernardo. Only one foreigner, in any case familiar in Venice, Francesco Solimena, with two small paintings. Only two alleged classic paintings: 'Bassano' with a *Noah's Ark* and 'Paolo' with a *Holy Family* of half-length figures. Continuing the inventory, in the third room in the house were other 'family portraits', two by Stefano Torelli and one by Fortunato Pasquetti. Stefano Torelli, born in Bologna, his father was from Verona, was at the Dresden court between 1740 and 1758, and must have been a friend of Bernardo. The two family portraits, or at least one of them, might have depicted Bernardo's own family.[13] Moreover, having been the student of Solimena for some time, this might explain the presence of the paintings by that Neapolitan painter, who was in any case highly celebrated. Torelli, who moved to St Petersburg in 1762, could have been Bellotto's contact there, for his planned trip to Russia in 1767. The curious *Livres de groupes d'Enfans Boucher*, apparently unexplainable as a repertoire of models for Bellotto, might be connected to his link to Torelli, who was a great passionate imitator of the French artist. Finally, there were a pair of portraits of the sovereigns of Saxony and Poland, which are listed as by anonymous painters in the inventory but might be traceable, given Bernardo's exacting nature, to the official court painter, Louis de Silvestre. Understandable and far-sighted gratitude, seeing that, a few years later when the Mengsian academics, headed by Hagedorn, tried to fire the painter in 1764, it was the court that saved him.

In other rooms, hurried note was made of '4 Quadri d'Inventione fatti da me con Cornici d'Orate' (4 fanciful paintings made by me in gilded frames) and, in the children's room, '7 Quadri Ritrati Antichi, con Cornici d'Orate' (7 old portraits, with gilded frames), evidently anonymous.

Unlike the library, the international character of the picture gallery was securely entrusted solely to the pair of heads by Rubens and Van Dyck, two well-known Italianate painters, while it of course extended liberally in the print collection. The composition of Bellotto's gallery in any case clearly intimated belief in the absolute superiority of the contemporary Venetian school of the European eighteenth century.

The seventy-three paintings all had a similar gilded frame, designed specially for them by their sophisticated owner, and this also confirms their final function as furnishing for the home.

There were then numerous drawings by the author himself collected in volumes: 400 sheets, a 'Cartela di vari studii ed altri celebri autori del numero 628 carte' (Volume of various studies by myself and other famous artists of 628 sheets), 'Abozzi di pittura, da 513 carte' (513 sheets of sketches for paintings), 215 autograph drawings, 304 sketches 'fatti dal Naturale' (made from life) – which would have been interesting for understanding how the painter worked – 'Studii di Gio: Batt:a Piazetta' (Studies by Gio: Batt:a Piazzetta) and 'Carte di Varii celebri Autori sotto 250. Stampe ~~legate in Libro~~' (Sheets by various famous artists in 250. Prints ~~bound in book~~). 1,260 landscape prints in two volumes. Another two volumes with 1,000 prints by 'famous' northern artists. And large or complete print collections by Lebrun, Natoire, Marco Ricci, Canaletto, from the Carracci, from Titian and Veronese. Tintoretto is missing. There is no trace of the painter Vanvitelli. Although in this case there is no specific description of the authors, it is clear that Bernardo Bellotto's collection of paintings and prints was of notable substance, even more select thanks to the eye of a confident specialist. Piranesi must have been present among the unnamed sheets, an artist copied many times by Bernardo and his son Lorenzo, in various similar and dissimilar aspects. Canaletto is present in a *corpus* of engravings, perhaps in drawings as well, but there were clearly none of his paintings. Of course in Dresden the painting of Canaletto was that of Bernardo and all that was preserved of his uncle, perhaps, however, devotedly, were the work tools of his youth. The loss of the sizeable bulk of Bernardo's drawings has instead compromised the definitive, secure understanding of the development of his language and his work.

And we cannot fail to note Bernardo's meticulous and scrupulous attention to his final note, which is revealing of his character and a sign of his love for his collection of prints, drawings and books: 'Tutti Questi Libri Legati Alcuni in Bergamina, et il Resto in Pele di Vitelo Marmorisati, con suoi Numeri, e la mia Marcha cioè B.B.C. Riposti in ~~una Bibliotecha~~ Ripostorii di Rimesso di mia Inventione, con Cornici, Frontespicii e Lastre di Vetro, con Scalini Pedestali e tiradori per Scrivere' (All of these books, some bound in parchment, and the rest in marbled calfskin, with their numbers, and my mark, B.B.C. Kept in ~~a Library~~ inlaid containers of my own design, with frames, frontispieces and sheets of glass, with steps pedestals and 'tiradolri' for writing). Even more than in other cases, this library must have been a self-portrait, signed by the author (B.B.C.), all of its details specified and refined, then lost in the flames ignited by the cannon fire immediately subsequent to its completion and description. It could be a story by Borges.

Even from just a few chance and fragmentary details it is clear that, through the book, a new universal culture of vast breadth was underpinning the Venetian eighteenth century. In 1730, Sebastiano Ricci was betrayed to the Holy Office by a presumed student, Felice Petricini, for circulating books, written in French, against the cult of the Virgin, the saints and the sacraments, books that were probably the work of Enlightenment thinkers, acquired on trips to London and Paris.[14] In the self-portrait of a painter, presumed to be Federico Bencovich, dating to about 1725 and in the Accademia in Venice, we read the names of Leonardo, Dürer and Accolti (Pietro?) emblazoned on the spines of the depicted books. On his death, Giambettino Cignaroli (1770) left his theoretical books to start an academy library in Verona, bearing his name. In 1794, again in Verona, in a painting of the noble Spolverini family in their library, the nephew of Cignaroli, Saverio Dalla Rosa, deliberately included the names of the Englishman Thompson (translated in French), Klopstock and Kleist, here, too, on the spines of books.[15] In the immediately subsequent years, even the apparently provincial and old-fashioned Agostino Ugolini painted his portraits of the most famous bishops, from Gualfardo Ridolfi to Agostino Liruti, against the background of a wall of books.

Nothing is known of the others, but this might also be purely chance. It is difficult to imagine that Giambattista Tiepolo, who so assiduously frequented Maffei and Algarotti, did not have his own library. In the inventory taken after Canaletto's death, published by Constable in 1989, there are instead no books at all. There was, however, in Venice a documented tradition of wide-ranging libraries among the more cultured artists, like Pietro Liberi, Carl Loth and Antonio Zanchi, as early as the late seventeenth century.[16]

And then the Venetian artists of the eighteenth century, Balestra, Tiepolo, Michelangelo Spada, Rotari, Piazzetta, Crosato, Gaspare Diziani, Antonio Visentini, Brida, Lorenzi, Giambettino and Giandomenico Cignaroli, Alessandro Longhi, Zompini, Pietro Antonio and Francesco Novelli and Saverio Dalla Rosa were almost all famously involved in the work of book illustration, for the most famous editions.

The description of the inventory of the library is not just an erudite exercise, an 'addition' of information to Bernardo's biography. Now that we know of it, it seems like a clear and inescapable key to understanding his art, lucid and cold, anti-rhetorical and critical but grandiose and powerful, and of absolute spiritual breadth. Apparently similar, but nevertheless far, removed from the magnificent Baroque decoration of his uncle, Canaletto, from whom he immediately distanced himself, even though he has been interpreted for centuries as his double, in part due to the name, and his dark twin. The decision to keep the name, while certainly an economic guarantee, in any case expresses a perhaps unconscious nostalgia for his family, which had caused him so much trouble and bitterness in his youth, and in the end for Venice. The precedents were there: Domenico Tintoretto, the much beloved son of Jacopo, never signed his own name, and his workshop was turning out 'Tintoretto' canvases until the end of the seventeenth century.

In the letters of his contemporary correspondents, in Warsaw and Dresden, Bernardo is simply 'il signor Canaletto'. All the worse for his poor wife, Maria Elisabetta Pizzorno, the most pathetic figure in the story, who as a logical consequence became, and without the irony that we might see in it, 'Madama Canaletta'. In reality, from the complex interweaving of work relationships, between drawings, paintings and prints, recently brought to light by Kowalczyk, we see that, at least so long as he was still in Venice, Bernardo was not a simple student, but must have instead felt himself to be a true part of a 'Canaletto' enterprise. His detachment, including his move to other countries, must have been psychologically necessary for recovering an identity that was nevertheless partially stopped at the name. But in substance he overturned all of the past of the tradition, perhaps in part thanks to the far-sighted and, in the end, benevolent advice from his uncle, who, according to Guarienti, was the first to encourage him to travel.

Paintings like *The Old Market of Dresden, from Seestrasse looking North* and *The Ruins of the Kreuzkirche*, are unthinkable, even with all of the conditioning of the 'spirit of the age', in the work of other artists.

The library confirms something that one already intuited about Bernardo's elusive character. 'The whole city [of Dresden] knows [his] beastly brain', were the words of his atrocious father Lorenzo, writing to the minister Brühl in 1754. In the letters from Giuseppe Rosa (Joseph Roos), a landscape painter in Dresden, to Marcello Bacciarelli, a painter at the Warsaw court, we find a request to reassure Bernardo's wife, who remained in Dresden, as to his psychological condition ('Madama Canaleta ... desidera ... di sapere se il marito sia libero dalla sua avuta malinconia, mentre nelle sue lettere non ne fanno nessuna menzione, ma non vorrebbe che lui ne sapesse niente di questa domanda' [Madama Canaleta ... would like ... to know whether her husband is now free of his melancholy, while in her letters no mention is made of it, she does not want him to know nothing of this query]). There is insinuation that Bernardo was horribly moody ('... essendo i quarti della luna differenti' [... being the four different quarters of the moon]) and even irony when Rosa sends his greeting to his friend ('Priego di fare i miei saluti al Signor Canaletto se pure in questo fratempo è diventato savio ...' [Please send my greetings to Signor Canaletto if in the meantime he has become sensible ...]). Meanwhile, for Bernardo, there was also the bashing of the French landscape painter Jean Pillement, a devoted creator of pseudo-Chinese and fantastical arcadias and also a court painter, who left Warsaw right at that moment, and perhaps in part for this reason.

The image one gets is of a difficult character, melancholic to say the least, a true artist. In any case, he was a solitary reader, not an assiduous presence at salons. In her umpteenth, plaintive plea to Stanisław Poniatowsky, always asking for money to pay debts, 'Madama Canaletta' recalled in passing, to excuse him and prevent rancorous refusals, that the deceased painter had also disobeyed his own king ('... restan a Varsovie contre la volonté de Son Roi' [... he remained in Warsaw even against the will of his King]).[17] Even the magnanimous sovereign had at a certain point tried to rid himself of Bernardo. And it is also from these details, of no small importance, that Bernardo's desire for freedom and independence from the prince emerges. As we also see from the contents of his library, Bernardo was the only Venetian painter ready for the age of the French Revolution.

I would like to thank Chiara Ceschi, Paolo Delorenzi and Maria Chiara Piva.

[1] On Bernardo Bellotto, see my own catalogue *Bernardo Bellotto*, Verona 1990, and in particular my essay 'I lumi e le ombre della città del principe', pp. 39–50. Also see all of the publications by Bożena Anna Kowalczyk, and, for the artist's early years, see G. Marini, '"Con la propria industria e sua professione". Nuovi documenti sulla giovinezza di Bellotto,' *Verona illustrata*, 6, 1993, pp. 125–140.
[2] The inventory, discovered in Vilnius, was published in E. Manikowska, 'The rediscovery of Bernardo Bellotto's inventory', *Burlington Magazine*, 154, 2012, 1, pp. 32–36, and *Bernardo Bellotto i jego drezdeński apartament. O tożsamości społecznej i artystycznej weneckiego wedutysty*, Warszawa 2014. The quotations from the *Catalogo de Danni* here reported respect the new philological transcription from the original made by Bożena Anna Kowalczyk.
[3] On Michele, see B.A. Kowalczyk, 'Il Bellotto veneziano nei documenti', *Arte Veneta*, 47, 1995, pp. 69–77; P. Scapecchi, 'Tipografia, erudizione e libri in un centro "minore" del '700. Michele Bellotti ad Arezzo e la stampa del Muratori', *Biblioteche oggi*, XVI, 1996, 8, pp. 52–62, where, among other things, the fact that Michele was Bernardo's brother is ignored. Michele printed the life of Muratori in 1767, after his brother had been reading this author for many years. One therefore wonders, here as well, whether this, too, might have been Bernardo's idea, given that the work was extraneous to the rest of the printer's catalogue. Like Michele and Bernardo, the third brother, Pietro, was also destined to the life of an immigrant, leaving Venice.
[4] The Bellotto's library cannot be compared with the vaster, more practical one of Antonio Maria Zanetti di Girolamo, partially published in B.A. Kowalczyk, 'Il "prezioso" manoscritto della collezione Bettagno: l'Indice della biblioteca di Anton Maria Zanetti', in *Venezia Settecento. Studi in memoria di Alessandro Bettagno*, ed. B.A. Kowalczyk, Cinisello Balsamo 2015, pp. 31–36, who was a dilettante artist and first and foremost an intellectual and merchant, of European prominence, with no equal in Italy. Canova's library by now belongs to a different century and was that of a culture minister; in this as well, however, it is less surprising. See G. Pavanello, *La biblioteca di Antonio Canova*, Possagno 2007.
[5] See P. Portoghesi, 'La biblioteca di Francesco Borromini', in *La festa delle Arti. Scritti in onore di Marcello Fagiolo per cinquant'anni di studi*, eds. V. Cazzato, S. Roberto, M. Bevilacqua, Rome 2014, I, pp. 358–364.
[6] In her commentaries, Manikowska seems to ignore that erotic side of Bellotto's library, and barely notes, even generically, its anti-clericalism and philosophical side, limiting herself to the art-historical aspect. Concerned with seeing what Bellotto had in common with the culture of his time, she misses what was different.
[7] The exact title is: *Nouvelle metode pour apprendre la langue italienne avec grande facilité; et en tres peu de tems.* Bernardo, who was very precise with the substance of the titles of the books, often recorded their formal wording imaginatively, as if by memory. This also leads one to think that he was the author the inventory, although it was possibly written down by others, taking dictation.
[8] When Bernardo died, his list of debts, incurred with almost every type of merchant and totalling 324 ducats, did not include any booksellers. At that time, therefore, he either paid for books or did not buy them.
[9] See F. Barbierato, *Politici e ateisti, percorsi nella miscredenza a Venezia fra Sei e Settecento*, Milan 2006, p. 267.
[10] 'Tiepoletto' in the sources is always Giambattista Tiepolo, a rather short man, and not his son Giandomenico, still very much in his father's shadow at the time, as interpreted by Manikowska. And Bellotto was not the type to make mistakes in the attributions of his paintings. The loss of the painting in any case makes it permanently impossible to confirm. It is possible that Bellotto had some connection to Tiepolo when they were working in far-off Würzburg, in 1751–1753. Giandomenico was judged 'mediocre' in his autobiographical text, by the malevolent, amateurish Giacomo Casanova, who abstained, luckily for him, from comments about his father, but left pages of vitriol about Mengs.
[11] An example of one of the two indicated themes, *Joseph Explaining his Dreams*, is found among the surviving works of Gaspare Diziani and preserved in the Aschaffenburg Gallery. Its dimensions (86.3 x 118.7 cm) could also possibly be confused with those of a sketch. The painting, however, has a pendant and dates to around 1755.
[12] It is preserved among the anonymous works from the Baroque period, in the Photo Library of the Kunsthistorisches Institut in Florence.
[13] See I. Graziani, *Sognare l'Arcadia. Stefano Torelli, 'peintre enchanteur' nelle grandi corti del Nord Europa,* Bologna 2013. The two group portraits of royal Saxon princelings, from the final chapter in Dresden and now in the city's Gallery, might provide an idea of the ones by Torelli for Bellotto.
[14] See Barbierato, *Politici e ateisti*, op. cit., pp. 271, 300.
[15] See S. Marinelli, 'La pittura del Settecento a Verona', in *La pittura in Italia. Il Settecento*, ed. G. Briganti, Milan 1989, I, pp. 136–146.
[16] See I. Chiappini di Sorio, 'L'inventario della casa di Pietro Liberi', *Arte Veneta*, 18, 1964, pp. 151–152. Liberi's library particularly stands out for its alchemical books. M. Lux, 'L'inventario di Johann Carl Loth', *Arte Veneta*, 54, 2000, pp. 146–164.
[17] The letters from Giuseppe Rosa, Karl De Perthées and Bernardo's widow are published in A. Rizzi, *La Varsavia di Bellotto*, Milan 1990, pp. 150–152.

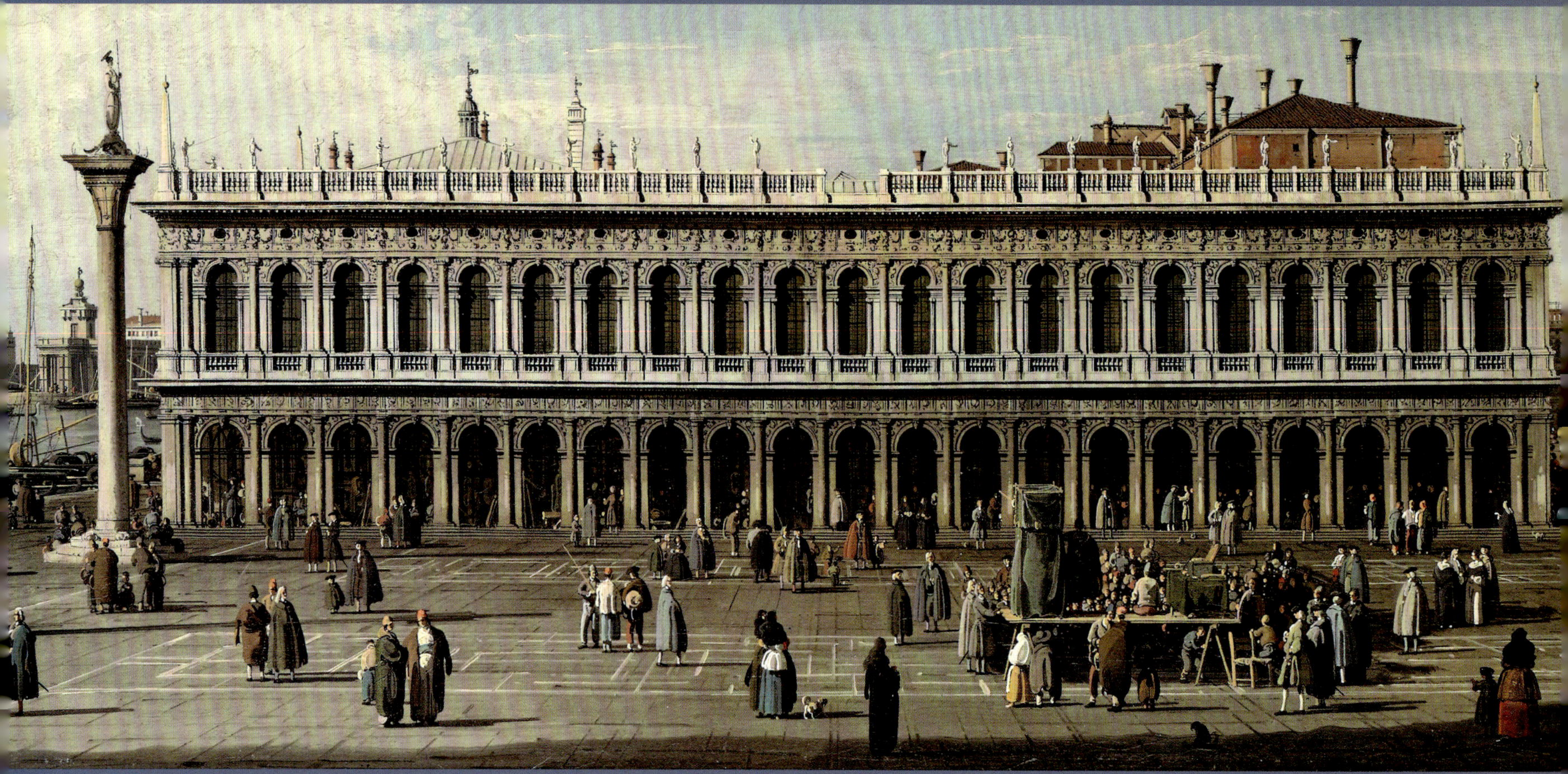

1. CANALETTO, BELLOTTO'S MASTER

When the young Bellotto entered his uncle Canaletto's atelier in around 1736, the master was at the height of his fame and success, under the aegis of his friend and merchant, Joseph Smith (circa 1674–1770), a passionate collector of his works. In Canaletto's paintings from that time – views of Venice, San Marco, the Grand Canal, public *Campo* and churches – Bellotto discovered a perfect balance between precision and pictorial quality and between rationality and poetry, resulting from more than a decade of study of technique and perspective composition. In order to cope with the commissions coming in one after the other at a frenetic rate, Canaletto had developed a rational, effective way of using the *camera optica* and the sketches he obtained, using them on multiple occasions. *The Campo Santi Giovanni e Paolo*, *Venice* painted between 1738 and 1739 (cat. 1) for Joseph Smith, is a perfect example of a composition created using the preparatory sketches preserved in the album now at the Accademia in Venice, and stands as a compendium of the technical methods that Bellotto, too, soon mastered: the precise drawing of architecture using a straight edge and compass, expert use of the technique of making incisions in the fresh paint in order to emphasise architectural details and enrich the painting's lighting, marking figures with touches of light and using dots for noses and eyes. Between 1736 and 1740, Bellotto, the only pupil of Canaletto who grasped and adopted his methods, used documentary sketches with more precision than the master himself, prepared the compositions for paintings and new drawings (cat. 3, 6), and even sketched from life the figures that Canaletto then used in his own paintings (cat. 10).

In 1738–39, he contributed fifteen paintings to the series of views of Venice ordered by Henry Howard, 4th Earl of Carlisle, a commission mediated by Anton Maria Zanetti di Girolamo (1680–1767). *The Grand Canal looking South from the Palazzi Foscari and Moro Lin to Santa Maria della Carità, Venice* (cat. 7), one of the first sent to Castle Howard, in Yorkshire, best exemplifies his abilities at his debut. Also for Castle Howard, the young painter made a copy of *The Libreria, looking North*, *Venice*, part of the series of four commissioned in 1738–39 by Thomas Brand of Hoo, one of the noble English Whigs, collectors of views, in contact with Smith during their stay in Venice. *The Molo looking West, the Column of Saint Theodore on the Right*, *Venice* (cat. 9) reveals the artist's achievement of full independence in the treatment of light and more precise rendering of details with respect to the 'model' provided by his uncle, now at the Castello Sforzesco in Milan. (cat. 8).

1

CANALETTO

(Venice 1697–1768)

The Campo Santi Giovanni e Paolo, Venice
ca. 1738–39

oil on canvas; 46 x 78.4 cm
The Royal Collection / HM Queen Elizabeth II, RCIN 400715

The Campo Santi Giovanni e Paolo was the subject of a series of works by Canaletto from his youth onwards, in which the fulcrum of the composition is the marble facade of the Scuola Grande di San Marco, the masterpiece of early Renaissance Venetian art finished in 1495 by Mauro Codussi (1440–1504).
This painting is unique in this series of views for the choice of point of view, from the Rio dei Mendicanti, opposite the monumental brick facade of the Dominican Basilica, built from about the middle of the thirteenth century in the particular Venetian version of the gothic style. It is also a unique piece as regards the collection of Canaletto works in the collection of Joseph Smith (1674 ca.–1770), sold to King George III in 1762: it is the only one for which the documentary sketches are known and the only one engraved by Antonio Visentini for second edition of the *Prospectus Magni Canalis Venetiarum* (1742, II, I).
The sketches, contained in the album of the Gallerie dell'Accademia in Venice called 'Quaderno', are two continuous drawings, of the view of the Basilica and of the nave with the monument to Bartolomeo Colleoni and the houses of the Calle del Forno, seen from two very different points of view in the *Campo* (Nepi Sciré 1997, pp. 149–53) (fig.a-d). There is no drawing of the Scuola di San Marco. A dashed line stresses the relationship between the height of the chimneys and the nave but this indication was ignored in the painting, where the chimneys appear higher. A shadow is indicated on the building standing next to the lateral apses, implying an impossible lighting from the north-west. J.G. Links thought that this detail suggests the composition derives from the print by Lovisa, in turn inspired by that of Carlevarijs (*Fabbriche, e vedute*, Venice 1703, no. 23). The drawings were effected using a *camera optica*, as was first demonstrated by D. Gioseffi (1959, pp. 41–49). In his painting, Canaletto created the illusion of a more distant and frontal viewpoint with regard to the facade of the church, and he brought together the two drawings of the Basilica as if they had been taken from only one point of view, integrating the Scuola di San Marco and depicting this too from an arbitrary viewpoint. The result is a highly sophisticated image, unreal in the proportions of the monuments and in the perspective views but of great beauty. The sharp divisions in the shadows cast by the two main buildings add structure to the space. The drawing of the details is delicate and the outlines of the architecture precise, marked out with a ruler incised into the fresh paint. The clear light adds lightness to the atmosphere and forms.
The rationality of the execution, the careful study of every detail of the composition and the precise technique, emblematic of the artist's maturity, resolve themselves in an image of great naturalness and poetry. Some of the figures portrayed are unusually humorous, each recorded at some task, making this a picture of daily life in Venice.
A number of versions and replicas of this compositions are known, accurately noted by W.G. Constable (308 [aa], [bb], [a]-[d]). The author was able to examine one, from a private collection. This was an autograph replica of larger size, dating to the period when the artist was in England (C/L 308-bb).
The *Campo* today is identical to the way it was depicted by Canaletto; only the windows of the Basilica di Santi Giovanni e Paolo are changed, having being returned to their original form during a restoration, and there is now a metal barrier around the Colleoni monument.

Bożena Anna Kowalczyk

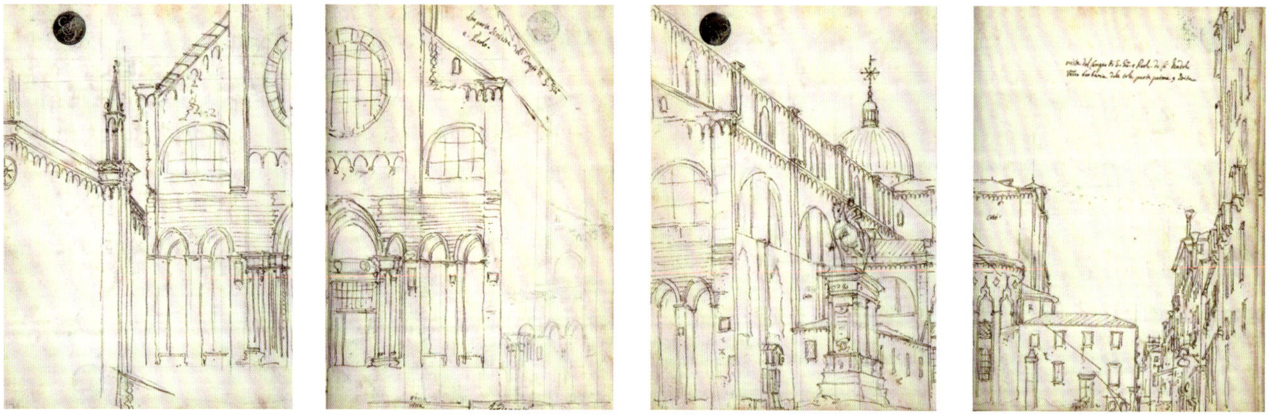

a-d Canaletto, *The Facade of the Basilica di Santi Giovanni e Paolo and Barbaria della Tole* (album of sketches, sheets 52*r*, 51*v*, 51, 50*v*), ca. 1738, pen and brown ink over pencil, 23 x 17 cm. Venice, Gallerie dell'Accademia, Gabinetto Stampe e Disegni, C1 III, n. 1785.

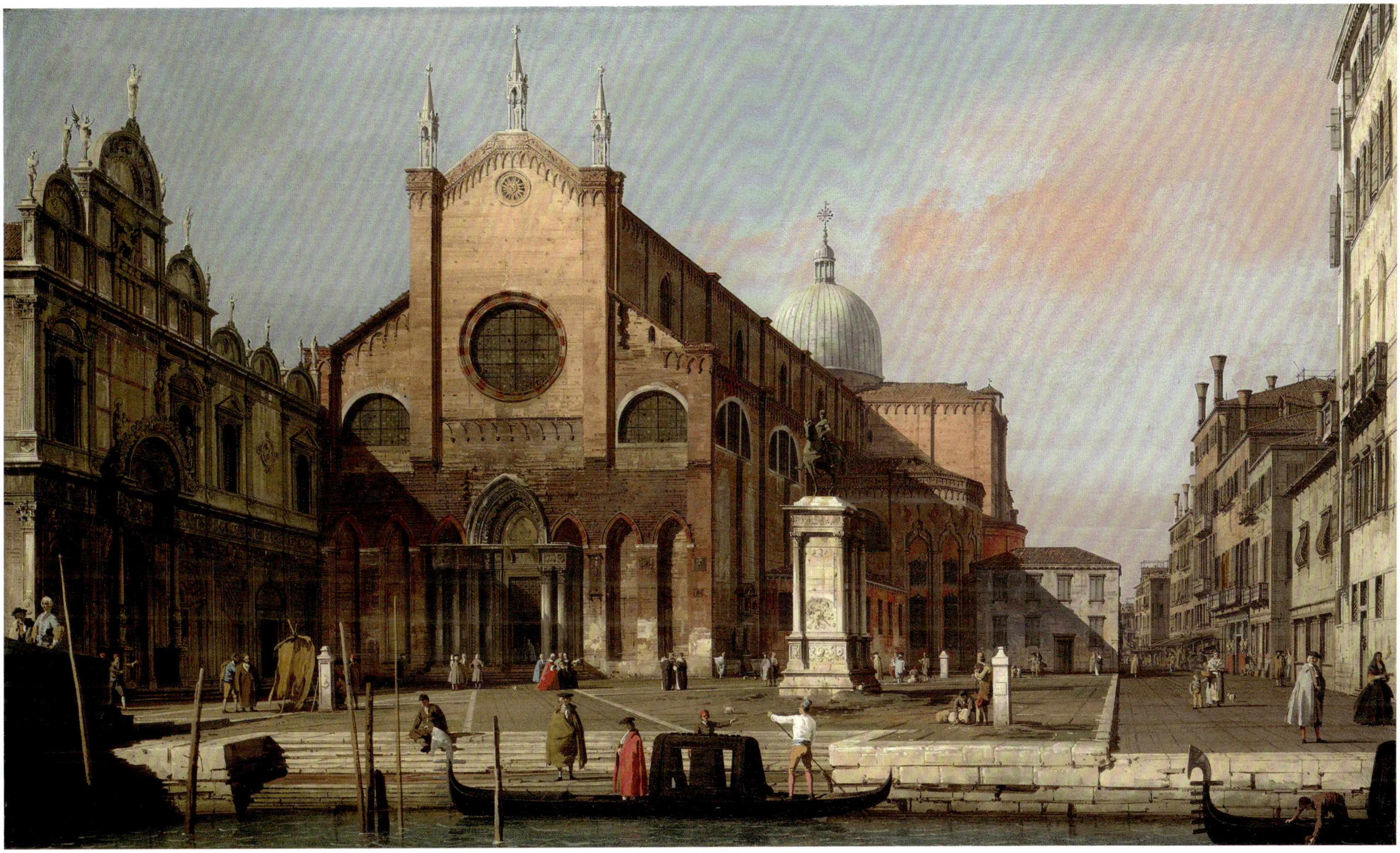

2

CANALETTO

(Venice 1697–1768)

The Piazzetta towards the Libreria, Venice
ca. 1739

oil on canvas; 47 x 78.2 cm
Private Collection

The Libreria was built between 1538 and 1591 by the Republic to a design by Jacopo Sansovino, in order to house the precious Greek and Byzantine codices left as a gift from 1468 by Cardinal Bessarione (1408–1472). The light brightly illuminates 'the richest and most ornate building that has perhaps been constructed since ancient times' (Palladio) and which Canaletto describes with precision and delicacy, noting the effects of the pluvial runoff differentiating the two floors of the building.
The image is especially harmonious, a studied composition of at least three views from various points located in the Loggia of the Doge's Palace, to frame the piazzetta to the left with the San Marco's columns, showing the Punta della Dogana and the Giudecca with the Redentore and Santa Eufemia, and to the right with the Campanile of San Marco and showing the Loggetta and a part of the Procuratie Vecchie. No sketches with studies for the picture survive.
In the Piazzetta, Venetian society is crystallised in the light around a puppet theatre, strolling and chatting, beyond the shadow in the foreground. Figures of gentlemen and common people, women and children, religious, Orientals and street vendors are skilfully distributed, and each described with a fluid, round brushstroke, each with a touch of light. The silhouettes of a procurator in wig and a little dog stand out against the shadows of the foreground.
The painting is part of a series of four, commissioned by Thomas Brand (ca. 1717–1770) of Hoo, in Hertfordshire, during his stay in Venice in the autumn months of 1738 (Ingamells 1997, p. 117), acting on the enthusiasm for the artist's works on the part of the Whig nobles, relatives or friends of John Russell (1710–1771), 4th Duke of Bedford. Woburn Abbey, the duke's residence, was decorated with twenty-four views by Canaletto, painted between 1732 and 1736; one subject was repeated for Brand, *The Grand Canal from Palazzo Corner towards the Palazzo Contarini degli Scrigni* (C/L 193a); another two paintings commissioned by Brand are *The Campo Santi Giovanni e Paolo* (C/L 306) and *Piazza San Marco from Campo San Basso* (C/L 40 note).
The paintings must have passed through the hands of Joseph Smith: the view of the Grand Canal was engraved by Antonio Visentini (1688–1788) for the second edition of the *Prospectus* (1742, II, 10), the publishing project sponsored by the future British Consul, while *The Campo Santi Giovanni e Paolo* was prepared in two drawings in outline (Venice, Correr Museum) and shaded with hatching (London, British Museum) but no engraving was ever made of it (B.A. Kowalczyk, *Rome 2005*, p. 280, no. 42). By 1738 already, Bernardo Bellotto was a painter with his own style and, particularly attracted by the paintings from the Brand series, he reproduced all the compositions on larger canvases (approximately 60 x 90 cm), expanding the foreground and lateral extension, using colder colours and accentuated contrasts of light; his figures are similar in type but are more elongated and sharp. The collector who commissioned the painting in this version was Henry Howard (1694–1758), 4th Duke of Carlisle, a member of the same Whig circle who was also in Venice in 1738–1739 (Ingamells 1997, p. 181); the painting is still preserved at his residence, Castle Howard in Yorkshire.
Canaletto painted another three versions of this composition: a painting in a private collection, which, from a photograph appears earlier, around 1735 (C/L 70), and two later ones: one formerly belonging to Thomas Neave, of circa 1755 – which brings the Libreria closer and includes only the column of Saint Theodore – and the other that used to belong to Champalimaud (Christie's, 6 July, 2005, lot 15, together with its pendant), typical of the production of the 1760s, in which the crowd in Piazzetta are brilliant dots of light and colour (C/L 71–72).
W.G. Constable links this painting to a drawing commissioned by Joseph Smith of circa 1740 (Parker 1948, n. 60). The Libreria is depicted in a similar way but the view is greatly expanded to give such a 'wide-angle' effect to form a *capriccio* as to include, on the right, the south end of the narthex of San Marco, an oblique glimpse of the Piazza and the Campanile depicted in all its height.

Bożena Anna Kowalczyk

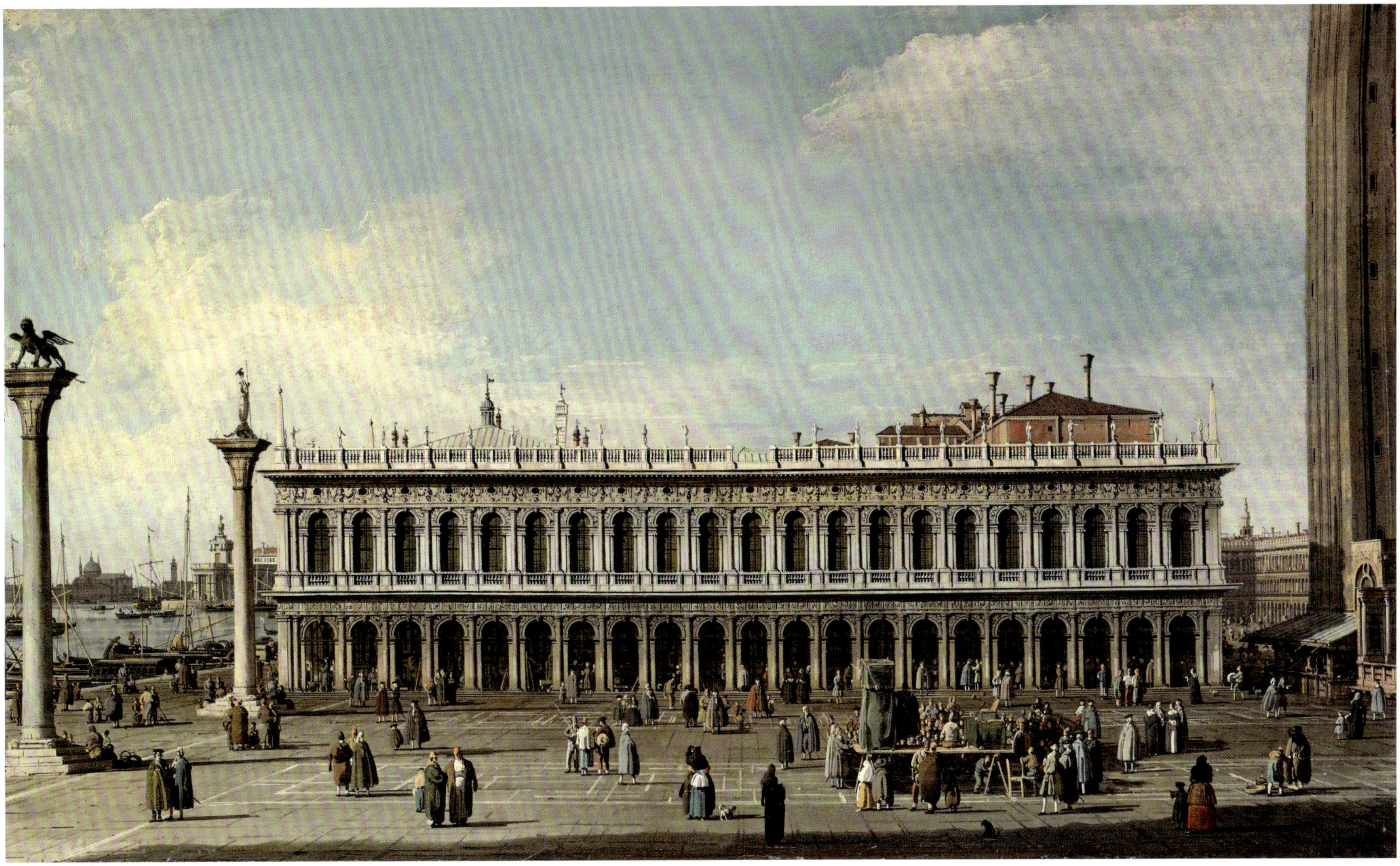

3

BERNARDO BELLOTTO

(Venice 1722 – Warsaw 1780)

The Campo Santa Maria Formosa, Venice (recto); Figures Studies (verso)
1738–39

pen and brown ink, over free and ruled pencil and pinpointing (*recto*); pencil (*verso*);
255 x 382 mm
Darmstadt, Hessisches Landesmuseum, AE 2210

Inscriptions: in the centre of the sky written with pen, 'S[ta] Maria Formosa'; up in to the right corner with red pencil, '20'; different writings and scrawls (*verso*).

According to tradition, the church of Santa Maria Formosa was founded in the seventh century by Saint Magnus, bishop of Oderzo, at the point where the Virgin allegedly appeared in *vaga forma*. After 1492, it was rebuilt by Mauro Codussi, respecting the building of the eleventh century, which had been built in imitation of the central part of Basilica di San Marco. The facade facing the *Campo* is of the early seventeenth century and was built at the expense of the Cappello family, as was the classical one facing the canal, constructed about half a century earlier. The fanciful seventeenth-century bell tower is a project by the monk Francesco Zucconi. The *Campo*, one of the largest and finest in Venice, is flanked on the left by the Donà buildings, of which the oldest one, with a fine Gothic portal, is described in the shade; the Venier House is shown behind and beyond the Rio and we can see the Renaissance Palazzo Malipiero Trevisa. The site, located near the homes of Canaletto and Bellotto, at San Lio, in Corte Perina and at Santa Marina, is one of their favourite subjects during the years they worked together.
This sketch is of fundamental importance in the sequence of drawings and paintings of the *Campo* by Canaletto and Bellotto. The calligraphic line, with a deliberate but responsive line, insistent in the details and disordered in the sky, is emblematic of the Venetian drawings of Bellotto which already around 1738 displayed a rigorous perspective framework.
S. Kozakiewicz published the sheet as 'one of the seven drawings by Bellotto executed on the basis of the sketches in Canaletto's album conserved in Venice at the Gallerie dell'Accademia and related to Canaletto's Windsor drawings'. The album, the famous 'Quaderno', is the most comprehensive document of the master's work in plein-air, using a *camera optica* along the Grand Canal and in the squares; these drawings formed the basis for paintings, especially those of the Bedford (1732–1735) and Harvey (1736–1738) series (Pignatti 1958; Nepi Sciré 1997; Venice 2012). In about 1736–1738, these same sketches were re-composed in the series of drawings by Canaletto, commissioned by Joseph Smith (British Royal Collection). These accurate drawings share many features with the rather elementary sheets by the student, but for the most part they are not identical. Scholars of Canaletto and Bellotto, Von Hadeln, Frtizsche, K.T. Parker, W.G. Constable, had no doubts that they were mere copies but some of Bellotto's drawings follow the indications of the sketches at times adopted by Canaletto with such fidelity as to corroborate the hypothesis of the Polish scholar who was the first to claim the student had an important role in the studio. In this case, the succession of sheets are, from left to right, 38*v*, 39, 37*v*, 38, 36*v* 37 (Nepi Sciré 1997 pp. 115–123).
In the sheet by Canaletto which corresponds in every detail to this sketch, we also find some typical Bellotto figures, such as the unmistakable backlit silhouette in the right foreground; also similar is the unusual hatching to indicate the shadow of the houses on the left. In his drawing, Bellotto uses the four vertical folds in the paper to set out the prospective drawn in pencil and ruler (the horizontal folds in the sky are later) and like Canaletto uses a pencil and ruler to mark the line of the horizon (here 66–68 mm from the bottom edge); the vanishing point marked with the compass is located between the apse of the church and Palazzo Malipiero Trevisan behind the bridge. We can note many *pentimenti* in the position of some figures, of the gentleman on the left of the group in the foreground, of the wanderer with his bag and stick, and in the seller with the basket. A larger portion of the buildings is visible here on both sides. The writing is from the eighteenth century but probably later in date. The red numbers were put later by the Darmstadt Museum.
Bellotto used the sketch in 1739–40 for the painting now in a private collection (B.A. Kowalczyk, in Venice–Houston 2001, no. 2; fig. a); in 1742, he made a larger version with a greater extension to the sides and inverted light, both long considered by Canaletto (B.A. Kowalczyk, in Turin 2008, n. 11).

Bożena Anna Kowalczyk

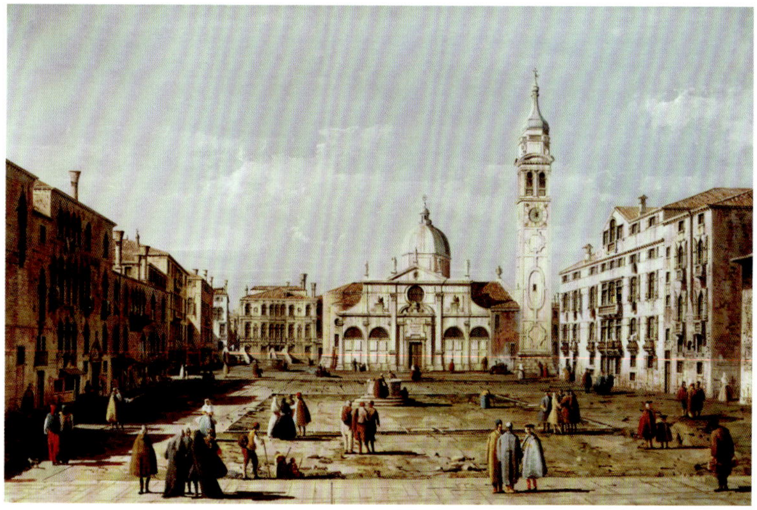

a. Bernardo Bellotto, *Campo di Santa Maria Formosa, Venice*, 1739–40, oil on canvas, 61 x 92.4 cm. Private Collection

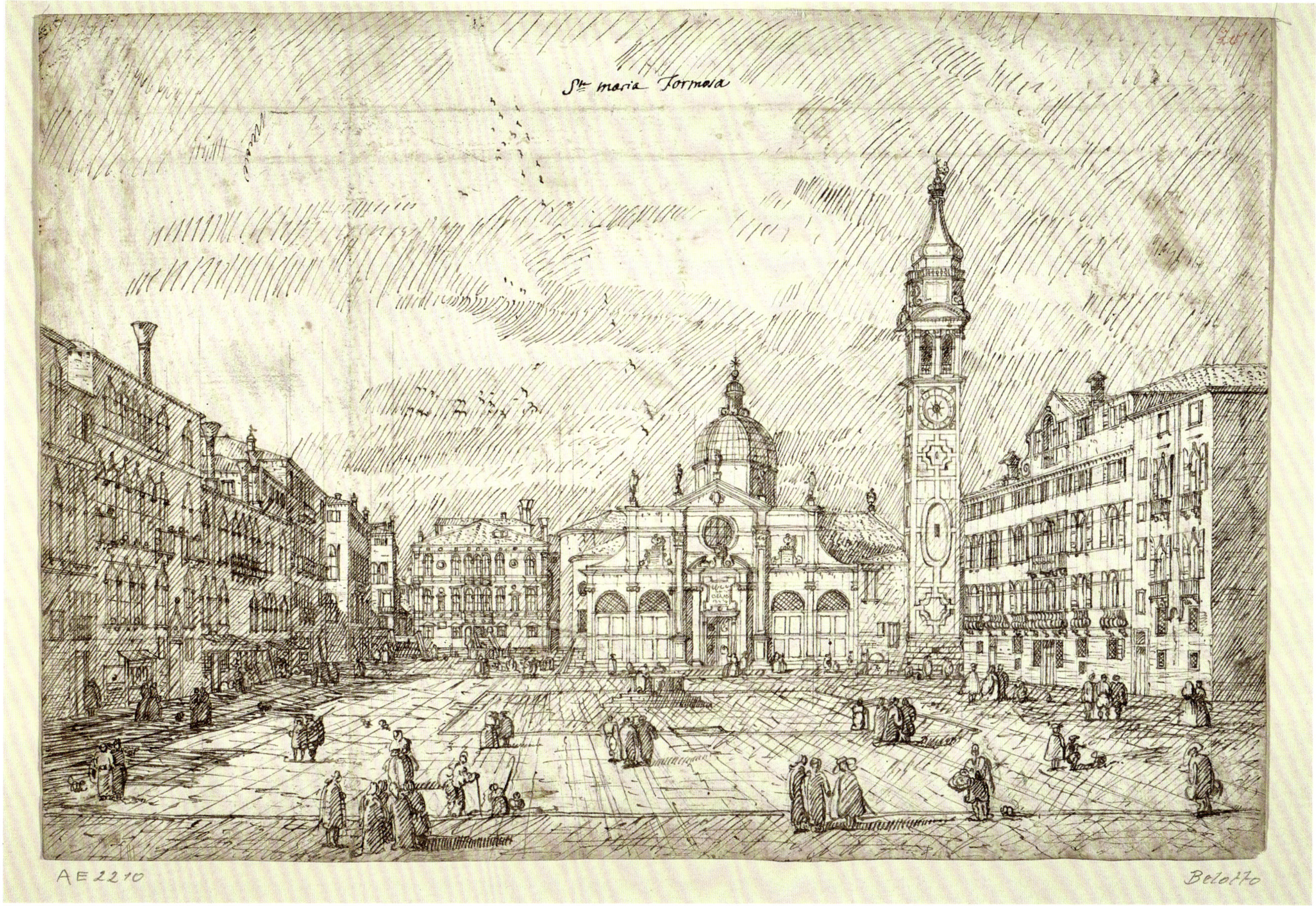
Sta maria Formosa
AE 2210
Belotto

4

CANALETTO

(Venice 1697–1768)

The Campo Santa Maria Formosa, Venice
1738–1740

pen and brown ink, over free and ruled pencil and pinpointing; 270 x 376 mm
The Royal Collection / HM Queen Elizabeth II, RCIN 907478

Of the sketches by Canaletto bound in the album of the Gallerie dell'Accademia in Venice, the six sheets dedicated to Campo Santa Maria Formosa are the most fascinating for the exemplary method of noting details and for their pictorial quality resulting from the use of red pencil. This drawing was suggested by K.T. Parker to be the first graphic composition and model for Bellotto's version of the work in the Darmstadt Museum (cat. 3). S. Kozakiewicz believes instead that this is a subsequent work to his pupil's drawing.

The two sheets, this one and the version by Bellotto (cat. 3), correspond exactly in the tracing of the lines and the same vanishing point is pricked with a compass. The shadows of the buildings on the left have the same extension and contours, achieved with an intense hatching of parallel lines laid, unusually, perpendicular to the buildings. The manner of depicting the tiles, with short curved lines, is also the same, as is the way of creating the shadows of the figures in the *Campo*, with quickly applied parallel lines. The two artists differ in the clouds, here marked like 'rain' with rather untidy lines, and instead bolder and lighter in the sheet in the Royal Collection.

The *modus operandi* is identical: even though the majority of accessory lines is deleted here, it is possible to make out the lines of pencil and ruler and the horizon line drawn from edge to edge. Small pinpointing from compass holes can be noted, used for the measurements and to draw the dome; a ruler has also been used for some of the lines of the paving in ink. A *pentimento* in the height of the houses on the left has been left visible. Given that one of the two drawings is a copy of the other, it is interesting to note that neither is a simple tracing but both stem from the same constructive process (see the graphic of the author in her catalogue essay).

The comparison of the two drawings suggests that the Bellotto sheet is the preparatory sketch, subsequently perfected by Canaletto. This is so close in the tracing of lines to the Darmstadt one, and in the hatching and silhouettes of figures, some typical of Bellotto, that the present writer had some doubts with regard to the attribution to Canaletto (B.A. Kowalczyk, in Turin 2008), but the line is more uniform and firmer, confirming the attribution.

Canaletto produced another version of this drawing for Smith, exactly the same in terms of size and with the same perspective composition but introducing a number of variations, and with greater care in the hatching and the finishing (The Royal Collection, RCIN 907479, fig. a). As in the other versions, the light comes from the left, but the shadow area in the *Campo* is more extensive and differently structured – the Ponte della Ruga Giuffa is in the light – and obtained with a different type of hatching, in the same direction as the lines shading the facades on the *Campo*. The view of the buildings on the right side is slightly more frontal and decreases the edge in shadow of the last house. The line is led with a light touch that assures precision in the details, and the hatching is in general more open and well spaced. The shadows of the figures in the *Campo* are marked as usual, with an unbroken spiral line, and not with tight parallel lines as in the version here attributed to Bellotto (cat. 3). The shadowed area in the foreground, typical of Bellotto, is here eliminated and the figures are more numerous and arranged in a more natural way, even though, as in the other version, they follow the main perspective lines. Canaletto does not stress the scroll with the inscription over the door of the church, and nor the appearance of the statues of the *Virtues* above, but hints at the state of neglect of the *Campo* around the well, and focuses on the round balustrades of the little terraces. The sky has an abundance of clouds, as in the Bellotto sheet, but they are lighter and outlined by an undulating line.

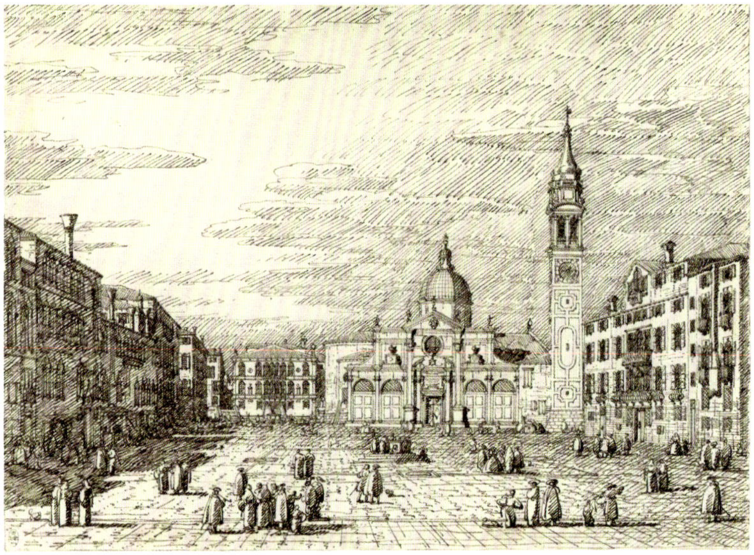

a. Canaletto, *Campo Santa Maria Formosa, Venice*, ca. 1740, pen and brown ink in two shades over pencil, 270 x 376 mm. The Royal Collection, RCIN 907479

Some paintings by Canaletto based on these sketches are known but with different perspective and figures; one belongs to the Duke of Bedford at Woburn Abbey, dating from 1734–35 (C/L 278), another was formerly in the Fonthill Collection (C/L 280), reproduced by Visentini (1742, II, 8), and there is a third in private collection, both of circa 1740 (Links 1998, no. 280*).

Bożena Anna Kowalczyk

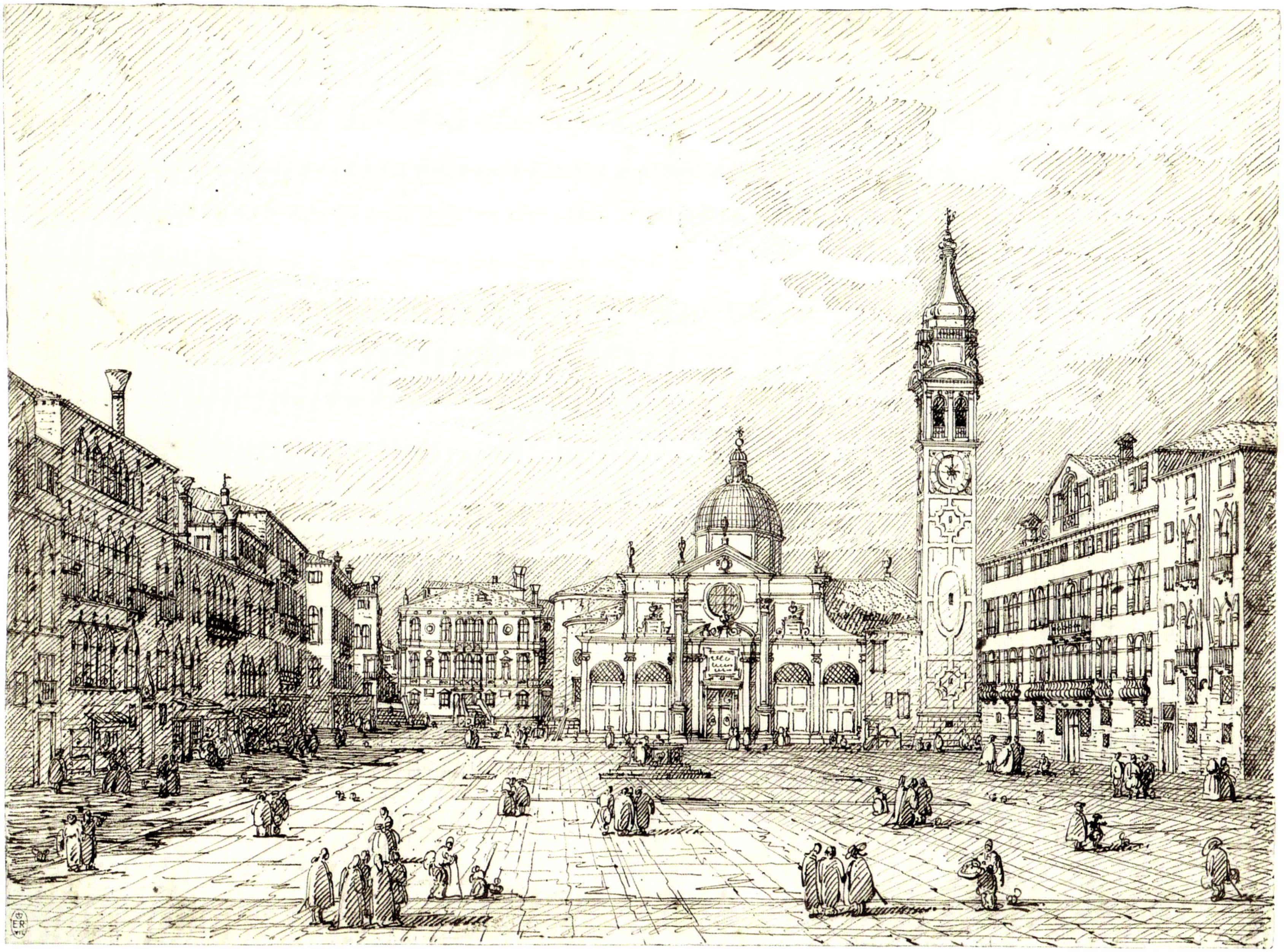

5

CANALETTO

(Venice 1697–1768)

The Rialto Bridge from the South, Venice
ca. 1740

oil on canvas; 45 x 76 cm
Paris, Institut de France, Musée Jacquemart-André, MJAP-P-577-1

The classical facade of Palazzo Dolfin-Manin, designed by Jacopo Sansovino and the future residence of the last Doge, Ludovico Manin, dominates this stretch of the Grand Canal, which proceeding from San Marco, arrives at the Rialto Bridge; beyond the bridge, to the right, there is the Fondaco dei Tedeschi, with traces of Giorgione's frescoes still visible, and on the left, the edge of the Palazzo dei Camerlenghi. A row of shops punctuates the Fondamenta del Vin, and boats used for the wine trade are berthed alongside, as required by the Serenissima's laws; in the right background, we see the Riva del Ferro, the centre of the metals market. This painting and its pendant, *The Piazza San Marco, looking East*, from the same collection, were attributed to Bernardo Bellotto when studies regarding the distinction between the two artists in their views of Venice were in their beginnings, and the cooler shades, greater contrasting shadows and figures with ball-shaped noses were universally considered the hallmarks of the younger *veduta* artist. The two pendants actually belong to Canaletto, at that stage of collaboration around 1740 when Bellotto was not only preparing the drawings for the compositions but was with his own interpretations influencing the master's painting. In the case of this work, the attribution to Bellotto was undoubtedly suggested by the rationality of the perspective composition and by the importance accorded the architecture. The composition follows two drawings by his pupil and collaborator in every detail, even down to the boats and figures: one in the Rijksmuseum, Amsterdam, and the other in a private collection (cat. 6).
A similar view in the Galleria Nazionale d'Arte Antica, Rome, formerly in the principe Giovanni Torlonia collection, has also been associated in the past to Bellotto, together with the series of four works to which it belongs (C/L 228a-4): in the larger size (68.5 x 92 cm) typical of Bellotto and not of Canaletto, it depicts a larger area of water and sky, and different boats arranged differently.
Bellotto painted another version of this view in the same period, now in the National Gallery of Victoria, Melbourne (B.A. Kowalczyk, in Turin 2008, p. 68, no. 7, fig. a). The architecture differs only in small details, such as the height and disposition of chimneys or the awnings and clothes from the windows, but the figures and vessels instead change altogether and are like those in another painting by Canaletto, formerly in the Arthur Bisgwood collection (C/L 228a-3), painted in 1738–1739.
Inexplicably, W.G. Constable catalogued the painting that used to be in the Rothschild collection, signed and dated 1744 (C/L 228) as being the main version of this view, but it has a different sky and variations in the type and disposition of the boats and figures. The painting, one of the many works of art dispossessed in World War II, has been deposited by the Musée du Louvre in 1957 to the Musée d'art et d'archéologie du Périgord at Périgueux and, recently restored, is now confirmed as an autograph work by Canaletto.

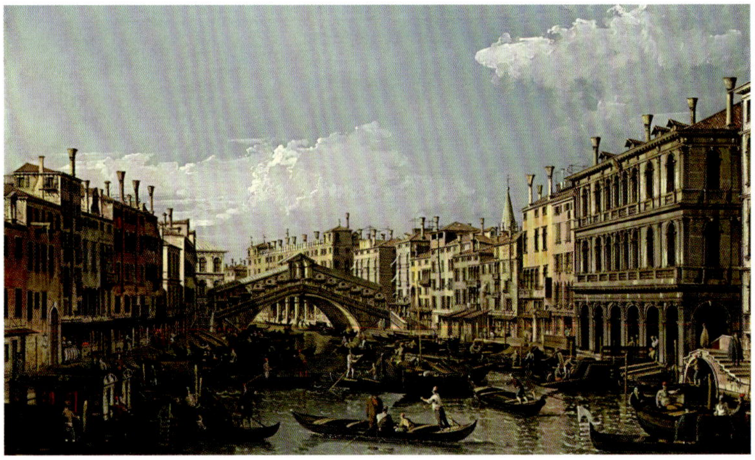

a. Bernardo Bellotto, *The Rialto Bridge from the South, Venice*, ca. 1739, oil on canvas, 61 x 92.2 cm. Melbourne, The National Gallery of Victoria, Felton Bequest, 1919, 965/3

J.G. Links (1998, no. 228-a) has published a larger version under the name of Canaletto, which presents some minor variations in the boats and figures. It was bought at Christie's (26 February, 1917, lot 35) by the Japanese Prince Matsukata and sold in 1983-1984 through the London art market.
The present painting was bought by Édouard André (1833–1894) with the pendant, *Piazza San Marco, looking East* (C/L 6) at the Charles Pillet sale, Hôtel Drouot, 12 April, 1865 (N. Saint Fare Garnot, in Paris 2012-2013, p. 54). The price of 18,500 francs gives a good idea of the esteem in which Canaletto and views of Venice were held, especially in comparison to the 285 francs paid by the same collector a year before for a beautiful gouache *capriccio* by Francesco Guardi, the only other work by a Venetian *vedutista* in the collection of the Musée Jacquemart-André (B.A. Kowalczyk, in Paris 2012–2013, no. 50).
Of the two pendants, only this one was engraved by Antonio Visentini and published for the first time in the 1742 edition of the *Prospectus*. For an indefinite period of time, the picture and its pendant hung in the Venetian home of Joseph Smith, as stated in the album's foreword.

Bożena Anna Kowalczyk

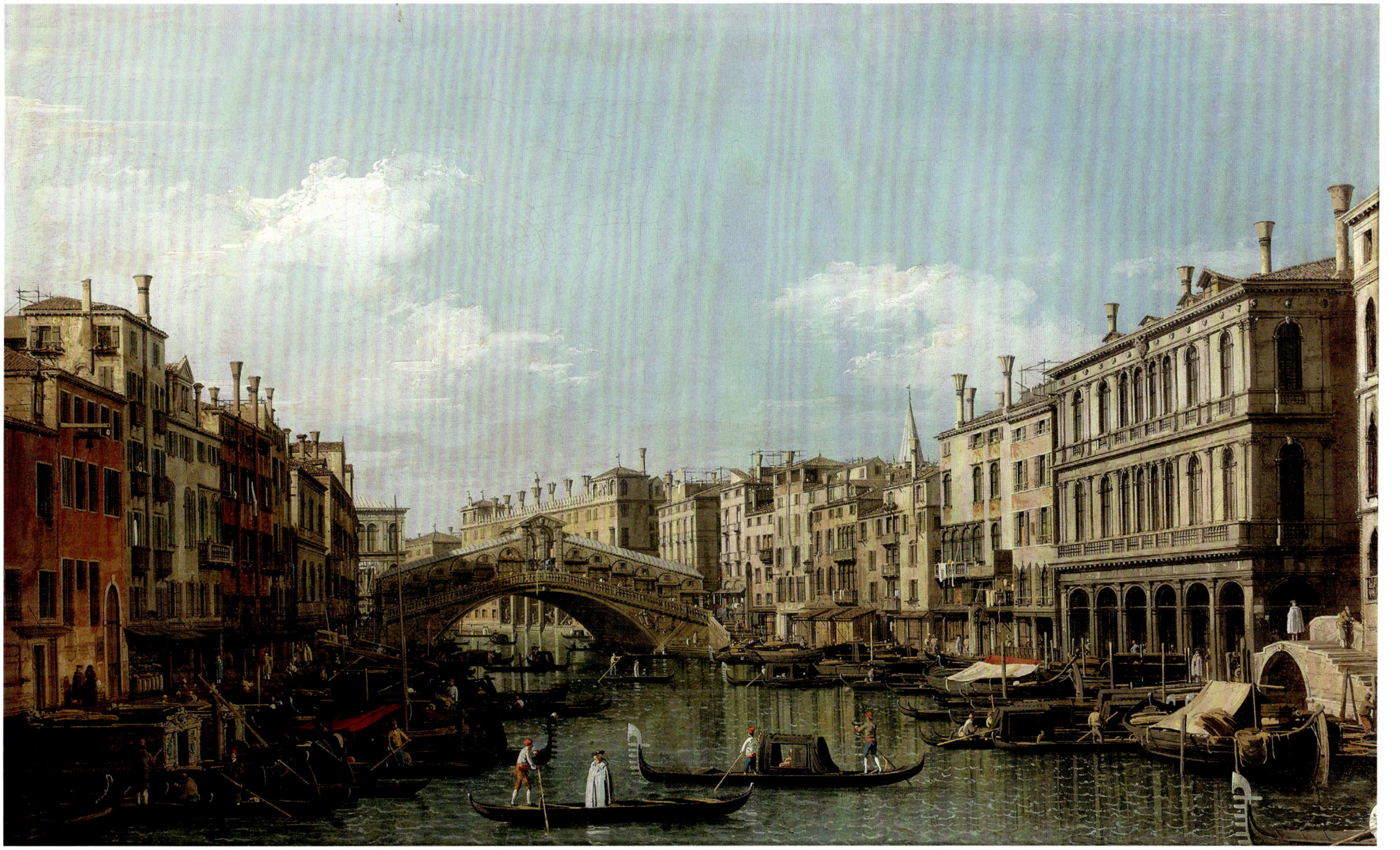

6

BERNARDO BELLOTTO

(Venice 1722 – Warsaw 1780)

The Rialto Bridge from the South, from the Palazzo Dolfin-Manin, Venice
1739–40

pen and two shades of brown ink over free and ruled pencil and pinpointing; 217 x 385 mm
Private Collection
work not on display

Of the various types of preparatory drawing that survive from Bellotto's early period, this sheet, together with one with a similar composition at the Rijksmuseum in Amsterdam (fig. a), comprises a unique case, representing distinct, already advanced, phases of preparatory work done for a painting. They are even more interesting for the fact that they were used for a painting by Canaletto – at the Musée Jacquemart-André (C/L 228a-1) (cat. 5) – offering clear evidence of the extremely close collaboration between the two around 1740, probably supported by Joseph Smith, who bought the painting. The transition from one drawing to the other and the subtlety of the 'corrections' and adjustments, which perfected the perspective, indicate the quality of Bellotto's training to that point and the accuracy of the preparatory work.

The two drawings were made using the same method of pure outline – the only small hatched area is in the present sheet, on the portico of the Fondaco dei Tedeschi. Both describe the outlines of the clouds and note the waves in the foreground and the reflections of the boats in the water. This was the first sketch and was produced in the studio based on four partial drawings, made using a *camera optica* on a boat on the canal. Bellotto used Canaletto's proceedings methods, but the composition of the sketches introduced a unique contribution of his own: he first folded the white sheet vertically, to divide it into four equal parts, and then reinforced the folds with a ruled pencil; like Canaletto, he marked the horizon line, to get the main reference points for his perspectival composition. He subsequently drew the architecture in pencil, using a straight edge and a compass, and then added the details, boats and figures freehand. He passed over the pencil drawing with pen, also using the straight edge, in two stages that are distinguished by the colour of the ink, starting with the background, from the Rialto Bridge and the nearby buildings, where the ink is darker. With few exceptions, the figures were drawn solely in pen, and last, above the other drawn lines. The style, which tends towards precise, synthetic indication of details, is unmistakable, from the nervous, literal, interrupted line used to delineate the figures, clouds and reflections in the water.

The two drawings have the same width but are of different heights. The one at the Rijksmuseum is trimmed at the top, following the horizontal fold along the upper margin of the present sketch. The differences in composition are very subtle and especially concern the angle of the Palazzo Dolfin-Manin, which dominates the image to the right, and some of the first houses on the Riva del Vin, less sharply rendered, with a consequential slight divergence of the vanishing point. The outlines of the figures follow those of the present sheet but were drawn prior to other marks in the background, small adjustments made to the boats.

The Jacquemart-André painting follows the Rijksmuseum drawing in every detail, but it has the same proportions as the present sheet and also picks up a few rare details omitted in the other sketch, like the tall chimney to the side of the roof of the Fondaco dei Tedeschi. Both note the frescoes by Giorgione on that building.

Bożena Anna Kowalczyk

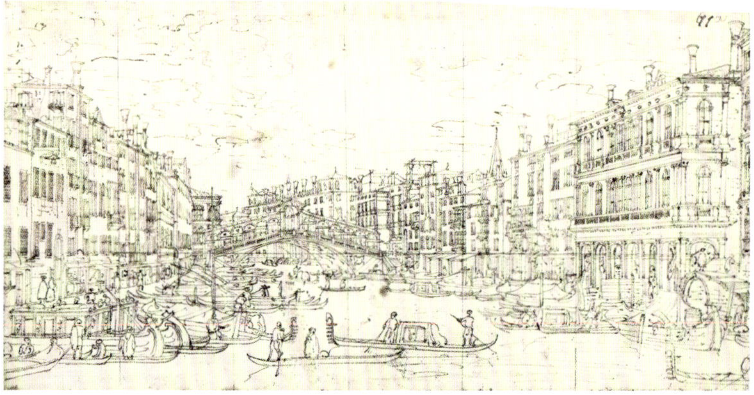

a. Bernardo Bellotto, *The Rialto Bridge from the South, from the Palazzo Dolfin-Manin, Venice*, 1740, pen and two shades of brown ink over free and ruled pencil and pinpointing, 196 x 385 mm. Amsterdam, Rijksmuseum, RP-T 1953-216

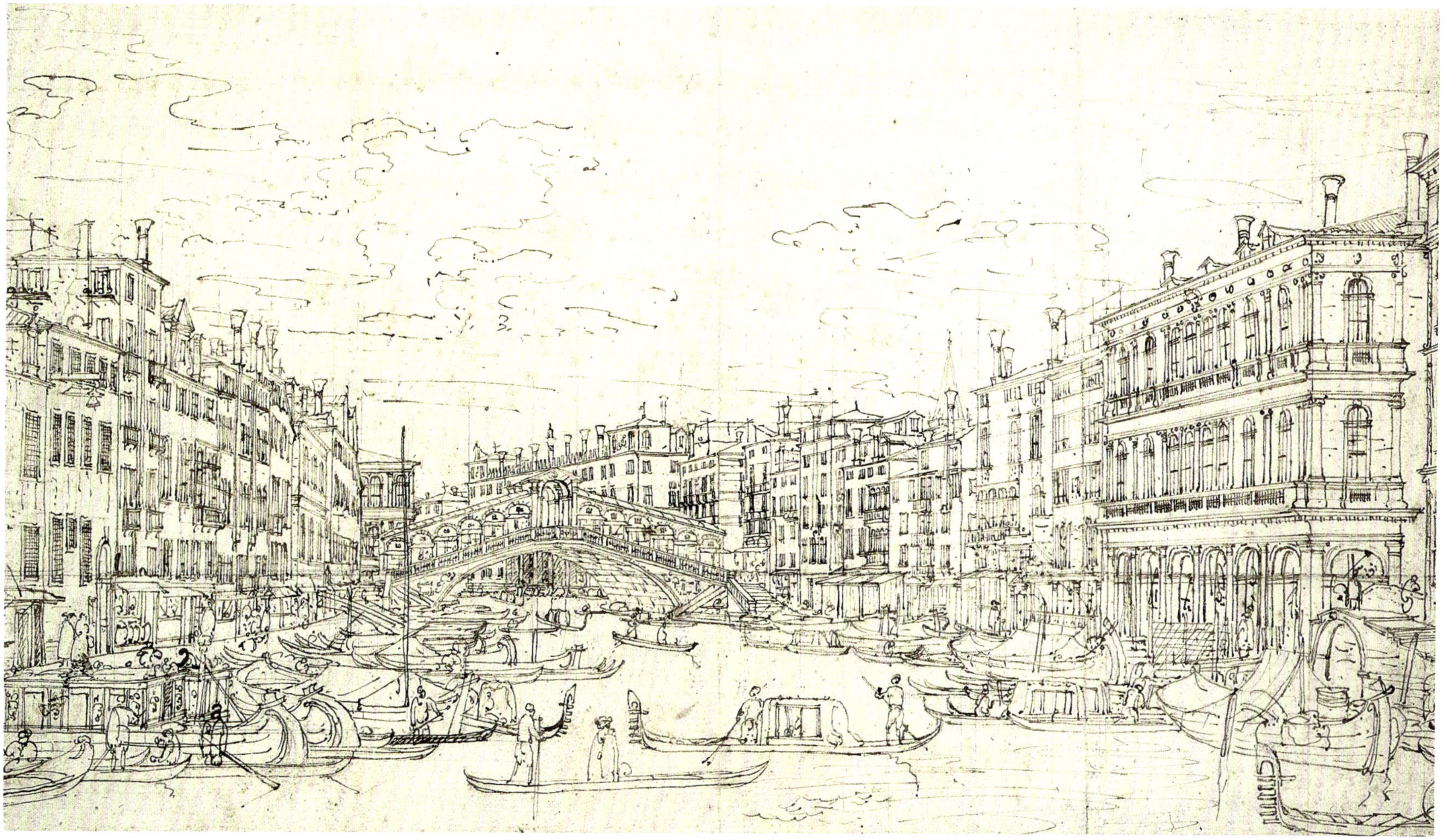

7

BERNARDO BELLOTTO

(Venice 1722 – Warsaw 1780)

The Grand Canal looking South from the Palazzi Foscari and Moro Lin to Santa Maria della Carità, Venice
1738–39

oil on canvas; 59.7 x 89.5 cm
Private Collection, courtesy Fabrizio Moretti Ltd., London

In 1739–40, the young Bellotto, then just seventeen, was present with fifteen paintings in the largest collection of Venetian views to be formed by a British tourist. Henry Howard (1694–1758), fourth Earl of Carlisle, is documented as being in Venice in November 1738 (Ingamells 1997, p. 181); he met Anton Maria Zanetti di Girolamo (1680–1767), as evidenced by subsequent correspondence (Scarsbrick 1987, p. 96) and certainly also Joseph Smith (1674 ca. –1770), who was a point of reference for British travellers in Venice. Before June 1740, the duke received the first views of Venice at Castle Howard, his sumptuous residence in Yorkshire; these were sent by Zanetti, who was without doubt the prime mover behind the commission. The years 1742–43, the date of the latest works – two pendant views of San Marco by Canaletto, now at the National Gallery of Art in Washington (C/L 50 and 154) – provide the *terminus ante quem* for the formation of the collection, comprising forty paintings. Canaletto is the only name mentioned in the inventories of Castle Howard until the early twentieth century; the correct attribution to four different artists – Canaletto, Bellotto, Michele Marieschi and Giambattista Cimaroli – is recent (D. Succi, in Mirano 1999; B. A. Kowalczyk, in Venice–Houston 2001). Three paintings by just Bellotto remain at Castle Howard.
For Bellotto, this was his first important commission and his first series of views of a city: two of the San Marco basin – one with the *Bucintoro at the Molo on Ascension Day* – eight of the Grand Canal and five of various *Campi* and churches. For the most part, they are replicas of works by Canaletto: a careful choice from the works that Howard might have seen in Venice, such as the paintings from the 1720s in the house of Joseph Smith – like the model for the present painting (fig. a) – and other contemporary or very recent ones painted for other British Whig noblemen, the Duke of Marlborough and Thomas Brand of The Hoo.
This fascinating painting could be one of the first to have been sent to Castle Howard. Bellotto was certainly required to paint like Canaletto. The ambitious execution is exemplary of the way Bellotto tackled the task, remaining strictly close to the composition of Canaletto, but returning to the location to investigate the details, and interpreting the chiaroscuro contrasts, tones and colour range in a wholly personal way, together with the rendering of the sky, water and figures. The viewpoint has been slightly shifted to the left, to attenuate the perspective view of the Foscari buildings and to show a greater portion of the lateral facades along the right bank of the canal; in order to increase the area of water in the foreground, the viewpoint has also been moved back, as evidenced by a boat exiting from the Rio di Ca' Foscari on the right, which is absent in the Canaletto version. This subtle intervention, that testifies to the deep training in the use of perspective already attained by Bellotto by that date, is joined by a number of other modification, starting from the boats and figures, which are different or differently positioned, with the exception of the large cargo barge in the foreground, in which only the details have been modified. Moreover, the chimneys have increased in number, the awnings have been eliminated here and there and elsewhere added, there are shadows cast on to the illuminated surfaces by protruding tiles, and some of the plasterwork is of a different colour; some liberties have also been taken, such as the fanciful description of Carità's bell tower and the curious omission of the roof of Palazzo Moro Lin. The technique is Canaletto's contemporary one, which Bellotto interpreted with conviction, accentuating its essential aspects – the incisions in the fresh paint, the three-dimensional drawing of the architectural details – and with masterful effect in the facades and in the Palazzi Foscari and Giustinian in the shade. Only Bellotto could have succeeded in rendering the texture of the stones, the dampness of the plasterwork, the wooden roof structures of Ca' Rezzonico, then left unfinished. The rendering of the sky and water are demonstrations of an ambitious virtuosity.
This creative interpretation anticipates many solutions of the second version of this view in the National Museum in Stockholm, painted by Bellotto in the early months of 1740, before his departure in April-May for Florence to commemorate the visit of the Electoral Prince of Saxony, Frederick Christian (Kowalczyk 1999).

Bożena Anna Kowalczyk

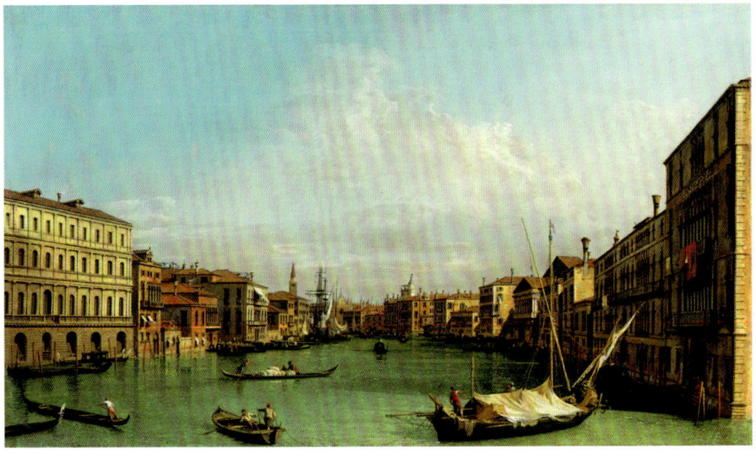

a. Canaletto, *The Grand Canal looking South, from the Palazzi Foscari and Moro Lin to Santa Maria della Carità, Venice*, 1726–27, oil on canvs, 49,9 x 80,3 cm.
The Royal Collection, RCIN 401404

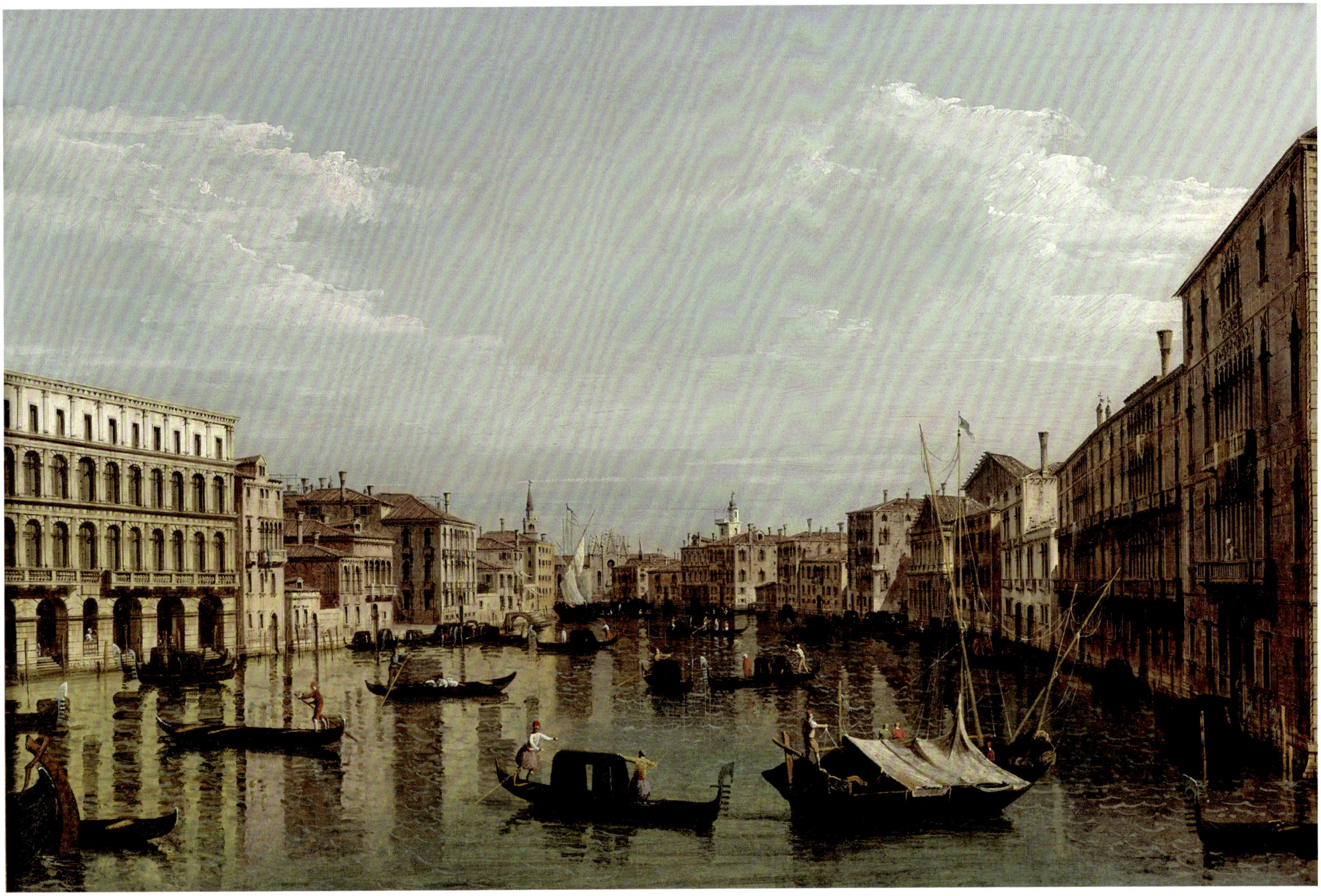

8

CANALETTO

(Venice 1679 – 1768)

The Molo looking West, the Column of Saint Theodore on the Right, Venice
ca. 1738

oil on canvas; 110.5 x 185.5 cm
Milan, Raccolte d'Arte Antica, Pinacoteca del Castello Sforzesco, 1474

This beautiful canvas and its pendant, *La Riva degli Schiavoni looking Est, Venice* (C/L 113), came from the sophisticated collection of the Dukes of Leeds at Hornby Castle, Bedale, Yorkshire. In 1882, John Murray notes the presence of eight paintings by Canaletto in the castle, in particular admiring the four in the Billiard Room: 'Canaletti: 4 very fine Venetian scenes, 2 of them festivals, with the Bucentaur conspicous. The 2 others are views from the head of Piazza San Marco. These are among the best Canalettis in England. The skies are especially clear and beautiful' (Murray 1882, 303). The two festival scenes are now at the National Gallery in London (C/L 333 and 350). The collection also included two views of Piazza San Marco (The Detroit Institute of Art and The Fogg Art Museum, Cambridge; C/L 14 and 24) and five other paintings, currently in private collections. In 1902, the Canaletto paintings were brought together in the Second Drawing Room, along with two spectacular views of Rome by van Wittel, acquired in 1737 at an auction in London (*Catalogue* 1902; Briganti 1996, nos. 14, 141) and an exceptional pair of pendants by Panini, *Interior of Saint Peter's* and *Interior of Saint Paul Outside-the-Walls*, both signed and dated 1741 (Christie's, London, 7 July 2004, lot 106).
In the absence of archival documents, there is no reason to doubt that the Canaletto collection was built by Thomas Osborne (1713–1789), 4th Duke of Leeds, who is documented to have been in Venice on his Grand Tour between March and June 1734. 'One of indispensable acts of English noblemen on the grand tour was to buy Venetian views of Canaletti' ('Athenaeum' 1878, p. 342), but the idea of commissioning or purchasing works by the artist, which might have emerged during that trip, was not acted upon until later, probably around 1738, in parallel to the collecting activity begun in 1738–1739 by Henry Howard, 4th Earl of Carlisle, at nearby Castle Howard, with the mediation of Joseph Smith who had etchings of this pair made by Antonio Visentini for the second series of the *Prospectus* (1742, II, XII and XI). Thomas Osborne's collecting of Canaletto and Panini was parallel to that of William, 3rd Earl of Fitzwilliam, who is documented to have been in Venice in April 1740. They were related through Mary Godolphin, who married Thomas that year. Between 1742 and 1744, Canaletto painted two similar scenes in smaller format for William (C/L 98 and 114).
In 1924, after the sale of the whole group of eleven Canalettos from Hornby Castle at a Christie's auction on 11 June 1920, this painting and its pendant were in the collection of the senator Luigi Albertini, representing Milanese collecting of Venetian views at its best. The successful compositions develop the themes already treated in the similarly formatted pairs at Chatsworth (ca. 1729) and Tatton Park (1730) (C/L 115, 149 and 111, 97), by boldly expanding the spaces. The narrative interest and variety of the scenes, with large, meticulously detailed figures, is completely anomalous in Canaletto's mature repertoire and contrasts with the sophisticated lighting solutions, explaining scholars' uncertainty about their chronology. I would argue that they were painted after 1735–36, when the splendid *Bacino di San Marco* at Sir John Soane's Museum was made, but before the *Bacino di San Marco* at Museum of Fine Arts, Boston, from 1738–39.
The view extends up to Santa Maria della Salute and the Giudecca Canal, with the Redentore, but converges on the scene at the Molo, with the fish and poultry market, while its pendant embraces the Riva degli Schiavoni, from the Column of San Marco and the Ducal Palace up to the Arsenale, described with admirable detail, but shifting the accent to the basin, with a profusion of boats brought to life by colourful, well characterised figures. Standing out in this painting is a Venetian nobleman wearing a tricorn, watching the scene on the Molo, while its pendant has a young foreigner, travelling in a gondola and gazing, enchanted, at the panorama laid out before him.

Bożena Anna Kowalczyk

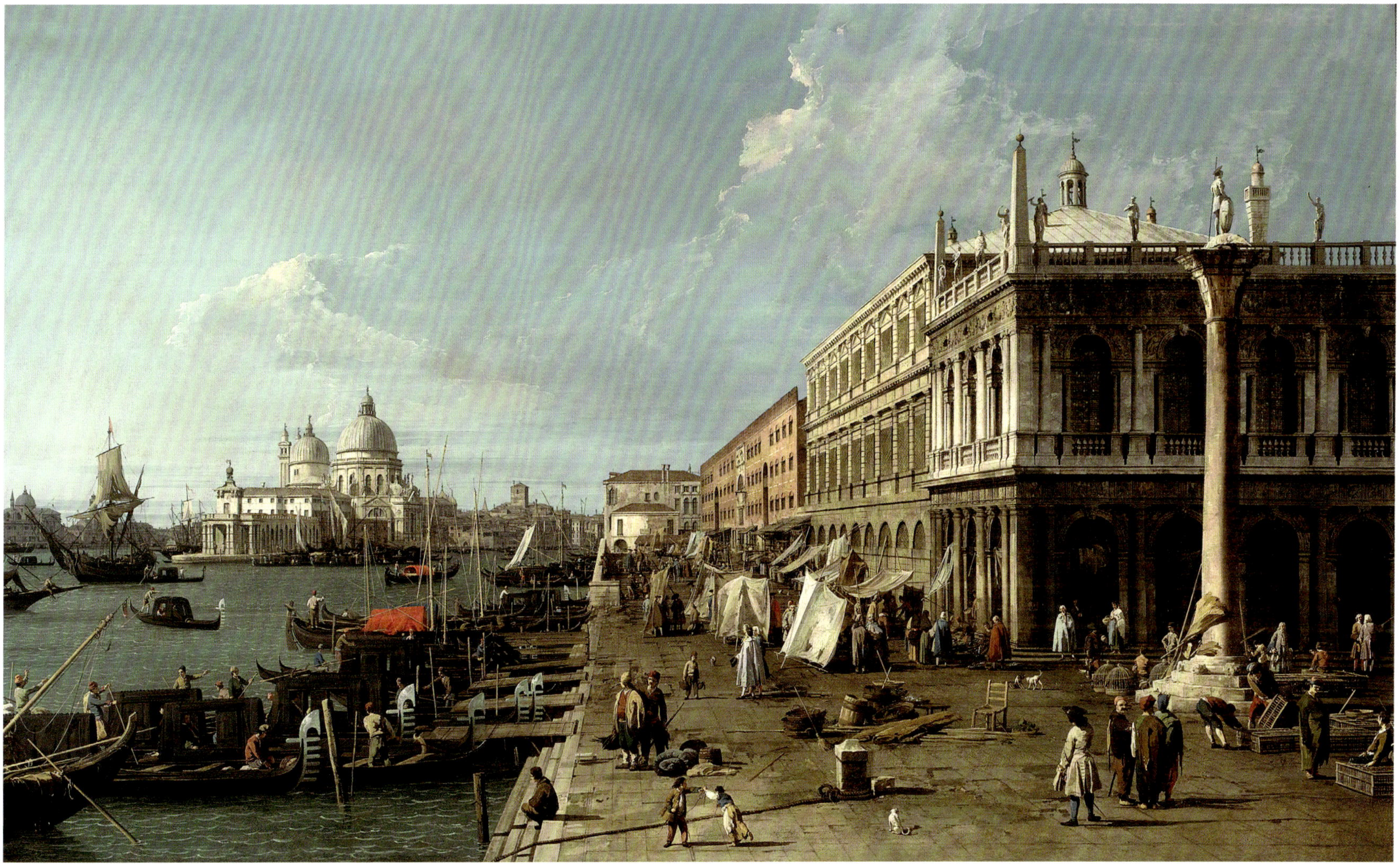

9

BERNARDO BELLOTTO

(Venice 1722 – Warsaw 1780)

The Molo looking West, the Column of Saint Theodore on the Right, Venice
ca. 1739

oil on canvas; 62.2 x 94 cm
Madrid, Abelló Collection

This view of the Molo is an ambitious response on the part of Bellotto to one of Canaletto's most important achievements during his years of training, the painting commissioned by Thomas Osborne, fourth Duke of Leeds (1713–1789) (cat. 8). Despite the general fidelity with regard to the perspective composition, Bellotto presents an original work, different in terms of its narrower format, and distinguished by a clear, silvery light, with a virtuoso play of reflections in the transparent water. The range of cold colours with a prevalence of various shades of ochre and blue in the clothes of the figures, and with rare touches of well-distributed red and the presence of lilac, never found in Canaletto, is typical. Another distinctive feature of Bellotto is that of bringing the background forward to show the details more clearly; in this case, we see this in the Punta della Dogana with the Salute; the architecture on the Molo, from the Fonteghetto della Farina to the old granaries, the Zecca and the Libreria are carefully rendered, and surpass Canaletto'a painting in the quantity and incisiveness of detail. The space in the foreground is slightly increased – another device used by Bellotto – and the figures in the boats in the foreground are larger than those in Canaletto's picture, which are of a typical elongated shape with small heads. The column of Saint Theodore is a vibrant patchwork of overlapping brushstrokes.

The painting is a recent, valuable addition to the catalogue of the young Bellotto, together with *The Grand Canal looking South-West from the Rialto Bridge to the Palazzo Foscari, Venice,* with which it has shared its history (C/L 219-a). Their recognition is symptomatic of the long reconstruction of the catalogue of Bellotto's Venetian works that increasingly reveals his breadth and quality. The traditional attribution to Canaletto was first questioned in 1962 by W.G. Constable who studied the two works in private collection in Boston and who proposed giving the view of the Grand Canal to Bellotto. However, basing himself on the photographs, S. Kozakiewicz preferred to define both as 'studio of Canaletto'. Only the recent changes of ownership have made the works available again for study, making it possible to detect the stylistic and technical characteristics of the younger landscape artist for both the paintings.

The painting by Canaletto (cat. 8) was probably already sold at the time it was commissioned but Bellotto may have had available the preparatory sketches and he was also aware of the print by Antonio Visentini, part of the second edition of 1742 of the *Prospectus Magni Canalis Venetiarum* (II, 12; fig. a): here the colours are different to those of the painting belonging to the Duke of Leeds, and the clouds carefully follow the frayed contours of the print's version and not the more nuanced ones of the canvas. The silhouette of a gentleman with cocked hat in the foreground is thinner than that of the painting, which is also close to the interpretation by Visentini. Visentini's album also included the print of *The Grand Canal looking South-West from the Rialto Bridge to the Palazzo Foscari, Venice* (I, 1), published for the first time in 1735. On browsing this approximation of a catalogue one might think that

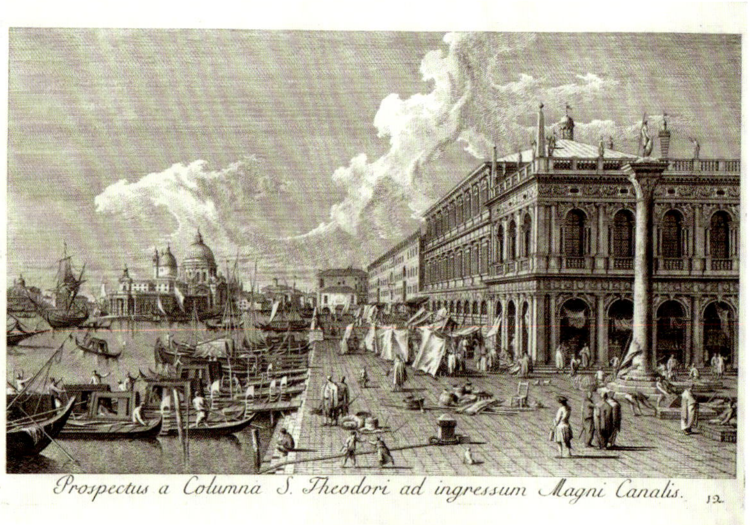

a. Antonio Visentini, *Prospectus a Columna S. Theodori as ingressum Magni Canalis*, 1742 (*Prospctus Magni Canalis Venetiarum*, 1742, II, 12), engraving, 250 x 419 mm.
Venice, Museo Correr, Gabinetto Disegni e Stampe

the two paintings were commissioned but in the case of the view of the Grand Canal, Bellotto had available Canaletto's actual painting, which hung in the Venetian home of Joseph Smith until 1762, and was the most 'dramatic' of the youthful series to which it belongs. Bellotto interpreted it in his own style and technique of the moment but maintained its contrasting brightness, which differs from the clear light of the present painting. The pair of works is unusual also for the slight difference in size, and this induces us to be prudent in considering them to be companion pieces.

The two paintings were purchased in 1860 as part of a group of Venetian views by Colonel The Hon. Edward Gordon-Douglas-Pennant (six years later, he became the first Baron Penrhyn), from one of the most important English collectors of the Victorian era, Edmund Higginson (1802–1871). Until their sale in 1924, they were preserved in Penrhyn Castle, the most important example of Norman revival in England, as part of an excellent Italian and Dutch painting collection that included some Canalettos and Rembrandts.

Bożena Anna Kowalczyk

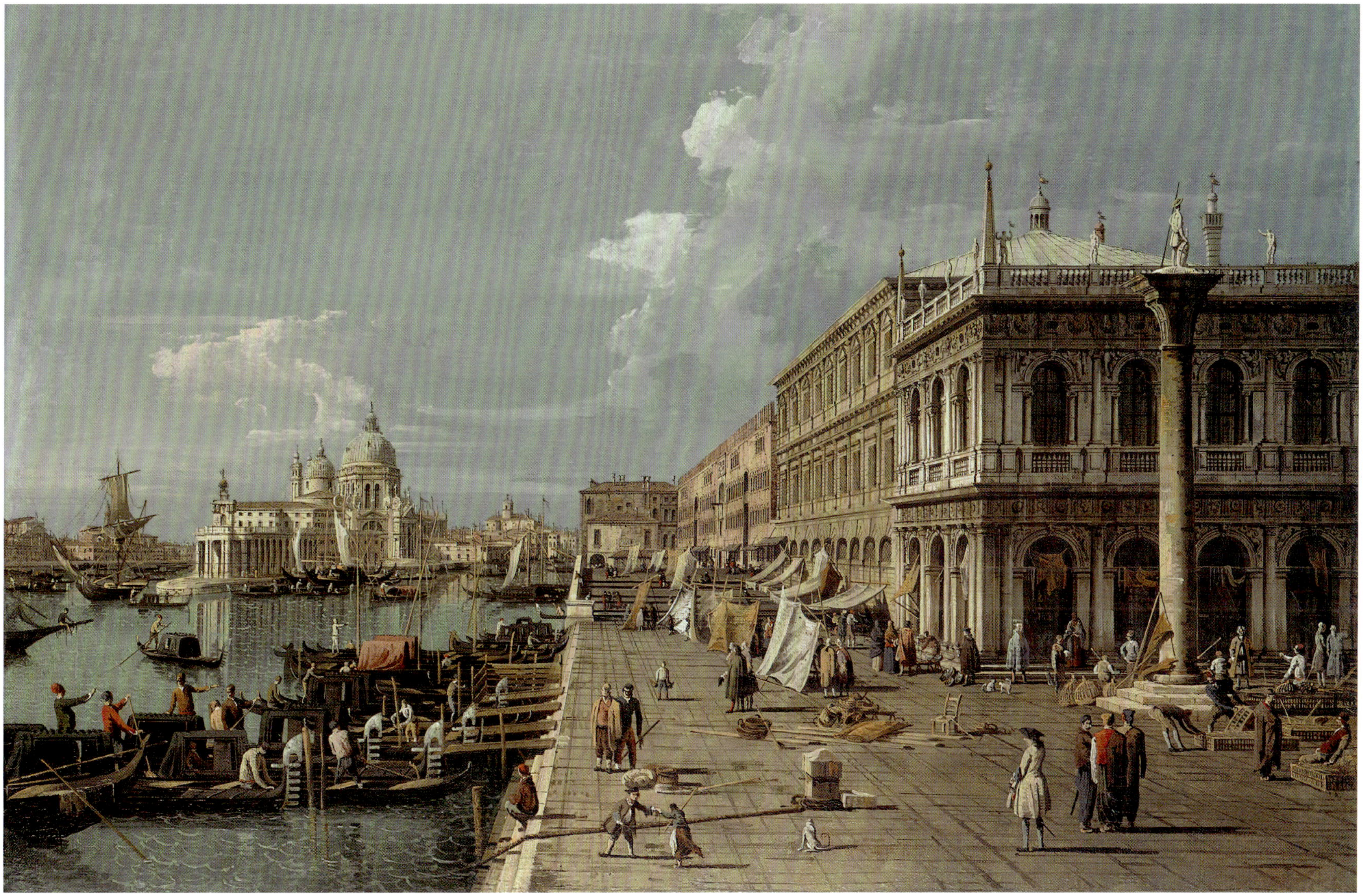

10

BERNARDO BELLOTTO

(Venice 1722 – Warsaw 1780)

Six Figures around Bird-Coops
1742–43

pen and brown ink over free and ruled pencil and pinpointing, on white paper;
210–208 x 293 mm
New York, The Metropolitan Museum of Art, Anonymous Gift, 1997.454

Inscriptions: numbered at top centre, with the same pen and ink as the drawing: '42'.

Watermark: difficult to make out, letters in a *cartouche*.

The bird market in the Piazzetta and the fish market on the Molo were part of daily life in San Marco in the eighteenth century, as is well illustrated the by Canaletto's paintings. The scene depicted on this sheet may have been recorded from life: in the *Catalogo de Danni* which includes the inventory of his library destroyed in Dresden in 1760 as a result of the Seven Years' War, entry no. 1078 states: 'Schizzi di figure fatti dal naturale dal medesimo da 304 carte legati' (Sketches of figures taken from the life by myself comprising 304 bound papers), confirming a precise working method. The few other Venetian figures studies by Bellotto that survive, part of one or more loose sketchbooks, are probably the ones left in Venice. This one has been used literally in a painting commissioned by Joseph Smith, *La Piazzetta, looking North, Venice* now in the British Royal Collections (fig. a), signed and dated 24 October, 1743, and used in England for the two figures on the right in the *Campo San Giacomo di Rialto, Venice* in the National Gallery of Canada, Ottawa, of about 1750, and then in Venice, and again the inspiration in 1758–1760 for the outline of the man sitting with tricorn and the woman with hat in *Piazza San Marco, looking east, Venice* in the National Gallery in London (C/L 68, 297, 21). A duplicate probably also existed: Bellotto also placed two figures on the right in a painting of Dresden, *The Old Market Square from Seestrasse* (Pantazzi).
A further ten sheets of figure studies in pure outline survive: some have occasional sporadic hatching, most of them are in pen and brown ink over pencil but two are just pen and ink; four are drawn on both sides and were catalogued by W.G. Constable as Canaletto; four, like this one, depict Venetian scenes of San Marco occupying the whole sheet, and are now in private collections (C/L 840.*, 840.***, 840.*****; Christie's, London, 10 December, 2015, lot 98); two of the most admired and strongly associated with Canaletto, with sketches of individual figures, at the Courtauld Institute of Art and Metropolitan Museum of Art (C/L 839 and 840), four others with various studio distributed over a single sheet, at the Kupferstichkabinett in Berlin, the Museum Boijmans van Beuningen, Rotterdam and the J. Paul Getty Museum, Los Angeles, designed in the last two with architecture studies on the verso (C/L 837, 839 and 541 verso); one unusual shows the upper half of figures wearing masks (Carnegie Institute, Pittsburgh C/L 840.****). All are numbered, with those drawn on the *verso* and *recto* marked with the word *uolta* (meaning 'turn') near the number, apparently in the hand of Canaletto, and some are of similar size and may be considered to have come from various loose sketchbooks. The manner of drawing, the distribution on the sheets and sometimes the types of the figures reveal a knowledge of drawings by Luca Carlevarijs. Canaletto placed other figures borrowed from those sheets in various paintings, and in *The Old Bridge over the Po River, Turin* (cat. 53), Bellotto used the studies on the Getty sheet of a woman sitting on a chair but from a different angle. However, the attribution to Canaletto cannot be supported. The strong propensity for a realistic rendering of the figures which often, as in this drawing, almost becomes caricature, the line that is marked and not supple, fluid and seductive as in Canaletto, are the dominant characteristics of these sheets which tend to suggest an attribution to Bellotto 'even though the nephew's line, unlike here, is always dashed' (Corboz). Canaletto was an exquisite draughtsman of figures as shown by his early ('prima maniera') paintings; and highly inventive and imaginative in his later canvases, in Venice as in London. The use of drawings used by Bellotto in the years they worked together must be seen as a studio practice to increase and diversify the artists' repertoire, in line with an ever broader-ranging and busy production.

Bożena Anna Kowalczyk

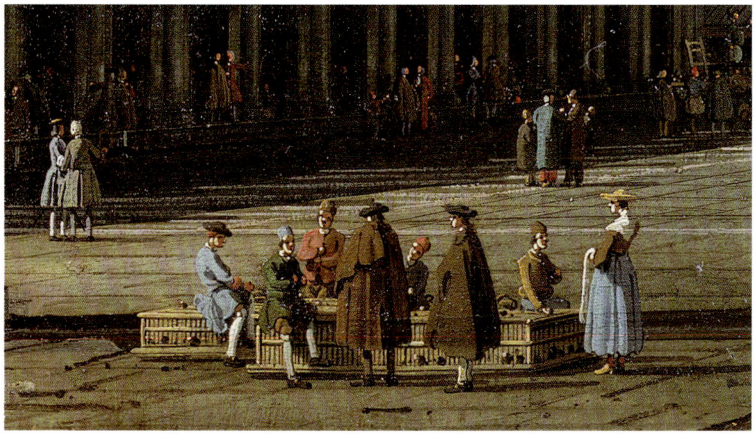

a. Canaletto, *The Piazzetta, looking North, Venice* (detail), 24 October 1743, oil on canvas, 60 x 95.6 cm. The Royal Collection, RCIN 400515

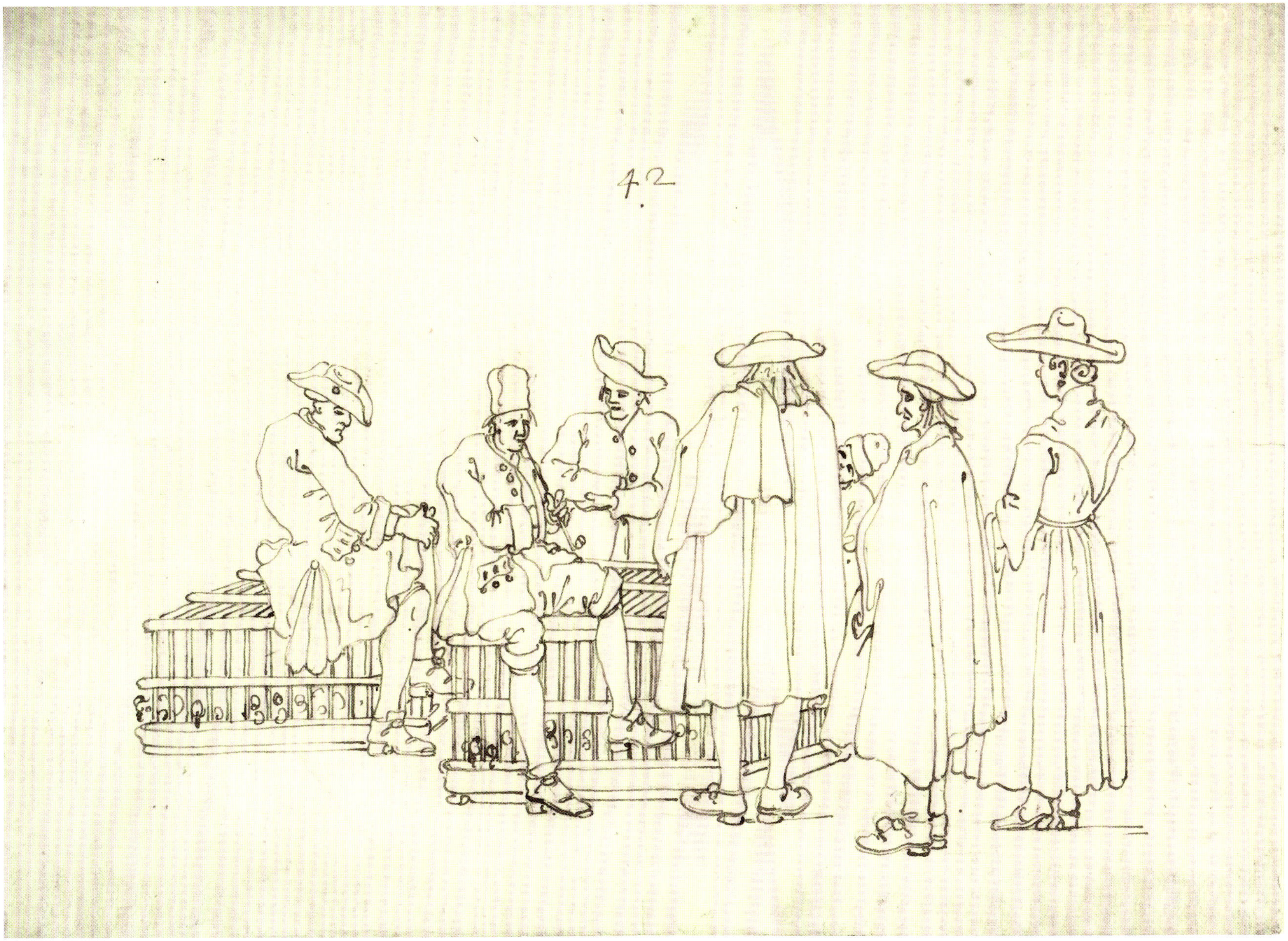
42

11

CANALETTO

(Venice 1679–1768)

Camera Optica

Venice, eighteenth century

wood, glass and mirror; 38 x 24.2 x 22.5 cm
Venice, Museo Correr, Cl. XXIX, s.n. 30

Inscriptions: engraved on the flap, 'A. CANAL'.

The *camera optica* is an instrument based on the principle of the projection of an image onto a surface lit through a hole fitted with a lens. The principle, the same as that of the human eye, has been known since Aristotle. Applied in the construction of optical devices, it has been used in surveying, science, the military and art since the first half of the fifteenth century. The development of these instruments went hand in hand with progress in the field of perspective and optics, from Leonardo da Vinci to Johannes Kepler. The seventeenth century saw the production of increasingly sophisticated equipment such as the *camera optica* with an internal operator and an external mirror, illustrated in Diderot and D'Alambert's *Encyclopédie* in 1753, or the portable 'book' version used by the painter Sir Joshua Reynolds, now kept at the Science Museum in London. We know that the inventor of photography – Nicéphore Niépce (1765–1833) – used in his research the method of fixing the image of two *camera optica* with concave lenses, purchased in Paris in 1826.
The *camera optica* in the Museo Correr in Venice, donated by Luigi Vason in 1901, bearing the inscription 'A.CANAL', which suggests it belonged to Canaletto, is a simple wooden box. Small in size, making it portable and easy to use outside, it is of the best-known type, with an internal mirror, used by landscape painters and *vedutisti* since the second half of the seventeenth century.
The internal mirror, angled at 45 degrees, reflects the image, introduced through the small pinhole fitted with a concave lens, onto the frosted opal glass located in the upper part of the box. By placing oiled, transparent paper on the glass, it is possible to draw the outlines of the image, with an inverted left/right reflection. Artists used this documentary evidence as their starting point, helping them to record details and perspective; the results nevertheless depended first and foremost on the artist's skill and preparation. The use of optical instruments, professed and even recommended by eighteenth-century art critics – see the writings of Anton Maria Zanetti di Alessandro (1771), Francesco Algarotti (1792) and Pierre-Jean Mariette (1851–1853) –, only led to the creation of original art if the artist was skilled at 'correcting the defects', as Canaletto famously was. The experiments carried out using the instrument in the Museo Correr – initiated by Terisio Pignatti – to compare the sketches in the album at the Gallerie dell'Accademia with images taken by the instrument, have cast doubt on whether it was in fact used by Canaletto.

Bożena Anna Kowalczyk

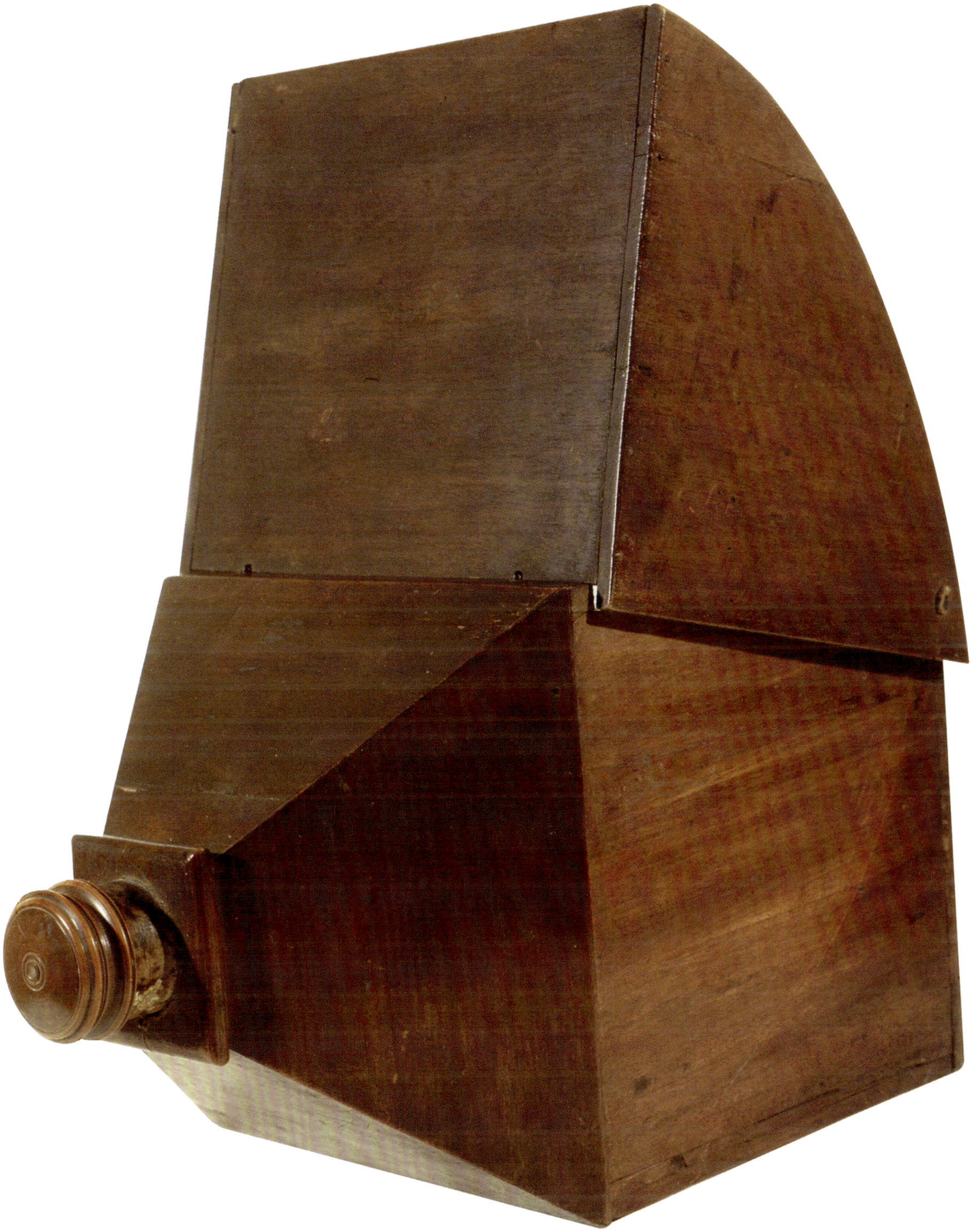

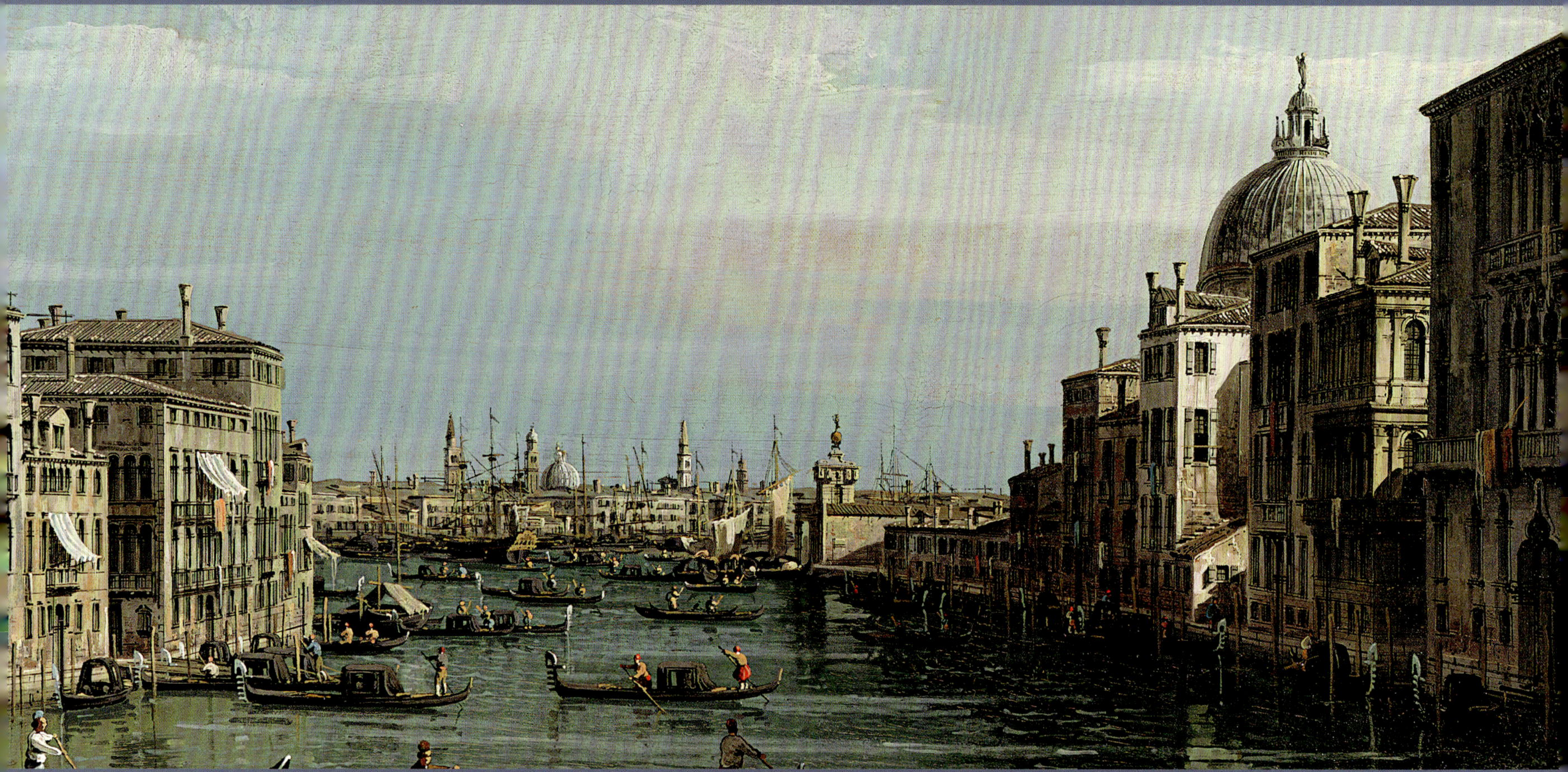

2.
BELLOTTO, CANALETTO'S *ALTER EGO*

In 1738, Bellotto joined the guild of Venetian painters and, in 1741, just before getting married, he could proudly state that he was able to support his family 'con la propria industria e sua professione' (with his own hard work and profession). Although his views of Venice, similar in composition to those of Canaletto, differ in their silvery-grey tonalities, strong contrasting light, caricatured figures, unusual tendency towards realism and marked perspectival rigour, his first biographer, his friend Pietro Guarienti, inspector of the Royal Gallery of Dresden, stated that 'un grande intendimento ricercasi in chi vuole distinguerle da quelle del Zio' (distinguishing them from those of his uncle would require a powerful intelligence) (Orlandi, Guarienti 1753, p. 101). In the early 1740s, Bellotto produced a few views, in complete compositional independence, of corners of Venice that had never before been portrayed by view painters. *Santa Maria dei Miracoli and the Apse of Santa Maria Nova* (cat. 12) is the most outstanding example of the realism and cold light that characterise his painting.
During those same years, Canaletto continued to paint for the English nobility, with Joseph Smith (1674 ca.–1770) as mediator. Smith also commissioned a series of paintings for his own residence in Venice. Among them, thirteen overdoor *capricci*, two of which were inspired by magnificent paintings of San Marco commissioned by Sir Hugh Smithson, who later became the Earl of Northumberland (cat. 16, 17).
Bellotto contributed to the workshop's production for the English market. The two large canvases *The Grand Canal with Santa Maria della Salute from Campo Santa Maria del Giglio, Venice*, and *The Piazza San Marco looking South-West, Venice*, marked by a perfected, mature technique and figures resembling those of Canaletto but with more characterisation, are from the collection of the Earls of Craven in Coombe Abbey, Warwickshire (cat. 14, 15). Reunited here for the first time since their sale in 1961, they are only two of the many paintings by Bellotto preserved in English collections that were attributed to Canaletto until recently. The discoveries continue, as we see in the case of *The Grand Canal looking East, from Palazzo Loredan Cini in Campo San Vio, Venice* (cat. 13), the attribution of which was only very recently changed from Canaletto to Bellotto.

12

BERNARDO BELLOTTO

(Venice 1722 – Warsaw 1780)

Santa Maria dei Miracoli and the Apse of Santa Maria Nova, Venice
ca. 1741

oil on canvas; 41.6 x 66 cm
Hanover, Niedersächsisches Landesmuseum, Landesgalerie, L 29
(on permanent loan from The Fritz Behrens Foundation)

In the Venetian repertoire of Bellotto, this charming painting is unique for a number of reasons. The view is faithful to the topography of the site only with regard to the foreground, where it shows the position vis-à-vis the canal and bridge of the apses of two churches: Santa Maria dei Miracoli, a jewel of the early Venetian Renaissance built by Pietro Lombardo, and Santa Maria Nuova, which no longer exists, together with the buildings beyond the shadow of the bridge. The houses along the canal, shown much wider than it is in reality, and the view that opens onto the lagoon – actually on the other side –, are pure fantasy, as are the two slender baroque bell towers, soaring above the island and behind the houses. A bright light illuminates the scene.

The choice of this site in the Castello district, near Bellotto's house in the parish of Santa Marina, was wholly overlooked by Canaletto and other Venetian *vedutisti* of the eighteenth century; this, plus its subtle transformation must have had a particular motivation, either for the artist himself or for the buyer, who was probably Venetian. The painting appears to date from soon after the view of a nearby location, the *Rio dei Mendicanti*, *Venice* now in the Gallerie dell'Accademia in Venice (Kozakiewicz 1972a, n. 23), which features another Renaissance masterpiece, the Scuola di San Marco, and which may have suggested the idea of a canal giving on to the lagoon. Both pictures share the solutions of diagonal dark shadows that follow each other to give a sense of space, as well as the figures emerging from the darkness and the highlighting of the atmospheric bleaching effects on the surfaces of the walls. While in *Rio dei Mendicanti*, Bellotto painted every detail of the facade of the Scuola di San Marco, here he deprives the church of the Miracoli of its sculpted bas-relief decoration, of its medallions, the reliefs inserted between the arches and the ornamental frieze at the top. The description of these Renaissance refinements was of no interest to him at this time; it was instead in rendering the discolouring of plaster, working the pasty material of the apse of Santa Maria Nuova, and forging the classic forms of the little altar that Bellotto saw the possibilities for a demonstration of virtuosity.

The figures in the foreground are real characters, similar to those of *Rio dei Mendicanti*: the old woman emerging from the shadows on the bridge, the two tatty servants, large and unusually three-dimensional figures in the foreground, and other rare apparitions, are all well orchestrated to create an air of melancholy. The thin outline of a backlit dog is a kind of signature, like the cypress growing alongside the church, the gondola that glides silently under the bridge, the flags waving on the top of the Miracoli church, and the stick leaning against the bridge and its shadow.

The first known owner was Count Gregory Stroganov (1829–1910), descendant of an important Russian family of collectors and patrons. Among the Venetian works in his Roman collection of European painting, apart from two *capricci* by Francesco Guardi, there was a rare portrait of Anton Maria Zanetti di Girolamo by Rosalba Carriera (Sani 2007, no. 14) but there is no evidence to assume that the presence of a work by Bellotto in the same collection as the portrait of his patron was anything but coincidental.

In the Stroganoff inventory, the painting is listed under the name of Bellotto, for the 'tonalité un peu sombre des couleurs dans les architectures' (Muñoz 1911), an attribution repeated by S. Kozakiewicz but opposed by W.G. Constable and J.G. Links. As in the case of *Rio dei Mendicanti* and many other works by the young Bellotto, Canaletto scholars have long tended to attribute the beauty and maturity of compositions such as shown here by his pupil to Canaletto himself.

Bożena Anna Kowalczyk

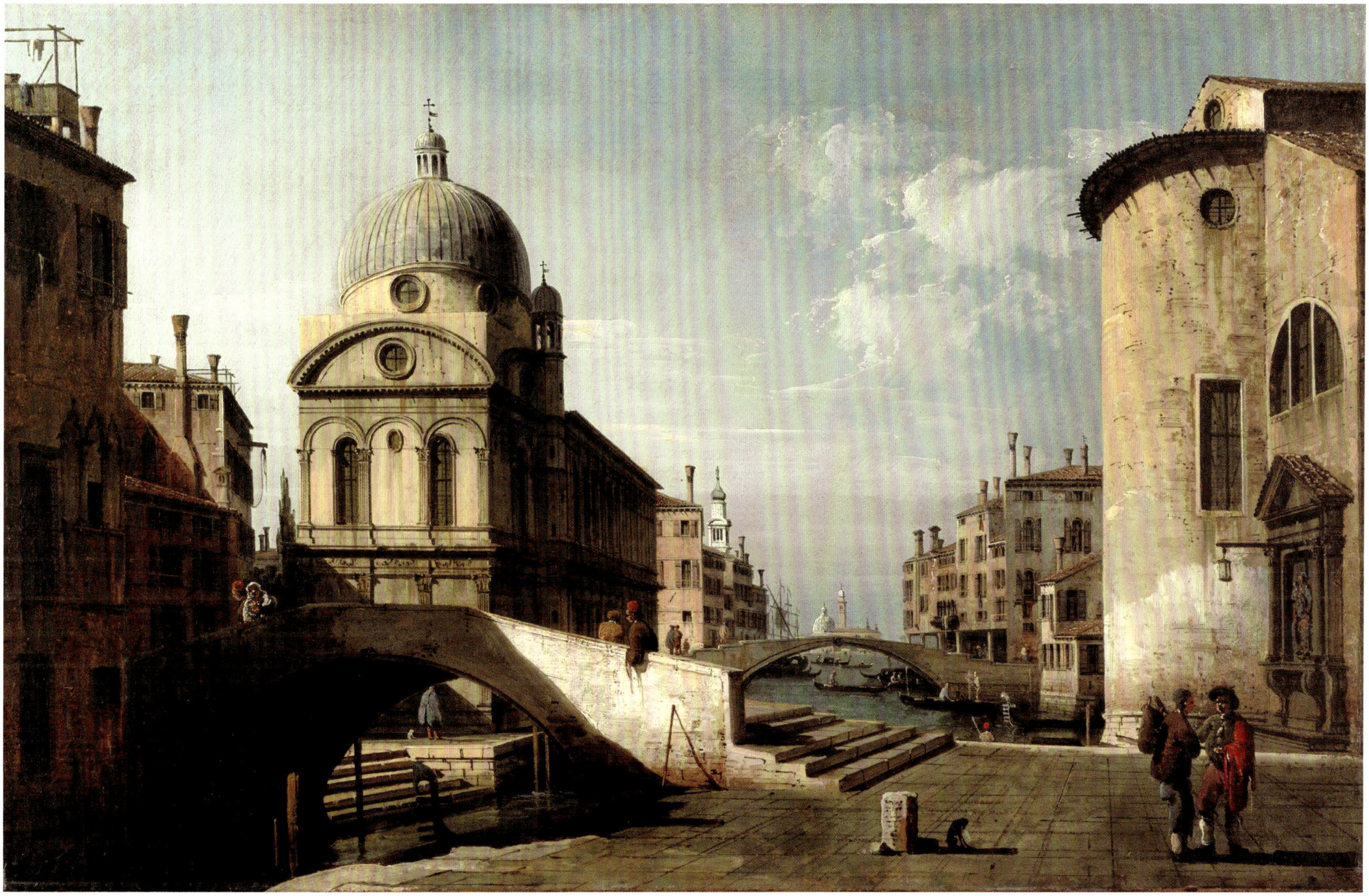

13

BERNARDO BELLOTTO

(Venice 1722 – Warsaw 1780)

The Grand Canal looking East, from the Palazzo Loredan Cini in Campo San Vio, Venice
ca. 1742

oil on canvas; 61 x 97.5 cm
London, Private Collection

In the broad field of Venetian view painting of the eighteenth century, discoveries are still possible, though rare. This beautiful painting was preserved for thirty years under the name of Canaletto – just at the time when studies of the master and pupil were advancing rapidly – in the dining room of the New York home of Alfred Taubmann, the well-known connoisseur and collector. Only with its recent appearance in the art market did a firm attribution to Bernardo Bellotto become evident, making the work a valuable addition to our knowledge of his work in Venice.
The view, taken from a window of the *piano nobile* of Palazzo Loredan Cini on the opposite side of the *Campo* with respect to Palazzo Barbarigo framing the view to the right, is Canaletto's invention. It was one of his most widely-used compositions, especially in the 1720s, with ever new solutions in terms of perspective and light, and with different figures and boats, the first two of which were the dramatic versions in the collections of the Duke of Wallenstein of Dux (1722–23) and of Prince Joseph Wenzel of Liechtenstein (1723–24) (C/L 182–193). In 1727–28, he showed the same view for Joseph Smith (ca. 1674–1770), in one of the series of twelve rational and bright views of the Grand Canal (fig. a). These paintings, engraved by Antonio Visentini for the famous *Prospectus Magni Canalis Venetiarum*, were published for the first time in 1735, and became standard compositions for Venetian view painting.
Bellotto used Smith's painting as a model, which like the rest of the series was preserved in his home on the Grand Canal until its sale to King George III in 1762 (C/L 184). It is possible that the artist was working on commission for the British Consul, who was known for his skill in handling the purchase of Venetian views for British tourists on the Grand Tour. The 'model' for Bellotto was just a starting point that he then transformed through his interpretation of space and light, conferring his own structural solidity to the architecture. With the increased size of the canvas, the artist has, by moving back and slightly lifting the viewpoint, expanded the foreground space but also brought the background closer, following the perspective layout and the description of the buildings, except for a few details, but changing the treatment of the sky, of some figures and boats. He replaced Canaletto's warm light in favour of a cold, clear one, alternating well-lit areas with hard-edged shadows, such as in the passage on the right, where the illuminated corners of the Palazzi Dario, Benzon and Barbaro, dominated by the dome of the Salute, emerge from the darkness. A typical feature is the swarm of boats in the distance in Basin San Marco, which are here increased in number and rendered with a few bright brushstrokes, and another curious tendency is to make higher the chimneys. The summary but precise description of the Riva degli Schiavoni is eye-catchingly successful, and in the distance one can make out the bell towers of San Martino, San Pietro di Castello and San Biagio on the horizon.
In his youth, Bellotto produced replicas of eight other paintings from Smith's series, some twice, adopting similar methods. Examples include, for instance, *The Grand Canal from Palazzi Foscari and Moro Lin*, *Venice* formerly at Castle

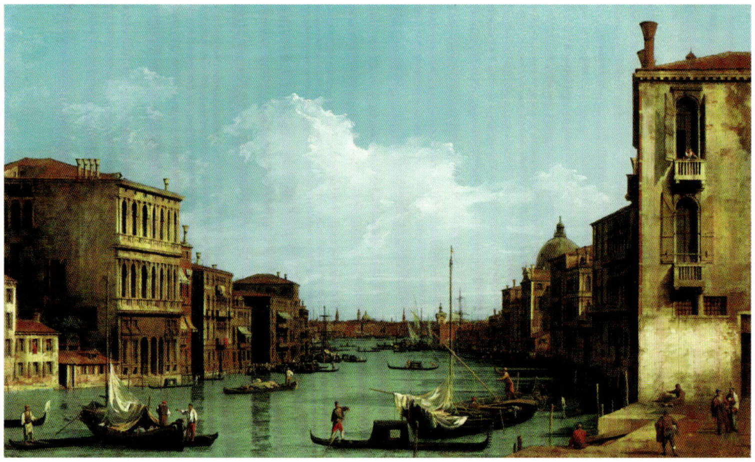

a. Canaletto, *The Grand Canal looking East from the Palazzo Loredan Cini in Campo San Vio, Venezia*, 1727–28, oil on canvas, 475 x 79.5 cm. The Royal Collection, RCIN 400518

Howard (1738–39) (cat. 7) and *The Grand Canal looking South, from the Rialto Bridge to Palazzo Foscari*, in a private collection (ca. 1739; cf. cat. 9).
The different hues of the architecture and the more vivid colours of the figures clothing suggest that Bellotto may have based himself instead on Visentini's print. This is an appealing suggestion but the serene progress of the clouds here is more similar to that of the painting, while in the print the skies are breezier and more dramatic. It is known that probably at the end of the 1730s, Canaletto repainted the skies to render the Smith series more uniform.
The work reveals all the features of Bellotto's manner around 1742, an interpretation marked by that of the mature Canaletto, with a heightened realism of the description, and dense use of viscous colour, laid in lumps in the highlights. The cracked wall and exposed brickwork on the side of Palazzo Barbarigo is a kind of signature, as is the solitary gentleman with tricorn on the *Fondamenta* in the foreground, who is similar to those that appear in other contemporary works, such as *The Dolo Watermills*, formerly in the collection of the Viscountess of Hambleden (Kozakiewicz 1972a, n. 29).
Bellotto painted the same view for Henry Howard, 4th Earl of Carlisle, probably in 1738–39, which was one of the fifteen paintings that adorned the rooms of Castle Howard in Yorkshire. Destroyed by the castle fire in 1940, this too was considered to be by Canaletto.

Bożena Anna Kowalczyk

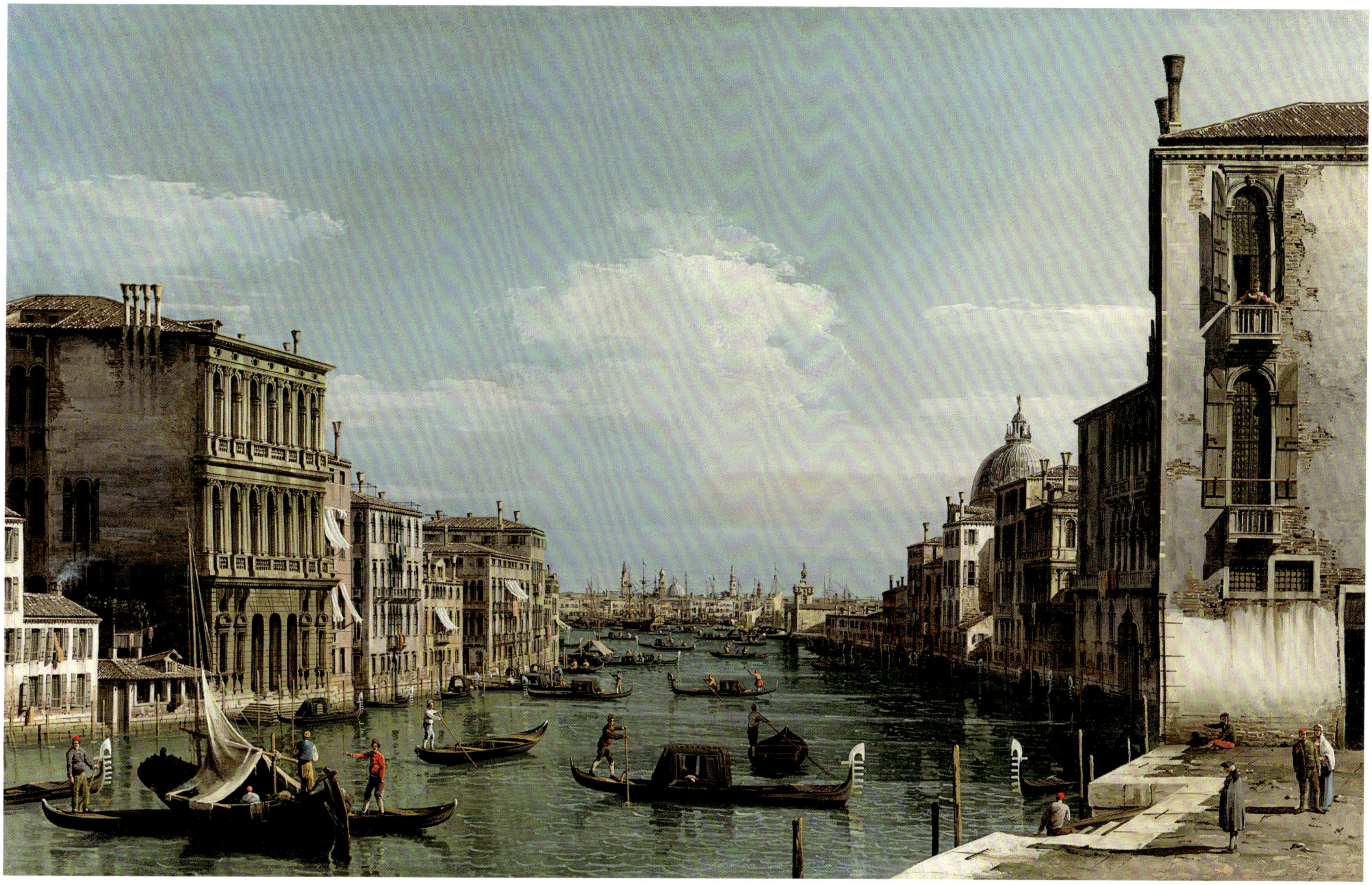

14

BERNARDO BELLOTTO

(Venice 1722 – Warsaw 1780)

The Grand Canal with Santa Maria della Salute from the Campo Santa Maria del Giglio, Venice
ca. 1743

oil on canvas; 135.5 x 232.5 cm
Los Angeles, The J. Paul Getty Museum, 91.PA.73

This impressive view, a pendant of *The Piazza San Marco looking South-West, Venice* at the Cleveland Museum of Art (cat. 15) is the widest depiction of the Grand Canal in the repertoire of Bellotto and in the contemporary one of Canaletto. The origin of the composition can be recognised from a print by Luca Carlevarijs entitled *Altra veduta della Salute* which shows, from a similar perspective and illumination, only the right bank of the Grand Canal, from the Abbazia di San Gregorio to the San Marco basin and the Riva degli Schiavoni in the distance (*Fabriche, e vedute*, Venice 1703, no. 5). Bellotto integrates the view with the church of San Gregorio in full sunlight beyond the abbey in the shade and the Renaissance facade of Palazzo Pisani-Gritti in the *Campo*; at the foot of the palazzo, we see the *traghetto*, which still exists today, at the end of the Riva degli Schiavoni, from the Pietà to the Abbazia di Sant'Antonio. The view, which is impossible to embrace from one point of view, a skilful composition of new sketches, appears for the first time in a smaller version in The Fitzwilliam Museum, Cambridge, canvas of ca. 1741, which it is suggested was part of a similarly composed pair of pendants (see cat. 15).
Here Bellotto accurately depicts the arrangement of the architecture but confers a broad sense of space to the view, pushing back the Riva degli Schiavoni, now visible in all its length, down to the Motta di Sant'Antonio; the artist has varied the details and introduces a number of figures. The Museum of Darmstadt drawing, carefully hatched but considered a preparatory work, is so faithful in the details and in the distribution of the lights as instead to be a record from the painting (AE 2243). With the quality of the description, Bellotto affirms his vocation for rendering architecture. Every detail of the Palazzo Pisani-Gritti – the sixteenth-century mullioned windows with sparkling glass, the colourful fresco frieze, the small altar, the writing on the wall, the cornerstones, the brickwork – acquires importance and consistency. The bulk of the basilica is shown in its magnificent volume, accurately described in detail and in different levels of light. The shadow that surrounds the ancient monastery of San Gregorio on the other hand offers an opportunity for a virtuoso depiction of the age and dampness of the walls, rendered with overlapping brushstrokes of browns, greys, oranges, and with thin incisions to mark the edges of the windows. There is a broad range of figures shown with pungent realism: true portraits and caricatures, from the elegant young gondolier in the foreground sporting bare feet to the man with a big belly on the boat to the right.
The painting, documented for the first time in 1831 as part of the collection of William, second Earl of Craven (1809–1866), at Combe Abbey in Warwickshire, has a particularly troubled critical history, from a firm attribution to Canaletto to attribution to Bellotto or Bellotto and studio. While the size of the canvas, as in the case of the pendant, may indicate the participation of assistants, as studies stand at the moment, there is no sign of their work: from the paintwork for the sky laid diagonally to the water that is full of reflections, all bears the mark of Bellotto's hand.
Bellotto also painted a third excellent version of this view, formerly in the Mrs. Stewart collection, New York (C/L 180-a) in which he introduced other figures in the *Campo* and in the boats, and brought the Riva degli Schiavoni nearer, making it visible only in part. Another painting, hitherto mentioned in literature as autograph, and formerly in the Otto Hirsch Collection (Kozakiewicz 1972a, no. 9), is definitively to be considered a non-autograph replica, already Stewart.
Canaletto painted this view only once, probably in about 1741 (The Fitzwilliam Museum, Cambridge; C/ L 180.-aa). His version has a different arrangement of figures and boats; in terms of the elongated format and of the proportions between the water, sky and architecture, it is closer to the Los Angeles painting than to other works by Bellotto; it stands out from all them for its delicate brightness and a considerably simplified description.
The success of this composition is confirmed by the large number of copies made, among which stand out those of Francesco Albotto, Apollonio Domenichini and of at least a couple of painters close to Bellotto.

Bożena Anna Kowalczyk

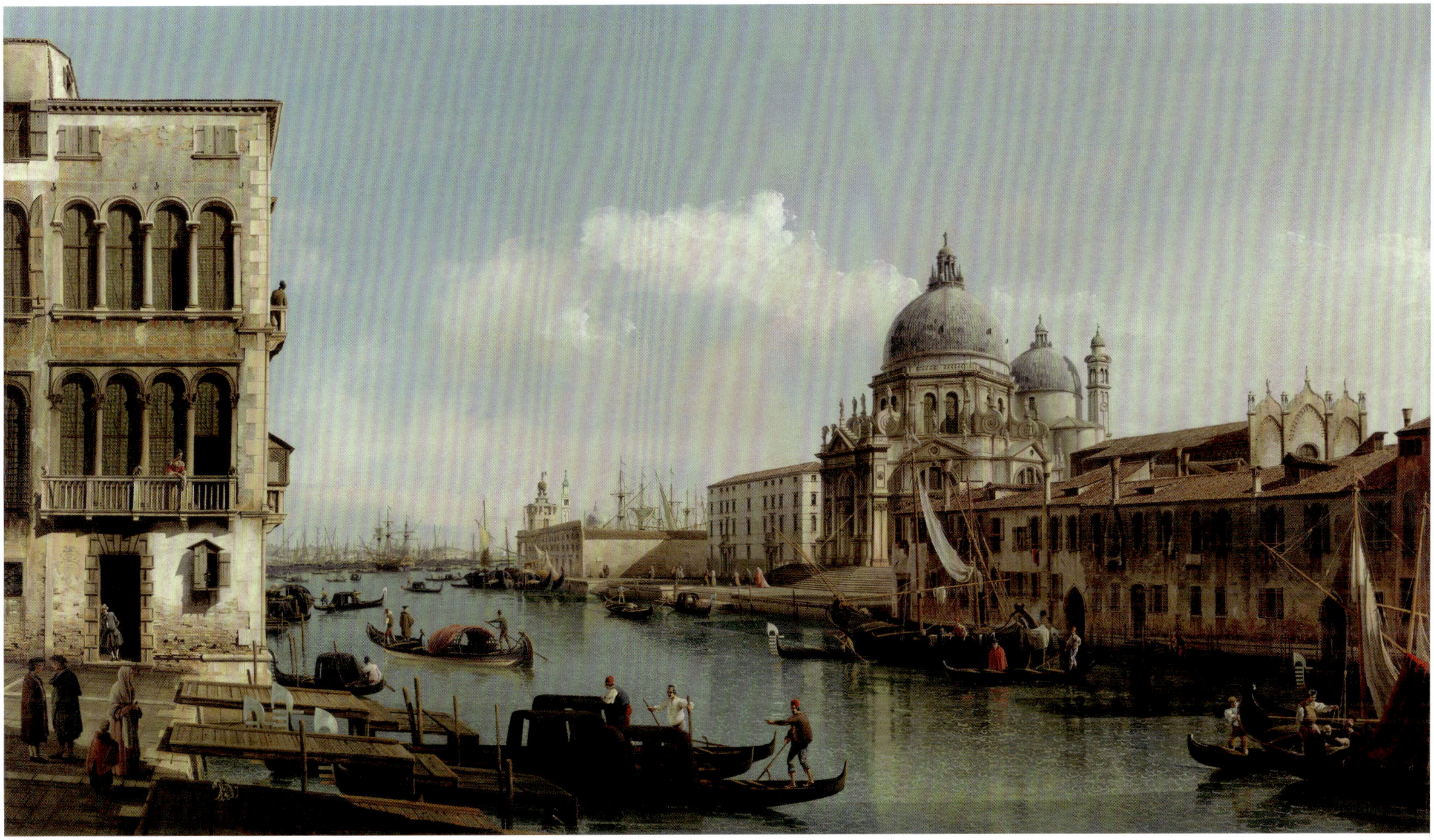

15

BERNARDO BELLOTTO

(Venice 1722 – Warsaw 1780)

The Piazza San Marco looking South-West, Venice
1742–43

oil on canvas; 136.2 x 232.5 cm
The Cleveland Museum of Art, Leonard C. Hanna, Jr Fund, 1962.169

With this great image of the Piazza San Marco, a pendant to *The Grand Canal with Santa Maria della Salute from the Campo Santa Maria del Giglio, Venice*, cat. 14), Bellotto highlighted the interest of Venetian painters for producing wide-angle views of the most iconic place in Venice, in the manner of Israel Sylvestre's prints. There are precedents for this view in the repertoire of Luca Carlevarijs and Domenico Lovisa (*Fabriche, e vedute*, Venice 1703, no. 50; *Gran Teatro*, t. I, no. 5) but it was especially Canaletto who developed this view in a drawing dated 1731 (C/L 357*), followed by the paintings in the Wadsworth Atheneum Museum of Art, Hartford, CT (C/L 54) and in the Sir John Soane's Museum, London, of circa 1734 (C/L 54-a). In these early versions, the Procuratie Nuove are seen in perspective, and not on a plane parallel to the viewer, as here, as the result of spatial distortion caused by the use of a *camera optica*, probably of the type fitted with mirrors, such as the portable model described and illustrated in detail in the *Encyclopédie* of Diderot and d'Alembert (vol. III, 1753). It is no coincidence that similar perspective solutions recur in the paintings of Michele Marieschi (1710–1743), who was notoriouslyfree in the use of optical instruments.

Around 1740, Canaletto, followed by Bellotto, constructed this view like a kind of photomontage, composing 'shots' of individual monuments to create a picture of the Piazza like the one that stays in the memory of a tourist. Typical of this are a drawing by Canaletto in the British Royal Collections (RL 7422) and two drawings by Bellotto, one in the Museum of Darmstadt (AE 2211) and the other in the Rijksmuseum in Amsterdam (53:217). The latter, autonomous and very elementary, served as an outline for this painting, both in the relations between the buildings – compare the perspective view of the Doge's Palace, the position of the Island of San Giorgio and of the flagpoles – and for the outlines of some of the figures; but it was first used for another painting, smaller in size and even more faithful to the drawing, formerly in the collection of Captain Samuel Cecil and now at the Fuji Art Museum, Tokyo (C/L 53-note), where it still bears the name of Canaletto. The latter is probably the pendant of *The Grand Canal with Santa Maria della Salute from the Campo Santa Maria del Giglio, Venice* in The Fitzwilliam Museum, Cambridge (cat. 14).

In the larger size of this canvas and its pendant, adopted here for the first time, Bellotto tended towards the same unitarity as in the first pair. The space in the foreground is expanded and the oblique shadows form a certain symmetry with the course of the Grand Canal in the pendant but the proportions of the architecture and the few figures are different. Common to both is the great care taken in depicting the facades in the foreground: here the basilica provides the most beautiful and intense detail, with the square of the Piazza San Marco also worthy of admiration.

An infrared photo highlights the careful construction of this picture and its pendant (fig. a) Will Real, Mellon Fellow in Painting Conservation at the Museum of Cleveland, has noted that the profiles of the architecture showing against the sky to the right and above the Piazzetta are those of the pendant that then belonged to the Lehman Collection. The painted sketch of the volumes might have been helpful for understanding the balance between the two compositions but more likely it was an initial and failed experiment: the San Gregorio facade is in fact too close to the edge of the canvas. The earlier date of the present painting is, however, confirmed and it was probably executed in 1742, before installation of the bronze gate of Antonio Gai's Loggetta and before the panelling in marble of its flank. The same photograph highlights some *pentimenti*, especially in the height of the slender chimneys, which Bellotto carefully lowered.

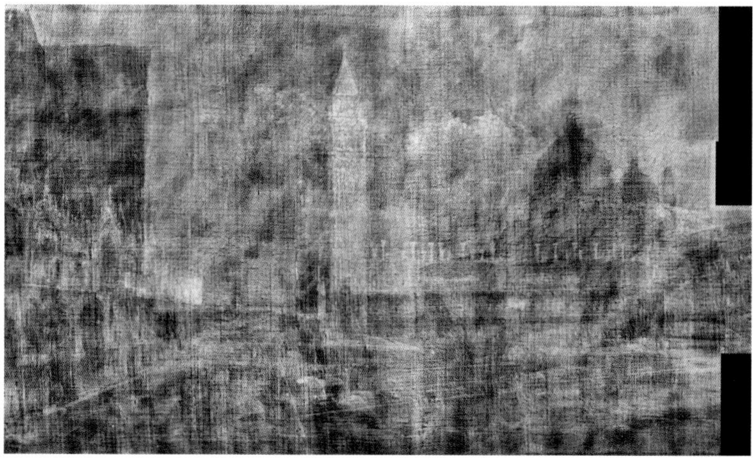

a. X-ray photograph

The shaded area in the foreground also appears in the oil version by Canaletto, formerly in the Lord Hillingdon collection, which must be slightly earlier, followed here in the type, proportions, and methodical disposition of the figures along the perspective lines; some are copied from the pendant, *The San Marco Basin from the Piazzetta, Venice* in a private collection (CL 53* and 129). Later, towards 1744 to 1746, Canaletto painted the version in the Art Gallery of New South Wales, Sydney (C/L 49c); none attains the same sense of space. Of the replicas, the closest to Bellotto are those formerly in the Bath Club collection and in the Musée des Beaux-Arts in Lille, but with no trace of his hand.

Bożena Anna Kowalczyk

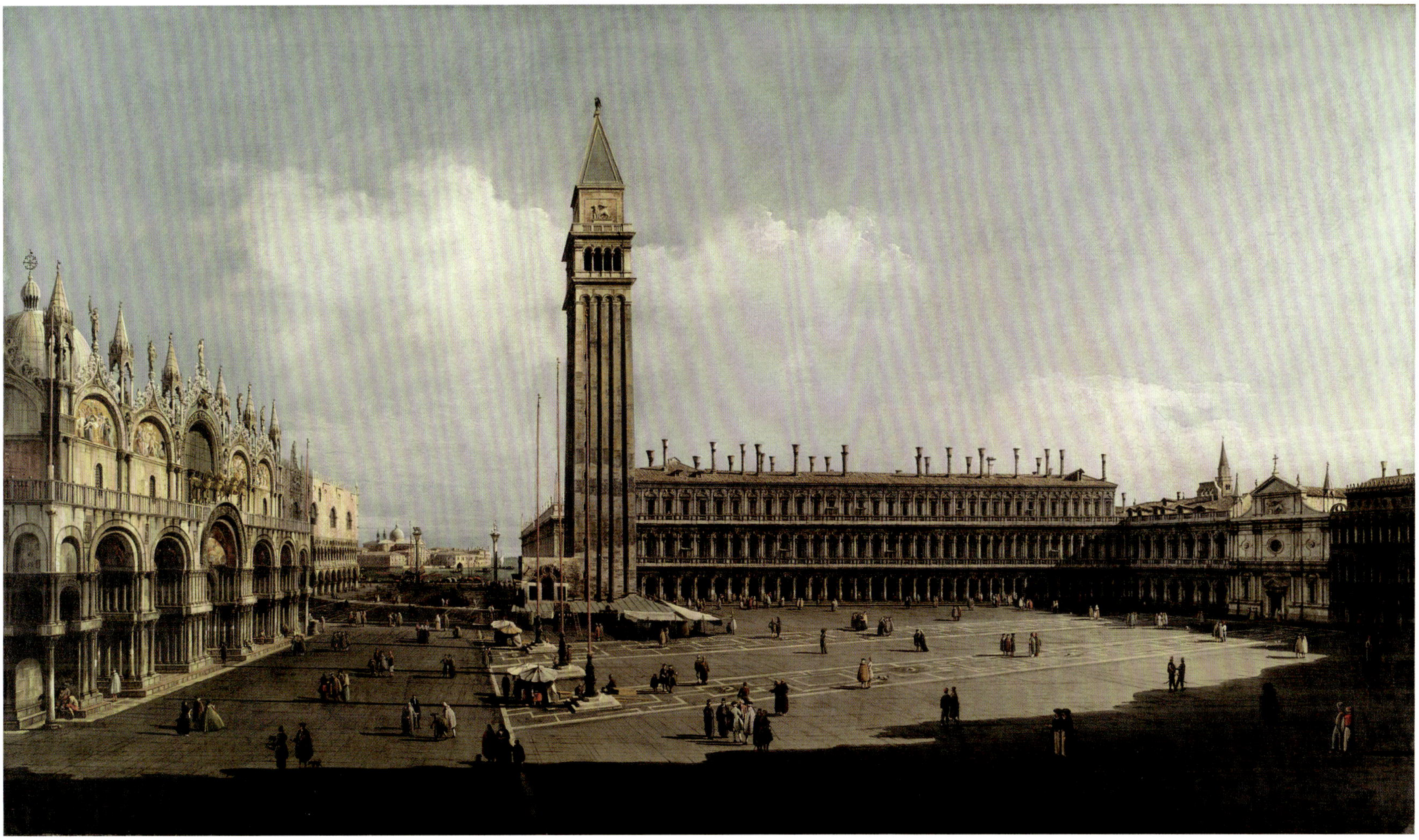

16

CANALETTO

(Venice 1697–1768)

The Ducal Palace: the Scala dei Ciganti, Vcnicc

ca. 1743

oil on canvas; 175.2 x 139.5 cm

Alnwick Castle, The Duke of Northumberland Collection, 03341

Canaletto leads the viewer in through the Porta della Carta – the formal entrance to the Ducal Palace – as far as the shadow cast by the Arco Foscari, to admire the elaborate Renaissance decoration of the east facade of the courtyard and the Scala dei Giganti; built in 1497 by Antonio Rizzo, the staircase is dominated by the statues of Mercury and Neptune by Jacopo Sansovino, completed in 1566. The setting for the coronation of the doges, this is also the main entrance to the palace. No detail of the rich sculptural decoration of the facade – rebuilt by Rizzo after the fire of 1483 and later finished by Pietro Lombardo – has been left out, nor of the staircase sculpted and decorated by Angelo Rusteghello in 1726–27; it is a profusion of marbles, reliefs and *niello* engravings. The right-hand side of the ground floor portico frames a darkened window: the prison in which state traitors were confined. The pointed arches of the first floor are what remains of the Gothic structures of the facade; the small courtyard on the left, known as the 'Cortile dei Senatori', is bordered by an elegant Renaissance building by Giorgio Spavento and Antonio Scarpagnino, the doge's private oratory; above, there is a terrace originally used as a hanging garden. In the two reliefs of the side balustrades at top of the staircase, *le Fame e le Vittorie* are holding two medallions with coats of arms, on the left those of Alvise Pisani (1735–June 1741), on the right the coat-of-arms with chevron of the Canal family. Sir Michael Levey, a scholar and connoisseur of Venetian painting, suggested that this symbol was reproduced in works of which the artist was particularly proud.

The framing of the arch, which suggests a transition from its shadow to the beautiful image flooded with light, gives the composition a marked theatrical character and enhances its decorative appearance. The scene is captured on an ordinary day: senators are conversing, figures stand at the window, and guardians are captured in the shade of the portico. The figures arranged in a zigzag from the bottom to the top of the staircase, carefully measured in diminishing size, suggest depth and height; the play of deep and nuanced shadows with bright and veiled light help set the scene.

The artist uses all the compositional and stylistic means at his disposal to convey the striking beauty and importance of the place; an extremely fine grid of drawn and incised lines constructs the perspective and defines the details of the architecture; the finely modulated and shaded layers of paint on the facade of the palace recreate the light colour of the marble, the floral relief decoration, and coloured marble *patera* reliefs; the lighting structure makes use of thin incisions, which surround the architectural details in shadow to reproduce delicate light reflections.

This picture and its pendant (cat. 17), monumental overdoor paintings in which architecture dominates, are among Canaletto's largest works, painted in the years just before his departure for London in May 1746. Their exceptional

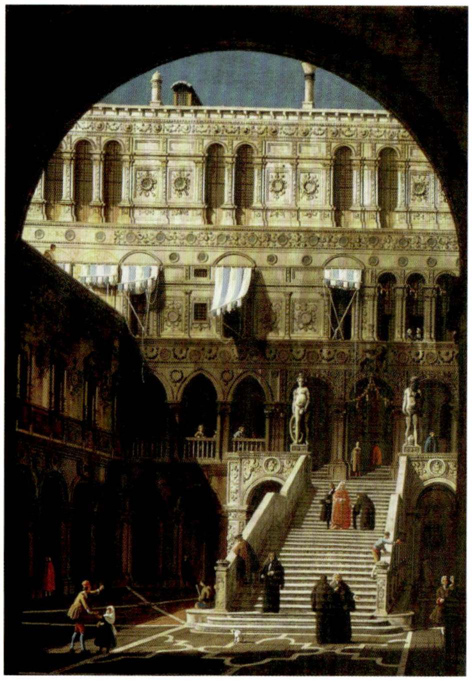

a. Canaletto, *The Ducal Palace: the Scala dei Giganti, Venice*, 1745, oil on canvas, 43 x 31 cm. Private Collection

nature in Canaletto's oeuvre points to a precise commission, defined not only in the size and verticality of the format, but also in the choice of subjects and details: this painting depicts a masterpiece of the early Renaissance. In complementary fashion, its pendant brings together with clearly forced perspective Jacopo Sansovino's three great achievements at the height of the sixteenth century: the Library, the Loggetta and the facade of San Geminiano.

The first reliable reference to this painting and its pendant is a lithograph of 1818 by Miss Martha Helen Davison that depicts the Renaissance-style Dining Room in the house at Stanwick that belonged to Hugh Smithson, Canaletto's main patron during the artist's stay in England. A large canvas is seen above the fireplace, perhaps *Mary Magdalene*, listed in the infantry of 1865 as 'copy by Guido of Carlo Maratta'; the Canalettos, this one and the *The Piazza San Marco looking West* (cat. 17), are hanging up high, above two landscape paintings, perhaps by Marco Ricci. The two canvases do not appear in the 1779 inventory,

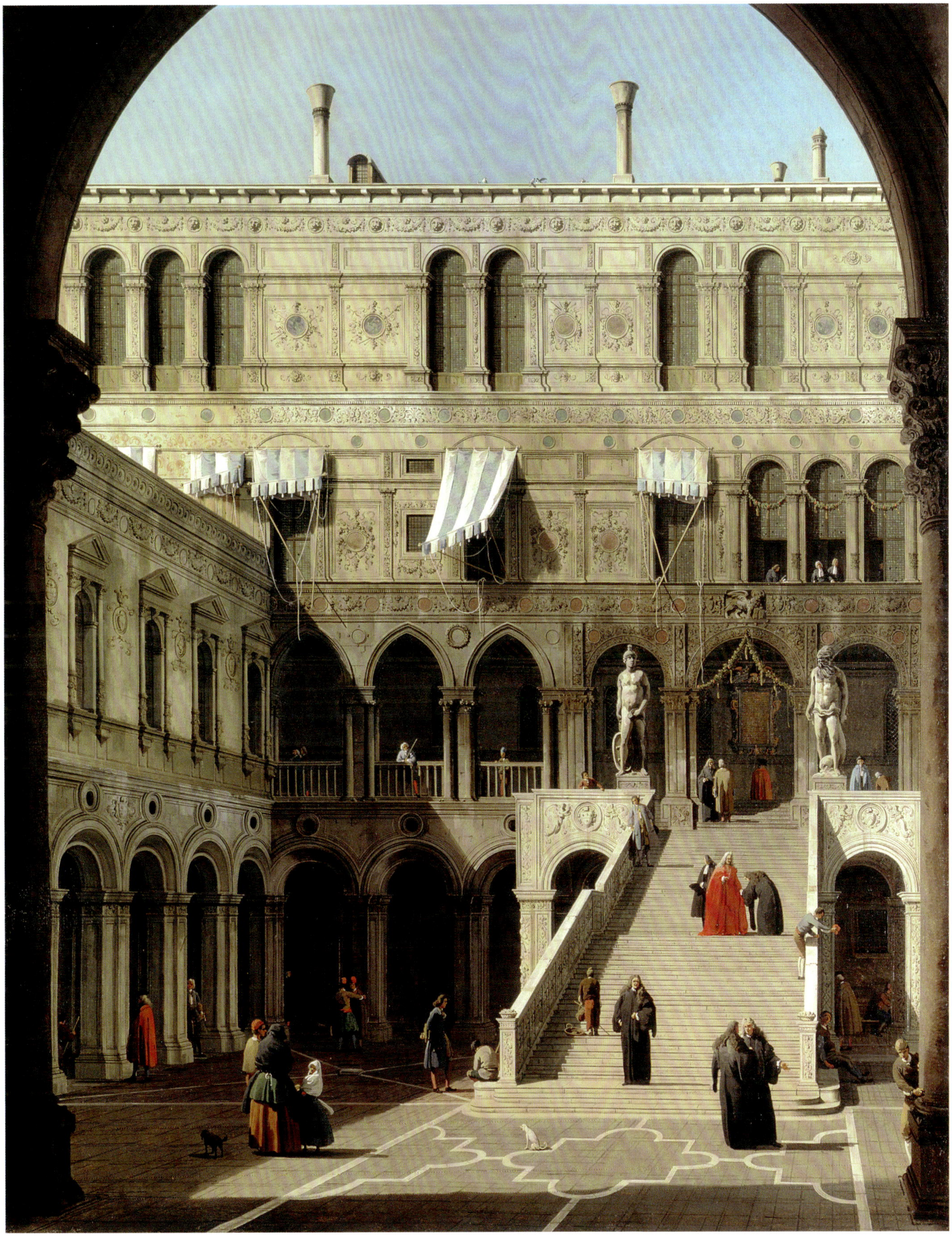

but this is summary and generic in nature; they are mentioned in the 1865 list, drawn up on the death of Algernon, fourth Duke Northumberland, in the same Dining Room, along with a series of landscapes, paintings of ruins and *capricci* by Giovanni Paolo Panini, Giuseppe Valeriani, Hendrik van Lint (Studio) and the aforementioned Marco Ricci, as well as a *Sacrifice of Isaac* by Pietro da Cortona and a *Mythological Scene* by Luca Giordano; this painting is called 'View of Saint Marks': 'A Grand Picture' (*An Inventory* 1865)*.
Hugh Smithson, one of Canaletto's most important patrons in England (cf. cat. 67), is documented as having been in Italy in 1733–34, in Florence, Venice and Rome; in 1736, in London he became a member of the Royal Society, the Society of Antiquaries and a founder member of the Society of Dilettanti; in 1773, he was again in Milan (Ingamells 1997, p. 873); a collection so profoundly marked by traditional Grand Tour purchases must have been formed during his travels. In a letter of 1741, Lady Hertford, mother-in-law of the English aristocrat, told her friend Lady Pomfert of her admiration for a large Canaletto canvas depicting the Doge's Palace, which by that time was already owned by Sir Hugh (Constable, Links 1989, I, pp. LXIV–LXV); there are no other known paintings to which this appreciation may refer, but the style of the painting does not allow us to recognise it as the object of Lady Hertford's admiration, as has been indicated by J.G. Links ('There can be little doubt that she was referring to *The Ducal Palace: the Scala dei Giganti…*'), accepted by the author, despite a number of doubts, until their appearance at the *Canaletto: il trionfo della veduta* exhibition at the Palazzo Giustiniani in Roma in 2005. The coat of arms of the doge Alvise Pisani seemed a further confirmation of a dating prior to 1741.
The style and technique of the two pendants are very similar to those of the series of thirteen overdoor paintings with 'most admir'd Buildings at Venice, elegantly Historiz'd with Figures & Adjacencys to the Painter's Fancy', commissioned in 1743–44 from Canaletto by Consul Smith, and the subjects anticipate two paintings in the series. In *Capriccio with the Courtyard of the Ducal Palace and the Scala dei Giganti*, Canaletto used the same drawings for a fantastical transformation; he frames the courtyard of the Doge's Palace with a twin-vaulted arch, supported by a double column, and gives the palace the feel of a Renaissance pavilion; in addition to the signature in cubic letters 'ANTO.C.F. / MDCCXLIV', he also affixes the coat of arms of the coat of arms with chevron (C/L 455). The large and solid figures in the foreground are patches of colour composed of opaque layers, as in this painting and its pendant, a technique different to that used by Canaletto until the very early 1740s, to define them with overlapping but transparent passages of colour. The two statues on the other hand, marked with bold brush strokes, represent anatomical study that is so convincing as to make us think of another painter.
W.G. Constable was the first to point out that this composition had been followed by Bernardo Bellotto in three *capricci*, painted in Dresden between 1762 and 1764, in the museums of Wörlitz and Schwerin, and in a private collection (Kozakiewicz 1972a, n. 307–309). It is likely Bellotto made use of a preparatory drawing by a studio assistant, taken from Venice and now kept at the Weimar Museum (B.A. Kowalczyk, in Rome 2005, n. 55).
In 1744–45, Canaletto painted a beautiful small version, commissioned in Venice by George Garnier (1703–1763), now in a private collection (C/L 81; fig. a). The Scala dei Giganti also appears in one of twelve drawings in the series of *Fasti Dogali*, painted in circa 1766, depicting the coronation of the doge Alvise Mocenigo IV (C/L 632).

Bożena Anna Kowalczyk

**Information from the Stanwick archives was kindly passed on to me by Miss Clare Baxter, The Northumberland Estates, Alnwick Castle, Collections Manager, and I would like to thank her warmly.*

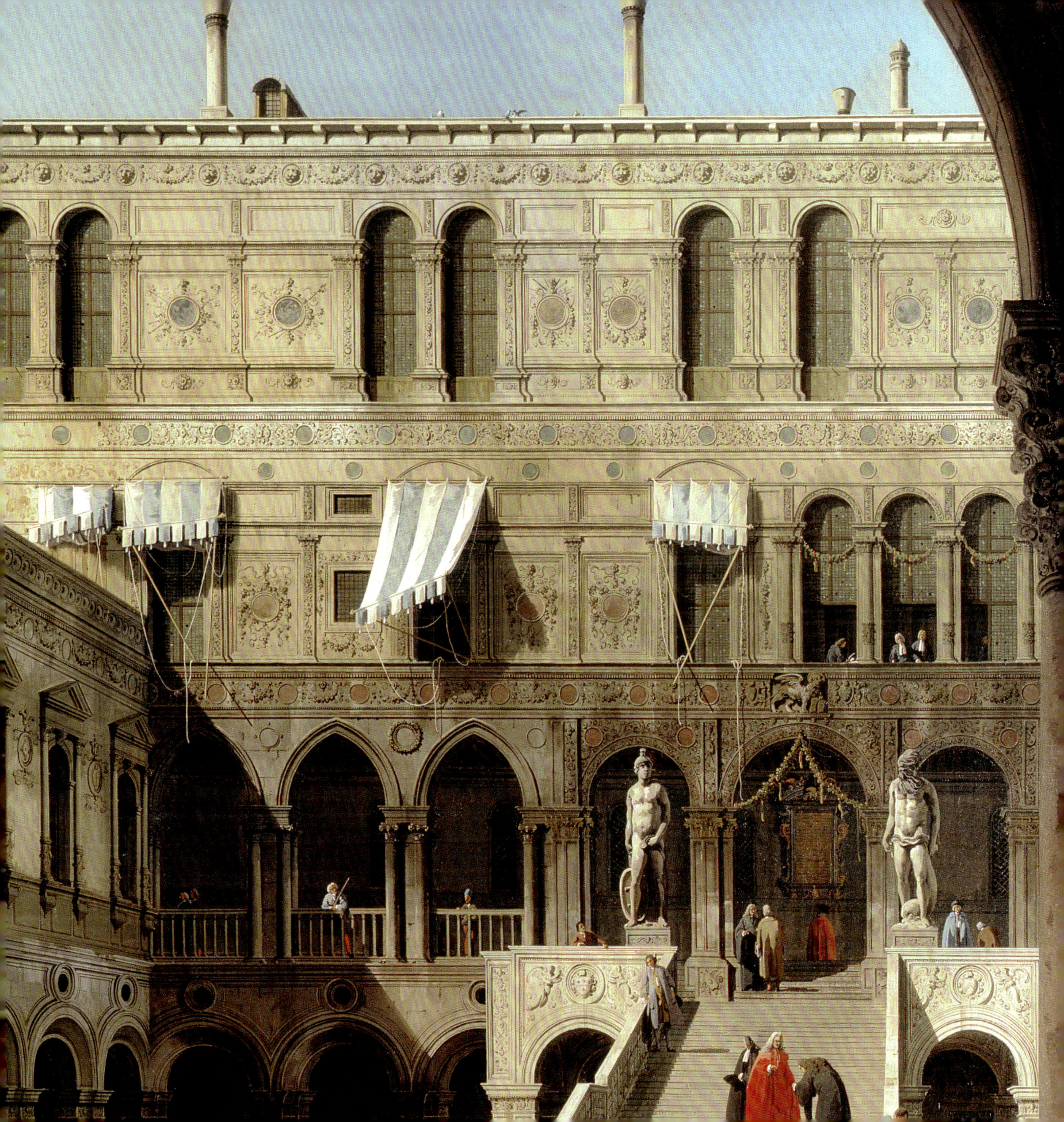

17

CANALETTO

(Venice 1697–1768)

The Piazza San Marco looking West, Venice
ca. 1743

oil on canvas; 175.2 x 139.5 cm
Alnwick Castle, The Duke of Northumberland Collection, 03327

This virtuoso angle shot of the Library, Loggetta and part of Sansovino's facade for the ancient church of San Geminiano is as pictorially exquisite as that of the Scala dei Giganti in the pendant (cat. 16). The two views are perfectly complementary: this one is taken from near the Ducal Palace's Porta della Carta, with the entrance and the Arco Foscari behind.

Canaletto was probably invited to create the two vertical overdoor pictures on the example of six decorative paintings of the architecture of San Marco, commissioned by Joseph Smith in 1722–23, of which four were vertical, kept at his Venice house in the parish of Santi Apostoli. These lively visions of the artist's youth – with monuments sketched out in broad strokes, sensitively modelled large figures and impetuous skies – next to the later works, 'traditional' views or *vedute*, provided a starting point for commissions made by English tourists who visited Venice and the house of the consul. William Holbech (1699 ca.–1771) of Farnborough Hall commissioned Canaletto to paint a series of four pictures almost equal in size to that of the Smith's horizontal canvases, including a *View of the Libreria and Campanile with the Loggetta* similar to this one. The Smith canvases were an example for the young Bellotto in circa 1742 when he painted four vertical format pictures for an English commission, three of San Marco and another of the Arsenale; two, now at the National Gallery of Canada *The Piazzetta, Venice* and *The Arsenal, Venice*, are documented in the Bouchier Cleeve Collection in Foots Cray Place, Kent (C/L 67) in 1760.

For this painting and its pendant, Canaletto used canvases of the same size as those belonging to Smith; he refers in the composition to one of his patron's paintings, as well as to one belonging to William Holbech, circa 1736–1738, now part of the Haberstock Foundation in the city of Augsburg in Bavaria (C/L 38). He forced the relationships between the architecture, thanks to the format undoubtedly requested by the patron, even involving, with the elevated view point, the Loggetta, which had a precise role as a theatrical wing in the perspectival structure of the canvas.

Like the pendant, this view was also developed into a *capriccio* in the series of thirteen overdoor views of the 'most admir'd buildings at Venice', commissioned from Canaletto always by Consul Smith in 1734–1744. In *Capriccio with the Libreria*, signed and dated 1744, Sansovino's monument is depicted as here, with the three arches, but seen more frontally, while the Loggetta appears in an angle of pure fantasy. The large figures in this series of *capricci*, similar to these of Alnwick Castle in technique, suggest a neighbouring execution date.

In a clear light, under a blue sky crossed by fluffy white clouds, the decorative details of the Library stand out, described with precision and delicacy; the glimpse of the Procuratie Nuove in shadow is a symphony of greys, contrasted by the pinkish tones of the Loggetta and the lively pink, orange and green tones of the figures, rare in Canaletto's Venetian scenes. The appearance of lovingly described costume masks – including noblewomen – that allude to the carnival, are unusual. This descriptive vein extends to the fixtures and fittings of a pharmacy in the shadow of the Library portico, as well as to the contents of the merchandise baskets in front of the Loggetta: various kinds of bread and buns, lettuce and quince.

We would like to think that the figure with the wig at the window is Anton Maria Zanetti di Alessandro (1706–1778), elected Custodian of the Biblioteca Marciana on 26 January 1737, an important and prestigious role he held throughout his life. It is to this younger cousin of the famous Anton Maria Zanetti di Girolamo (1680–1767) that we owe the first illuminating biography of Canaletto (Zanetti 1771).

Bożena Anna Kowalczyk

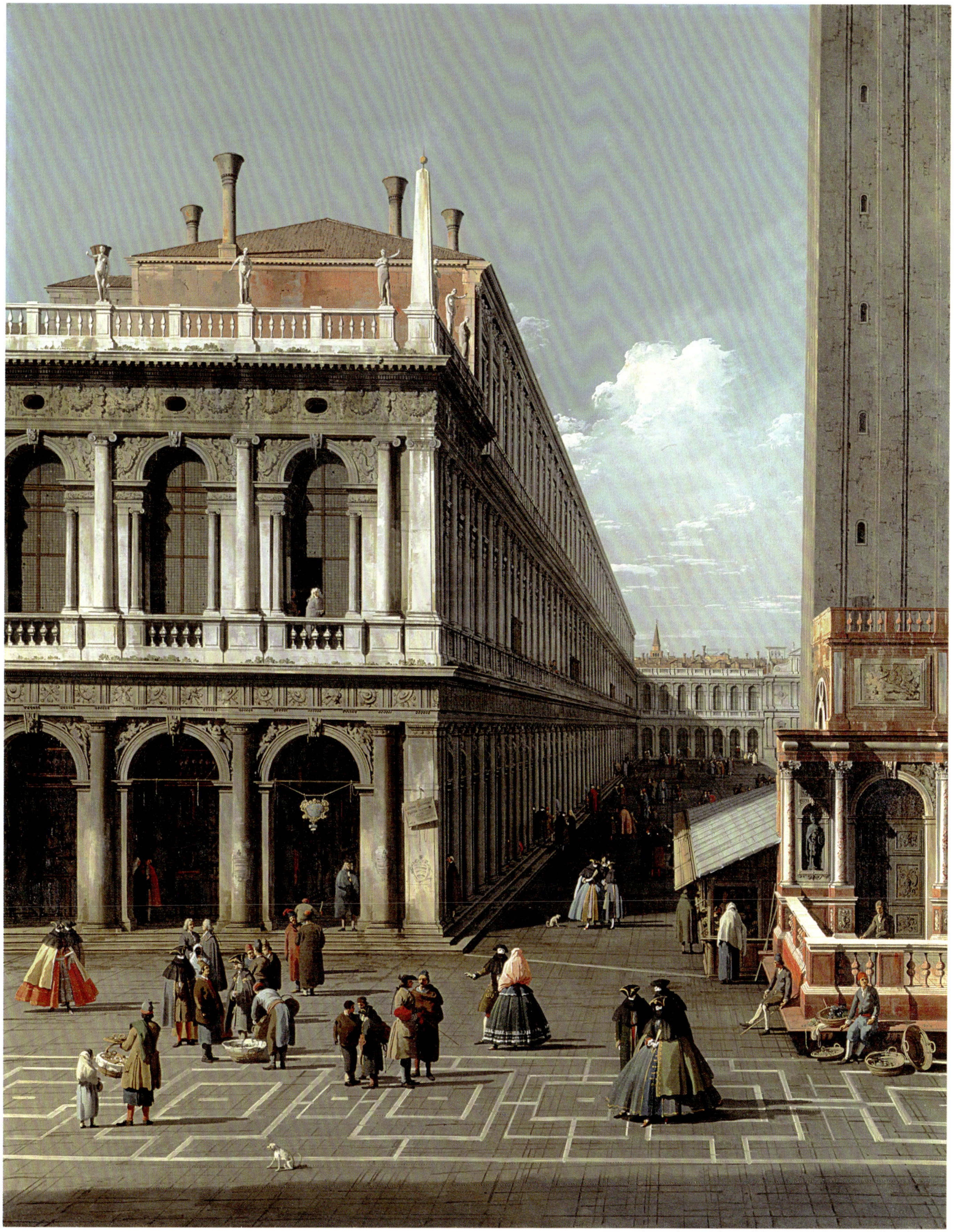

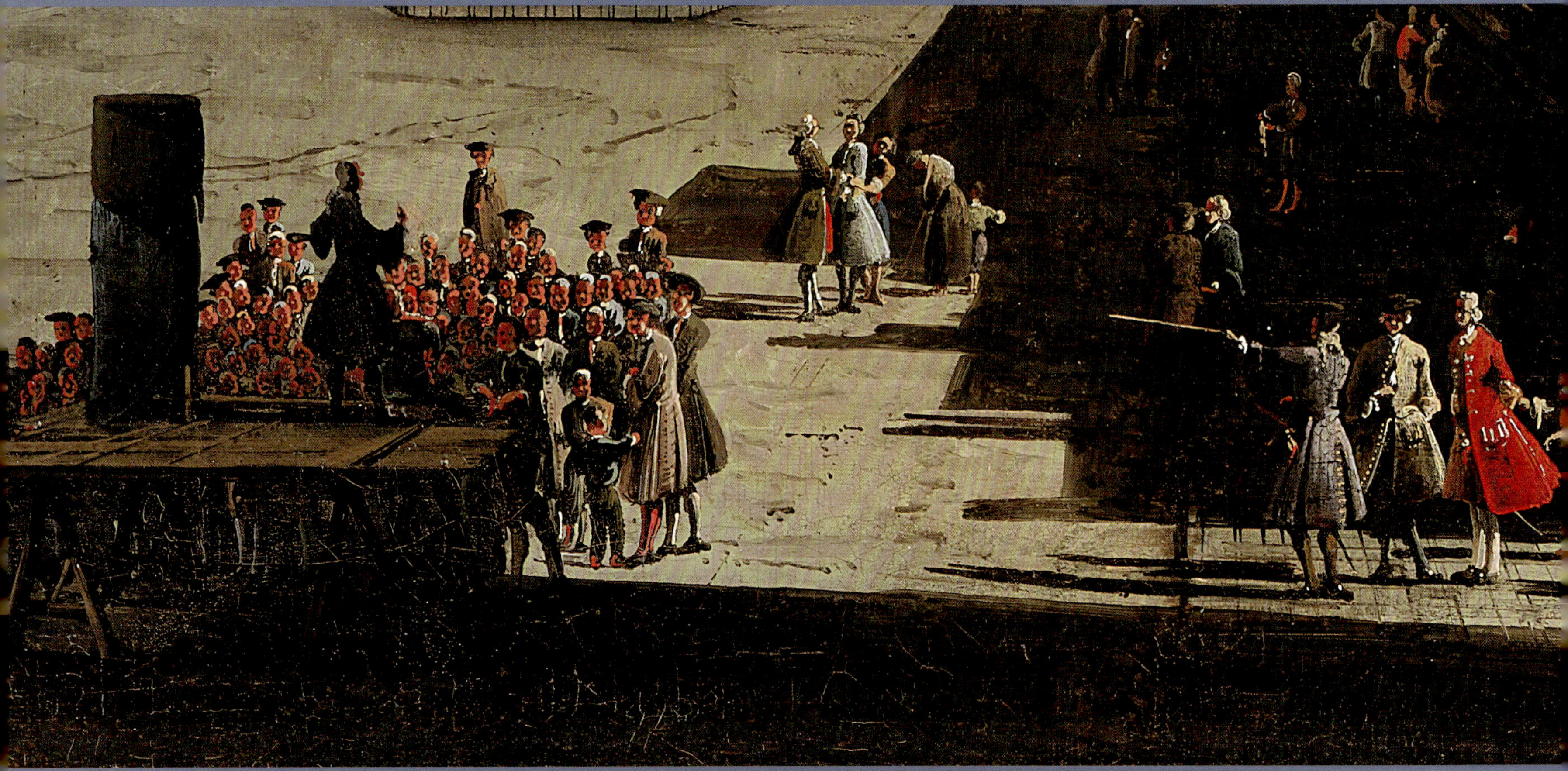

3.
BELLOTTO: FAR FROM VENICE

On 22 April 1740, Bernardo Bellotto received thirty-six 'Filippi' silver coins, just over the price of a small painting by Canaletto, from Anton Maria Zanetti di Girolamo (1680–1767) on behalf of the Marquis Andrea Gerini (1691–1766), who invited him to Florence. This is the earliest document of Zanetti's patronage, who organized the young view painter's trip to Florence, where he painted views for the Marquis Andrea Gerini and Vincenzo Riccardi – two of the most important Florentine collectors of the eighteenth century – already signing himself 'Bernardo B. detto il Canaletto'. During his stay in Florence, which lasted from the end of April to 30 September 1740, Bellotto met Giuseppe Zocchi (1717–1767), a painter for the Gerini family, who was entrusted with introducing view painting in Florence, in the wake of Venice, Rome and Naples. Bellotto taught Zocchi what he had learned from Canaletto about technique and perspective composition. Two sketches by Bellotto, one from the Museo Correr and the other in a private collection (cat. 20, 25), are evidence of the importance of their relationship: Zocchi used them for his own paintings, from which Fabio Berardi (1736–1788) in turn drew his own fine engravings (cat. 21, 22, 23, 24). This is how we know that on Bellotto's subsequent trip to Rome he passed through Rota, a small village built on a tufaceous rock near Tolfa, recognisable in this group of works by Bellotto, Zocchi and Berardi.

The sketch of the Porta della Carta del Palazzo Ducale (cat. 27), traditionally attributed to Canaletto, is paired for comparison with the perspective drawings of the south facade of Basilica di San Marco, perhaps contemporary, on the versos of Bellotto's two drawings of Rota.

The relationship between Gerini and Bellotto seems to have been satisfactory to both parties: the marquis sent the artist a gift of two volumes of prints by Zocchi, *Scelta di XXIV vedute delle principali contrade, piazze, chiese e palazzi della città di Firenze* and *Vedute delle ville e d'altri luoghi della Toscana*, published in Florence in 1744–45, and in exchange, Canaletto's nephew sent him 'two little pictures' which we think might have been the *Capriccio with a Bridge on a River* (cat. 28) and its lost pendant, of which Zocchi made copies.

The Archibishop of Milan, Giuseppe Pozzobonelli, also became one of Bellotto's patrons, commissioning in 1744 *San Paolo Converso and Sant'Eufemia, Milan* (cat. 50) and a view of Vaprio. In 1754, the Archbishop received two landscapes by Zocchi, one of which designed by the Venetian, as a gift from the Marquis Gerini (cat. 25).

18

GIUSEPPE ZOCCHI

(Florence 1717–1767)

Anton Maria Zanetti di Girolamo and Andrea Gerini
1740–1744

oil on copper; 37 x 28 cm
Venice, Ca' Rezzonico, Museo del Settecento Veneziano, Cl. I no. 144

Inscriptions: on the letter, 'ILL.MO SIG. A.M. ZANETTI Q. JER.VENEZIA.'.

In 1960, Terisio Pignatti published this small oval on copper with an attribution to an 'eighteenth-century Venetian painter' in the style of Jean Jacques Flipart (1719–1782); Anton Maria Zanetti di Girolamo (1680–1767) was recognised as the figure on the left, with Anton Maria Zanetti di Alessandro (1706–1778), his cousin of the same name and Custodian of the Biblioteca Marciana, on the right. Also in 1960, Francis Haskell, in a short article on artistic relationships between Venice and Florence, linked the work with a painting in the collection of Gian Maria Sasso that had been put up for sale shortly after the death of the Venetian collector and antiquarian in 1803 and described as follows in the catalogue: 'Copper oval, with portrait of the famous Anton-Maria Zanetti, in the company of the Marquis Gerini, looking at cameos, by Zocchi, an oval 1 foot high and 10 inches long' (*Catalogo de' quadri*, no. 381). The fact that the cameos and medals are at the centre of the pair's attention suggested to Haskell a date close to the publication of Zanetti's *Dactyliotheca* in 1750. M. Ingendaay also supports this date, believing the figure of Gerini to be a repetition from another work by Zocchi, *Portrait of a group of gentlemen*, in a private collection, dated by her to 1749 on the basis of an identification of one of the figures, Abbot Lorenzo Lorenzi (?–1797/8), whose arrival in Florence 'was pinpointed by historiography' to that year (Ingendaay 2013, pp. 91, 113–114). A. Tosi however, based on the physiognomy of Andrea Gerini (1691–1766) 'more in his 50s than 60s', believed that the portrait was painted in 1740–41 on commission by the marquis and sent to Venice as 'a sign of gratitude for a generous gift', a volume of the *Chiaroscuri*, the arrival of which is recorded in the *Novelle Letterarie* in June 1741.
A keen-eyed self-portrait of Zocchi, drawn before his departure for Rome in July 1744 and engraved by Johann Gottfried Seuter for the frontispiece of *Vedute delle ville, e d'altri luoghi della Toscana* in 1745, is the only portrait that can be securely dated.
This double portrait, in which the physiognomies are depicted with liveliness and finesse, may have been painted during the work on the two series of prints, both publishing ventures by Gerini with the help of Zocchi, the aforementioned *Vedute delle ville* and the *Scelta di XXIV vedute delle principali contrade, piazze, chiese e palazzi della città di Firenze*, of 1744.
In this informal conversation piece Zanetti is depicted at a similar angle to which he had portrayed Rosalba Carriera in the 1720s for the well-known print by Giovanni Antonio Faldoni that appeared in the *Chiaroscuri* album. The scene is imaginary, an affectionate tribute to Zanetti by the Florentine marquis: no part of it indicates a Venetian setting. The atmosphere is intimate and familiar, pointing to an already consolidated friendship.
From the last months of 1737, Zanetti, himself a refined collector, is documented as an agent for Gerini, instigator of the commissions and purchases of contemporary Venetian paintings for his collection, by Francesco Zuccarelli, Michele Marieschi, Bernardo Bellotto, Bartolomeo Nazzari and Giambattista Pittoni; their works would significantly enrich the collection of the marquis from the first half of the 1740s. By mutual agreement they came up with the idea of bringing Bellotto to Venice to introduce *vedute* painting to the Tuscan capital; the young Venetian taught Giuseppe Zocchi during this period. In Gerini's aforementioned publishing venture, Zanetti was the point of reference in Venice for the project that he both prepared and led in detail, employing Venetian engravers such as Pietro Monaco, Giuseppe Filosi, Giuliano Giampiccoli and Giuseppe Wagner, including two unusual appearances by the young Giambattista Piranesi and the *peintre-graveur* Michele Marieschi (Kowalczyk 2012).

Bożena Anna Kowalczyk

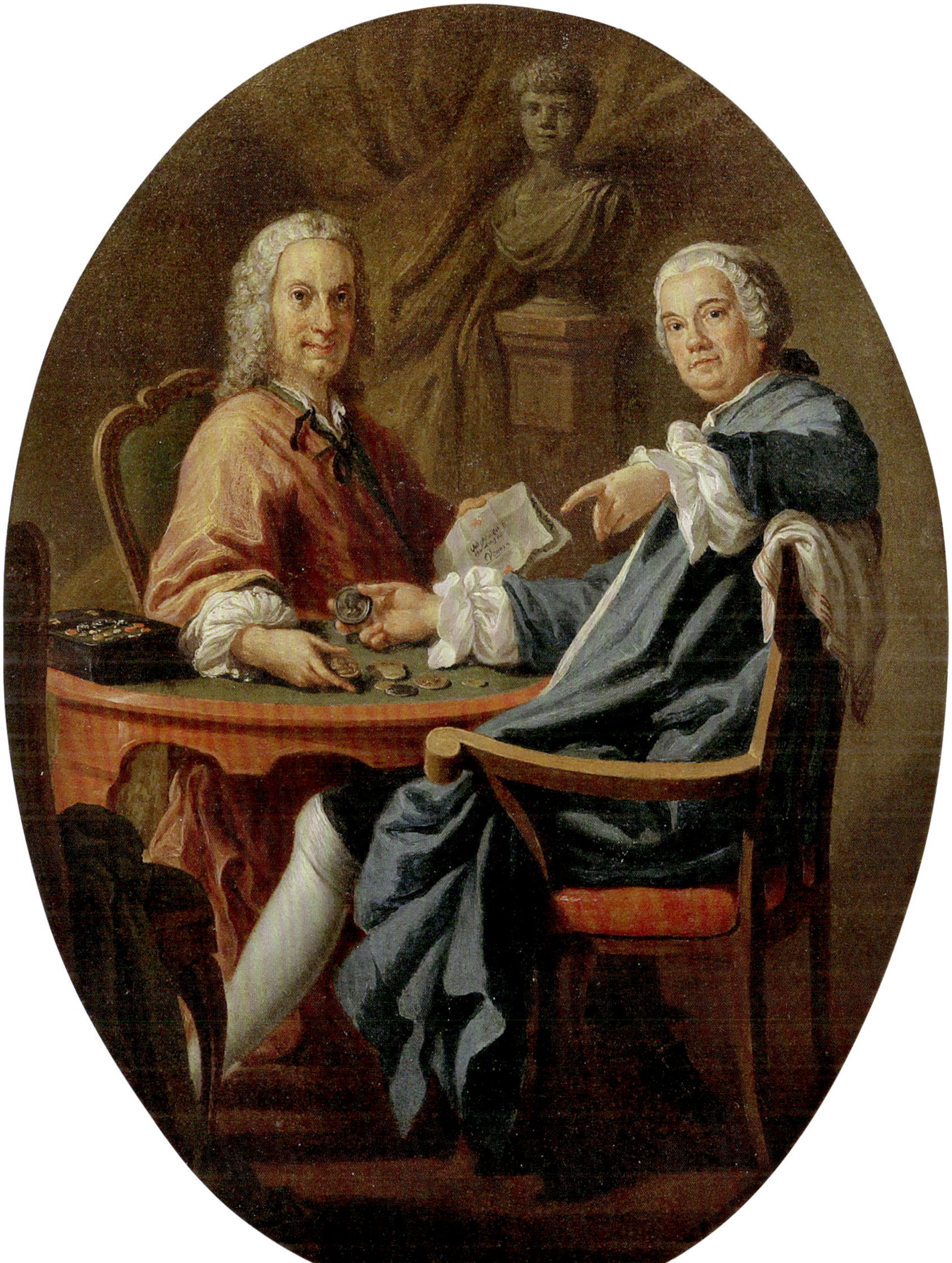

19

BERNARDO BELLOTTO

(Venice 1722 – Warsaw 1780)

The Piazza della Signoria looking East, Florence
1740

oil on canvas; 61 x 90 cm
Budapest, Szépművészeti Múzeum, 645

The two views of Florence at the Szépmúvészeti Múzeum, this one of *The Piazza della Signoria* and its pendant, *Florence, The River Arno looking towards the Ponte Santa Trinita*, both in the same collection (inv. 647), are the earliest documented paintings by Bellotto. Works with extraordinary expressive force, they reveal the ambitious personality of the young view painter on his first trip outside Venice. They are a manifesto of his artistic precociousness, and fundamental for all consideration of his early activity as a painter in Venice.

The two paintings are listed under the name Canaletto in the inventory taken in 1741 of the personal collection of the Marquis Vincenzo Riccardi (1704–1752) 'Due Quadri compagni con cornice intagliati, e dorati alla Salvador Rosa rappresentante L'uno La Piazza del Granduca, e L'altro La veduta de Ponti coll'Arno, porta dal Ponte Vecchio verso Ponente' (two pendant paintings with carved frames, gilded in the manner of Salvador Rosa, one representing the Piazza of the Gran Duke, and the other a View of the Bridges with the Arno, from the Ponte Vecchio looking West) (Kowalczyk 2012, pp. 29–30). Bellotto probably arrived in Florence shortly after 22 April 1740. Invited there by Andrea Gerini, his stay was orchestrated by Anton Maria Zanetti di Girolamo (1680–1767), who sponsored his activity. He painted a further four views of the city for the Florentine marquis, which have not yet been identified. Gerini, from an old Florentine family of merchants and bankers and closely connected to the Medici court and, later, the Lorraine, was probably the one who transmitted his interest in contemporary Venetian painting and views to Riccardi, the husband of one of his nieces.

Bellotto painted this exceptional image of the Piazza della Signoria, the only one of his known views of Florence that is not of the Arno, for the young Marquis Riccardi, who served as extraordinary ambassador in Rome between 1738 and 1739 and was a passionate collector of landscapes, seascapes, battle scenes and Italian, Flemish and Dutch works. The main square of the Tuscan capital, decorated with famous Renaissance sculptures outside the Palazzo Vecchio, with the Loggia dei Lanzi in shadow, is described through a play of light and shadow, with incomparable coherence and narrative force. The use of the red-brown shade for the architecture strengthens the chiaroscuro effects, while the delicate sky is laid out on a layer of warm grey. Bellotto deliberately presented himself as an avant-garde artist and also shows, through the story that unfolds in parallel in the foreground and the grotesque backlit figures, his admiration for the prints of Jacques Callot (1592–1635), who was in Florence between 1612 and 1621, working for Christina of Lorraine.

This same compositional model, with the foreground immersed in shadow and elongated figures, was also used for the view of *Piazza San Martino, Lucca* (York Art Gallery, Museums Trust; Kozakiewicz 1972a, no. 58), from just a little later, and *The Campo Santi Giovanni e Paolo*, *Venice* at the Museum of Fine Art, Springfield, which was painted upon his return from his successful trip in Tuscany, as confirmed by the date of 8 December 1740 on the preparatory drawing at the Hessisches Landesmuseum in Darmstadt (Kozakiewicz 1972a, no. 24–25).

Two other pairs of views of Florence by Bellotto are known, but none from the documented eighteenth-century history. The two pendants at the Alfred Beit Foundation, Roussborough House, Wicklow in Ireland, *The Arno from the Vaga Loggia and the Arno with the Ponte Vecchio*, can be dated to 1740 through their stylistic similarity to the Budapest paintings and were therefore possibly part of the Gerini series. Two others, at The Fitzwilliam Museum in Cambridge, have a stylistic maturity datable to around 1744 (cat. 36, 37).). The only known drawing of Florence, *The River Arno, looking towards the Ponte alla Carraia*, from around 1740, at the Uffizi, might have been a preparatory drawing for one of the lost Gerini views, before also being used for the version in Cambridge.

Bellotto's Florentine paintings served as a school of technique and chiaroscuro for Giuseppe Zocchi (1717–1767), who painted for Gerini and was busy from 1740 on drawing views of Florence and villas for two famous print series, *Scelta di XXIV vedute … della Città di Firenze* and *Vedute delle ville, e d'altri luoghi della Toscana*, published in 1744–45. He is documented to have painted some of them in oil in 1741.

Bożena Anna Kowalczyk

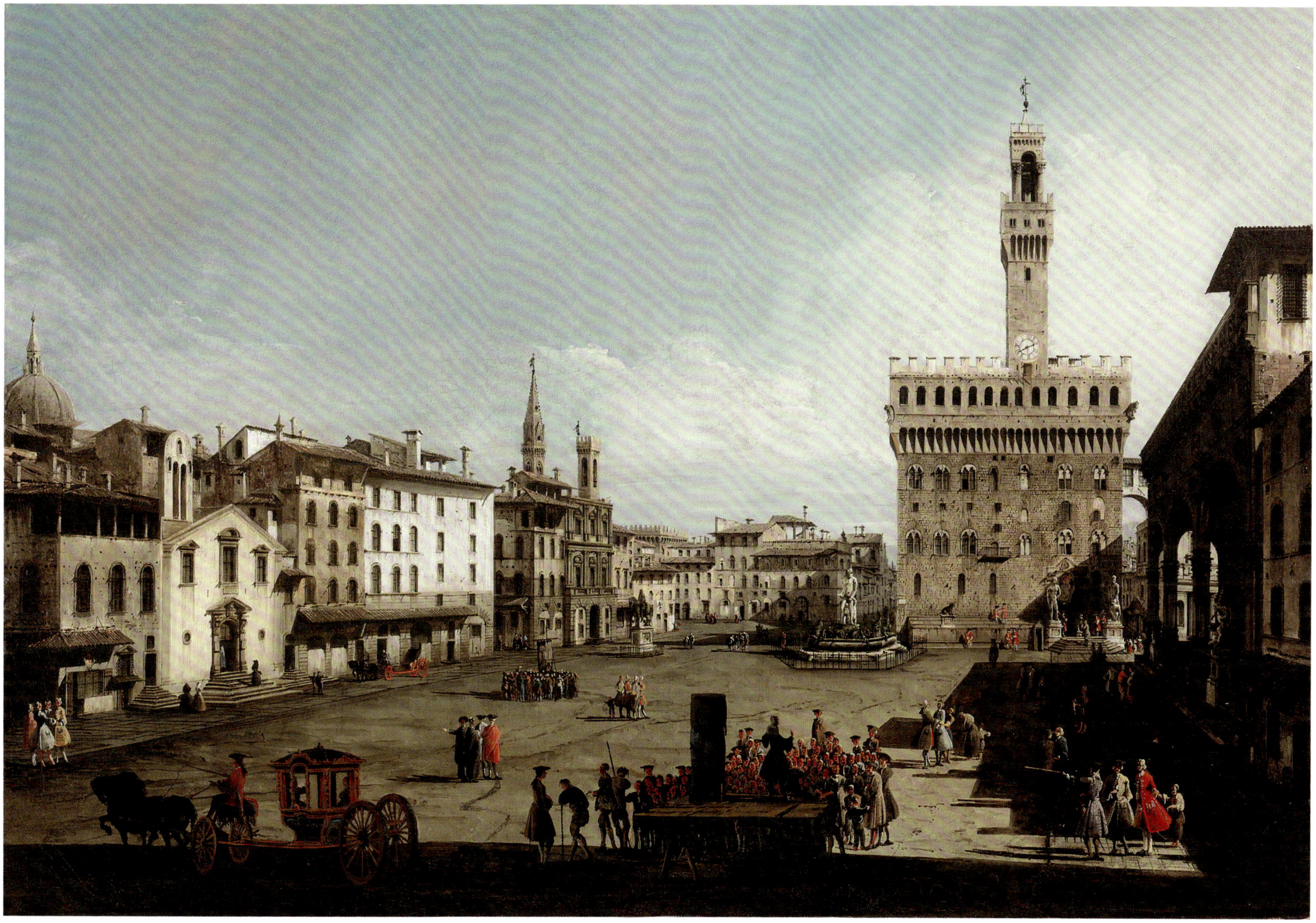

20

BERNARDO BELLOTTO

(Venice 1722 – Warsaw 1780)

Landscape with Motifs of Rota, near Tolfa (recto)
Basilica di San Marco, Venice. Studies of the South Front (verso)
1743–44

pen and brown link over over free and ruled pencil and pinpointing; 278 x 305 mm
Venice, Museo Correr, Gabinetto dei Disegni e delle Stampe, C1. III n. 8633

Watermark: three crescent moons.

Marks: below on the *recto* a brown oval with an intertwined F and C, not present in Lugt.

'The landscape appears real, and the buildings on the hilltop and the bell tower seem to be drawn from life; the descriptions range from general to analytical, seeking to record the most characteristic aspects, the buttresses of the rustic hillside homes, the tiled roofs and the structure of the simple country bell tower' (Kowalczyk 1987–88, p. II–328). Only recently it has been possible in this image to recognise the typical motifs of central Italy that Bellotto had crossed while travelling to Rome along the Via Francigena, from Pistoia and Lucca towards Viterbo and Bracciano. The small villages on their tufa rocks and the buttressed houses are often found in those areas but the 'Etruscan' archway leading to the village, the small church, the square and partially collapsed tower, are details that are found in Rota, near Tolfa, on the Via Claudia-Braccianese, a small detour from the Via Francigena. The viewpoint is from a nearby hill and offers a view along the road leading downhill and then uphill, where in the drawing there is a capital, the traces of which can still be seen today. The composition of the individual elements, however, is a kind of montage that leaves room for other elements to be identified: the old church of San Girolamo in the centre of the village has never had the high bell tower that appears in the drawing. The owner of the fiefdom since 1703 was Domenico Grillo (1682–1756), Duke of Monterotondo and Giuliano, a cousin of Clelia Grillo Borromeo Arese (1684–1777), the famous protagonist of the cultural and scientific life of Milan and from 1763 his heir in Rota.
The village of Rota – if the identification is correct – is depicted in reverse, as though the sketches had been drawn with a portable *camera optica*, and then drawn from memory. The brief but effective lines record every detail of the houses, revealing their uneven structure, supported by three buttresses, together with the special shape of the fireplace – there are still some similar ones to be seen today – and the gable of the roofs.
The drawing was executed on the same paper – with identical watermark – as a sketch taken from life of *The Watermill on a River, probably Mignone* (cat. 25), and which likewise has pencil sketches on the *verso* of the south side of Basilica di San Marco (fig. a). They both stand out for the vibrant line of a particular intensity, pure outline, laid over a tangle of pencil sketches and a number of *pentimenti* – the most obvious here being the position and height of the cypress near the small bell tower of the church. Both are also unusual in Bellotto's Italian repertoire in terms of their being 'village' subjects, but they are entirely consistent with his way of sketching compositions.
They also share the fact that they were used by the Florentine painter Giuseppe Zocchi (1717–1767), supported by Marquis Andrea Gerini (1691–1766) and engraved by Fabio Berardi (1736–1788) in prints produced in the Venetian printing house of Giuseppe Wagner (1708–1786) in the series of four rural images annotated 'Zocchi dipinse' (painted by Zocchi); the other sheet was printed in two states, with different texts on the lower margin (cat. 26).
The painting for which this is a preparatory sketch (cat. 21), and its pendant, *Landscape with Motifs of Rota with the Brick-Kiln, near Tolfa* (cat. 22), were made to commission for Marquis Andrea Gerini, probably in 1746–1750; the 'companion' drawing served for one of the 'pendants' sent by the marquis to his friend Giuseppe Pozzobonelli, Archbishop of Milan (cat. 25). It should be noted that in the associated print (cat. 23), aligned in the same direction as this sheet, Fabio Berardi showed three buttresses as in this drawing (in Zocchi's painting there are only two). He also made the windows the same size, whereas they are smaller in the Zocchi picture (cat. 21). This may suggest that the sheet was available to him in Wagner's print shop.

Bożena Anna Kowalczyk

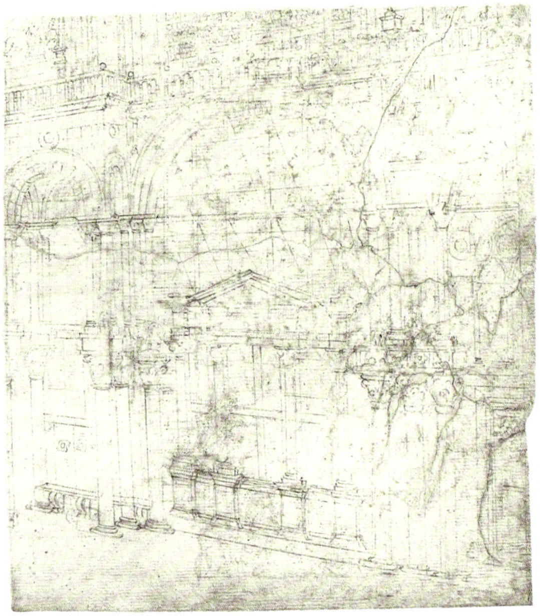

a. Bernardo Bellotto, *Basilica di San Marco, Venice. Studies of the South Front* (*verso* of cat. 20)

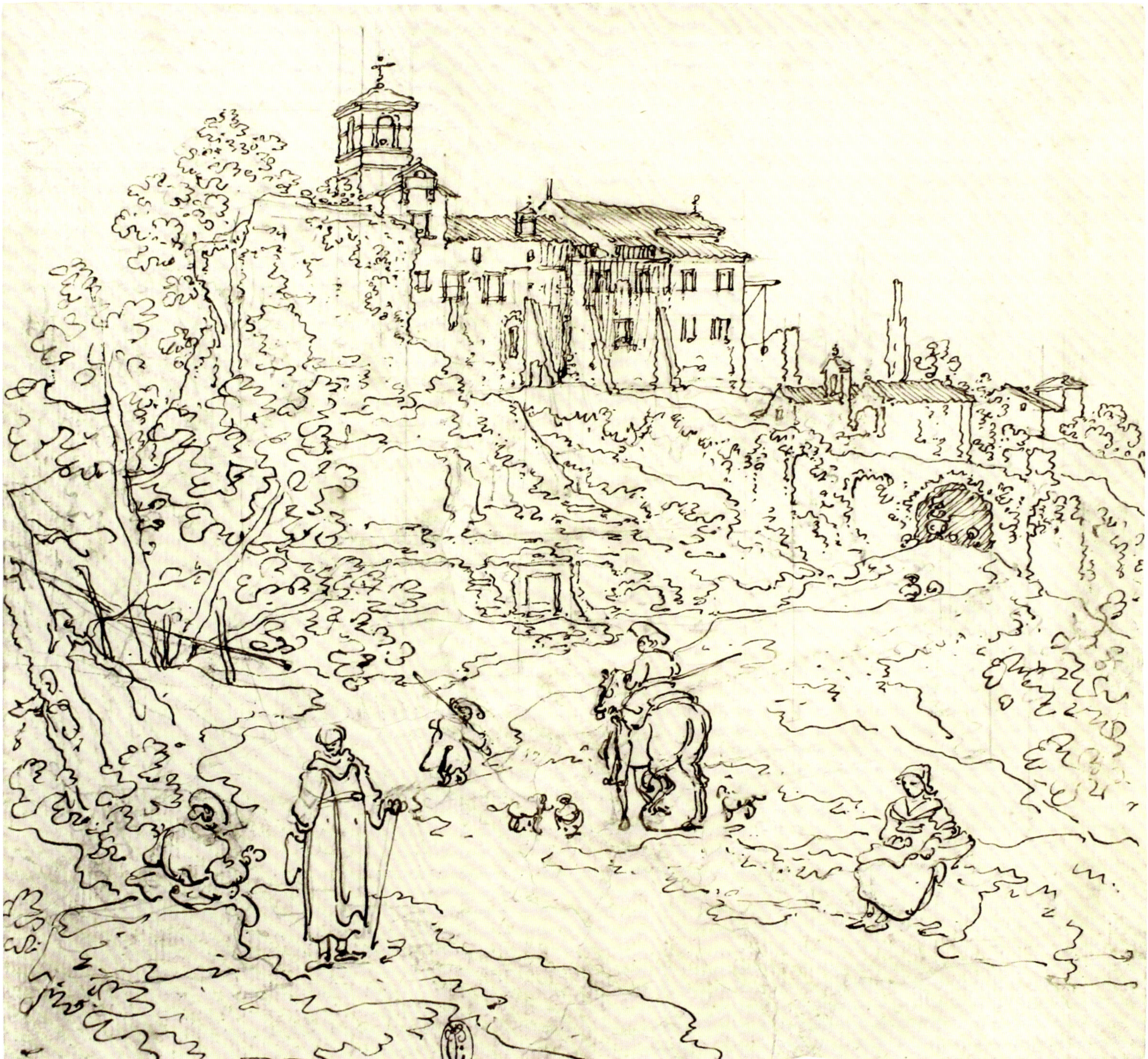

21

GIUSEPPE ZOCCHI

(Florence 1717–1767)

Landscape with Motifs of Rota, near Tolfa
1746–1750

oil on canvas; 83 x 53.5 cm
Private Collection, courtesy Jean-Luc Baroni Ltd., London

22

GIUSEPPE ZOCCHI

(Florence 1717–1767)

Landscape with Motifs of Rota with the Brick-Kiln, near Tolfa
1746–1750

oil on canvas; 83 x 53.5 cm
Private Collection, courtesy Jean-Luc Baroni Ltd., London

Giuseppe Zocchi, author of preparatory drawings and engraver of some plates for the *Scelta di XXIV vedute … della Città di Firenze* e *Vedute delle ville, e d'altri luoghi della Toscana*, the most important publishing venture in Florence in the eighteenth century, sponsored by the Marquis Andrea Gerini (1691–1766), was the finest and the most versatile Florentine painter of the mid-century years. His background was as a painter of figures – his first biographer and patron, Francesco Maria Nicolò Gabburri (1676–1742) mentions an apprenticeship in the studio of Ranieri del Pace – but in 1740 he began to paint views of Florence and Tuscany; Pierre-Jean Mariette remembers him as a landscape painter, a pupil of Claude-Joseph Vernet (*Abecedario* 1851-1853, vol. VI, p. 158). From November 1732, the young Zocchi drew a salary as resident artist to Marquis Andrea Gerini (Ingendaay 2013, vol. I, p. 105); it was the latter who guided his artistic choices and planned his international debut as a landscape artist and *vedutista* in collaboration with Anton Maria Zanetti di Girolamo (1680–1767), an illustrious Venetian antiques dealer and collector, patron of Bernardo Bellotto, Michele Marieschi (1710–1743) and Francesco Zuccarelli (1702–1788) (Kowalczyk 2012). In this regard, the relationship with Bellotto, hitherto only assumed and misinterpreted, is made clearer. Bellotto was active in Florence as early as the late spring of 1740, the guest not of the Marquis Vincenzo Riccardi, as believed, but of Andrea Gerini. Zocchi learned Canaletto's technique for the description of city monuments and atmosphere from the young Bellotto; he learned this in Florence and not in Venice, which he visited only in 1749, and his contact with Bellotto is closely linked to his debut as a landscape painter, with his views of Florence often in the past being attributed to the Venetian painter, who was five years younger. In Florence, he also studied the works of Canaletto, Marieschi, Giovanni Paolo Panini and Gaspar van Wittel to be found in the important Florentine collections of Francesco Nicolò Gabburri, Vincenzo Riccardi and Gerini. In his training as a landscape artist, an important role was also played by the Venetian landscape painting of Francesco Zuccarelli and Marco Ricci, and the Roman school represented since 1732 in the Gerini Collection with works by Andrea Locatelli and Paolo Anesi, and from 1743 with works by Vernet. He also had direct experience of the Roman manner after visiting the city, where he is documented on 4 July 1744 (on 9 March 1746 he was back in Florence; Ingendaay, vol. I, p. 109).
These two paintings, known only through the prints of Fabio Berardi (1736–1788) (cat. 23, 24) until their appearance in the art market in 2003, represent the finest examples of Giuseppe Zocchi as a painter of landscapes. The splendid compositions, partly invented, combine elements of the village and castle of Rota, near Tolfa, on the via Claudia Braccianese, from 1703 to 1756 the property of the Genoese aristocrat Domenico Grillo (1682–1756), Duca di Monterotondo e Giuliano, who also had properties in Venice, and was a scholar of literature and theatre. The dating can be narrowed down to 1746–1750, after his return from Rome: the *terminus ante quem* is the date of the other two paintings which were probably planned as a 'village' series – and all four of them were engraved by Berardi – which are recorded as 'accomplished' by Gerini before 6 January 1750 for Pozzobonelli (1696–1783), Archbishop of Milan (cat. 25, 26). The idea was to compete with Francesco Zuccarelli, whose paintings were collected by the same Florentine marquis and also by Pozzobonelli through Zanetti, but Zocchi's interpretation reflects his experiences in Rome, in the use a clear light, and in the concreteness of the description, of the nature, architecture and figures that are reminiscent of Panini and Vernet.
The first painting, *Landscape with Motifs of Rota, near Tolfa*, framing the hillside hamlet with tall trees in the foreground, has a clear correspondence with a sketch by Bellotto in the Museo Correr (cat. 20) although it reproduces it the other way around – Berardi's print is set the same way as the drawing – which better reflects the topography of Rota, if indeed it is this village: the 'Etruscan' arch along the 'new road' – there is also another one in the village, on the 'old road', which had been abandoned by the eighteenth century – appears correctly on the left and the tufa rock with the collapsed tower on the right, high above the cliff. That the sketch precedes the painting is confirmed by observing the rendering of the architecture: with the precision that is typical of him, Bellotto noted the rough form and age of the houses, supported by three buttresses, the exact shape of the chimney place and the gap in the roof; Zocchi neglects or generalises these details, as if unaware of the place. The pendant, for which no preparatory sketch survives, adds further elements of the Rota landscape: the furnace, recorded in archive papers – the old structure still stands on the slope – and the river flowing at the foot of the hill, the Mignone.
Bellotto was also the author of the preparatory sketch for one of Pozzobonelli's paintings, *The Watermill on a River, probably Mignone* (cat. 25). The note added to the second state of the related print states the painting belonged to the Pozzobonelli's collection (cat. 26).
The two Bellotto drawings connect the two pairs of pendant as a series of landscapes of the same place, confirming the Marquis Gerini commission indicated albeit without documentary proof by D. Tosi; even now, after the publication of the entire, rich and carefully ordered Gerini archive, which since 2004 belongs to the Archivio di Stato of Florence, it is impossible to identify the associated payments. The prints made by Giuseppe's son, Cosimo Zocchi, show that Gerini also owned two other vertical format landscapes but of wilder scenes, with waterfalls and a bridge suspended between the rocks (Tosi 1997, pp. 276, 278); these must be the 'rural views with figures' mentioned in the catalogue of the collection of Giovanni Gerini (1770–1825) – the son of Carlo Francesco, nephew and heir of Marquis Andrea – drawn up in 1825 for a sale; and the dimensions also correspond (*Catalogo* 1825, nos. 67, 68).
The name of Bellotto is associated once again – but through Zocchi and subjects from those identified with him so far – to those of Andrea Gerini and Pozzobonelli, collectors who were guided in their artistic choices by Anton Maria Zanetti di Girolamo (1680–1767).

Bożena Anna Kowalczyk

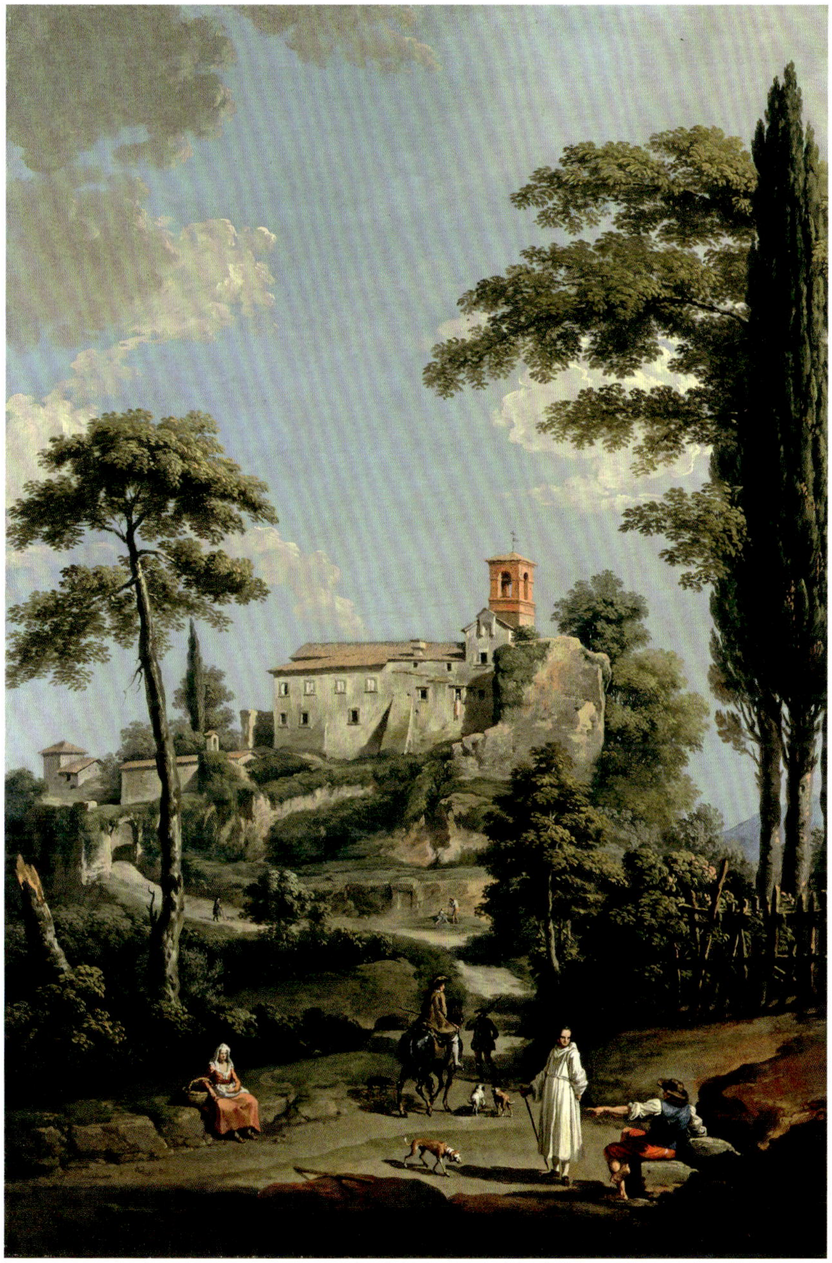

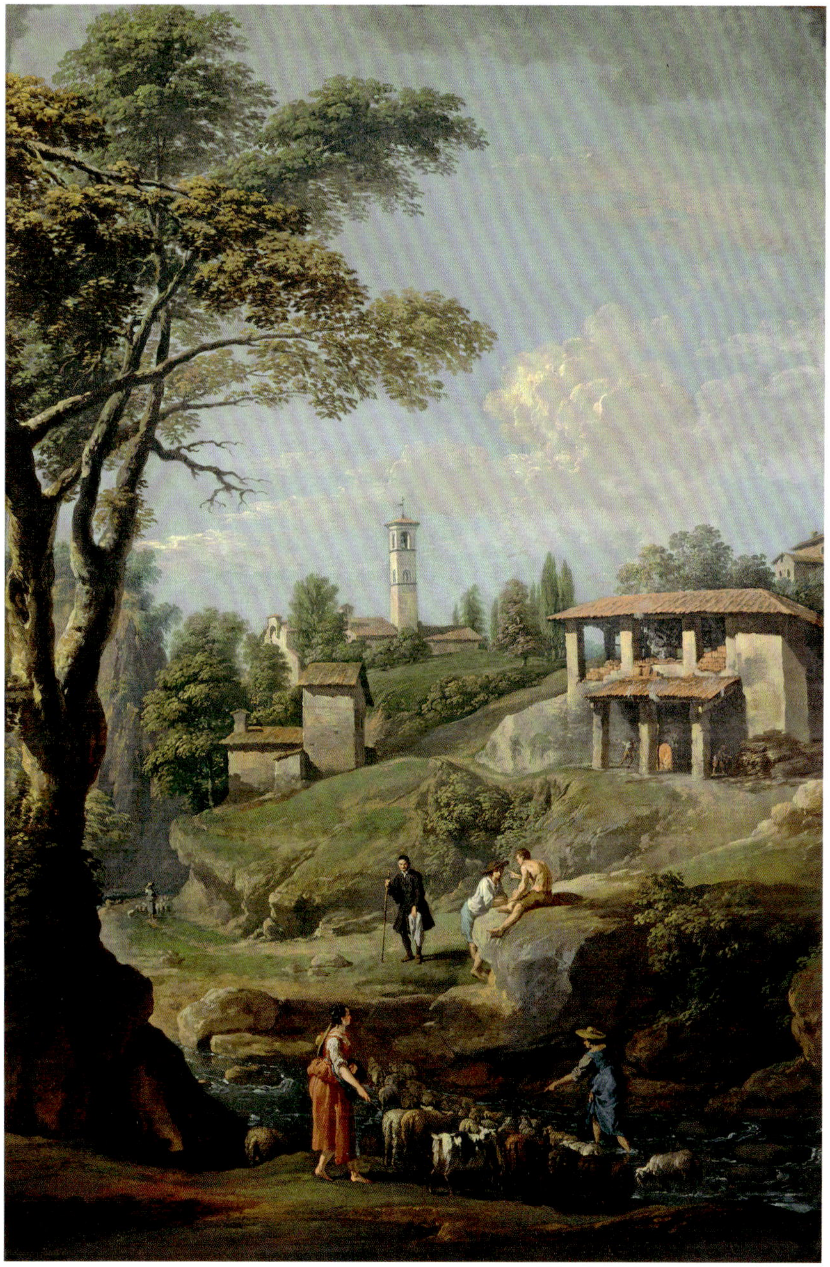

23

FABIO BERARDI

(Siena 1736 – Venice 1788)

Landscape with Motifs of Rota, near Tolfa
1765–1770

etching and engraving, II state of two; 343 x 496 mm
Private Collection

Inscriptions: in the margin, 'Zocchi dipinse Fabio Berardi Scol. appo Wagner Venezia C.P.E.S/ Anco in mezzo a dirupi in valle oscura/ Trovan conforto de' mortali i cuori, / I passeggi, le caccie, ed i lavori/ Sono dell'uom trattenimento e cura'; fragment of number lower left '[N° 60.2]'.

Fabio Berardi, one of the best engravers reproducing paintings in the Venetian tipography of Joseph Wagner (1706–1786), was born in Siena where he was baptised on 24 May 1736 (Dri 2004–2005, p. 5). When he arrived in Venice, probably in 1754, he already had some experience as engraver but it was in the lagoon city that he developed his soft and ductile manner of engraving, of French origin, with a combination of etching and engraving that he learned from Wagner, himself a pupil of Jacopo Amigoni (1682–1752) in London.
Wagner had arrived in Venice with Amigoni in 1739, and was an engraver of a precise and elegant manner and also a renowned and much sought-after typographer. For the most part, he was involved in reproductions: his print shop at San Lio, and later at San Zulian, saw the publication of about fifteen hundred prints, and he was in close contact with Anton Maria Zanetti di Girolamo, a refined connoisseur, who suggested him in 1742–43 as an engraver for the six plates of the *Vedute delle ville, e d'altri luoghi della Toscana* (1744–45), an important publishing project undertaken by Marquis Andrea Gerini (1691–1766), followed by the *Scelta di XXIV vedute … della Città di Firenze*, published in 1744 at the printing house of Giuseppe Allegrini. It is in the association of Wagner with Zanetti and Gerini that we should seek the idea of commissioning Fabio Berardi to engrave the four plates of 'rural views' by Giuseppe Zocchi (numbered from 60.1 to 60.4), two for Marquis Gerini, and two more for his friend Giuseppe Pozzobonelli, Archbishop of Milan.
Fabio Berardi was also in direct contact with Zocchi, whose compositions were used in Wagner's printing shop from the 1740s. It has been suggested (Ingendaay) but not corroborated by documentation that Berardi based his prints on drawings sent to him in Venice between 1760 and 1766 by the Florentine painter. Given that in 1765–66 the engraver is documented in Florence – shortly before the death of Marquis Andrea on 25 April 1766 – and soon after, in 1767 in Milan, it is likely that the idea of the commission for the four prints cropped up during these two trips. The refined technique that increases the picturesqueness and charm of the compositions suggests a fairly late date of execution in Berardi's career: A. Dri, author of the first catalogue raisonné of the Sienese engraver's oeuvre considers it to date from the second half of the seventies on the basis of style, subsequent to the famous series of prints after Canaletto (p. 17). Pierre-Jean Mariette instead writes: 'Un graveur, nommé Berardi, a aussi gravé dans ces derniers temps quelques uns de ses tableaux, et c'est ce qui a été fait mieux d'après lui' (*Abecedario* 1851-1853, vol. VI, p. 158).
Like the present one, all four plates bear a text stressing their village character. This one, which presents the most beautiful and complex composition of the series – based on a sketch by Bernardo Bellotto (cf. cat. 20) – is distinguished by a particular finesse in rendering chiaroscuro passages, especially in the sections dedicated to nature, translated in the print with some dense cross-hatching mitigating the harshness of the light effects of Zocchi, influenced by Roman art.
The changes from the first to the second of the print reflect a pictorial and free manner that is wholly Venetian, highlighted here for the first time: the height of the cypresses, slim and slender in Zocchi, and reproduced as such in the first state, is limited here to underline the soft crown of the tree behind; in both, there is a greater importance than in the painting accorded to the fencing at the foot of the backlit cypresses, which is significant for the chiaroscuro. The worried monk in Zocchi becomes softer under burin of Fabio, renowned for his benevolent and serene character.

Bożena Anna Kowalczyk

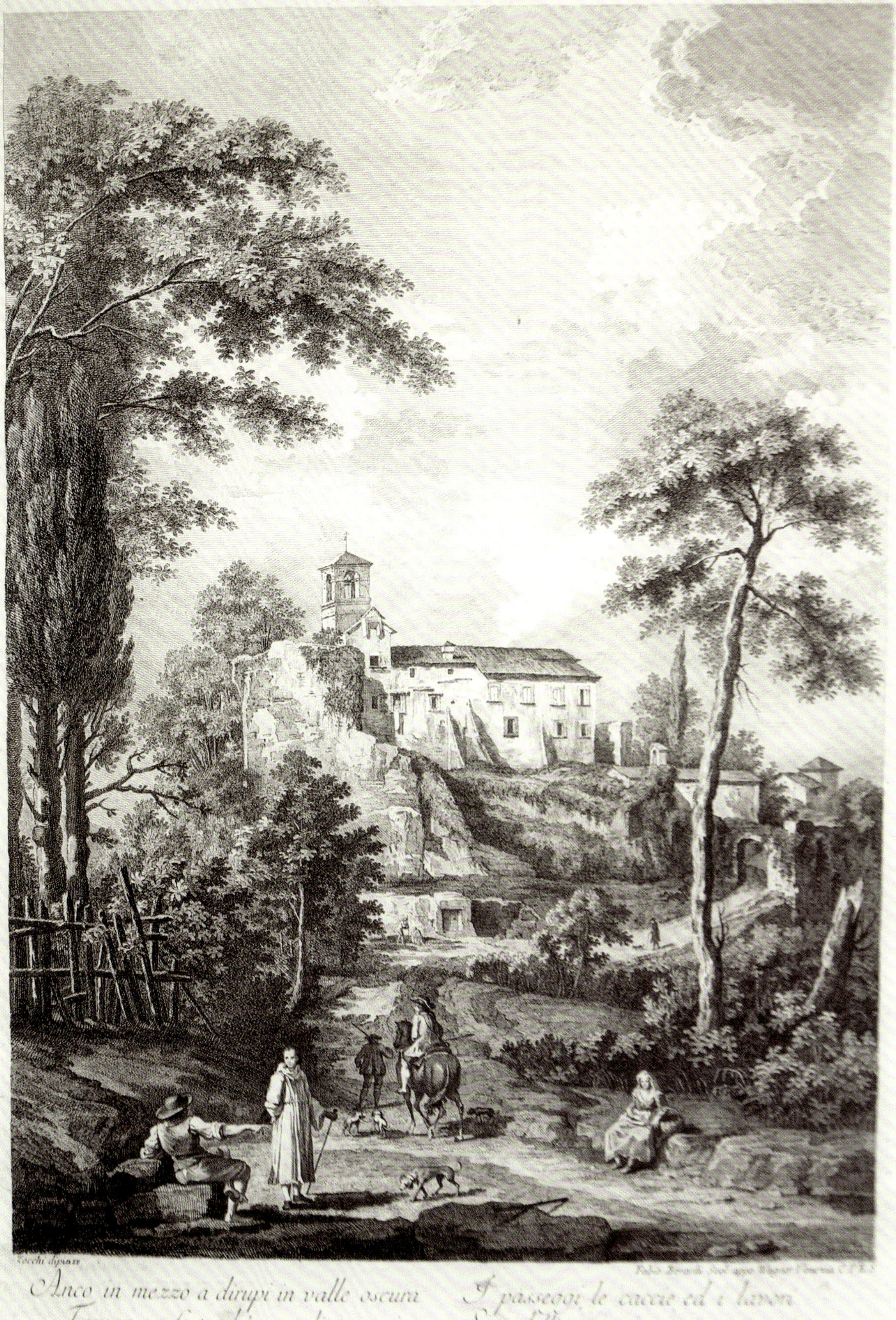

Zocchi dipinse

Fabio Berardi Scol. appo Wagner Venezia C.P.E.S.

Anco in mezzo a dirupi in valle oscura
Trovan conforto de' mortali i cuori,
I passeggi, le caccie ed i lavori
Sono dell'uom trattenimento e cura

24

FABIO BERARDI

(Siena 1736 – Venice 1788)

Landscape with Motifs of Rota with the Brick-Kiln, near Tolfa
1765–1770

etching and engraving, single state; 328 x 452 mm
Venice, Fondazione Querini Stampalia, cart. XVI, no. 1

Inscriptions: on the margin, 'Zocchi dipinse Fabio Berardi Scol. appo Wagner Venezia C.P.E.S / Quando il sole è all'occaso ha per costume / Che della greggia è alla custodia intento/ Guidar dal pasco il satolato armento/ A qualche fonte, ad un ruscello, a un fiume /'; lower left, 'N°60.1'.

The etching is part of the series of four 'village' subjects, numbered from 60.1 to 60.4, which reproduce in reverse two pairs of paintings by Giuseppe Zocchi (1717–1767), commissioned by Marquis Andrea Gerini (1691–1766), a patron of the painter. This print corresponds to one of the companion pieces, mentioned as 'rural views' in the inventory of Giovanni Gerini (1770–1825), son of Carlo Francesco, the nephew and heir of Marquis Andrea (*Catalogo* 1825, nos. 66- 67; cf. cat. 21, 22). The pendant, *Landscape with Motifs of Rota, near Tolfa*, makes use of motifs of the same village, situated on a tufa rock on the via Claudia Braccianese, near Tolfa: namely, the 'Etruscan' arch, the little church, the severed tower of the castle and the house with buttresses (cat. 21). In this view, taken from the road now used as the main access to the village and the castle, new elements of the Rota landscape appear, such as the furnace, recorded in the archives – the ancient structure is still present on the slope – and the river that runs at the foot of the hill, the Mignone. The bell tower standing behind the houses is an invented detail.
The river is also present in the second pair of paintings engraved in the same series by Berardi, for what was probably a gift to Giuseppe Pozzobonelli from Gerini (1696–1783). These paintings are known only through the prints and are *The Watermill on a River, probably Mignone* and *Country Scene with Fisherman* (Tosi 1997, fig. p. 61); these prints are known in two states different for the text in the lower margin: in the first appears the legend that explains the position of the 'original', in the second there is a verse in a 'village' taste, as here (cat. 23). The collection of the Fondazione Querini Stampalia also possesses the second state of the *Country Scene with Fisherman*, annotated 'Zocchi dipinse Fabio Berardi scol. appo Wagner Venezia C.P.E.S. / Mentre per le campagne errando vanno / Pastorelle e Pastor col bianco armento, / In riva al fiume il pescator è intent / Per tenere alla preda insidie e inganno. /'; lower left 'n°60.4'.
These are among the most beautiful prints Fabio Berardi ever produced, in which the softness of his style of engraving and the ductility of the line – parallel, cross-hatched, light or firm – create a delicate effect of light and space in a Venetian interpretation of the models. The sky too is remarkable, as in the other prints in the series.
The relationship between the Sienese engraver and the Gerinis – the Marquis Andrea and his nephew Carlo Francesco (1738–1796) – is well documented by receipts for payments and various notes bearing witness to esteem and trust, in particular with regard to his participation in the second part of *Raccolta di ottanta Stampe rappresentanti i quadri più scelti de' Signori Marchesi Gerini di Firenze*, with prints taken from paintings by Giovanni di San Giovanni, Carlo Dolci, Salvador Rosa, Piazzetta and Vernet, and which was published in 1786, but it is not possible to identify the papers concerning his work for the two 'rural views' (Ingendaay 2013, vol. I, pp. 93–96).

Bożena Anna Kowalczyk

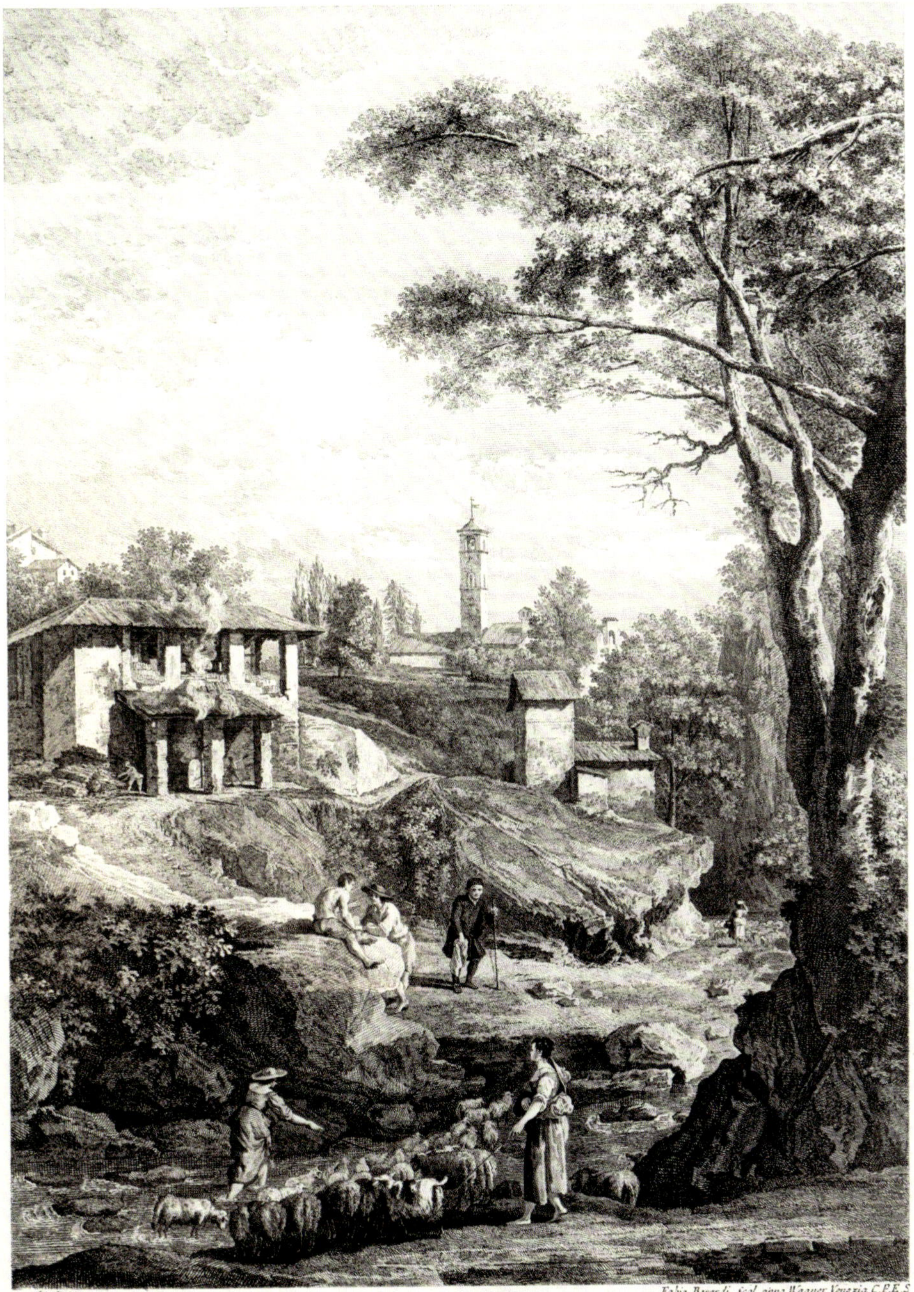

Zocchi dipinse | Fabio Berardi Scol. appo Wagner Venezia C.P.E.S.

Quando il Sole è all'occaso ha per costume
Chi della greggia è alla custodia intento
Guidar dal pasco il satolato armento
A qualche fonte, ad un ruscello, a un fiume.

25

BERNARDO BELLOTTO

(Venice 1722 – Warsaw 1780)

The Watermill on a River, probably Mignone; Study of the Torre dell'Orologio, Venice (recto)
The Basilica di San Marco, Venice: the Upper Part of the South Front; the West Facade in Perspective (verso)
1743–44

pen and brown ink over a lightly sketched pencil, only free and ruled pencil with pinpointing (*recto*); pencil (*verso*); 323 x 290 mm
Private Collection, courtesy Jean-Luc Baroni Ltd., London

Watermark: three crescent moons.

The drawing presents an unusual subject, that of a watermill, with farmers as protagonists and a wanderer with his horse atop a high bridge; on the horizon, a hilly landscape and the outline of a village. The undulating line over the preliminary work in pencil, worked freely and presenting a series of *pentimenti*, the 'ticked' foliage, the type of figures and, finally, the very character of the drawing, an overall study of pure outline, all conform to Bellotto's well-known graphic output between 1740 and 1744.
The drawing has a sort of companion piece in *Landscape with the Motifs of Rota, near Tolfa* (cat. 20) from a series of sketches made during his journey to Rome, while halting at the castle of Rota, on the Via Claudia-Braccianese, a minor detour from the Via Francigena. This sketch, drawn on paper of the same ream, is stylistically close and probably depicts the mill documented in the vicinity of the castle on the Mignone river, together with the old bridge indicated in maps of the property, which like the mill itself was probably built in the Middle Ages with an ogival arch, in like manner to others in central Italy, and over Roman foundations, detailed here down to the pontaie holes.
As with its companion sheet, this one too is laid over earlier pencil sketches that appear here on both sides. Below the drawing, and in part on the sky, we can see a view taken from life: a very slight pencil sketch, laid horizontally on the paper. The trace of ruled and freehand lines enable us to recognise the facade of the clock tower in Piazza San Marco in Venice. The tower, designed by Mauro Codussi in 1496–1499, emerges from the white part of the paper, with the little semicircular balcony and, hinted at, the statue of the *Virgin with Child*, two rectangular niches to the side, the underlying arch, and the little Corinthian columns. The pen drawing only partly conceals one of the side wings, and the roofs of the workshops, whose contours are used for the base of the bridge in the final drawing, are quite visible.
Other views of San Marco can be seen on the verso. We can recognise the upper part of the south facade of the Basilica, the one facing the Piazzetta, with the arch above the Zen Chapel, the two side aediculae, the balustrade and the top of the arch of the chapel itself. The main facade is depicted in a quick sketch, but we can also make out the horses of San Marco. These sketches are linked with those of the 'pendant's' verso, which are probably contemporary to the drawing of the *The Ducal Palace: the Porta della Carta, Venice* (cat. 27). The drawing was copied faithfully in a print by Fabio Berardi which, as the inscription on the margin of the first state of the print states, reproduces a painting, now lost, from the collection of Giuseppe Pozzobonelli (cat. 26). The print embraces a larger portion of the tree to the right, where the sketch appears clipped. None of the drawings were instead followed up in Bellotto's oeuvre: neither the landscape view in ink, nor the architectural sketches of San Marco. The southern facade of Basilica di San Marco and Torre dell'Orologio appear in a painting by Canaletto in the Royal Collection, *The Piazzetta from the North*, signed and dated 'A. Canal Fecit XXIV Octobris MDCCXLIII' (M. Levey, Levey 1991, no. 405). It is possible that the pencil studies were done for this painting. In particular, the perspective of the Torre dell'Orologio agrees, although that of the south facade of the Basilica, which is itself shown frontally in the canvas, changes. Bellotto is certainly the author of the study of the group of figures in the foreground, with baskets of birds (cf. cat. 10), which is probably contemporary.

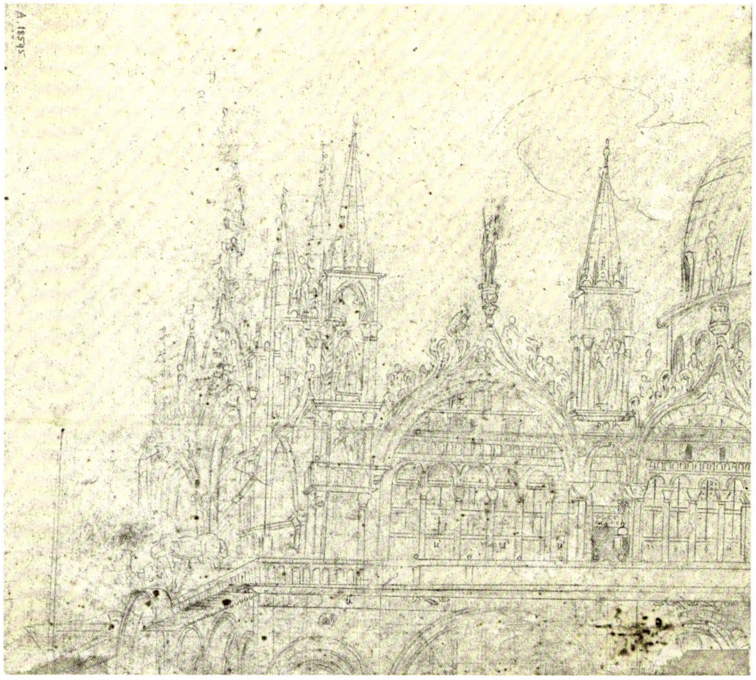

a. Bernardo Bellotto, *The Basilica di San Marco, Venice: the Upper Part of the South Front; the West Facade in Perspective* (*verso* of cat. 25)

Bożena Anna Kowalczyk

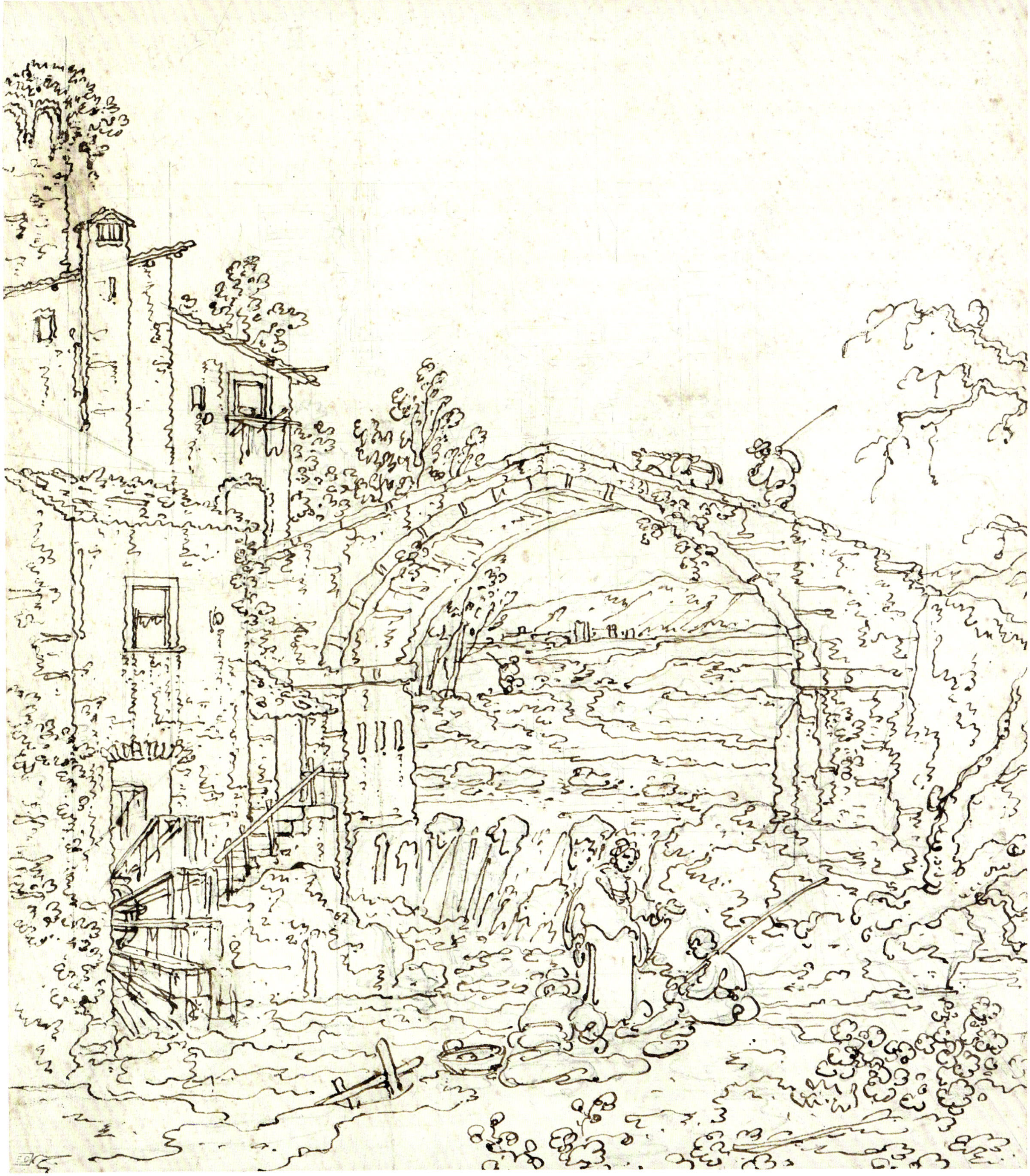

26

FABIO BERARDI

(Siena 1736 – Venice 1788)

The Watermill on a River, probably Mignone
1765–1770

etching and engraving, I state of two; 345 x 504 mm,
Milan, Civica Raccolta delle Stampe 'Achille Bertarelli', Art. g 2-17

Inscriptions: on lower margin, 'Zocchi dipinse Fabio Berardi incise / L'Originale è appresso -- L'Eminentissimo Signore /Cardinale Pozzobonelli -- Arcivescovo di Milano'.

Cataloguing the collection of Giuseppe Pozzobonelli (1696–1783) in 1802, painters Andrea Appiani and Alessandro Bellinzaghi did not recognise the hand of Giuseppe Zocchi (1717–1767) in the two 'Landscapes with waterfall, one of which with bridge and various boats, the other with a figure fishing', and attributed the two paintings to the Roman school (Bona Castellotti 1991, p. 102). The painter had died in Florence in 1767, shortly after his patron, the Marquis Andrea Gerini; the well-informed Pierre-Jean Mariette lamented that '... a peinne songeoit-on à lui pendant qu'il vivoit; ses compatriotes le laissoient sans occupation et mourant de faim' (*Abecedario* 1851-1853, vol. VI, p. 158). It is the rare reproduction prints by Fabio Berardi, this one and its companion piece, *Country Scene with Fisherman* in the edition including a text indicating the name of the collector, adorned by the cardinal's coat of arms, to offer the immediate attribution to the artist (Tosi).
Giuseppe Pozzobonelli, a cultured Milanese nobleman, was elected Archbishop of Milan on 14 June 1743; his work in the pastoral and political field for the Archdiocese of the Lombard capital has been compared to that of Carlo and Federigo Borromeo. He left his art collection to the Archdiocese – he loved Arcadian landscapes – but only a part is preserved today in the Diocesan Museum: some important works were sold, others lost, including those relative to the two prints. Anton Maria Zanetti di Girolamo (1680–1767) was his adviser in purchasing and commissions: Pozzobonelli's inventory includes the works of Bernardo Bellotto and Francesco Zuccarelli, both of whom he sponsored (cf. cat. 50).
There is no doubt that the two paintings by Zocchi are the same mentioned in Andrea Gerini's 'paperwork' before 6 January 1750, as stated by the painter himself in the receipt of payment; they were sent to Milan in 1754, probably as a gift to the Archbishop (Ingendaay 2013, vol. I, pp. 110–111; vol. II, p. 73, doc. 14 and 15). One may think that they originally formed a series of four with the pair of 'rural views' belonging to Gerini, since the two pairs have motifs of the same place, the property of Rota, a fiefdom in the hands of the Genoese nobleman, Domenico Grillo (1682–1756) (Kowalczyk 2015); they do form a series of four reproduction prints by Fabio Berardi, numbered 60.1 to 60.4, published by the Venetian printing house of Giuseppe Wagner (cf. cat. 23, 24).
This print should be considered the first state of two; the copies of the second are numbered 60.3 and annotated 'Zocchi dipinse Fabio Berardi Scol. appo Wagner Venezia C.P.E.S./ È gran ristoro negli estivi ardori/ Giacer di folte piante all'ombre amene/ seder presso i torrenti e sull'arene/ Agli affannati stanchi agricoltori'. The fact that Berardi signed himself here with just his name, without indicating the publisher of the printing plate as Wagner, as in his works published in the second part of the *Raccolta di ottanta Stampe rappresentanti i quadri più scelti de' Signori Marchesi Gerini di Firenze*, published in 1786, may mean that he was working on commission from Pozzobonelli or Gerini himself. It is also likely he made the drawings for the prints directly from the paintings himself, perhaps during his stay in Florence and Milan in 1766–1767: usually in his reproductions from paintings the name of the artist reproducing the picture is indicated, but here it just states 'Zocchi dipinse' (Zocchi painted). As in the case of the numbered print – 60.2 – reproducing one of the Gerini paintings, there is a preparatory sketch of the composition of Bellotto (cat. 25).
The particular attention to the depiction of the irregularities in the surfaces of the wall that Berardi reproduces from the lost original, stressing the effects of the atmospheric leaching, suggests that the influence of Bernardo Bellotto's technique was so strong as to impress Zocchi's work for a long time.

Bożena Anna Kowalczyk

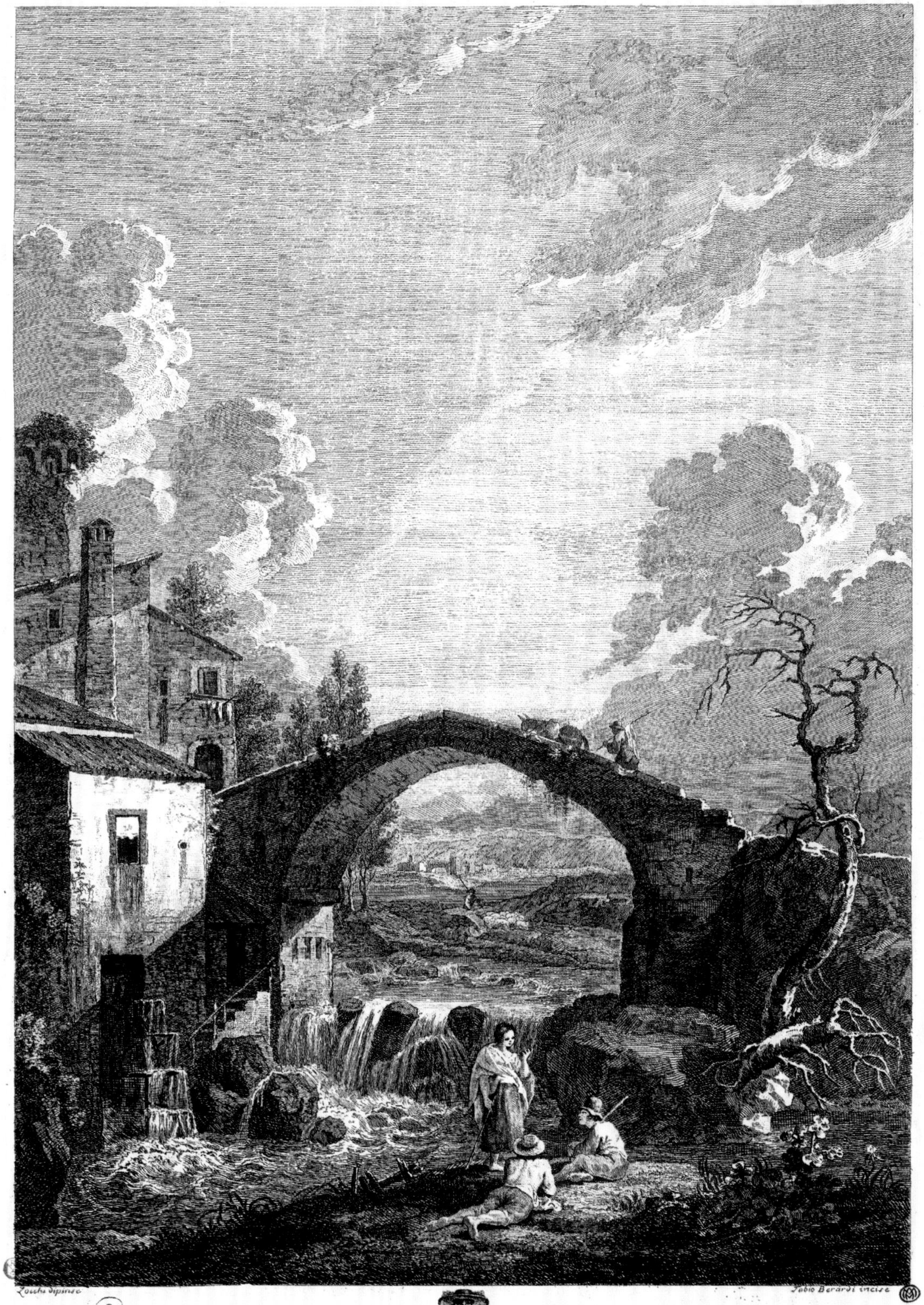

Zocchi dipinse — Fabio Berardi incise

L' Originale e' appresso L' Eminentissimo Signore Cardinale Pozzobonelli Arcivescovo di Milano

27

BERNARDO BELLOTTO

(Venice 1722 – Warsaw 1780)

The Ducal Palace: the Porta della Carta, Venice
1740–1743

pen and brown ink over traces of pencil; 432 x 192 mm
Leipzig, Museum für Bildende Künste, I2198/c

Inscriptions: '60 parte della metà della porta dela Carta con il rimanente del folio 61'; a horizontal line drawn in pencil with a ruler.

The Porta della Carta, the monumental entrance to the Ducal Palace in Venice, is summarised here in its essential elements and sculptural Gothic and Renaissance decoration. The line, albeit synthetic and offering only an outline, renders the idea of the magnificence of the design by the Bon father and son team of Venetian sculptors, who were commissioned in 1438 and were responsible for some of the sculptures, including the *Justice* with sword and scales dominating the top – here sketched in at the height of the window through lack of space at the top of the sheet – and of the *Saint Mark* just below at the centre but here omitted; Pietro Lamberti and Antonio Bregno instead sculpted the figures of the four *Virtues* in the niches of the side pillars. The Porticato Foscari can just be discerned through the open door; on the right margin, there is a corner of the Doge's Palace.
Four other architectural studies on numbered sheets like this one are known, similar in size and in the technique of simple outline: at the Berlin Kupferstichkabinett, drawn on both sides ('59'); a further two in the J. Paul Getty Museum ('58/uolta') and the Boijmans Van Beuningen Museum, Rotterdam ('57/uolta') with sketches of figures on the *verso*. All focus on Campo San Basso, sketches of the clock tower and of the north facade of the Basilica, come from the same album and were probably executed on the same day, in the order indicated by the numbers (C/L 540, 541, 555). Their attribution to Bellotto, widely questioned, is correct at the present state of the studies.
This drawing, which is probably contemporary to the others, as suggested also by Alice Binion who published it in 1980, joins the other sketches in the same notebook; of the same height as the Berlin, Rotterdam and Los Angeles sheets, it is missing a section on the left, as mentioned in the hand-written note (on which, maybe, was sketched the *tondo* with *Saint Mark* in bas-relief, apparently by Canaletto). The same series of views may include the pencil sketches on *The Watermill on a River, probably Mignone*and *Landscape with Motifs of Rota, near Tolfa* (cat. 25, 20) and of the clock tower on the recto of the first sheet and of the south facade of the Basilica, in the versos of both.
Traditionally attributed to his master, and each bearing a text in his own hand, these are perhaps the type of drawings referred to by the Venetian dealer and collector Gianmaria Sasso in a letter of 19 May 1781 to the British resident in Venice, John Strange, 'about 20 other large sketches by Canaletto but what then are these sketches other than pure contours in pen drawn from the life ... and although they are only outlines they give a true idea of the site since these are the best and the most beautiful views of Venice. These were used by Canaletto to paint his beautiful views but they served him as cartoons. Here I send two that were lent me so you may see them. They are on light paper since they were used to lay over the outline for pouncing with some needle tip or other tool. But the lines are very black and exact and I am amazed at Canaletto's bravura because the paper is so spongy that no one could draw a line on it, yet he has done so in pen and with such frankness that the paper was not spoiled [?] at all, and the lines are drawn to perfection as if they were on coarse paper' (Mattioli Rossi 1980, p. 87).
It has been suggested that these sketches were made with the help of a *camera optica*, but Constable notes that '... the treatment of the perspective does not support this'. The Rotterdam sheet in particular is a composition of views from various points of view, and the use of a ruler for the main constructive lines in pencil in all the drawings is a indication that these are works executed in the studio, on the basis of sketches *en plein-air*.
No painted works are known to have been based on these drawings.

Bożena Anna Kowalczyk

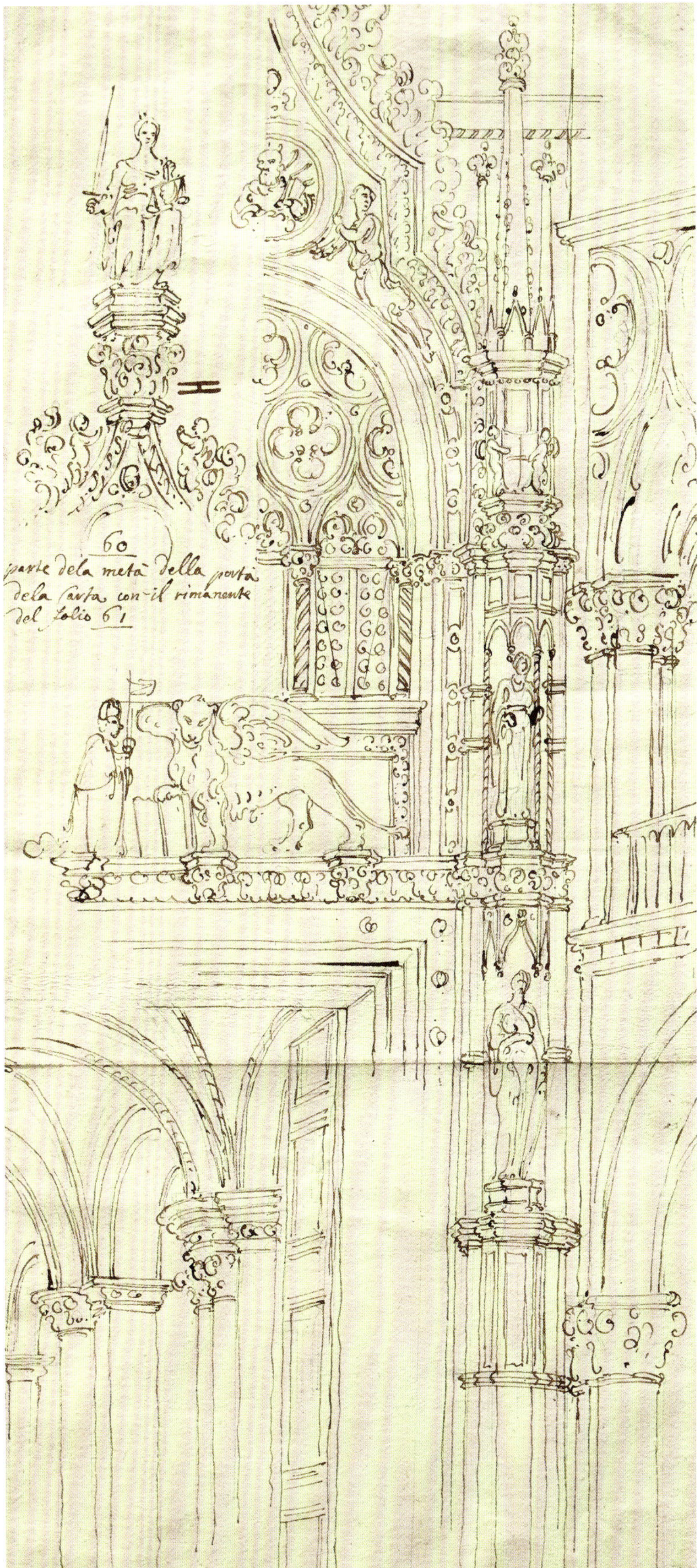
60
parte dela metà della porta
dela carta con il rimanente
del folio 61

28

BERNARDO BELLOTTO

(Venice 1722 – Warsaw 1780)

Capriccio with a Bridge on a River
1745

oil on canvas; 48.5 x 73 cm
Madrid, Museo Thyssen Bornemisza, 40, 1934.2

This splendid *capriccio* is one of the most complex works in the young Bellotto's oeuvre. The composition is an assemblage of several motifs taken from various places visited during his travels in Italy, and the style and technique make it difficult to attribute to a specific period, leading to some hesitation about the possible dating. The figures – not just those in the right foreground, as previously thought, but unusually all the others as well – are by another Venetian hand. Exceptionally, there are three earlier drawings, from circa 1742–1743, used as a basis for this composition but then decidedly left behind: the sketch with just outlines in the Boijmans Van Beuningen Museum in Rotterdam (I. 146) and two sheets with wash in the British Royal Collections (Parker 1948, nos. 85–86). Rarely for early paintings by Bellotto, there are also two good copies, one of which by Giuseppe Zocchi.

Elements copied from the Veneto prevail: the villa at the foot of the bridge on the left, with nearby houses, surrounded by tall trees behind a wall, might have been drawn from life along the river Brenta between Venice and Padua, and also the fusion of the house with sarcophagus and the roof terrace with the high medieval tower alludes to the Porta Portello on the Canale del Piovego in Padua which gave access to the city for those arriving from Venice by boat. Behind the bridge which is partly invented, we see some woodland in the distance, together with a few houses and a high mountain.

Bellotto also ingeniously mixes elements from his trip through northern Italy, which are absent in the drawings: the tower is similar in proportions to the Ezzelino tower in Padua, depicted in the drawings in the distance, behind the bridge, but also to the Bona di Savoia tower in the Cortile delle Armi of the Castello Sforzesco in Milan, and the mountain could be a mountain peak sketched on that trip; the idea of the bridge dominated by a tower could instead be inspired by the Ponte delle Navi, Verona (G. Marini).

There is no doubt that the style dates from after his journey to Rome, because of the clear description of the architecture, because of the shape and rendering of the masses of clouds in the sky and of the water, expertly modulated in various hues and shades, with wavelets in the foreground and a flatter field of colour in the background; the aerial perspective of the landscape in the distance is difficult to assess because of the less-than-perfect state of preservation of the picture. These elements, plus the manner of painting the foliage in the foreground, are comparable to the first pair of views of Vaprio, of 1744, and to that of Verona, dated 1745–46.

That a pendant once existed is indicated by the two pairs of copies, one by the Florentine painter Giuseppe Zocchi (1717–1767) and the other by another painter (formerly in the Aldo Borletti Collection, Milan; Kozakiewicz 1972a no. A 417 and A 430), comprising – apart from a view similar to the present one – a *capriccio* with *A River, with a Bridge and Town* following another drawing by Bellotto, now in the Kupferstichkabinett in Berlin (Kozakiewicz 1972a, no. 122). The copies are connected with this painting but also with the drawings and in some details also between them, indicating – as already noticed by S. Kozakiewicz regarding the former Borletti pair, the only ones he saw – a close relationship between the three artists.

Among the Gerini papers in the Florence State Archives, the list of recipients of the volumes of prints sent as a gift by the Marquis Andrea – the *Scelta di XXIV vedute … di Firenze* and the *Vedute delle ville, e d'altri luoghi della Toscana*, of which he was the promoter – included some lucky individuals who received both books, one of whom was the 'nephew of Canaletto', who in exchange sent 'two little pictures' (M. Guidetti, in Florence 2009, p. 294) (Fondo Gerini 1409, string 47, file n. 5, paper 10). This painting and its lost companion piece are the most credible candidates from Bellotto's known repertoire to be the gift to Marquis Andrea Gerini; a spirited Veneto-Lombard response to the views of the Tuscan villas drawn and some engraved by Giuseppe Zocchi (1717– 1767). The figures could be by Francesco Zuccarelli (1702–1788), another Tuscan artist sponsored by Anton Maria Zanetti di Girolamo, collected by Gerini; he would have been the best choice as collaborator.

Bożena Anna Kowalczyk

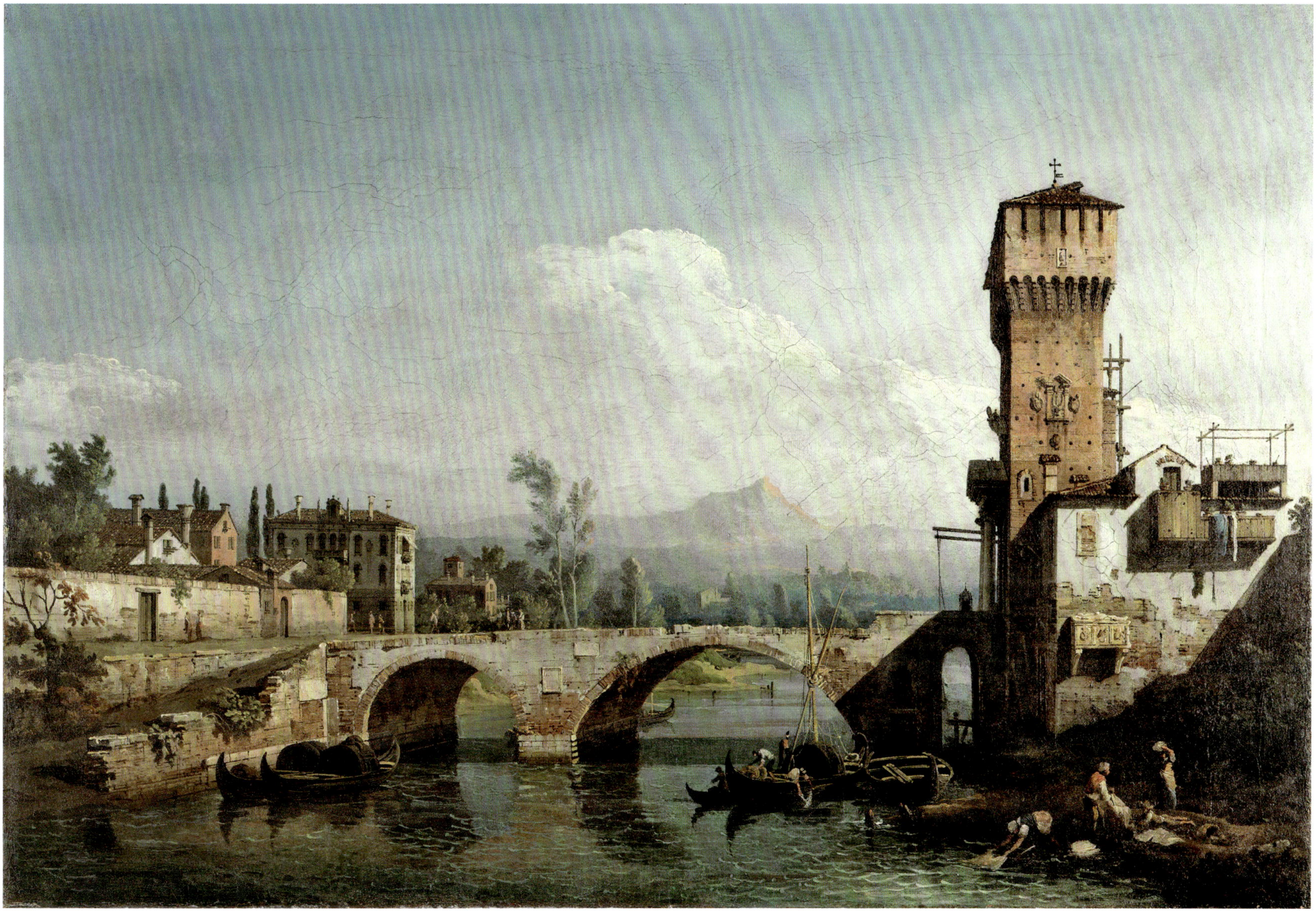

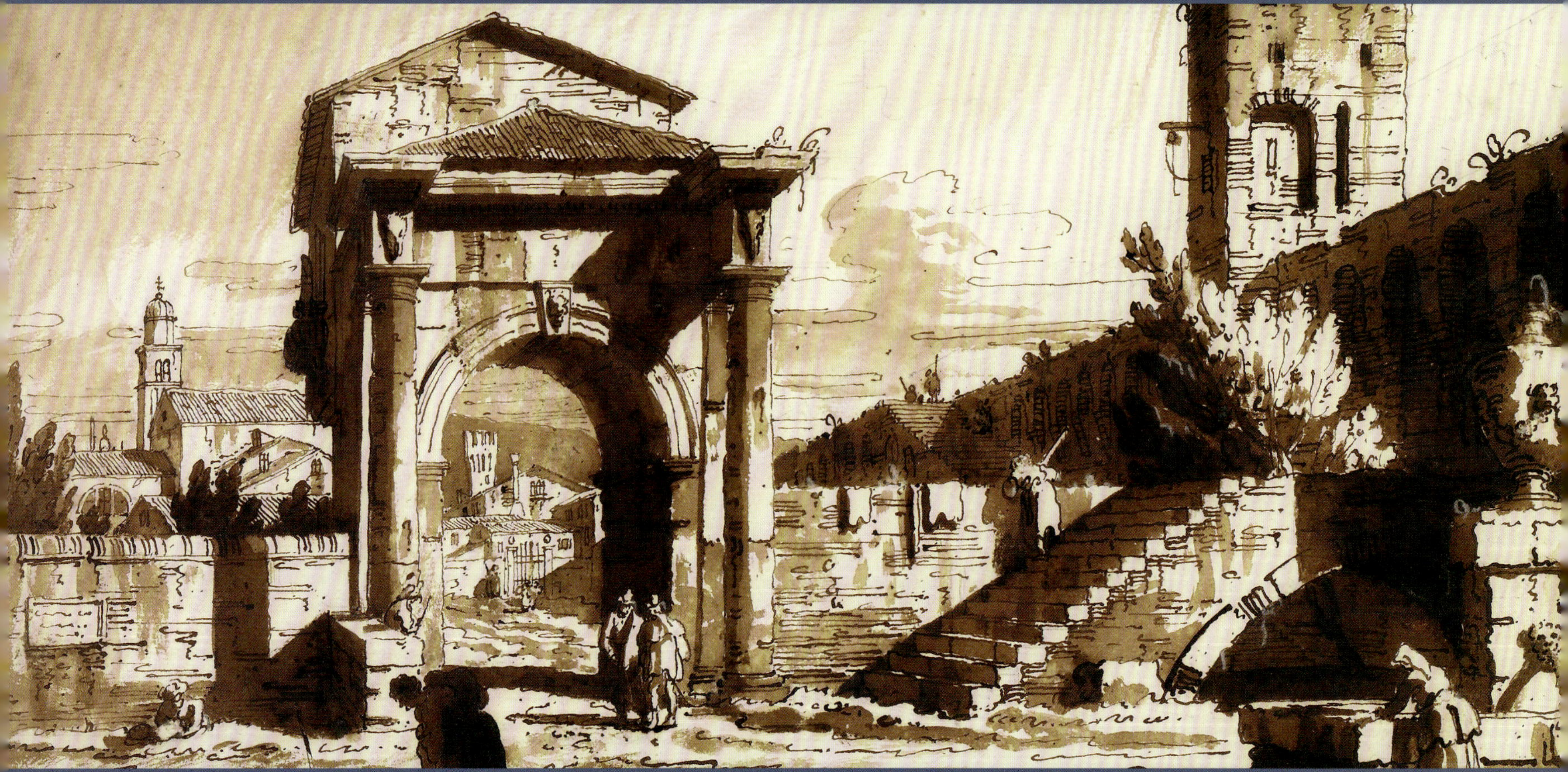

4.
THE CAPRICCIO

As in the case of their views of real places, Canaletto and Bellotto exchanged motifs and subjects in their *capricci*, but they differed in their conception of the artistic genre, which reached the height of its expression in eighteenth-century Venetian art, as in theatre and music. In Canaletto, the *capriccio* has a dimension of pure fantasy: evidence of this is found in the drawings that he made for Joseph Smith and the prints in the series *Vedute Altre prese da i Luoghi altre ideate*, which he began engraving in around 1740 and that were published after Smith's appointment to the post of British Consul in Venice in 1744. Whereas for Bellotto, this expressive genre was nourished by real subjects, recorded in Venice and during his travels, but then put together 'at whim'.

In the *Capriccio with a Ruined Triumphal Arch on the Shores of the Lagoon* in the Museo di Asolo (cat. 29), Bellotto combined Roman and Venetian motifs according to his own taste. The drawing that Canaletto made for Smith with a similar composition, exquisite for its delicate use of grey-blue watercolour (cat. 30), follows a preparatory drawing by Bellotto for the painted *Capriccio*, perfecting its line. Bellotto's drawing *Capriccio with a Ruined Roman Temple and a Isolated Column* (cat. 32), an early idea for the second pendant in Asolo, departs from Canaletto's style through the use of pure contour and a short, nervous line. It was, however, used as a model for another sheet by Canaletto, with hatched shading, in the British Royal Collection. Later, in the 1740s, Bellotto drew the superb *Capriccio with a Classical Gate and Reminiscents from Padua and Verona* for Joseph Smith (cat. 34), demonstrating his full mastery of the brown watercolour subjected to his dramatic expressiveness.

In their etchings, the compositional elements shared by the two artists are just as frequent and clear. The motifs found in some of Canaletto's beautiful prints, including *The Portic with a Lantern* (cat. 33a) and *The Cart on the Bridge* (cat. 33b), appear in Bellotto's youthful engravings, in his drawings and in his paintings, up to his late period. In *Capriccio with a Paduan Villa* (cat. 35), made by Bellotto in around 1760, not only do we find the cart with the bulls on the bridge, but we can also recognise elements from the drawings made in the 1740s: in the foreground, there is a Paduan Renaissance villa, the subject of another splendid sheet by Canaletto (cf. cat. 35).

29

BERNARDO BELLOTTO

(Venice 1722 – Warsaw 1780)

Capriccio with a Ruined Triumphal Arch on the Shores of the Lagoon
1743

oil on canvas; 40.5 x 49 cm.
Asolo (Treviso), Museo Civico, 470

The peculiar sharp realism that distinguishes Bellotto's *vedute* from those of Canaletto also pervades the composition of his *capricci*, a well-thought-out assembly of mostly real recognisable motifs taken from drawings made in Venice, on the mainland and while travelling throughout Italy and Europe.
The two Venetian landscapes with Roman ruins on the shores of the Lagoon, this painting and its pendant, also from the Asolo museum (cat. 31), best illustrate Bellotto's process, which remained unchanged until his last known *capricci* from his second period in Dresden (1762–1766).
The arch in the foreground, decorated with a Christian *patera*, seems to be an ingenious blend of the Porta Santo Spirito and the arch of Titus, captured in drawing during a visit to Rome, probably in 1742; while the high wall on the left replicates in profile the bastions built by Pius IV, depicted by Bellotto in the topographical view of the porta designed Antonio da Sangallo the Younger, in a private collection (cat. 42, 43, 41).
In the outline drawing at the Darmstadt museum that precedes this painting, and the version by Canaletto in the British Royal Collection, which features similar outlines carefully shaded with watercolour (cat. 30), the opening of the ruin frames the arch of Titus in the distance, while in this picture we see a Venetian village with a Palladian church and two medieval bell towers; further to the right, we can also see the Basilica di Santa Maria della Salute on the shores of the Lagoon. The intention may have been to suggest the continuation of the Roman architecture in Palladio and Longhena, in the spirit of Joseph Smith's (1674 ca.–1770) neo-Palladian setting. The symbolic motifs of the Masonic lodges, the pilgrim with his rake in this painting, the pyramid and the grave diggers seen in the pendant are the same as those found in works by Canaletto, while some are also used by Guardi (see, for Canaletto, Corboz 1985, pp. 437–470).
The two sailing ships on the Lagoon that appear in these drawings instead form part of the pendant, however (cat. 31).
The pair of paintings joined the collection at the Asolo museum in 1910, bequeathed by Canon Giacomo Bertoldi (Salzano 1846 – Asolo 1910), an esteemed connoisseur, scholar and poet. His collection of 177 paintings, the nucleus of the museum, was formed in the Treviso area – home to numerous villas belonging to noble families – when he was the parish priest in Carpenedo (Mestre) and Scandolara (Zero Branco), and then Asolo, where he was appointed provost in 1894 (the biographical information is taken from L. Comacchio 1979, pp. 102–105).
They were thought to be by Francesco Guardi, thanks to the theme of the ruins, but in 1946 they were definitively attributed to Bellotto by Rodolfo Pallucchini, despite the fact that Constable and J.G. Links continued to consider them 'characteristic of one phase of Canaletto's work', so fine was the pictorial quality of the handling.
A comparison with Canaletto's drawing in the British Royal Collection tells us much about the different vision of the two artists: the arch in this canvas has a remarkable consistency, and in raking light its prominent structures leave dark shadows with well-defined outlines; in the drawing, the same ruins form a gentle theatrical wing, shaped by delicate and vague shadows (cat. 30).

Bożena Anna Kowalczyk

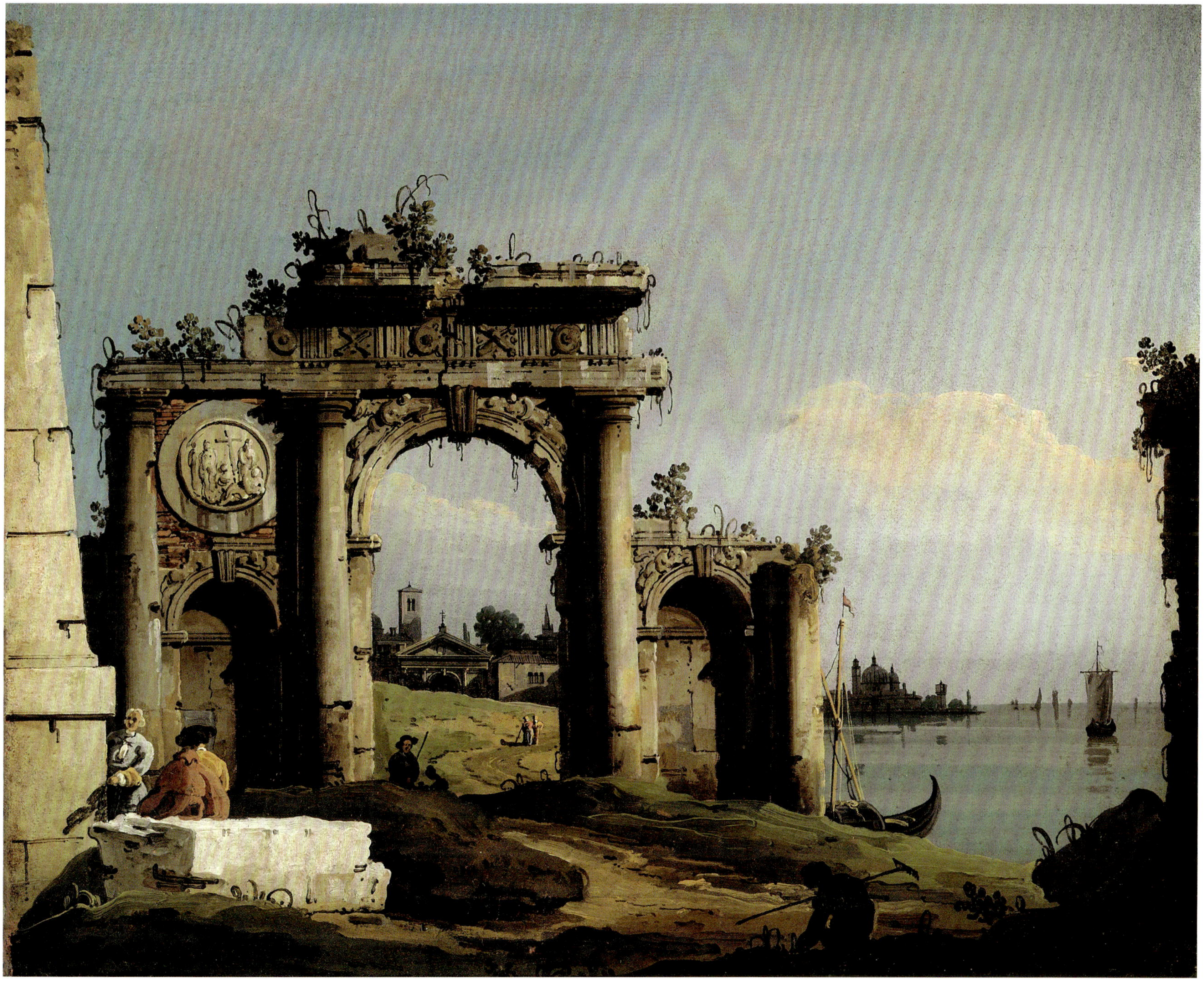

30

CANALETTO

(Venice 1697–1768)

Capriccio with a Ruined Triumphal Arch on the Shores of the Lagoon
1742–43

pen and brown ink with blue-grey wash over pinpricked pencil drawn freehand, with a ruler and pinpointing; the arches and medallion are pinpricked; the drawing appears within a ruled ink line; 198 x 278 mm
The Royal Collection / HM Queen Elizabeth II, RCIN 907533

K.T. Parker distinguishes three different types of soft pen, from a very flexible reed for the foreground, vegetation and profiles in shadow, a quill (probably goose), for the contours exposed to light and, finally, a thin stylus sign with a very delicate line, for the buildings on the horizon, which the scholar believes to be a metal nib. The effect is of great refinement and is enhanced by the use of a sensitive wash of varying depth, applied with one or more brush passes, which we find in some twenty *capricci* made with this technique and commissioned by Joseph Smith before Canaletto's departure for London in May 1746.
The composition is linked to two works by Bernardo Bellotto, the canvas in the Museo Civico di Asolo (cat. 29) and an outline drawing in the Darmstadt Museum, which was also made with two types of pen: this drawing is very similar in size and like the present one, is contoured with a ruled ink line (AE 2221; fig. a). The two drawings are similar but not identical in the pen lines. The present one, beautiful work of art, is firmer and more relaxed in line, both in the straight lines and in the rounder ones of the decorations of the arch and in the foliage, and in the lines describing the steep terrain. The Darmstadt sketch in some points appears more hesitant, more complicated, especially in the curved lines, and the sign is generally shorter, and here and there interrupted. There are small differences in the foreground terrain, where the grass in the Bellotto is less luxuriant; the wavy hat of the figure on the far left is more regular in shape, but round in the Canaletto; the foliage does not correspond exactly and the second arch in the distance seems to be seen by Bellotto from a different angle. Canaletto left some *pentimenti* visible: the double arch in pencil and compass to the left of the monument, a wild herb above the architrave in just pencil. Both sheets present a framework applied in ruled pencil lines and the arches drawn with a compass.
In the long dispute over which drawing came first, there are two camps: the traditional one, which starts with Baron von Hadeln followed by Fritzsche, Parker, Constable up to Martin Clayton, who argue that the Bellotto sheet is a copy, or rather 'an exact facsimile', and the view so far only put forward by S. Kozakiewicz and myself, who believe that the Bellotto sketch is a preparatory drawing for Canaletto's work. It is impossible to make a direct comparison because of problems of preservation in the Darmstadt sheet, resulting from the use of iron gall ink which with time and light has strongly corroded the paper; but the digital processing of the two overlapping patterns was performed (see the essay of whom is writing). In the Royal Collection, there are four similar cases of perfectly finished drawings by Canaletto that match Bellotto's sketches: for one there seems to be agreement: both sketch and drawing are attributed to Bellotto's hand (*Capriccio with a Bridge over a River*, Kozakiewicz 1972a, no. 110 and Parker 1948, no. 86). The composition, in that case, reappears adapted for a painting in the Thyssen Bornemisza Museum, to conclude the creative cycle of the younger artist (cat. 28).

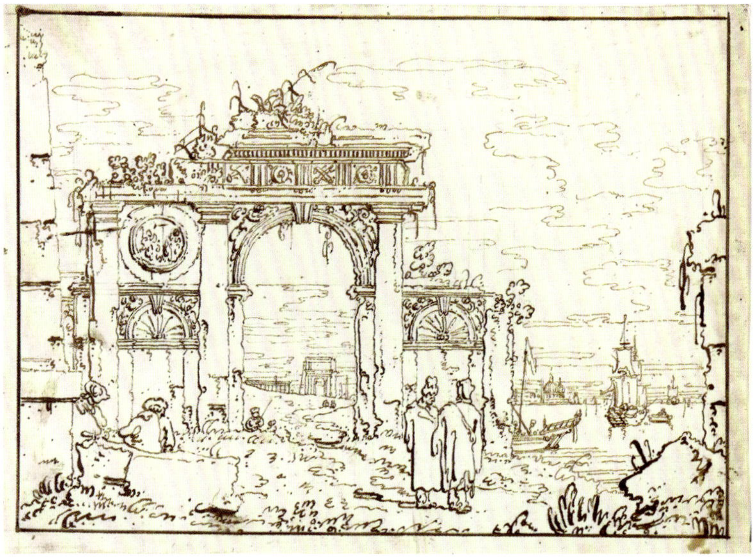

a. Bernardo Bellotto, *Capriccio of a Ruined Arch on the Shores of the Lagoon*, 1742–43, pen and brown ink over pinpricked pencil drawn freehand, with a ruler and pinpointing, 206 x 284 mm. Darmstadt, Hessisches Landesmuseum, AE 2221

In this case too, only Bellotto used the composition for a painting, in the *capriccio* at the Museo Civico di Asolo; in fact, he used it in two works, given that the two sailing boats on the lagoon appear also in the pendant (cat. 29, 31). But the attribution of this drawing cannot be doubted, for the fluidity and softness of the line. Evidently, even in 1742–43, the collaboration between the two artists and the exchange of ideas were still very strong.
In Asolo painting, Bellotto introduced a gentleman in the place of the figure with hat. He also eliminated the two soldiers, preferring a mysterious silhouette shown against the light, and he replaced the arch in the distance with a Veneto town.

Bożena Anna Kowalczyk

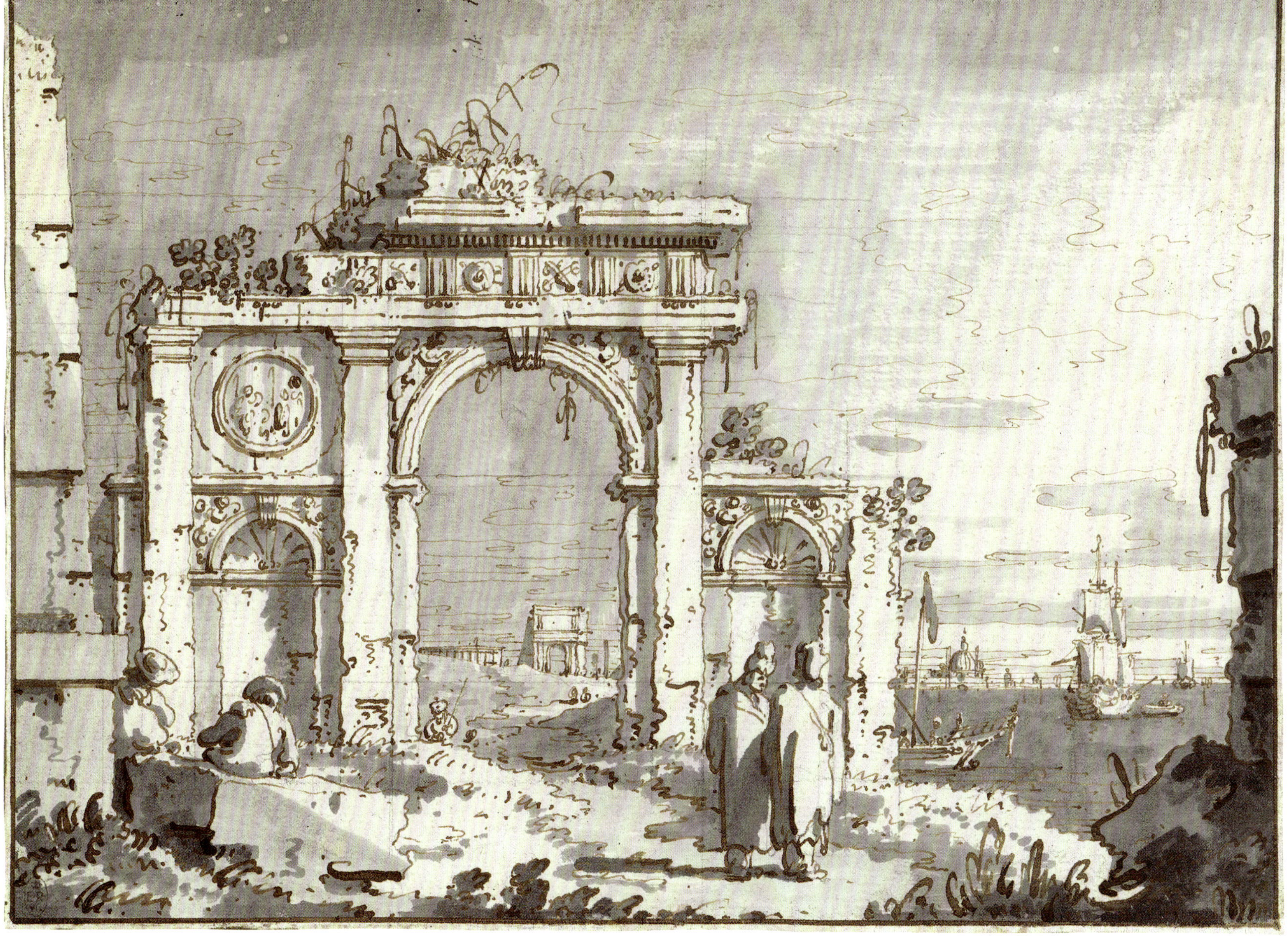

31

BERNARDO BELLOTTO

(Venice 1722 – Warsaw 1780)

Capriccio with the Ruins of a Roman Temple on the Banks of the Lagoon
1743

oil on canvas; 40.5 x 49 cm
Asolo (Treviso), Museo Civico, 471

On the rugged edge of an island in the Lagoon, as in its pendant (cat. 29), Bellotto imagined the ruins of a Roman temple and archaeologists (before they were known as such), 'grave diggers' in action. In the distance he places the pyramid of Caius Cestius and Venetian buildings, dominated by the dome of Santa Maria della Salute, as well as a medieval bell tower, partially enveloped by the shadow of the large grey-white cloud. The white sails of a galleon, an apparition of rare beauty, are reflected in the stagnant waters of the lagoon. In the foreground, as in the pendant, at the edge of the shadow, the curved silhouette of a pilgrim with a quiff and a long stick or rake had become a sort of signature for Bellotto since his visit to Rome; in the oblique shadow of unknown origin, to the left, the statue of a soldier stands out against the light.
Both compositions, well-balanced in their lighting choices and organisation of space, appear to be projections of an archaeological dream onto the site of the lagoon. When they arrived at the museum they were attributed to Francesco Guardi, the painter *par excellence* of *capricci* with ruins, but were then attributed to Bellotto in 1946 by Rodolfo Pallucchini, who met surprising resistance from the most influential Canaletto scholars of the twentieth century, W.G. Constable and J.G. Links, and isolated support for the hand of the master.
The extremely high quality of the handling and the evocative atmospheric rendering indicate a period after his trip to Rome in 1742 and shortly before his departure for Lombardy in 1744, when the young Bellotto was experimenting with the gradual mastery of a personal technique through new Roman subjects. The broad, thick brushstrokes that define the terrain are already similar to those of his views of Lombardy and Turin.
The painting does not have precise graphic precedents like those of its pendant, but the left-hand side of the composition and the buildings in the distance are studied in two outline drawings in the Darmstadt museum; the first, more elaborate and sophisticated in both its draughtsmanship and composition (cat. 32), responds in its handling of the lines to a drawing with hatched shading by Canaletto in the British Royal Collection (RCIN 907520; see the comparison figure cat. 32); the second is a later elaboration, in which the colonnade has been simplified and is closer to the one in this painting (AE 2222). K.T. Parker believed that the first sheet was a copy of the drawing by Canaletto, but its sketchy nature suggests an earlier invention by Bellotto. The fact that the two paintings have remained in the Veneto region would most likely point to a local patron. The marble soldier in shadow here traces its origins back to similar ornaments in eighteenth-century gardens of the Veneto; and an entire company of *schiavoni* in the service of the Republic populates the garden and access terrace of the villa Giustinian in Roncade, which was also frequented by Canaletto. The statue in this *capriccio* has the same outline as those located in front of the portico, looking at people gazing out from the house. The owner of the villa at that time was the Venetian patrician Marc'Antonio Giustinian, son of Girolamo, who has already been suggested by scholars as a possible patron (2001). Found in other works by Bellotto and in many by Canaletto, the presence of various emblematic motifs of the Masonic lodges, pyramid, grave diggers, and pilgrims with rakes is mysterious.

Bożena Anna Kowalczyk

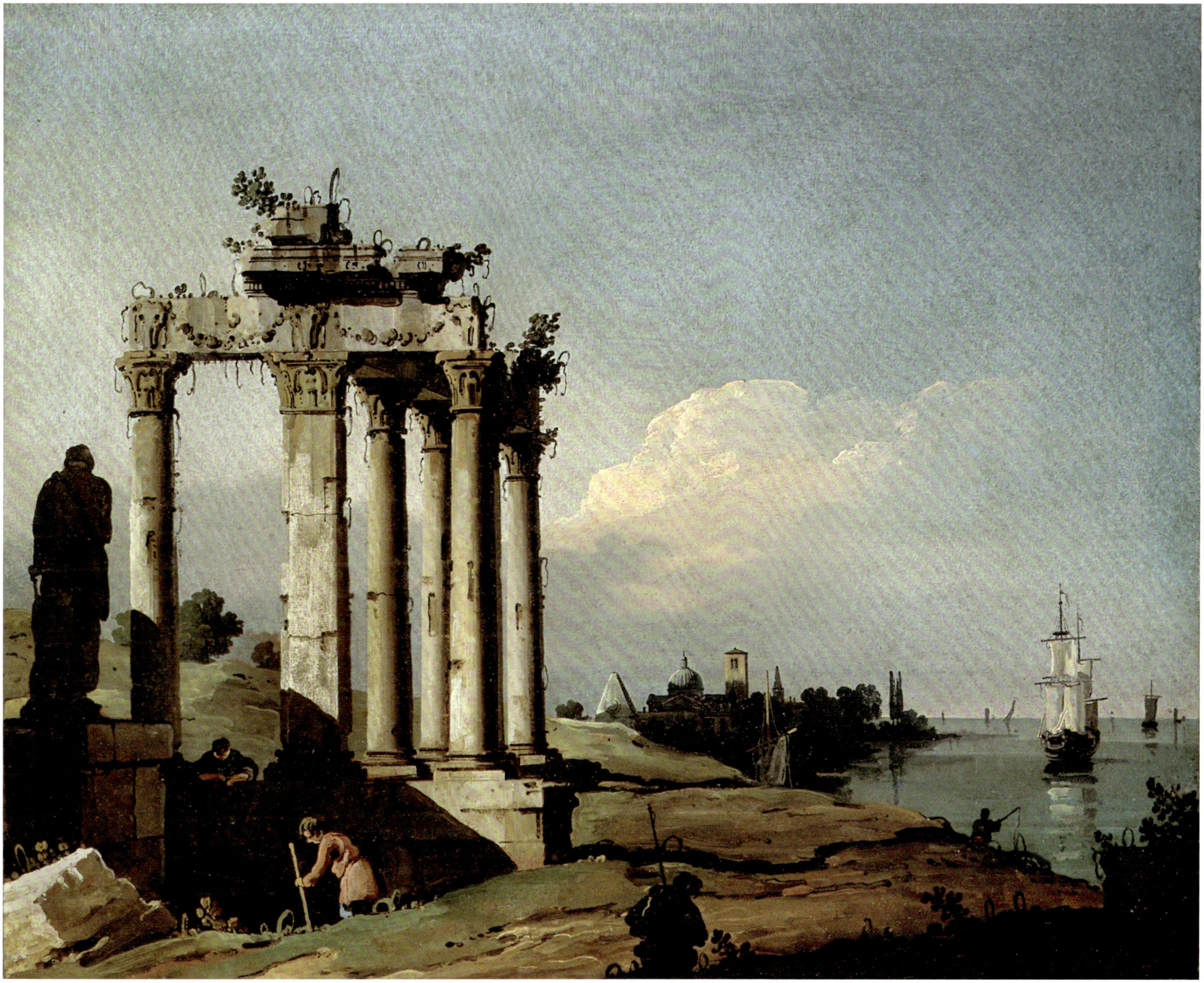

32

BERNARDO BELLOTTO

(Venice 1722 – Warsaw 1780)

Capriccio with a Ruined Roman Temple and a Isolated Column
1742–43

pen in brown ink, over freehand and ruled pencil and pinpointing; traces of contour line at top and bottom;
259 x 377 mm
Darmstadt, Hessisches Landesmuseum, AE 2185

Inscriptions: numbered at top in pen, '19'; above, a '15' in red pencil; inscribed on the verso in pencil, 'A.C.'.

This delicate outline drawing brings together a series of fanciful motifs inspired by the ruins of the Roman Forum: the Ionic colonnade in ruins, shown in a perspective similar to that of Saturn's portico in *The Forum towards the Capitol* (cat. 40), the solitary column, a transposition into the Ionic style of the Corinthian column of Phocas, fragments of marble on the ground. But it also includes other motifs, from the Veneto, in the form of the bridge and the domed building resembling Palladio's Rotunda but with arched pilasters from the Pantheon.
The composition underlies the invention of the *Capriccio with the Ruins of a Roman Temple on the Banks of the Lagoon* from the Museo di Asolo (cat. 31) and of the *Capriccio with the Ruins of a Rotunda*, one of the eight Italian etchings (Kozakiewicz 1972a, n. 120). The colonnade in these works is shown with the same perspective but already rethought and redrawn as a Corinthian order on another sheet in Darmstadt, *Capriccio with the Ruins of a Rotunda* (AE 2222), which introduces the statue of the soldier on the left and various elements on the right side; this is the drawing that was translated into an etching (mentioned above). The motif of the tree rising from behind the colonnade is present in all three works. In the *capriccio* from the Museo di Asolo, the colonnade is set on an island in the lagoon, and two beautiful sailing ships appear on the water, borrowed from another of the Darmstadt drawings, *Capriccio with a Ruined Triumphal Arch on the Shores of a Lagoon*, in turn a preparatory work for the second Asolo pendant (cf. cat. 29).
In this fast-paced sequence of ideas starting from this drawing, there is also another drawing, this time by Canaletto, in the British Royal Collections, that faithfully repeats the linear outline of the architecture and the figures but is carefully hatched (RCIN 907520; fig. a). As in other similar cases of two versions of similar composition by Bellotto and Canaletto, the pupil sketch has, until the studies of S. Kozakiewicz, always been considered a copy of the master's drawing; H.A. Fritzsche, K.T. Parker and W.G. Constable all concur on this point. The Polish scholar, however, noted that 'Bellotto's drawing is more detailed and it appears unlikely to be a copy of Canaletto's version'. In this case, his opinion is fully justified by a particularly dense and intense hatching that erases the details carefully drawn by Bellotto, such as the emblem on the monument to the left or the decoration of one of the lintels of the temple.
The drawing by Canaletto attains a sophisticated atmospheric effect; in the Royal Collection, it is flanked by two other sheets preceded by sketches by Bellotto, which are stylistically close and certainly contemporary: *The Temple of Antoninus and Faustina, Rome* and *The Arch of Septimius Severus, Rome* (Parker 1948, nos. 104 and 103).
The version by Bellotto is without a chiaroscuro definition and has its own stylistic autonomy, applied with great sensitivity. Employing a subtle and precise use of a pen dipped in dark ink, the ornamental values of the architecture in the foreground are enhanced, together with the fine play of the friezes, and the form of the Ionic capitals and cornices. The staffage that are the figures of pilgrims, have a strong realistic value. To H.A. Fritzsche (who confused it with the Pantheon), the rotunda in the background, drawn with a lighter touch, suggested a link with another print from the youthful series, *Capriccio with a Domed Church*, but this was studied in another sketch from the Landesmuseum in Darmstadt (Kozakiewicz 1972a, nos. 124, 123). This last composition was literally reproduced, even for the central figures, in a painting by Canaletto in England in 1754–55, now at the Worcester Art Museum, Massachusetts, and in a probably contemporary drawing now at the Fogg Art Museum (C/L 508 and 830).
The blue and dark red coloured patches here, on this sheet lower left, testify to the fact that the drawing was handled while the artist was working on a painting, as is the case of some other drawings in the Hessisches Landesmuseum.

Bożena Anna Kowalczyk

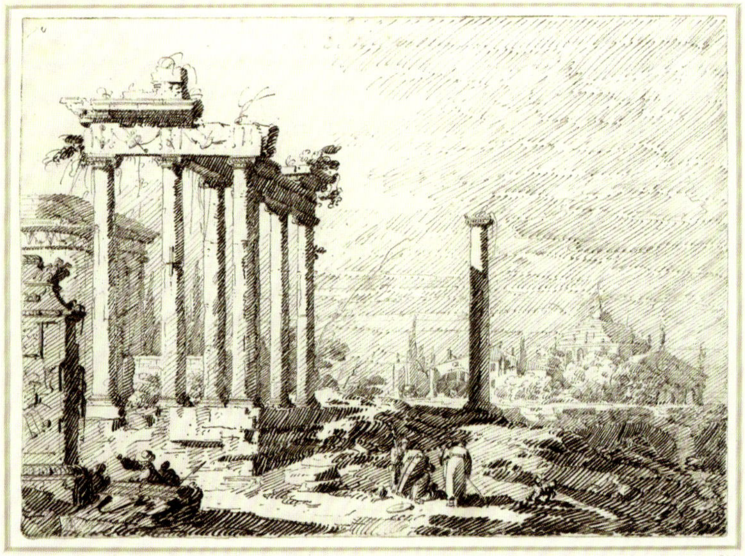

a. Canaletto, *Capriccio with a Ruined Roman Temple and Isolated Column*, 1742–43, pen in dark brown ink, over freehand and ruled pencil and pinpointing, 270 x 376 mm. The Royal Collection, RCIN 907520

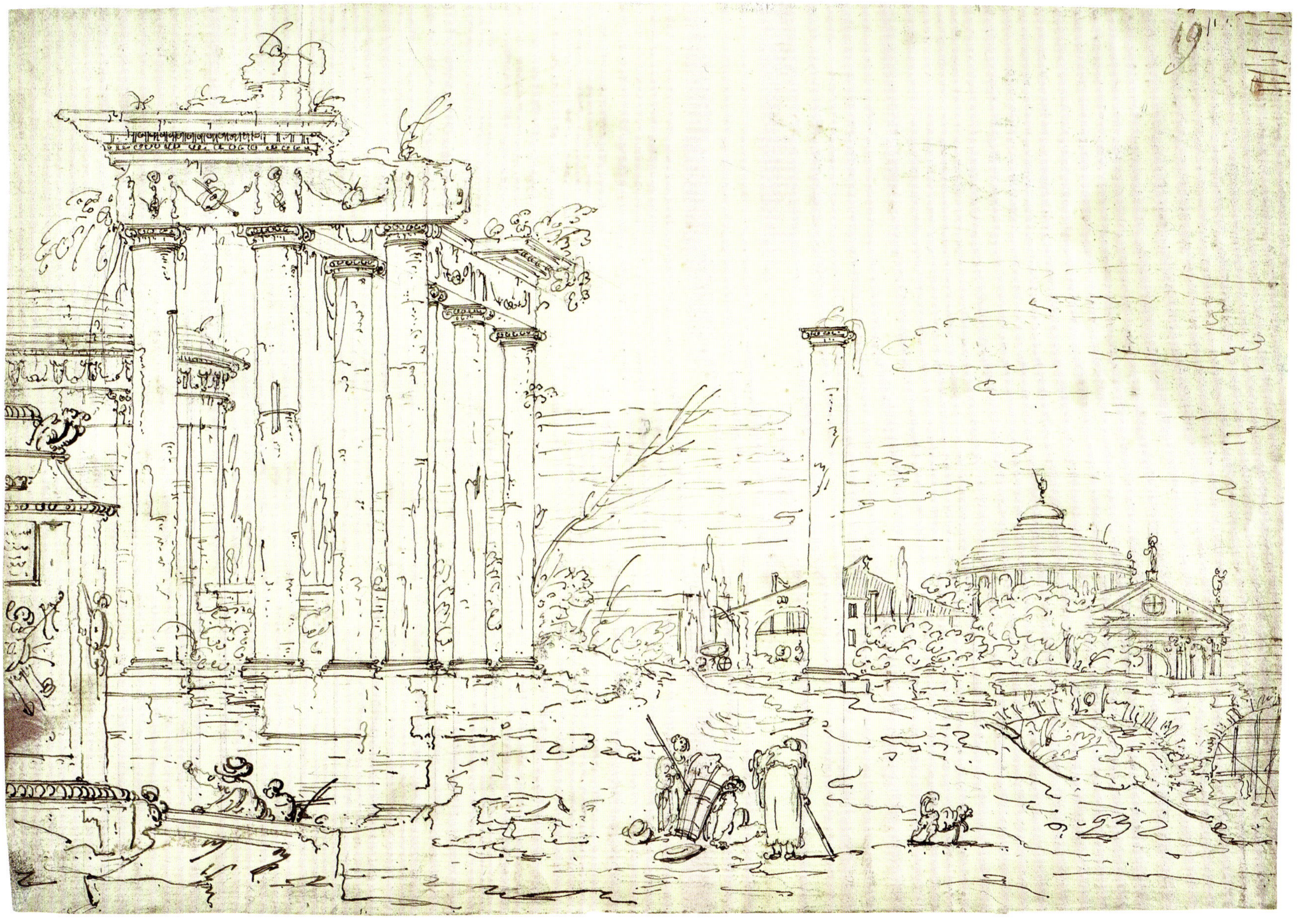

33a

CANALETTO

(Venice 1697–1768)

The Portico with a Lantern
ca. 1742–43

etching, proof; 300 x 434 mm (plate), 303 x 439 mm (sheet)
Rome, Istituto Centrale per la Grafica, on deposit at the Accademia Nazionale dei Lincei, F.C. 37701

33b

CANALETTO

(Venice 1697–1768)

The Cart on the Bridge
1742–43 ca.

etching, proof; 141 x 129 mm (plate), 143 x 129 mm (sheet)
Roma, Istituto Centrale per la Grafica F.C. 37714

Inscriptions: (cat. 33a) beneath the image, in the centre, 'A. Canal. f. V.'; (cat. 33b) beneath the image, on the right, 'A. Canal. f.'.

In eighteenth-century Venice, etched *capriccio* images – using a technique that was in itself already unpredictable – expressed genius and creative imagination through their immediacy. The thirty-one plates of *Vedute Altre prese da i Luoghi altre ideate* were engraved by Canaletto in the early 1740s, at the same time and shortly after the *Capricci* and *Scherzi* worked on by Giambattista Tiepolo, under the aegis of Zanetti (Bettagno 1998). The two *peintres-graveurs* created absolute masterpieces of eighteenth-century Venetian engraving, which are comparable for their delicacy of touch, light and imagination. Canaletto's etchings embark on an imaginary journey from Venice and the Lagoon along the Brenta to Padua, through enchanting real or invented landscapes, recreated with attention to the most delicate atmospheric effects, crystallised with a meticulous and sensitive touch, with a 'particular stamp of poignant melancholy' (A. Bettagno, in Venice 1982, p. 26). Joseph Smith published the series with his typographer Giambattista Pasquali at an unspecified date following his appointment to the British Consul on 6 June 1744, but certainly prior to circa 1755, when Francesco Guardi began copying some of the prints.
The two etchings displayed here, *The Portico with a Lantern* and *The Cart on the Bridge*, are extremely rare impressions, from an album belonging to an unknown eighteenth-century collector. Only Joseph Smith had the same edition of *The Cart on the Bridge*, now kept at the Royal Library at Windsor Castle, while *The Portico with a Lantern* is also present in this state at the Courtauld Institute, London and in two private collections. They were considered the first states until Federico Montecuccoli degli Erri introduced the concept of exhibiting precious pre-publication impressions.

The Portico with a Lantern is perhaps the most poetic of Canaletto's inventions, the one that most demonstrates his unpredictable imagination. A porch with three arches and a lantern at its centre, as in a Venetian arcade, is framed by an ideal city; on the right stands a classical temple and a triumphal arch on the shores of the Lagoon; on the left, houses and a tomb, with the statue of a bishop and, above the door of the house with the turret, the crest of the Canal family, the chevron. Sailing ships can be seen in the background on the Lagoon.
Montecuccoli identifies three states of this print, two of which are contemporary, published by Pasquali, with the correction in the first state of the profile of the classical temple on the right and numerous enhancements; the second was also published by Remondini of Bassano, in the first posthumous edition, from 1772. The writing 'FF4' appears at the base of the column on the left in the third state, published later by Remondini.
The Cart on the Bridge is the left part of a plate cut by Canaletto into three parts, for unknown reasons, before printing. The right part, entitled *The Small Monument*, shows the base of the arch of the bridge, the monument near a tree and a town on the horizon, with a pyramid, bell tower and the dome of a church. The third fragment of the plate, with the sky above the monument, is missing. Montecuccoli identified a single state for the published printing of this engraving, distinct from this one thanks to the addition of vertical lines on the right arch of the bridge and enhancements on the ground beneath the arch to the right.
Both prints inspired Bellotto. The same motifs appear transformed in his contemporary Italian engravings (see the essay by the author of this entry). A cart with oxen on a bridge is a motif he used often in his *capricci*, and Canaletto also used the motif in *Capriccio with Reminiscences of Padua* in the British Royal Collection (C/L 495).

Bożena Anna Kowalczyk

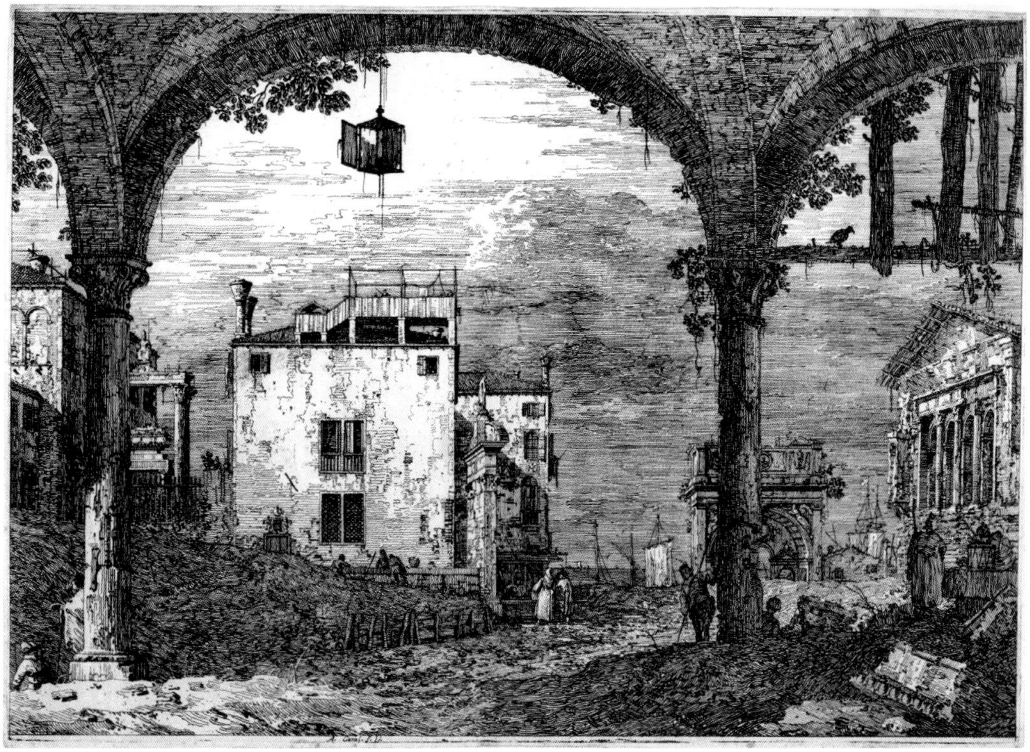

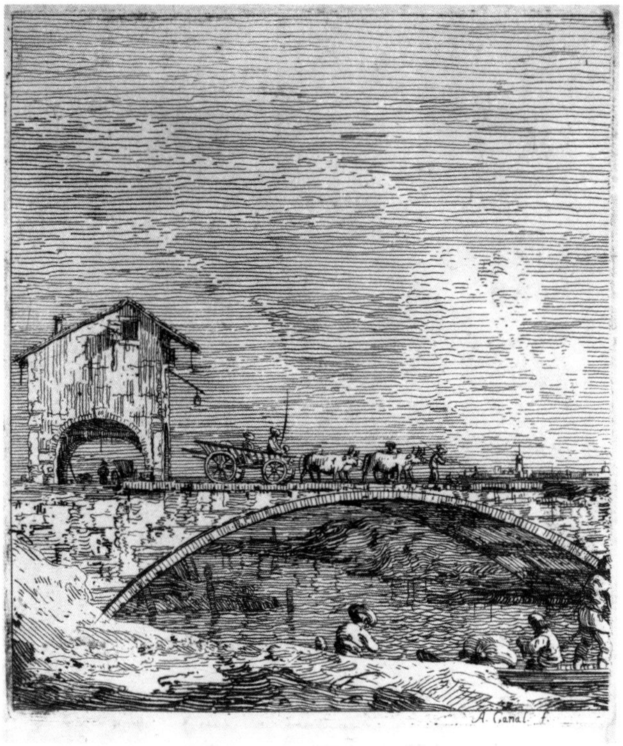

34

BERNARDO BELLOTTO

(Venice 1722 – 1780 Warsaw)

Capriccio with a Classical Gate and Reminiscences of Padua and Verona
1746

pen in brown ink with brown wash and heightening in body-colour, over freehand and ruled pencil and pinpointing; 270 x 379 mm
The Royal Collection / HM Queen Elisabeth II, RCIN 907508

The sheet arrived at the Royal Collection in 1762 with the collection of Joseph Smith in the album of Antonio Visentini, together with two other drawings catalogued in 1948 by K.T. Parker as Canaletto: *Capriccio with the Ponte delle Navi in Verona* and the *The Statue of Hercules in the Bonavides Garden in Padua* (P [C] 123 and P [C] 143). The recognition of the subjects and the relationship of the two compositions – this one and the Veronese capriccio – with paintings by Bellotto, led A. Corboz (1985) to suggest the attribution to Canaletto's nephew, despite making no stylistic justification: there was no known drawing by Bellotto comparable to these. But it was the style motifs and unusual techniques – already commented by Von Hadeln and K.T. Parker – to convince C. Miller (1983) that the attribution of the two sheets (and of two other *capricci*, P [C] 085 and 086) 'can justifiably be queried' and the name of Bellotto is mentioned for the first time, but while G. Marini (in Verona 1990) explained the topographical, stylistic reasons and the relationship with the paintings in support of an attribution to Bellotto, the second edition of the catalogue by K.T. Parker, of 1990 edited by C. Miller (Parker, Crawley 1990), confirmed the attribution to Canaletto of all the 142 drawings at Windsor.
The sheet is linked with one of the four *capricci* in the Gallerie Nazionali di Parma from the Sanvitale collection (cf. cat. 45, 46); the composition recalls the Roman Forum with a gate and surrounding wall, but the gateway is Renaissance and beneath the arch appear the houses of Padua with the Ezzelino tower; these same elements appear in Bellotto's *Capriccio* in the Victoria and Albert Museum (B.A. Kowalczyk, in Torino 2008, no. 79), in one of his Darmstadt drawings and in a print, as well as in two drawings by Canaletto, but shown from a different angle (Kozakiewicz 1972a, nos. 44, 45; P [C] 81; C/L 685). The unusual mixture of Roman, Veneto memories, ideas drawn from Marco Ricci and others from Canaletto, is so harmonious and ingenious, yet Canaletto-like in the details – in this regard, note the tiny figures with sticks at the top of the stairs or the laundry laid carefully on the wall – as to divert from its proper attribution; it probably represents a first draft, which would be extensively altered in the pictorial version.
Yet from the foreground in the shade onwards, the sheet contains stylistic elements typical of Bellotto, expressed with such force as to make them even exciting: note the figures of the pilgrims and the tall weeds shown against the light, the low-angled light in beams, contrasting with dark shadows, the walls stained from atmospheric wash-off, the insistent, interrupted and nervy line in the contours of the figures and clouds. The dramatic impact, carefully planned in every detail, is increased by the use of brown wash, which is never present in Canaletto. This and the contemporary *Capriccio with the Ponte delle Navi in Verona* are the only specimens of 'collectible' drawings by Bellotto from 1745–1746 to represent his graphic style on the eve of his departure from Italy (one of the towers of the Castelvecchio that rises over high walls is evidence of his stay in Verona). The fact that these sheets belonged to the Smith Collection testifies to the uninterrupted patronage of the British Consul.
The use of lead white – here used on the finish of the vase, in the dark parts of the bush, and beneath the arch – can also be noted in Canaletto, but in the drawings produced at least ten years later. Despite the awkward effect of the great figure of the hero, the third sheet from the Visentini album, *The Statue of Hercules in the Bonavides Garden in Padua*, leaves no doubt regarding the attribution to Canaletto, but the unusual circumstance that it was cut from a larger composition, *Paduan Capriccio with the Triumphal arch in the Garden Bonavides in Padua*, may confirm C. Miller's idea that the three drawings were detached from Canaletto's context because of their different aesthetic impact (P [C] 142).

Bożena Anna Kowalczyk

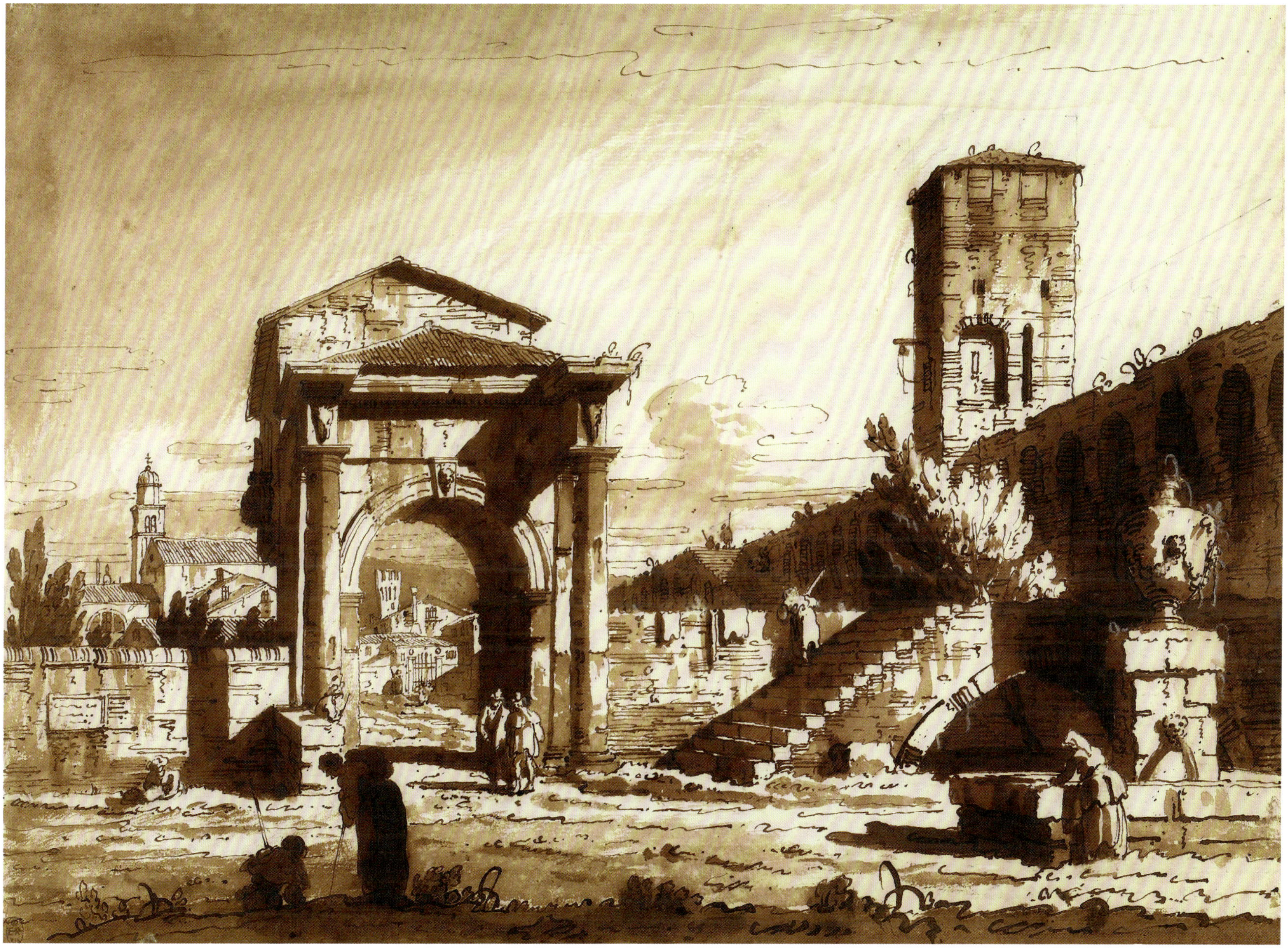

35

BERNARDO BELLOTTO

(Venice 1722 – Warsaw 1780)

Capriccio with a Paduan Villa
1760

oil on canvas; 48 x 79 cm
Private Collection, courtesy Fabrizio Moretti Ltd., London

Upon arrival in Dresden from Venice in April 1747, Bellotto appeared before Augustus Frederick II, Elector of Saxony and King of Poland with the name of August III (1696–1763), with two pairs of works showing Italian motifs: the first consisting of views of Verona, *The Adige from Ponte Nuovo towards the Castel San Pietro* and *The Ponte delle Navi on the Adige* (Kozakiewicz 1972a, nos. 99 and 102), and the second of *capricci*, *The Dolo Lock* and *Capriccio with a Paduan Villa*, constituting the first version of the present painting (Kozakiewicz 1972a no. 245). The views of Verona replicated those painted before his departure for a British collector, now at Powis Castle (National Trust) and the National Gallery of Scotland, Edinburgh, based on specific drawings that are preserved respectively in Darmstadt and in the Muzeum Narodowe in Warsaw (Kozakiewicz 1972a, nos. 98 and 100, 101 and 103); the *capricci* were instead new compositions, based on motifs drawn from his own works and from those of Canaletto. Both pairs are large, of the same size as used by Bellotto for the series of views of Dresden and other European cities.

After a space of some years, this painting takes up the composition of the *Capriccio with a Paduan Villa*, supplementing it with motifs of Dresden. The stone bridge on the river in the first version has a Venetian look, whereas here it recalls the arches and buttresses of the Augustus Bridge by Matthäus Daniel Pöppelmann (1662–1736), built on the Elbe in Dresden between 1727 and 1731. Bellotto could not resist including a wagon with oxen on the bridge, a much-loved motif in the prints (cf. cat. 33b).

The composition recalls the *capricci* of recent years in Italy, like the *Capriccio with a Roman Arch* in the Columbia Museum of Art which in its first draft had, as here, a colonnade in ruins on the left, subsequently repainted (Kozakiewicz 1972a, no. 133); but the collection of memories for the most part already used in the Italian works, is even more intense here, and the finest example of the 'combinatorial' approach for which Bellotto is renowned. It is striking that the Renaissance villa dominating the left side is only known from a drawing by Canaletto, *Capriccio with a Paduan Villa*, one of his most beautiful ones and commissioned by Joseph Smith, who kept it in Venice until the sale to the British crown in 1762 (fig. a). The villa, which no longer exists, must have had a special significance for Canaletto who used the drawing in England, transforming it into a *capriccio* in one of the paintings commissioned by the fourth Earl of Chesterfield before February 1752 (C/L 514*). But it must also have been important for Bellotto, who certainly possessed another, detailed sketch that is now lost: the villa is depicted in its most likely Veneto form, with the two little lateral towers, shown in the same perspective and position with regard to the road and with similar and masterfully replicated effects of light. Bellotto confirmed the location of the villa outside the walls of Padua, which can be identified with the ramparts around the invented town entered by the Porta Portello at the foot of the bridge (B.A. Kowalczyk, in Aix-en-Provence 2015). Another Canaletto motif is the cottage at the lowest level of the road, like in his famous print that Bellotto possessed of *An Imaginary View of Padua* but here with a greater portion of the facade (Bromberg 1974, n. 11). At the end, between the walls, one can recognise fragments of paintings and drawings by both artists: the portico of Saturn, the turreted citadel, the pyramid of Caius Cestius, the Punta della Dogana, and perhaps the Pantheon with its portico and two turrets by Bernini but with a typical Dresden roof; behind the Porta Portello there is a detail of the Zwinger Palace. On the road, a Turk is shown; he was already present in the first version and appears here again, maybe just at the same time as work was being done of the print *Le Turc généreux*, 1759 (cat. 89). In view of the style and the contrasting light, the bright tones of the colours and the intense sky, we might suggest that the painting was produced in Vienna in 1759–1760, a date that is also valid for the pendant, from which it parted company in 1961: *The Breite Gasse, Pirna*. This is the only replica of the painting made for Augustus III in 1753–1756 (Kozakiewicz 1972a, no. 206), and like the present canvas, it reveals an excellent and clear execution. Bellotto could have built up this view using the drawings he brought with him to Vienna, leaving Dresden in December 1758 and with fresh memories of the Saxon capital. The drawings whose motifs can be recognised here are those that were saved from the Prussian bombardment of Dresden in July 1760 that destroyed his other sheets, lovingly collected and bound in albums (*Catalogo de Danni*, cat. 83). There is still the hope of finding the sketch of the Paduan villa and of Pirna at the Breite Gasse which were evidently saved.

Bożena Anna Kowalczyk

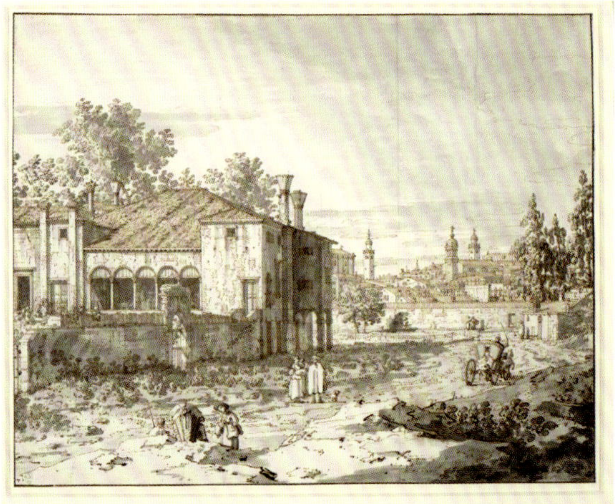

a. Canaletto, *Capriccio with Villa of Padua*, pen in dark brown ink with grey wash, over freehand and ruled pencil and pinpointing, 314 x 399 mm, The Royal Collection, RCIN 907514

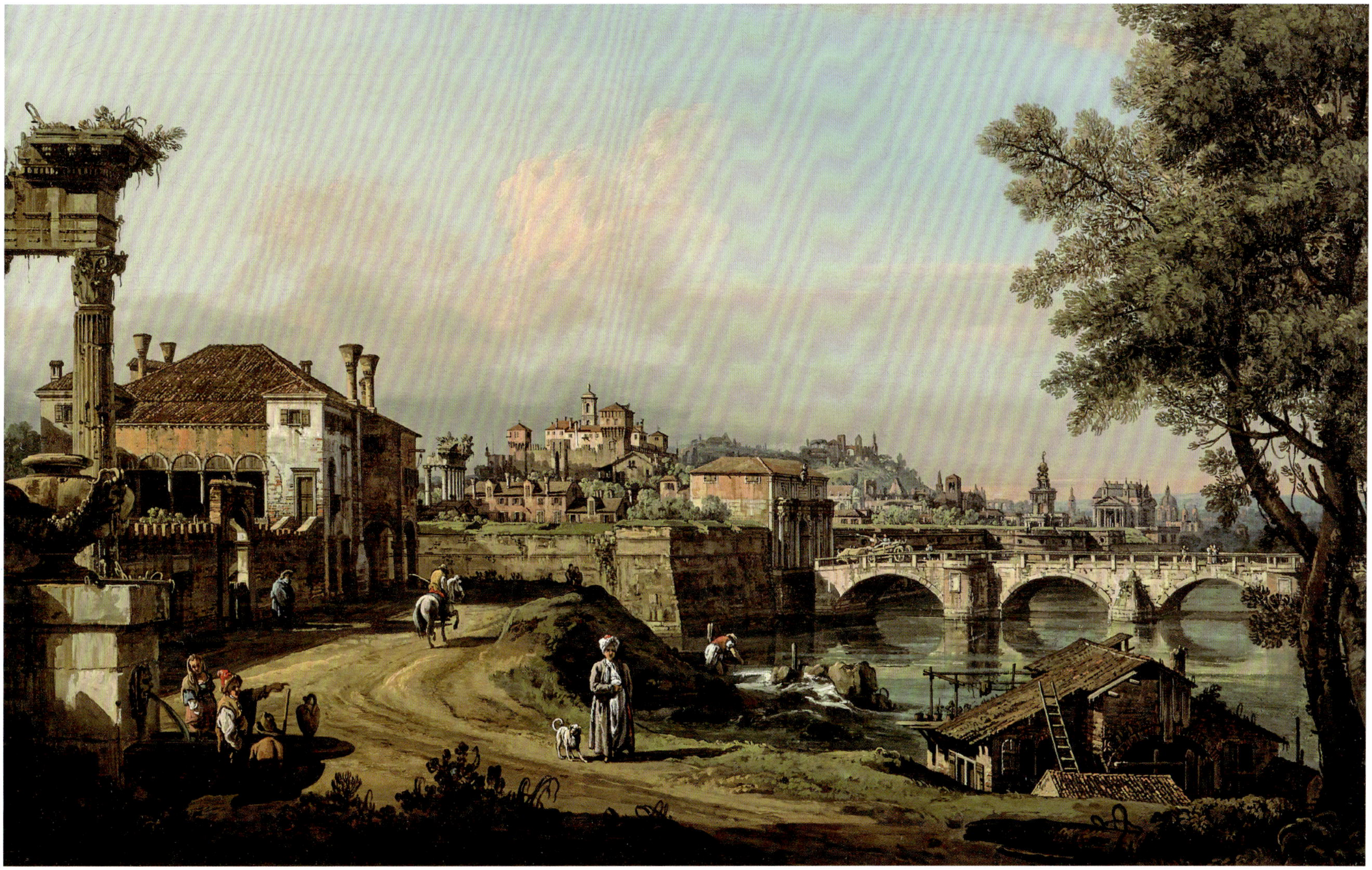

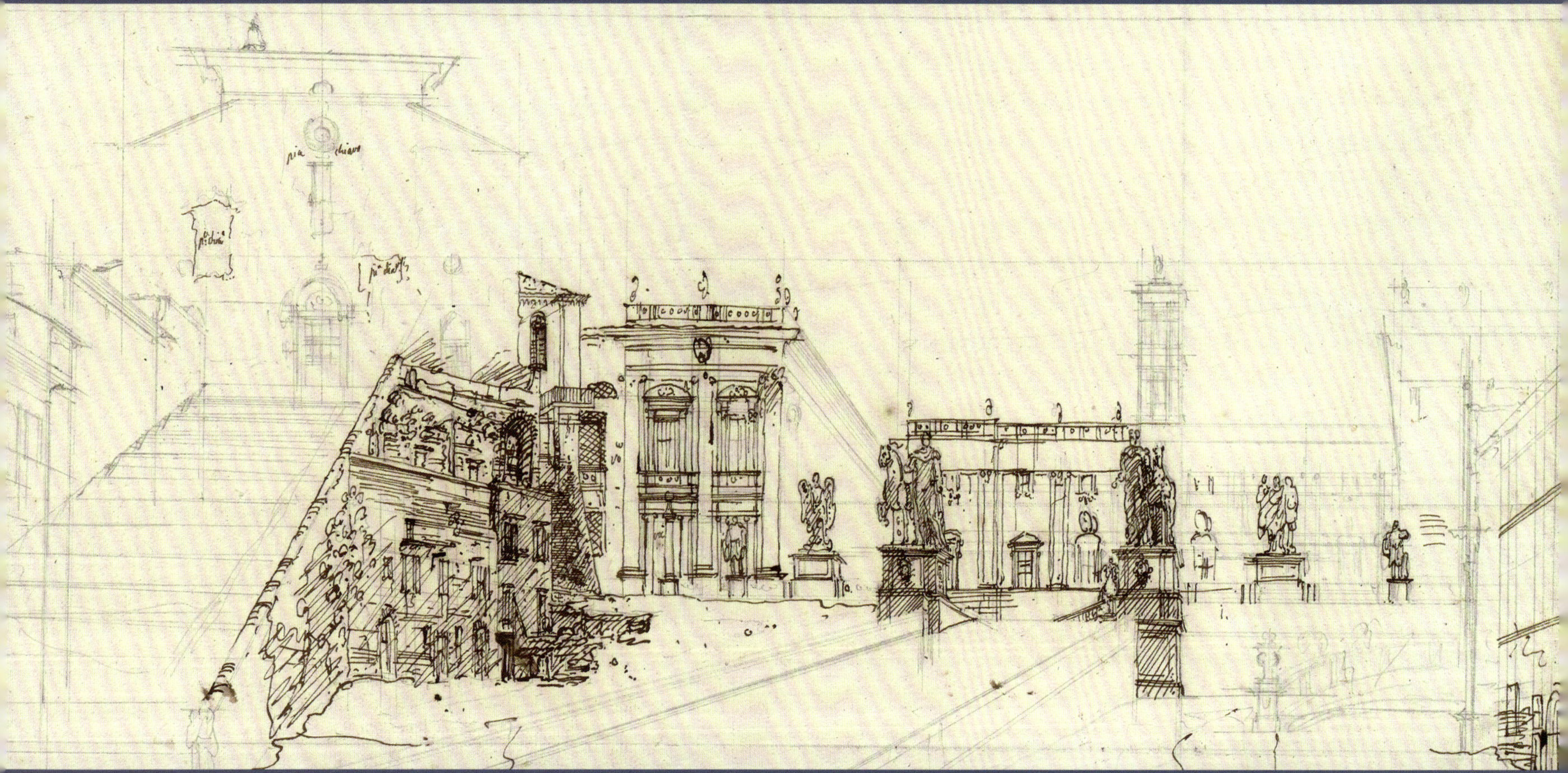

5.
TOWARDS ROME

'Bei soggetti ei trovò quivi nel genere spezialmente dell'antichità' (he found beautiful subjects there, particularly in the genre of Roman antiquity), we read in the famous passage by Anton Maria Zanetti di Alessandro (1706–1778), Canaletto's biographer, writing about the artist's sojourn in Rome between 1719 and 1720, when he transformed from a stage designer into a painter of views and *capricci*. The twenty-three small sheets that he made during that trip (now at the British Museum and the Hessisches Landesmuseum in Darmstadt) served as a valuable repertory that Canaletto used on various occasions. Some of them also guided Bellotto's choice of subjects when he made his own trip to Rome, a journey documented solely by his works and imagined to have taken place between late spring and early summer 1742. On the basis of those drawings, Canaletto painted Rome: *The Temple of Antoninus and Faustina, Rome* (cat. 39) and *The Roman Forum towards the Capitol with the Temple of Castor and Pollux, Rome* (cat. 38), which Bellotto, prior to going to Rome, made faithful replicas of for Smith (now in a private collection). On his return from Rome, the nephew, in the larger version of *The Roman Forum towards the Capitol with the Temple of Castor and Pollux, Rome* (cat. 40), corrected a series of architectural details – the shape of chimneys, now Roman, the height of the columns of the Temple of the Castor and Pollux, the distances between the windows of the Palazzo Senatorio – while keeping the same perspective composition, a synthesis of the site that would be impossible to take in from a single point of view.

'In his Roman paintings and drawings, architecture was given a degree of prominence that Bellotto had only exceptionally granted previously and would only exceptionally grant subsequently' (Kozakiewicz 1972a, vol. I, p. 37). *The Piazza Navona looking North, Rome* (cat. 49) and *The Porta Santo Spirito looking North-West, Rome* (cat. 41) – the pendant to *The Arch of Titus, Rome* (cat. 42) – clearly exemplify Bellotto's authentic and independent interest in the modern works by Borromini and Sangallo the Younger, in addition to those of antiquity. Roman motifs were from that point forward an important element of his *capricci* (cat. 45, 46, 29, 31).

The Arno towards Ponte alla Carraia, Florence (cat. 37) and *The Arno towards Ponte Vecchio, Florence* (cat. 36) show such a maturity of technique and such a rendering of light studied at different times of day as to suggest that Bellotto made a second trip to the Tuscan capital, certainly after the one in the summer of 1740 – documented by a sketch of the view looking towards the Ponte alla Carraia, now at the Uffizi – perhaps on the occasion of his trip to Rome.

36

BERNARDO BELLOTTO

(Venice 1722 – Warsaw 1780)

The Arno towards Ponte Vecchio, Florence
1744

oil on canvas; 73.3 x 105.7 cm
Cambridge, The Fitzwilliam Museum, 192

This beautiful view of the Arno, rendered in broad, parallel brushstrokes of emerald colour, sparkling with enchanting reflections, is shown from the parapet of the Santa Trinita bridge looking upstream, towards the Ponte Vecchio and the Oltrarno; to the right, we can see the apse and the bell tower of San Jacopo sopr'Arno, and to the left the Lungarno Acciaioli in the shade. The pendant in the same museum depicts *The Arno towards Ponte alla Carraia, Florence* (cat. 37). This is the complementary view, shown from the same point in the opposite direction and the ideal continuation of a painting in the Museum of Budapest – *The Arno towards Ponte Santa Trinita, Florence* – the pendant of the *The Piazza della Signoria looking East, Florence* on display in the present exhibition (cat. 19). There are two more Florentine companion pieces known, one in the Alfred Beit Foundation, Russborough House Wicklow, depicting the Arno towards the Ponte alla Carraia, with San Frediano in Cestello in the right and towards the Ponte Vecchio, but from the Tiratoio (Kozakiewicz 1972a, nos. 52 and 56). With the five views of the Arno in Florence, Bellotto depicted the river in every stretch in the city, showing it from different directions, studying the effects of light at different times of the day.

A greater stylistic maturity has always been noted for the Cambridge pair. The similarity to the Roman views, and in particular to *Santa Maria d'Aracoeli and the Capitol*, Petworth House, Sussex, The National Trust, the painting exhibited in Venice on 16 August, 1743 (cf. cat. 44), suggests a similar date. The recently established chronology of the other two pairs of 1740, raises the question of a second trip to Florence (Kowalczyk 2012).

The fact that a preparatory drawing in the Uffizi (M. Chiarini, in Verona 1990, no. 6) is known for the pendant, and firmly dated to around 1740 for reasons of style, might indicate that Bellotto executed the Cambridge paintings using drawings made a few years earlier; but, as noted by M. Chiarini, the effects of light studied in the drawing were not used in the pendant which instead captures a moment of morning light and accurately records the effects on the bridge and in the long shadows reflected in the water, and this suggests a new survey undertaken on site. Elsewhere, I have indicated the possible provenance of this painting and its pendant, donated to the museum in 1876 by the British scholar Arthur Augustus Vansittart, from the Florentine Borri collection, auctioned at Mr. Kents in London on 29–30 March 1759. As lots 34 and 35, they appear as two pendants of 'Canaletto': *'View of the Arno, with the Ponte Vecchio'* and *'its companion, with the ponte Carraia'* (Sale Catalogue 1760, pp. 173–178). Borri must have been in close contact with Andrea Gerini and Anton Maria Zanetti di Girolamo: he possessed six paintings by Francesco Zuccarelli, two views of Venice and two *capricci* by Michele Marieschi, four paintings by Giuseppe Zocchi and four other curious ones, depicting 'Florentine feasts' attributed to Zocchi and Marieschi; two *'Architetture'* by Zocchi were displayed by Giuseppe Borri at the 1767 exhibition (Borroni Salvatori 1974, p. 136 and 140).

In support of the notion of a Florentine commission and of the artist's stay in the city for at least a few years is the existence of a copy, with variations and smaller in size, painted by a follower of Giuseppe Zocchi (1717–1767). The picture is held by the Museum of Fine Arts, Boston where, for long attributed to Bellotto, it is now attributed to his circle and dated 1740–1780 (Kozakiewicz 1972a, no. A 311).

Bożena Anna Kowalczyk

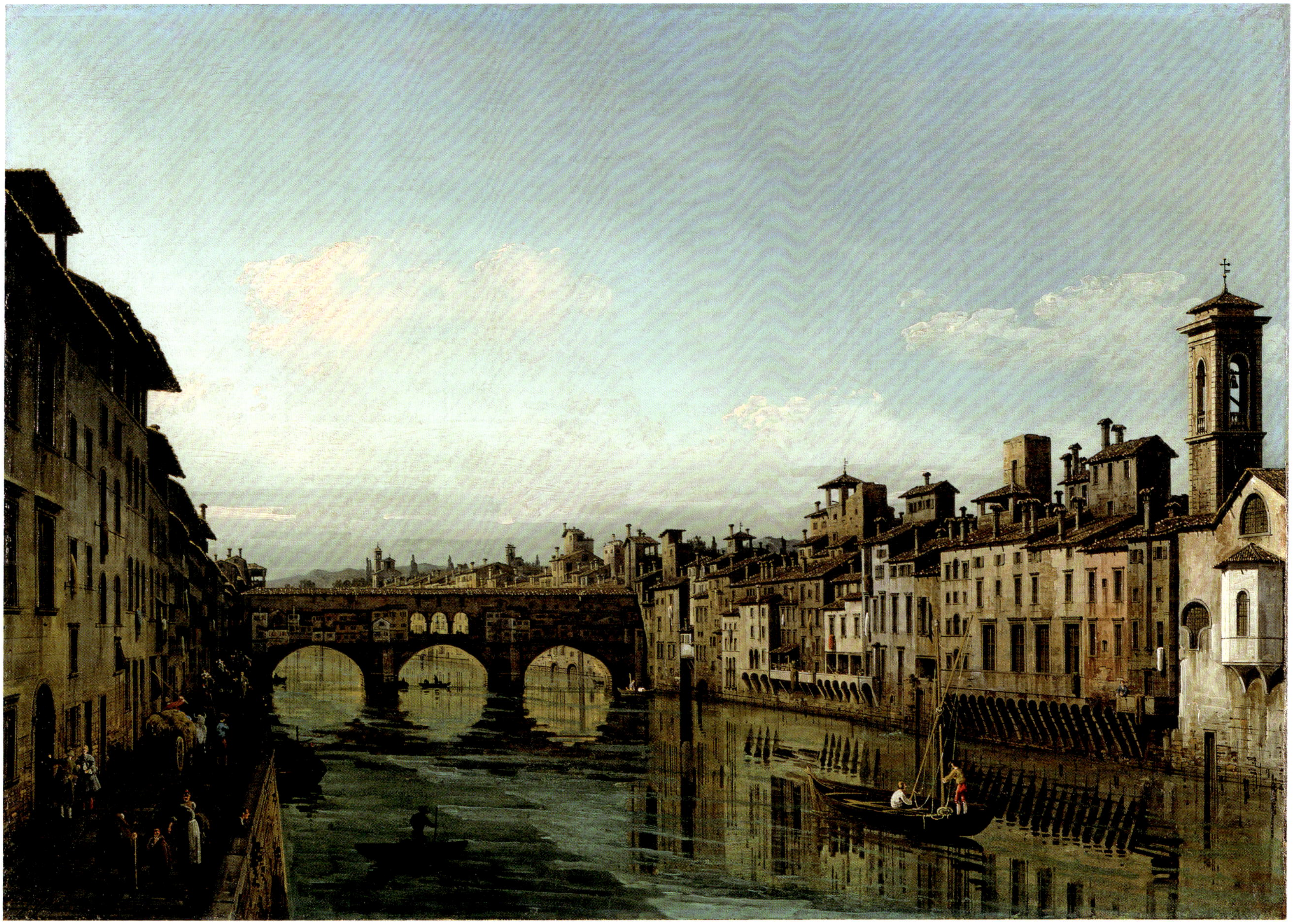

37

BERNARDO BELLOTTO

(Venice 1722 – Warsaw 1780)

The Arno towards Ponte alla Carraia, Florence
1744

oil on canvas; 73.7 x 105.4 cm
Cambridge, Fitzwilliam Museum, 195

From the Ponte Santa Trinita, looking in the opposite direction to the view towards the Ponte Vecchio seen in the pendant (cat. 36), Bellotto depicts Lungarno Corsini on the right and Lungarno Guicciardini on the opposite side of the river, from Santo Spirito to San Frediano, with the hills in the distance. The view was studied in a drawing kept at the Uffizi, from circa 1740, that differs not only in its lighting – an area of light in the right foreground and the Ponte alla Carraia without shadows – handling of the sky and water, but also includes a horse in the right foreground, bathers in the river and a boat with a couple using a parasol to protect themselves from the sun. The scratchy style of the drawing is far removed from the soft way in which the paint has been applied in this picture. Giuseppe Zocchi used the sketch for one of his own drawings, kept at the Hessisches Landesmuseum in Darmstadt in the file containing Bellotto's drawings (AE 2197).
E.P. Bowron expressed concerns about the chronology with regard to these two views of Florence: 'The greyish-brown buildings, warmer in the roofs and greenish in the shadows, the green-grey water, and greenish-blue sky with slightly rosy clouds share much greater affinity with Bellotto's various views of Rome and even Verona than his earlier views of Florence now in Budapest' (2001).
With a current understanding of the evolution of Bellotto's painting style and technique, we are able to confirm a later dating with certainty. The dense paint, the unique handling of the shimmering water full of reflections, with broad parallel emerald green brush strokes, and the sky with even white clouds, grey at the horizon, created with horizontal relief brush strokes, combine to express the maturity acquired in Rome and then enriched by the observation of nature in Lombardy. This idea also confirms the way of painting the trees in the distance outlined against the hills, the distinct touches of light on the tiles and the edges of the roofs, the walls painted with dense overlapping paint layers, and the figures drawn with confident and rounded brush strokes. It was in Lombardy that Bellotto painted two complementary views such as these for the first time: the two pendants of Vaprio, in a private collection (cat. 57, 59) and the views of Gazzada (cat. 60, 61).

Bożena Anna Kowalczyk

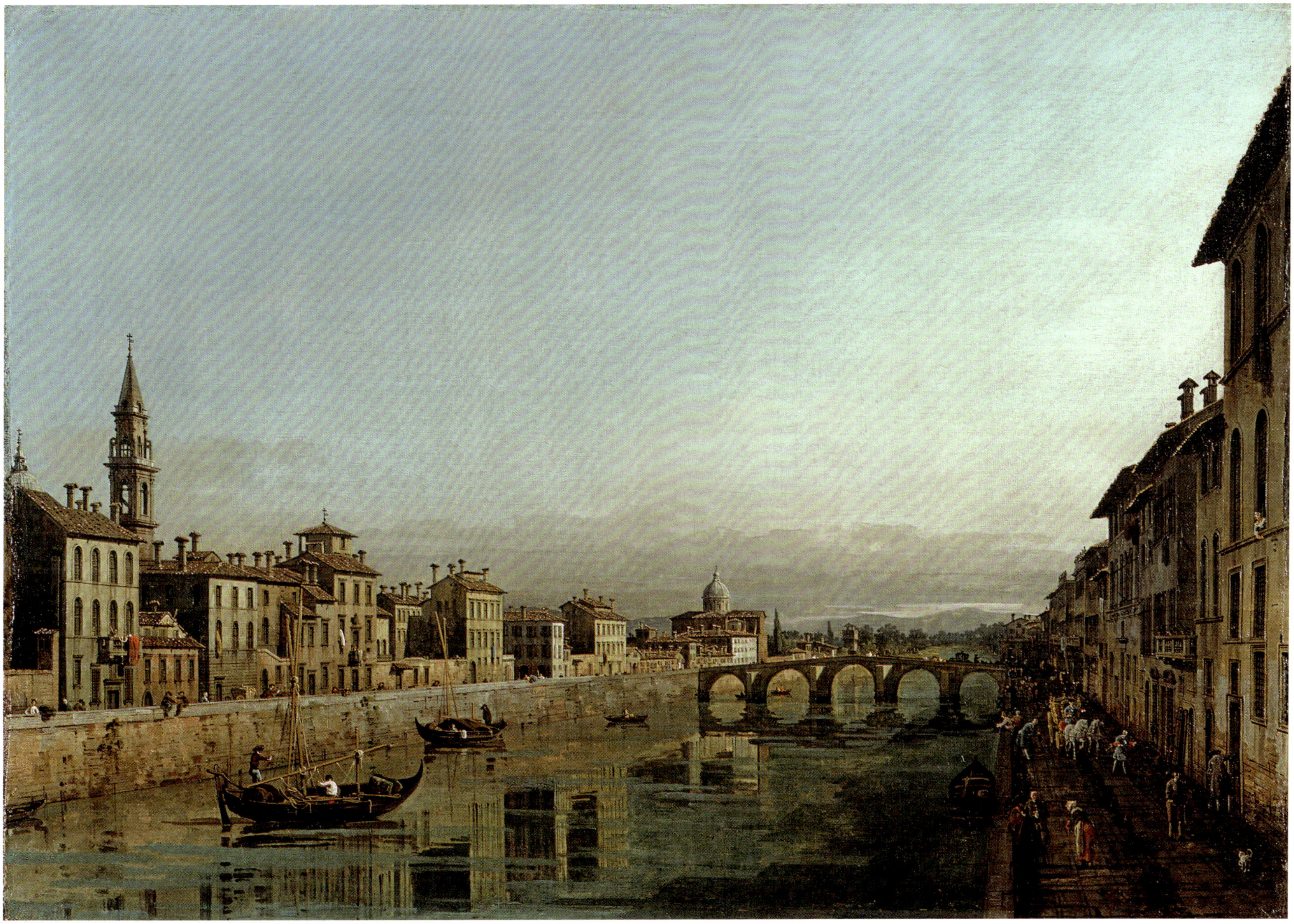

38

CANALETTO

(Venice 1697–1768)

The Roman Forum towards the Capitol with the Temple of Castor and Pollux, Rome
ca. 1742

oil on canvas; 61.9 x 95.3 cm
The Royal Collection / HM Queen Elisabeth II, RCIN 409047

The pair of paintings – this one and its pendant, *The Temple of Antoninus and Faustina in the Roman Forum, Rome* (cat. 39), bequeathed by James Henly Batty (1868–1946) to King George VI (1895–1952), are the only works by Canaletto to have arrived in the Royal Collection from a direction other than from the British Consul, Joseph Smith. Gustaw Waagen was the first to attribute them to Canaletto in 1857 during his survey of the British collections, describing the present picture as 'powerful and warm in tone, and very careful'.
The seventeenth-century church of Santa Maria Liberatrice, demolished in 1900 to make room for Santa Maria Antiqua, frames the view of Campo Vaccino, with the three columns of the Corinthian temple of Castor and Pollux, built in 484 BC and the portico of the temple of Saturn, one of the most revered monuments of the Roman Republic. In the background, on the Capitol, we see the Palazzo Senatorio. An artist is drawing and some tourists with a guide wander through the Parian marble columns of the temple.
In this painting, with the exception of the figures, Canaletto followed the composition of a early drawing executed in Rome in 1719–20, one of the series of twenty-three, often used many years after the journey (C/L 713–224); the perspective composition is the same, as are the relationships between the buildings, the details, even the vegetation which grows in the same spots as in the drawing: for example, on top of the Lacus Juturnae and on the portico of Saturn. One can also observe that the three columns of the temple of Castor and Pollux are equally low, as in the drawing and the cracks in the marble match. The tower of Palazzo Senatorio is, as in the drawing, without openings.
The attribution of the two pendants has long been questioned, with the idea of a possible participation of Bellotto not shared by S. Kozakiewicz; finally in 1998, J.G. Links exclaimed: 'There can be little doubt, after cleaning, that … ex-Batty pair, which entered the Royal Collection fortuitously and for which there is no early history, are mainly, if not wholly, by Canaletto'. The conservation status of the two works is not optimal, but the delicacy in the execution of the architectural structures and of the sky allow us to believe that the attribution to Canaletto be correct. The figures are an example of the fluidity of touch and finesse of type of which Canaletto was a master. The unusual brown lines in the garment of the figure in red near the spring are – as explained by Claire Chorley, curator of the paintings in the Royal Collection – the effect of the medium-rich painting becoming more transparent with time, where the artist has pressed the brush to describe the folds.
The existence of replicas by Bellotto, commissioned by Joseph Smith and conserved in the part of the collection excluded from the sale to King George III in 1762, suggests that this pair was a commission from Smith, replaced after its sale by the 'records' of his nephew. Frances Vivian has explained that the two paintings – which he thought to be by Canaletto – preserved until about 1925 at Paxton House, Berwickshire, Scotland, were a purchase made in Venice by Patrick Home of Wedderburn (1728–1808) and noted in his diary on 16 June 1773: the Scottish Parliamentarian bought them as Canaletto along with a couple of views of piazza San Marco (C/L 129a and 135) from the widow of Joseph Smith, Elizabeth Murray (Vivian 1971, pp. 143–144). Only recently has it been possible to identify them (C. Beddington, in Venice-Houston 2001, nos. 18, 19): published with incorrect provenance by S. Kozakiewicz (1972).
The comparison between the two pairs is the most intriguing in the field of the studies and of the two artists. It is a unique case in that the size, rare for Canaletto, customary for Bellotto, is almost exactly the same. The delicacy of tone and softly diffused light that softly shapes the smooth forms in Canaletto, is contrasted by Bellotto with a strong three-dimensional impact for every detail in the architecture and figures, painted with a packed brush and in more vivid colours, which can also be appreciated thanks to the perfect preservation of the paint layer.
Despite the general similarity of every detail, the pictures are distinguished by the different solution for the tower of the Palazzo Senatorio, which in the Canaletto is like the drawing in the British Museum, without openings, while in the Bellotto it is correctly open on two floors. The chimneys are everywhere of a Venetian form.
After the trip to Rome, Bellotto painted another version of this view (cat. 40) in 1743, which introduces many more elements observed from life.

Bożena Anna Kowalczyk

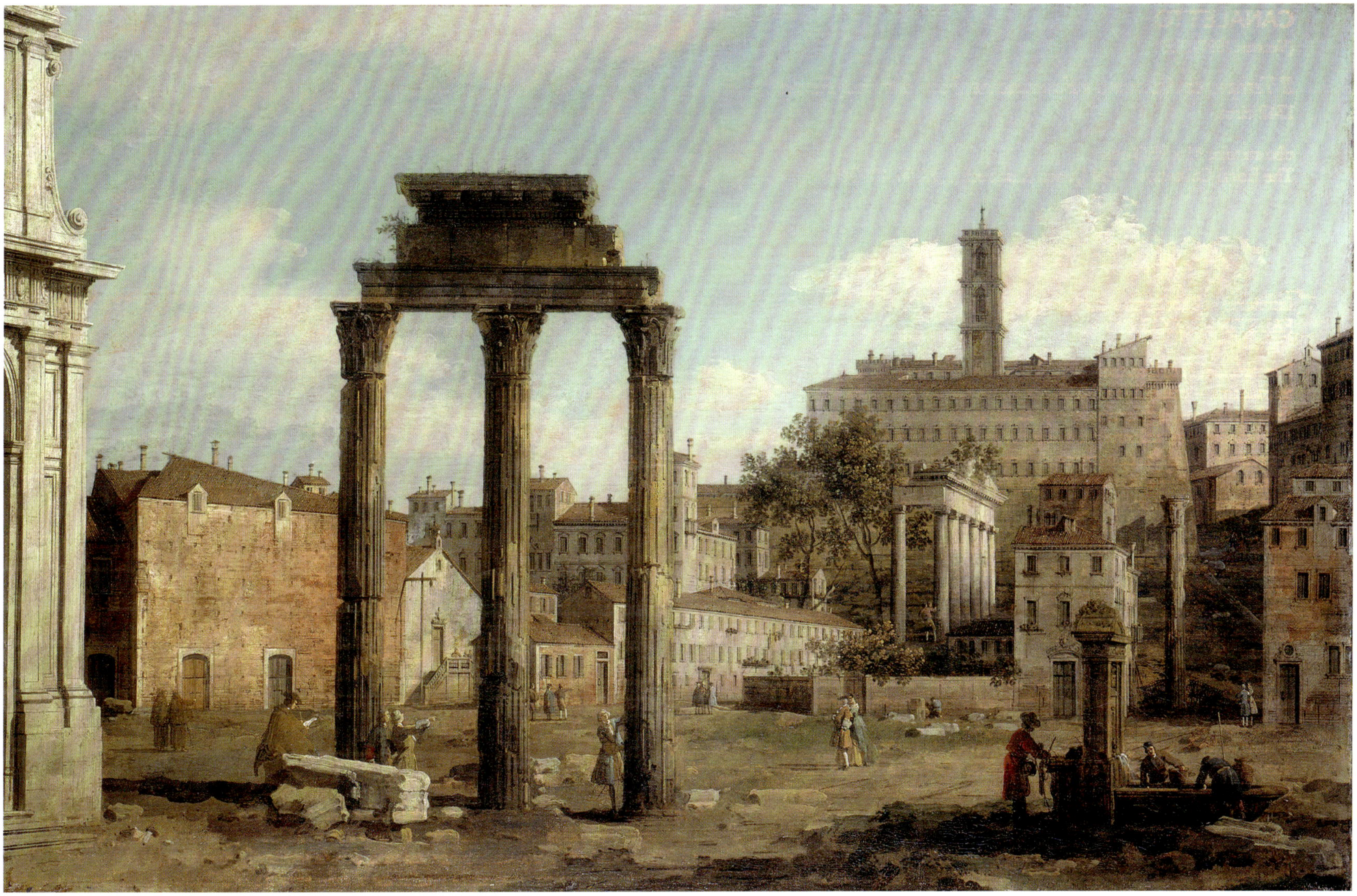

39

CANALETTO

(Venice 1697–1768)

The Temple of Antoninus and Faustina in the Roman Forum, Rome
ca. 1742

oil on canvas; 61 x 95.3 cm
The Royal Collection / HM Queen Elisabeth II, RCIN 409046

Inscriptions: on the temple architrave, 'DIVO. ANTONINO. ET. / DIVAE. FAUSTINAE. EX. S.C.'.

The temple in the Forum dedicated in AD 141 by Antoninus Pius to his deified wife Faustina – and which the Senate also consecrated to the memory of the emperor after his death in 161, adding the upper row on the lintel – was reduced to ten magnificent monolithic columns harbouring the ancient church of San Lorenzo in Miranda within, rebuilt in baroque style in 1602–1606 by Orazio Torriani but left unfinished in the facade.

This was this situation when Canaletto recorded the church on his visit to Rome in 1719–20, in one of the drawings signed 'Antonio Canal delineò in Roma' in the series of twenty-three small works now in the British Museum. The drawing was then used as the basis for this painting (C/L 713–255); another drawing of the same series was used for the pendant, *The Roman Forum towards the Capitol with the Temple of Castor and Pollux, Rome* (cat. 38). The second order of the church facade and the pediment are a design by Matteo Sassi (1647–1723), who worked with Carlo Fontana, dating from 1721–23; during his trip to Rome in 1742–43, Bellotto devoted a special study to these new architectural details in his drawing entitled *The Forum from the Temple of Castor and Pollux towards Santa Francesca Romana, Rome*, which was a study for a painting now in a private collection (Kozakiewicz 1972a, nos. 68, 67). In this painting, Canaletto left the same coat of arms of the reigning pope as noted in the drawing executed in his youth, that of Clement XI Albani, shown on the house next to the temple. Clement XI was Pope from 1700 to 1721, and this fixes the canvas to that particular moment in the past.

Discussing the presence of the pair of Canaletto pictures in the collection of Lord Caledon, of which this painting is one, Gustaw Waagen was less enthusiastic about its quality than of that of the pendant (cat. 38): 'This is much poorer in composition, and heavier in tone'. His opinion was certainly influenced by the looming and undecorated architecture, but Waagen did not note the delicacy of the brown-toned brushwork in the most sophisticated reflections, nor the elegant figures of the gentlemen and that of a page in livery, finely drawn with bright colours and fluid touches of the brush.

Sir Michael Levey believed Bellotto participated in the painting of both pictures, considered in 1964 to be 'Studio of Canaletto', and in 1991 'Canaletto and studio', but S. Kozakiewicz disagreed with this suggestion. Bellotto's version, which came from the collection of Joseph Smith, and is now, along with the companion piece, *The Forum with the Temple of Castor and Pollux towards the Capitol*, in a private collection (cf. cat. 38), clearly shows a series of differences in the manner of applying colour and marking the architectural details. In this regard, it is worth comparing the shape of the facade of the church, with the niches and pilasters softly modulated in diffused light in Canaletto's version, and recorded with highlights by Bellotto (fig. a). The figure of the backlit pilgrim monk with stick and lock of hair, introduced in the foreground in this painting, is found in several subsequent works by Bellotto, suggesting the possibility that it was his own invention, and confirming that the two pairs of paintings were made at the time of their collaboration, almost certainly before Bellotto's voyage to Rome in 1742 to 1743.

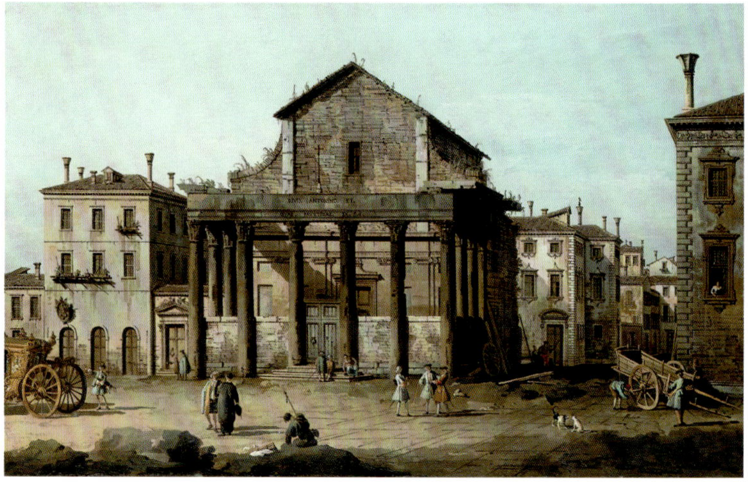

a. Bernardo Bellotto, *The Temple of Antoninus and Faustina, Rome*, 1742, oil on canvas, 61.9 x 96.8 cm. Private Collection

The Temple of Antoninus and Faustina must have fascinated Canaletto and Bellotto with its history. The hatched drawing by Canaletto commissioned by Smith, and the sketch by Bellotto, executed after an engraving by Étienne du Pérac in *Vestigi delle Antichità di Roma*, published for the first time in 1575 and showing the temple before the baroque reconstruction of the church within (B.A. Kowalczyk, in Turin 2008, no. 36) are probably contemporary with this series of paintings. A version belonging to Lord Sandwich that W.G. Constable mentioned for the first time with the name of Canaletto in the impressive article written in 1925 in collaboration with T. Ashby dedicated to the Roman subjects of Canaletto and Bellotto, is certainly the work of a follower (C/L 381-a).

Bożena Anna Kowalczyk

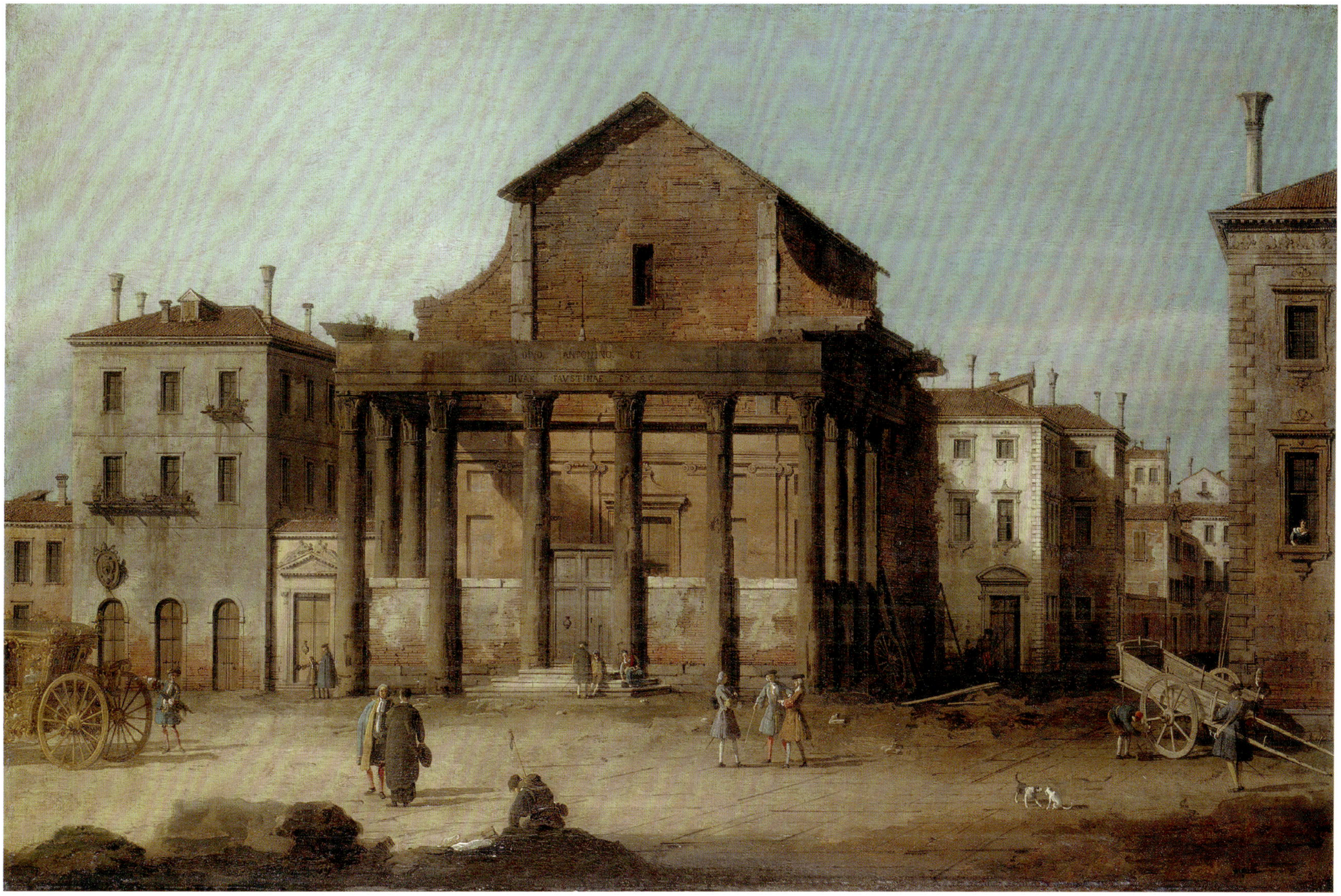

BERNARDO BELLOTTO

(Venice 1722 – Warsaw 1780)

The Roman Forum towards the Capitol with the Temple of Castor and Pollux, Rome
1743

oil on canvas; 87 x 148 cm
Melbourne, National Gallery of Victoria, Felton Bequest, 964-3

This splendid view of the Forum is one of seven known Roman paintings by Bellotto of the same large size, stylistically similar and dated to 1743–44. C. Villis (2000) has shown how they were planned in pairs of pendants; because of the symmetry of the composition which converges towards the palazzo Senatorio, this painting was allegedly planned together with *The Capitol with Santa Maria d'Aracoeli* belonging to the National Trust, Petworth House, Sussex (cf. cat. 44), the only two of the series to follow youthful drawings by Canaletto.
In the series, this is the only painting of ancient Rome. Unlike Canaletto who in his trip as a youth to Rome in 1719–20, was fascinated mostly by the ruined monuments, Bellotto explored modern Rome, the Rome of the popes, Sixtus V and Innocent X Pamphili, of Michelangelo, Sangallo the Younger and Borromini, from the Quirinale to Piazza Navona (cf. cat. 49), the Capitol, the Tiber with Castel Sant'Angelo and San Giovanni dei Fiorentini, and on to the port of Ripetta, anticipating a sense of monumentality in Roman landscape painting that Giambattista Piranesi made his own.
The precision and sensitivity in the rendering of the Roman monuments, the details and atmosphere bear witness to his otherwise undocumented journey. It is assumed the pictures were actually painted in Venice on the basis of drawings and notes, probably on commission but the series was soon dispersed in various English collections. All seven paintings were attributed to Canaletto until recently. This one was first attributed to Bellotto by Sir Michael Levey (1964) – who considers it superior to the version in the Royal Collection (cat. 38) – but Stefan Kozakiewicz, author of the Bellotto monograph, prefers not to express an opinion on the basis of a photograph, instead favouring another version, from the Consul Smith and then Paxton House collection, which he mistakenly presents with the photographs of a good copy (1972).
The peculiarities of Bellotto's style and technique shortly before his departure for Lombardy in 1744 are here clearly expressed, with the silver-grey tone, the purple hues in the sky, the strong lighting contrasted with dark shadows, the precision of the strokes packed with paint. The strong imprint of Canaletto's style, especially in the figures and in their attitudes (note the traveller taking notes or the another one led by a guide), dissolves here in the dense atmosphere peculiar to Bellotto, created from the exact, material description of every thing in a play that is here overtly theatrical of lighting that reveals and obscures, between highlights and deep shadows. The fountain in the right foreground, shown backlit with slow-moving figures around it, acts as a signature.
In an excellent study of the paintings of Bellotto and Canaletto preserved at the National Gallery of Victoria, this one, *The Rialto Bridge from the South, with Palazzo Dolfin Manin, Venice* by Bellotto, of about 1739–40, and *The San Marco Basin from the Piazzetta, Venice* by Canaletto, painted before 1750, Carl Villis, curator of the Melbourne Gallery, explains, through an analysis of the processes and pigments, how Bellotto arrives at a different expression despite mainly maintaining the processes learned from Canaletto and using the same pigments, which were common to those used by other artists in the eighteenth century: white lead and Prussian blue for the skies, coal black for much of the architecture and earth colours for the browns; yellow, red, vermilion and Naples yellow for figures, and water painted in *terre verte* and Prussian blue (2008). This was a gradual process that led away from Canaletto and towards the development of executive techniques ever more closely tied to the purposes of depiction, starting from the most complex preparation of the canvas; 'in three layers, with the first layer of red ochre, covered with an initial ground of yellow ochre, followed by a dense light-coloured field composed principally of white lead', and unlike Canaletto who expanded the different areas – architecture, water and sky – Bellotto's third layer 'is a veritable primer that covers the entire surface of the canvas', mostly left rough (fig. a). The sky is painted in a 'calm and controlled' manner (which Carl Villis believes similar to that of Canaletto), but with a more substantial painting, with the peculiar grey clouds on the horizon; in their movements, the figures mimic Canaletto's brushstrokes but their implementation is more 'troubled'.

Bożena Anna Kowalczyk

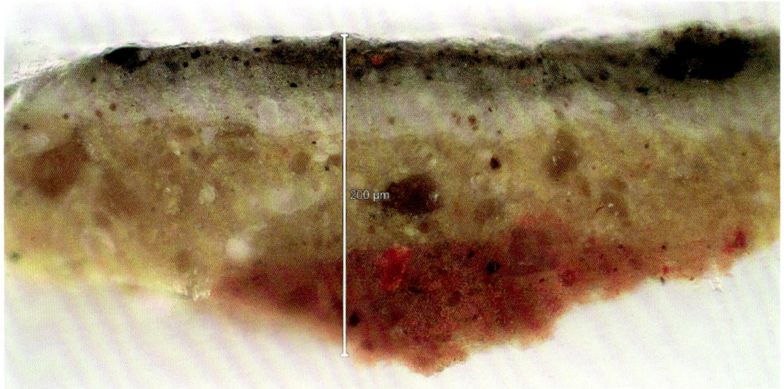

a. Cross section of a colour sample taken from the bottom left corner of *The Roman Forum towards the Capitol with the Temple of Castor and Pollux, Rome*, of Melbourne (cat. 40)

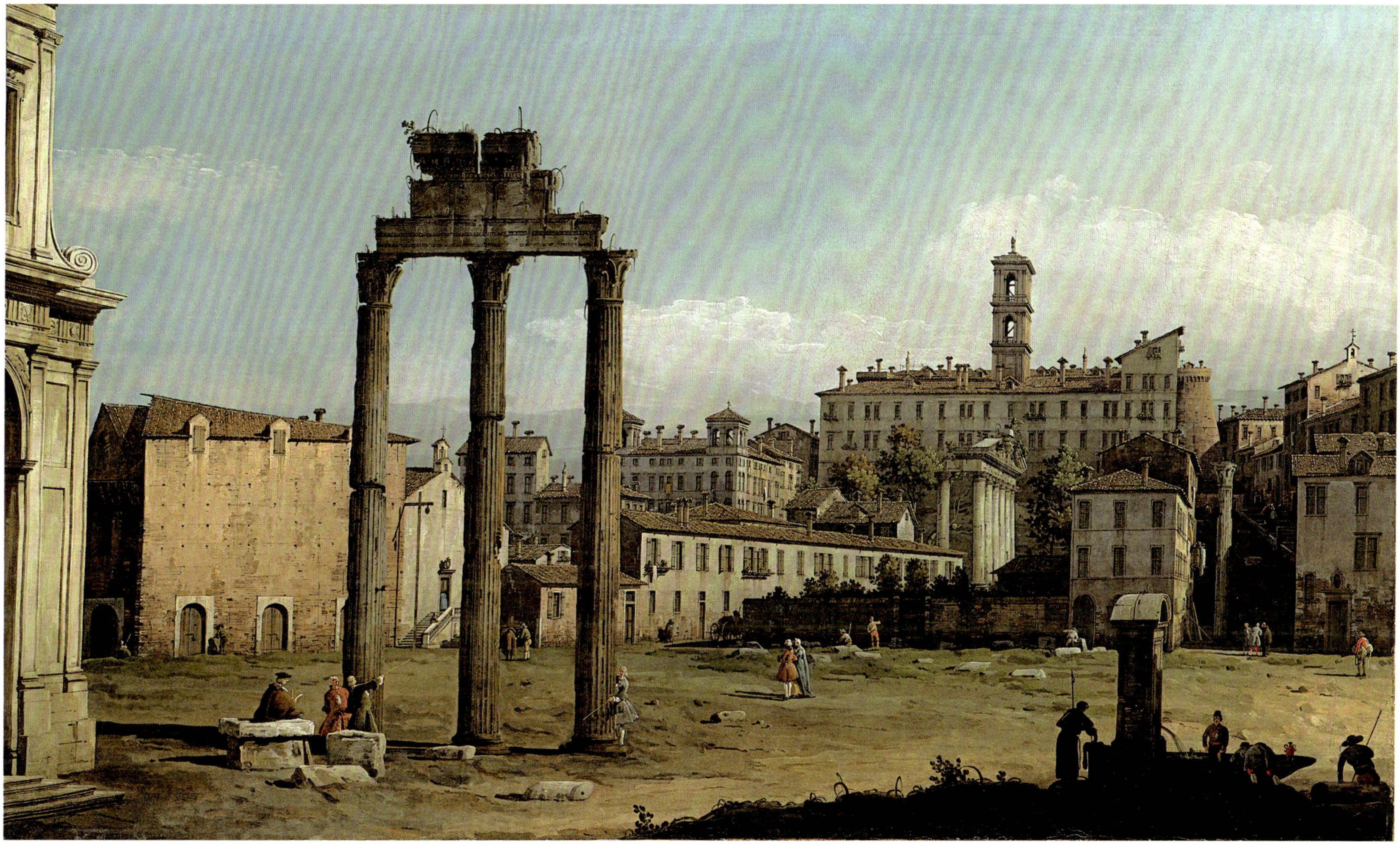

41

BERNARDO BELLOTTO

(Venice 1722 – Warsaw 1780)

The Porta Santo Spirito looking North-West, Rome
1743–44

oil on canvas; 98.5 x 75 cm
Private Collection, courtesy Pym's Gallery, London

In 1540, as part of the improvement and modernisation of the Leonine Wall, Pope Paul III commissioned Antonio da Sangallo the Younger (1484–1546) to reconstruct the ancient *posterula Saxonum*, the only door connecting San Pietro and the Trastevere. When, in 1545, Michelangelo (1475–1564) was appointed architect for the papal fortifications, Sangallo abandoned his project and the door, which took its name from the nearby church of Santo Spirito in Sassia, remained unfinished, despite some intervention by Michelangelo after his death. It is worth recalling Giorgio Vasari's well-known comment: 'It was done with order and to the design of Antonio da Sangallo, with rustic travertine ornament, in a very firm, and very rare manner, with so much magnificence, that it was the equal of antique things' (Vasari [1569] 1943, vol. II, pp. 565–566).

Bellotto must have known this passage by Vasari when he painted this canvas as a companion piece to *The Arch of Titus, Rome* (cat. 42). Fascinated by its unfinished appearance, he analysed the structure as though it were a modern ruin. He accurately rendered the constructive elements in travertine over the brickwork, demonstrating a perfect mastery of architectural design; he engaged in a realistic description of the abandoned fragment of the second order on the left, barred with wooden planks, and of the vases of wild plants arranged on a shelf to replace the top of the door.

The oblique shadow falls on the monument from the powerful bastion on the left, completed by Pius IV in 1564, highlighting the large empty niches; above, a fragment of the eighteenth-century villa Barberini; the arch of the door frames the via dei Penitenzieri that leads to the Vatican; the slender fifteenth-century bell tower is that of the church of Santo Spirito in Sassia, attributed to Baccio Pontelli (1450–1492).

In the preparatory study, one of the eight Roman sheets that survive, Bellotto accurately copies the architecture, the spatial relationships and the sky, but his main interest lay with the chiaroscuro passages which he masterfully resolved with a dense hatching of lines; two silhouettes can just be made out against the dense pattern of lines (Kozakiewicz 1972a, no. 75). The adjustments the artist introduced in the painting are subtle and measured, effected by modulating the intensity of the shadows and making the contours more slender; he also adjusted some details, making the edge of the roof of the house loom less over the garret on the right, the bush on top of the bastion less dense and the figures smaller; less understandable is his motive for making the bell tower of Santo Spirito in Sassia thinner.

From a place nearby along the Lungotevere, and perhaps on the same day, he portrayed another monument by Sangallo the Younger, the church of San Giovanni dei Fiorentini, in a similar luministic study for two paintings, now in the Toledo Museum of Art and in a private collection (Kozakiewicz 1972a, nos. 66–67; G. Marini, in Verona 1990, no. 9).

The painting and its companion show that the interest for Rome's architecture is not matched by one in the city's life: the figures in the Roman views are mere 'staffage': here a man urinating under the ramparts, there a beggar and a carriage passing through the gate, are all literal quotations from early works by Canaletto, and in particular from some of the 23 drawings he made during the trip to Rome in 1719–1720. But it is in Rome that the application of colour becomes more dense and doughy, the tones deeper and the skies bluer and brighter, crossed by white clouds; there is always a small touch of red on the clothing (Kozakiewicz 1972a, vol. I, p. 38).

The motif of the Porta Santo Spirito reappears, albeit transformed, in one of the four *Capricci* of circa 1746 in the National Gallery of Parma (cf. cat. 45).

Bożena Anna Kowalczyk

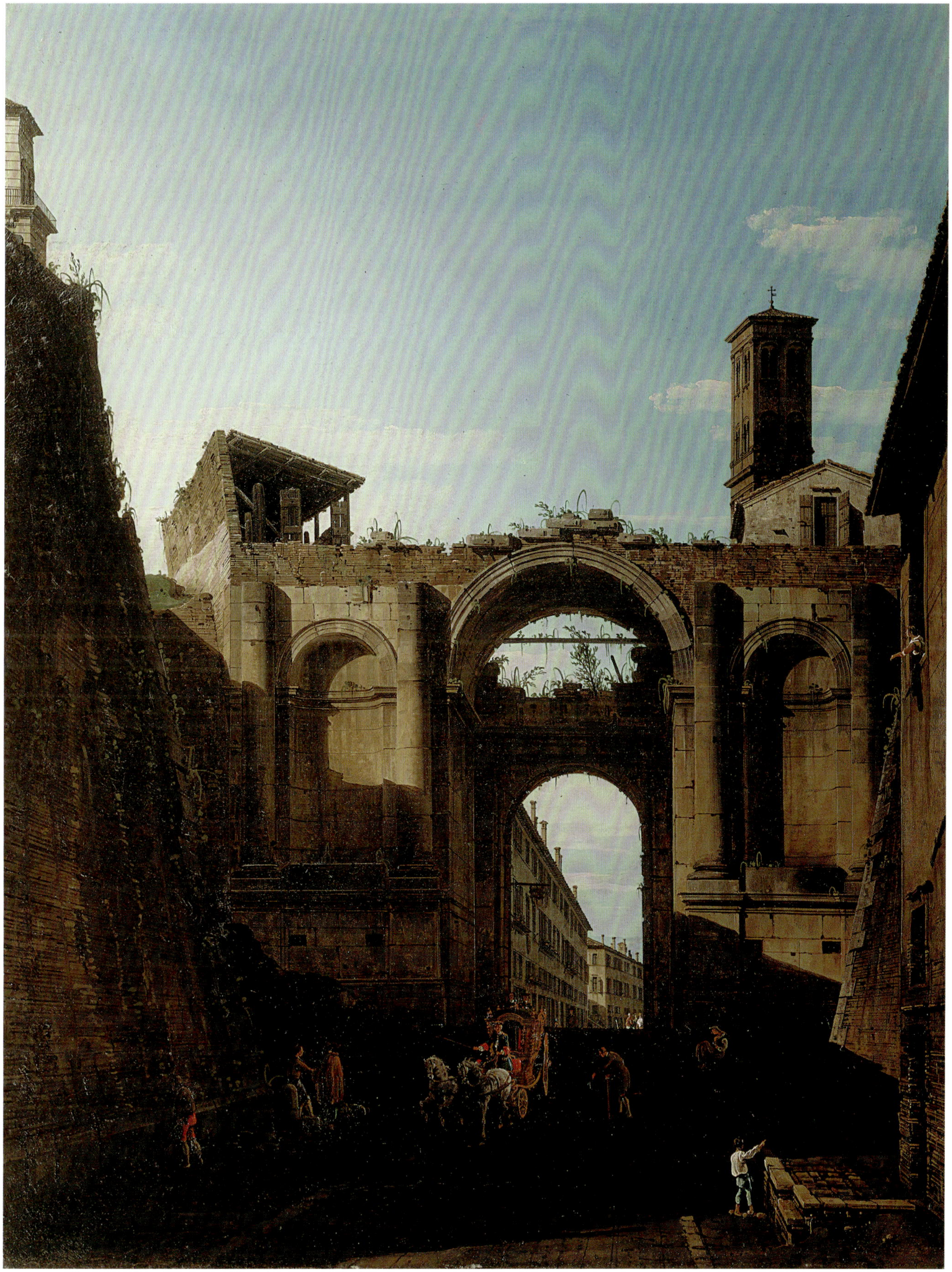

42

BERNARDO BELLOTTO

(Venice 1722 – Warsaw 1780)

The Arch of Titus, Rome
1743–44

oil on canvas; 98.5 x 75 cm
Private Collection, courtesy Pym's Gallery, London

Inscriptions: on the pediment, 'SENATUS./POPULUSQUE. ROMANUS./DIVO. TITO. DIVI. VESPASIANI. F.[ILIO]/VESPASIANO. AUGUSTO.'.

Ever since its appearance in the art market with the name of Bellotto in 1937, the authorship of this painting and its pendant, *The Porta Santo Spirito looking North-West, Rome* (cat. 41) has never been questioned, so strong is the impression of the painter's personal style. The crisp and precise rendition of the monuments, protagonists of the two vertical canvases, illuminated by oblique light and marked by dark shadows that shape the space in the foreground with their sharp edges and lead the eye inward to the light in the background, highlight the perfect mastery of the stylistic and technical skills attained by Bellotto after returning from Rome around 1743–44.

The arch of Titus, erected by the Senate on the Via Sacra at the end of the first century AD to commemorate the victories of Titus Flavius Vespasianus Augustus, Roman emperor from the year 79 to 81, in the war against the Jews and in the conquest of Jerusalem in AD 70, was still partly attached to the medieval walls of the Frangipane in the eighteenth century, from which it was freed and largely recovered in the restoration conducted by Raffaele Stern and Giuseppe Valdier in 1823. Bellotto depicts the monument with the Colosseum behind him; to the right, there is the Santa Francesca Romana convent and to the left a rustic house that was part of the vineyards pertaining to the Abadia di San Sebastiano; the archway itself frames the boundary wall of the Farnese gardens, demolished in the nineteenth century, with the majestic Vignola gateway, rebuilt in the south-east side of the Palatine hill. Ancient symbol of Rome in the Flavian era, the arch was in ruins and formed one of the favourite themes in the Roman landscape painting of the seventeenth and eighteenth centuries. It was here painted by Bellotto as a pendant for the unfinished *Porta Santo Spirito* (cat. 41), a monument of papal and modern Rome, overlooked as a subject worthy of depiction by Gaspar van Wittel (1652/1653–1736); Bellotto's choice marked an intellectual and innovative attitude that was wholly new to the canons of Roman landscape painting. This pair of companion pieces is an ambitious response by the young painter to the series of five Roman paintings in vertical format, including three of the triumphal arches – of Constantine, of Septimius Severus and of Titus – painted by Canaletto in 1742 on commission to Joseph Smith, the future British Consul (circa 1674–1770) (C/L 386, 378, 382, 384 and 390). Canaletto's *Arch of Titus* (fig. a) depicts the monument in a similar situation as regards perspective and lighting but at its most advanced state of ruin, with the marble covering full of cracks and crumbling. As noted by Sir Michael Levey, the house on the left is more Venetian in character than Roman and the inscription on the pediment erroneously divides the word 'POPULUSQUE'. The compositional bond between the two paintings is undeniable and confirmed by the shared imaginary framing beneath the arch of all three pillars of the temple of Castor and Pollux in the Campo Vaccino, and by the omission of the Capitoline hill with the Palazzo Senatorio and its bell tower, which is instead more accurately present in the seven paintings and two drawings of the area by van Wittel (Briganti 1996, nos. 76–81; D 167 and D 260). The author believes it was Canaletto, who was highly skilled in using various visual sources, to have suggested the idea of the composition to Bellotto and not the other way around, as has been speculated.

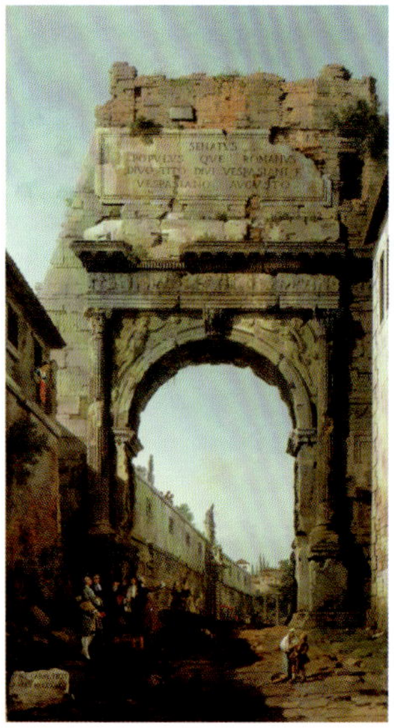

a. Canaletto, *The Arch of Titus, Rome*, 1742,
oil con canvas, 192.2 x 106.5 cm.
The Royal Collection, RCIN 401002

In his painting – as in the others of the series – Canaletto presented the ancient myth of Rome admired by elegant tourists, wearing colourful and fashionable garments, like in the paintings by Panini. Bellotto went to Rome to study the reality of the sites on 'the recommendation of Uncle' who visited the Eternal City only once, in his youth. In his description, the monument acquires a precise material consistency, both in the marble facing, and in the medieval brickwork added on top. The decorative details emerge in the thick paint: the fluted columns and the frieze on the high-relief entablature depicting scenes of sacrifice, with human and animal figures, the two victories at the sides of the arch. On the stone bearing the inscription in honour of Titus, Bellotto has recorded the marks caused by pluvial runoff. The viewpoint is slightly to the right of those chosen by Canaletto and van Wittel, and with the foreshortened perspective of the wall of the Farnese Gardens in the shade, this gives the painting a special perspective rigour and dynamism. A smaller version belongs to the Accademia Carrara, Bergamo (cat. 43).The Arch of Titus is often present in Bellotto *capricci*.

Bożena Anna Kowalczyk

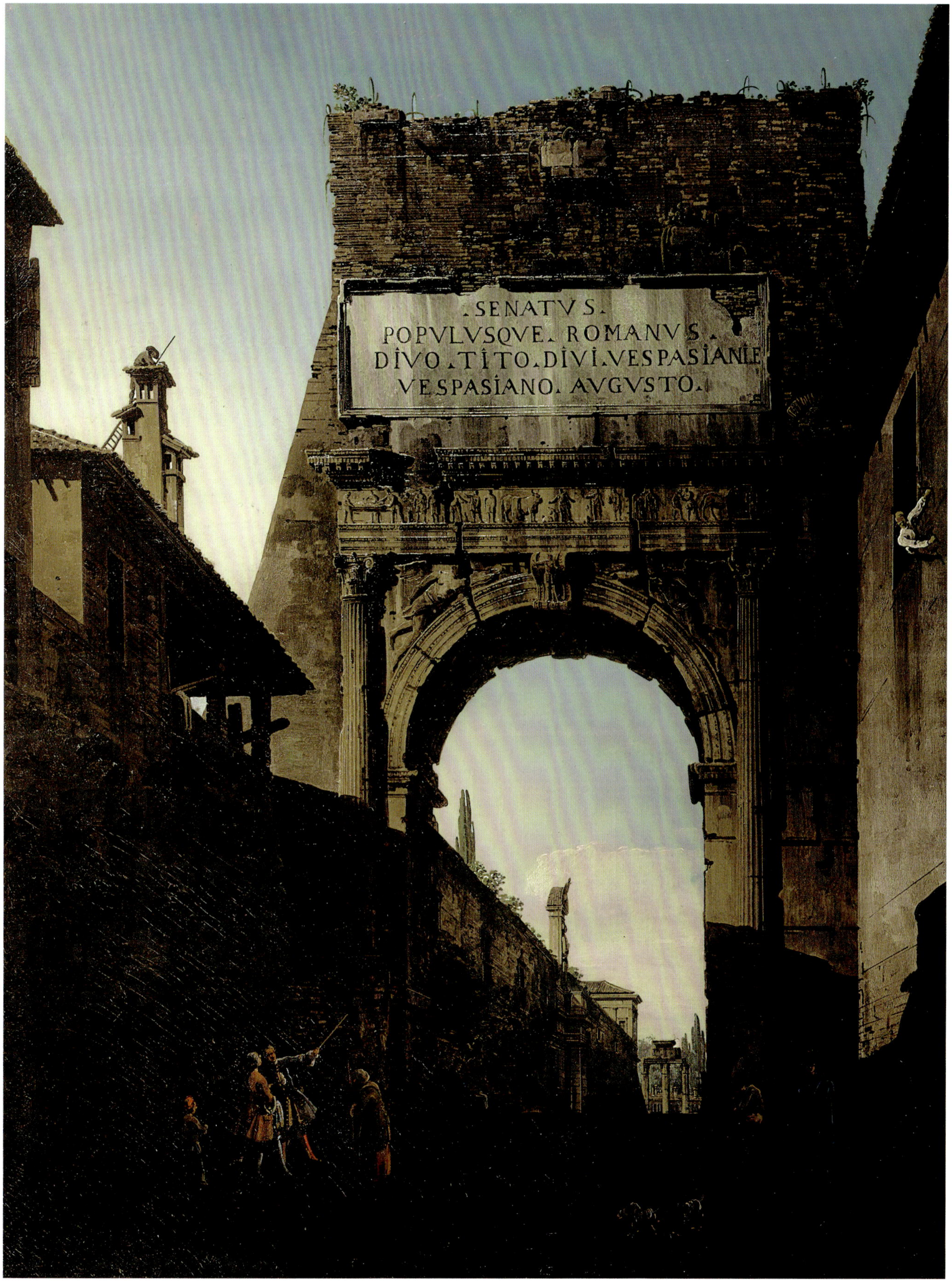
SENATVS
POPVLVSQVE ROMANVS
DIVO TITO DIVI VESPASIANI F
VESPASIANO AVGVSTO

43

BERNARDO BELLOTTO

(Venice 1722 – Warsaw 1780)

The Arch of Titus, Rome
ca. 1744

oil on canvas; 38 x 28 cm
Bergamo, Accademia Carrara, 240, 58AC00149

Inscription: on the pediment 'SENATUS POPULUSQUE ROMA[...] / DIVO TITO DIVI VESPASIANI F./VESPASIANO AUGUSTO'.

A warm glow floods the triumphal arch erected on the Via Sacra in honour of Emperor Titus Flavius Vespasianus Augustus, son of Vespasian, shortly after his death in AD 81. The soft and mellow brushwork describes the monument, effectively sketching out its decorative details, broadly repeating the depiction in the painting formerly in the Lovelace collection, which is larger and was painted in 1743–44 with its companion piece *The Porta Santo Spirito looking North-West, Rome* (cat. 41). No pendant is known for the present work, and indeed it probably never existed.

The style and technique of the brushwork, with overlapping layers, patches and light dabs, diagonal brushstrokes in the sky, energetic and in various directions in the clouds, are of such a sureness and freedom as to suggest that the picture was painted after the trip to Rome, datable to between the two *capricci* of Asolo and the views of Gazzada (cat. 29, 31 and 60, 61). This makes it unlikely as a model for the former Lovelace canvas, as suggested by E.P. Bowron, as the latter is carefully finished and highly detailed. The differences between the two images confirm the idea that Bellotto, using the same drawings, improved and corrected the composition of the details: he made the majestic portal of the Orti Farnesiani of Vignola emerge from the shadows and moved the cypress rising behind the wall further along; he made the descent to Campo Vaccino more evident; the view at the end, between the arch, is sketched with strokes of light and colour, forming a 'picture within a picture'. However, the presence of the two columns of the temple of Castor and Pollux at that location remains arbitrary, even further removed from reality than in the former Lovelace painting. The edges of the shadow in the foreground have been revised and refined. The freedom shown in laying the commemorative inscription on the pediment – on three lines instead of four – and in 'cutting' the word *Romanus* with an imaginary breach in the stone, is best explained by seeing this picture as a fanciful and later version rather than as a preparatory model.

The patron was probably Italian, given the documented presence of the picture in Bergamo a few years after it was painted. The existence of two non-autograph copies testifies to its success. One of these, from the collection of Sir Evan Edward Charteris (1864–1940) in London, seemed so successful to W.G. Constable that the latter wrote: 'Has been attributed to Canaletto; the colour and the handling of the figures is more like that of Bellotto' (C/L-386c). Another version belonged in 1947 to the collection of Gino Cesura (1947; 37.5 x 28.5 cm; photograph Fototeca Pallucchini, Fondazione Giorgio Cini).

Bożena Anna Kowalczyk

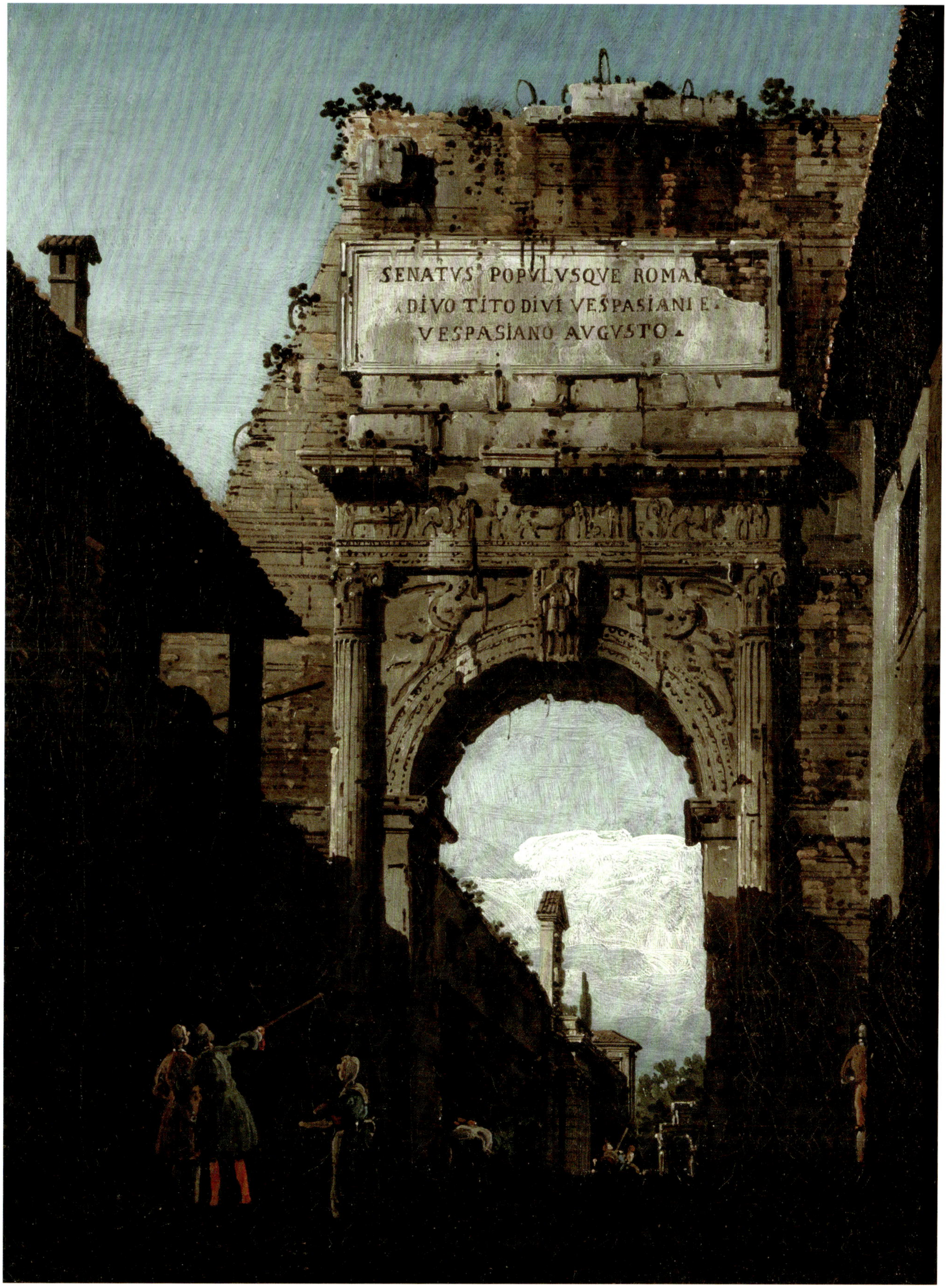
SENATVS POPVLVSQVE ROMA
DIVO TITO DIVI VESPASIANI
VESPASIANO AVGVSTO

BERNARDO BELLOTTO

(Venice 1722 – Warsaw 1780)

Santa Maria d'Aracoeli and the Capitol, Rome
1742–43

pencil freehand and ruled with pinpointing; the central part finished in pen in dark-brown ink, applied freehand
310 x 538 mm
Warsaw, Muzeum Narodowe, Rys. Pol. 2040

Inscriptions: words 'più chiaro' (lighter) added repeatedly over the facade of Santa Maria d'Aracoeli; numbers and text in pencil on the stairs leading to the church ('quinte di 8', 'da 8 quindeci'; 'da 4..'...).

Watermark: a fragment, 'IV'.

The journey to Rome, undertaken 'on the recommendation of [his] Uncle', was crucial for the pictorial formation of Bellotto. Some twenty views of Rome, including seven large ones, testify to the rapid progress made in terms of composition and technique in the years between 1742 and 1744 during his travels. On 16 August 1743, Bellotto exhibited a view of the Capitol in Venice for the annual feast of San Rocco, which has been identified as being the painting of Petworth House in Sussex (Kozakiewicz 1972a, no. 77, fig. a). The ambitious composition was carefully prepared with the present drawing.
This view of the Capitol, taken from the foot of the hill, to the left of the Cordonata stairway, was a popular one reproduced in the prints of Lieven Cruyl (1640–1720), Israel Silvestre (1621–1691) and Giambattista Falda (1643–1678). Bellotto was also in possession of a small drawing by Canaletto from the series of twenty-three 'delineated' on the journey to Rome in 1719–20, which showed a similar view. Removed from the group now in the British Museum, this sheet arrived at the Museum of Darmstadt with a group of his own drawings (AE 2186). Bellotto used these sources as compositional ideas but built his own rigorous structure of perspective and light, and updated the topographical details.
The drawing, done in the studio, is a scenic composition of other sketches done *in loco*. Bellotto clearly shows he has mastered the processes employed by Canaletto but in manner that is wholly his, he begins at the vertical folds that divide the sheet into four equal parts. The line in pencil and ruler, left in view, with the exception of the central area and some details on the right side, has been gone over in pen and ink highlighting the two Dioscuri at the top of Cordonata stairs while the equestrian statue of Marcus Aurelius, barely visible, allows one to follow the logic and precision of the work in view of the pictorial realization, to which the horizontal lines in pencil and ruler covering the sheet allude. The *pentimento* at the top of the Santa Maria d'Aracoeli church is clearly visible, as is the construction of the facade using measurements made with a compass, starting with the central vertical line, which is dotted with pinpricks. Using the same tool, the artist has outlined the round clock on top of the facade, which was moved in 1728 from lower down, where it was to be found at the time Canaletto depicted it (Marini 1991, p. 150). There are some cryptic pencil marks on the stairs leading to the church, probably indicating the number of steps within each space marked in the drawing; in the spirit of Canaletto, those instructions on the discoloured areas on the fifteenth-century facade ('lighter'), have been followed in the painting. The contour line of the shadow area which crosses the bottom of the sheet obliquely, has been tossed down, in part in ink, in part in pencil; in the painting, this was rethought and better articulated, especially on the right side.
The rapid work in ink over the pencil drawing, which reveals the precise knowledge of the architectural structures, is indicative of the graphic style which separates the young Bellotto from Canaletto.
Slightly changing the perspective view, the central part of the sheet was used for *Capriccio with the Capitol*, of 1746, in the Gallerie Nazionali di Parma (cat. 45).

Bożena Anna Kowalczyk

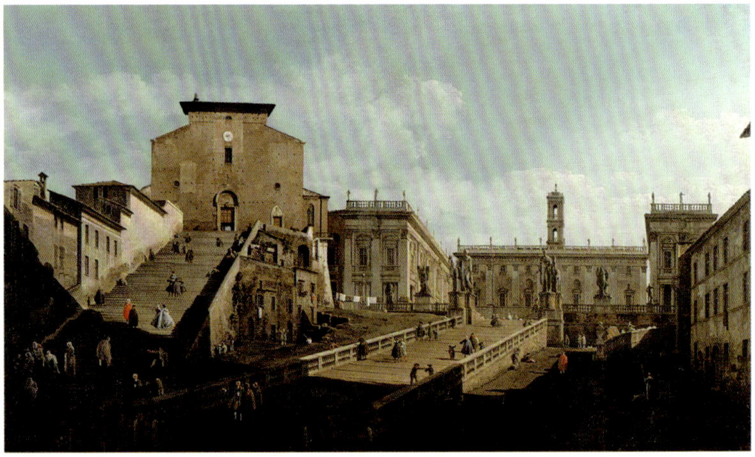

a. Bernardo Bellotto, *Santa Maria d'Aracoeli and the Capitol*, Rome, 1743, oil on canvas, 86.4 x 148.6 cm, Petworth House, The Egremont Collection (The National Trust)

Rj.Pd. 2040

45

BERNARDO BELLOTTO

(Venice 1722 – Warsaw 1780)

Capriccio with the Capitol
1746

oil on canvas, 117 x 132 cm
Parma, Galleria Nazionale, 237

An eccentric horseman, wrapped in a red cloak with his nightcap on his head, is about to climb the ramp of stairs designed by Michelangelo for both men and horses, before passing under the imposing arch that resembles the Porta Santo Spirito in Rome. Bellotto shows us only a part of the Capitol and Santa Maria d'Aracoeli, the Palazzo Nuovo and one of the statues of the Dioscuri, with the Palazzo Senatorio in the background. The view between the arch is taken, with a slight perspectival modification, from a drawing in the Muzeum Narodowe in Warsaw, probably carried out on his visit to Rome, in 1742 or shortly afterwards, in 1743, and partially gone over in pen (cat. 44). The houses built against the staircase of Santa Maria d'Aracoeli, with visible brickwork and under siege from vegetation, are subject to scrupulous detail in both the drawing and the painting. This picture is the pendant to *Capriccio with the Coliseum* (cat. 46); similar in size and with the same vertical format and monumentality, it also represents a transformed Roman site, featuring images described in the same analytical and lucid way, as well as strong *chiaroscuro* contrasts, all of which are typical of Bellotto's work. Another two paintings from the gallery are part of the same series, *Capriccio, a classical gate and reminiscences of Padua and Verona* and *Capriccio, with a civic gate* (inv. 235 and 236), but these are horizontal in format and iconographically more complex, combining motifs from both Rome and the Veneto. The large and well-defined figures in the foreground of both pairs denote a choice that was unusual during that period but much more common during the 1760s in Dresden; it has, however, been ascertained that only the figures in the vertical paintings are by Bellotto himself, while those in the horizontal pair are by Francesco Zuccarelli (1702–1788). The beautiful horse, painted with a knowledge of equine anatomy, is the first in a series that would continue in Warsaw in the 1770s.
The four canvases were acquired in 1835 by Earl Stefano II Sanvitale (1764–1838), a member of an illustrious family from Parma with a reputation for fine collecting (A. Talignani, in Ceschi Lavagnetto, Talignani 2006). No documentary evidence of the commission or purchase has yet come to light but we know that his grandfather, Marquis Giacomo Antonio II Sanvitale (1699–1780), a diplomat to the Viennese court, moved to Venice in the 1740s. He is also remembered by Giacomo Casanova in his *Memoirs* for squandering his fortune for Giulia Ursula Preato, a courtesan famous across Europe. It is interesting to note that the same 'Sig. Giulia Preati' and 'il Sig. Co. Jacopo Sanvitale' appear in the list of subscribers to the second volume of *Delle Antiche Statue Greche e Romane* by Anton Maria Zanetti di Girolamo (1680–1767), published in 1743, guaranteeing the relationship with the artist's patron.

Bożena Anna Kowalczyk

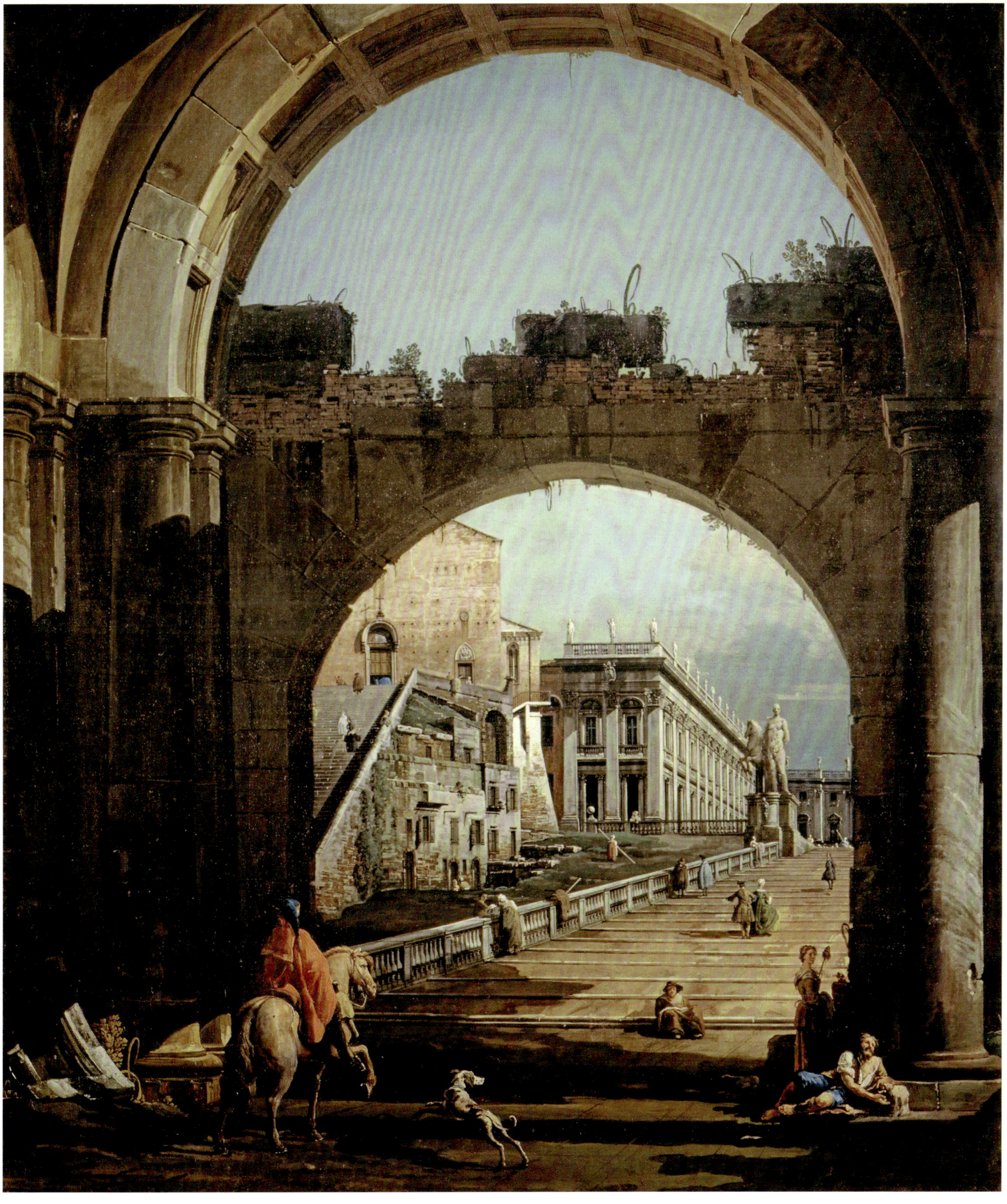

46

BERNARDO BELLOTTO

(Venice 1722 – Warsaw 1780)

Capriccio with the Coliseum
1746

oil on canvas; 134 x 119 cm
Parma, Galleria Nazionale, 238

The magnificent series of four *capricci* kept at the Galleria Nazionale in Parma, to which this painting belongs, was Bellotto's greatest achievement before his departure for Dresden in April 1747. The completeness of his pictorial skill is expressed by the careful drafting of these paintings and the confident use of space; the technical processes applied here to describe the architecture, ground and sky are those he would use with different tones throughout his career. The primary role given to the architecture and the means of formulating space, of managing the raking light that is theatrical in nature in the large *capricci* can be compared in Bellotto's oeuvre with the works painted in around 1765, *Architectural Capriccio with Self-Portrait* (cat. 82), the pendant that accompanies two of the three versions, *The Expulsion of the Money Changers from the Temple*, and *The Portrait of Polish Noblemen* in the El Paso Museum of Art (Kozakiewicz 1972a, no. 337). A composition similar to this series, with two vertical and two horizontal formats, would be repeated in 1773 in Warsaw with the four equestrian portraits (cat. 98). As in the Polish series, the different format pendants are marked out by their compositions, and in this case also by their figures. In this painting, as in the vertical pendant, *Capriccio with the Capitol* (cat. 45), the figures are by Bellotto's hand, painted with substantial brush strokes and rich in impasto; with an admirable capacity for emulation, they are reminiscent of the Arcadian typologies used by Francesco Zuccarelli in two other pendants. This is quite unusual in Bellotto's repertoire, only those in the background correspond with his usual silhouettes, acquired from Canaletto's repertoire. This is the only painting in the series of four that clearly competes with the *capricci* of ruins by Giovanni Paolo Panini, without precise spatial framing. At the same time, however, it makes its mark through the use of entirely recognisable architectural elements that are faithful to the real appearance of the monuments in the Roman Forum.
On his visit to Rome, Bellotto understood the fascination of the three ruined columns of the temple of Castor and Pollux in the Campo Vaccino; already present in a series of paintings and a drawing at the Hessisches Museum in Darmstadt, carried out between 1742 and 1744 (cf. cat. 40), they form a transparent barrier here that allows the space to be organised and introduces the view of the Colosseum and the pyramid of Caius Cestius in the distance; nearby, almost as it is in reality, stands the Juturna fountain. The attention and freedom with which Bellotto describes each of the three nicked Corinthian columns in a different way is notable, as they support a fragment of architrave covered in wild vegetation. The Coliseum, rarer in Bellotto's work, is depicted from a different angle in a painting kept in a private collection, of 1743 (C/L 388*). The amphitheatre may never have been portrayed in paint with such similar ambition to record every stone and brick, and every pilaster in light or shade. The painting is involved in a sort of competition with one by Canaletto depicting the monument that was painted for Joseph Smith, signed and dated 1743 (nevertheless attributed by Waagen to Bellotto; Levey 1991, n. 373).
The organisation of the space using light, from the foreground in shadow, had now become typical of Bellotto. The strong raking light allows for the investigation of every column flute and crack, with some exaggeration of the damage. The stones are an opportunity for a majestic description, in the architectural fragments in the left foreground and the architrave of the ruined temple, where various shades of brown and grey alternate. The way in which Bellotto creates his crisp and expressive images becomes clear, adding and overlaying layers and touches of colour as he works.
The four *capricci* were acquired from the collection of Earl Sanvitale (Cattani 2000) with an attribution to Francesco Guardi. They may have been commissioned by his ancestor, Earl Giacomo Antonio II Sanvitale (1699–1780), in contact with Anton Maria Zanetti di Girolamo in Venice; the lion of Pireo, which appears as an important compositional element in one of the horizontal pendants that must have been painted first, part of Statuario Publico della Serenissima, is engraved in the second volume of *Delle Antiche Statue Greche e Romane*, the magnificent publishing achievement of the two Zanetti cousins, to which the nobleman from Parma was a subscriber.

Bożena Anna Kowalczyk

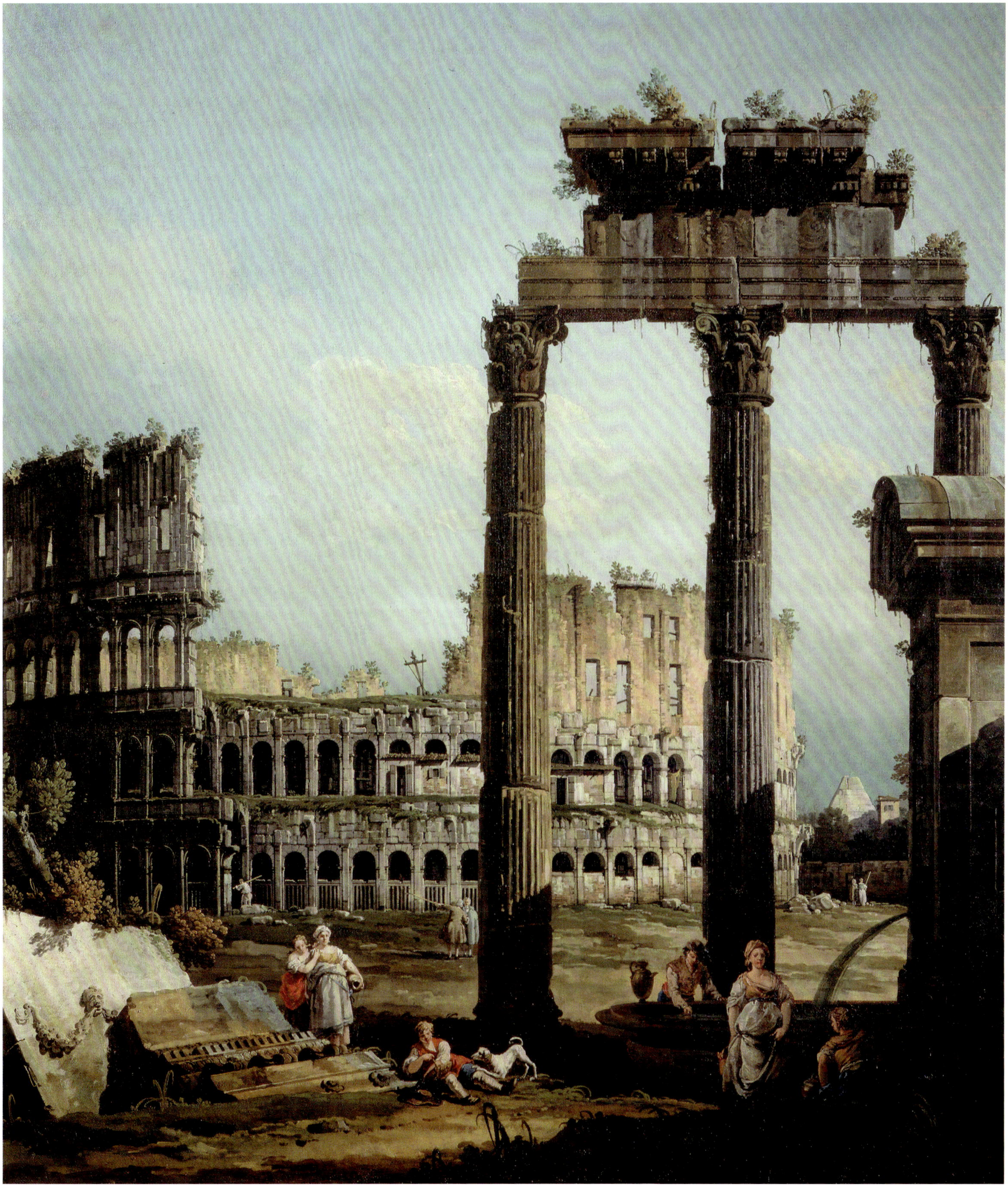

47

BERNARDO BELLOTTO

(Venice 1722 – Warsaw 1780)

The Piazza San Giovanni in Laterano, Rome
1743–44

oil on canvas; 63.5 x 98.5 cm
Private Collection, courtesy Robilant+Voena, London

The obelisk from the Temple of Amun in Thebes is the highest and oldest of Rome and divides the space into two parts: on the right is the Palzzo Laterano, built in 1586 by Domenico Fontana as a summer residence for Sixtus V; on the left, Nero's aqueduct and the Scala Santa. The Loggia delle Benedizioni of the Basilica di San Giovanni in Laterano, designed by the same architect, with all five arches of the portico on two floors and one of the two Romanesque towers that surmount it, sinks into the shadow on the far right that extends obliquely along the palace. Near the obelisk – rediscovered in 1588 in three pieces in the Circus Maximus, where it has been erected in 357 by Emperor Constantius II and moved to this site by Pope Sixtus V – stands the Saint John the Evangelist fountain, also designed by Fontana as part of the project to re-order the piazza; at the time, this square – as is clear from the drawings by Canaletto and Bellotto – was without the Medici lilies that have flanked the figure of the Evangelist since 1605. The artist has portrayed himself in the foreground, sketchbook in hand, drawing the facade of the church, with an assistant or servant gesticulating emphatically. The strong light comes from the right.
The painting was considered to be by Canaletto when it appeared in 1937 at the Lovelace sale in a group of ten paintings, including seven masterpieces by Canaletto commissioned from the artist at the end of his stay in England, in circa 1754, and two Roman companion pieces by Bellotto, *The Porta Santo Spirito looking North-West* and *The Arch of Titus* (cat. 41, 42). It was attributed to Bellotto in 1955 by Francis J.B. Watson, an opinion not supported by W.G. Constable and J.G. Links, and firmly rejected by S. Kozakiewicz.
In 1993–1996, the present author attributed the painting to Bellotto 'for the clear description of the architecture, for the clear and sharp shadows in which the details of the church and of the carriage in the square are merely discerned, for the quality of the brushwork that lingers to depict the unevenness of the terrain'; the attribution was confirmed at the *Bernardo Bellotto and the Capitals of Europe* exhibition in Houston, through a comparison with contemporary works by the artist.

The painting is one of the six views of Rome by Bellotto that are based on a drawing by Canaletto, belonging to the series of twenty-three executed during his visit to Rome in 1719 to 1720; in this case, the drawing is C/L 713–241; for the other works, see cat. 38, 39, 40, 44, 46. The oil differs from the drawing not only in the figures and in the carriage which is depicted only here, but also for the inclusion of a greater portion of the Lateran church; in the form of the gables over the ground-floor windows of the building (and which is correct); in the open space between the palace and the Scala Santa, in the hills that show in the distance only here. The 'corrections' and the added details reveal that Bellotto actually visited the site. His drawing of the same composition in the British Royal Collection is more faithful to Canaletto's view (cat. 48).
Rationality as well as the compositional choices are also evident in the style and technique but the effect is one of poetic melancholy, created by the silvery range of colours in various shades of beige, grey and green, with clear contours to the shadows, and the sky crossed by leaden and pink clouds on the horizon and purple outlines of the hills. The description of the Loggia delle Benedizioni is a veritable signature of the artist, marked by a concentrated quest to make clear every shade of the architectural structures shrouded in shadow.
The minute and lively figures are part of the scene in the square, and are rendered with the typical colours of Bellotto's pallet: blue, lilac and mustard yellow. Their contours are highlighted with dense brushstrokes of white lead, and they are of a type so close to those of Canaletto as to justify the attribution to Bellotto's master for a long time.
The pendant to this work has not been identified with certainty; it is perhaps lost, and was probably the view of *The Basilica di Santi Domenico e Sisto, Rome,* depicted in the drawing now in the British Royal Collections, which was a pendant, in turn, of the sheet with the composition for this painting (cf. cat. 48).

Bożena Anna Kowalczyk

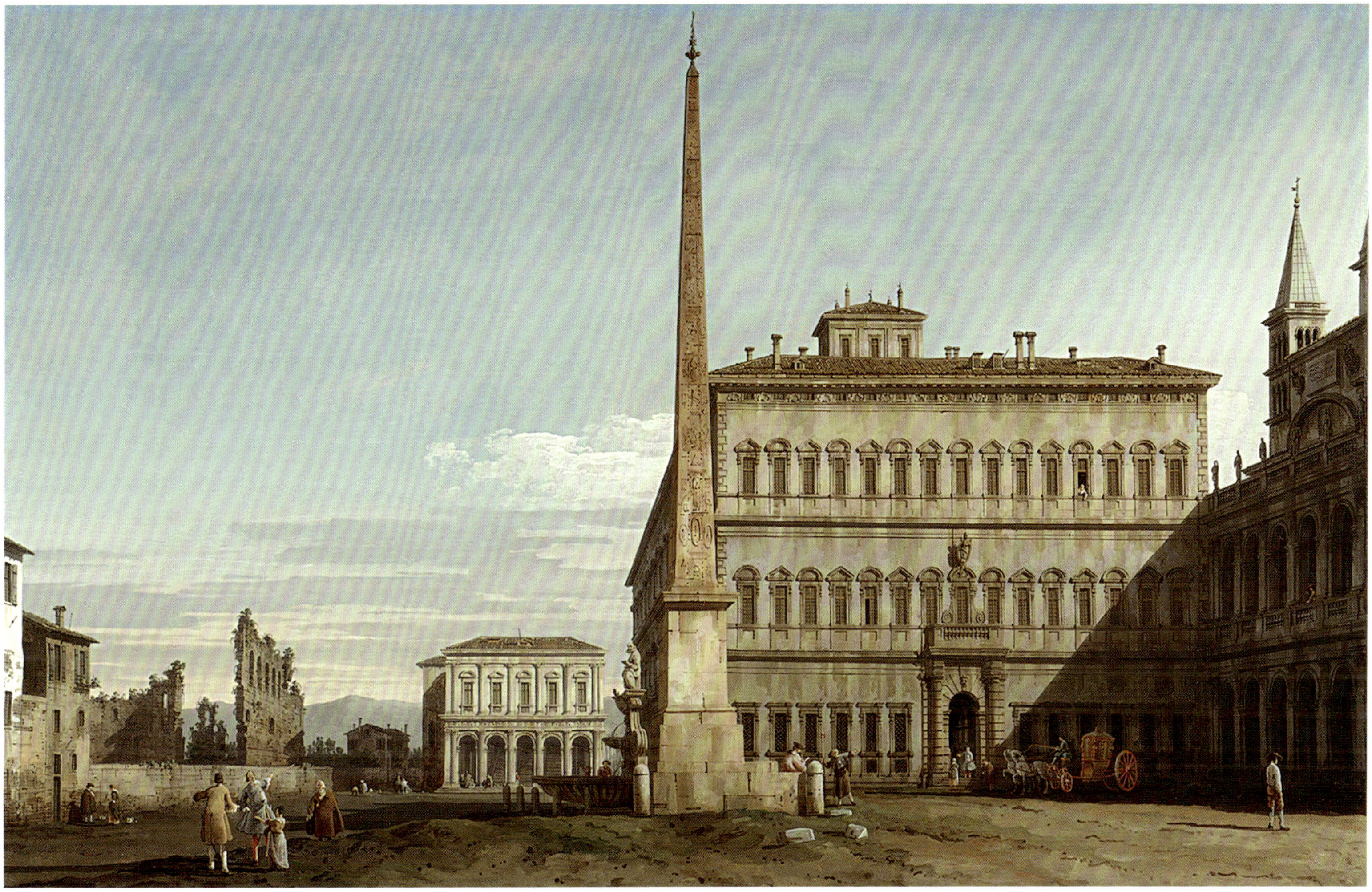

BERNARDO BELLOTTO

(Venice 1722 – Warsaw 1780)

The Piazza San Giovanni in Laterano, Rome
1743

pen and dark grey ink with grey wash over pencil, free and ruled pencil and pinpointing; first outlined in pencil and ruler, then reinforced in pen; 199 x 284 mm
The Royal Collection / HM Queen Elizabeth II, RCIN 907517

K.T. Parker noted that this drawing is the pendant to the sheet depicting *The Basilica di Santi Domenico e Sisto, Rome* in terms of size, style and technique, and like the latter commissioned by Joseph Smith and today part of the Royal Collection in Britain with an attribution to Canaletto (P [C] 110); the compositions of both derive from the early drawings by Canaletto from the series of twenty-three drawings brought home from the journey to Rome in 1719–1720 and now conserved, with the exception of one, in the British Museum, London (C/L 713–241 and 234). However, a painted version (cat. 47) is known only of the present drawing. Studying the drawings in the British Museum for the *Canaletto prima maniera* exhibition – which displayed twelve of them – H. Chapman recognised the hand of Bellotto in this drawing. The composition introduces a few changes with respect to the drawing by Canaletto: the Lateran Palace is less vertical, the diagonal shadow on its facade longer and some new figures make an appearance. Moved from the Circus Maximus in 1588, the ancient Egyptian obelisk constitutes the vertical axis of the view, like in Canaletto's drawings, and arranged to fit together with the corner of the Lateran Palace, flanked by the fountain with the statue of the seated Saint John but without the Medici lilies added by Taddeo Landini in 1605 on commission to Pope Leo XI; the Scala Santa is extended and the tympanum above the lower order of windows do not correspond to reality. These free adaptations and inaccuracies were then corrected in the painting.
Originating from the Lovelace Collection and traditionally attributed to Canaletto, the picture was given to Bellotto by the present writer in a PhD thesis (1993–1996). The artist introduces a space between the Palazzo Laterano and the Scala Santa and presents all five arches of the Loggia delle Benedizioni of the Basilica di San Giovanni in Laterano; he also inserts new figures and a carriage. The diagonal shadow is the same length as that of the British Museum drawing.
In this sheet, the stylistic proximity to Canaletto is disconcerting, especially in the figures, but it is typical Bellotto with his excessive and zealous graphic stress in the description of the hieroglyphs, in the nervously frayed contours of the clouds, and in the swaying lines of the ruins of Nero's aqueduct. The careful drawing in pencil and ruler, with the aid of a compass – clearly visible on the facade of the Lateran Palace, but also on the obelisk, vertically, to give order to the hieroglyphics – expresses Bellotto's approach to precision in the construction of a work. The grey wash creates an opaque effect which also come across in other drawings shaded with this technique; it is interesting to note that the diagonal shadow on the Lateran Palace is twice outlined.
The attribution of some drawings to Bellotto among the 139 sheets sold – like this one – by Joseph Smith in 1762 to the British crown in the album of *Experimenta et Schedae (Volume di Dissegni di Antonio Canale…)* is an achievement of studies conducted in recent years. It seems impossible that it should have been Canaletto himself to present Smith with some drawings by Bellotto under his own name; we are therefore tempted to believe, with A. Corboz who first posed the question, 'that in the packet of Canalettos ... Smith slipped in a few sheets by Bellotto'. Today we can be certain that the British Consul was able to distinguish between the two hands not only as a patron of Canaletto but also of his young nephew. This drawing and its companion piece, *The Basilica di Santi Domenico e Sisto, Rome*, may have been commissioned in memory of paintings sold, in like manner to some drawings by Canaletto in his collection.

Bożena Anna Kowalczyk

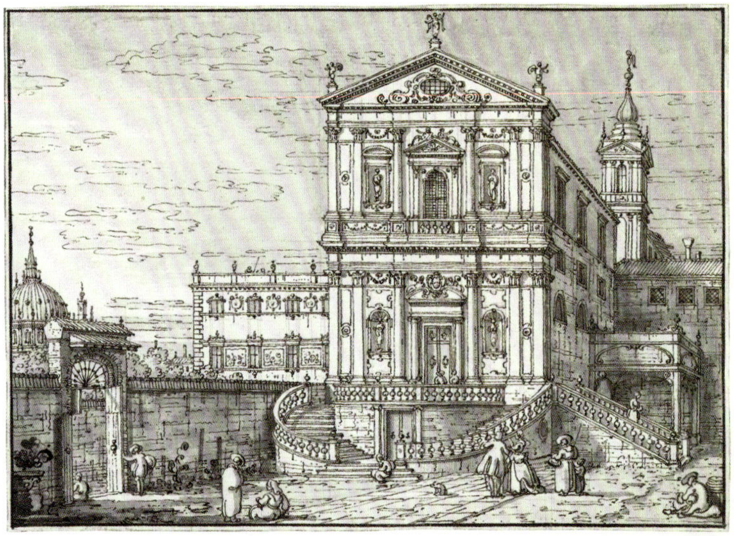

a. Bernardo Bellotto, *The Basilica di Santi Domenico e Sisto, Rome*, 1742–1745, pen and black ink with grey wash over pencil, 199 x 282 mm.
The Royal Collection, RCIN 907518

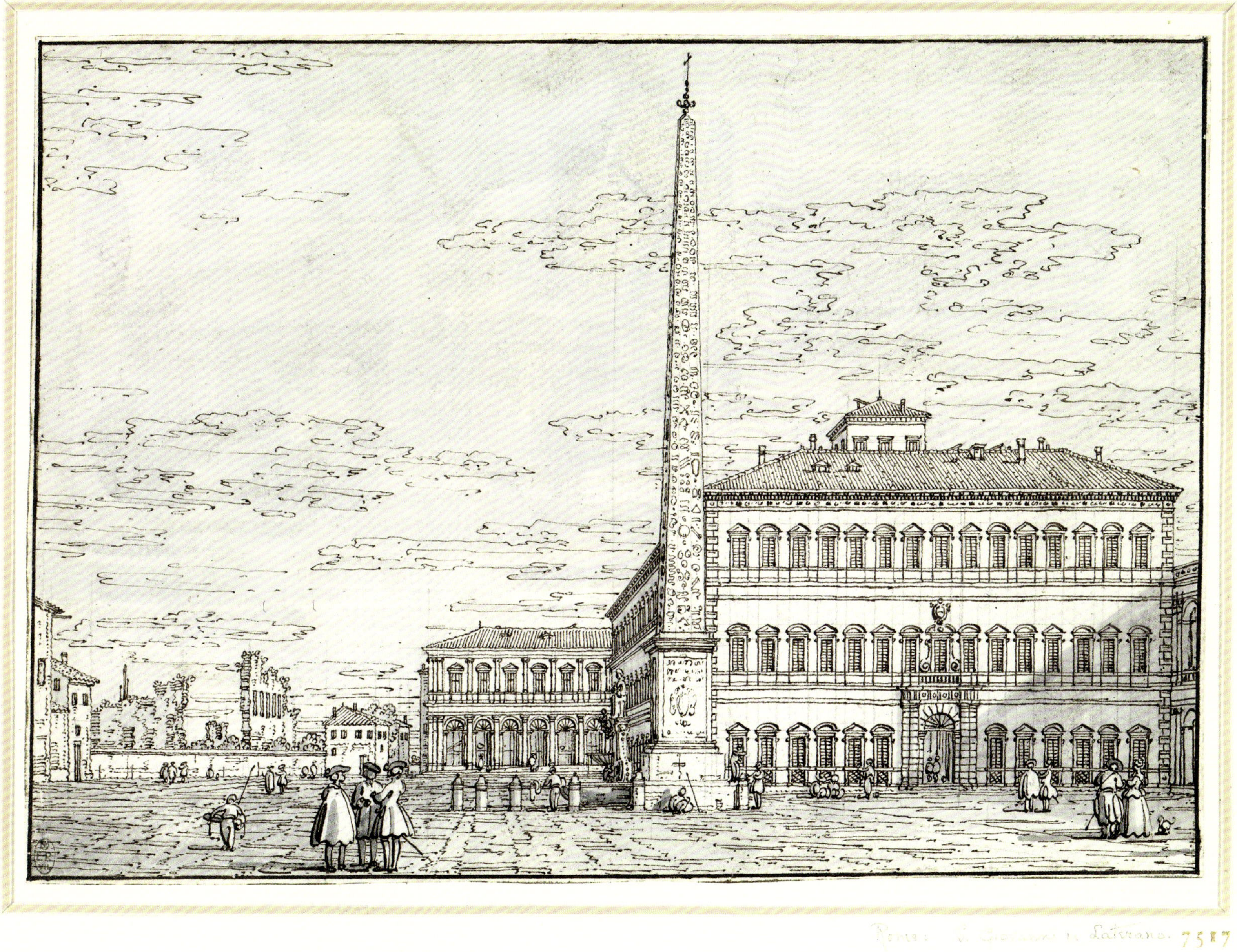
in Laterano. 7587

49

BERNARDO BELLOTTO

(Venice 1722 – Warsaw 1780)

The Piazza Navona looking North, Rome
1743

oil on canvas; 88 x 149 cm
Private Collection

The Piazza Navona, the ancient stadium of Domitian – unavoidable subject of Roman landscape painting, defined by etchings by Giambattista Falda (1675) and Gomar Wouters (1693) – appears in a series of paintings by Gaspar van Wittel (1652/1653–1736), which he began to paint starting from 1688, all based on the same drawing (Briganti 1996, p. 145, nos. 36–34 and pp. 394–395, no. D 312). Bellotto portrays the *piazza* from a perspective similar to that of the Dutch landscape painter, from the same window of Palazzo Lancellotti – focusing, however, on Bernini's fountain of the Four Rivers, which is surmounted by a Roman obelisk from the circus of Maxentius. Bellotto omits the fountain of the Moor, in the foreground in van Wittel's work. With the rigorous perspective and ironclad logic that distinguish him, he highlights other important monuments in the square, those built or planned during the papacy of Innocent X Pamphili (1644–1655): Palazzo Pamphili, completed by Gerolamo Rainaldi around 1652, and the church of Sant'Agnese in Agone, designed by Francesco Borromini, who oversaw the works until 1657.
The composition was prepared in an accurate overview sketch housed in the Darmstadt Museum, produced in the atelier but completed 'in the sky' by detailed studies of one of the church towers and a window of Palazzo Pamphili. The sheet of squared paper, with no figures drawn, indicates the shaded areas and writings that mark the various architectural elements – doors, overdoors, steps and columns – and their frequency. When von Hadeln was amongst the first to study Bellotto's drawings at the Darmstadt Museum, this very drawing and the view of the Forum represented the focal points in style and method to tell the difference from Canaletto (Hadeln 1929, p. 8).
In the painting, exactly four times as large as the drawing, Bellotto recalls the indications set out on paper. However, he attaches more importance to the church of Sant'Agnese, raising its towers and describing it in minute detail, in the morning light and against the shadow falling – from the buildings on the right – almost to brush against the flight of steps in front of the church. Bellotto's vivid interest in the sensitive, restless Borromini – quite surprising in a Venetian landscape painter – is our favourite explanation for his particularly dramatic and spectacular view of the *piazza*, with its succession of shadow and light, a colour change in the shadow cast against the houses in the background giving way to the beam of light cast from a side street on the right, which illuminates the figures in the *piazza* as if they were actors in a puppet theatre. It was probably in Rome that Bellotto purchased Borromini's volume of plans and drawings. Published in 1720, it was part of his Dresden library (cat. 83).
The recent high-resolution imaging by infrared scanner carried out by the Italian National Institute of Optics – supervised by Raffaella Fontana and analysed and interpreted by Maurizio Zecchini – highlight the extraordinary pictorial quality of Bellotto's techniques. Bellotto completed the details of the architectures, mouldings, gables and bas-relief decorations freehand, over the precise design of architectural lines – only visible in certain parts, and probably done in graphite with the aid of a ruler and later gone over again with a very fine brush. The several small figures which clearly follow the Canaletto's patterns, were painted after the architectures were finished, as shown by the appearance of the latter against the light, but the use of pigments that do not always feature infrared permeability makes it difficult to pinpoint the phase in which they were realized. While the drawing presents the obelisk drawn in ink above the houses in pencil, in the painting, instead, Bellotto uses colour freehand over the already finished architectures (fig. a, b). The most astonishing part is the facade of the church of San Giacomo degli Spagnoli, to the far right. It was painted last of all, freehand and almost irrespective of the drawing (fig. c, d).
Canaletto painted a view of piazza Navona towards the end of his English sojourn, in 1754–55, based – like its pendant, *Il Quirinale, Rome* – on Wouters' prints (now at the Tokyo Fuji Museum; C/L 401). Interestingly, he includes the same pair of friars seen here near Bernini's fountain.

Bożena Anna Kowalczyk

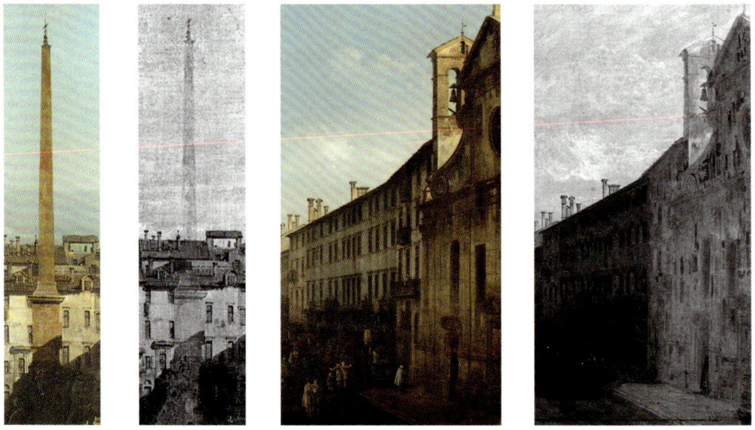

a-d. Detail photographed in natural light and in infrared light at 1830 nm.

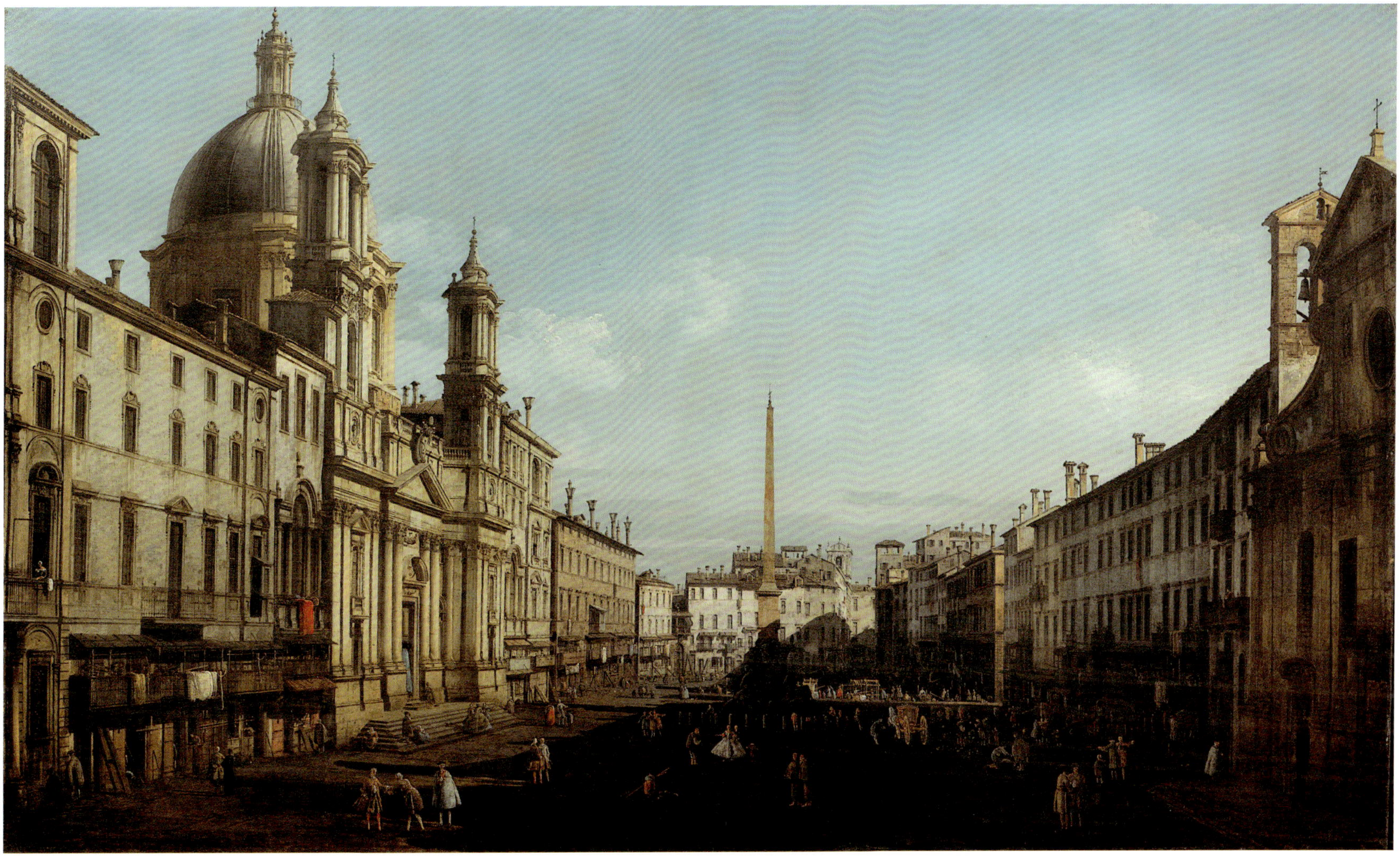

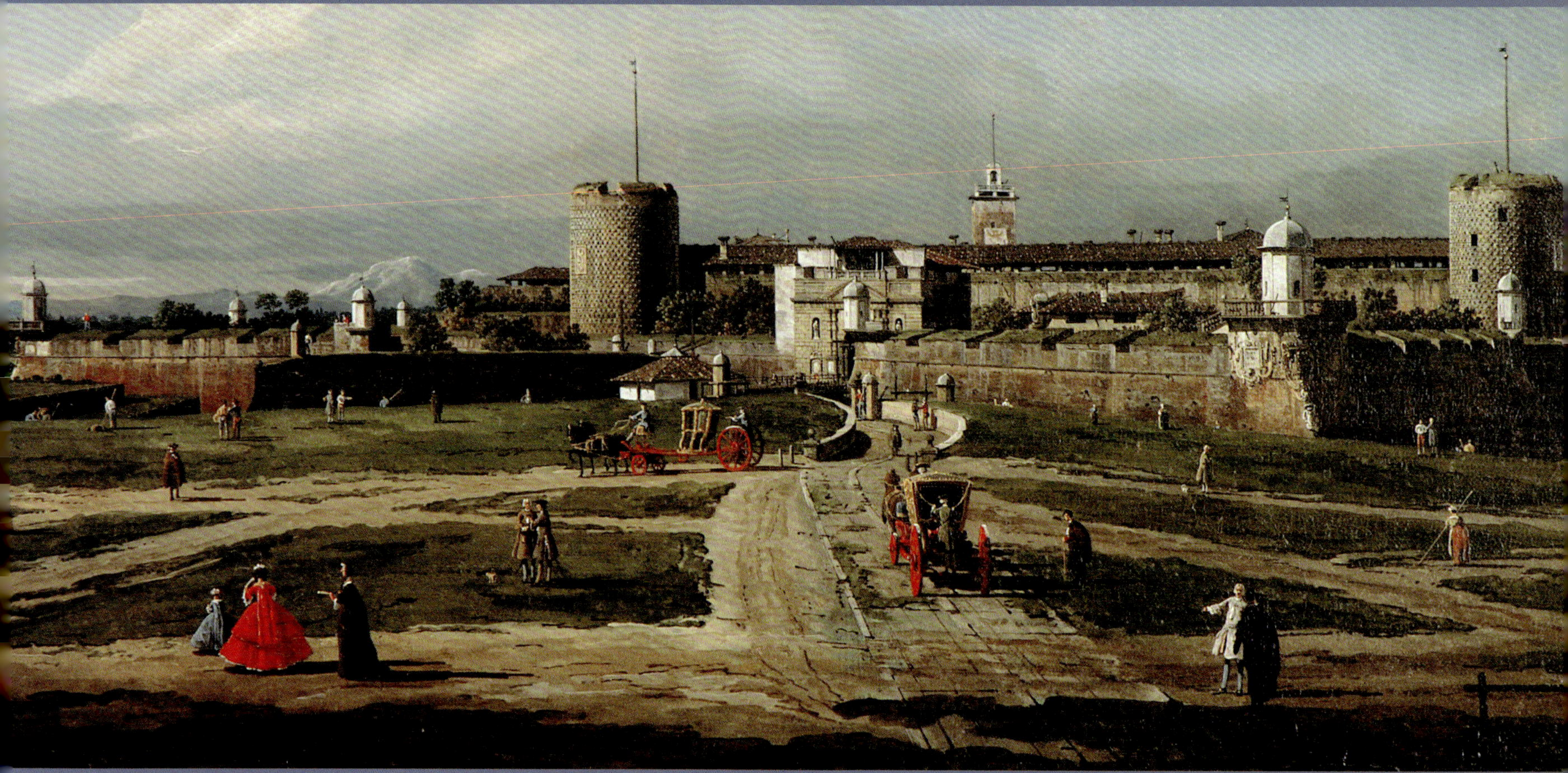

6.
BELLOTTO: BOLD PERSPECTIVES

After Rome and Florence, in the mid-1740s Bellotto confirmed his compositional independence in his views of Milan, Turin and Verona. 'Le più cospicue prospettive' (The more substantial views) of these cities, depicted from carefully considered points of view and documenting aspects that are now changed, are valuable documents for the cities they portray. In the beautiful *Castello Sforzesco, Milan* (cat. 51), the castle, with its towers and fortifications, spreads out to the horizon, serving as the backdrop for a field furrowed by strips of beaten earth, in a composition that recalls the Paduan houses and churches in Canaletto's print *Prà della Valle*. But the idea to depict the castle from the less-representative side, the Piazza d'Armi, projecting it against the city, was a wholly original, intentional choice.
The perspective chosen for *The Palazzo dei Giureconsulti and the Broletto Nuovo, Milan* (cat. 52), with the cathedral far off in the distance, cramped in the background, is stunning. Even if the canvas was cut, as some believe (although I do not believe that it necessarily was), its view of the Palazzo dei Giureconsulti, with the corner of the Palazzo della Ragione in the foreground, is a demonstration of virtuosity and beyond comparison.
The telescope perspective of the churches of *San Paolo Converso and Sant'Eufemia, Milan* (cat. 50) recalls that of *Piazza San Martino with the Cathedral, Lucca*, which Bellotto painted in 1740. But the emphasis on the facade of San Paolo crowned by statues of angels is an element of new, exuberant creativity.
In *The Old Bridge over the Po River, Turin* (cat. 53) the choice of perspective is the most brilliant of Bellotto's entire repertoire up to that point. It was his most carefully considered and prepared painting to date, the work of an Enlightenment painter and historian who wanted to reveal a city, even at the cost of forcing the perspective. With this work and the amazing pendant, *The Royal Palace, from the Garden Side*, followed shortly after by the *Castelvecchio and the Ponte Scaligero, Verona* (cat. 54) depicted from an ideal spot on the Regaste di San Zeno in order to capture the two military structures in their full extension and beauty, Bellotto demonstrated his readiness to take on the great cities of Europe, in his role as a fully independent view painter.

50

BERNARDO BELLOTTO

(Venice 1722 – Warsaw 1780)

San Paolo Converso and Sant'Eufemia, Milan
1744

oil on canvas; 61 x 97 cm
Private Collection

The stay in Lombardy marks one of the most felicitous moments in Bernardo Bellotto's career. New light has been shed in recent years on patronage in Lombardy and on the circumstances of the commissions. It was an Enlightenment Milan that invited and welcomed this emerging painter; already European, he was not selected as a replacement for Canaletto, his uncle, but for his own qualities, as proven by the views of Venice, Rome and Florence. The Lombard collecting world was a special one that sought pictures of their villas and loved sites, a tradition already established with Gaspar van Wittel, invited during his journey of 1694 to paint Vaprio and Isola Bella, and which would continue with Francesco Zuccarelli (1702–1788), who in ca. 1750 painted a series of bucolic images of the Borromeo properties.

It was the Milanese friendships of Anton Maria Zanetti di Girolamo that facilitated the journey. The Archbishop of Milan, Giuseppe Pozzobonelli, who was in contact with the marchese Andrea Gerini, responsible for commissioning four views of Florence from Bellotto, was probably the main artifice. And it was he who commissioned this painting, perhaps the first of the three noted views of Milan, and its pendant, *Vaprio and Canonica on the Adda, looking North-West, Lombardy* mentioned in 1802 by Andrea Appiani and Alessandro Bellinzaghi in the inventory of the Pozzobonelli collection in the Archbishop's Palace: 'Two paintings, one depicting a view of the monastery of the Monache di San Paolo, the other a view of Vaprio with boats' (Bona Castellotti 1991). Still Venetian in compositional structure, also tested in the Tuscan views of 1740 (cf. cat. 19), with the shadowed area in the foreground and figures seen against the light, it stands apart in its mature technique and a fascinating structuring of light, first tested in the views of Rome. It offers an extraordinary picture of eighteenth-century Milan, with the earthen square adorned with two churches, the early Christian church of Sant'Eufemia with its basilica-like facade and medieval bell tower, and the Baroque San Paolo Converso, with the side in shade punctuated by Corinthian pilasters and the facade of 1611–1619 by Giovanni Battista Crespi (1573–1632).

The low-angled light shapes the architectural elements of the two facades, giving a three-dimensional sense to the play of timpani, columns, capitals and the three dramatic statues of angels on top of San Paolo Converso. The site was of particular importance for the archbishop: in comparing the picture with the print by Marcantonio Dal Re (1697–1766), made perhaps a few years earlier, the binocular-like perspective pushes back the basilica – it was here that Federigo Borromeo, nephew of Charles, his predecessor at the archdiocese of Milan, was baptised – to highlight San Paolo Converso, where his brother Gian Claudio was a regular cleric and two nieces nuns in the convent of La Maddalena, to which the open door leads. One of the painter's finest effects of light accompanies the entry of a noblewoman in a luxurious carriage preceded by a rider; this is probably his sister, Innocenza Pozzobonelli, the wife of Gregorio Visconti. If this is correct, her presence would explain the choice of pendant, in which the Visconti villa of Vaprio, a country retreat belonging to the family, is depicted in the foreground on the Naviglio (Olivari, in Milan 1999–2000). Bellotto attaches such importance to this episode, showing it in every detail and passage of light, as to make the other rare figures in the square mere walk-on extras.

In the pendant, for the first time, the artist proudly adds his signature: 'Bernard.° Bellott.° det.° Canaletto'; the two paintings share their history until the sale at Christie's in 1971; on 3 December 1997, again at Christie's (lot 90), the Vaprio view was purchased by an American collector.

San Paolo Converso appears today as it does in the painting by Bellotto, apart from the three angels that have disappeared, but Sant'Eufemia was extensively rebuilt and added to by Enrico Terzaghi, and now has a neo-Romanesque facade dating from 1870; corso Italia was opened at the beginning of the twentieth century.

Bożena Anna Kowalczyk

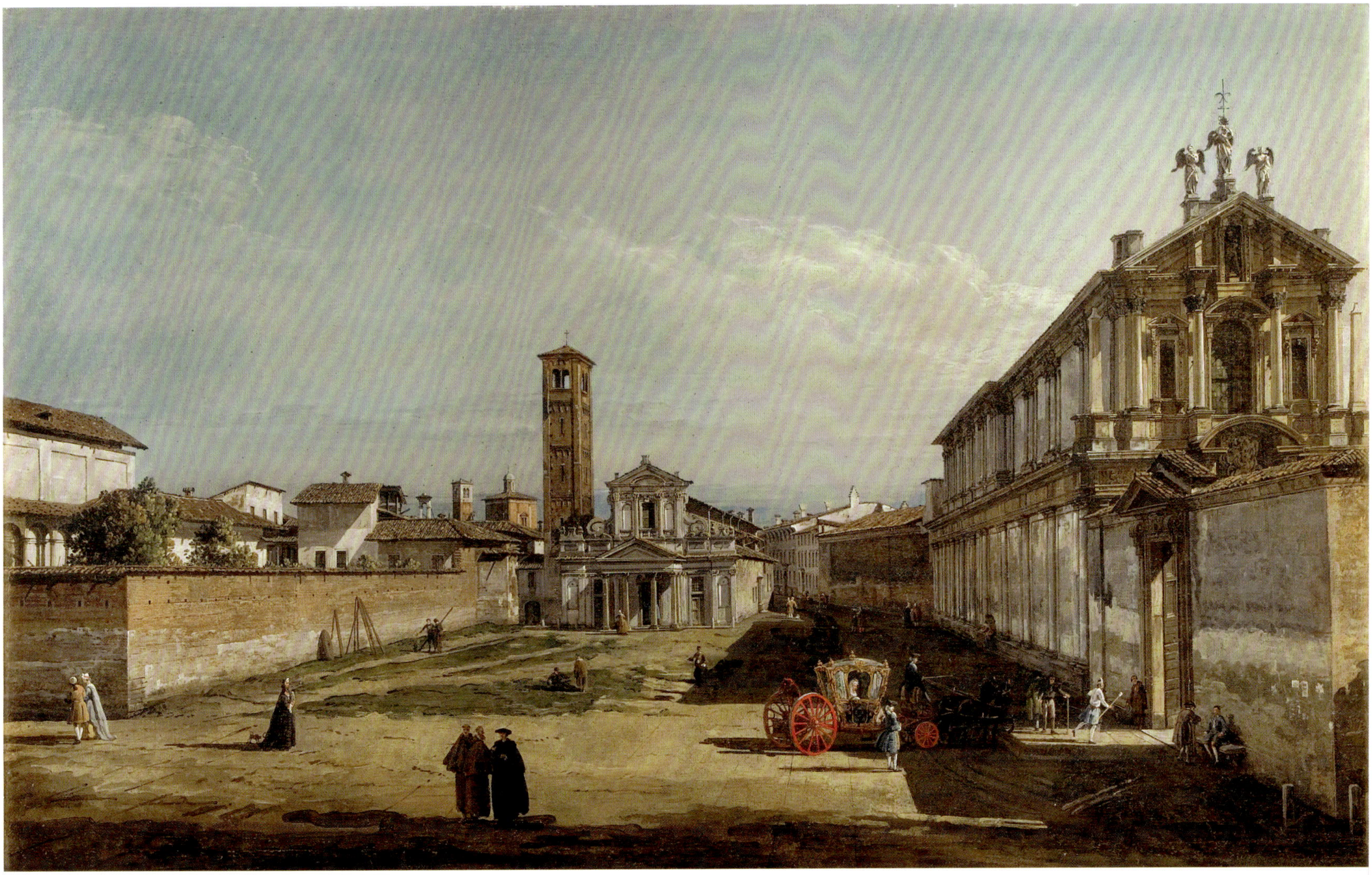

51

BERNARDO BELLOTTO

(Venice 1722 – Warsaw 1780)

The Castello Sforzesco, Milan
1744

oil on canvas; 61 x 97.5 cm
Castle Náměšť nad Oslavou (Czech Republic), The National Heritage Institute, Regional Historic Sites Management in České Budějovice

This sharp image of the Castello Sforzesco, as seen from the parade ground on the opposite side to the entrance through the Filarete tower, is the only one of this major monument and symbol of the history of Milan to show its appearance stone by stone before the destruction of the Spanish ramparts in 1802 under Napoleon and the renovation and alteration works, undertaken in 1890–1900 by architect Luca Beltrami. The sleepy Austrian garrison at the time of Bellotto betrays its military function through the presence of a soldier in Imperial uniform in front of the gatehouse controlling access via the drawbridge over the moat. A tranquil everyday scene takes place in the large area in front, which is partly of earth, partly lawn. This and the churches of *San Paolo Converso and Sant'Eufemia, Milan* in a private collection, of which the present work was considered the companion piece before the discovery of Archbishop Pozzobonelli's inventory (cf. cat. 50), must have been the first paintings produced in Lombardy, because of the proximity of their style to Canaletto, in the way the figures are dotted around the large square, and the space created and in the manner the eye is drawn in via the little red and blue patches of the clothes, together with the luminosity of the scene, and the use of paint that is not yet thick and lumpy. However, the rigour with which the image of the castle has been constructed is typical of Bellotto, as is the livid sky, with low clouds on the horizon and the mountain range with a snowy peak.
The castle, defined in space and down to the tiniest detail through a fine play of light and shadow, appears on the horizon between the two powerful circular towers dating from the times of the Sforzas, adorned with rusticated stones and crests, and distinguished by the amazingly tall flagpoles like the entrance tower. Bellotto deliberately ignored aerial perspective in the rendering of the architecture, seeking effects of a telescopic sharpness, to convey all the details, colour and shape of the terracotta rendering, of the white of the plastering of the turrets, of the coats of arms on the ramparts, in what is a true historical documentation. The castle is projected against the city that appears beyond, like in *The Old Bridge on the Po River, Turin* (cat. 53). The space proceeds from the shaded foreground with the curving of the strip of beaten earth and the other, diagonal, strips that cross each other, like in the paintings of the Venetian *Campi*.
This painting was discovered by S. Kozakiewicz. It belonged to the Haugwitz family, and was housed first in the Plaveč Castle, and later in its current location. Prince Eugene Haugwitz, who distinguished himself in the service of the Habsburg court in Vienna, has been suggested as the potential buyer of the painting when he was in Brescia in 1848 and then in Verona, as commander of an Austrian battalion (M. Olivari, in Verona 1990).

Bożena Anna Kowalczyk

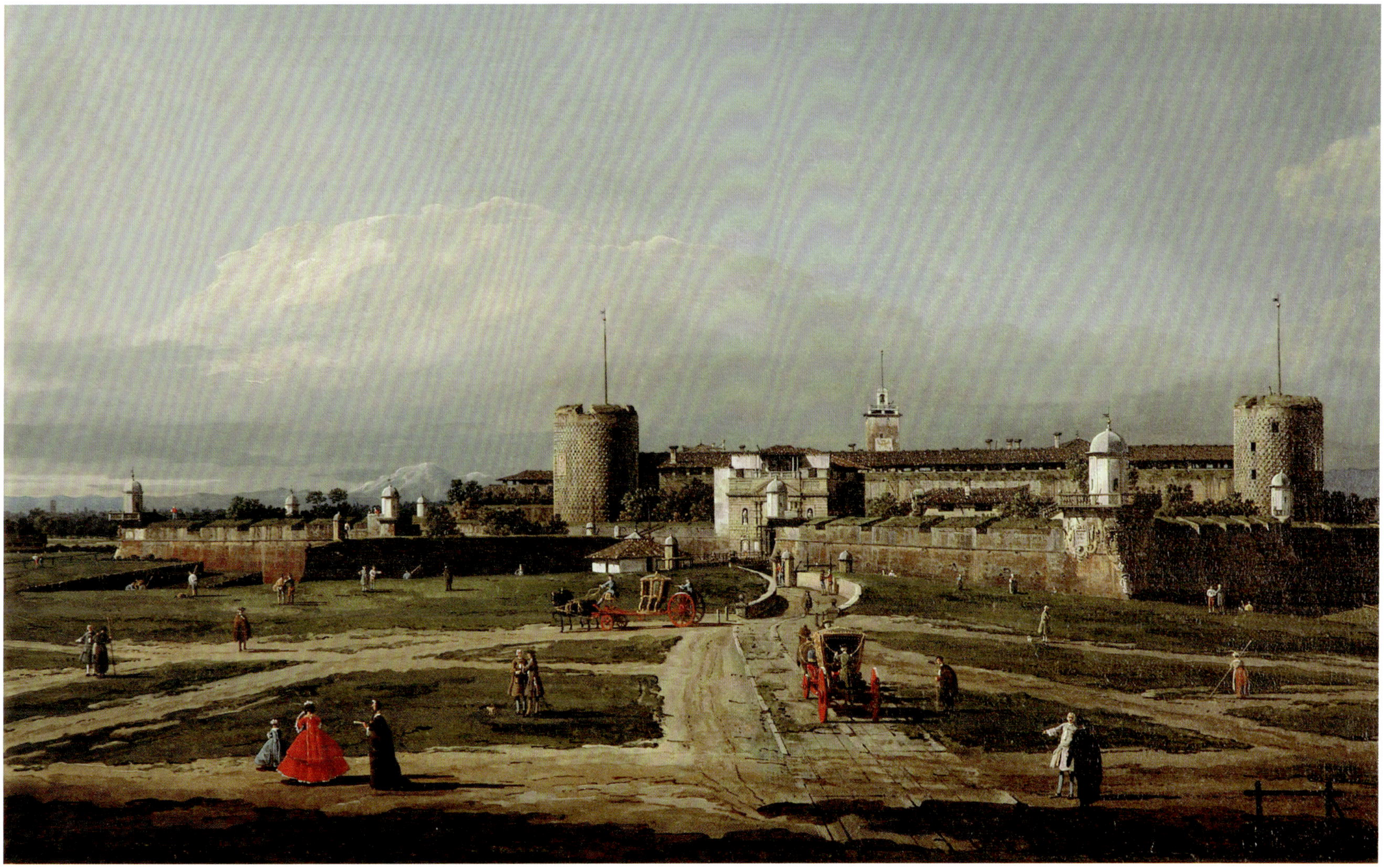

52

BERNARDO BELLOTTO

(Venice 1722 – Warsaw 1780)

The Palazzo dei Giureconsulti and the Broletto Nuovo, Milan
1744

oil on canvas; 71 x 56 cm
Milan, Raccolte d'Arte Antica, Pinacoteca del Castello Sforzesco, 1506

This jewel of Milanese landscape painting makes use of a vertical format to embrace the Palazzo dei Giureconsulti (Dei Nobili Dottori), built starting in 1562 and designed by Vincenzo Seregni. It is depicted in foreshortened perspective offset to the right by the side of the Palazzo della Ragione. The two buildings were the main parts of the Broletto Nuovo, the centre of commerce and city life, closed off by the Pescheria Vecchia at the end. On his visit to Milan, Bellotto noted every detail of the location in this medium-sized canvas, before substantial architectural and urban transformations definitively changed that area of Piazza dei Mercanti. The tower looms above the main entrance; this civic monument was commissioned in 1272 by Napo Torriani, and is shown as it appeared until the renovation of the facade by Enrico Terzaghi in 1859. The monument to Philip II of Spain still had its statue, which was removed in 1799 and replaced in 1833 by the figure of Saint Ambrose. In the shadows on the right, once can see the 'pietra dei falliti', a sixteenth-century well-head replaced in 1767 with a classical base, and in the background there is the bell tower and the old lantern tower of the cathedral, demolished in 1765–1768, to give rise to the pinnacle on which the Madonnina was placed in 1774. In 1867, the Via dei Mercanti between Cordusio and the Duomo was opened.
Bellotto's picture boasts a notable virtuosity. The deep shadow that surrounds the Piazza leaves the higher orders of the two facades to emerge, with the rich decoration of the Palazzo dei Giureconsulti and an essential brick lining of the Palazzo della Ragione, perhaps the finest feature of this work for its the severe beauty. There is a metaphysical lighting of the houses and parts of the Duomo destined to disappear. Bellotto is a master at conveying the appeal of areas in the shade by describing the darkened details here and there, illuminated by sudden flashes of light. The two hajduks in the foreground in their garish red capes, remind us that the Lombard city was under Austrian control.
The first known owner of this fascinating unique work in Bellotto's Milanese repertoire – of the Lombard paintings, this one is the closest to the two views of Gazzada (cat. 60, 61) – was the English nobleman, Thomas Hollis (1720–1774). Francis Haskell draws a profile of him, gleaning information from the two volumes of Francis Blackbourne, *Memoirs of Thomas Hollis, Esq*, published in London in 1780 and from six other volumes of unpublished memoirs in the Houghton Library at Harvard (F. Haskell, in Venice 1982, pp. 77–78). Hollis was 'a rich and eccentric English gentleman of considerable intellectual gifts, who devoted his life to the idea of freedom, fighting strenuously against regimes and absolutist theories in the various European countries'. He collected books, medals and commemorative prints of Republican heroes of the civil war. He travelled twice to Italy, in 1748–49 and in 1750–1753. He also visited Milan and met Joseph Smith, Winckelmann, Francesco Alagarotti and Piranesi.
The canvas appeared with the name of Canaletto – but without a companion piece that must have existed – in a sale at Christie's on 3 May, 1884, under lot 134, consigned by the widow of Edgar Disney, heiress of the English gentleman's collection, with a group of six other views commissioned from Canaletto in London in 1754 and in 1755: *The Interior of the Rotunda at Ranelagh*, in the National Gallery, London, *Saint Paul's Cathedral*, now in the Yale Center for British Art, Paul Mellon Collection, *The Old Bridge in Walton*, the Dulwich Picture Gallery, London, and three others now in several private collections: *The Capitol*, *Westminster Bridge*, *Banqueting House and Holbein Gate, Whitehall* (C/L 420, 422, 441, 396, 437–b, 472). Despite the quality and beauty of these works, Francis Haskell could not understand 'what could have induced a character so out of the ordinary to commission no less than six paintings from the Venetian artist'.
If Hollis had bought this painting by Bellotto during one of his trips in Italy, as it is reasonable to believe, this image of Milanese civic life anticipates the series of Canaletto in his collection and it may be reasonable to suppose that it provided the spark that triggered the intellectual's passion for landscape paintings. It is still unknown who commissioned the work in the first instance, but he must have been Milanese.

Bożena Anna Kowalczyk

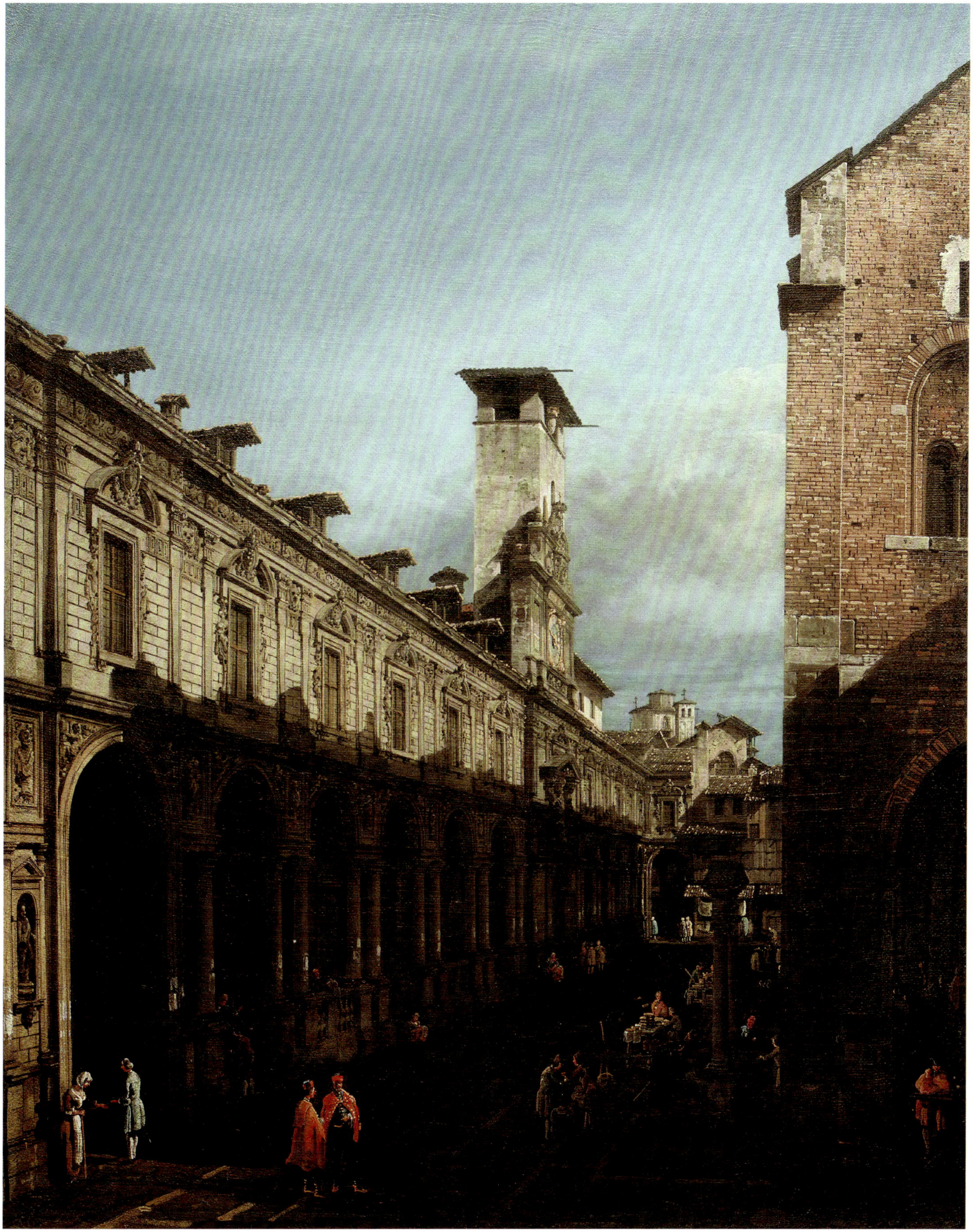

53

BERNARDO BELLOTTO

(Venice 1722 – Warsaw 1780)

The Old Bridge over the Po River, Turin
1745

oil on canvas; 128.5 x 173 cm
Turin, Galleria Sabauda, 469

Inscriptions: signed at lower left, 'BERNARDO. BELLOTO/ D.° IL CANALETTO/ F.e.'.

Bellotto must have arrived in Turin at the very latest during the early months of 1745 to paint the present work and its pendant, *The Palazzo Reale, from the Side of the Garden, Turin*, in the same collection, both of which are of extremely high quality. The vast store of documentary information presented by the Venetian painter in the two canvases – his first panoramas of a European capital – reveals his deep knowledge of the city's architecture and the historical moment. The present painting was documented first on 21 June 1745, with an expense note kept in the accounts of the Real Casa, already known to Baudi de Vesme, totalling 975 liras and specifying the name of the painter, 'Bernardo Bellotto detto il Canaletto', the patron, his majesty, the subject, 'una veduta di questa città' (a view of this city), and the date it was made, 'nel corrente anno' (this year). A similar expense note was issued on 17 July for the pendant, 'una veduta di questa capitale verso li reali giardini e palazzo et altre adiacenze' (a view of this capital city looking towards the royal gardens and palace and other adjacent buildings). For his first royal commission, Bellotto chose a large format and did not hesitate to depict himself in this canvas while making the drawings, a delightful figure, in the company of an ecclesiastic and one thinks of Filippo Juvarra; in this same area he also signed his full name.
In Turin, perhaps more than elsewhere, the Venetian painter acted as a historiographer, not just representing, but also investigating, distinguishing and presenting. The choice of subject for the pendant, the Palazzo Reale, might seem obvious, but the vantage point is brilliant 'from the side of the garden' – where work was humming away for the *Rimodernamento de Reali Appartamenti*, an important and costly project, recorded in the accounts of the Real Casa between 1742 and 1747 –, the expanse of fields with cows and hanging laundry in the foreground, and the city on the horizon. There was a also a specific reason for the choice of the view of the Po river, with the old bridge, the only entry to the city from the hill and from Genoa, built in masonry starting in 1406 and partially destroyed by a flood in 1706. The river was of key importance to the royal house, which built a trade port there, around which emerged in turn the Borgo Po, a residential quarter that supported port activity. Bellotto took pleasure in describing the modest houses on the bank, but the notably extensive view also included noble architecture, the Capuchin monastery on the hill and the sunny road leading up to it, and the far-off Valentino Castle, surrounded by scaffolding.
In both cases, the subjects are closely related to the interests of the painter, who offers us captivating descriptions of the workers on the scaffolding set up in the water of the moat and of the ruined arches of the bridge. He did not omit such picturesque details as the workhorses and the washerwomen, also recording the specifics of the construction of the boats, which have been appreciated by naval historians.
The splendid, dense painting is rich in vignettes and colour, beneath an intense blue sky. The few figures are already charismatic, the subject of careful study, like the produce seller with a yellow hat, sketched multiple times and from different angles on the *verso* of two sheets, one at the J. Paul Getty Museum and the other at the Boymans Museum, Rotterdam, settling in the end for the pose with her back turned to the viewer (C/L 542 and 838). The trees with their tops painted in varied shades of green were rendered with a sensibility that draws on his experience in Gazzada and here as well the freehand outlines stand out in the distance. The architecture and even the stones of the arches were planned out in a precise drawing, as revealed by X-ray photography.
I am convinced that Bellotto's call to Turin – which was of inestimable importance for the city and the artist's career – was engineered by the omnipresent Anton Maria Zanetti di Girolamo (1680–1767), who was in contact with the Sabauda and Vienna courts for the acquisition of the collection of Prince Eugene of Savoy, concluded in 1741.

Bożena Anna Kowalczyk

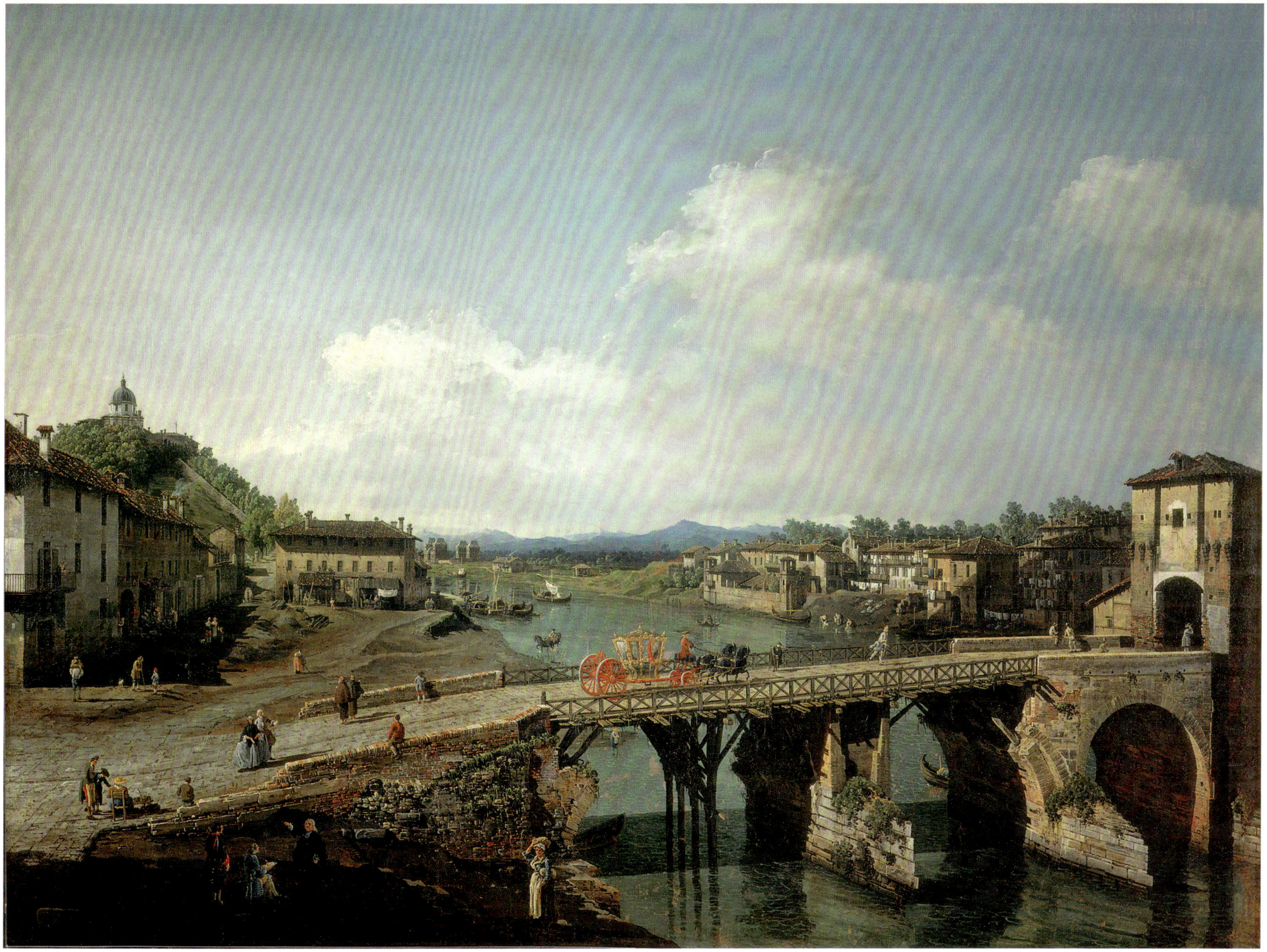

54

BERNARDO BELLOTTO

(Venice 1722 – Warsaw 1780)

Castelvecchio and the Ponte Scaligero, Verona
1745

oil on canvas; 84.5 x 137.5 cm
Verona, Fondazione Cassa di Risparmio di Verona Vicenza Belluno e Ancona, Fondazione Cariverona Collection

Bellotto carefully chose the vantage point on the Regaste di San Zeno in order to depict the Ponte Scaligero from a nearly frontal position and capture its full monumentality. The Castelvecchio and the brown brick bridge spread out majestically, continuing to the horizon, but the city is also present, with the church of Sant'Eufemia to the left in the distance, and, behind the arches of the bridge, the tower of the Lamberti, the bell tower of San Lorenzo and the Palazzo Canossa. The church of San Martino in Aquaro, after which the castle was originally named, is represented by the top of its cusp, which can be seen behind the crenellation. Dramatically lit, with a dark, brooding sky and the river and the houses on its bank invaded by shadows, every detail of the two fortified complexes and the city is presented in its reaction to light, in a play of masterful light transitions typical of Bellotto.
Bellotto's trip to Verona was attested by his first biographer, the Verona painter Pietro Guarienti. The seven views of the river Adige, including the present painting, which is the only one preserved in the city, and their respective drawings provide secure confirmation of this trip, even though one can only hypothesise about the circumstances surrounding it. It was his last trip before his definitive departure for Dresden in April 1747. It is possible that Bellotto stopped in the city – to pick up his drawings – on his return to Turin, in the second half of 1745. As with the other cities he visited, Bellotto's images of Verona were so fascinating and descriptively complete that they became a part of its history. In Verona in particular, he let loose the most lyrical qualities of his painting, which we can also see in his *capricci* with motifs typical of the city, examples being the two drawings attributed to him in the British Royal Collections (cf. cat. 34).
Upon the sale of the collection to Earl Alexis Orlov in Paris in 1920, the painting was separated from its pendant, *Verona with the Castelvecchio and the Ponte Scaligero towards the Adige River*, which is lost (Kozakiewicz 1972a, no. 96). The left side of another view of the bridge at the Philadelphia Museum of Art, initially conceived as a larger version – clearly indicated in the X-ray photo published in Verona 1990, p. 122 – introduces Venetian elements added on a whim and memories of trips to Lucca and Milan on top of the first pictorial layer (Kozakiewicz 1972a, no. 97). In addition to these three images of the fortified city, there are also two monumental panoramas of the River Adige, from the Ponte Nuovo and looking towards the Ponte delle Navi, true masterpieces that were painted 'for England', as Bellotto noted in Italian on the drawing for one of them (Powis Castle, The National Trust, anonymous loan to the National Gallery of Scotland, Edinburgh; Kozakiewicz 1972a, nos. 98 and 101). Bellotto made copies of the panoramas of Verona in the same large format when he arrived in Dresden – the perfect calling card at the Saxon court.

The preparatory drawing for the present painting, preserved at the Hessisches Landesmuseum in Darmstadt (AE 2196), is a precise, richly detailed outline of the composition. A line drawing with no shading, it meticulously records the mills on the river and the reflections of the houses in the water. In the painting, Bellotto eliminated the side of the house to the right, rendering the composition more dynamic, and in place of the knight watering his horse he painted two washerwomen, the same ones that he put in the foreground of the *Capriccio with a triumphal arch* of Columbia Museum of Art (Samuel H. Kress Foundation), which must have been painted just slightly later, considering the memories of Verona it includes and the same dense theme (Kozakiewicz 1972a, n. 133).

Bożena Anna Kowalczyk

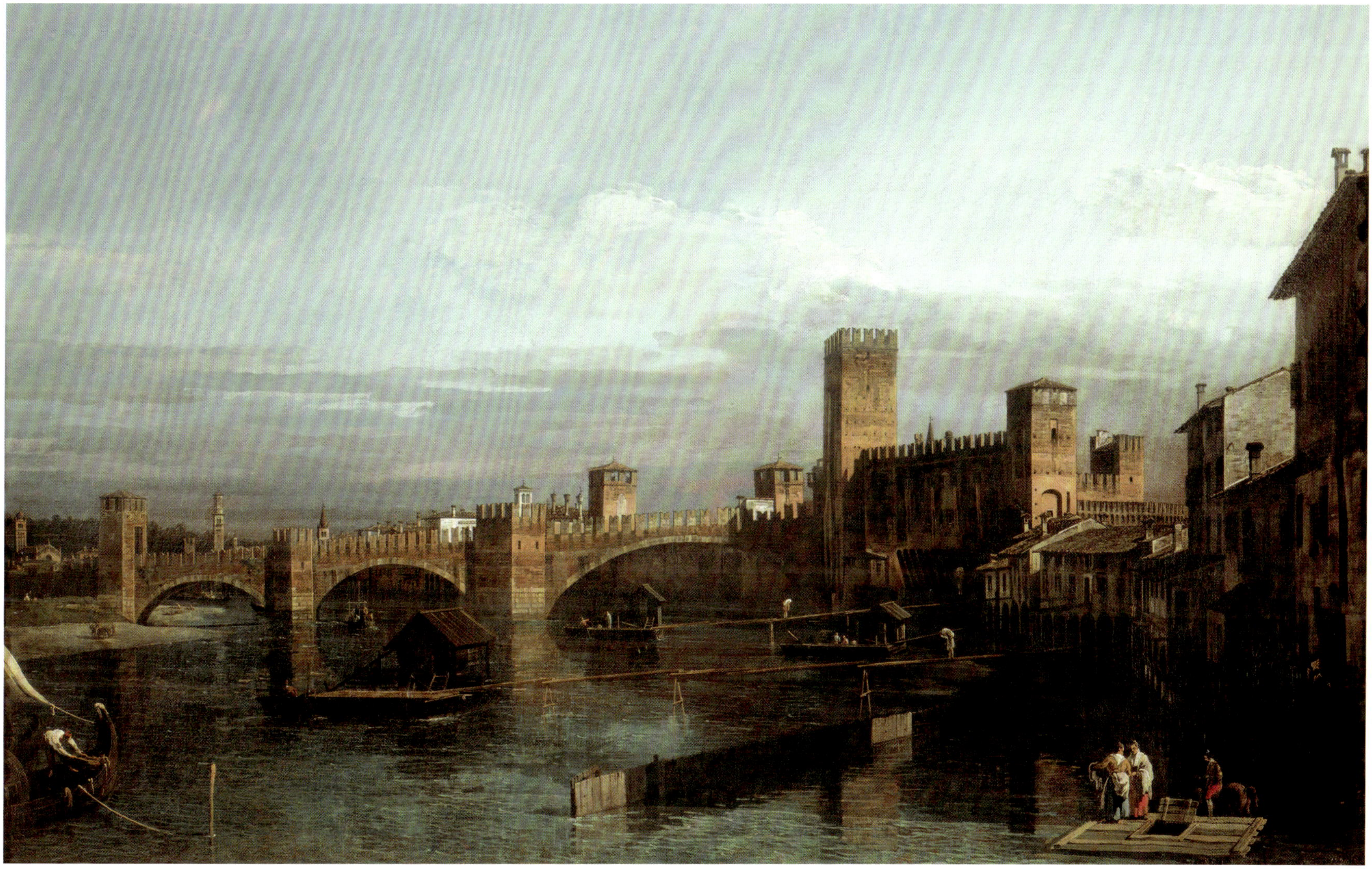

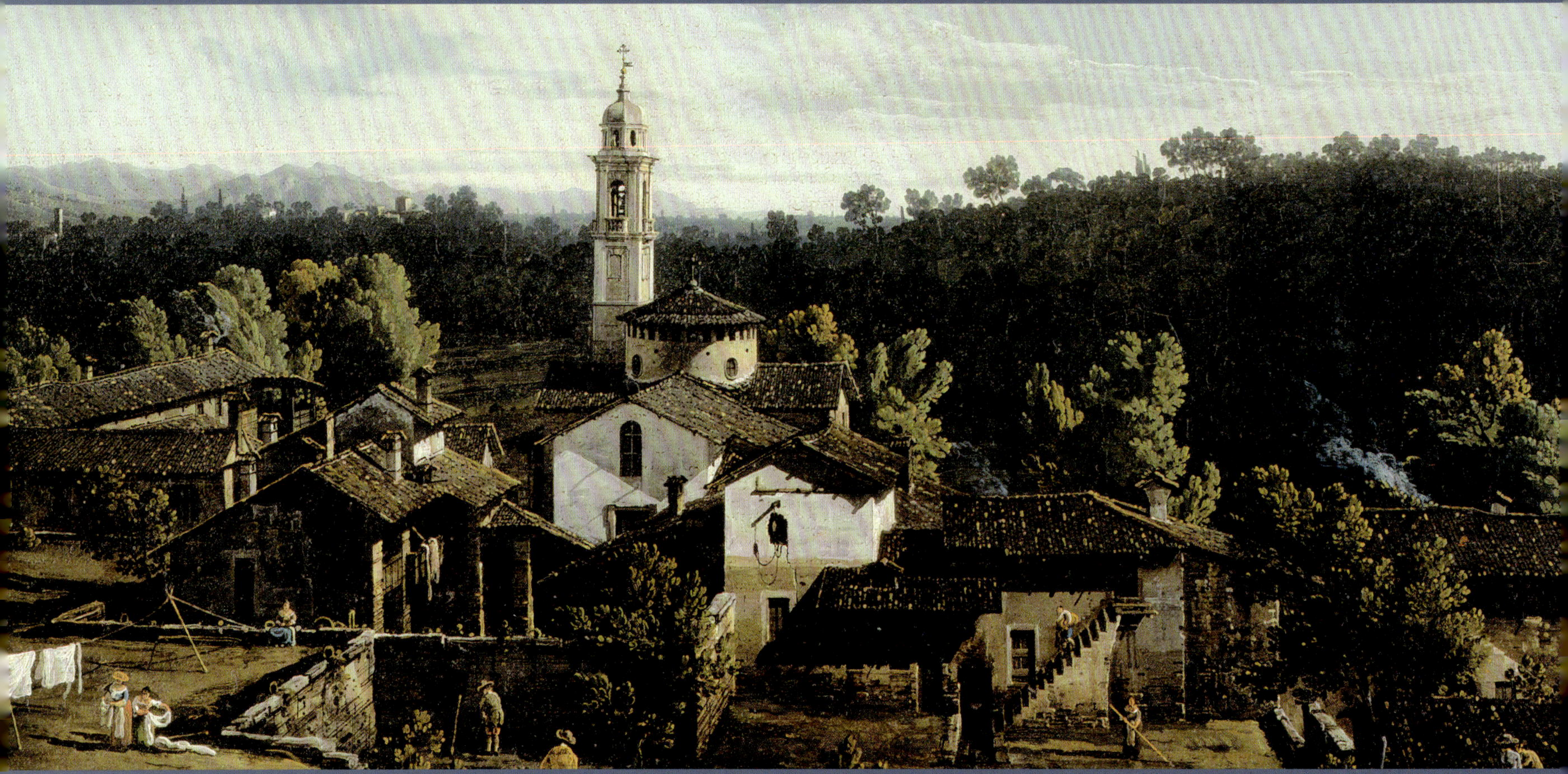

7.
LANDSCAPE

During his sojourn in England (ca. 1746–1755), Canaletto showed himself to be sensitive to the beauty of the landscape around the castles, along the Thames, in Windsor and in Eton, giving it a stylised appearance that complements the sophisticated look of the architecture (cat. 66).
For Bellotto, the commissions for views of Lombardy in 1744 were his first opportunity to live in close contact with nature. Fascinated by the natural beauty of the places, he studied their forms and reaction to light. He was keenly interested in the tall cypresses and bushes along the Adda, and in Gazzada he recorded the varied shades of green around the villa and village and on the hills in the distance and reproduced the rows of trees against the light profile of the hills and the ones standing out on the hilltops (cat. 60, 61). Throughout his travels in Europe, he continued his close observation of the landscape, which became a unavoidable backdrop for his rendering of the panoramas of cities and castles, in Dresden, Vienna and Nymphenburg, almost like a lyrical escape from the foregrounds. In Pirna, a Saxon city south-east of Dresden, he searched for points of view and compositional solutions that gave the landscape an importance equal to that of the architecture. He depicted the real shapes of the trees, studied the reflections on the water and also introduced cows and flocks of sheep, borrowing the motif from the prints of Nicolaes Berchem. His compositions were unprecedented, but his depiction of boundless panoramas and the play of light and shadows projected by the high clouds suggests that he must have studied paintings by the seventeenth-century Dutch painters Jan van den Goyen (1596–1656), Philiphs Koninck (1619–1688) and Jacob van Ruisdael (1628/29–1682), all of whom were represented in collections in Saxony. In his final years, in Warsaw, landscape was the subject of two large views – *The Wilanów Meadows, Warsaw* (cat. 97) and its pendant, *Warsaw, View of Ujazdów* – and four paintings of the castle of Wilanów, in which the garden is the main focus, a symphony of green (cat. 65). Green was his favourite colour, a preference that emerges in his descriptions of his flat in Dresden (*Catalogo de Danni*, cat. 83). Comparing these final masterpieces with the early Gazzada landscapes, we see that Bellotto had developed a deep feeling of participation in nature and achieved the faithful rendering of its true forms.

55

BERNARDO BELLOTTO

(Venice 1722 – Warsaw 1780)

Vaprio and Canonica on the Adda, looking North-West, Lombardy
1744

oil on canvas; 4.1 x 99.7 cm
New York, The Metropolitan Museum, Joseph Pulitzer Bequest, 1939, 39.142

Vaprio, Canonica and Monasterolo, picturesquely situated between Bergamo and Milan on the river Adda where the Brembo joins it, and from which the Naviglio Martesana leads all the way to Milan, were the favourite resorts of the Milanese aristocracy at the time of Bellotto.

Bellotto was called on to paint the beauties of the site not in the place of Canaletto but as a popular emerging artist, on the recommendation of Anton Maria Zanetti di Girolamo and of the Florentine Marquis Andrea Gerini, his first patrons. Earl Antonio Simonetta (1759), the Habsburgs' chamberlain in Milan and owner of a large estate in Monasterolo, Villa Contessa, commissioned a pair of paintings, this one and its pendant, *Vaprio and Canonica on the Adda, looking South, Lombardy* (cat. 56). The Archbishop of Milan, Giuseppe Pozzobonelli (1696–1783), commissioned the view of *Vaprio and Canonica on the Adda, looking North-West, Lombardy*, from the promenade along the Naviglio (canal) that runs alongside the Adda at a higher level, here in the shade, now in a private collection in New York, together with a view of Milan (cf. cat. 50). Bellotto then repeated the compositions for another client, perhaps a traveller on the Grand Tour, delighted by the picturesqueness of the location, as was Mme du Bocage in the famous passage in her works cited by M. Olivari (in Verona 1990) (cat. 57, 59).

From the east bank of the Adda the view extends to Monasterolo behind the row of cypresses and on to the Alps behind Bergamo on the horizon; Vaprio can be seen on the left, with the Villa Visconti Archinto near the river, and the Villa Melzi dominating the heights above the hanging gardens, its facade in shadow; on the opposite bank, there are the houses and bell tower of Canonica. A clear, lunar light illuminates the facades of the houses and steeples, leaving the thick vegetation in the shade and slipping over the tops of the trees along the river. Various shades of green prevail. There is a solitary boat on the gleaming, gloomy water.

In all his Lombard views, Bellotto surprises for his boldness and innovation. Here, we are struck by the simplicity of the construction of space through the alternation of areas that are illuminated and others immersed in shadow. Once again, the precision of the landscape artist is confirmed, accompanied here by an admirable participation and contemplation of the spectacle of nature.

As Pietro Zampetti first noticed, the colourful group of noblemen under the tree with silvery leaves, and the peasant woman standing on the boat are an addition by another painter, suggested by Sergio Marinelli to be Mattia Bortoloni (1695–1750), who at the time was working in the nearby Villa Rasmi at Cavenago (M. Olivari, in Milan 1999–2000). The intervention is in exquisite colours, and in a rococo style with an Arcadian flavour, and perhaps intended by the client to recall that this was a place of leisure and entertainment; the addition of a military encampment in the pendant instead remembers the war that was then under way. The sky has also been attributed to another hand: the romantic look, which is unusual for Bellotto, is due in large part to extensive restoration.

An exceptional documentation accompanies the two pendants, the drawings that are signed and dated 1744 and indicate the name of the buyer. The two sheets at the Darmstadt Museum (AE 2215 and 2216) along with another of Warsaw (cat. 58) represent the Italian views that Bellotto considered to be among the most important and appealing; indeed, he took them with him to Vienna in a folder of selected drawings, thereby saving them from destruction. Each is called a 'copia dela vista di Vaver' (copy of the view of Vaver, dialectal name of Vaprio). In the case of this painting and of the pendant, it is important to know if Bellotto really painted the figures that were sketched in the drawings, and which were subsequently covered by Bortoloni. The trace is clearly visible to the naked eye against the water, in the same position as in the Darmstadt drawing (fig. a), and some residues of colour can be made out at the same point as the sketched figures in the sheet, between the two gentlemen on the shore and between the lady and the knight to her left. Only a thorough technical investigation will confirm what we can already sense with the naked eye.

Bożena Anna Kowalczyk

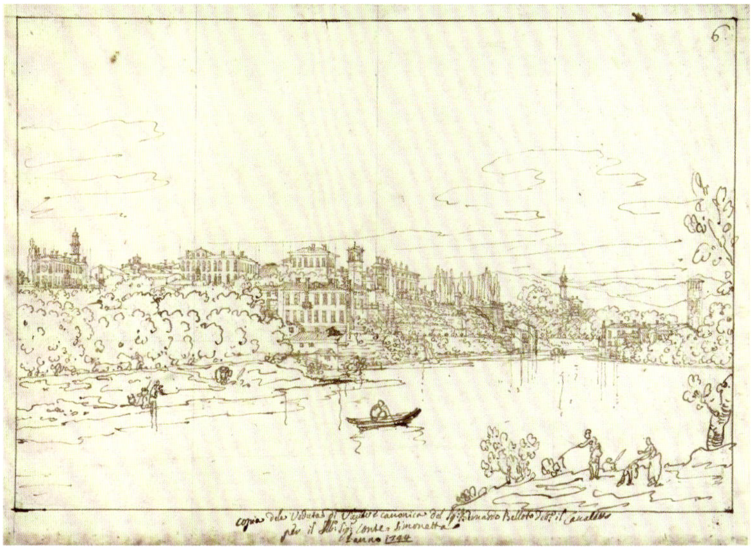

a-Bernardo Bellotto, *Vaprio and Canonica looking North-West, from the Adda Eastern Bank*, 1744, pen and brown ink over pencil, 364 x 508 mm.
Darmstadt, Hessisches Landesmuseum, no. AE 2215

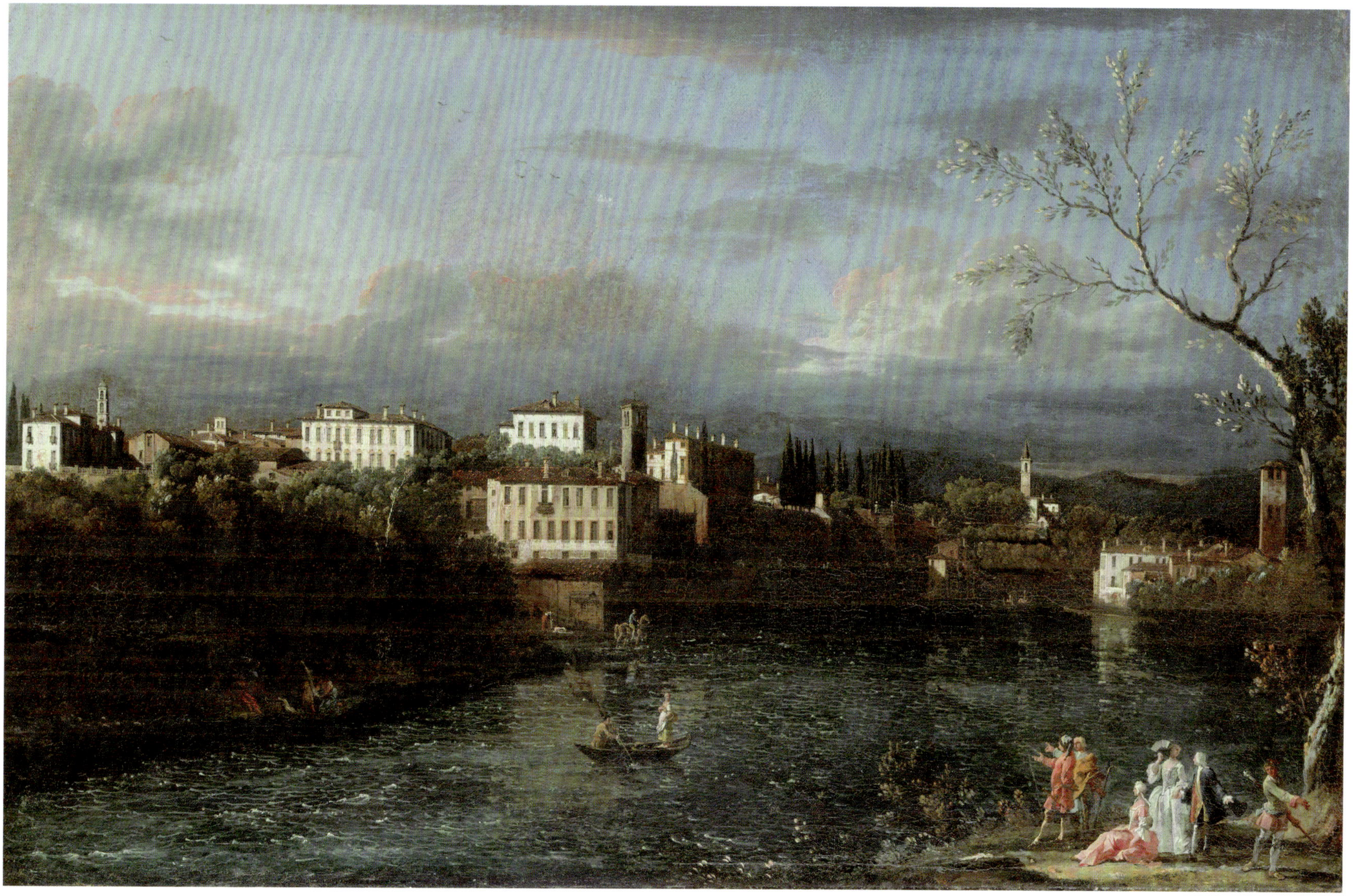

56

BERNARDO BELLOTTO

(Venice 1722 – Warsaw 1780)

Vaprio and Canonica on the Adda, looking South, Lombardy
1744

Oil on canvas; 64 x 99 cm
Naples, Museo di Capodimonte, Q 1829

This extraordinary picture, a wide bird's-eye view of the river Adda flanked by the Naviglio Martesana (canal), with Canonica and Vaprio on either bank, under a high sky stained with intense rosy colours, is a pendant to *Vaprio and Canonica on the Adda, looking North-West, Lombardy* (cat. 55), where the light is almost nocturnal. The two views are perfectly complementary: this one shown from Monasterolo, the other from a point downline of the two villages. The commission is of a singular refinement: Earl Antonio Simonetta, the Habsburg chamberlain in Milan, did not seek a view of his family's country retreat in Monasterolo, the villa Contessa, but preferred panoramic images of the area: this one similar to a view from his window, the other taken from the promenade along the Adda which he probably loved to stroll, looking towards the house in the distance, which can only be guessed at behind the row of cypresses. The encampment of soldiers dominating the foreground on a small island in the river, is an element of topicality in Bellotto's timeless scene – the war of Austrian Succession was then under way in the Milan – and is actually the work of the Venetian artist Mattia Bortoloni, who was responsible for the figures in the pendant.
Bortoloni is also the author of the two figures at the top right of the wall; other figures in the foreground are not by the hand of Bellotto. The infrared survey conducted by Carlo Falcucci shows that the islet is an addition painted on top of the water with its ripples; the *craquelure* is uniform, and thus indicates that the addition by Bortoloni was painted soon after the original. The infrared does not, however, make it possible to distinguish the painted parts with figures beneath the curtain, as is instead possible in the pendant, but the shrubs that grow nearby and the unnatural position of the islet make one sense that this is an overlaid addition to the pre-existing painted surface beneath.
The client is indicated by Bellotto himself in the text in the margin of the two studies for these compositions, which also specifies the date, 1744; these precise outline drawings reveals the artist's original ideas even as regards the figures (Hessisches Landesmuseum, Darmstadt, AE 2015 and 2016). The drawing of this composition was used literally by Bellotto also for one of the pendants formerly in the Duke of Abercorn collection at Baron's Court, now in a private collection which, like the drawing, shows two figures with a basket on the islet busy collecting stones for building (and not with a *camera optica* as used to be stated) and replaced in this picture by soldiers (cf. cat. 59). All the secondary figures in the drawing can be found in this painting: those on the river near the bank, the outlines on the terrace at top right (unlike the Abercorn version that omits some); the couple strolling on the embankment has only a parasol here and the Emilian Apennines are low on the horizon, as in the drawing.
This exact correspondence can confirm its role as 'copy of the view of Vaver', as 'souvenir' which Bellotto himself attributed to all three of the Vaprio drawings (cat. 55, 58). The drawings add evidence in establishing the chronological sequence of the five known views of Vaprio: first the Simonetta pair, then that of the Archbishop Pozzobonelli which combined *Vaprio and Canonica on the Adda, looking North-West, Lombardy* with a view of Milan, the churches of *San Paolo Converso and Sant'Eufemia, Milan* (cat. 50), and finally the two pendants in a private collection, the only pair not to have been divided, closest to the views of Gazzada (cat. 60, 61).
The two Simonetta pendants appear separated at the beginning of the twentieth century, when he was in Vienna; but many details of their history are still unknown.

Bożena Anna Kowalczyk

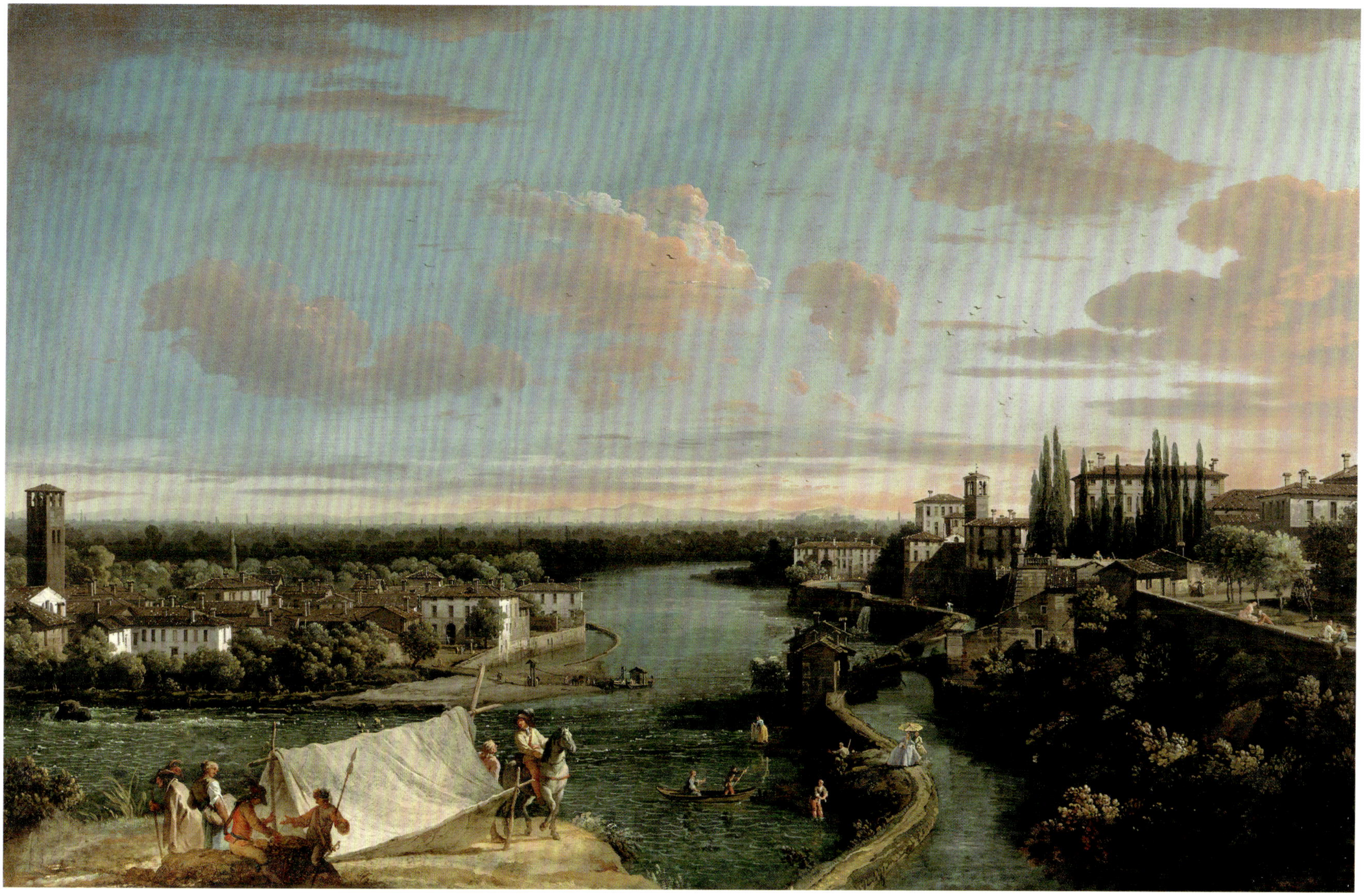

57

BERNARDO BELLOTTO

(Venice 1722 – Warsaw 1780)

Vaprio and Canonica on the Adda, looking North-West, Lombardy
ca. 1744

oil on canvas; 47 x 71 cm
Private Collection

The Villa Melzi enjoys a dominant position in this painting. Above the hanging gardens, in full light, a boat pulled by a horse crosses the Naviglio Martesana (canal). The ferry in the distance on the river, moved along a cord stretched between the two banks, and the Naviglio itself, are both inventions by Leonardo, which Bellotto clearly emphasised. Francesco Melzi (1491 ca.–1568/70?), one of Leonardo's pupils, was the testamentary heir of all of the artist's drawings and manuscripts, which he preserved until his death at the villa in Vaprio. In the eighteenth century, the site was visited by view painters, the first was Gaspar van Wittel, who portrayed it in at least seven paintings, all with a composition similar to this one, with the villa in a dominant position; three are dated 1717, 1719 and 1722.
The villa was owned by Don Antonio Maria Melzi (1672–1748), a Milanese patrician, important figure in the cultural and political life of Lombardy, royal steward general and postal administrator in 1724, under Charles VI and then in 1733, under Maria Theresa. He was undoubtedly in contact with Bellotto's patrons in Lombardy: Earl Antonio Simonetta (died 1773), owner of a large estate in Monasterolo, the Villa Contessa, the Archbishop of Milan, Giuseppe Pozzobonelli (1696-1783) and the brothers Gabrio and Giuseppe Perabò, owners of the villa and town of Gazzada (cat. 60, 61). Melzi was the patron of the composer Christoph Gluck, like Bellotto's future Viennese patrons, the Princes Kaunitz and Liechtenstein and Earl Giacomo Durazzo. And yet no documentation of his patronage of Bellotto had emerged until now. It is known that this painting and its pendant, *Vaprio and Canonica on the Adda, looking South, Lombardy* (cat. 59), the only pair of views of Vaprio that has not been separated, were in the collection of the Dukes of Abercorn at Baron's Court in Ireland, but their commission and eighteenth-century history are unknown. Nor is there a known explanation for the note on the preparatory drawing at the Warsaw Museum that this painting followed, with small differences in the details, 'the painting in Dresden' (cat. 58). Its execution seems later than that of the Pozzobonelli and Simonetta canvases, in terms of the compositional balance of the present painting, the style and the extraordinary creative confidence. Bellotto found the most favourable vantage points – elevated and opposed – to create a perfectly complementary pair of views and describe the place in its entirety. The appeal and historical importance of the location, the beauty of its sunny, lush landscape, just like those who stayed there for pleasure would have wanted, are perfectly expressed. Small in scale, similar to the size used by Canaletto for paintings for English clients, the two paintings could have also fascinated an English tourist of the Grand Tour.

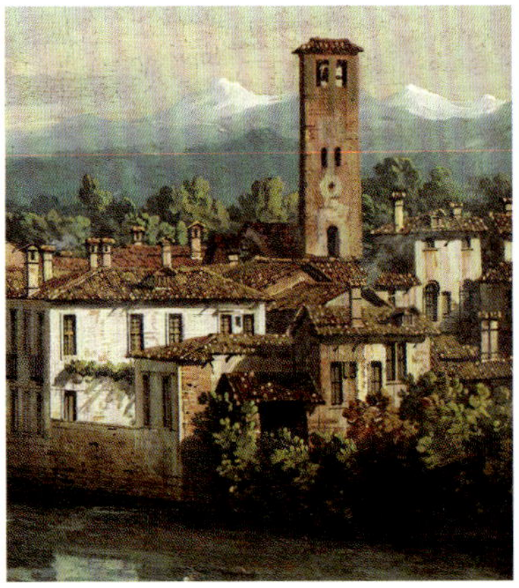

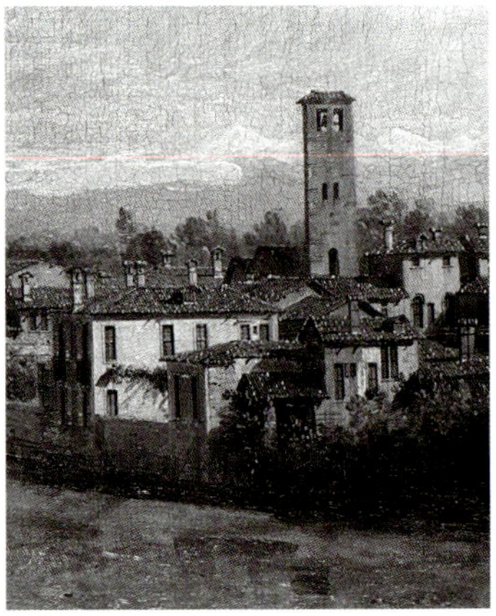

a-b. Detail photographed in natural light and in infrared light at 1600 nm

The recent infrared studies, carried out in Florence by the Istituto Nazionale di Ottica, headed by Raffaella Fontana and read and interpreted by Maurizio Zecchini and Ezio Buzzegoli, underlined the importance of the drawing for planning the architecture and figures and, at the same time, Bellotto's creativity as a painter of landscape produced in one go, painting in layers for the leaves of the trees and the rendering of the ripples of the water, the sky and the snow-covered mountains (figs. a and b). All of the basic architectural elements – the outline of the houses and the bell towers, that of the windows, horizontally and vertically, the chimney tops – were marked out with a kind of natural graphite, soft, unlike a modern pencil, and perhaps a straight edge, and then gone back over with a brush at the painting stage. On the contrary, other architectural elements, like the pillars and the gables of the windows of the palazzo Visconti Archinto, on the left, were painted directly, with no drawing. The rigorous structural base was then completed with overlapping layers of fluid colour. The architecture was completed before the landscape: the two cypresses in front of the villa cover the carefully defined details, which are clearly visible under the 1600 nm wavelength.

Bożena Anna Kowalczyk

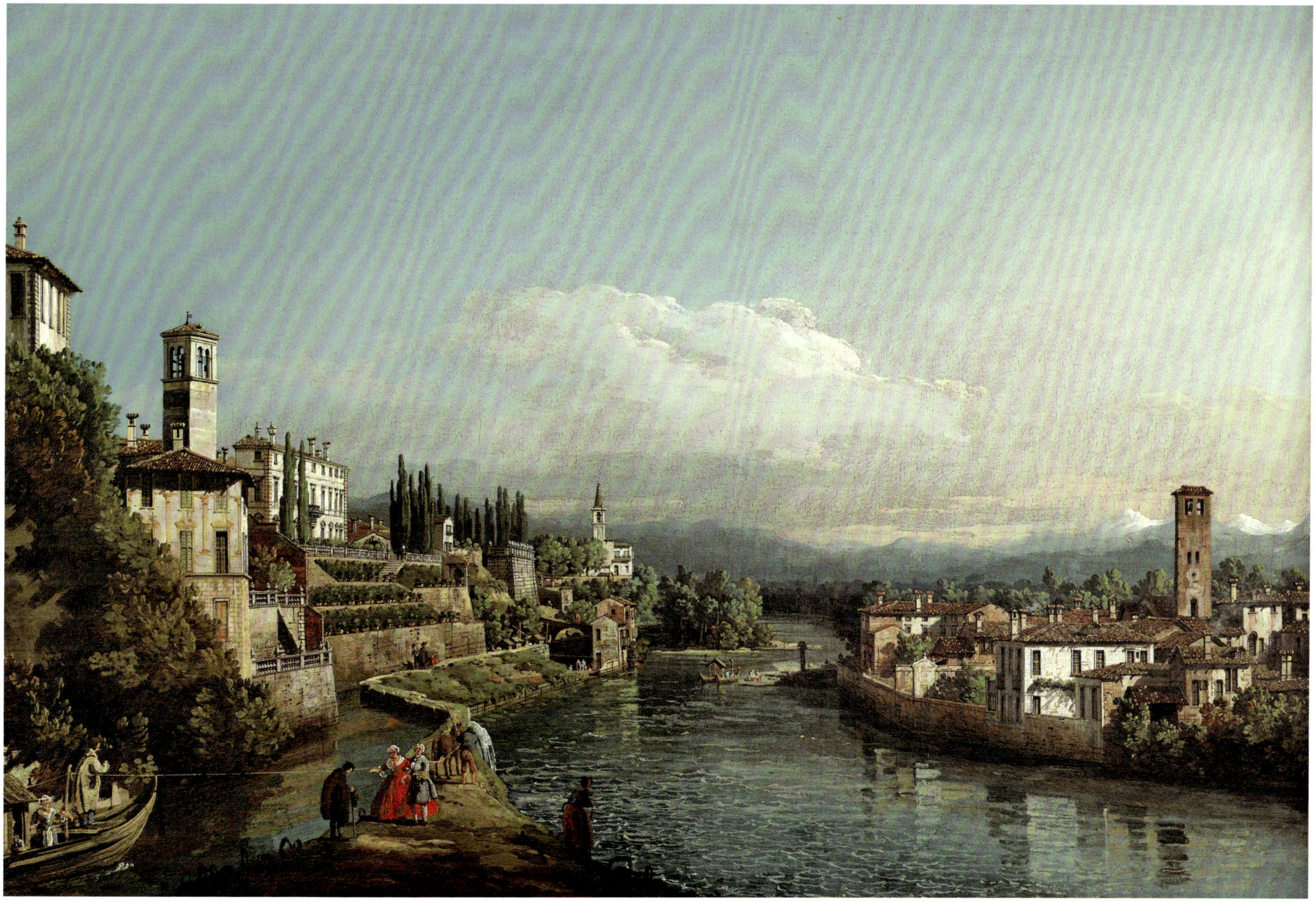

58

BERNARDO BELLOTTO

(Venice 1722 – Warsaw 1780)

Vaprio and Canonica on the Adda, looking North-West, Lombardy
1744

pen and brown ink over pencil line, free and ruled pencil, marked with a compass, thick white paper; the drawing is outlined in pen with a ruler; the horizon line is marked at 12.3 cm from the outline; divided into four equal parts with four thin vertical lines in pencil and with a ruler; 337 x 502 mm
Warsaw, Muzeum Narodowe, Rys. Pol. 2039

Inscriptions: written between the outline and the edge of the sheet, to the left, in pencil, 'quadro si trova a Dresda'; in the centre, in pen and ink, 'Copia dela Vista di Vaver Fatta dal S. (?) Bernardo Bellotto de:o il Canaletto'; on the facade of the building on the left, in pen and brown ink: 'depento'; in the background on the right, at the foot of the mountains, in pen with the same ink: 'bergamo'.

Watermark: trefoil dominating a sphere containing three balls.

In the three known drawings of Vaprio, this one – seen from the west bank of the Adda – and two sheets in the Hessisches Landesmuseum in Darmstadt – one that extends from the east bank towards Monasterolo (AE 2015) and the pendant in the opposite direction (AE 2016) – Bellotto includes a sentence written in the space left intentionally beneath the outline. Such documentation is exceptional, and in the Darmstadt drawings, described as 'copie della veduta di Vaver', he specifies the date of 1744 and the name of the patron, Earl Antonio Simonetta. This sheet, cut down along its lower edge, bears only the name of the place and the signature, but seen on the Black light it reveals to be inscribed like other two, classified by Bellotto as a 'copia' or copy ('Copia dela Vista di Vaver Fatta dal S. (?) Bernardo Bellotto de:° il Canaletto'). The caption has been discussed at length and for the most part understood as a 'true image' of the place, given the seemingly preparatory nature of the drawing, even as compared to the first versions.
Two other drawings feature this definition – *The Adige from the Ponte Nuovo, towards the Castel San Pietro, Verona*, Darmstadt Museum (HZ 160), and *The Adige with the Ponte delle Navi, Verona*, in the Muzeum Narodowe in Warsaw (Rys. Pol. 2042); the second of these two was carried out on paper from the same ream that is equally thick and marked with the same watermark. All five have two pictorial versions, one contemporary to the drawing and another later. In this case, the painting that corresponds exactly to the drawing was commissioned by Giuseppe Pozzobonelli, Archbishop of Milan, linked to the location through one of his sisters, the wife of a member of the Visconti family to whom the first house on the river belonged. The view, catalogued in 1802 in his Milanese palace as 'Canaletti', with the pendant, *San Paolo Converso and Santa Eufemia, Milan* (cat. 50), includes all the figures sketched here, the same profile of the mountains and the diagonal movement of the clouds, as well as the couple in the foreground flaunting an umbrella to protect themselves from the sun. The signature 'BERNARD.°BELLOTT.° DET.° IL/CANALETO' is very similar to that of the drawing, which may indeed be later, a 'copy' for subsequent repetitions.
The early pencil writing on the drawing – 'il quadro si trova a Dresda' – can only refer to the single known autograph version, kept until 1972 at Baron's Court, Ireland, in the collection of the Dukes of Abercorn (cat. 57). There is no doubt that this particular drawing has a preparatory function for that painting, which, in terms of surety of hand is, in addition to the pendant, later than other views of Vaprio and closer to the paintings of Gazzada (cat. 60, 61).
The purely outline drawing differs from the astonishing fluidity applied using a soft pen that lingers with an almost obsessive care in the myriad details.
From the section of the artist's legacy that merges with the collection of Earl Konstanty Tyszkiewicz in Łohojsk, Belarus, it is found in 1939 in the collection of Andrea Boni (1894–1962), a Tuscan architect active in Poland, who sells it to the Muzeum Narodowe in Warsaw.

Bożena Anna Kowalczyk

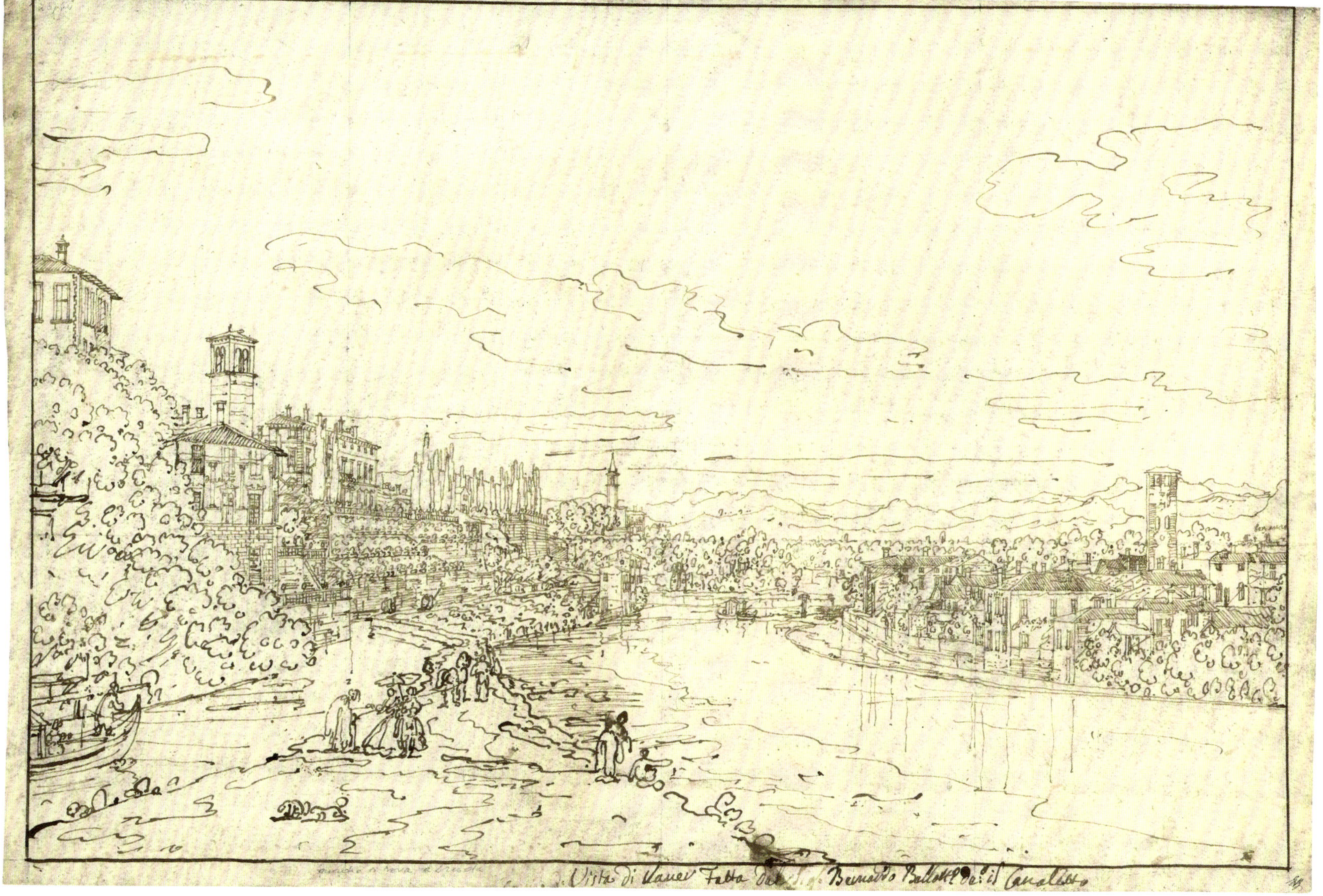

59

BERNARDO BELLOTTO

(Venice 1722 – Warsaw 1780)

Vaprio and Canonica on the Adda, looking South, Lombardy
1744

oil on canvas; 47 x 71 cm
Private Collection

This view from above of the hill of the estate of Earl Antonio Simonetta in Monasterolo, the preparatory drawing for which is in Darmstadt (AE 2016), has, unlike its pendant, no precedents in the repertoire of Gaspar van Wittel. Bellotto alone depicted Vaprio in its entirety, in two pairs on canvas: this one and the one commissioned by Earl Antonio Simonetta (cat. 55, 56), expressing his unusual ambition, already clear in the views of Florence from 1740, to study the places he had visited from two opposing directions and in different lighting, stone by stone and including every last detail of the landscape.
The views of Vaprio are the first strong expression of Bellotto's interest in nature. On a clear day, when the air is crisp, perhaps in the spring given the snowy mountaintops, you can see, as here, the profiles of the Emilian Apennines on the horizon from up high on the Simonetta estate in Monasterolo. The shadows are long and solid, getting thicker in the distance. The light on the bushes is clear, it reflects on the walls and renders the emerald water crystal clear. The lady wearing a bonnet walking along the bank, accompanied by a gentleman – the same couple as that in the pendant – has no parasol, unlike the drawings and the early versions of this view, formerly belonging to the Simonetta family, and in that of the pendant, commissioned by the Archbishop Pozzobonelli (cat. 50). There are other small differences with respect to the Darmstadt drawing – the peaks of the Apennines are much higher here.
The contrasting light and density of the bright colours – the lacquer red garment of the lady walking along the bank of the Naviglio (canal) leaps out – stand out on the red-brown background, which was rarely used by Bellotto, and apparently only in Italy. The type of canvas employed here was acquired ready for use, the primer being not only inexpensive, but also versatile, as explained by the painter Francesco Simonini (1686–1766) in a letter of August 1757 (Zecchini 2008, pp. 40-41).
Traces of the drawing like natural graphite, visible in the outlines of the buildings, which are so precise as to suggest use of a straight edge, are legible under infrared light in some areas, as is the case with the pendant, beneath the ink drawing made over them with a fine brush, a technique unique to the artist, in spite of the brown background that famously makes them difficult to read. The colours of the buildings were applied in stages, first the backgrounds and then in overlapping layers to define the tonal and light values. The infrared studies reveal Bellotto's extraordinary creativity, starting with a rigorously constructed base and then continuing freehand, creatively improvising and shaping the material, adding touches of colour until reaching the desired effect. The landscape, trees and leaves were painted with colours of different thickness, darker and thicker in the shadows. As was customary, the figures were painted last, but the dense coat of paint – in particular the intense red of the garment of the lady on the bank – not only conceals the view of the landscape beneath it but is impenetrable under all wavelengths
Before being presented at the Christie's auction in London in 1991, the two paintings were on display from 1979 on at Kenwood House, managed by English Heritage, in Hampstead, London. Faithful but not autograph contemporary copies recently appeared on the antiquarian market and stand as evidence of the success of the two compositions.

Bożena Anna Kowalczyk

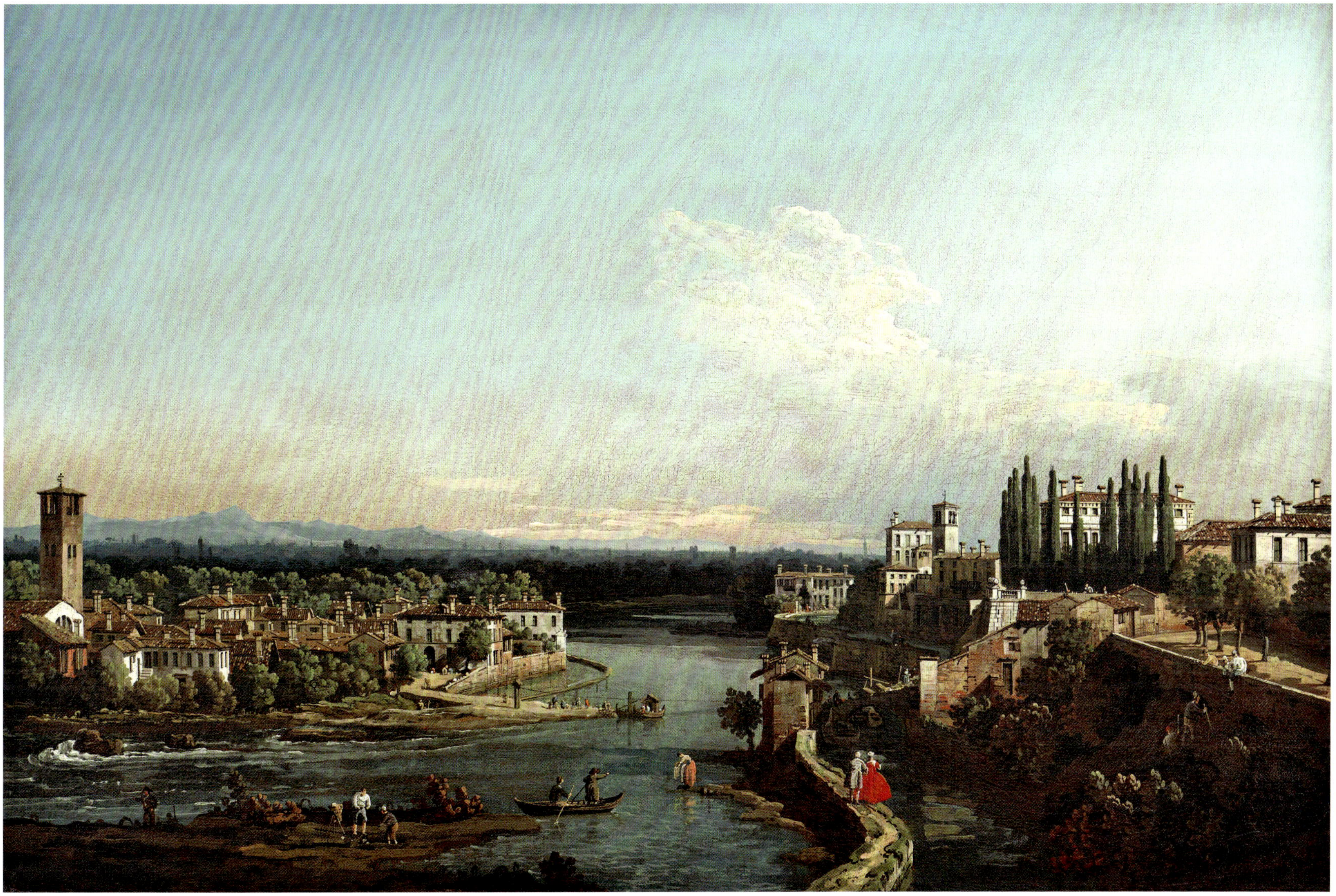

60

BERNARDO BELLOTTO

(Venice 1722 – Warsaw 1780)

Villa Perabò, Gazzada, Lombardy
1744

oil on canvas; 65 x 100 cm
Milano, Pinacoteca di Brera, 235

The two paintings of Gazzada, this one of the villa and the complementary *veduta* of the village (cat. 61), are among Bellotto's most admired works and are quite rightly considered milestones in his painting. The lucid realism that characterises the works of the young artist from the very beginning finds in these subjects – a noble villa and its surrounding landscape, rustic houses and nature – a perfect environment in which to express itself.

The wonderful balance between the architecture and the landscape, the story of life in the village and the nature perceived with a lyrical emotion – as already mentioned by S. Kozakiewicz – suggests a prolonged stay by the artist, supported by his patron or patrons. Nothing is known of the collecting interests of Gabrio and Giuseppe Perabò, owners of the villa at the time of Bellotto's visit, members of a powerful family from Varese and senior officials in the government of the city and of the Duchy of Milan; but their patronage alone can explain the origin and complex, rational structure of the paintings. Related to Bellotto's godfather, Francesco Perabò, secretary of the Procuratia de *Supra* of the Venetian Republic, and on friendly terms with the Archbishop Giuseppe Pozzobonelli, they undoubtedly had a role to play in the artist's trip to Milan.

The villa on the hill is seen from the village; a farm building in the foreground is described stone by stone; a cart pulled by oxen travels along the road. The villa is still asleep in the white light of the morning that picks out its simple architecture and encircling citrus garden. Activity in the village has already begun. This was the period in which the Perabò brothers brought their landed property in Gazzada and the villa to its most beautiful best, as interpreted by Bellotto. The skilful and well-thought-out composition is like a photomontage, defining the position of the villa in its surroundings – with Monte Rosa in the distance and the lake with the village of Bodio – in a way that is impossible to see from the chosen viewpoint. If an understanding of place was an instinctive quality for Bellotto, only careful contemplation could lead him to understand and interpret the interaction of light and shade with the porous walls of the farm building and smooth white plaster, with the foliage of the trees, both nearby and in the distance, and with the various shades of green, lawns and the lake. Such an appeal to the emotions is possible because, for the first time, the passionate observer of real-life prevails over perspectival preparation in the artist's studio, which is nevertheless present in the constructive base of the picture, as demonstrated by the X-ray photographies taken in 1989 in the Photoradiographic Laboratory of the Soprintendenza di Brera, directed by Dante Pini during, the restoration. This shows a precise ruled outline in the construction of the villa, similar to that which appears in his drawings; the

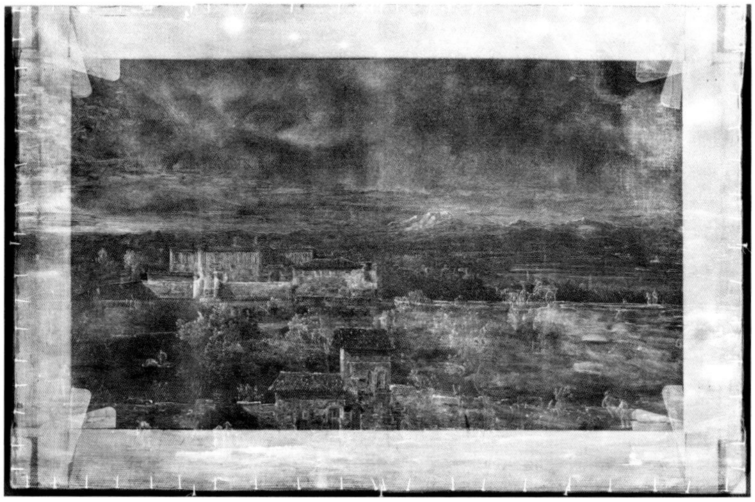

a. Ray-X photograph

arch above the main entrance of the villa is marked with a compass (fig. a). In the radiographic investigation, the drawing appears to have been spread with a thin brush, probably over a graphite line, which is not perfectly consistent. The landscape is constructed with the same attention, firstly the ground and the architecture, with the trees and figures above. All the outlines, including those of the trees and individual leaves, from the mountains to the horizon, are marked with a colour that absorbs X-rays, demonstrating the extraordinary ability of the artist.

Studies of Bellotto's Lombard period carried out during the last two decades – by M. Olivari and S. Marinelli – deal primarily with his patrons; they highlight the lack of information on the history of the paintings from the time of the commission until 1831, when the antiquarian Alessandro Brison sold them to the Accademia di Brera for 1,000 lire each, certain that they were by Bellotto's hand and proud to own paintings by 'this extremely rare painter' (M. Olivari, in Pinacoteca di Brera 1990).

Bożena Anna Kowalczyk

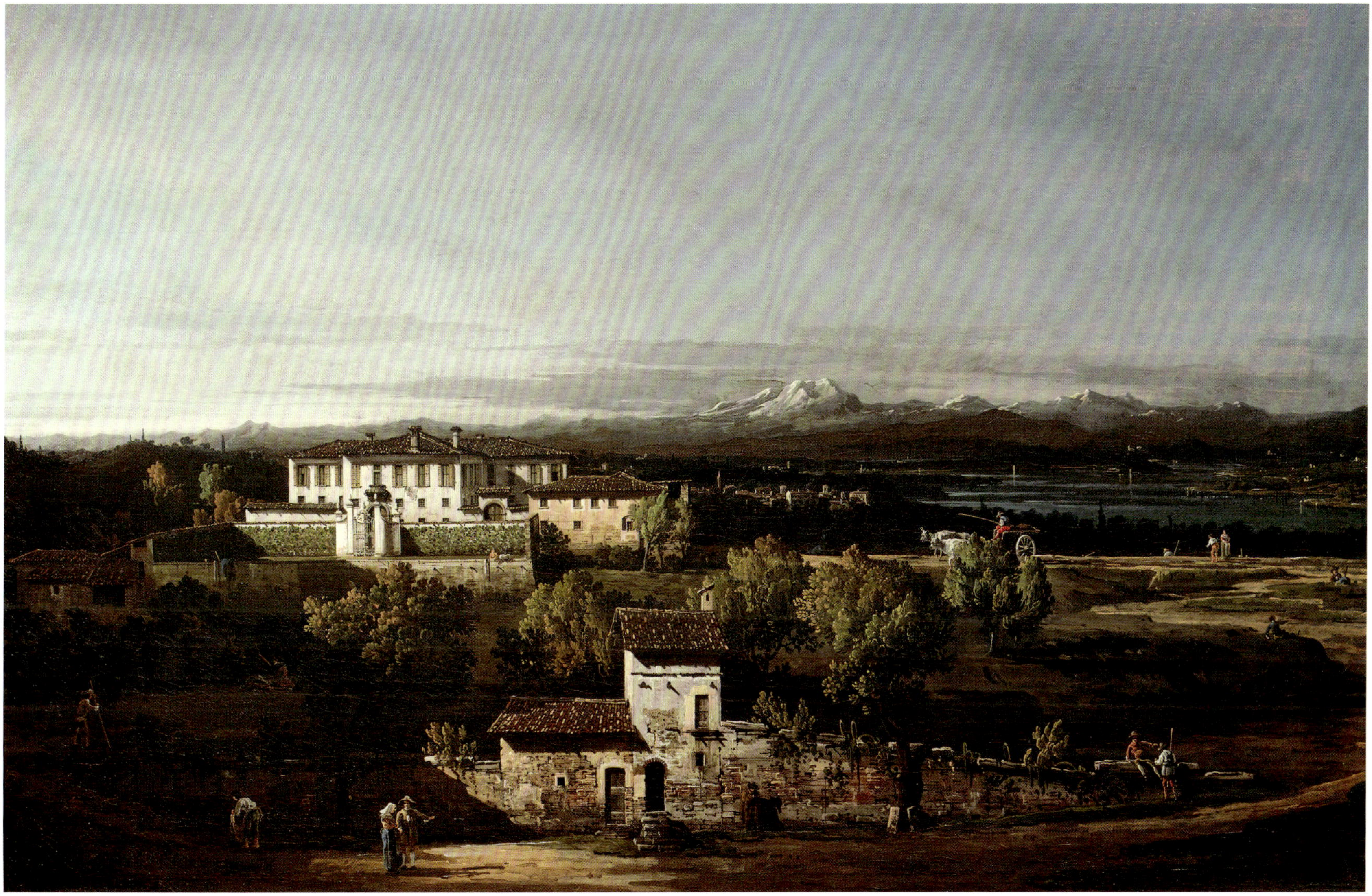

61

BERNARDO BELLOTTO

(Venice 1722 – Warsaw 1780)

The Village of Gazzada, Lombardy
1744

oil on canvas; 65 x 100 cm
Milan, Pinacoteca di Brera, 236

The view of the village is seen from the top of the low wall that runs along the road overlooking the villa on the hill, to the left of the gate (cat. 60). The houses cluster around the small church of Santa Croce with its cylindrical dome, a sequence of sloping roofs and simple rustic buildings in various shades of brown, interrupted by the dazzling whiteness of the two houses near the church; some of these buildings can still be recognised today. The low afternoon light illuminates the scene; a handful of small figures involved in everyday activities appear between the houses. The alternating green tones are astonishing. Hills and tiny villages can be seen in the distance.

Bellotto arrived in Gazzada at the end of his visit to Lombardy, invited by the brothers Gabrio and Giuseppe Perabò, owners of the villa and the village. The two complementary views he painted in this location – one of the main villa, the other of the village – provided a breath-taking change with regard to the Venetian painting of the time. These were not the elegant, Arcadian landscapes of Francesco Zuccarelli, nor those with peasant undertones by Giuseppe Zais, but two rational views, rigorously constructed on parallel planes, in which the subjects are an intrinsic part and not a decorative element. One of these, the village, is depicted literally, as it appeared to the naked eye; the other is assembled intelligently from distant viewpoints: one from higher up, the other from lower down, with the horizon raised in both. The light is the most extraordinary new element, a 'metaphysical' light that reveals that the nature of the motifs, a source of admiration for the two works has never waned.

The two drawings must have been preceded by a series of sketches, taken with a *camera optica* and a drawing of the whole, similar to the drawings in Vaprio, and particularly the one in Warsaw, the richest in terms of detail (cat. 58). The X-ray photography carried out during the 1989 restoration shows an intricate interweaving of the outlines of the roofs, houses, trees and peaks in the distance, but no *pentimenti*; every element corresponds to those of the painting. Traces of geometric drawing can also be seen here, despite the immediacy of the handling, in the wall on the right and in the profiles of the roofs, which were probably painted with a small, thin brush. The paint has been applied thickly, sometimes in clumps. The fluency of the drawing of the figures is remarkable. The stormy appearance of the sky, with diagonal brush strokes, is more evident here than in the pendant, as is the more visible *craquelure* of a thick mesh; a different ground has clearly been used in the two pictures (M. Olivari, in *Pinacoteca di Brera* 1990). The row of tree silhouettes on the hill that stand out against the sky in the distance is a final touch by Bellotto, a sort of signature. The importance of these two views to the *plein-air* painting of nineteenth-century Lombard landscape painters has been highlighted.

Bożena Anna Kowalczyk

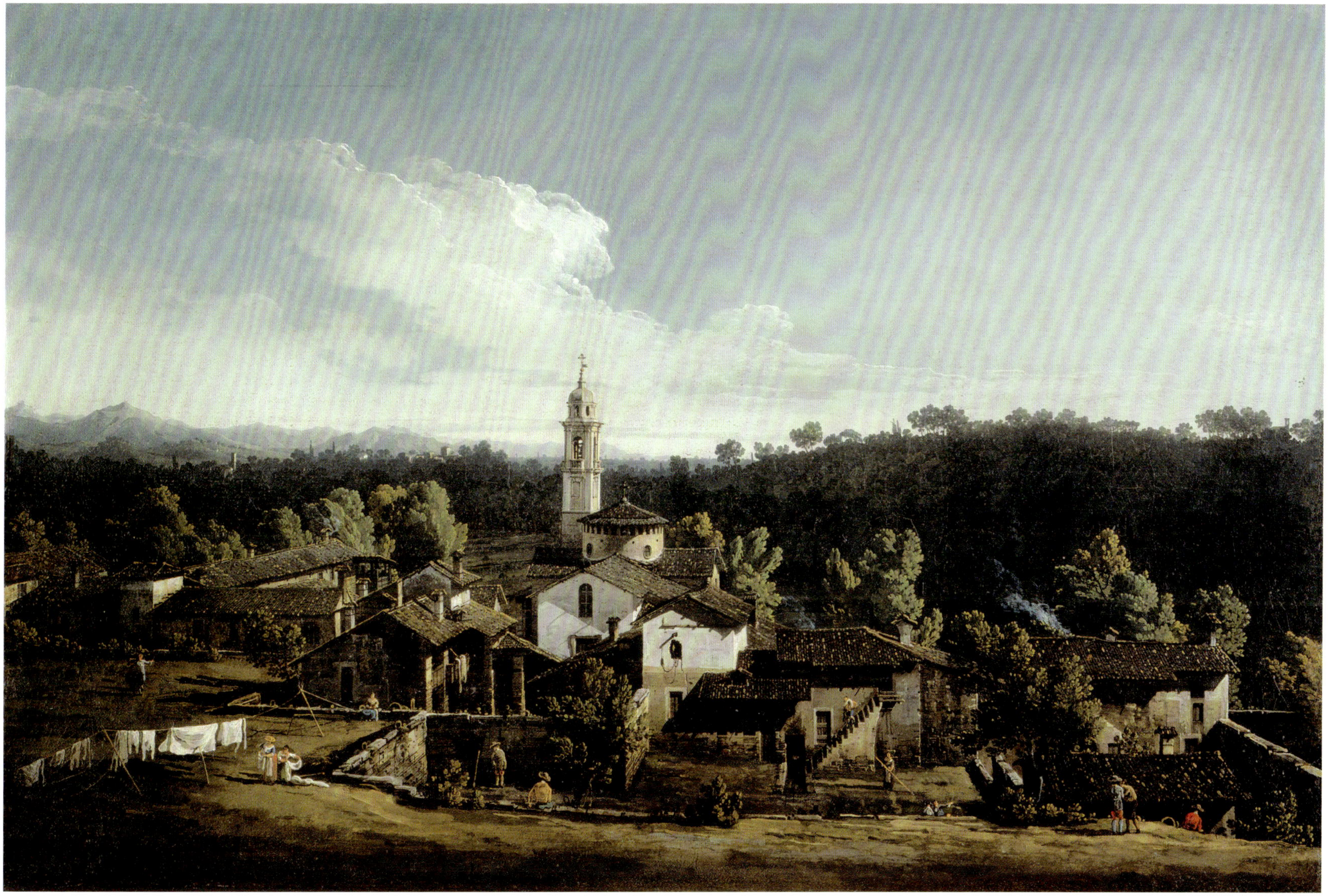

62

BERNARDO BELLOTTO

(Venice 1722 – Warsaw 1780)

Pirna from the Boatmen's Village
1753–1755

oil on canvas; 36 x 237 cm
Dresden, Staatliche Kunstsammlungen, Gemäldegalerie Alte Meister, 626

Of the eleven views of Pirna, small town 20 km south-east of Dresden, and made for that Court, this one was born 'under a particularly happy star', like the two views of Gazzada (cat. 60, 61). Inscribed in the margin of the etching that reproduces the composition, Bellotto indicated that this was a view of the suburbs of the town, 'devant la Porte des Bateliers', with the prospect of Sonnenstein Castle on one side and, on the other, rocks and vineyards. The description is accurate and, as in the other prints, shows the essential elements of the view. This was a very special Pirna suburb, and Bellotto devoted a lyrical focus to it, showing the old harbour and access to the river for the barges, and the houses of the Elbe boatmen, built partly of brick and partly wood and latticework. These closely-packed houses, shown from the front beyond the expanse of water, some in shade, others barely lit – with high gabled roofs, awnings, cracked walls and latrines in wooden boards on the bank – were a new and fascinating subject for Bellotto, just as the village of Gazzada had been on his trip to Lombardy. The fortress stands on a hill in full sunlight, characterised in its essential lines, revealing the barracks with two lateral towers; a tree-lined road leads to the town, and in the distance we can see the roof of the Marienkirche and the bell tower; to the right, among the vineyards, there is the village of Posta, dominated by the brownish rocks that intrigued Bellotto and which are typical of this area. Along the river, in the distance, lies the point from which he depicted the view in *Pirna Seen from Kopitz* (cat. 64). A boat has already passed through customs – the house on the right, next to the wooden bridge – and is about to moor, drawn by a man on the shore, while others are already at the berth.

That Bellotto in Dresden had been fascinated by the painting of the Dutch Golden Age is more than ever evident in this painting. It is the landscapes of Jacob van Ruisdael and Philips Koninck that taught him how to show the idea of the changeability of light, with clouds that glide through the sky, casting shadows on the landscape and leaving other areas in the sun, as yet unaffected by the clouds. Other artists were Meindert Hobbema who preceded him in choosing to depict half-derelict houses set in nature, and Aelbert Cuyp, whose clear light was used to delineate the outlines of things. Bellotto confirmed Nicholas Berchem's use of prints, published by Giuseppe Wagner in Venice: the small group of cows drinking water next to the shepherd and the dog comes from a print entitled 'Senza pensier sol della Mandria ho cura' (Without care, I am responsible only for the herd) (G.J.M. Weber, in Venice-Houston 2001). We know that Bellotto collected prints voraciously, amassing 1,260 of them in two bound albums from 'Paesi di Varii celebri Autori Ital: Fran: e Fiamengi' (countries with various celebrated artists: Italian, French and Flemish) (*Catalogo de Danni*, cat. 83).

As in all the other views of Pirna, the observation of nature lies at the basis of the depiction. The two trees in the foreground holding up a rope for the laundry convinced Bellotto to effect a realistic description, but not so much of the trees themselves, whose species remains unclear, as of the pollarding done in the countryside to assure a mass of flexible branches. The makeshift tent to protect the merchandise is described with its curtains applied carelessly as though this were a kind of 'still life'. Bellotto suggests it is evening, as there are long shadows cast by two the washerwomen on the bank in the foreground, but it has been observed that the light comes from the North, another subtle poetic licence in this depiction.

The etching made from this painting, one of the six known of Pirna, bears the emblem of the union of Saxony with Poland (Kozakiewicz 1972a, no. 219). Like the others in the series, it must have been produced before the painter's departure for Bayreuth and Vienna in December 1758 and before the destruction of the plates themselves in the bombing of Dresden: *Catalogo de Danni* lists '6. [Rami] più Pichioli Vedute di Pirna' ('6. [Coppers] plus other small views of Pirna') (p. 17*r*). But this seems to be contradicted by the fact that one of the series, *Pirna from the Posta Vineyards*, is certainly dated 1764 (Kozakiewicz 1972a, no. 192).

Bożena Anna Kowalczyk

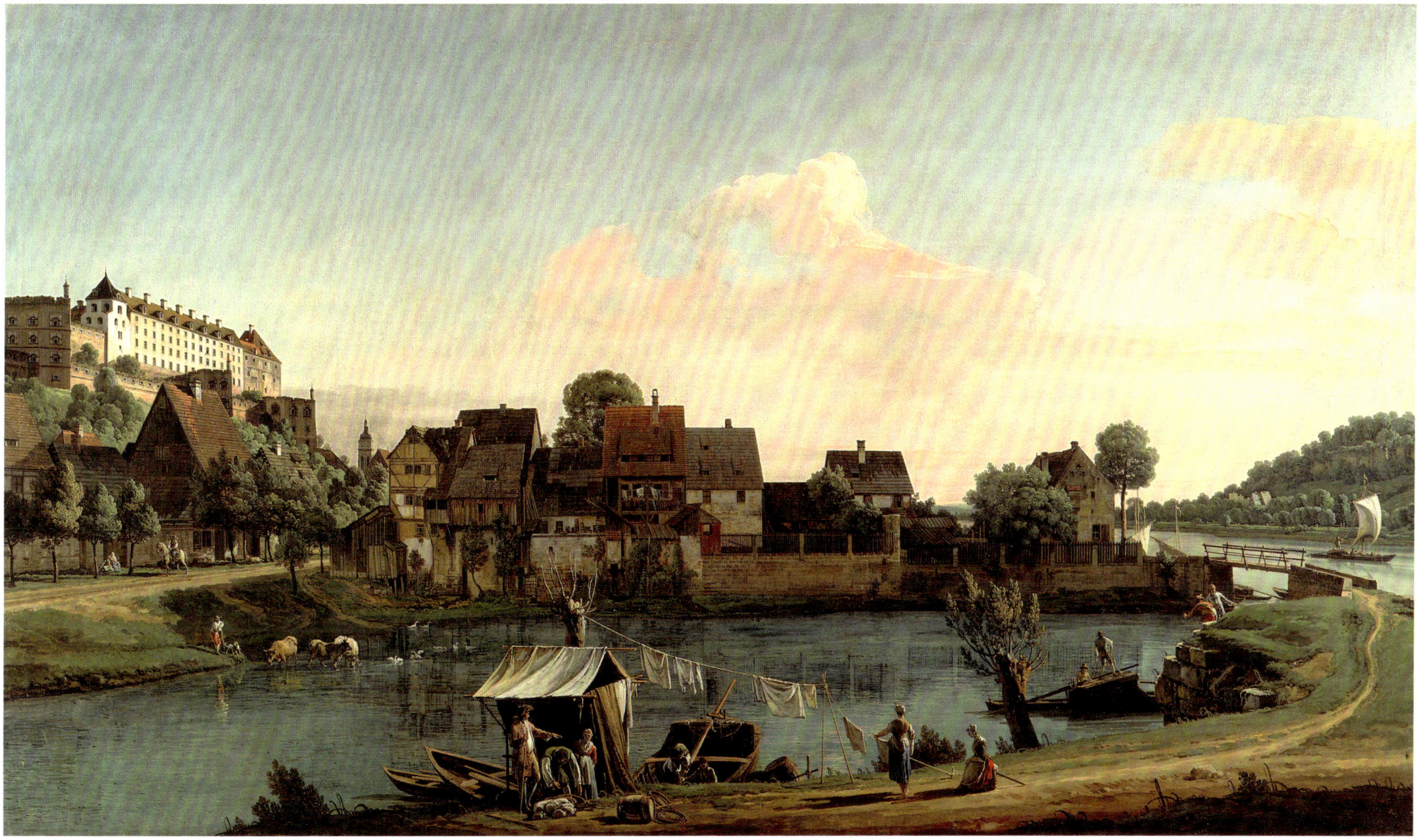

63

BERNARDO BELLOTTO

(Venice 1722 – Warsaw 1780)

Pirna from the Sonnenstein Fortress
1753–1755

oil on canvas; 133 x 234 cm
Dresden, Staatliche Kunstsammlungen, Gemäldegalerie Alte Meister, 625

In the eleven views of Pirna, south-east of Dresden painted by Bellotto between the spring of 1753 and 1755 on commission to Augustus III, the Sonnenstein Fortress invariably appears. This was a powerful castle-like construction completed in the sixteenth century dominating the Saxon town from the top of a hill. With his pass issued by Augustus III on 26 April, 1753, the Venetian painter was allowed to climb to the circle of the rampart and, from close-to, sketch the oldest tower of the fortress, mentioned as early as the thirteenth century (and demolished in 1859), as well as the new 'horn' bastion built in 1701, and the old promenade. The tall, austere building on the far right is the home of the commander and the two-storey one on the corner is the castle's inn, which still exists. The oblique structure with tiled roof is the 'Klappe', which conceals a staircase leading from the basement to the upper floors of the fortress. A tranquil atmosphere reigns: there is a woman with children, a sleeping dog, a soldier peeking inside the tavern, while another, rather scruffy one in the foreground guards an old cannon, in what is a beautiful still life. It has been observed that no one here seems to be expecting the imminent outbreak of the Seven Years' War that would overwhelm the peace of this region.
Bellotto found the most favourable viewpoints to embrace both the fortress and the town surrounded by hills, in the middle of meadows on the banks of the wide river; this painting marks perhaps his most surprising and boldest use of perspective. The viewpoint chosen made it possible to render the idea of the massive power of the rampart and at the same time was useful for showing the broad view of the landscape of the Elbe valley, from the houses of Kopitz surrounded by greenery to the hills above Pillnitz and on to the horizon. At the foot of the fortress, the town's houses huddle around the Marienkirche with its red pitched roof and incorporated tower that act as a counterpoint to the massive walls of the fortress. Evening is approaching, and the shadows have already spread over the town, and are climbing the roof of the church, but the fort is still in full sunlight. A solitary boat crosses the river, offering 'a picture within a picture' admired by all writers, and considered the inspiration for Friedrich. It is this extraordinary ability Bellotto had to grasp the beauty of a moment, a fleeting instant of light, the passage of a cloud which, as here, obscures the distant hills, that completes and brings alive the poignant realism of his depictions.
The distant landscapes that lead the eye to the horizon are an indispensable element in Bellotto's views of Dresden, Vienna and Munich; in Warsaw, the landscape and nature would become protagonists in the views of the meadows and of Wilanów near the capital.
The print made from this painting, with a more extensive view to the left and changes in the figures, adorned with the emblem of the Saxon-Polish union (Kozakiewicz 1972a, no. 229), must have been etched before the departure of Bellotto for Bayreuth and Vienna in December 1758, as documented in the manuscript inventory of the artist's goods that mentions all six plates of Pirna being left in the house at Dresden (*Catalogo de Danni*, p. 17*r*). Four copies of this print are recorded as being delivered to the Kupferstich-Kabinett on 2 June 1766 (Journal beym Churfürstlichen Kupferstich-Cabinet de Anno 1766, held by Christian Friedrich Wenzel, c. 22*v* and 23*r*; Ms., Kupferstich-Kabinett, no. 94); these were probably sheets that the artist had brought with him to Vienna, thereby saving them from destruction.

Bożena Anna Kowalczyk

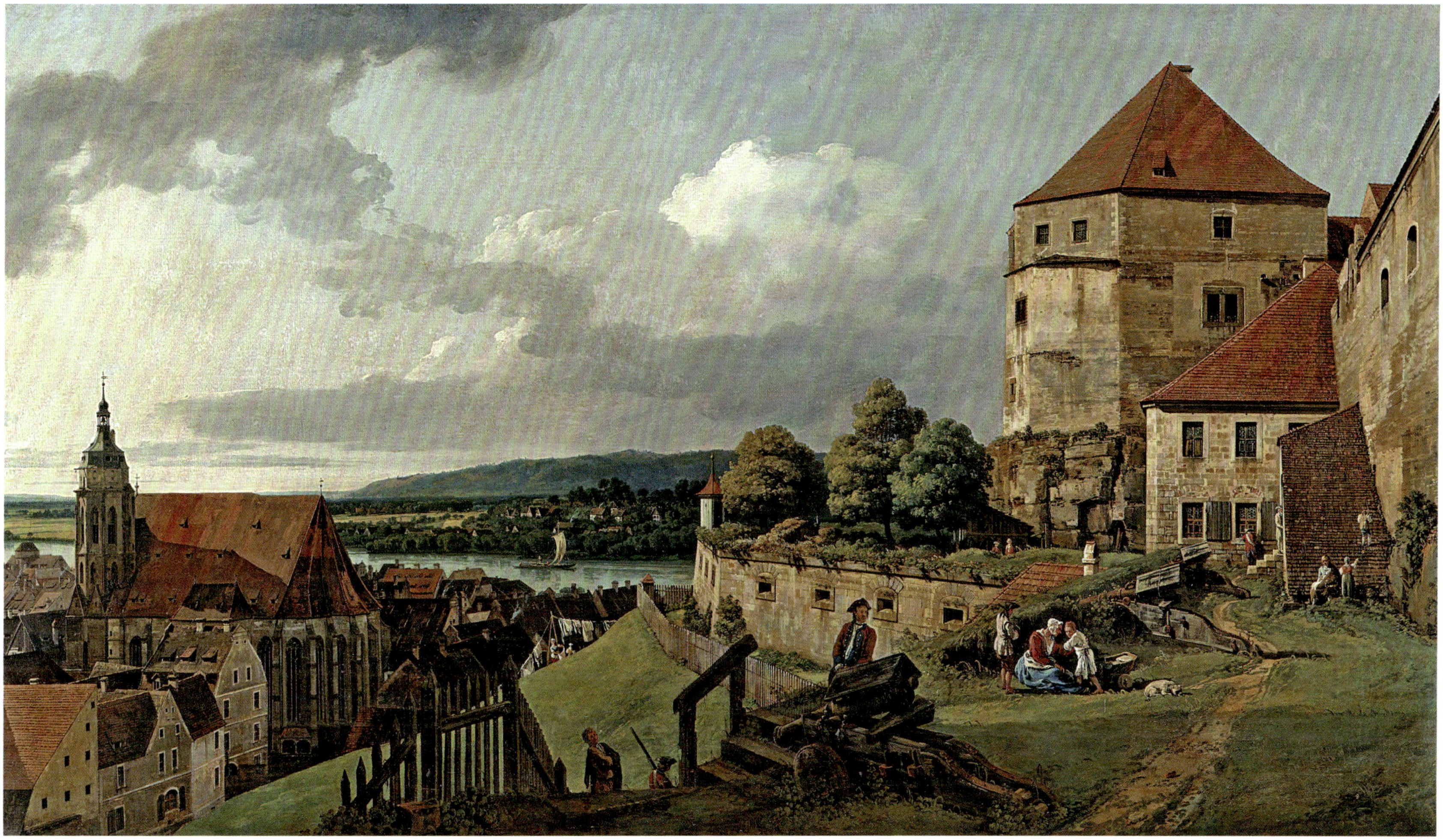

64

BERNARDO BELLOTTO

(Venice 1722 – Warsaw 1780)

Pirna from the Right Bank of the Elbe near Kopitz
1753–1755

oil on canvas; 133 x 237.5 cm
San Petersburg, The State Hermitage Museum, GE 208

Bernardo Bellotto arrived in Dresden in April 1747 and was appointed court painter the following year. Between 1747 and 1755, he provided the Royal Gallery with twenty-five large-scale paintings – 14 *vedute* of Dresden and 11 of Pirna. In the same period, he made replicas on the same scale for Heinrich, Earl von Brühl (1700-1763), prime minister of the Saxon Court; we know of 13 *vedute* of Dresden and 8 of Pirna. Five years after the collector's death, Tsarina Catherine the Great bought his picture gallery, which featured over 600 paintings – amongst them the Pirna series, including this canvas and only seven city views – for 80,000 thalers (Levinson-Lessing 1985, p. 260). Five more *vedute* turned up at a Christie's auction on 3 May 1946, from the collection of Arthur, 3rd Baron Hillingdon, (1891-1952), Hassocks, Sussex (cat. 71), whilst one has not yet been recovered: *The Moat of the Zwinger, Dresden* or *The Frauenkirche, Dresden*. Bellotto worked for Brühl without remuneration, supposedly to repay him for the invitation to Dresden, for which the prime minister – along with Anton Maria Zanetti, the artist's Venetian patron – was probably responsible. Brühl, a shrewd yet rash politician, was in charge of the disastrous Saxon foreign policy that led to the Seven Years' War, which Bellotto himself was a victim of – the artist lost all his possessions (his house with all its furnishings, his library and collections, see cat. 83) in the Prussian bombing of Dresden in 1760. Bellotto turned to Brühl's heirs, requesting 200 thalers per painting, only after this severe loss, but there is no record that he was ever paid.
In April 1753, Augustus III assigned Bellotto the task of painting the *vedute* of Pirna, located about twenty kilometres from Dresden in the Elbe valley, dominated by the Sonnenstein fortress – one of the strongholds of the Saxon defence system. This was the Venetian painter's chance to return to painting nature. The royal version of this *veduta* and its pendant, *Pirna from the Right Bank of the Elbe near Posta*, both taken from the narrow path that zigzags amongst the vineyards along the river, between Kopitz and Posta, are believed to be the first four versions painted in Pirna and presented to the Royal Gallery in 1754, by virtue of their compositional similarity to the pair of views of the Elbe carried out upon Bellotto's arrival in Dresden (J.G.M. Weber, in Venice-Houston 2001, p. 184; Oesterreich 1754, I 546-549).
Bellotto captures a majestic image of the town and of life along the river, which flows by slowly, taking up half the painting. Two young farmers with a dog stand by the riverside, talking; a sailboat is transporting a cart and horses; still more horses are fording the river, pulling a cart with a barrel towards the shore; a washerwoman is folding her laundry; the town is bathed in the crystalline light reflecting in the clear river waters – a 'painting within the painting'. From right to left, we recognise the Dominican Klosterkirche with its unfinished belfry, a fortified tower known as the 'Crown', the Marienkirche with its belfry – the marketplace is behind, where the tower of the town hall stands out (see cat. 80) – and the entire fortress complex, with its four-storey main body intended as military barracks, the 'Old Walkway' to the front, the four ramparts and the commandant's home. The stone arch illuminated near the riverbank is a remnant of a military structure. To the left is a singularly beautiful landscape – the treetops, in different shades of green, in contrast with the rock formations, typical of the area, on the other side of the river; pale and dark greens alternate; certain shapes on the hilltop stand out against the sky, in an effect much loved by Bellotto.
The canvas sailed up the Elbe to Lübeck along with the Brühl's picture gallery; Jacob von Stählin (1709–1785), scientist and chronicler at the court of Russia, tells that the journey upriver caused paintings to mould, calling for restoration immediately upon arrival in Saint Petersburg. The empress's interest was aroused as she was present during the restoration work (I. Artemieva, in Venice-Houston 2001, p. 160).
There are few differences in the details compared to the first version for Augustus III, but the sky is entirely original, crossed by well-defined grey clouds, while the treetops, looking like cotton wool, are more contrasted in light. The shapes reflected in the water are recreated with even greater care, making the river the true protagonist of this representation. We have no knowledge of preparatory drawings, and no prints were made.

Bożena Anna Kowalczyk

Many thanks to Irina Artemieva for giving me kindly assisted in the study of the Hermitage's Bellotos.

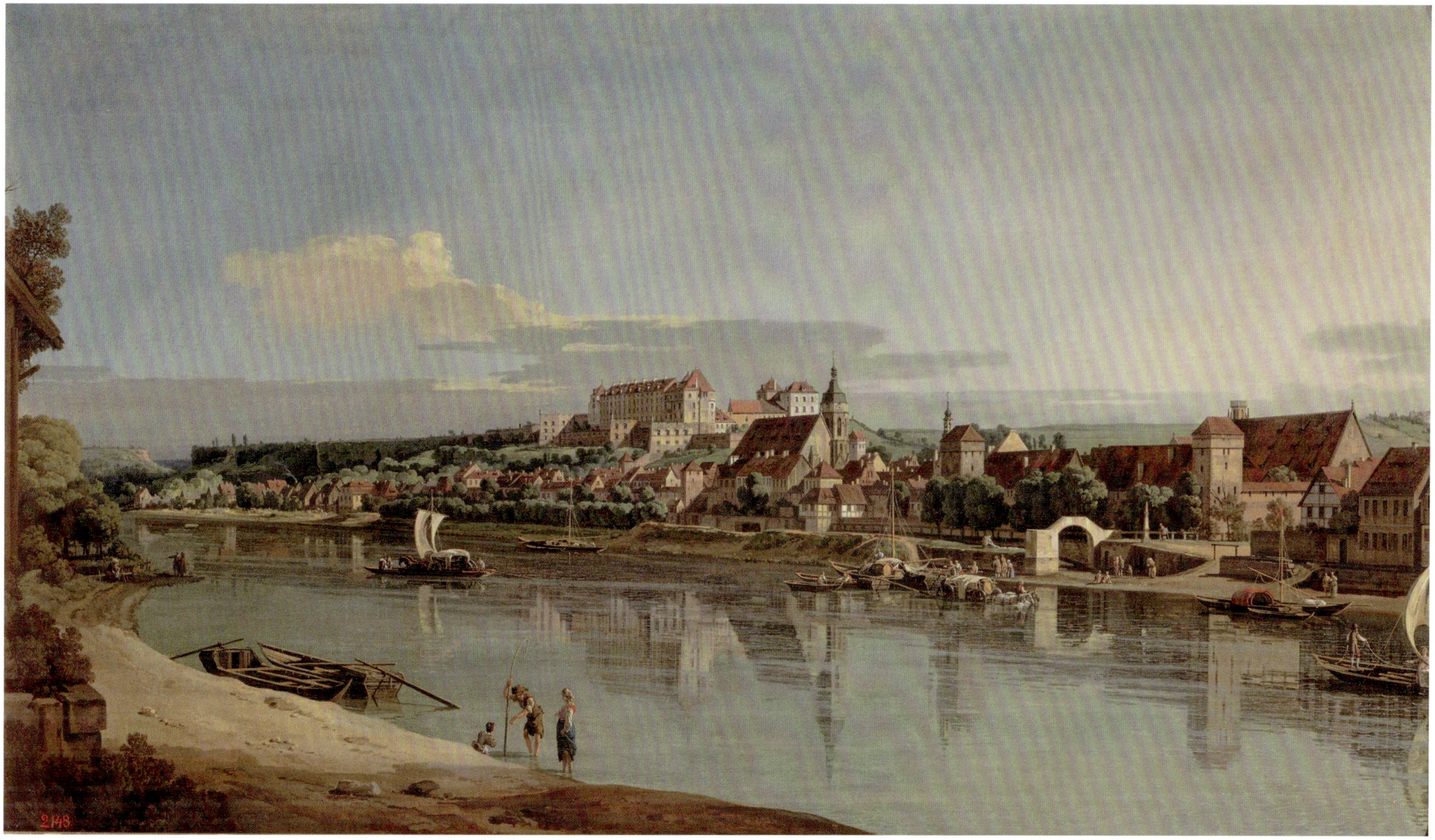

65

BERNARDO BELLOTTO

(Venice 1722 – Warsaw 1780)

Wilanòw Palace from the Garden, Warsaw
1777

oil on canvas; 117 x 164 cm
Warsaw, Royal Castle, Museum, ZKW / 460

Arriving in Warsaw in January 1767, Bellotto found a situation of serious political decline but a great cultural openness towards the Western world, which was manifested by a munificent patronage and the enlightened collecting of King Stanisław II August Poniatowski, and of the Polish and Lithuanian aristocratic families. The series of twenty-six views of Warsaw commissioned by the king and painted between 1768 and 1780 is Bellotto's last masterpiece. In 1776, the king decided to decorate the antechamber of the Senate in the Royal Castle with a series of paintings by Bellotto, using those already executed and commissioning others to complete the series. Among the other views of Warsaw, the views of Wilanów, 'with all the surrounding area' (A. Rottermund, in Venice-Houston 2001, p. 36) were installed in the panelling at the end of 1777. Thus was born the 'Canaletto Room', which the King gave the role of representing his reign in a suitably prestigious manner.
The Wilanów Palace (New Villa), rebuilt in the original Baroque style, with the respect for the Polish tradition of a noble countryside residence, by the Dutch architect Tylman van Gameren and the Italian Vincenzo Agostino Locci for King Jan Sobieski (1629–1696), was the subject of two pairs of pendants, depicting it from different sides. The first, painted in 1776 in a small format, *Wilanòw Palace from the entrance, Warsaw* and *Wilanòw Palace from the garden looking west, Warsaw* are two frontal views, constructed in parallel planes, looking toward distant horizons, as often occurs in the work of Bellotto (Kozkiewicz 1972, no. 424 and 425). The second pair, from 1777, of medium format, includes the present and *Wilanòw Palace from the Garden looking North, Warsaw* (Kozakiewicz 1972a, no. 426); these represent a break in compositional terms also from all his previous works: 'Mighty and massive trees, ancient pines dominate the scene of the picture, with the castle itself deliberately shifted from the centre to the side, deep in a forest of trees, intersected by the distant horizon…' (Fritzsche 1936). In this painting, the protagonist is the Italian garden, its two levels, with the refined design of the flowerbeds, bordered on the left by the French hedges and dominated by a dense row of wild trees. The tall uncultivated pines remind us that we are in a North European country. In the second painting, the thick forest of mighty trees with light-coloured bark occupies almost half of the picture near the pond with swans. All four views of Wilanów are the culmination of Bellotto as landscape painter, and show his modernity and knowledge of contemporary developments in European painting, which as we know from the inventory of his library, he avidly studied also through prints (*Catalogo de Danni*, cat. 83).
In these paintings, S. Kozakiewicz perceives a note of melancholy and a light that he defines metaphysical, as in the paintings of Gazzada. A number of elements goes beyond reality: the northern wing appears increased by a section, the Belvedere rooftop sculptures are an invention, and the fountain at the centre seems never to have existed, as also the decoration on the wall of the terrace. Bellotto must have made use of the unrealised projects that the Polish scholar has found in the archives of the castle. The point of view, defined as 'artificial', with a high horizon, is adapted to the requirements of the picture's position at the lower end of the 'Canaletto Room'. It is probable that for these special views Bellotto had a wooden tower built, similar to that documented and used in Nymphenburg (P.O. Krückmann, in Munich 2014–2015, pp. 314–315).
Among the figures in the foreground in *Wilanòw Palace from the Garden looking West*, the owner of the castle, Prince August Aleksander Czartoryski has been recognised, together with his daughter and heir, Izabela Lubomirski, famous for having enriched the castle with art collections. As in that painting, here too the few figures are described with a considerable attention to human types and costumes.

Bożena Anna Kowalczyk

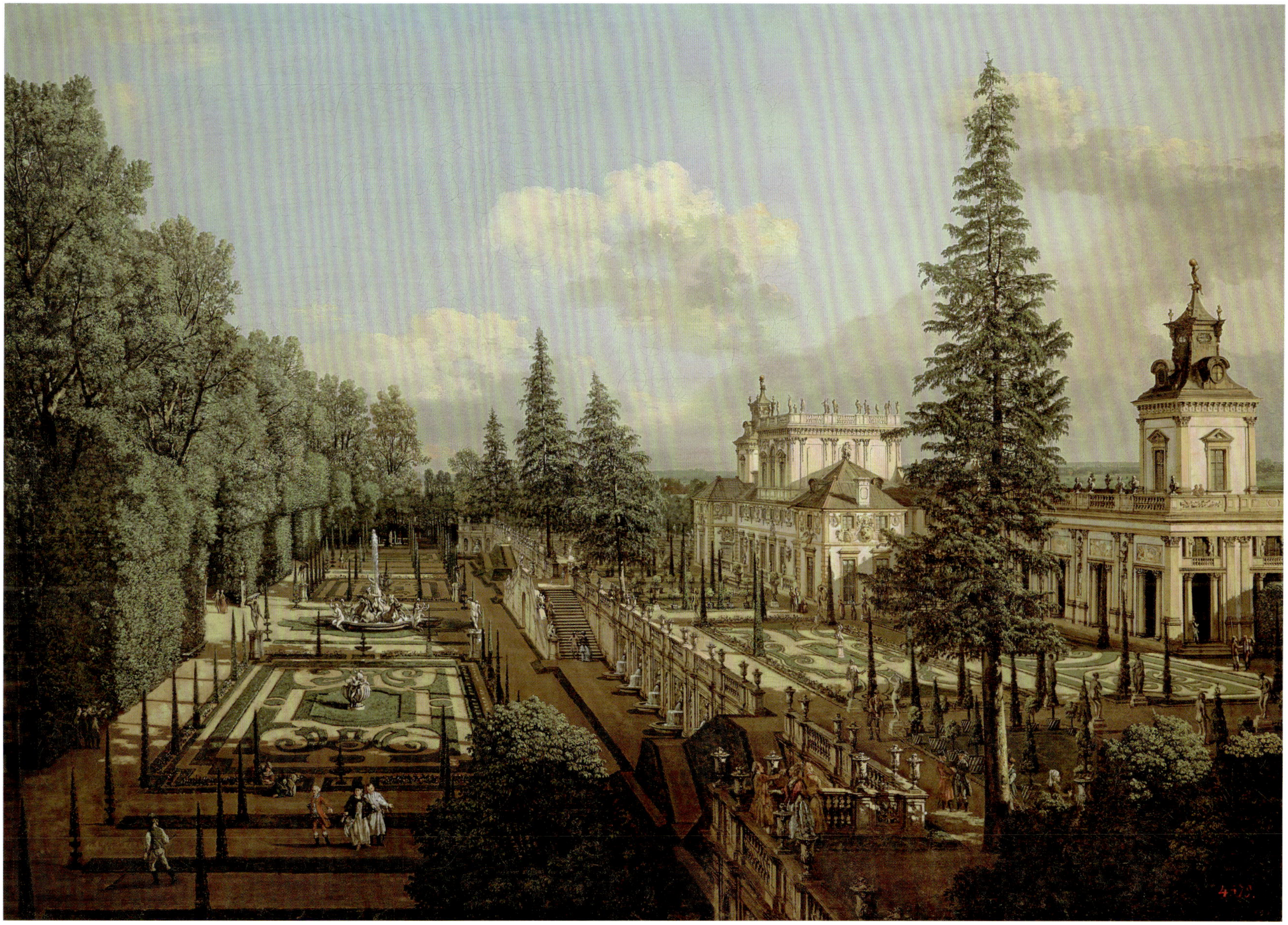

66

CANALETTO

(Venice 1697–1768)

Eton College
ca. 1754

oil on canvas; 61.6 x 107.7 cm
London, The National Gallery, Wynn Ellis Bequest, NG 942

Eton College, the most famous public school in England, was founded by Henry VI in 1440 near Windsor Castle, on the other side of the river Thames. The bridge which is not shown here but appears in Canaletto's painting of *Windsor Castle* in the collection of the Duke of Northumberland (C/L 449) connects Eton to the castle. The dominant building is the chapel, completed in 1482; M. Levey supposes that the small building shown in front used to contain the kitchens; on the right, it is possible to recognise the Cloister Court, of 1441 to 1460. With a rare pictorial licence, Canaletto placed buildings that have never existed along the riverbanks, such as the churches on the left, none of which resembles the parish church of Windsor or that of Eton which was anyway built later (Levey); he endowed Eton Chapel with minutely described invented details, such as the towers with little cupolas, a statue on top and two rows of narrow four-lobed arches in the large window of the facade. Other buildings, real or fictional, are carefully defined as to the volumes and colours created by the light. The slender saplings at Eton, shown with their shadows, have a realistic air, but the mannered nature on the Windsor side does not; here we see a tall tree growing with generic foliage, together with some bushes of undefined specials, depicted with rounded brushstrokes; the one on the right is crowned by a giant red flower. Yet the topographical inaccuracies and vague description of nature are part of the beauty of this painting, a dreamy and crystalised image in a slightly dimmed light. The horizon is low and the sky delicate, marked by grey tones, occupying more than half of the picture.
Studies of this painting have always stressed the lack of topographical accuracy, to the point of questioning its attribution or have assumed that the painting was painted on the basis of an inaccurate engraving; J.G. Links notes that drawing Windsor Castle before the month of June 1747 from Mr. Crowle's cottage on Romney island, Canaletto needed only to turn his chair to the right to see Eton College in front of him; but there are seven years between the Duke of Northumberland's painting and the drawing, which was produced in a 'markedly more mannered style' and was rightly dated by Sir Michael Levey to the end of the English period, in the same style as the *Interior of the Rotunda at Ranelagh, London*, 1754 (C/L 420). It has also been assumed that Canaletto used drawings made hastily during his visit to Windsor but this idea does not seem to me to be consistent with Canaletto's manner; it is more likely that this was a special commission. A trial for the composition takes the form of the drawing that used to belong to Lord Harmsworth, Mereworth Castle, in which the horizon is even lower but the buildings correspond in detail to those of the painting, apart from the highest bell tower of one of the churches. In the painting, Canaletto enriched the scene on the Windsor riverbank with a greater number of figures and on the Eton side with tiny characters on the lawns. The idea advanced by Constable and repeated in the catalogue of the latest Christie's sale of both works having possibly been produced after the artist's return to Venice is not possible (Christie's, London, 4 July, 2004, lot 69).
Eton chapel is one of the few Gothic buildings to have impressed Canaletto, who then pictured it in more or less fanciful ways in a series of *capriccio* drawings and paintings, executed in England and shortly after returning to Venice.

Bożena Anna Kowalczyk

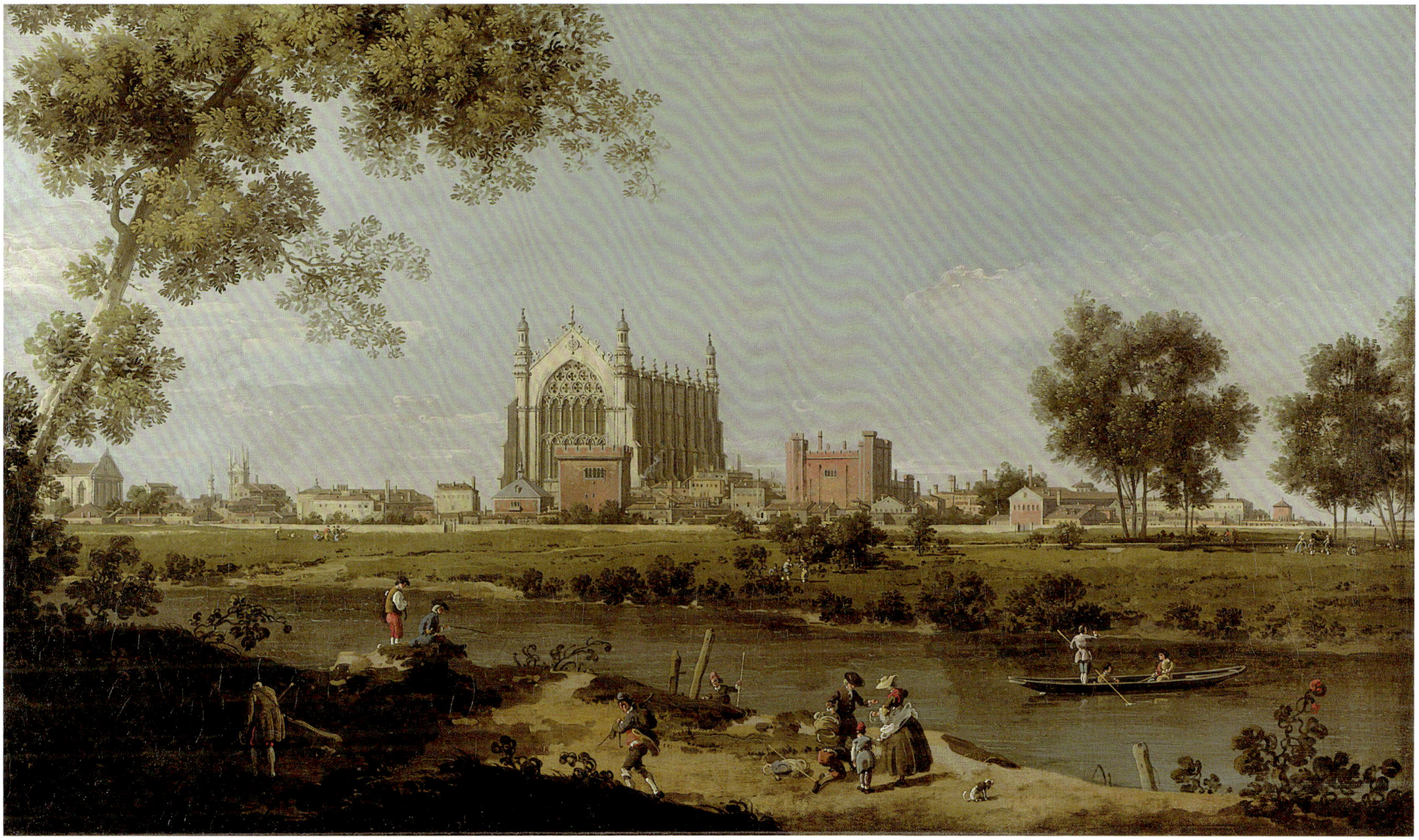

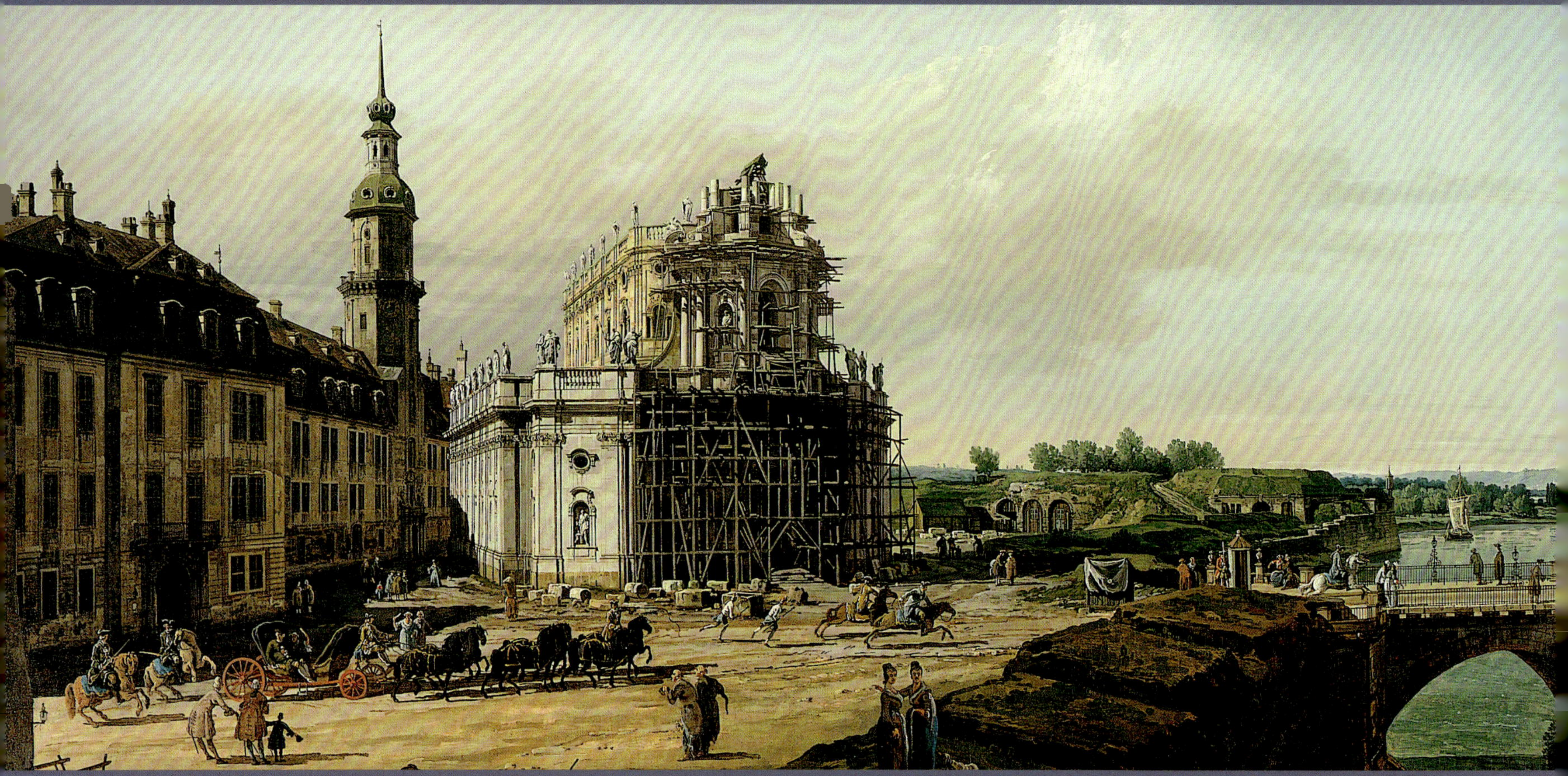

8.
CANALETTO IN LONDON, BELLOTTO IN DRESDEN

Canaletto's departure for London in 1746 and Bellotto's for Dresden in April 1747, also marked the definitive separation of their figurative worlds. In London, Canaletto was able to devote himself to the increasingly sophisticated stylisation of his painting, aided by the delicate English light and the shapes and colours of the architecture and landscape, whereas Bellotto's task in Dresden was instead to concretely depict the splendour of the city and its Baroque buildings. Both Canaletto and Bellotto proved to have an admirable ability to understand the nature of their new surroundings, and their artistic training and Enlightenment perspective led them to share the same mental outlook in dealing with the cultures they were portraying. The sophisticated *Northumberland House, London* (cat. 67), in which Canaletto recreates myriad of details with his light touch (this is the most 'Venetian' of the views from Canaletto's time in England, for the lively street life, workshops and inns, and the perspective close to a lagoon city Campo), reveals the quintessence of English civilisation, just as Bellotto's *The Neumarkt from the Jüdenhof, Dresden* (cat. 68) reveals that of Saxony. Both are works that fully met their patrons' expectations.

With the fourteen views of the city of Dresden, painted for August III (1697–1763) between 1747 and 1752, Bellotto created his first major cycle, a masterpiece. The views of the river Elba, the fortifications, the court of the Zwinger, the public squares and the churches were painted in pairs of pendants. And while painting the versions for the court, Bellotto also created replicas for the Prime Minister, Earl Heinrich Brühl (1700–1763). Identical in size, the replicas differ in the tonality of the sky, water and architecture and in the small details, particularly the figures (cat. 68, 71, 75, 77). The two versions of the view of *Dresden from the Left Bank of the Elbe, the Palace on the Left, the Catholic Hofkirche Streight Ahead* (cat. 71), compared here for the first time and united with the pendant in the Royal Collection, *Dresden from the Left Bank of the Elbe, below the Fortifications* (cat. 69), are the sole exception, due to their different depictions of the Hofkirche, which was being built at the time: in the version for the king, the tower is already in place, in accordance with the architect Gaetano Chiaveri's plans, whereas the version for Brühl mirrors the actual situation at the time when the painting was made.

While producing his first paintings in Dresden, Bellotto also created etchings of them, admirably recreating their details and light. The only surviving autograph drawings are from his period in Pirna, based on the paintings and used for the replicas and engravings. Presented here with the paintings, and also, in the case of *Kreuzkirche, Dresden* with a magnificent print, they clearly illustrate Bellotto's rigorous working methods.

67

CANALETTO

(Venice 1697–1768)

Northumberland House, London
1752–53

oil on canvas; 84 × 137 cm
Alnwick Castle, The Duke of Northumberland Collection, 03327

In February 1750, after the death of Algernon Seymour, 7th Duke of Somerset (1684–1750), Northumberland House and other properties belonging to the Percy family were inherited by Hugh Smithson (1712–1786), as well as the title of Earl of Northumberland. Sir Hugh and his wife, Elizabeth Seymour Percy (1716–1776), continued the reconstruction work begun by the Duke of Somerset on his London residence, built in the early years of the reign of James I and located at Charing Cross, between the Strand and St. Martin's Lane; on completion of the work they commissioned this painting from Canaletto. In 1753, the publisher Robert Sayer published a printed reproduction signed by Thomas Bowles, indicating that the picture must have been carried out before this date.

Sir Hugh Smithson was already in possession of the magnificent paintings of San Marco (cat. 16, 17), and during Canaletto's nine-year stay in England the Earl and his wife's family completed their collection with a further six paintings by the artist. In 1747, shortly after his arrival in London, Canaletto painted two innovative *vedute* for Smithson of *Westminster Bridge under Construction, London* (C/L 412 and 434); and in the same year, for the Duke of Somerset, *Windsor Castle* and in 1749, *Syon House* (C/L). The view of *Alnwick Castle*, Smithson's Northumberland residence, which documents the condition of the manor house before the construction work (C/L), was painted in circa 1752. The collection kept by the family has been perfectly preserved.

This painting is one of Canaletto's masterpieces. The renovated, bright facade of Northumberland House, with its two lateral towers and carefully rendered subtle decoration, occupies half of the picture. The lead lion that crowns the central section of the house, the emblem of the Percy family, was transferred to Syon House in Middlesex, the family's principal residence in 1873, when the building was demolished to make way for Northumberland Avenue. The statue of Charles I, by Hubert Le Suer (1633), to the right of the painting, is seen here on its second place, from 1675, near its current site in Trafalgar Square (laid out in the early nineteenth century). In the background a carriage is about to enter the Strand, which teems with shops. In the transparent shadow that envelops the houses to the left, the signs of the Golden Cross Inn and other inns and shops can be seen; in the well-lit open space, amidst a certain amount of chaos of which Canaletto was fond, we can make out wooden axles and wheels. The figures are handled delicately in keeping with the painting's other details, using yellows, blues and reds; light, fluid touches that reveal the position of the light create the soldier, hunchback beggar and running child, charismatic figures that were studied for this painting. The rosy clouds in the clear sky cast warm reflections.

We know of a drawing of this subject by Canaletto but it presents notable differences in both the perspective and figures, with the facade of Northumberland House relegated to the background (The Minneapolis Institute of Art, C/L 740). It may have been created as a 'modello' for this painting and then 'corrected' by Canaletto, as requested by Sir Hugh, to give the residence greater importance (C. Beddington, in New Haven-London 2006–2007, no. 14).

This painting, as well as the views of the Thames and castles painted in England for the Whig aristocracy, make Canaletto the most sensitive interpreter of mid-eighteenth century British society. The success of this composition was extraordinary, with an impressive number of replicas by other artists taken from the print, listed by Finberg and W.G. Constable. While in England Canaletto used finely woven canvases that contrasted with the thicker ones he used in Venice; he painted on a very light grey ground with subtle layers of colours in order to recreate the delicate light of English landscapes.

Bożena Anna Kowalczyk

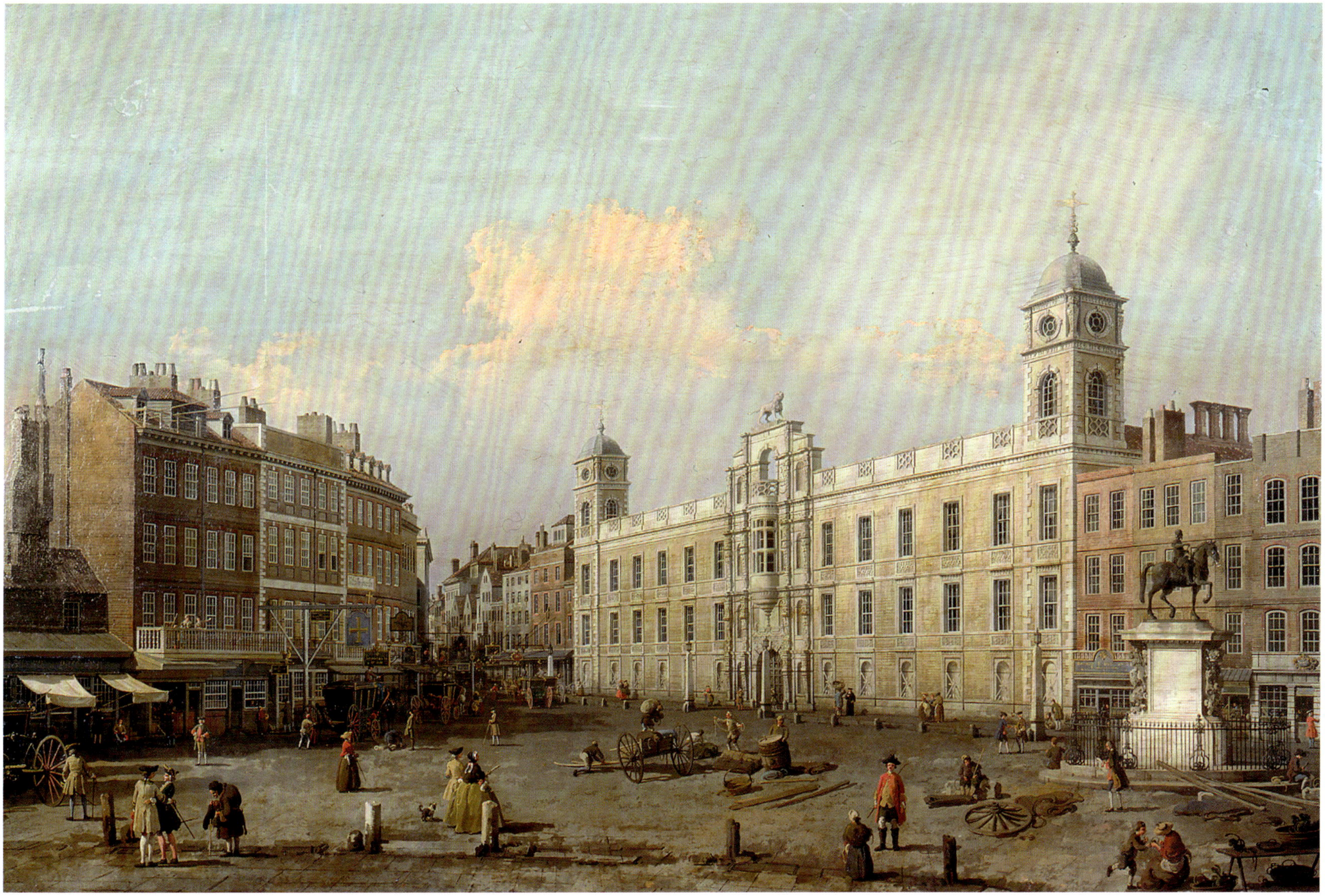

BERNARDO BELLOTTO

(Venice 1722 – Warsaw 1780)

The Neumarkt from the Jüdenhof, Dresden
1749–1752

oil on canvas; 134.5 x 236.5 cm
San Petersburg, The State Hermitage Museum, GE 203

The royal coach, drawn by six white horses, is crossing Neumarkt, the main square in the Old Town of Dresden. The rider at the head of the convoy stops it; his horse rears and the coach comes to a swaying halt. Augustus III (1697–1763), King of Poland and Elector of Saxony, where he was known as Frederick Augustus II, is on his way to visit his picture gallery, housed in the building on the left. Once the seat of the old stables, it was built between 1586 and 1591 by architect Paul Buchner and refurbished as royal picture gallery under Augustus II the Strong (1670–1733) in successive stages, beginning in 1722. In 1746, Augustus III was finally able to arrange the royal collection there, eliminating the partition between the two floors to house the larger paintings as well, thus earning the admiration of visitors such as Winckelmann and Goethe. He himself, as well as his father before him, had added to the royal collection considerably – the purchase of a hundred masterpieces from the Duke of Modena's collection dates back to that very year. The stately Frauenkirche, built between 1726 and 1743 by architect and city master carpenter George Bähr – the most beautiful example of Protestant Baroque in Saxony, it towers above the rooftops of the houses –, is also a credit to Augustus III. To evoke the ruler's power, Bellotto has the convoy come from the Pirnaische Gasse that leads to Pirna and Koenigstein, home to his impressive fortresses. Along the porticoes of the Old Town Guardhouse, a row of soldiers lines up to salute their ruler; some passers-by bow to the coach whilst others carry on with their activities – it seems like a scene from everyday life.
Comparing this *veduta* with its pendant, *The Neumarkt from the Moritzstrasse, Dresden* (Kozakiewicz 1972a, n. 171) we notice the forced perspective with which Bellotto introduces, on the right, the building with the Renaissance pediment – the artisans' warehouse built in 1591 by Buchner, which frames its companion on the left. These two *vedute*, the first town squares painted after the ones depicted around three years before in Italy – *The Piazza Navona* in Rome and the churches of *San Paolo Converso e Sant'Eufemia* in Milan (cat. 49, 59) – clearly show the extraordinary artistic maturity attained in Dresden. The rules of representation remain the same, but here Bellotto asserts himself with skill and prospective and luminist sureness that do not fear wide spaces or imposing architectural structures. The architectural structures are drawn with extreme precision, the main lines are drawn with a ruler and engraved in the fresh paint – a technique that Bellotto uses skilfully in favour of pictorial quality. The pavement lines, drawn with a ruler and colour, are 'masked' by light touches of paint. Bellotto's depiction of the Frauenkirche expresses his admiration for the powerful edifice, capturing every detail – enhanced by the lighting – and thus proving his extraordinary vocation as painter of architectural structures.
The present painting belongs to the series commissioned by Heinrich, Earl von Brühl, prime minister of the Saxon court – replicas on the same scale and in the same format as the royal series, fifteen of which were bought by Tsarina Catherine the Great in 1768. This double commission, two series on the same scale, is a truly exceptional artistic event. Bellotto became an expert in replicas during his apprenticeship in Canaletto's workshop, and knows how to skilfully use drawings. As in his early years, Bellotto's replicas are works of art in their own right for his use of light and colours.The magnificent canvas showcases Bellotto's idea of also replicating the quality and degree of finishing. We perceive the colours more vivid – the browns and greens of the cobblestones, the blues and ochres in the garments of the figures, the grey-streaked blue of the sky – but the comparison of this aspect is still under the study, due to the different state of preservation (see cat. 74). The lighting is intense, the sharply-outlined dark shadows stand out against the illuminated areas, the white hints scattered amongst the figures appear clearly, as do the nervous, undulating strokes of the riders' uniforms and the horses depicted with solid touches, studied in different poses compared to the royal version. The opulent coach, depicted in its pictorial decoration of pale blue, red and white, with wheels in bright green and hints of yellow, adds a joyful note of colour. A beautiful print made from the royal version is dated 1749.

Bożena Anna Kowalczyk

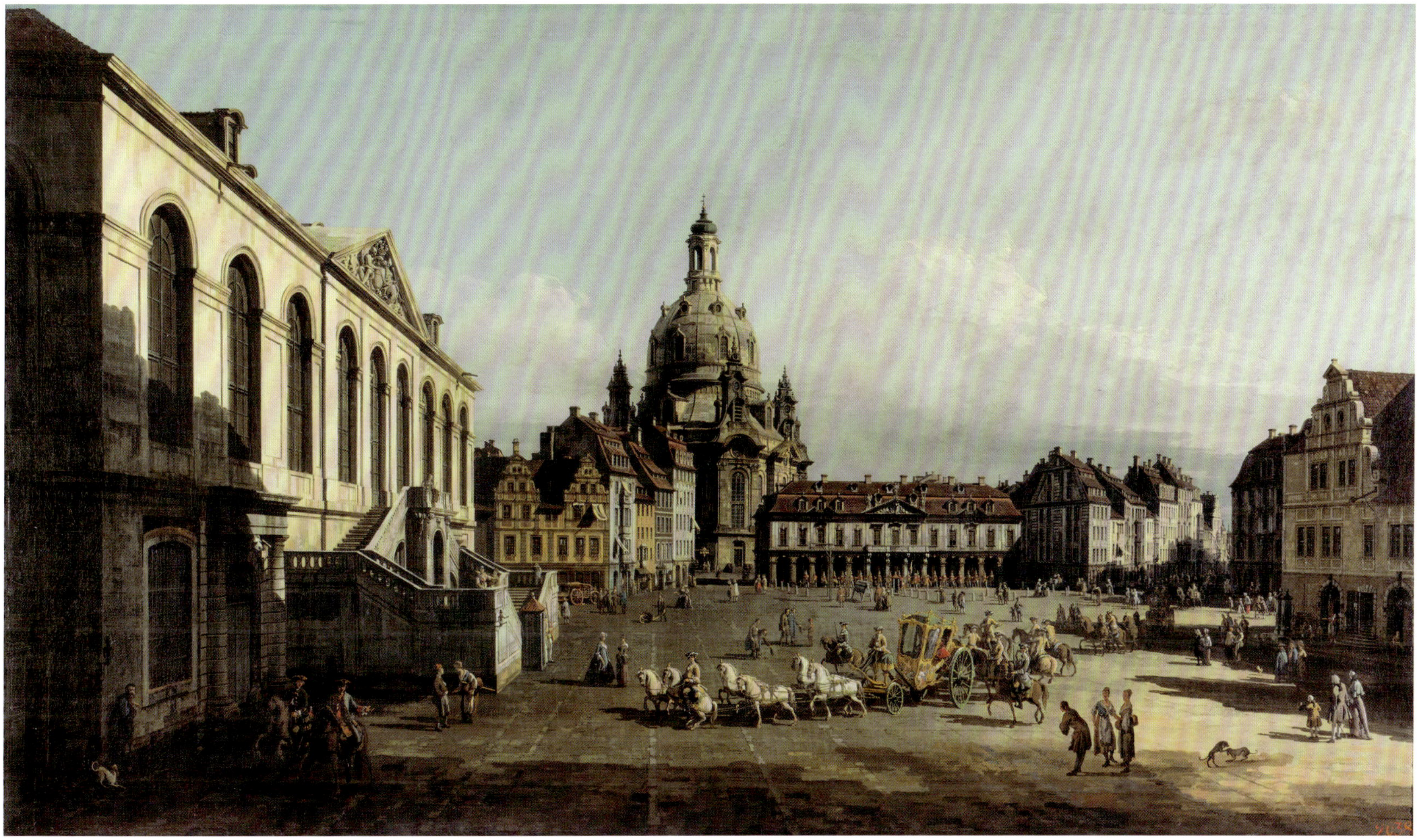

69

BERNARDO BELLOTTO

(Venice 1722 – Warsaw 1780)

Dresden from the Left Bank of the Elbe, below the Fortifications
1748

oil on canvas; 133 x 235 cm
signed at the bottom, slightly to the left 'BERNARD.º BELOTO DETTO / CANALETO. F. AN.º 1748'
Dresden, Staatliche Kunstsammlungen, Gemäldegalerie Alte Meister, 608

This view of the Catholic Hofkirche was one of Bellotto's first works in Dresden following his arrival in the city in 1747. As in the two views of the city from the Elbe that he painted soon after arriving in Dresden (Dresden, Gallery nos. 602 and 606), as well as the river view from the bank of the New Town (Dresden, Gallery no. 607; cat. 72), the artist signed and dated this work. Bellotto subsequently stopped this practice, but then began signing and dating his works again after the Seven Years' War.

This picture shows the view of the Schloßplatz with the Hofkirche from the Brühlsche Terrasse. This church was one of the most important architectural projects built in Dresden by the Prince Elector Frederick Augustus II of Saxony (in office from 1733 to 1763). It is therefore not by chance that the artist depicts the ruler passing in front of the church in his official coach drawn by six horses. Like his father, Augustus, known as the Saxon, he had converted to Catholicism in order to also reign over Poland – with the title of Augustus III of Poland.

The painter's viewpoint is located in the garden of Earl Brühl, prime minister of Saxony, inside the Jungfernbastei (Venus fortifications). The Schloßplatz was built in 1737, following the destruction of the Elbtor, the mint and the foundry, as well as the filling in of two former bridge pillars. This created sufficient space to erect the church. Its architect was Gaetano Chiaveri, from Rome, who had the first stone laid in 1739. Inside the main nave, a 3.5-metre circular route was also created to allow for the processions that would otherwise have been impossible to carry out in the Protestant city. The seventy-eight 3 metre-high statues of saints located on the parapet of the church are by the sculptor Lorenzo Mattielli from Vicenza. The fact remains that the church was not yet finished when Bellotto painted this view. The tower above the main facade only reached as far as the upper roof. To simulate the eventual appearance of the building, Bellotto used the architect's plans (the tower did not reach its height of 85.5 metre until 1755), painting scaffolding around the tower to mask the pretence. Although in the etching of the same year inspired by the painting (cat. 70) the artist abandoned the scaffolding, in the copy painted for the prime minister of Saxony, Earl Brühl (cat. 71), Bellotto showed the tower as it was in 1748.

To the left of the church we can see the Residenzschloss, or rather the castle built between 1547 and 1555 for the Prince Elector Maurice I, with its so-called Hausmannsturm, built between 1674 and 1678. To the left stands the Georgenbau, built between 1530 and 1535 to honour the Prince Elector George the Bearded, with the Georgentor, which led into the city.

The bridge over the Elbe was extended between 1727 and 1731 for reasons of prestige during the reign of the Prince Elector Frederick Augustus I, known as The Strong (in office from 1694 to 1733), father of Frederick Augustus II, by the architect Matthäus Daniel Pöppelmann. For precision, pedestrian walkways were added on both sides and lanterns were fitted. Panoramic viewpoints with a number of benches were also created above the pillars, and the bridge was surrounded by a wrought iron balustrade that was an invitation to strolling, as can be seen in the painting.

Behind the bridge we can see the Sol Bastion with its casemates, and on the other bank the Japanese Palace that housed Augustus the Strong's extensive collection of porcelain. The panorama along the course of the Elbe reaches as far as the high ground of the Lößnitz.

Andreas Henning

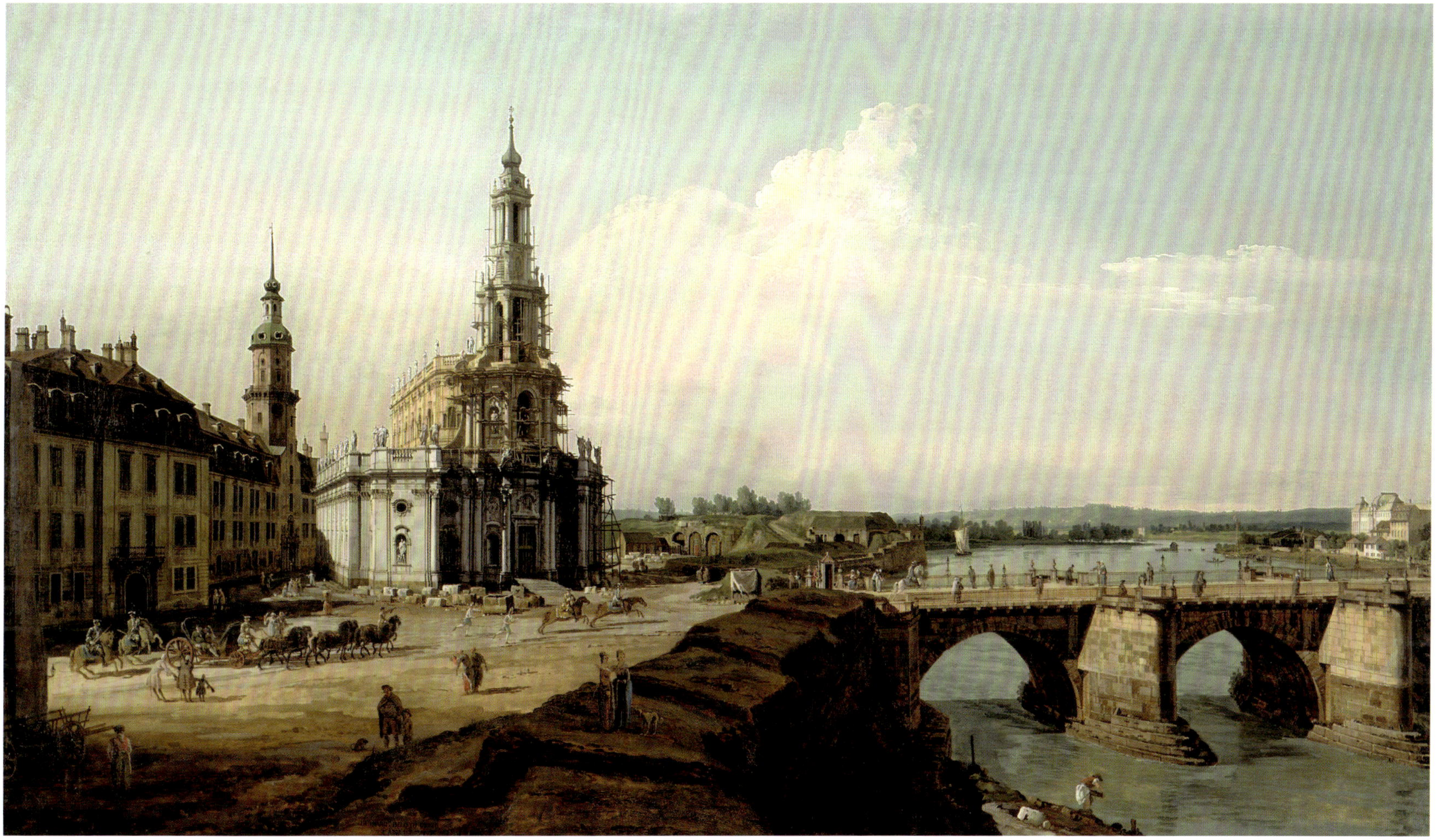

BERNARDO BELLOTTO

(Venice 1722 – Warsaw 1780)

Dresden from the left Bank of the Elbe, the Palace on the left, the Hofkirche Straight Ahead
1748

etching; I state of two; 544 x 837 mm
signed on the bottom left, inside the image, 'CANALETO. F.'
Milan, Civica Raccolta delle Stampe 'Achille Bertarelli', vol. FF 25, tab. 3.

*Inscription*s: on lower margin, 'Perspective de la Façade de la Roïale -- Eglise Catolique, avec une part du Palais / de S.M. et des Environs de Neudorff sur l'Elbe, tirée -- du Jardin de S.E.ce Mgr. Le Comte de Brühl Le Pre.r Ministre. / Ce Tableau fait par ordre de S.M. le Roy de Pologne et Elec. De Sax. &.&.&. -- Peint, dessiné, et gravé par Bernard Belloto dit Canaletto. 1748'.

In terms of its breadth and quality, the series of fourteen large etchings taken from the *vedute* of Dresden, with six smaller ones of Pirna, are a unique undertaking for an eighteenth-century *peintre-graveur*. The handwritten inventory in the Dresden apartment tells us that the artist had a proper printing press set up in one of the rooms, allowing him to follow every stage of the development of the plates, from engraving to printing; even the French inscription underneath, describing the subjects, are by his hand, as confirmed by a comparison with the polished writing of the manuscript (*Catalogo dei Danni*, cat. 83).
Bellotto engraved the views of Dresden in two periods: 1747–1750 and 1757–1758, before leaving for Vienna. The dating of the first views of Dresden, specified by the painter in the inscriptions, mostly agrees with that of the paintings, where indicated, and in one case printing preceded completion of the canvas, once again indicating the close relationship between painting and engraving (cf. cat. 72). The later engraved prints are of such beauty and adherence to every *chiaroscuro* passage of the canvases as to confirm H.A. Fritzsche's idea that the work for the etchings was carried out in front of the paintings. An accurate perspectival drawing of the details, such as the one that survives of the *Kreuzkirche, Dresden* (cat. 78), a one-of-a-kind, would undoubtedly have also been required.
The prints of Pirna are undated, but some of them must have been carried out before 1758; Bellotto lists all six of them in his inventory, but amends the number: at least one of these, in fact, *Pirna from the Vineyards of Posta*, belongs to his second period in Dresden, in 1764 (Kozakiewicz 1972a, n. 192); the inventory also includes sixteen prints of Dresden of the fourteen completed (*Catalogo de Danni*, cat. 83).
In the first Dresden period, in the 1750s, Bellotto engraved a painting by Jan van den Heyden in the gallery of Earl Brühl, probably for the never realised second volume of *Recueil* (Kozakiewicz 1972a, n. 247); he completed the elegant theatrical etching in Vienna in 1759 (cat. 89). After the Prussian bombing of July 1760, all that remained of his plates were, in his own words: 'Some coppers, only good to be sold for scrap copper' (*Catalogo de Danni*, p. 18*v*); but Moritz Stübel, the scholar who has made an essential contribution to the study of Bellotto's engravings, discovered one that had been saved, despite being damaged (Stübel 1911, n. 12). In the following years, Bellotto continued to take some prints dated 1758 to the Kupferstich-Kabinett, along with his freshly engraved prints, *The Courtyard of the Zwinger, Dresden* and *The Moat of the Zwinger, Dresden* and those of Pirna (see G. Metze, in Dresden 2011). Only *The Königstein Fortress with the Lilienstein* (cat. 91), *The Ruins of the Kreuzkirche, Dresden* (cat. 93) and *The Ruins of the Suburb Pirna, Dresden* (cat. 92), have precise matches in the archive of the Kupferstich-Kabinett – which keeps the registers from 1764 – confirming their execution in 1765 and 1766, shortly before delivery (G. Metze, in Dresda 2011).
This etching is one of the first made in Dresden and the only one to contain a signature engraved between the image, as in the Italian prints (see the essay by the author of this entry). The composition differs from both the painting in the royal series and that of Earl Brühl (cat. 69, 71) due to the extended width at the sides and the appearance of the Hofkirche, devoid of scaffolding; the figures, the riders and the silhouettes of the horses in particular, most resemble those of the Brühl version, only the two women in the centre of both paintings, in shadow, are replaced here by a small group of three, taken as a mirror image from a print by Canaletto (Bromberg 1974, no. 11).
The example in the exhibition is a beautiful first state, with the emblem of the union between Saxony and Poland printed on a small separate plate. In the rendering of the shadow on the path that runs diagonally up to the bridge Bellotto demonstrates real virtuosity and a strong link with Canaletto's engraving technique.

Bożena Anna Kowalczyk

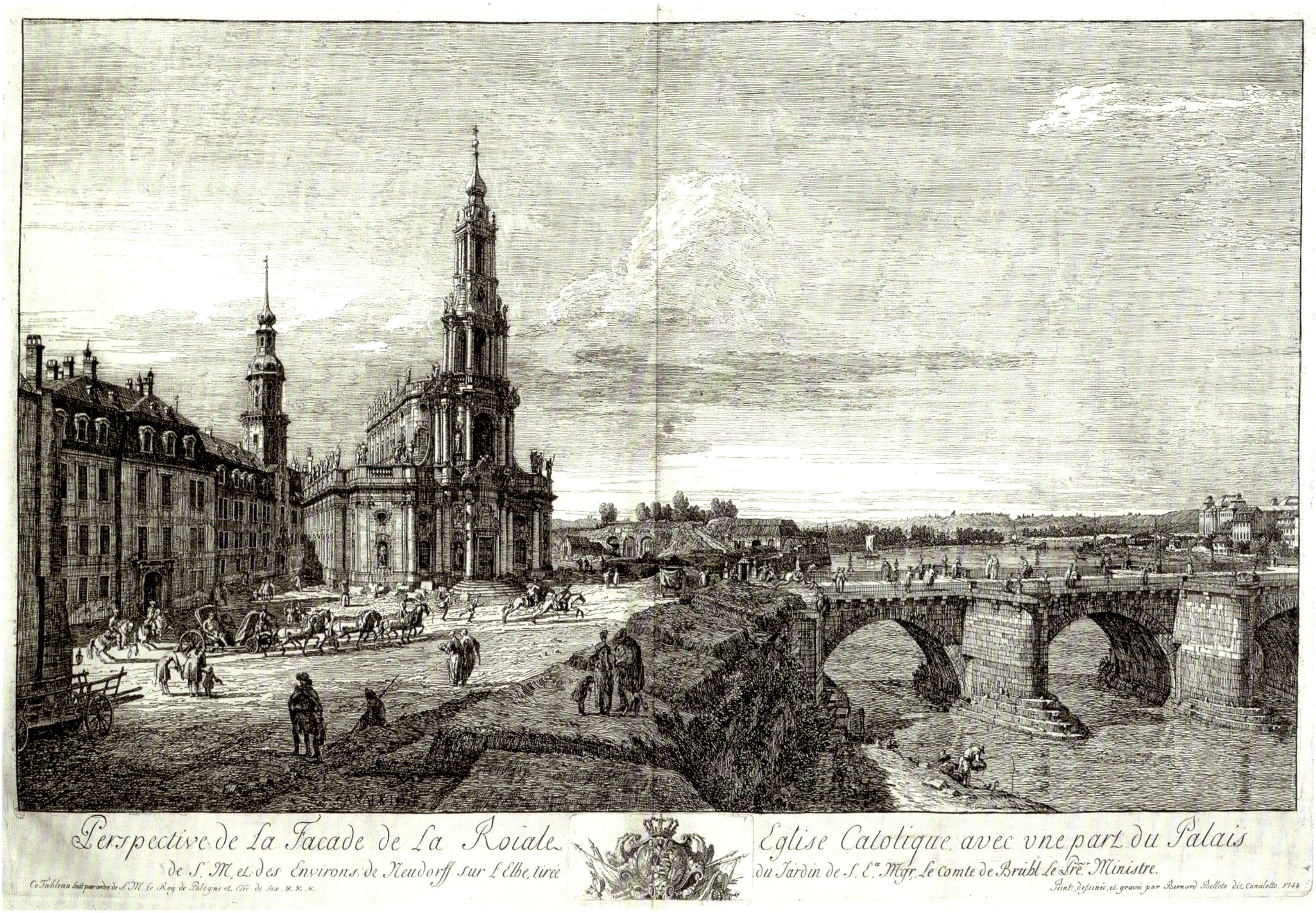
Perspective de la Facade de la Roiale Eglise Catolique, avec vne part du Palais
de S. M. et des Environs de Neudorff sur l'Elbe, tirée du Jardin de S. E. Mgr. Le Comte de Brühl Le Pre. Ministre.
Ce Tableau fait par ordre de S. M. le Roy de Pologne et Elec. de Sax. &c. &c. &c.
Peint, dessinés, et gravés par Bernard Belloto dit Canaletto. 1748

71

BERNARDO BELLOTTO
(Venice 1722 – Warsaw 1780)

Dresden from the Left Bank of the Elbe, the Palace on the Left, the Catholic Hofkirche Streight Ahead
1748

oil on canvas; 134 x 231 cm
signed lower left, 'BERNARDO BELOTTO DE.o / CANALETO F A.o 1748'
Pinacoteca Giovanni e Marella Agnelli, Turin

Gaetano Chiaveri (1689–1770), a Roman architect originating from Bergamo, arrived in Dresden in 1737, after working since his youth at the courts of Saint Petersburg and Warsaw, distinguishing himself for bold solutions and an intelligent eclecticism, while respecting local traditions. In 1738, Frederick Augustus II commissioned him for the building of the court church, the Hofkirche; this was to be a Catholic church, to which faith he had converted in 1712 and observed as King of Poland under the title of Augustus III. The first stone was laid on 28 June, 1739, and the church was consecrated in 1751, but the facade tower – a tribute to the German Westwerk – remained unfinished until 1755 when it reached its planned height of 85.5 metres. The Hofkirche was Chiaveri's masterpiece that triumphed over the difficulties of the high ground by the Elbe near the castle, and it was built at an oblique position with respect to the Augustus Bridge, appearing in the panorama of the Dresden Altstadt as a brilliant counterpoint to the majestic dome of the Protestant Frauenkirche, built between 1727 and 1743, to a design by George Bähr.
On his arrival in Dresden in April 1747, Bellotto found the body of the church already built, decorated on the outside with the 78 sculptures of saints, each three metres high, by sculptor Lorenzo Mattielli from Vicenza and the Dresden stonemasons Paul and Jakob Mayer. The tower had been raised to the second floor, with scaffolding covering only the first, and so, as a good student of Canaletto, he described it in his first view of the Saxon capital, *Dresden from the Right Bank of the Elbe, upstream of the Augustus Bridge*, signed and dated 1747, and in the replica of the same year for Earl Heinrich Brühl (Kozakiewicz 1972a, nos. 140, 141). The pendant, *Dresden from the Right Bank of the Elbe, downstream of the Augustus Bridge*, painted in 1748 and constituting the first version of this view, was executed in the same year for Augustus III (cat. 69), and instead showed the tower at full height, very slender but still with scaffolding, which was omitted in the print after the picture of 1748 (Kozakiewicz 1972a, no. 146).
It is certainly Frederick Augustus II who wanted to see the Hofkirche already finished in line with the architect's design; with the renovation of the Royal Gallery, this was his greatest architectural feat and glory. In the final realisation, the project was changed and the shape of the belfry and the clock were never to have the same appearance as in Bellotto's pictures. In London in 1746–47, Canaletto followed the design drawings for the last phases in the construction of Westminster Bridge in one of his first English paintings, *Westminster Bridge from the North with the Lord Mayor's Procession, 29 October 1746* (New Haven, Yale Center for British Art, Paul Mellon Collection, C/L 435), but the bridge opened in 1750 with so many changes to it as to make Canaletto's image a *capriccio*.
Earl Heinrich Brühl, who commissioned the painting, evidently left the artist free to choose. Bellotto took the opportunity to bring together his greatest interests in a single canvas: he depicted the real elements, the work in progress, a bridge over the river, the landscape in the distance. In this canvas, shown from the gardens of Earl Brühl – the current Brühlsche Terrasse – he combined the motifs of the two views of Turin, of the scaffolding and of the bridge, on the Elbe, rebuilt by Frederick Augustus I (1670–1733), shown at a similar angle to the crumbling one on the Po river (cat. 53). The scaffolding covers the entire facade, the building materials are scattered on the ground and the sandstone used for the lower nave are already plastered, as in the real view. The royal carriage is about to cross the bridge, escorted by two horsemen shown in the studied racing poses.
To the left, there is a part of the castle, the Georgenbau and, behind, Moritzbau with the Sentinel tower; to the right, beyond the bridge, the Japanese Palace. The Elbe is lost in the distance, running towards the hills of Lössnitz, where Bellotto conveys the poetry of the distant landscape. The viewpoint of the pendant, *Dresden from the Left Bank of the Elbe below the Fortifications*, now at the North Carolina Museum of Art, Raleigh (Kozakiewicz 1972a, no. 155), was in the meadows behind the Hofkirche. The two paintings were together until Christie's sale of 3 May 1946 in which they were sold along with three other Brühl paintings by Arthur Robert Mills, the third Baron Hillingdon (1891–1952).

Bożena Anna Kowalczyk

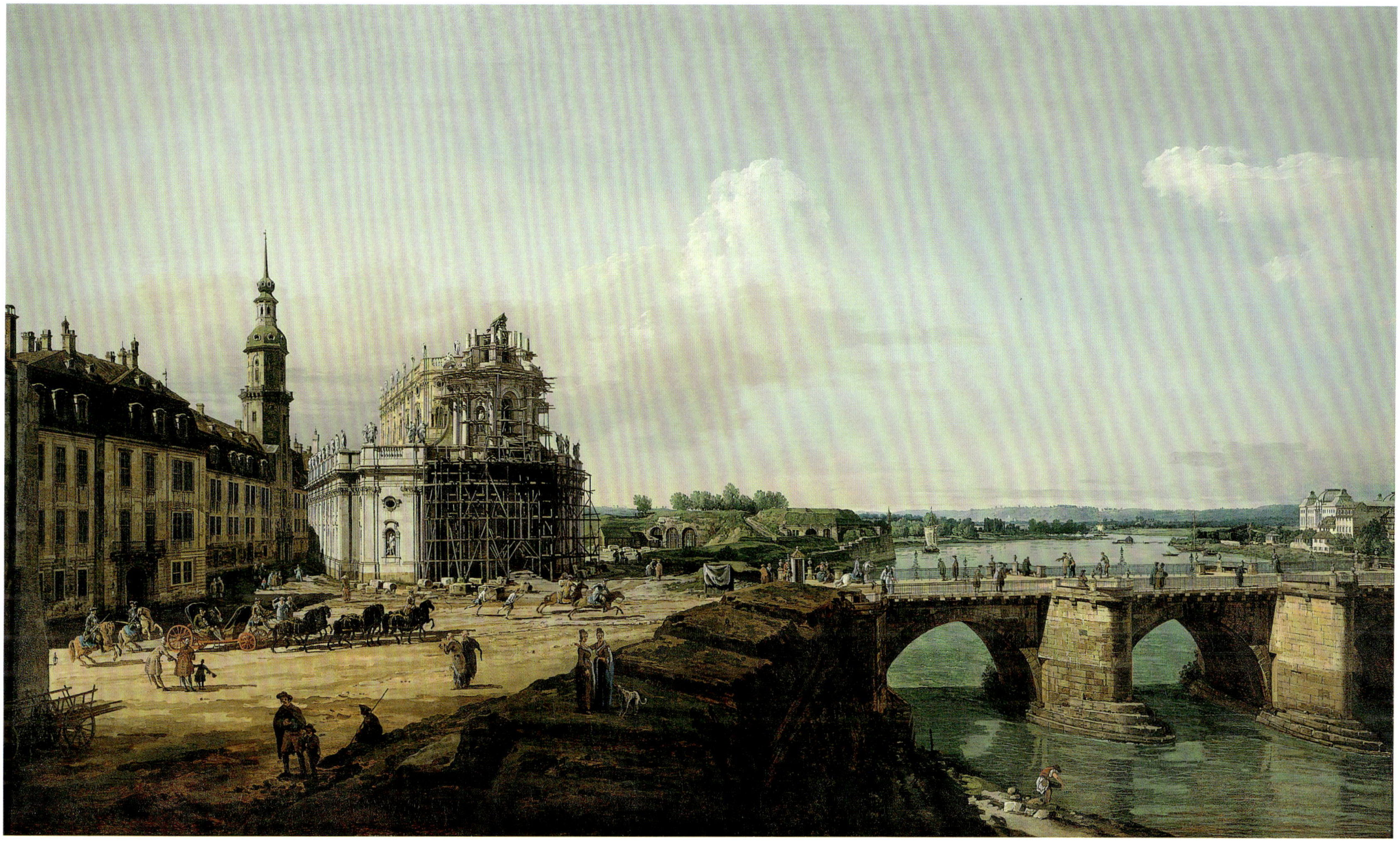

72

BERNARDO BELLOTTO

(Venice 1722–1780 Warsaw)

Dresden from the Left Bank of the Elbe, below the Fortifications
1748

oil on canvas; 133 x 234 cm
signed lower left on the stone block, 'Bernardo Bellotto detto Canaletto F.An.° 1748'
Dresden, Staatliche Kunstsammlungen, Gemäldegalerie Alte Meister, 607

73

BERNARDO BELLOTTO

(Venice 1722–1780 Warsaw)

Dresden from the Left Bank of the Elbe, below the Fortifications
1747

etching, III state of five; 538 x 850 mm (plate)
Milan, Civica Raccolta delle Stampe 'Achille Bertarelli', vol. FF 25, pl. 1

Inscriptions: (cat. 73) on lower margin, 'Perspective de La ville neuve, et du Palais -- de S.M. dit d'hollande et des Environs de / la Campagne de Loschùwitz, avec une partie de La -- Roïale Eglise Catolique et des Bastions de la ville de / Dresde, prise de la prairie Joignante aux Ecuries Roïales et à L'orangerie -- Ce tableau fait par ordre de Sa Majeste Le Roy de Pologne et Elẽc: de Sax. &.&.&. / Peint, dessiné et grave par Ber: Bellotto dit Canaletto Pein:R.le/1747'.

From the late spring of 1747, Bernardo Bellotto was in the service of Augustus III (1696–1763), Elector of Saxony and King of Poland (with the name of Frederick Augustus II), who continued the architectural transformation of Dresden started by his father, Augustus II the Strong (1670–1733). The artist, who was appointed court painter in 1748, depicted the different panoramic views and the city centre, built between 1747 and 1755, showing the city renewed and improved by the most recent constructions, the Augustus Brücke, the bridge over the Elbe (rebuilt between 1727 and 1731 by Matthäus Daniel Pöppelmann and Johann Gottfried Fehre), the Frauenkirche by George Bähr consecrated in 1743, the Hofkirche designed by Gaetano Chiaveri built between 1739 and 1755, and the Royal Gallery, transformed from the old stables and opened in 1746. The fourteen views of the city for the Royal Gallery were planned as pairs of pendants, as evidenced by the order in which they are mentioned in the inventory drawn up by Matthias Oesterreich in 1754, and as the similar perspective arrangement and choice of subjects also demonstrate. In Bellotto's second Dresden period, between 1762 and 1766, the artist painted three views of the city, *The Ruins of the Kreuzkirche, Dresden* (Gemäldegalerie Alte Meister, Dresden), *The Ruins of the Suburb Pirna, Dresden* (Musée des Beaux Arts, Troyes) and *The Old City from the Fort, Dresden* (Staatliche Kunsthalle, Karlsruhe).
The present painting, a pendant of the view of *Dresden from the Left Bank of the Elbe, the Palace on the left, the Catholic Hofkirche Streight Ahead* (cat. 69) stands out particularly, offering a panorama over the New Town beyond the Elbe, from the meadows near the old fortifications that take up more than half of the view. This compositional choice best expresses the particular ambition of a 'historian', an enlightenment approach already apparent in the last Italian views in embracing the reality of the places in all its aspects. It is also a legacy of Dutch painting of the seventeenth century, which Bellotto would have seen in the royal and Brühl collections, supporting his own interests.
The stretch of water of the moat at the foot of the fortified wall turns right to skirt the Zwinger after the collapsing wooden hut on stilts, shown with some gearing whose function remains unknown but of great beauty as painterly detail, and acting as counterpoint to the elegant Hofkirche; to the left of centre, on the bank of the Elbe, there is a sluice system ensuring the supply of the moat with water from the river. A rustic four-horse cart in the foreground attracts attention with its red cover and masterly characterisation; in Dresden, Bellotto carefully studied the elegant racehorses in the royal stables, depicting them in different positions, and in this case he shows that he also observed workhorses. Women, peasants, fishermen, cows, dogs and laundry all appear in the meadow.
It must have been by order of the patron commissioning the work that in this extraordinary extract of reality the Hofkirche should appear with the tower facade already shown full height, albeit behind scaffolding; it was actually completed in 1755 but did not soar upwards so much and was depicted in the royal series and in replicas for Earl Brühl – with a few exceptions – in line with the drawings or wooden model of its architect (cat. 71), Gaetano Chiaveri (1689–1770). The Frauenkirche appears behind with the top of the tower with the lantern.
The New Town is reflected in the transparent water of the river; between the town houses we can make out two buildings in particular: the impressive Japanese building on the left, built and commissioned by Augustus the Strong to house his collection of porcelain, and the Blockhause at the foot of the bridge, designed in 1730 by the architect Zacharias Longuelune, on the roof of which as equestrian statue of the sovereign was to have been placed, until a decision in 1736 moved it to the centre of the New Town's square. The clouds gather over the hills of Loschwitz in the distance, in another detail of great beauty.
The brilliant idea of reproducing the views of Dresden in etching must have arisen with the first paintings of the Elbe. Pierre-Jean Mariette, the first critic of Bellotto as engraver attributes this idea to the sovereign, who 'lui a fait peindre

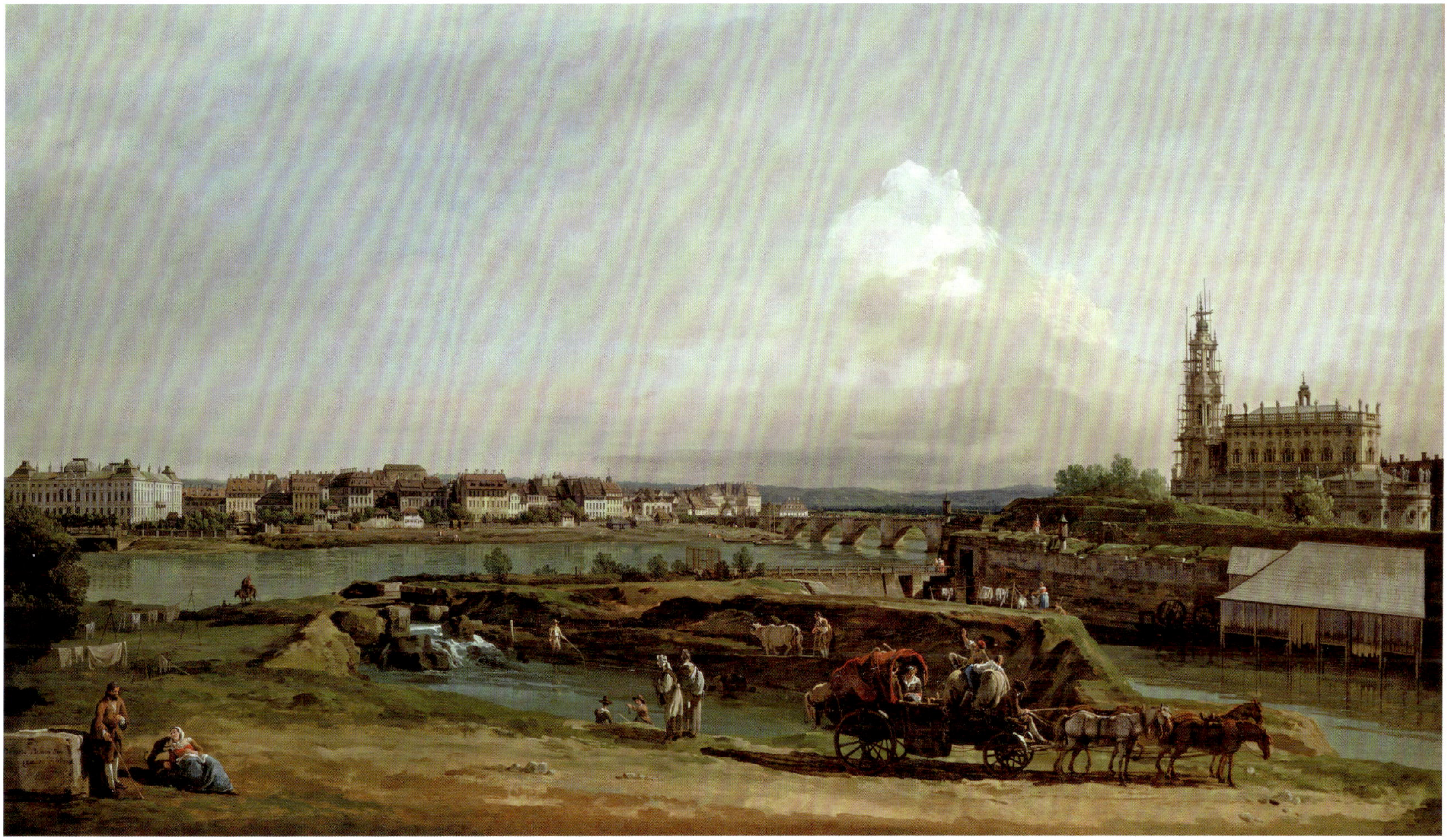

les principales veuës de la ville de Dresde, et il les lui a ensuite fait graver', and then commented: 'on les croiroit gravées par Ant. Canal même, tant elles sont ressemblantes par la touche, à ce qui a été gravé à Venise par ce dernier. C'est la même fermeté de pointe, on y trouve de même à redire trop d'égalité dans la touche et des dégradations de lumières pas assez sensibles' (*Abecedario* 1851-1853, t. 1, p. 115).
A room in the house of Bellotto when he lived in Dresden, in Salzgasse near the Neumarkt and the Frauenkirche, was used as a printing shop. Nothing was missing there to carve and print, from table 'per bagnare la carta' (to wet the paper), and 'ferramenti per Sciugar le Stampe' (ironware to dry the prints) to 'Torchi per stampare' (printing presses), reams of large and small paper, 'barile con color' (barrels of colour) and several bottles of 'Dura e tenera' (hard and soft) varnish (see *Catalogo de Danni*, cat. 83). The discovery that Bellotto was the creator of every productive phase of his prints makes us appreciate his great work even more.
This is one of the first etchings to be produced in Dresden, the most divergent from the painting, and the most 'corrected' in the various states; the present sheet is a rare third state with the coat of arms with the emblem of the Saxon-Polish union printed on a second small plate. In every state, the Hofkirche appears without the scaffolding and with the Hausmann tower of the castle on the far right, which was not included in the canvas, and with a dog prancing in front of the horses. The third state differs from the first and second also by the small text beneath the edge of the print; in the first state read: 'Peint, dessiné et gravé par Ber: Bellotto dit Canaletto 1747'; in the second state, only the date changed, becoming '1748'. Here Bellotto wanted to highlight his title as court painter which he had in the meantime received, but the date '1747' carried over from the first state cannot be explained as the error of the author of the inscription, as proposed by Stübel, and supported by Kozakiewicz: we now know that this was Bellotto himself. We must therefore conclude that the painting and the print were produced at the same time, with the print being finished first.
In the subsequent states, the coat of arms was part a single plate. In the fourth, the stone at lower left was reworked and the first horse on the right was given two reins; in the fifth, the windows of the Japanese palace and the roof of the neighbouring house were retouched.

Bożena Anna Kowalczyk

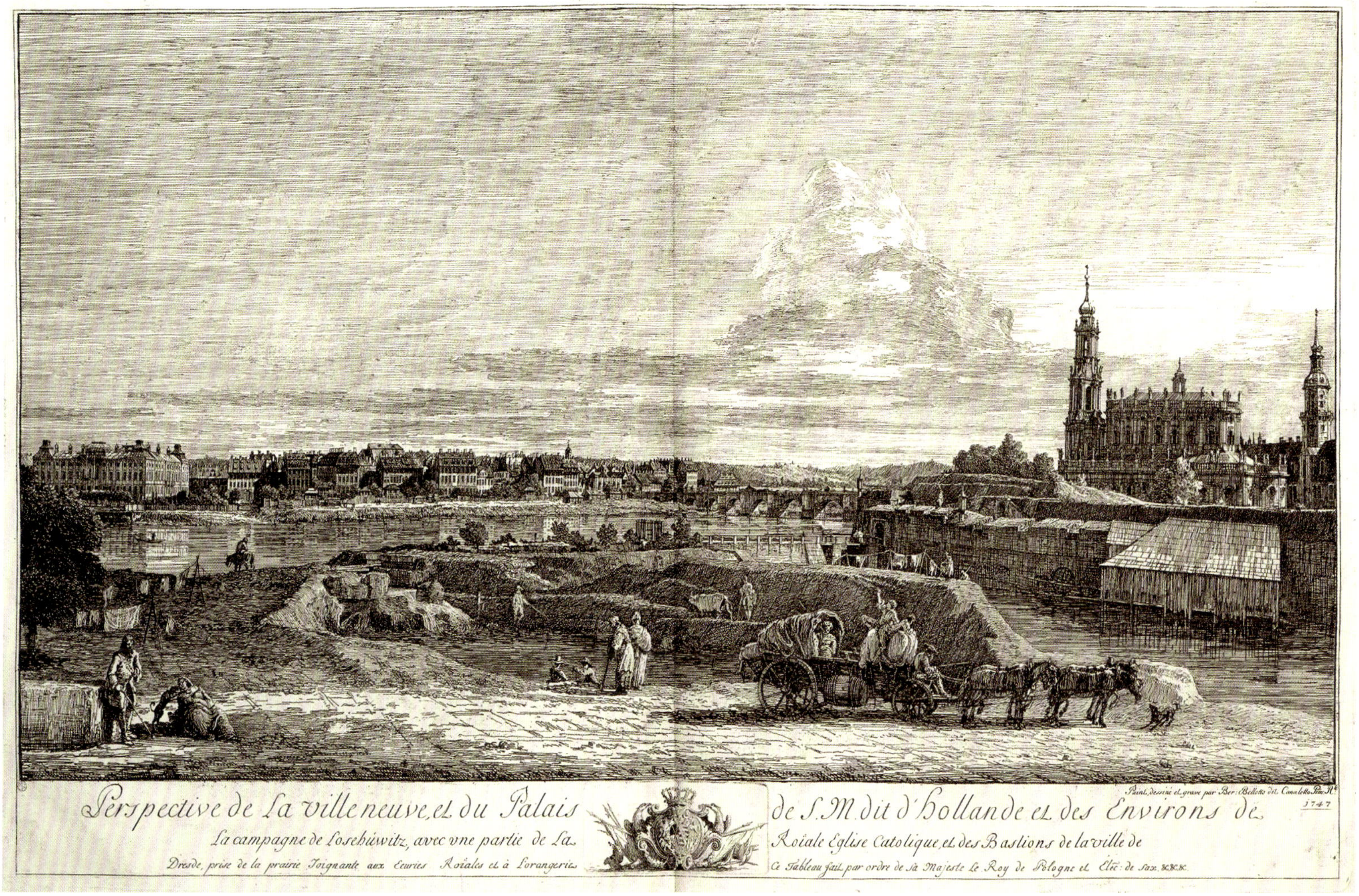

BERNARDO BELLOTTO

(Venice 1722 – Warsaw 1780)

The Courtyard of the Zwinger, Dresden
1751–52

oil on canvas; 134 x 237 cm
Dresden, Staatliche Kunstsammlungen, Gemäldegalerie Alte Meister, 629

From an urban planning perspective, the Zwinger in Dresden was one of the most important projects implemented by the Prince Elector Frederick Augustus I of Saxony, known as The Strong (in office from 1694 to 1733). It is located in the east of the city, between the fortress and the Residenzschloss. It was built as a place of celebration ahead of the wedding between the Prince Elector Augustus the Strong and Maria Josepha, archduchess of Austria, planned for 1719. The union of the Saxon prince with a daughter of Joseph I of Habsburg was a decisive political move, through which the electoral principality of Saxony expressed a desire for greater importance in Europe.

The architect Matthäus Daniel Pöppelmann built the Zwinger between 1710 and 1728 with the sculptor Balthasar Permoser. Six pavilions with galleries were specially built. From 1727, as part of a reorganisation of his collection of artworks, Augustus the Strong began arranging some of the sections of the Kunstkammer in the rooms of the Zwinger, creating a 'Palais des Sciences'. The Zwinger is now one of the most important Baroque buildings in Europe.

Bellotto looks out from the Wallpavillon at the 204-metre long Zwinger, towards the east of the city. Opposite the painter's viewpoint is the elegant Stadtpavillon (now known as the Glockenspielpavillon), flanked by two two-storey pavilions. In Bellotto's day, the pavilion on the left was home to the cabinet of engravings on the ground floor, with the library on the first floor. The pavilion on the right, as well as the neighbouring galleries, housed the Kunstkammer's zoological and natural sciences collections. As in the Glockenspielpavillon, the upper floor was home to some sections of the library. The natural sciences pavilion was connected to the so-called Langgalerie, above the centre of which stood to the Kronentor, topped by a gold-plated royal crown, carried by four Polish eagles. This was because both Augustus the Strong and his son Frederick Augustus II (in office from 1733 to 1763) also reigned over Poland. Towards the right-hand edge stands the pavilion housing the mathematics and physics hall, which is still home to instruments, globes and clocks. Along the left-hand edge we can see the French pavilion, the upper floors of which at that time were part of the Kunstkammer, dominated by the so-called Marmorsaal. In the light of projects aimed at doubling the surface area of the Zwinger, a wall instead of a Langgalerie had been built on the north side between the French and German pavilions. When this idea was abandoned in 1732, a simple painted wall (replaced in the mid-nineteenth century by Gottfried Semper's Gemäldegalerie) was built.

Glimpses of the city can be seen behind the Zwinger. A Renaissance tympanum of the Residenzschloss, for example, appears at the extreme left, behind the French pavilion. It is partially covered by the Komödienhaus, used from 1751 as a Ballhaus (and demolished in 1896). Above the roof of the German pavilion we

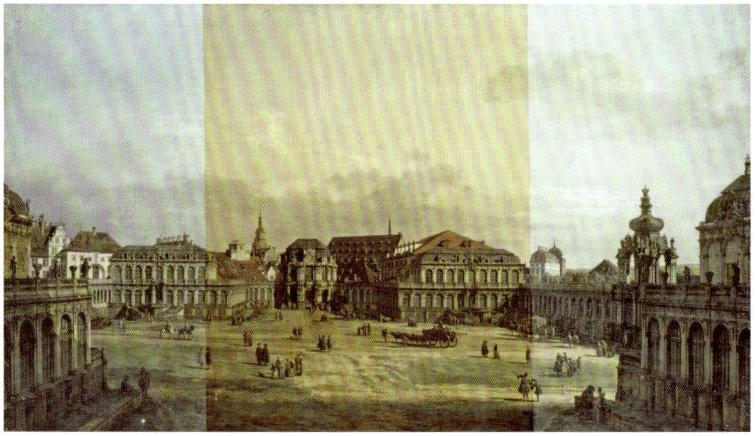

a. State of the painting during the removal of the protective layer, 2011–2012

b. Traces of the original blue of the sky

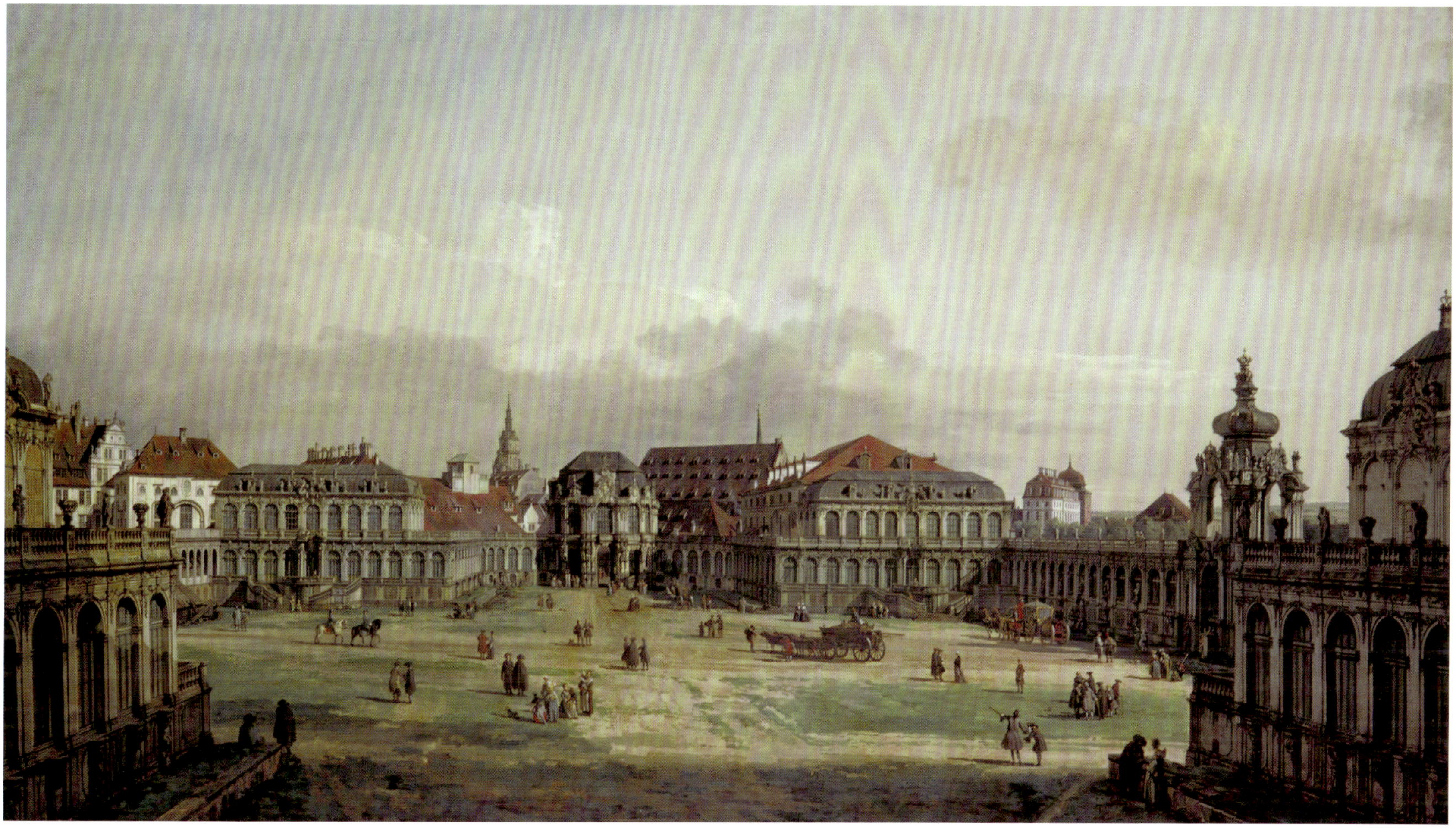

can see the series of chimney pots belonging to the Taschenbergpalais. Above the Bogengalerie that leads to the Glockenspielpavillon we can see the red roof of the Redoutenhaus (demolished in 1756), with the tower of the Kreuzkirche behind (collapsed in 1765). To the right, next to the Glockenspielpavillon, rises the sloping roof of the Sophienkirche, opened in 1602 (and demolished in 1963). The imposing building behind the pavilion on the right-hand side is the Pöppelmann Opera House (built between 1718 and 1719, destroyed by fire in 1849). The tall white building behind the Langgalerie, built in 1744, belonged to the secretary of the Landbauamt. Behind this we catch a glimpse of the Wilsdruffer Tor, with the large water tank on its roof (built in 1548, demolished in 1811).
As part of the campaign undertaken by the Gemäldegalerie Alte Meister to restore Bellotto's views, which began in 2009, the view of the Zwinger was restored between 2011 and 2012 by the laboratory of the Staatliche Kunstsammlungen in Dresden. It was worked on by Sabine Bendfeldt, with the occasional assistance of Kathleen Hohenstein. A thick layer of yellowed and streaked protective varnish, as well as harmful retouching, had long ruined the aesthetic impact of the picture. By removing these interventions, it was possible to bring a layer of stable and finely cracked paint back to the surface (fig. 1). The texture of the painting was perfectly maintained. The most obvious damage were partial scratches to the surface of the sky, caused by external interference. Although limited, areas of abraded colour could clearly be seen in the grey skies above the architecture. These were caused by structural changes linked to earlier methods of handling the paintings, which led to the formation of microscopic bubbles and subsequently to breakage in the painted layer.
Following the removal of the protective varnish a colder colourway, which does not correspond to Bellotto's original choices, jumps out. The colours bear clear signs of ageing. This is a more general problem, which affects Bellotto's views in particular. For his skies, the artist used the Prussian blue pigment, which had just been discovered and was unfortunately very unstable, so much so that over time it has faded considerably. The more intense blue tones, well preserved in the covered areas of the margins, reveal the original colour (fig. 2). This discolouration is irreversible. Using our imagination we can at least understand how Bellotto, contrary to what has been claimed by many scholars, did not use a Northern European coldness for his views of Dresden but, on the contrary, replicated all the light of a summer day in Saxony.
The serial nature of the views of Dresden also reveals some compositional similarities. As was usually the case, Bellotto employed a simply bound canvas of approximately 12 x 15 threads per square centimetre with a stuccoed lower edge for his view of the Zwinger. The original frame is now held by a fixed nineteenth century support with starch glue, and was strengthened in 1958 using the resin technique.
Bellotto's composition is multilayered. He followed a red ground used to level the structure of the canvas with a grey imprimatura, the real base for the paint. A further reddish-grey layer, intended as a background colour as well as an integral part of the painting, is used only in the sky. The colour is very thin, almost hazy in this area, but still applied with vigour. The painting is rapid, often with diagonal hatching, and the reddish-grey background is revealed in several areas. It was this method that allowed Bellotto to achieve the typical atmosphere of his skies. The paint is applied to the buildings in a subtle and very rational way. When viewed by X-ray, the thin layers of paint absorb very little. This method is therefore unsuitable for collecting information on the painting process, as it does not allow the preparatory drawings on the *imprimitura* to be identified. The topographical accuracy of the painting as a whole points to the fact that the painter must have subdivided the surface of the canvas, with a drawing possibly covered by the first layer of paint. It is likely that Bellotto then divided the surfaces to make the details of the facades clearer, although a preparatory drawing, however meticulous, drawn onto the ground under the first painted layer would not have helped significantly. It is interesting to note that incised lines are also a characteristic feature. Incisions were used by Bellotto to demarcate the work that had been started and as a stylistic device for articulating the facades. The final element, applied to the already dried surface of the painting, is the ornamentation. Thanks to the restoration we can now appreciate the painter's ability to fully render the play of light on the buildings. Using extremely delicate and well-balanced contrasts between light and shade, the sculptural beauty of the Zwinger takes shape. The depth of the perspective can also now be enjoyed once more.

The dating of this painting has long been debated in academic circles. Kozakiewicz proposed a period between 1749 and 1753; Rizzi dated it to around 1751; while Camesasca believed it to have been painted in circa 1752. Thanks to an inventory begun in 1747 but now lost, Gregor J.M. Weber has been able to pinpoint 1752 as the date when the painting first appeared in the inventory of the Gemäldegalerie in Dresden. It therefore follows that it must have been painted between 1751 and 1752.

Sabine Bendfeldt / Andreas Henning

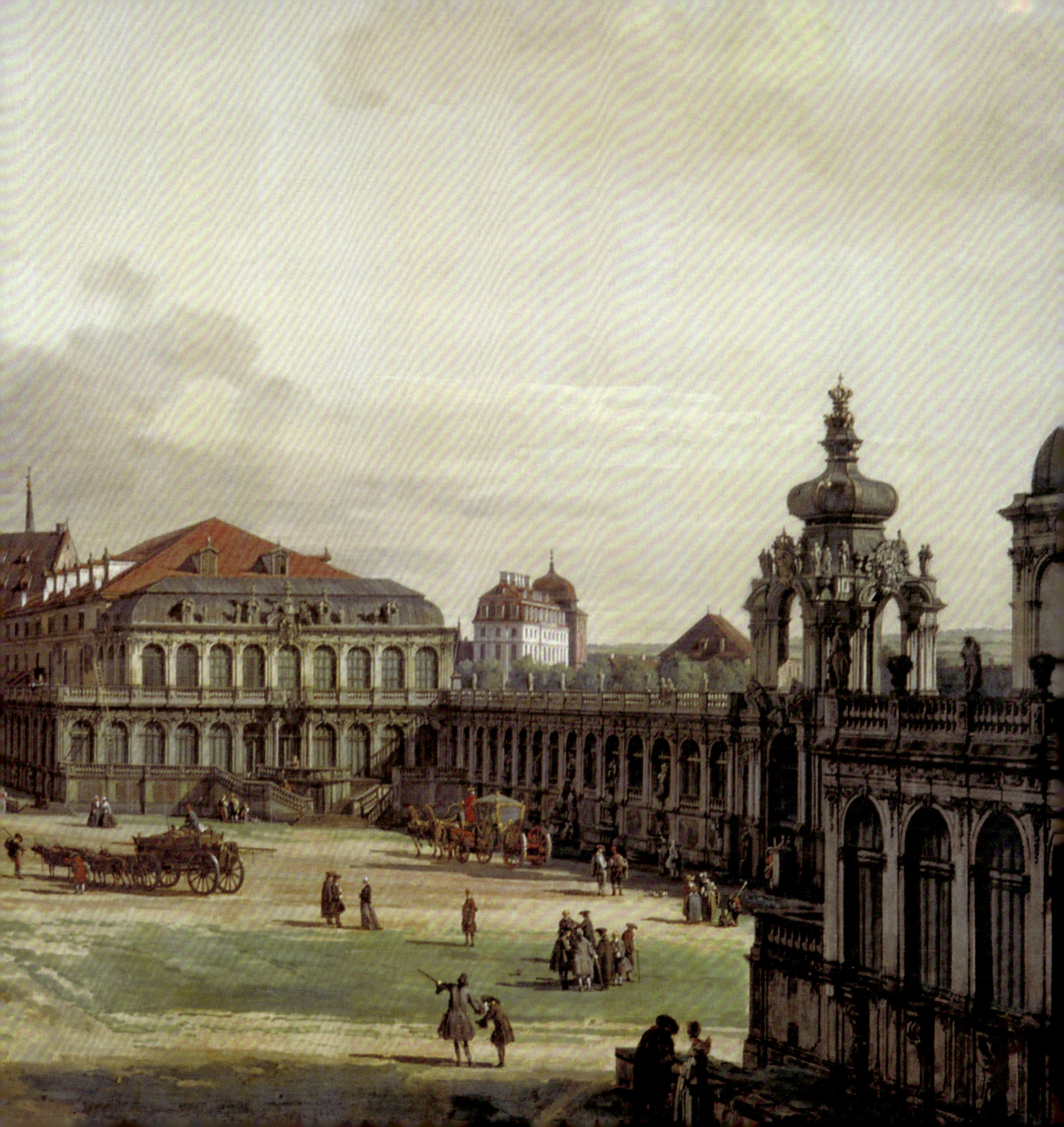

75

BERNARDO BELLOTTO

(Venice 1722 – Warsaw 1780)

The Old Fortifications of Dresden South of the Zwinger (the Saturn Bastion)
1749–1752

oil on canvas; 130 x 236.5 cm
San Petersburg, The State Hermitage Museum, GE 207

76

BERNARDO BELLOTTO

(Venezia 1722 - Varsavia 1780)

The Old Fortifications of Dresden South of the Zwinger (the Saturn Bastion)
1750

etching; 544 x 841 mm (plate); 522 x 820 (sheet)
II state of two
Milan, Civica Raccolta delle Stampe 'Achille Bertarelli', vol. FF 25, pl. 8

Inscriptions: (cat. 76) lower margin, 'Vue exterieure de la Porte dte Wilsche Thor -- Rempars de la Ville de Dresden et de / partie des magnifiques Pavillons où sont actuelle -- ment la Biblioteque Roïale et le Théatre de l'Opera / Peint et gravé par Ber: Bellotto, dit Canaletto, Peintre Du: Roi. 1750'.

Amongst the *vedute* of Dresden painted by Bellotto during his first sojourn in the Saxon capital between 1747 and 1753, this one shows the most innovative and daring composition. Though vividly reminiscent of the drawings he made in Padua of the Porta Portello along the Piovego canal, with the town houses and churches in the distance, here the originality lies in Bellotto's depicting the wooden houses of the town of Wilsdruff in the foreground. These modest homes with their sloping roofs, one of which is actually being built, are immersed in a deep shadow that spreads slantwise along the moat, in contrast with the brightness that spreads through the old town, which is surrounded by ramparts. A shaft of light filters through the scaffolding, highlighting the figures of the masons at work, and is reflected off the upper part of the obelisk. Erected in the centre of the passageway along the canal, this is one of the hundred scattered throughout Saxony, placed in front of the city gates as part of the ingenious system introduced by Augustus the Strong (1670–1733), from 1722 onwards, to indicate the distances in hours of a carriage's route between the main towns.
Amongst the works from the Brühl series acquired by Catherine the Great and commented by Count Ernest Muňich upon their arrival in Saint Petersburg, this is the one that best illustrates his view on aerial perspective:

> Ce Tableau considéré du côté du Travail mérite des éloges, mais il a le défaut ordinaire de la plupart des ouvrages de ce Maitre, d'être d'un pinceau maniéré et de manquer du côté de la perspective aérienne, qui est l'art de faire avancer, ou faire reculer, les objets par le moien du renforcement, ou de la dégradation des Couleurs (Muňich 1773–1783, no. 413).

The first critic of Bellotto's Saxon *vedute* didn't realise that the avoidance of the effects of aerial perspective is one of the very qualities contributing to the monumentality of these works. The fortified city is captured in the clear, still light which makes its shapes and colours stand out sharply. A bridge leading to a tunnel bored into the fortifications links it to the outlying town. From right to left, we recognise: the massive Wilsdruffer Tor (at the time known as Wilsches Tor), the three-storey white house belonging to agricultural clerk Adam, behind which appear a tympanum and the small tower of the Sophienkirche; the austere Opera House built in 1713–1719 by Matthäus Daniel Pöppelmann (1662–1736) and the Zwinger zoological pavilion. The two towers rising in the distance are those of the castle and the Hofkirche. As has been remarked, the latter is of exaggerated height and incorrectly placed to the left of the former, rather than to the right – it was not yet finished at the time the painting was done. The Saturn rampart depicted here, one of the six surrounding the historic centre of Dresden, was located south of the Zwinger – its moat is depicted in the pendant painting (Kozakiewicz 1972a, no. 156). Bellotto skilfully conveys its accurate rustication and the two side watchtowers on the mown grass. Beyond the bridge, he also portrays the bas-relief of Hans Walther II (1526–1586), sculptor and mayor of Dresden, which was done in 1573 to commemorate the union between Saxony and Denmark, sanctioned in 1548 upon the marriage between Augustus I of Saxony (1526–1586) and Anna, daughter of King Christian III of Denmark.
Bellotto delivered the first version of this *veduta* to the Royal Gallery in February 1751 (Kozakiewicz 1972a, n. 161). The differences in tonality and brightness notoriously detected between the two versions, the royal one and the Brühl replica, are impossible to point out in this case, due to the yellowed paint that still darkens the Dresden canvas – the standard omission of just a few figures such as, in this case, the man leaning against the balustrade in contemplation of the rampart and the dog barking at the beggar woman seated at the foot of the obelisk with the little girl, one of Bellotto's favourite episodes.
The print made from the royal version is dated 1750; Bellotto, therefore, only delivered the painting after having completed it. In the extremely rare first state, the inscription 'Porte d'Italie des' appears erroneously, to be promptly amended in the second – presented here – to 'Porte dte Wilsche'. In both states, the coat of arms is engraved directly on the main plate. The etching, less contrasted compared to the painting, highlights the details in the deep shadow of the painting with the small close signs.

Bożena Anna Kowalczyk

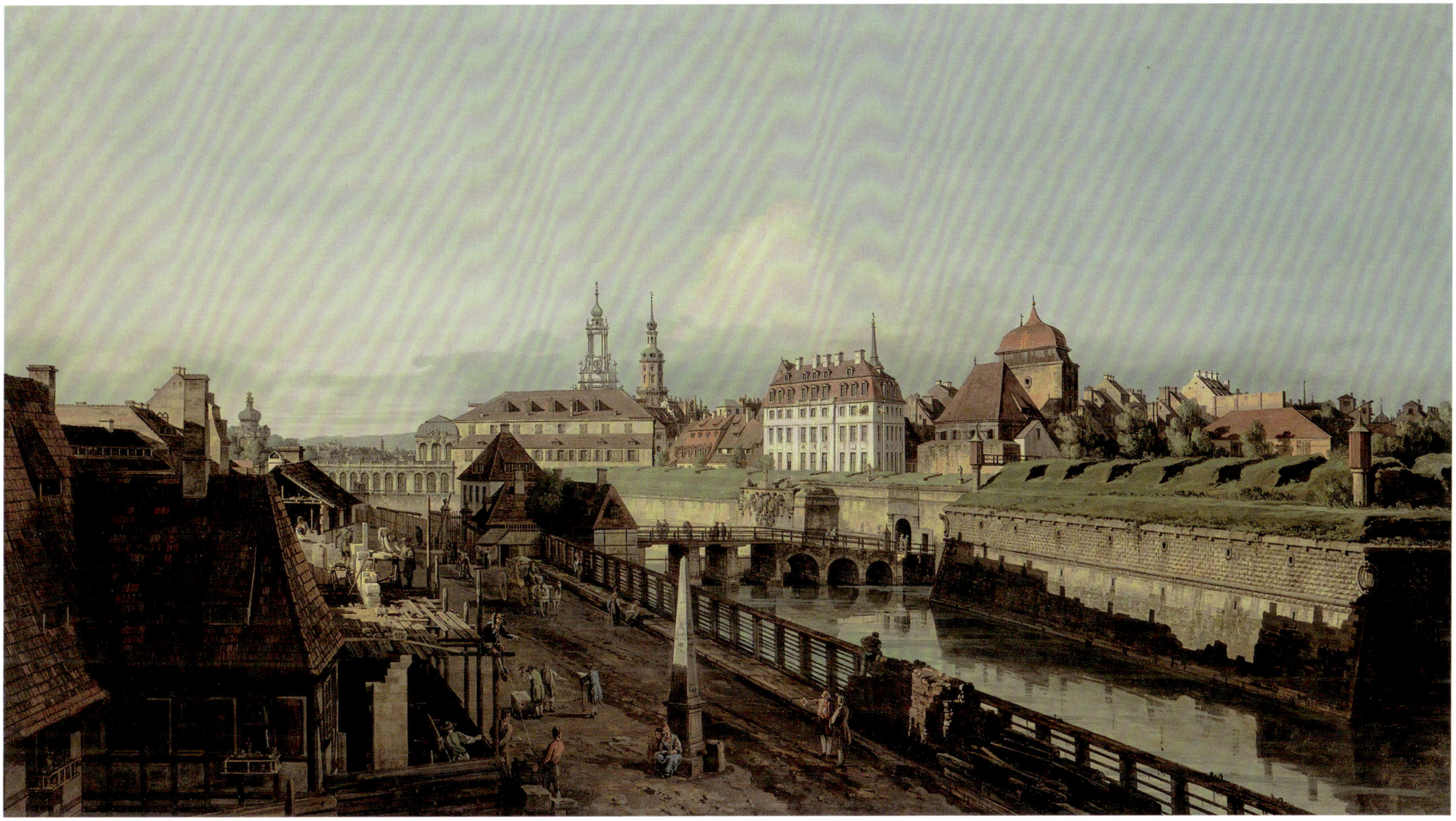

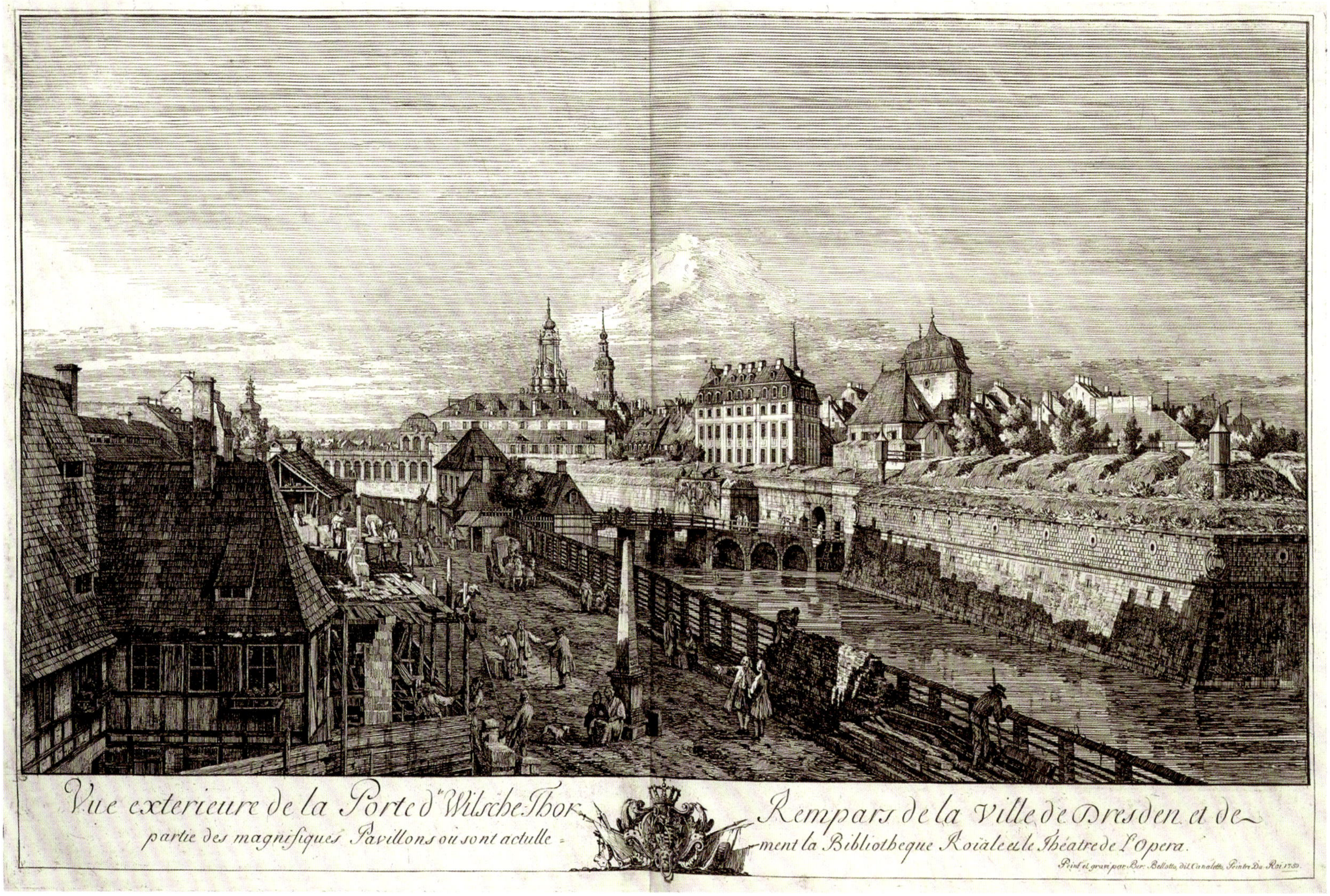
Vue exterieure de la Porte d'Wilsche-Thor Rempars de la Ville de Dresden et de=
partie des magnifiques Pavillons où sont actulle= ment la Bibliotheque Roïale et le Théatre de l'Opera.
Peint et gravé par Ber: Bellotto, dit Canaletto, Peintre du Roi 1750.

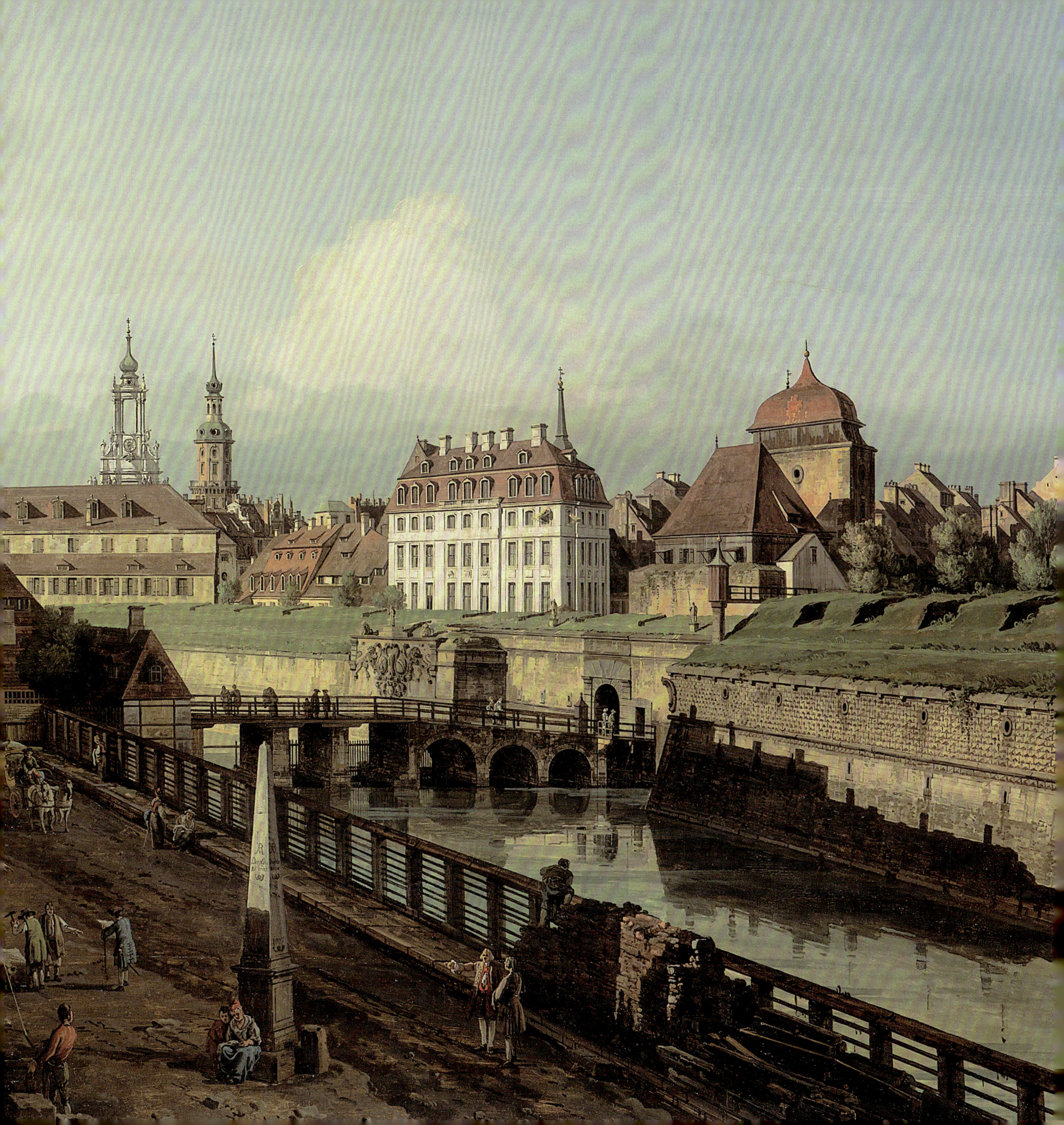

BERNARDO BELLOTTO

(Venice 1722 – 1780 Warsaw)

The Kreuzkirche, Dresden
ca. 1753

oil on canvas; 197 x 187 cm
San Petersburg, The State Hermitage Museum, GE 203

The Kreuzkirche, Dresden
ca. 1756

pen and grayish ink over pencil free and ruled, some red pencil lines and pinpointing; 586 x 480 mm
Warsaw, Muzeum Narodowe, Rys. Pol. 2042

The Kreuzkirche, Dresden
1757

engraving, only state; 770 x 620 mm (plate)
Dresden, Staatliche Kunstsammlungen, Kupferstich-Kabinett, A 85868

Inscriptions: (cat. 79) on the margin, 'Vuë, de l'Eglise et de la -- Rue de Sainte Croix, / ainsi que d'une partie de l'Hôtel de S: E: -- Mons.[gr] le Comte Rutowski, Feld Marechal General / Peint et gravé par Ber:[d] Bellotto dit Canaletto Pein.[r] - R 1757'.

Marks: (cat. 79) letters FAR [Fridericus Augustus Rex], on the top the crown; shared by the old Property but not present in Lugt.

Among Bernardo Bellotto's creations in Dresden this and the depiction of the *Frauenkirche* stand out for the importance conferred on the architecture, the protagonists of the foreground; this is large and of a vertical, almost square format. In all of Bellotto's pictorial repertoire in which architecture plays a prominent role, never has the description of each stone, of each detail, of each small passage of light attained such an intensity of expression.
Two paintings, a drawing and a print, executed by Bellotto in the space of about five years bear witness to the appearance of the *westwerk* – the western tower – of the most important Evangelical Lutheran Church of Saxony, after the reconstruction and completion in the late Renaissance style of the previously medieval structure. A quick glimpse of the building shows the side of the late-Gothic main nave with the side entrance, completed in 1499 by Conrad Pflüger (1450–1506/7), in the place of a medieval shrine dedicated to Saint Nicholas, destroyed in the great city fire of 1491. The severe structure of the tower was crowned between 1579 and 1584 with a two-storey belfry and a spacious balcony that surrounds the facade, built to a design by a group of Saxon architects led by the mayor and sculptor Hans Walther II (1526–1586). In 1589, the great sculpted portal with the life-size figures in relief and lush decorative elements was put in place, the project having been undertaken by Hans's son, Christopher Walther IV (1572–1619), and his brother-in-law Melchior Jobst.
The high, square and austere mass of the tower forms a counterpoint to the Kreuzgasse on the north side of the church, with its important Baroque buildings in sunlight. In the background, behind the area of shadow, one can make out the Vitzthum-Rutowski palace, with its high chimneys and the facade decorated with a carved pediment. This was the residence of General Field Marshal Earl Friedrich August Rutowski, the natural son of Augustus the Strong, and was designed by Matthäus Daniel Pöppelmann (1662–1736), being built between 1720 and 1724. On the other side is the Pfarrgasse.
This view was in reality impossible to embrace: as is evident in view of *The Old Market Square from Schloss-Strasse*, the space in front of the church was narrower, closed off by a building, as it still is today. Bellotto adopted the same solution as Canaletto in some of his Venetian views, such as that of *Campo Santa Maria del Giglio* (C/L 313), creating an imaginary space, with the shadowed area in the foreground.
The present painting is a replica of the version commissioned in 1751–1752 by Augustus III (1696–1763), King of Poland and Elector of Saxony, executed with twelve other views of Dresden and eleven of Pirna for Earl Heinrich Brühl (1700–1763), the prime minister of the Saxon court and a keen collector. It is not known why the Brühl series lacks the view of the *Frauenkirche*, the companion piece of the royal version (Kozakiewicz 1972a, no. 179).
The similarity of the two versions is astonishing. The quality of the replica is very high, without any lowering of creative skill. While considering the different state of preservation, it is clear that in this painting, as in other works belonging to the prime minister, Bellotto accentuated the contrasts of light and shadow and strengthened the brown tones, giving more emphasis to the illuminated edges and to the effects of atmospheric wash-off, conferring a menacing look to the sky, with contrasting purple and white cumulus clouds. There are small differences in the number and arrangement of the figures: the two gentlemen who were on the right margin in the royal version are missing, the tourist with his cicerone have

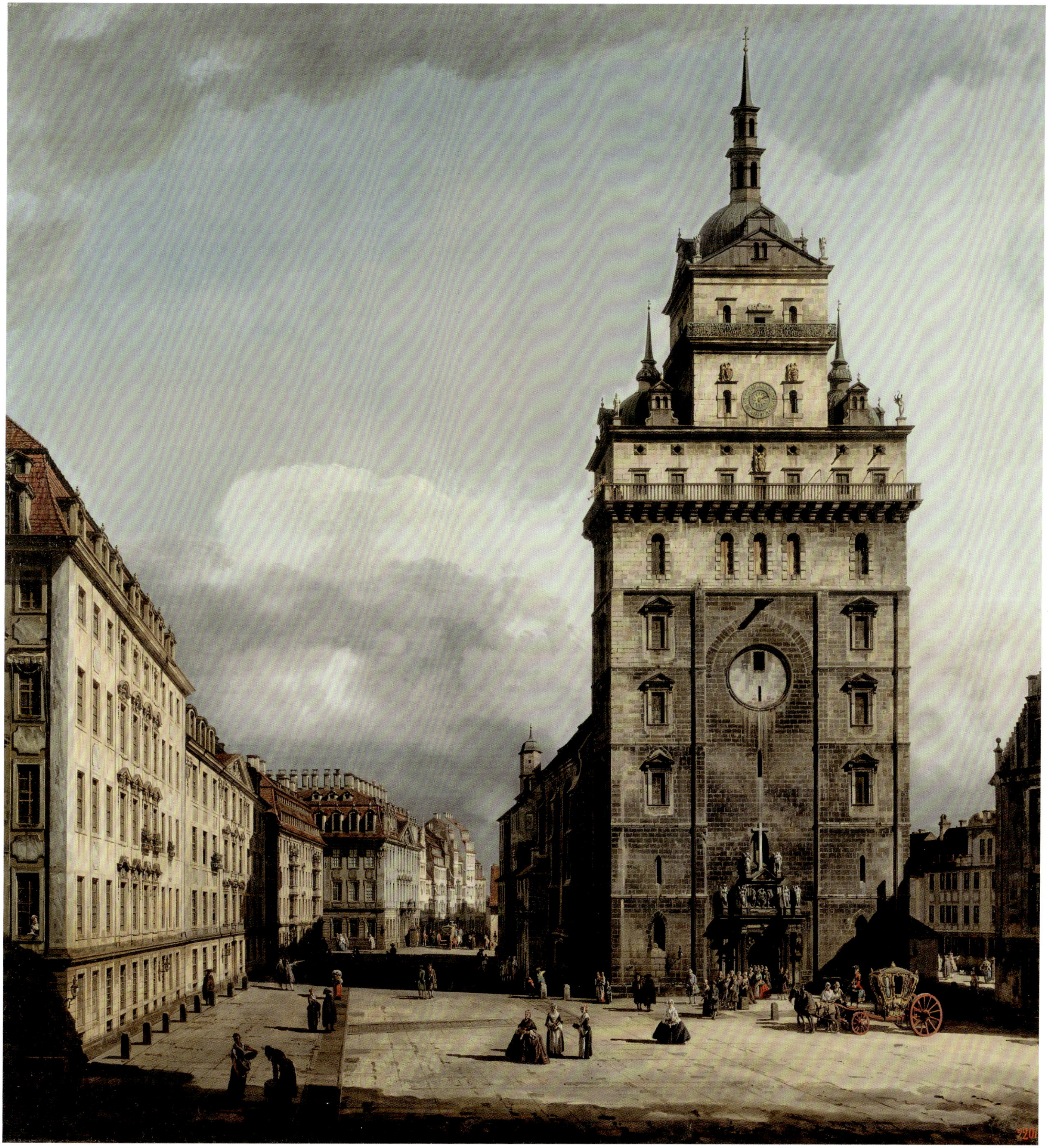

moved towards the houses, the group in centre background has partly dispersed but the procession leaving the church has slightly swelled in numbers; a woman looks out of the window of the corner building. The clock in both versions shows two o'clock and two tiny and colourful trumpeters appear on the terrace.
The Museum of Warsaw drawing, from the artist's personal holdings, is considered preparatory to the two paintings and print, published in 1757. It shows evident signs of measurements, marked in pencil and indicated by compass holes, a precise perspective construction, drawn with pencil and ruler, gone over in carbon-black ink in the main constructive lines. A grid is visible in the sky. The sketch has been completed freehand, later, with the figures, the profiles of clouds and shadows, as well as the decorative details of the architecture, drawn with the typical nervy line and a softer pen dipped in lighter ink. There is a *pentimento* in the height of the house on the left.
The first draft of this composition can be found in the verso of the *The Market Square, Pirna* sheet (cat. 81). The sketch was noted by A. Rizzi but erroneously considered the first draft of the recto. The sheet was first used in a vertical format, prepared exactly the same way as the present one, with four joined and glued sheets. The size must originally have been very similar, but both have been cut down significantly, here along the right side, and the other at the top. The perspective construction is drawn in pencil with a ruler; only the side of the Vitzthum-Rutowski palace and the facade of the house that precedes it on Kreuzgasse are retouched with a pen, with the same dark ink as was used for the architecture of the present drawing. As here, the vanishing point of the composition is on the edge of the building.
This find suggests the two sheets were drawn at the same time, or at least one soon after the other, even though the papers used, both very thin, are different: for the drawing of the *Kreuzkirche*, *Dresden*, Bellotto used the paper produced by the Dutch factory of Dirk and Cornelis Blauw, as indicated by the evident watermark, repeated twice (there are no other examples in the artist's known corpus), and another type of Dutch paper for *The Market Square, Pirna* made by the Honig company. Consequently, the question arises of the date of the present sheet which involves its function. Bellotto arrived in Pirna after 26 April of that year, when the king signed a pass for him; the painting of the royal version of the *Kreuzkirche, Dresden* must have been already completed and presumably the Brühl version too, but it is unlikely the drawing had been. I am inclined to believe that both this drawing of the *Kreuzkirche* and that of *The Market Square, Pirna* were made in 1756 or so, when the artist returned to Dresden. Bellotto needed to see the paintings in order to be able to make engravings from them. This drawing thus appears as a study for the print, published in 1757. The smoke-black colour for the ink appears only in these sheets, and appears a deliberate choice that anticipates the effects offered by etching.
The drawing is faithful in detail to the royal version but increases the foreground with the oblique area of shadow and introduces the figure of the gentleman with a three-cornered hat, a dog at his feet. It was believed that this was a later addition, added with a view to the print, but it was actually probably part of the project; this was a special case for Bellotto who often omitted the figures in his engravings.
In the text accompanying the etching, the only palace mentioned is that of Field Marshal Rutowski. The print, in a single state, is one of the most impressive of Bellotto's prints, both for its size and for the magnificent chiaroscuro and rendering of details. The increased space in the foreground follows the layout of the drawing.

Bożena Anna Kowalczyk

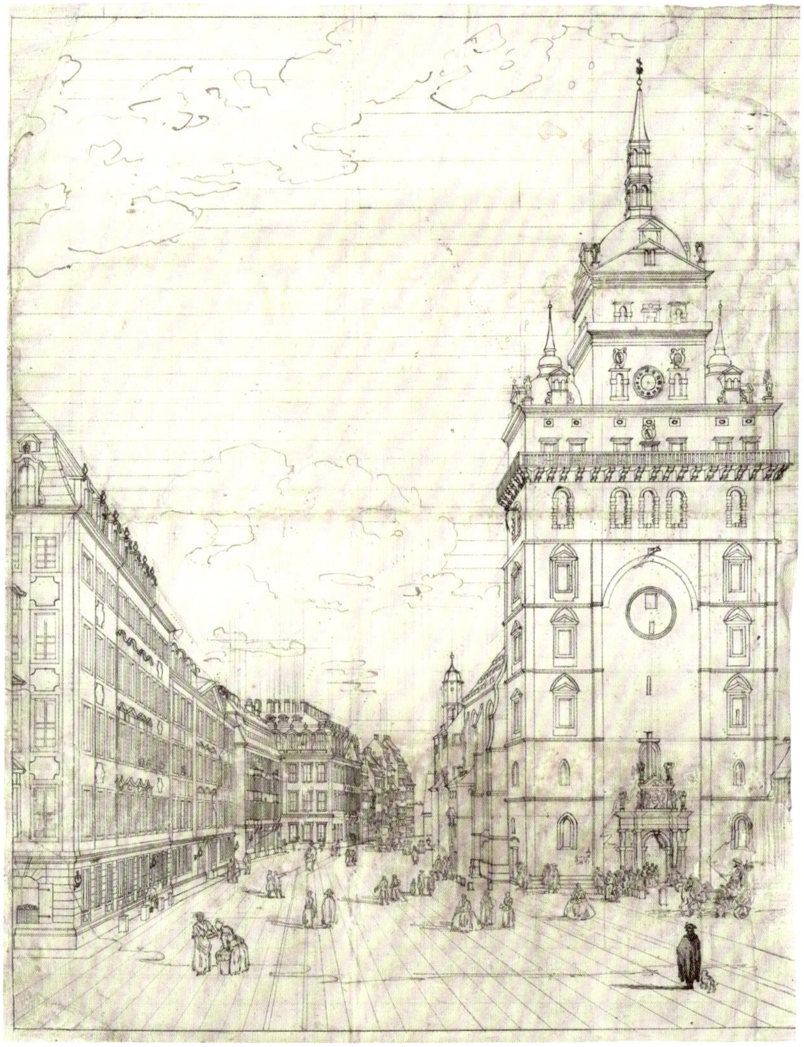

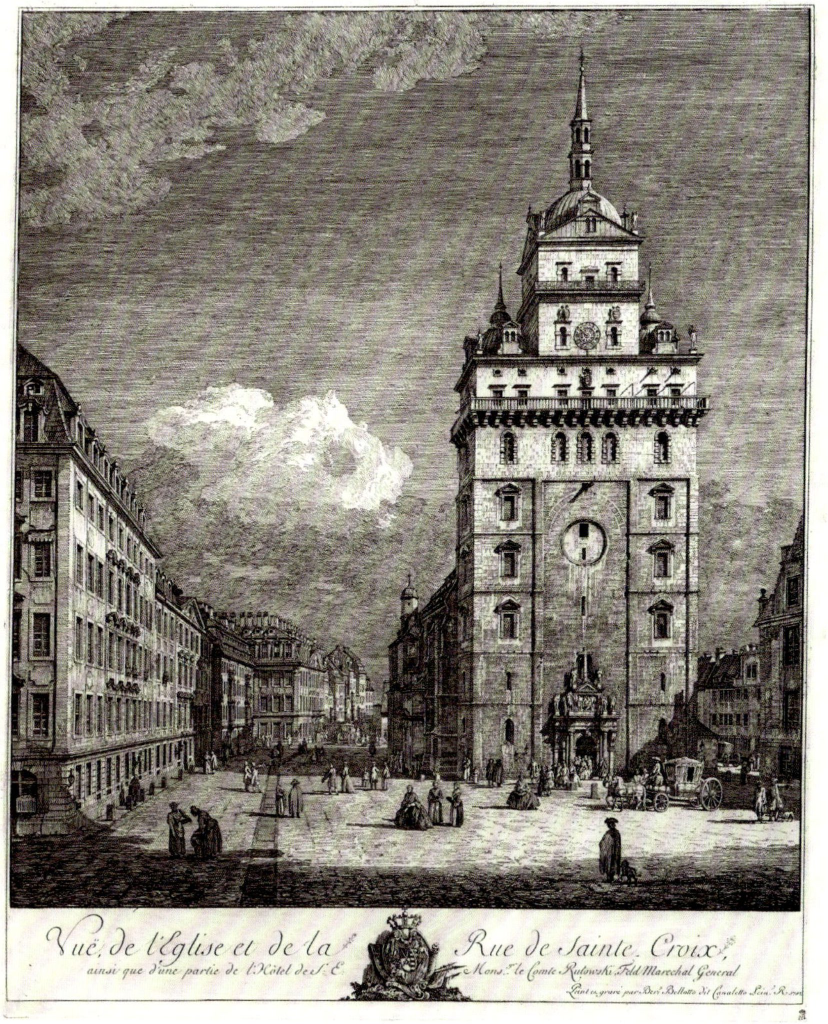
Vuë, de l'Eglise et de la Rue de Sainte Croix,
ainsi que d'une partie de l'Hôtel de S. E. Mons.r le Comte Rutowski Feld Marechal General

80

BERNARDO BELLOTTO

(Venice 1722 – Warsaw 1780)

The Market Square, Pirna
1753–54

oil on canvas; 134 x 238 cm
Dresden, Gemäldegalerie Alte Meister, Staatliche Kunstsammlungen, 623

The panoramic view of *The Market Square, Pirna* is the most admired of the eleven views of the Saxon town dominated by the Sonnenstein fortress on the hill, painted by Bernardo Bellotto between 1753 and 1755 on commission to Augustus III (1696–1763). Bellotto himself painted several replicas, and a series of copies are also known. At Pirna, Bellotto found new and happy inspiration. The series of views of the town depicted from various points, like part of the enchanting landscape of the Elbe valley, is crowned by this serene image of the main square, documented as being one of the first four to have been painted, and the only one identifiable in the inventory of the Royal Gallery drawn up in 1754 by Matthias Oesterreich.
Placing himself at a first-floor window of the house today at Schuhgasse 16 – as indicated by W. Schmidt – Bellotto shows the square in all its extent, going beyond left and right – this *veduta* is impossible to see from a single point of view. As usual, the drawings made on site using a *camera optica* has been done with the greatest care: the buildings are subjected to a precise perspective order, along the diagonals, leading the eye from the rooftops of the houses to the Lunenturm and Antique Walk on the hill. G.J.M. Weber points out some details prepared for this, such as the disposition on planes parallel to the field of vision of the two fine ornamental gables of the town hall and the increased height of the tower compared to the steeple of the Marienkirche, with their two peaks aligned on a diagonal that leads precipitously toward the fortress. Bellotto was fascinated by the mixture of serene medieval and Gothic architecture. He emphasises the Town Hall, shown in broad daylight in the middle of the square, an example of an unusual urban layout that Pirna shared with cities such as Padua, Krakòw, Wrocław and Lemberg; he renders the simplicity and beauty of its Renaissance style, the result of reconstruction in 1581 of the earlier fourteenth-century building destroyed by fire. The houses that line the square date back to the sixteenth century but the painted trompe-l'oeil decoration that enlivens the surfaces of the walls and surroundings of the windows dates from the early decades of the eighteenth century, and was executed just before the arrival of Bellotto. Only the building at the end, with the high-pitched roof and gable truss (now the tourist office headquarters and called the 'house of Canaletto') 'could really do with repainting' (G.J.M. Weber). The painter, a passionate chronicler of the various aspects of civil and commercial life of the places he visited, peeps at the stalls of the butchers in the low building to the left of the town hall, barely visible in the darkness of the open door and traditionally present in that place since 1386; he notes the public weigh station in the doorway, observes the market in the square, shown in bright patches of colour, and, finally, the two wooden water troughs, a meeting place in the square, which still exist today but were bricked in in 1774 and 1789. With his special predilection for turning the spotlight on distant and dark corners, he reveals other houses with high gables and little figures on the busy streets leading to the Marienkirche and fortress.
In the Earl Brühl replica, now in the Pushkin Museum in Moscow, unusually there is no market scene and the picture is 10 cm wider (Kozakiewicz 1972a, no. 212).

81

BERNARDO BELLOTTO

(Venice 1722 – Warsaw 1780)

The Market Square, Pirna (recto)
Study for a View of the Kreuzkirche, Dresden
ca. 1756

pen and gray ink; 377 x 650 mm
Warsaw, Muzeum Narodowe, no. Rys.Pol. 2044

The perspective rigour of the scene is highlighted by the drawing from Bellotto's personal collection, a reproduction in a pen of just the contours, outlines of the shadows and of the clouds, but complete with figures. Its purpose has long been a topic of discussion. S. Kozakiewicz sees it as a 'sketch of the paintings', and W. Schmidt agrees while G.J.M. Weber believes it to have been made in 1761 after the return to Dresden, and perhaps by his son Lorenzo, with the notion of producing an etching that was never printed. It is one of two drawings conserved showing Pirna. The other, *Pirna Seen from Posta*, is certainly the work of an assistant in the studio, perhaps his young son Lorenzo (1742–1770), and shows painting with a similar composition on which it is based (B.A. Kowalczyk, in Munich 2014–2015, no. 47). The present drawing, which here I attribute firmly to Bellotto on the basis of the infallible perspective composition, the edgy yet effective line in delineating the figures and in the contours of the clouds, is a reproduction with a view to producing a print but must have been made prior to 1757. The preparatory sketch on the verso for the print of *The Kreuzkirche, Dresden* (cat. 78) has recognised by myself; the very structure of the sheets, similarly composed of four pieces of glued paper, and even the same ink, suggests they were made almost together and hence prior to the publication of the print, dated 1757.
The sheet is a Dutch paper by the Honig company, whose watermark (J. HONIG & ZOON; Heawood 1957) appears twice; the *Pirna seen from Posta* drawing mentioned above, which is most probably contemporary, is made by the same paper. The paper from the same manufacturer but with a different watermark (the letters C & I Honig surmounted by a Strasbourg lily, Churchill 329) is found in two Viennese drawings preserved at the Museum of Warsaw, used as preparatory studies for the figures in the view of the *Liechtenstein Palace at Rossau,Vienna, the Garden*, of 1759–1760 (Kozakiewicz 1972a, no. 271; Rys. Pol. 2054 and 2057).
Bellotto brought a sheaf of selected drawings with him to Vienna, which were saved from the destruction of his home in Dresden in 1760, and it included the present one. At least one of the autograph replicas, the brightly coloured one belonging to the Batthyány-Strattmann collection, damaged in World War II, must have been made in the Habsburg capital around 1760 (Kozakiewicz 1972a, no. A 497). Of the other three known ones, all similar in size (about 48 x 80 cm), only two survive, one formerly Mrs. J.F. Guire, New York (Christie's, New York, 24 January, 2003, lot 163) and another at the Museum of Fine Arts, Houston. The painting in the Kaiser-Friedrich Museum, Berlin disappeared in 1945 (Kozakiewicz 1972a, nos. A 497 and 214–216).
The square has remained as it was at the time of Bellotto times but without those architectural and decorative details the Venetian painter portrayed with such charm, and without the Renaissance decorated gables, the murals or the portico of the town hall. Bellotto has stopped time with his serene view of the square and city life, one of emblematic value for the people of Pirna and Saxony.

Bożena Anna Kowalczyk

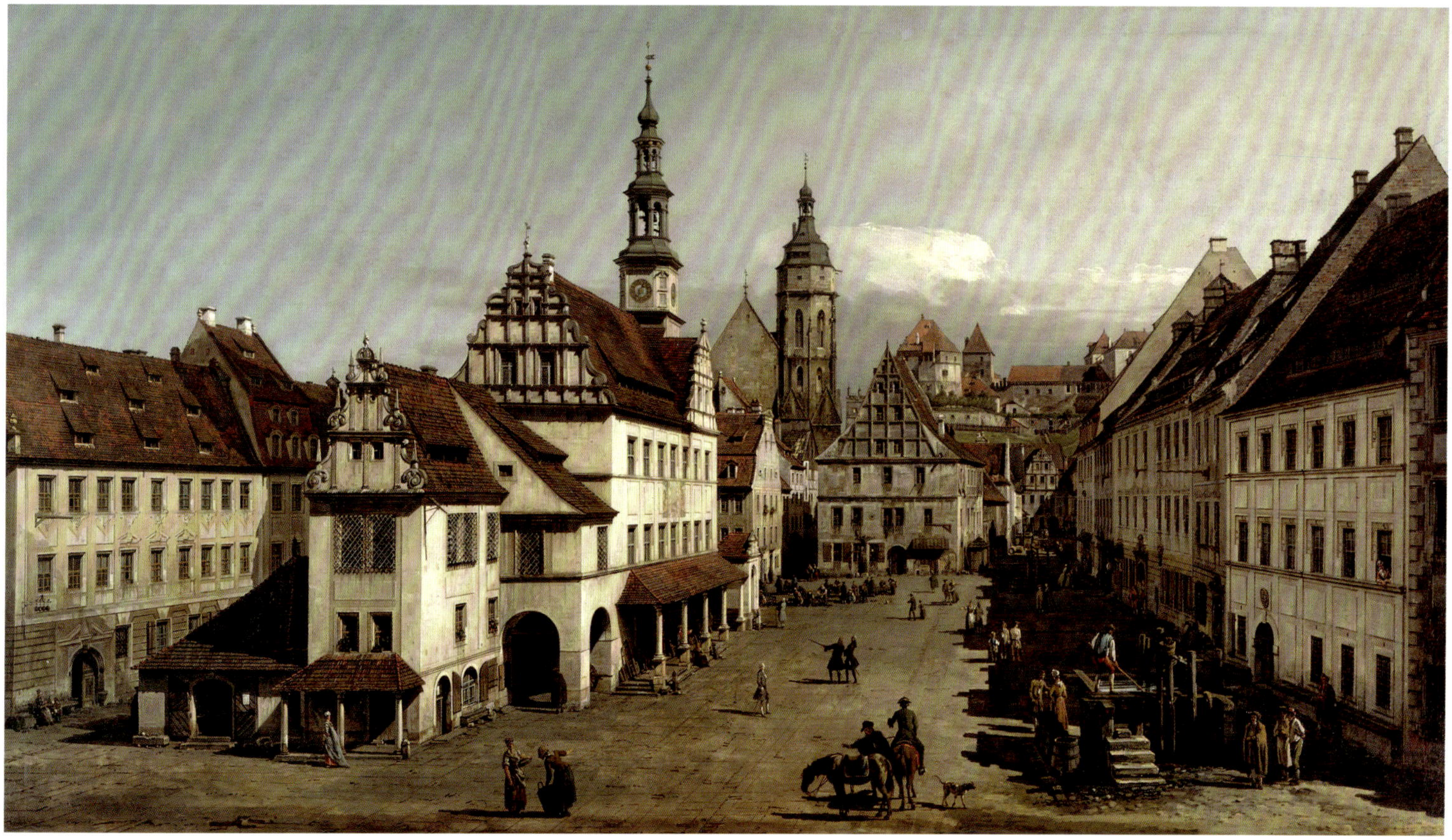

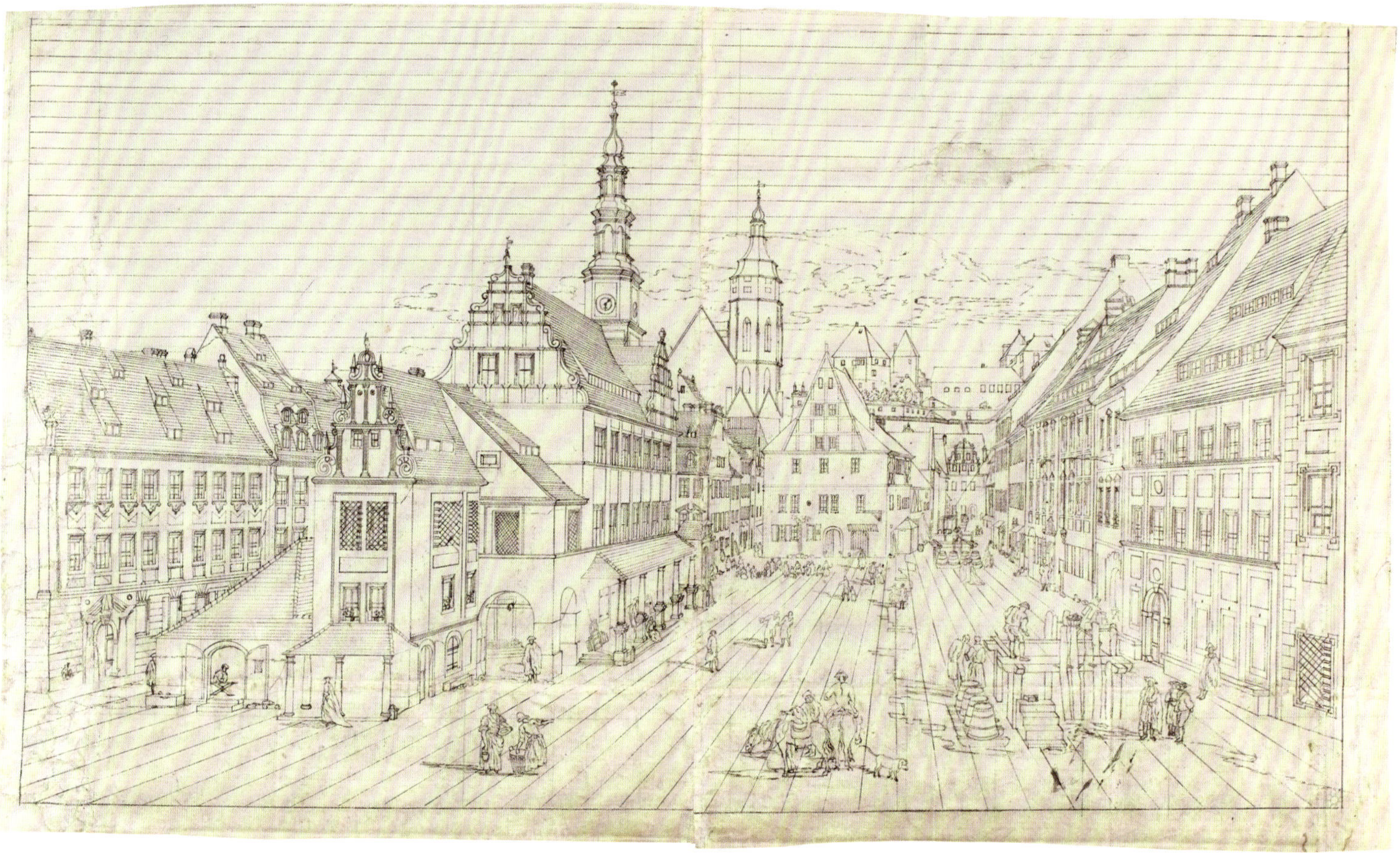

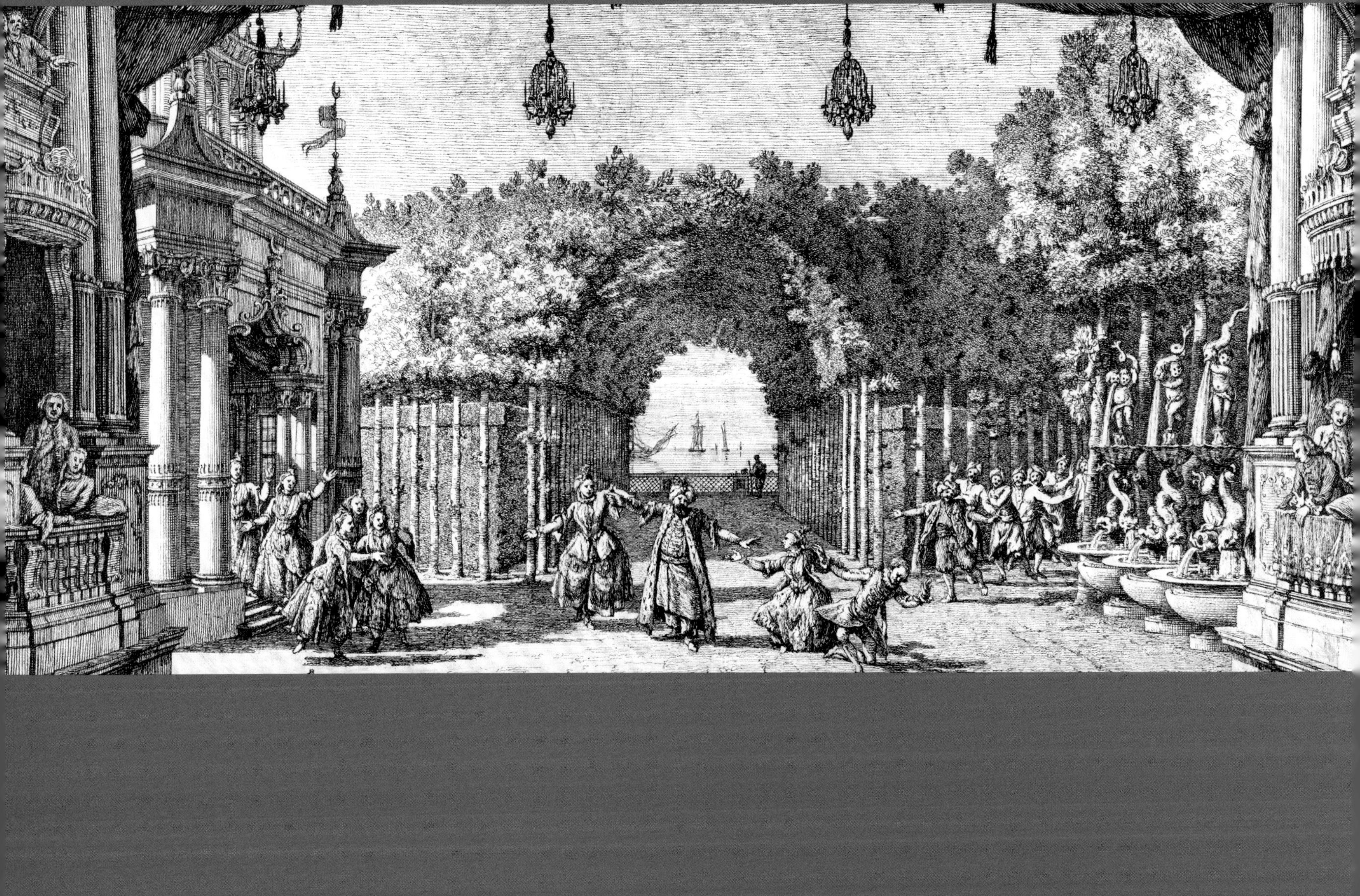

9.
PRIVATE PASSIONS

The inventory of Bellotto's personal library, part of the important, recently discovered *Catalogo de Danni* (cat. 83) lists 1,078 works, distinguished for their incredible variety. The twenty-eight titles selected for display in the exhibition, in the same editions as those owned by Bellotto, were chosen to reveal the artist's interests, which are even more surprising. Some of the texts are 'predictable', but useful for confirming his seriousness, like the volumes by Andrea Pozzo, Ferdinando Bibiena and Cesare Vecellio (displayed with studies of Polish and Balkan costumes, in poses and in perspective styles inspired by the figures in the book; cat. 85, 86), and the unexpected Francesco Borromini, whom Bellotto also studied first-hand, as evidenced by *The Piazza Navona looking North, Rome* (cat. 49) and a drawing in the collection of the Muzeum Narodowe in Warsaw (see fig. 20, p. 34), but also the refined George Berkeley, explaining the theory of perception.
The substantial collection of classical authors is represented here by the French edition of Horace (freely cited in Latin in the *Architectural Capriccio with Self-Portrait;* cat. 82); the collection that we might consider the most striking of all for its breadth and quality is the one of philosophical texts, which included such authors as Voltaire, Montesquieu and Hume.
And then there was his interest in 'current affairs publishing', including volumes added to the Index and censured, with works by Paolo Sarpi, Gregorio Leti and Giovan Francesco Loredan; his passion for reading, with texts by Marino (*Adone*) and Cervantes but also *Tom Jones, Pamela or The Virtue Rewarded,* and the scandalous *Papesse Jeanne* by Spenheim, still fresh from the printer; licentious works, which Bellotto did not disdain (Pietro Aretino) and the ultra-current Goudar and his description of the Lisbon earthquake. And then there were the proponents of the Enlightenment, Muratori and Maffei, which demonstrate his deep background, the fruit of keeping himself current and study.
The idea that Bellotto was passionate about theatre and had contacts in that sphere in Vienna and Dresden was already suggested by the print made in Vienna, dedicated to Earl Durazzo, *Le Turc généréux* (cat. 89), the two *Architectural Capricci* of 1764, in the style of Giuseppe Galli Bibiena (cat. 87, 88), and a whole series of architectural *capricci* from his second period in Dresden, the quality of which is represented in the exhibition by the first version of his celebrated self-portrait (cat. 82). But the book inventory allows us to clarify the breadth of his interest in the theatre, with volumes of the classics and the moderns, in complete editions, represented in the exhibition by Molière, Goldoni and Metastasio and one special volume, the *Opere* of Giovanni Claudio Pasquini, published by Bernardo's brother Michele Bellotti in Arezzo and dedicated to Earl Brühl. It has also been a pleasure to show that while in London Canaletto was also in some way linked to the theatre, considering his exquisite *Theatral Set Design* (cat. 90).

82

BERNARDO BELLOTTO

(Venice 1722 – Warsaw 1780)

Architectural Capriccio with Self-Portrait
1764–65

oil on canvas; 156.2 x 112.4 cm

This monumental architectural scene with figures posing in the foreground like actors is one of the most famous and enigmatic images of eighteenth-century Venice. Bellotto painted it in three versions, each time retouching the physiognomy, the costumes of the secondary figures and the colours of the sky. The version on display here is recognised as the first. Unlike the other two – kept at the Royal Castle in Warsaw and the Terruzzi Collection in Bordighera (Kozakiewicz 1972a, nos. 333–334), it does not have a pendant. The writing on the poster affixed to the column, above two theatrical playbills – the quotation from Horace's *Ars poetica* – is incorrect but is the same as the one that appears in the preparatory drawing at the Hessisches Landesmuseum in Darmstadt (AE 2174), almost as if it had been remembered by memory: 'Pictores / ac Poetae Facultatem / Habent / pingendi et Scribendi / Quidquid liberent. / Horatii Flaccidi / de Arte Poetica'. On one of the playbills, ripped picturesquely, the title of the play can be made out, *L'enfant prodigue* by Voltaire, staged at the Dresden court theatre in 1764; the column further back announces *Rodogune* by Corneille. Bellotto knew both of these plays well and they formed part of his library. In the other two versions the writing reads: 'Pictores / ac Poetae Facultatem / Habent / pingendi et Scribendi / Quidquid liberent. / Horatii Flaccidi / de Arte Poetica' (*Ars poetica*, 9–10).
The architecture, a Venetian *capriccio*, is recognisable as a composition of arches, columns and bas-reliefs taken from Jacopo Sansovino's Libreria, and the Procuratie Nuove by Vincenzo Scamozzi, with Piazza San Marco from the rounded corner – that this is a tribute to the court of the Zwinger is corroborated by the play of water – between the spans of the arches, the central one with a lantern, as in the torre dell'Orologio that inspired both the print by Canaletto and the version by Bellotto (cat. 33a). The low-relief marble *patera* comes from the repertoire of *capricci* with Roman motifs, while the vases are studied from life in two drawings at the Muzeum Narodowe in Warsaw, although oddly these have not been recognised (Kozakiewicz 1972a, nos. 374–375). The power of the structures and the illusion of the architectural setting surpass the authority of theatrical set designers and approach that of architects. 'These paintings lead to a comparison with the grandiose "perspective" stage sets of the Bibbienas and Servandoni. Only, when it comes to spatial reality, Bellotto's perspectives are more disciplined than theatrical stage sets' (Fritzsche 1936, p. 76). In addition to a volume by Ferdinando Bibbiena, Bellotto also had books by Andrea Pozzo, Borromini and Vignola in his library. The strong lighting provides an intentional theatrical effect.
The figure dressed as a Venetian nobleman was identified as Bernardo Bellotto for the first time in 1795 in the catalogue of the gallery of King Stanisław II Augustus, King of Poland, with reference to the version kept in that country: *Architecture de fantaisie, ou l'auteur s'est peint dans l'habit de noble Vénitien* (Mańkowski 1932, no. 461). The signature 'B BELOTTO DE CANALETTO' is in keeping with the figure's dress in its allusion to the artist's nobility. Bellotto must

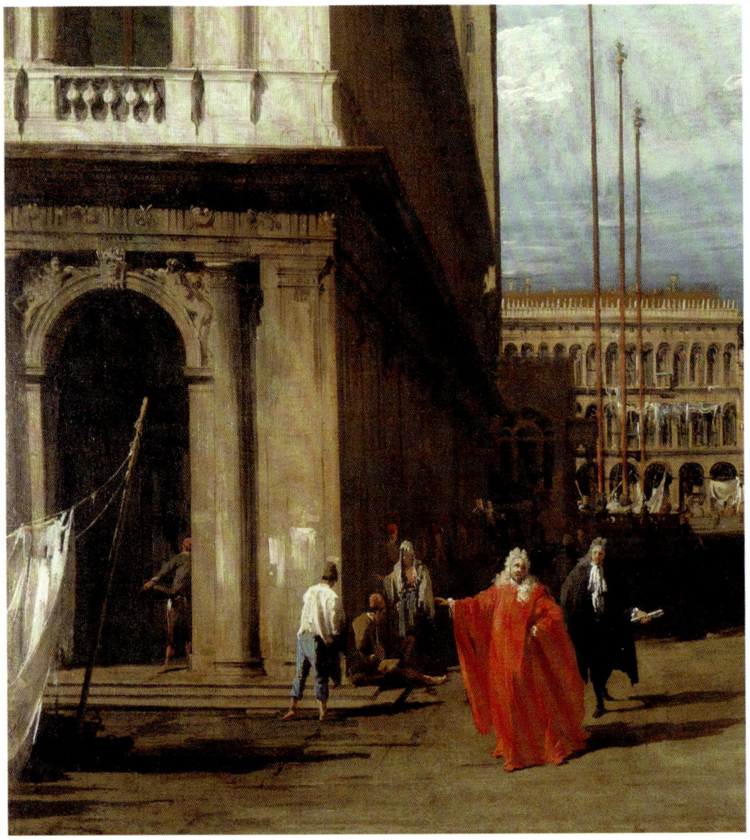

b. Canaletto, *The Piazzetta looking North, Venice*, 1722–23, oil on canvas, 172.8 x 135.2 cm. The Royal Collection, RCIN 405074

have approached his self-portrait as a theatrical game, and the subject of the pendant of the other two versions – *The Expulsion of the Money Changers from the Temple* – which may have also accompanied this painting, faithfully depicted in accordance with the *Gospel of Saint Matthew* and in keeping with the manner of Francesco Fontebasso, was one of the sacred themes included in Giuseppe

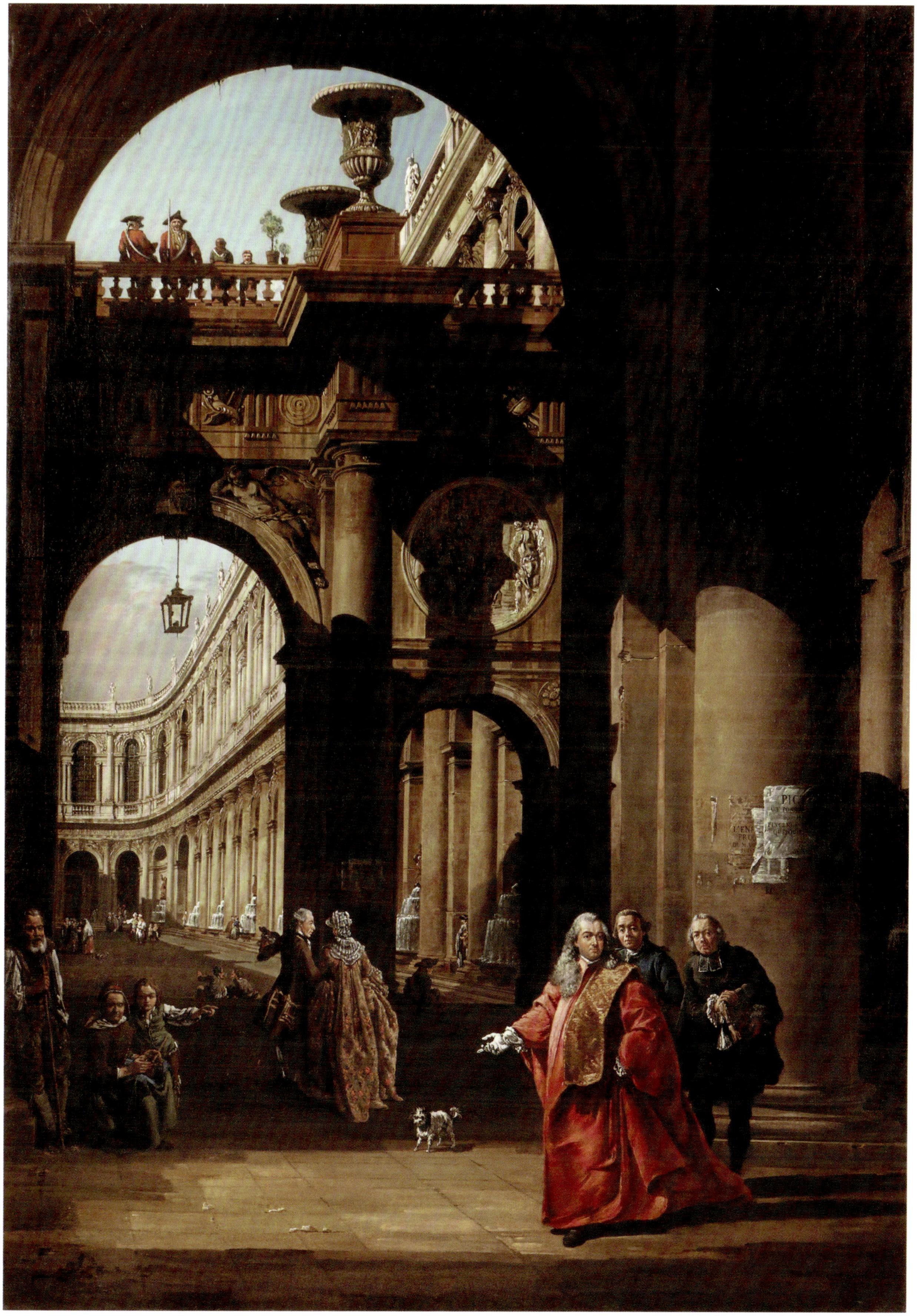

Galli-Bibbiena's theatrical engravings (1696–1757). He is identifying here with the incredibly tangible 'memory' of the nobleman attired in red near an arcade of the Libreria in one of the six pictures commissioned in 1722–23 by Joseph Smith (1674 ca. 1770), *The Piazzetta looking North, Venice* (C/L 63) (fig. a).
With the Horace quote, Bellotto is declaring his freedom as a painter by comparing himself to poets. In this context there is no doubt that the poets in question are those of the theatre. The Italian abbot following Bellotto with a sheaf of papers must be one of these, known in the theatres of the court. The first hypothesis identifying him as Giovanni Claudio Pasquini (1695–1763), whose works, dedicated to Earl Brühl, were published in 1751 by the painter's brother Michele Bellotti, a typographer in Arezzo, shared initially with Sergio Marinelli (see essay in this volume), is unconvincing. I would now like to suggest he be identified as Pietro Metastasio (1698–1782), court poet, who may have already been working on the poetry of Horace. Bellotto must have met him in Vienna; he was one of the subscribers to the first volume of *Delle Antiche Statue Greche e Romane* by Anton Maria Zanetti di Girolamo (1680–1767), a mutual friend. In another, now lost, contemporary *capriccio*, Bellotto portrays himself in the company of 'other very important people' (Kozakiewicz 1972a, no. 361; see the essay by the author of this entry).
Only Bellotto could turn this imposing architecture into a piece of poetry; only he could succeed in painting the walls, columns and friezes in such a way that provides an idea of their material consistency and structural certainty. The portraits – we will not question here whether the young man behind Bellotto is his servant Checo – are portrayed with a creative and attentive touch in both their faces and hands.

Bożena Anna Kowalczyk

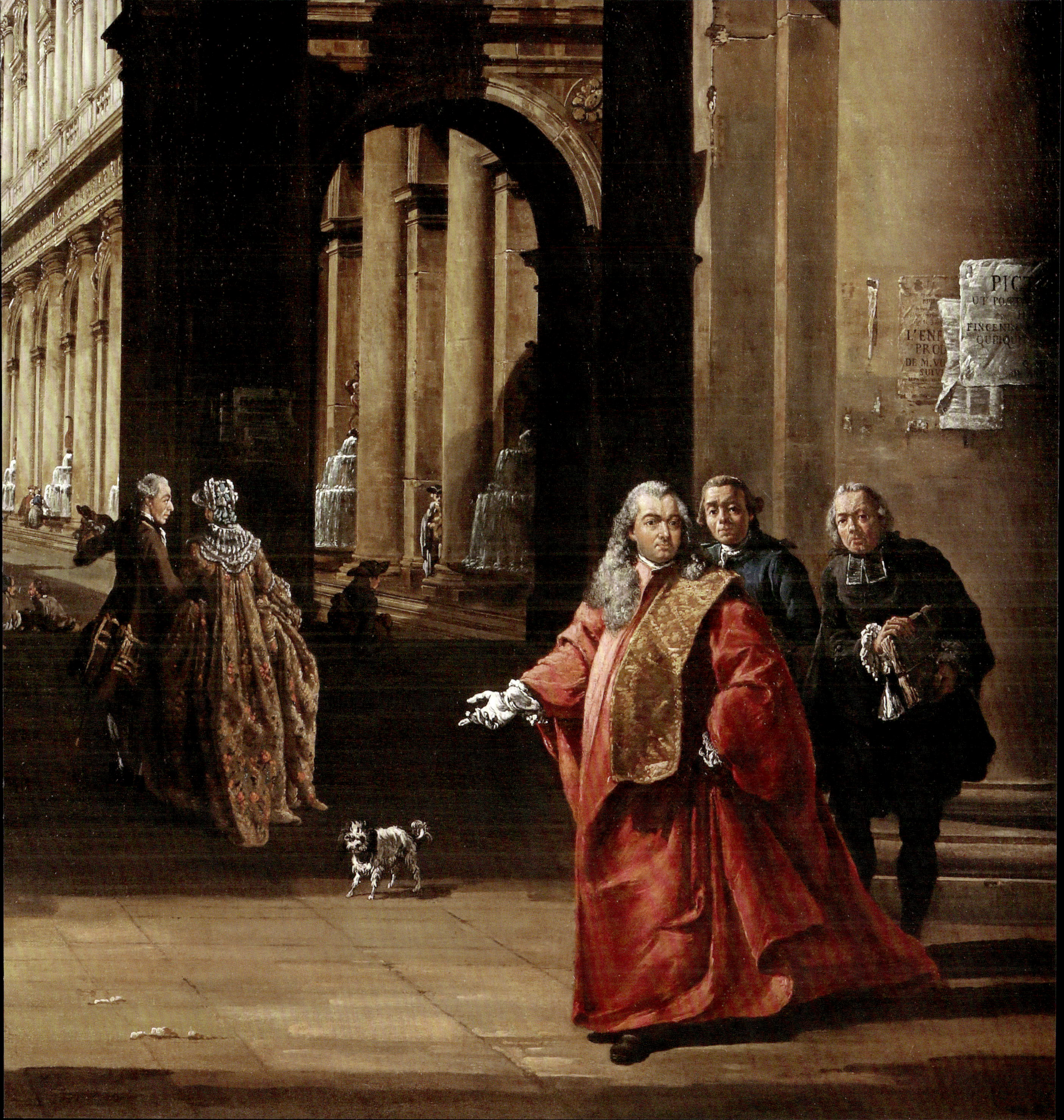
PIC
UT PO
FINGENI
QUIDQ
L'ENF
PROD
DE M. V
SUIV

83

BERNARDO BELLOTTO

(Venice 1722 – Warsaw 1780)

Catalogo de Danni
ch'ho' avuto, io, Bernardo Belotto de Canaletto: L'Anno. 1760.
(Nel Bombardamento, che fece il Re di Prussia) nel mio Alogio
Nella Salz:Gassen, in Casa del Sig.re Caesar. del. Valore:
Di Talleri Cinquanta Mille. dicco.........T: 50000.

July 1760–February 1762
manuscript; 33.5 x 20.3 cm

Vilnius, The Wróblewski Library of the Lithuanian Academy of Sciences,
The Manuscript Department, inv. F 22-26

Watermark: not identified.

This extraordinary document is the inventory of Bellotto's possessions in his house in Salzgasse, Dresden, near the Frauenkirche. The document is in a good state of preservation, apart from a tear along the fold at the top, which does not, however, impinge on the written part. It is twenty-one pages, nineteen of which written, all with the same watermark and numbered in pencil at a later date. The first page has a note at the top, with 'N 9' written in brown ink and '31' and '51' in blue pencil, but the handwriting is not that of Bellotto. Further down is the round stamp of the Library of the Lithuanian Academy of Sciences, with 26.Bx-IV written in purple ink. On sheet 20*v*, the same stamp and a stylised, nineteenth-century note in Polish: 'Ruża / Chinska / Prawda / Nie' [Rose / Chinese / Truth / No]. On sheet 21*v*, two lines of calculations. A later note in Polish is found on sheet 9*r*: 'Zaczeto r: 1828' (Begun year: 1828), providing the terminus *ante quem* for its purchase from the artist's heirs by Earl Konstanty Tyszkiewicz in Vilnius.

The *Catalogo de Danni*, drawn up by the artist himself for an appraisal in view of a claim for damages, documents the goods lost in the Prussian bombing which took place in July 1760, during the Seven Years' War, written by the artist to assess his losses in preparation for the compensation request. Before leaving Dresden for Vienna and Munich with his son Lorenzo (1742–1770) at the end of 1758 (the passport for Bayreuth is dated 5 December), Bellotto packed up his possessions in 'large boxes', witnessed by the owner of the building, Johann Karl Caesar, and his neighbours, all Italian, including other artists, the painter Francesco Gandini, a student of Pierre Subleyras in Rome and collaborator of Stefano Torelli in Dresden, and the court soprano Maria Rosa Negri, the wife of the painter from Friuli, Francesco Pavona, celebrated for his pastel portraits (ca. 1695–1777).

On his return in February 1762, he could only note that 'di tutto questo, non si è trovato altro che alquanti rami buoni da vendere, per rame vecchio' (out of all of this, all that remains are some coppers, only good to be sold for scrap copper) (sheet 19*r*).

Opening up the document, we expect to find a breathless, agitated Bellotto, his hand trembling as he compiled the list of lost possessions acquired with years of hard work. On the contrary, the inventory was written with a steady hand, in minute, careful handwriting laid out in precise lines, with sophisticated little waves marking the spaces. There are a few stylised, decorative lines between the paragraphs and very few erasures and changes. This leads us to believe, therefore, that Bellotto conceived the catalogue in Vienna, where he first heard the news of the bombing, or in Munich, and had already drafted it upon his return to Dresden. First the library, then the picture gallery and the house, another nine rooms, three for servants. One room was used as a printery and contained professional tools and equipment for engraving and printing his own etchings.

The long list of books – 1,078 entries, including albums of drawings and prints, both his own and those by others (and including *Vedute Altre prese da i luoghi altre ideate* by Canaletto, who Bellotto calls 'Antonio Canal') – records the volumes organised by size, from the small 'duodecimos' to the sixteen large albums 'In Carta Real', together with a celestial globe, a terrestrial one, a compass and a large telescope (sheet 15*v*). Bellotto aimed to list the title, author and edition, but the titles are rarely complete and the author's names are often omitted. As a rule, the editions are correct, but sometimes the publication location or date are missing. There is some naivety in the citation of proper names and places. Bellotto had clearly brought some notes with him, perhaps written quickly, without picking up each book one by one, and so partially from memory. There are no German titles, but there are a lot in French, a language that he must have known well, making no spelling mistakes, although he did leave out the accents. It is clear that he aimed for an orderly, standardised treatment of the citations and abbreviations, although he was not always successful. In listing tomes, he used the language they were written in for the abbreviation of the numbers. He made liberal use of capital letters, which predominate, although many proper names begin with small letters. Some of the titles are written on strips of glued-on paper, for example numbers 121, 211, 212, 222 and 223. It is more than a little surprising to find a book published in 1759, when in theory the library could no longer be expanded; the volume was listed as *Leg islateur Moderne, Memoires de Mailcourt*, Amst. 1759 (no. 110). 'Tutti Questi Libri Legati Alcuni in Bergamina, ed il Resto, in Pele di Vitelo Marmorisati, con suoi Numeri, e la mia Marcha cioè B: B: C. Riposti in Ripostorii di Rimesso di mia

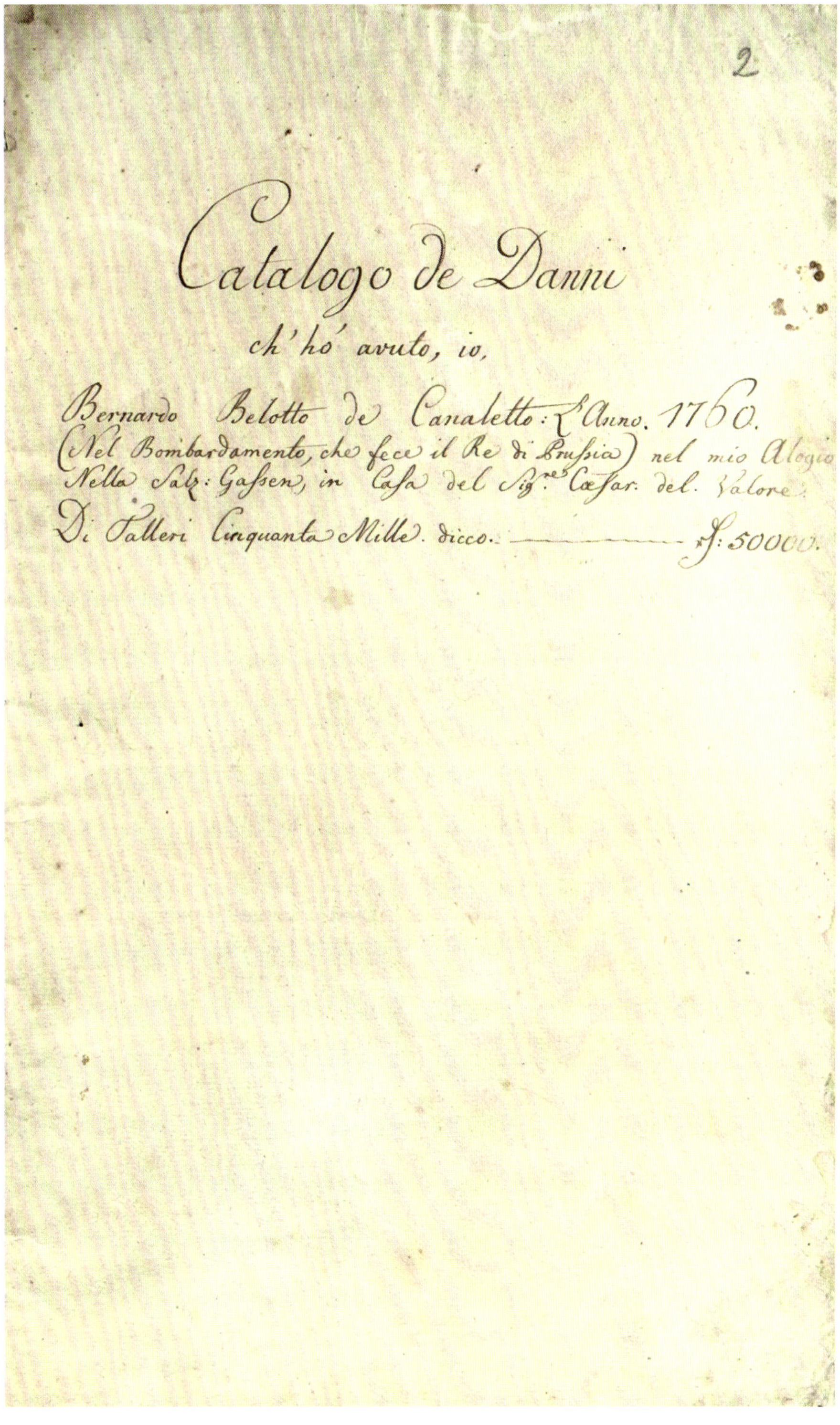

2

Catalogo de Danni
ch'hó avuto, io,
Bernardo Belotto de Canaletto: L'Anno. 1760.
(Nel Bombardamento, che fece il Re di Prussia) nel mio Alogio
Nella Salz: Gassen, in Casa del Sig.re Cæsar. del. Valore:
Di Talleri Cinquanta Mille. dicco. ——— Th: 50000.

Inventione, con Cornici, Frontespicii, e Lastre di Vetro, con Scalini Pedestali, e tiradori per Scrivere' (All of these books, some bound in parchment, and the rest in marbled calfskin, with their numbers, and my mark, and so B.B.C. Kept in inlaid containers of my own design, with frames, frontispieces and sheets of glass, with steps, pedestals and 'tiradori' for writing) (sheet 15*v*).
It was easier to remember the small, select collection of contemporary Venetian paintinsg, which included, except Rosalba Carriera and Canaletto, all of the important painters of his time, along with a few sixteenth- and seventeenth-century works and paintings by Bellotto himself, including four architectural *capricci*, four views of Königstein, two of Dresden and ten of Pirna. There was also sculpture, including 'Pezi di Bracii, Teste, Piedi, e Busti, Necesarii per il Studio. Attachati sopra le Tre Porte che erano nell'detto Gabinetto' (fragmentary arms, heads, feet and busts, necessary for study purposes. Mounted above the three doors in the Gallery) (sheet 16*v*).
The rooms where the family lived – his wife Elisabetta Pizzorno (Venice ca. 1724 – Warsaw 1785), adolescent son and three little girls – were recorded with nostalgia and gratification, room by room, with descriptions of the curtains, the colours of the upholstery 'verde con fiori naturali e ornamenti dorati' (green with natural flowers and golden embellishments); 'di tela gialla, con uccelli, e figure al naturale' (in yellow canvas with birds and nudes), mirrors, his own paintings and prints hung on the walls and furnishings, up to the china – a valuable set of Meissen given to him by Earl Brühl – kitchen porcelain.
Bellotto estimated the value of the goods listed at 50,000 thalers. There is no evidence of the sum – in total or at least in part – having ever been paid to him. The manuscript became part of his collections, travelling with him to Warsaw. In 1911, it could still be found in the Tyszkiewicz family residence in Łahoysk, Belarus, where it was seen by M. Stübel, the earliest Bellotto scholar. Recently rediscovered, it was published by E. Manikowska (2012 and 2014). The Polish scholar transcribed the list of books with great patience, completing and correcting it in order to help readers more easily identify the volumes.
The *Catalogo de Danni* is accompanied, in this exhibition, by a fragment of the draft of Bellotto's letter, probably addressed to King Augustus III, detailing his claim for damages (cat. 84), and by a selection of books, the very editions that once belonged to his library.

Listed below are the selected and exhibited editions.

Cesare Vecellio
De gli habiti antichi, et moderni di diuerse parti del mondo libri due, fatti da Cesare Vecellio, & con discorsi da lui dichiarati...
In Venetia, presso Damian Zenaro, 1590
Venice, Istituto di Storia dell'Arte, Fondazione Giorgio Cini

Pietro Aretino
Capricciosi & piaceuoli Ragionamenti di M. Pietro Aretino... Nuoua editione...
Cosmopoli, [Jan Elzevier, Leyden], 1660
Milan, Archivio Storico Civico e Biblioteca Trivulziana (Triv. L 1463)

Giovanni Francesco Loredan
Bizzarrie academiche, Parte prima, con altre compositioni del medesimo
Venezia, 1662
Venice, Biblioteca Nazionale Marciana, 69 C 239

Gregorio Leti
Il Puttanismo Romano, nuovamente ristampato con l'aggiunta d'un dialogo tra Pasquino e Marforio sopra lo stesso sogetto, et insieme, con il Nuovo parlatorio delle Monache, satira comica di Baltassaro Sultanini bresciano
In Londar, per Tomaso Buet, 1669
Torino, Biblioteca Nazionale Universitaria, Ris.99.2

Giambattista Marino
L'Adone, poema heroico del C. Marino con gli argomenti del Conte [Fortuniano] Sanvitale, e l'allegorie di Don Lorenzo Scoto...
Amsterdam, 1678
t. I
Venice, Biblioteca Nazionale Marciana, 221 C 203

Paolo Sarpi
Opere del padre Paolo Sarpi
Venezia, 1687
t. I
Venice, Biblioteca Nazionale Marciana, 146 D 257

Andrea Pozzo
Perspectiva pictorum et architectorum Andreae Putei e Societate Jesu. Pars prima
Romae, typis Joannis Jacobi Komarek Bohemi apud S. Angelum Custodem, 1693
Venice, Biblioteca Nazionale Marciana, 42.D.14

Ferdinando Galli Bibiena
L'architettura civile preparata su la geometria, e ridotta alle prospettive. Considerazioni pratiche di Ferdinando Galli Bibiena... dissegnate, e descritte in cinque parti...
In Parma, per Paolo Monti; in Bologna, appresso il Longhi, MCDCCXI [i.e. 1711]
Venice, Biblioteca Nazionale Marciana, 88 D 18

Erasmus of Rotterdam
L'Éloge de la folie
Leyde, P. Vander Aa, 1715
Naples, Biblioteca Nazionale "Vittorio Emanuele III", BNN, Fondo Doria 9.116

Francesco Borromini
Opera... cavata da suoi originali; cioè, la chiesa, e fabrica della sapienza di Roma, con le vedute in prospettiva, e con lo studio delle proporzni geometriche, piante, alzate, profili, e spaccati...
Roma, 1720
Rome, Biblioteca Romana Sarti, BRS 03063

Miguel de Cervantes
Histoire de l'admirable Don Quichotte de la Manche, traduite de l'espagnol de Michel de Cervantès (par Filleau de Saint-Martin)
Lyon, T. Amaulry, 1723
t. I and II
Naples, Biblioteca della Società Napoletana di Storia Patria

Scipione Maffei
Verona illustrata parte prima...
In Verona, per Jacopo Vallarsi, e Pierantonio Berno, 1731-1732
Venice, Biblioteca Nazionale Marciana, 70 D 16

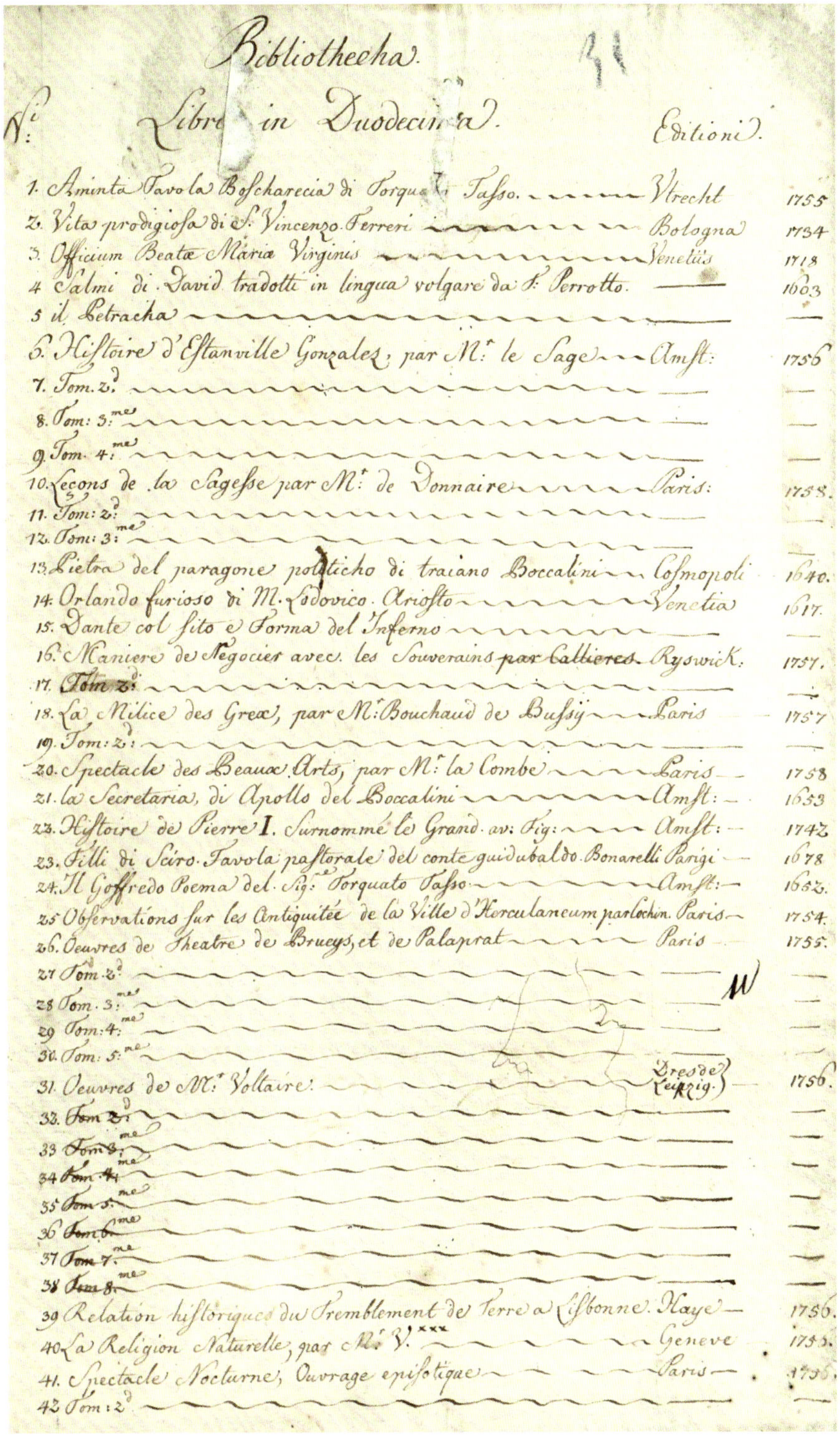

Bibliotheeha

N.i Libri in Duodecima. Editioni.

1. Aminta Favola Boschareccia di Torquato Tasso. — Vtrecht 1755
2. Vita prodigiosa di S. Vincenzo Ferreri — Bologna 1734
3. Officium Beatæ Mariæ Virginis — Venetiis 1718
4. Salmi di David tradotti in lingua volgare da F. Perrotto. — 1603
5. il Petracha — —
6. Histoire d'Estanville Gonzales; par Mr. le Sage — Amst: 1756
7. Tom. 2.d — —
8. Tom: 3.me — —
9. Tom. 4.me — —
10. Leçons de la Sagesse par Mr. de Donnaire — Paris: 1758.
11. Tom: 2.d — —
12. Tom: 3.me — —
13. Pietra del paragone politicho di traiano Boccalini — Cosmopoli 1640.
14. Orlando furioso di M. Lodovico Ariosto — Venetia 1617.
15. Dante col sito e forma del Inferno — —
16. Maniere de Negocier avec les Souverains par Callieres. Ryswick. 1757.
17. Tom. 2.d — —
18. La Milice des Grecs, par Mr. Bouchaud de Bussy — Paris 1757
19. Tom: 2.d — —
20. Spectacle des Beaux Arts, par Mr. la Combe — Paris 1758
21. la Secretaria, di Apollo del Boccalini — Amst: 1653
22. Histoire de Pierre I. Surnommé le Grand. av: Fig: — Amst: 1742
23. Filli di Sciro. Favola pastorale del conte guidubaldo Bonarelli Parigi — 1678
24. Il Goffredo Poema del Sig.r Torquato Tasso — Amst: 1652.
25. Observations sur les Antiquitée de la Ville d'Herculaneum par Cochin. Paris — 1754.
26. Oeuvres de Theatre de Brueys, et de Palaprat — Paris 1755.
27. Tom. 2.d — —
28. Tom. 3.me — —
29. Tom: 4.me — —
30. Tom: 5.me — —
31. Oeuvres de Mr. Voltaire: — Dresde Leipzig. 1756.
32. Tom. 2.d — —
33. Tom. 3.me — —
34. Tom. 4.me — —
35. Tom. 5.me — —
36. Tom. 6.me — —
37. Tom. 7.me — —
38. Tom. 8.me — —
39. Relation historiques du Tremblement de Terre a Lisbonne. Haye — 1756.
40. La Religion Naturelle, par Mr. V.xxx — Geneve 1755.
41. Spectacle Nocturne, Ouvrage episotique — Paris — 1755.
42. Tom: 2.d — —

George Berkley
Alciphron, ou le Petit Philosophe en sept dialogues, contenant une apologie de la religion chrétienne contre ceux qu'on nomme esprits-forts
La Haye, B. Gibert, 1734
t. II
Florence, Biblioteca Nazionale Centrale, MAGL.10.6.27, vol. II

Samuel Richardson
Paméla ou la Vertu récompensée
Amsterdam, aux dépens de la Compagnie, 1743
Private Collection

Ludovico Antonio Muratori
Annali d'Italia dal principio dell'era volgare sino all'anno 1500. Compilati da Lodovico Antonio Muratori bibliotecario del serenissimo Duca di Modena
In Milano [ma Venezia], a spese di Giovambatista Pasquali libraro in Venezia, 1744-1749
tomo IX
Milan, Archivio Storico Civico e Biblioteca Trivulziana, Triv. D 336/IX

Il Corano
L'Alcoran de Mohamet, traduit de l'arabe par André Du Ryer... Nouvelle édition
Amsterdam, P. Martier, 1746
t. II
Venice, Biblioteca Nazionale Marciana, 49 T 229

Montesquieu
Considérations sur les causes de la grandeur des Romains, et de leur décadence
A Lausanne, chez Marc-Michel Bousquet & compagnie, 1749
Naples, Biblioteca Nazionale "Vittorio Emanuele III", BNN, Racc. Villarosa. A 613

Henry Fielding
Histoire de Tom Jones ou l'Enfant trouvé
Londres, J. Nourse, 1750
t. I
Naples, Biblioteca Nazionale "Vittorio Emanuele III", BNN, Palat.48.92(1)

Pietro Leone Ghezzi
Les caricatures du célèbre *cavalier Ghezzi*
Dresde, 1750
Milan, Archivio Storico Civico e Biblioteca Trivulziana, Triv. ATL 119

Pietro Metastasio
Opere drammatiche del sig. abate Pietro Metastasio romano poeta cesareo. Nona edizione notabilmente accresciuta, e corretta
Venezia, al Secolo delle lettere, presso Giuseppe Bettinelli, 1750-1752
t. II
Milan, Archivio Storico Civico e Biblioteca Trivulziana, Triv. L 3588/II

Giovanni Claudio Pasquini
Opere del signor Gio. Claudio Pasquini senese cav. del Sacro Romano Imperio e poeta di sua maestà il re di Polonia elettore di Sassonia...
In Arezzo, per Michele Bellotti stampatore vescovile, 1751
t. I
Private Collection

Voltaire
Oeuvres de Mr. de Voltaire. Tome premier - Nouvelle édition *revue, corrigée et considerablement augmentée par l'auteur enrichie de figures en taille-douce*
A Dresde, chez George Conrad Walther, libraire du Roi, 1752
Venice, Biblioteca Nazionale Marciana, 195 C 135

Carlo Goldoni
Le commedie del dottore Carlo Goldoni avvocato veneziano
In Firenze, 1756
Venice, Biblioteca del Museo Correr, Ravà 3.4.8

Horace
Les Poësies d'Horace traduites en françois. Avec des remarques et des dissertations critiques. Par le R. P. Sanadon
tomo VII
Amsterdam, Leipzic 1756
Florence, Biblioteca Nazionale Centrale, Palat. 18.5.2.7, vol. 7°

David Hume
Essais philosophiques sur l'entendement humain, par Mr. Hume, avec les quatre philosophes du même auteur. Traduit de l'anglois
Amsterdam, chez J.H. Schneider, 1758
Milan, Biblioteca Comunale Centrale, Palazzo Sormani, F VET 815

Friedrich Spanheim
Histoire de la papesse Jeanne... Nouvelle édition...
La Haye, 1758
Milan, Biblioteca Centro Apice

Thanks to Sergio Marinelli for our conversations on Bellotto library and for valuable suggestions on the choice of books.

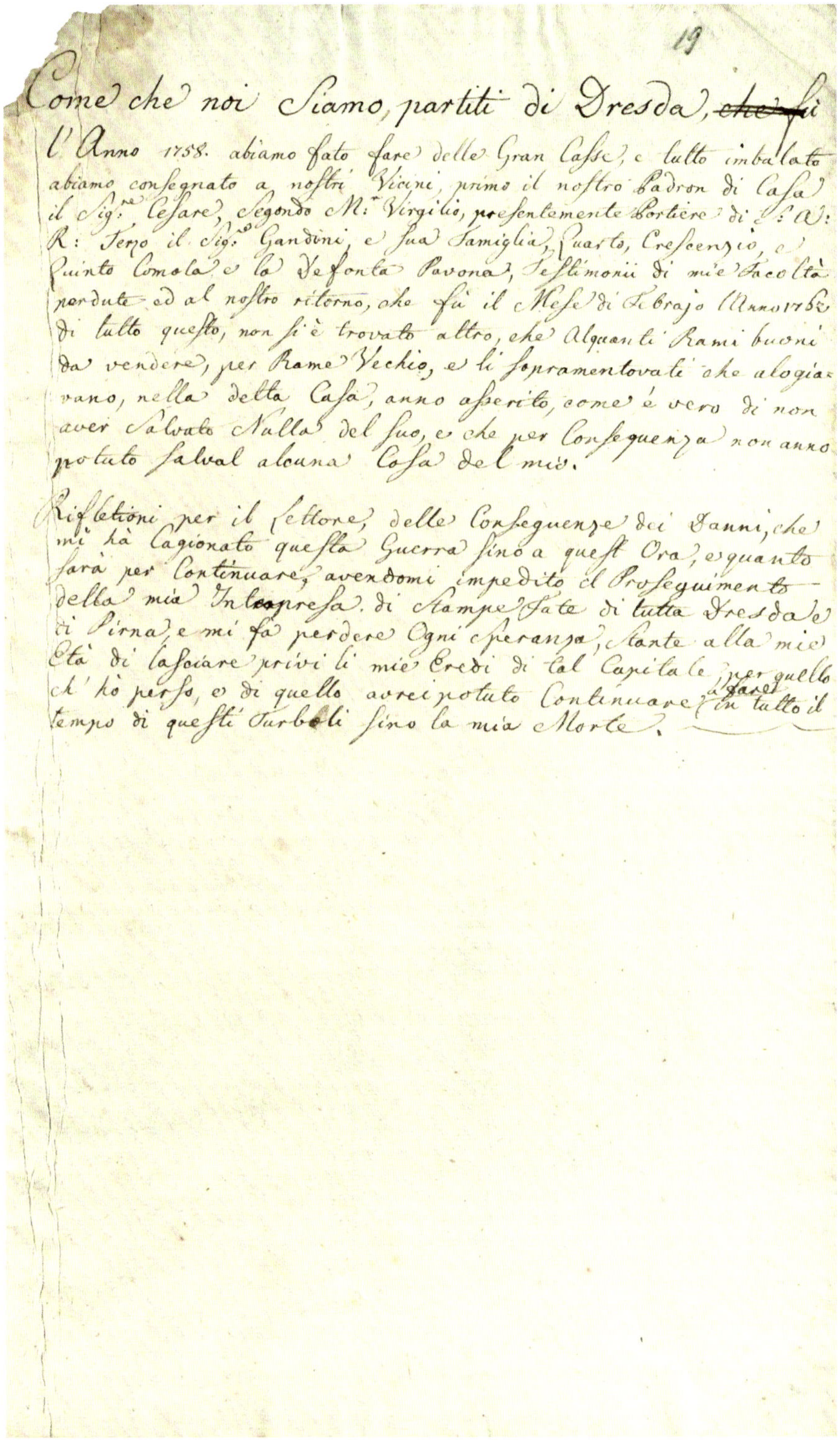

19

Come che noi Siamo, partiti di Dresda, ~~che~~ fù l'Anno 1758. abiamo fato fare delle Gran Casse, e tutto imbalato abiamo consegnato a nostri Vicini, primo il nostro Padron di Casa il Sig.re Cesare, Segondo M.r Virgilio, presentemente Portiere di S: A: R: Terzo il Sig.r Gandini, e sua Famiglia, Quarto, Crescenzio, e Quinto Comola e la Defonta Pavona, Testimonii di mie Facoltà perdute, ed al nostro ritorno, che fù il Mese di Febrajo l'Anno 1763 di tutto questo, non si è trovato altro, che Alquanti Rami buoni da vendere, per Rame Vechio, e li sopramentovati che alogiavano, nella detta Casa, anno asserito, come è vero di non aver Salvato Nulla del suo, e che per Consequenza non anno potuto salval alcuna Cosa del mio.

Riflettioni per il Lettore, delle Consequenze dei Danni, che mi hà Cagionato questa Guerra fino a quest Ora, e quanto sarà per Continuare, avendomi impedito il Proseguimento della mia In~~to~~presa. di Stampe Sate di tutta Dresda e di Pirna, e mi fa perdere Ogni Speranza, Stante alla mie Età di lasciare privi li mie Eredi di tal Capitale per quello ch'hò perso, e di quello averei potuto Continuare a fare in tutto il tempo di questi Turboli fino la mia Morte.

BERNARDO BELLOTTO

(Venice 1722 – Warsaw 1780)

Snippet of a Letter (verso)
Statue of Saint John Evangelist in a Niche (recto)
1762

pen and brown ink; 145 x 80 mm
Warsaw, Muzeum Narodowe, Rys. Pol. 2064

The sketch of a statue of Saint John the Evangelist in a niche on the *recto* of this sheet belongs to the large series of preparatory studies preserved at the Muzeum Narodowe in Warsaw and is related to the *Capriccio of ruins and a temple* at the State Museum of Western and Eastern Art in Kiev (Kozakiewicz 1972a, no. 347). The fragment of writing on the *verso*, which Kozakiewicz and Rizzi interpreted as a receipt of use for dating the painting, has been identified here for the first time as a draft of the letter that Bellotto addressed, probably, to King August III, requesting compensation for the damage caused by the Prussian bombardment in July 1760 that destroyed his home in the centre of Dresden, in the Salzgasse, along with his library and collection.
In the small fragment of the letter, written in Bellotto's clear hand, we read:

…li (?) auti nel Ocasione [effaced]
…a fatto il Re di di P …
…Hab [effaced]li 26 Fevraro 1762
…Dani che ho auti Io [?]

…o de Canaleto l'ann…
…damento che fece il …alogiamento nella di
…Sig. Cesare ad…

The letter, a dramatic plea for compensation for the serious losses he had sustained, must have accompanied the *Catalogo de Danni* (cat. 83), the inventory of possessions lost when the home was destroyed, written by the artist himself to justify the considerable sum requested of 50,000 thalers. In the fragment, we recognise the words of the heading of the manuscript: 'Re di P[russia]', 'Dani', 'Io …[Bellott]o de Canaleto, [bombar]damento', 'Sig. Cesare'; in spite of its fragmentary state, the similarity of the layout of the sheet is clear.
The original letter has not yet been found. The date is of great value, 26 February 1762. The *Catalogo de Danni* had already been compiled, probably in Vienna or Munich, before his return to Dresden that same month. The neat hand and very length of the manuscript suggest that he was not in a hurry.
The request for compensation came to nothing. After the Seven Years War, Dresden was a fragile city and the court's financial resources were exhausted. In October 1763, both of Bellotto's patrons died within three weeks of one another: King August III, who guaranteed the union between Saxony and Poland, and Earl Heinrich Brühl, the imprudent policies of whom led the small State to that devastating war. Bellotto found himself in grave economic difficulty, as well as disheartened by the lost of the plates for his engravings. After four years of work in a profoundly changed city, where even the cultural climate, with the first signs of Neoclassicism, was unfavourable to the artist,

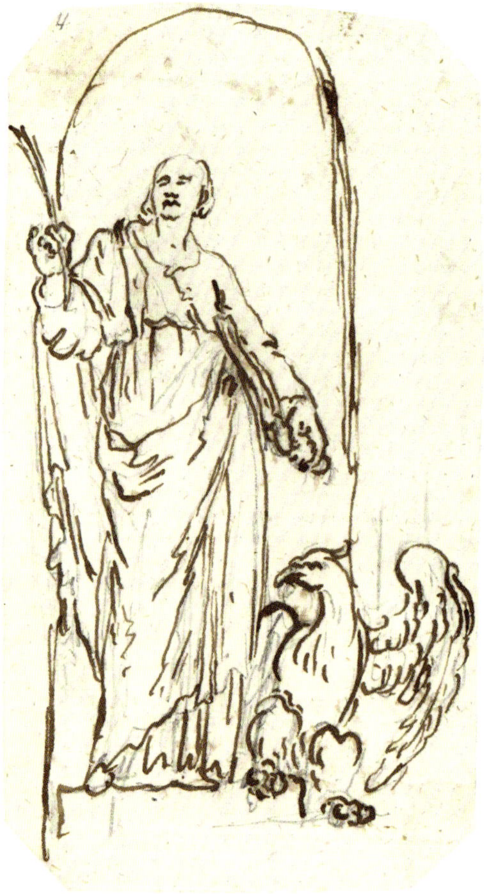

a. Bernardo Bellotto,
Saint John Evangelist,
(*recto* of cat. 84)

Bellotto left Dresden in January 1767, and headed to the Saint Petersburg court with his son Lorenzo (1742–1770). He stopped in Warsaw, where he was presented by the Roman painter Marcello Bacciarelli (1731–1818) to the new king, Stanisław II August Poniatowski (1731–1798), who invited him to remain in Poland.

Bożena Anna Kowalczyk

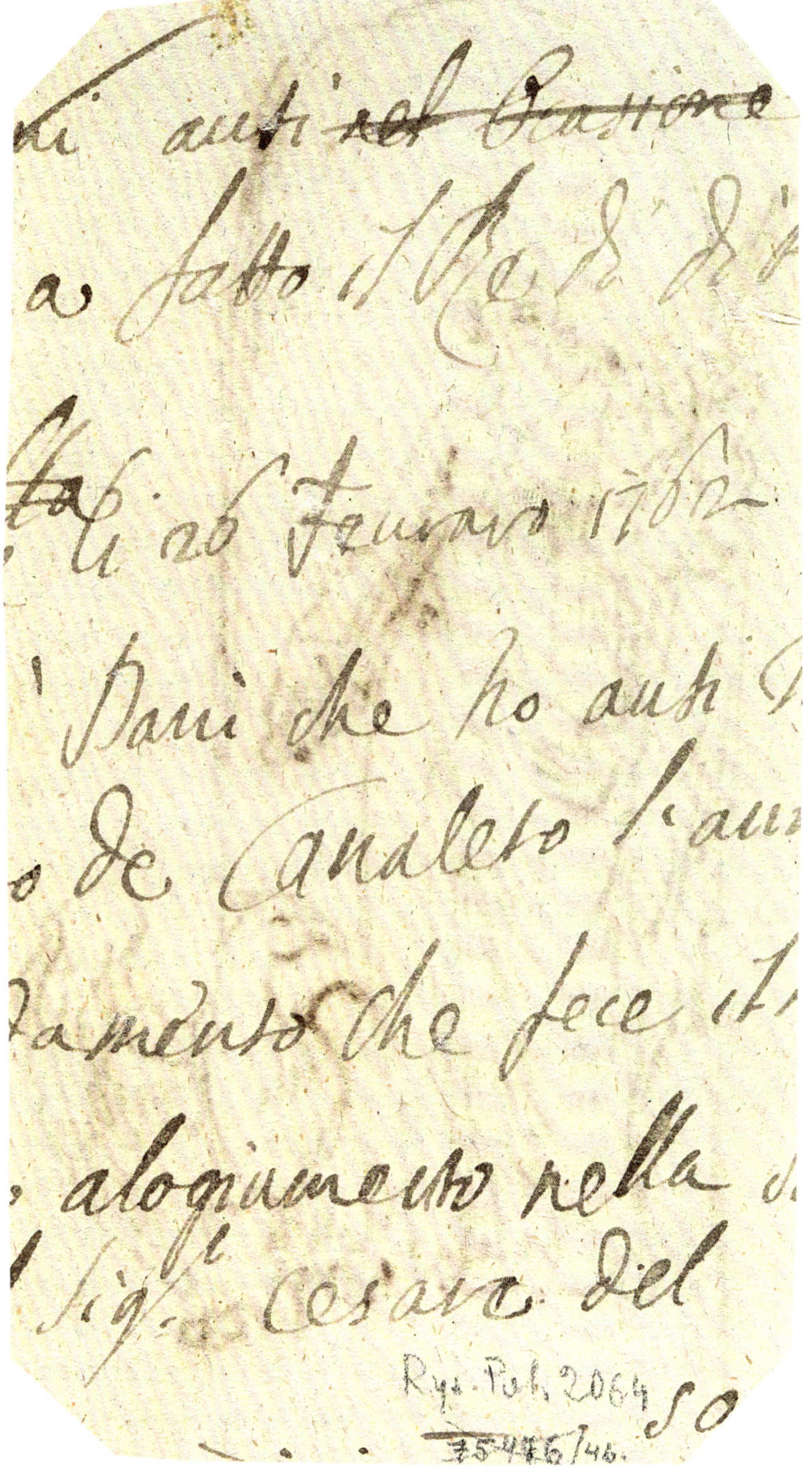
ni auti ~~nel Passione~~
a fatto il Re di P
ta li 26 Febraro 1762
Dani che ho auti
o de Canaleto l'ann
amento che fece il
alogiamento nella
l Sig.r Cesare del
Ryc. Pol. 2064
so
~~75476/46.~~

85

BERNARDO BELLOTTO
(Venice 1722 – Warsaw 1780)

Two Polish Hussars
1762

pen and brown ink over pencil; 561–562 x 322–320 mm
Warsaw, Muzeum Narodowe, Rys. Pol. 2082

86

BERNARDO BELLOTTO
(Venice 1722 – Warsaw 1780)

Two Balkan Hajduks and a Man with Cocked Hat
1762

pen and brown ink over pencil; 560 x 320 mm
Warsaw, Muzeum Narodowe, Rys. Pol. 2075

Inscriptions: (cat. 85) on the left-hand figure, 'Pele, Ple, mani/ca Pio; Roso, R so'; on the right-hand figure, 'Pele, Zolobin, Zolo no, Zb no'; (cat. 86) in pen, over the cape of the left-hand figures, 'roso sporcho' (dirty pink); above the central one: on the hat, 'Gialato' (yellowish), on the garments: 'Rso', and repeatedly, 'B' and 'R'; above the cape of the man with cocked hat: 'lacheta (?) sporcha'.

Watermark: (both) right-hand profile of a galloping unicorn with a monogram of 'L' in its body, not identified.

The Cabinet of Drawings and Prints at the Muzeum Narodowe of Warsaw preserves sixty-two drawings by Bellotto, with few exceptions executed in Vienna in 1759–60 and in the second Dresden period between 1762 and 1766. For most, they are groups of preparatory sketches for the same few paintings. There are forty drawings from the Dresden period executed on different kinds of paper. The examination of the paper, facilitated by the presence of very evident watermarks, provides an important help in the determination of the chronology.
These two large drawings of soldiers, Polish hussars and Balkan hajduks, perhaps the most well-known examples of the mature Bellotto's graphic work, belong to the group of sketches used for the three over-door cartouches at the Gemäldegalerie in Dresden (nos. 634, 635 and 636), whose dating has long been discussed: among the proposals was one claiming they were made in Poland, as suggested by their mention in the inventory of the Gallery's holdings, drawn up before 1841, as 'Canaletto. Views of the castle of King of Poland and Elector of Saxony in Warsaw' but perhaps also by the presence of Polish hussars. G.J.M. Weber considers the three paintings to be part of the decoration of a room, containing also the two *Allegories* of the same arched shape (Gemäldegalerie, Dresden, nos. 632, 633), one dated 1762, and so alleging the same date for the panels over the door.
The suggested date of 1762 for the three paintings and for the group of preparatory studies is confirmed now with the study of the watermarks. The two drawings have been executed on the same paper with the unicorn watermark as other sketches of the same cycle, *Sentinel* and two architectural backgrounds (Warsaw, Muzeum Narodowe, Rys. Pol. 2083, 2077 and 2081).
The fact that the same paper with the unicorn is found among the preparatory sketches for a *Capriccio with the Ruins of a Temple* in the State Museum of Western and Eastern Art in Kiev (Kozakiewicz 1972a, no. 347), in turn painted after February 1762 – the date on the verso of one of the preparatory drawings to this composition (cat. 84) – indicates a *post quem* date for this group of drawings too. But another element appears to circumscribe the time frame for its execution: the same watermark also appears in the preliminary sketch for the whole scene of the *Architectural Capriccio* at the Hamburg Kunsthalle (Rys. Pol. 2074), of which one of the over-door panels is a reduced replica, bearing the original words 'Canaletto...e... 1762'. The whole group of drawings marked with this watermark was therefore produced by the end of the same year.
The two drawings were used in the same size for the foregrounds in two different over-door panels; the figures of the two hajduks, smaller in size, also appear in the mentioned Hamburg *capriccio*. Bellotto prepared his paintings in every detail: while introducing the figures in the various paintings, he would draw their outlines in various sizes, depending on each canvas; in the drawing with the hajduks, as in the painting of Dresden (fig. a), behind the right soldier he added a man with a cocked hat, already in scale, given his location on the grand staircase in the distance.
The notes on the colours of the uniforms and the cloak worn by the gentleman

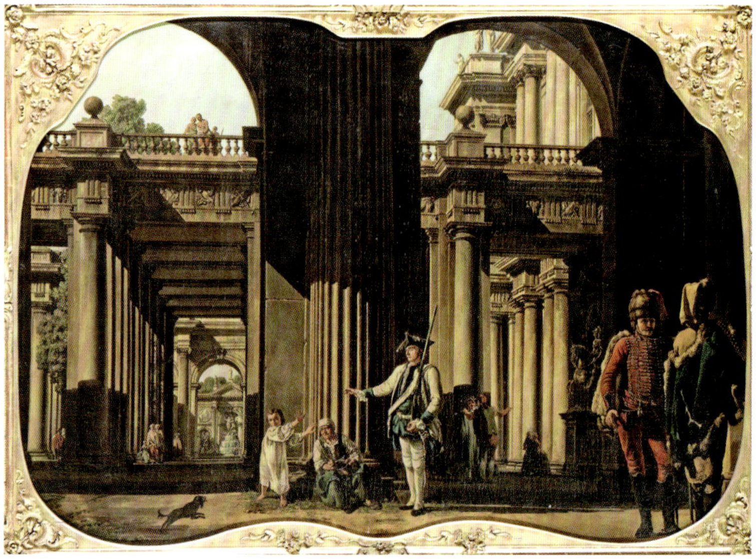

b. Bernardo Bellotto, *Architectural Capriccio*, oil on canvas, 104 x 146 cm. Dresden, Gemäldegalerie, 635

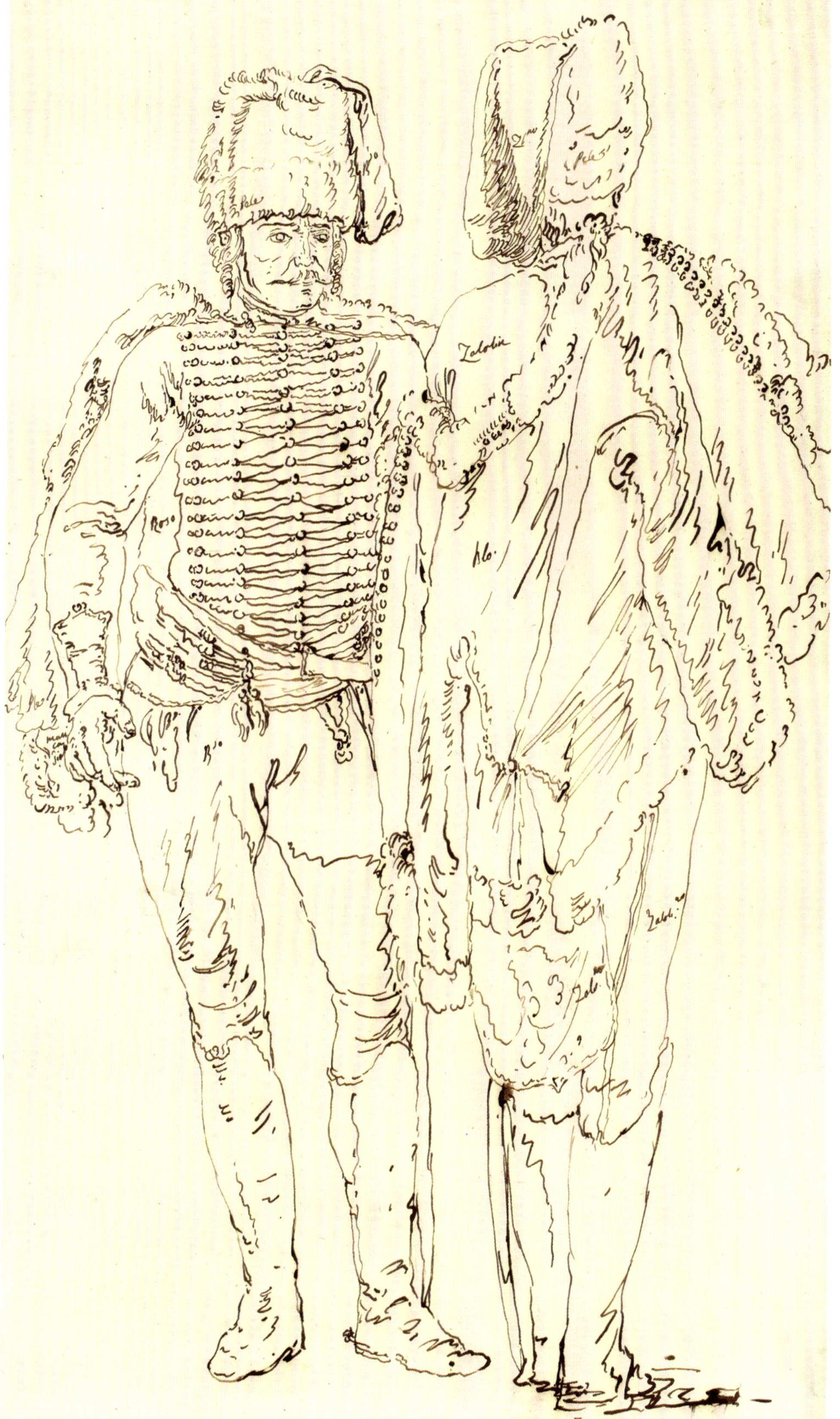

with the tricorn hat are reminders, as was Canaletto's wont; we find these same hues used for the garments in the Dresden and Hamburg canvases.
At the Muzeum Narodowe in Warsaw there are two other drawings of figures, intended for foreground details and from the same preparatory series for over-door panels in Dresden, *Arrotino* and *Woman with child*; like the present drawings, they are sketched on individual sheets in the manner of Luca Carlevarijs, already adopted in his youth in Venice, as seen in the drawings in the Courtauld Institute of Art and the Metropolitan Museum of Art (C / L 839. And 840). Other drawings in Warsaw show secondary figures and statues, small but effective outlines that were copied with care in the paintings.
These drawings emphasise the originality of Bellotto in his recording of reality and his theatrical taste. Large figures like these, mostly of ordinary people, soldiers, beggars, craftsmen, which then appear in the foregrounds of his *capricci* of the second Dresden period like actors on a stage, are ennobled by the painter, described with a genuine interest, and are of excellent quality in painting. The portrait of the old hussar offers a number of psychological details, but the focus concentrates on the description of the uniform with its complicated decoration of buttons and the soft fur of the soldier's cape seen from behind; the two hajduks are investigated with equal curiosity.
This interest could have drawn inspiration from the images of Venetian costumes and those worn by different peoples depicted in the plates in Cesare Vecellio's volume *De gli habiti antichi, et moderni di diverse parti del mondo*, a copy of which was to be found in our Bellotto's library.
The nervous outline and shorts, interrupted strokes mark the extreme development of his graphic style.

Bożena Anna Kowalczyk

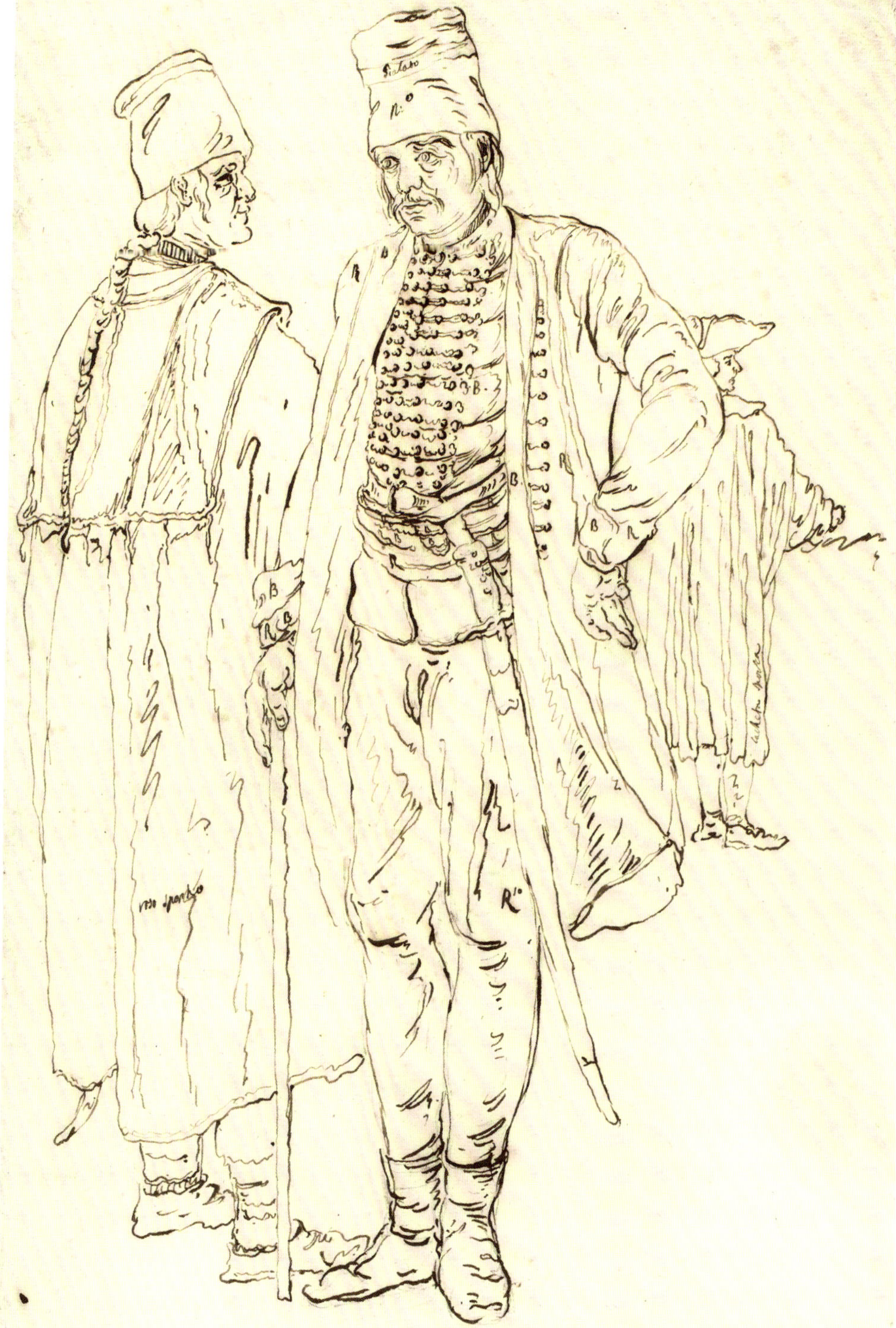

87

BERNARDO BELLOTTO

(Venice 1722 – Warsaw 1780)

Architectural Capriccio with an Equestrian Monument
1764

pen and grey-black and brown ink, grey wash, over free and ruled pencil with pinpointing; the design is outlined in pen and ruler; 443 x 619 mm
signed at lower left in brown ink, 'Bernardo Belotto/ de' Canaletto inv: et Fec. 1764'.
London, Victoria and Albert Museum, E. 30-1939

88

BERNARDO BELLOTTO

(Venice 1722 – Warsaw 1780)

Architectural Capriccio with the Dioscuri from the Capitol
1764

pen and grey-black and brown ink, grey wash, over pencil, over free and ruled pencil with pinpointing; the design is outlined in pen and ruler; 439 x 622 mm
signed at lower left in brown ink, 'Bernardo Belotto/ de Canaletto Inv: et Fec. 1764'.
London, Victoria and Albert Museum, E. 31.1939

In a letter dated 27 June 1927, in the Wallace Collection, George A. Simonson, author of the first monograph on Francesco Guardi (1904), informed the reader that he had 'two large pen & ink sepia drawings by Bellotto, signed and dated 1764'. Von Hadeln mentioned the sheets in the note dedicated to Bellotto's drawings but declared that 'owing to the certain weaknesses in the execution, it appears doubtful whether they are original'. S. Kozakiewicz quoted the letter but did not know the drawings. They were attributed to Bellotto by P. Ward-Jackson. The two carefully finished architectural *capricci*, planned as companion pieces as though they were a pair of paintings, represent the genre in which Bellotto regularly worked in second Dresden period, between 1762 and 1766; the date shown, 1764, express a connection with the appointment in the same year as an aggregate member for perspective at the Dresden Academy. They stand out for their character as a true theatrical drawing in like manner to those by Giuseppe Galli Bibiena (1696–1757), whose work he saw in the first Dresden period, but also for the structuring of space and the way he puts together the various compositional elements. The cold perspective correctness, the clarity of every detail and a theatrical luminosity, are elements by which Bellotto stressed his distance from Canaletto, who in the 1760s was devoting himself to drawings with a greater freedom and fantasy, but the masterful technique and the modulated use of grey wash constitute a veritable master class. Venetian and Paduan elements intersect in the two sheets at a frantic pace with those collected on his travels to Rome and Tuscany and with motifs drawn from the prints. The two drawings were preceded by detailed sketches of the composition, preserved in Warsaw and Darmstadt (Kozakiewicz 1972a, nos. 304, 305), in which the hand of an assistant can be made out, maybe his son Lorenzo (1742–1770), in accordance with the custom of Canaletto's studio.
In the two wings of the first sheet, one can recognise the edges of the Libreria Marciana, followed on the right by a few arches of Sansovino's building, to the left of the portico of the Prigioni, surmounted by a loggia similar to that of the Doge's Palace, but with twin columns; further back is a boatyard with a boat being repaired. At the centre are the ruins of a triumphal arch, similar to that of the Sergii arch in Pula, dominated by a medieval tower; beneath the arch, a round temple can be seen, together with a city in the distance on the lagoon, dominated by a high round tower, adapted from the print published in 1740 by Giuseppe Galli Bibiena (G. Marini, in London-Washington 1994-1995), with the Palladian church of San Francesco della Vigna and the dome of the Basilica della Salute with one tower. The base of the monument near the Libreria is inspired by the Venetian one of Bartolomeo Colleoni, but the equestrian statue is reminiscent of that of Augustus III in Dresden Neustadt, while the statue of slaves at the base are a reminder of those sculpted by Pietro Tacca and placed in 1624 on the monument to Ferdinand I de' Medici in Livorno (F.J.B. Watson, in London 1957); they reappear in a Bellotto oil at the State Museum of Western and Eastern Art in Kiev (Kozakiewicz 1972a, n. 347). Two Venetian *bissone* are berthing. There are dazzling light effects on the left to offset the atmospheric grey background and the shadow that surrounds the base of the monument. Masterful use of wash. Typical touches of parallel grey lines to mark the waves, the sky barely darkened, with the contours of the clouds rapidly marked out.
Two bridges meet over a body of water in the second sheet, one of which stretches from the right towards a triumphal arch, surmounted by the four horses of San Marco located on the high pedestal; beyond the bridge, there are two twin buildings, similar to Sansovino's Ca' Corner della Ca' Grande, set against a medieval tower, similar to that of Ezzelino near Padua; the dome of the Pantheon and the pyramid of Caius Cestius stand in the background, and further right, behind a garden, there is a Venetian *fondamenta*, with a Renaissance house and a building to the Prigioni; Trajan's column stands in the garden. Two sets of arcades frame the image, with the statues of the Dioscuri on pedestals. This is a carefully calculated world, frozen in perfect technicality, an intellectual exercise but perhaps also a *divertimento*.

Bożena Anna Kowalczyk

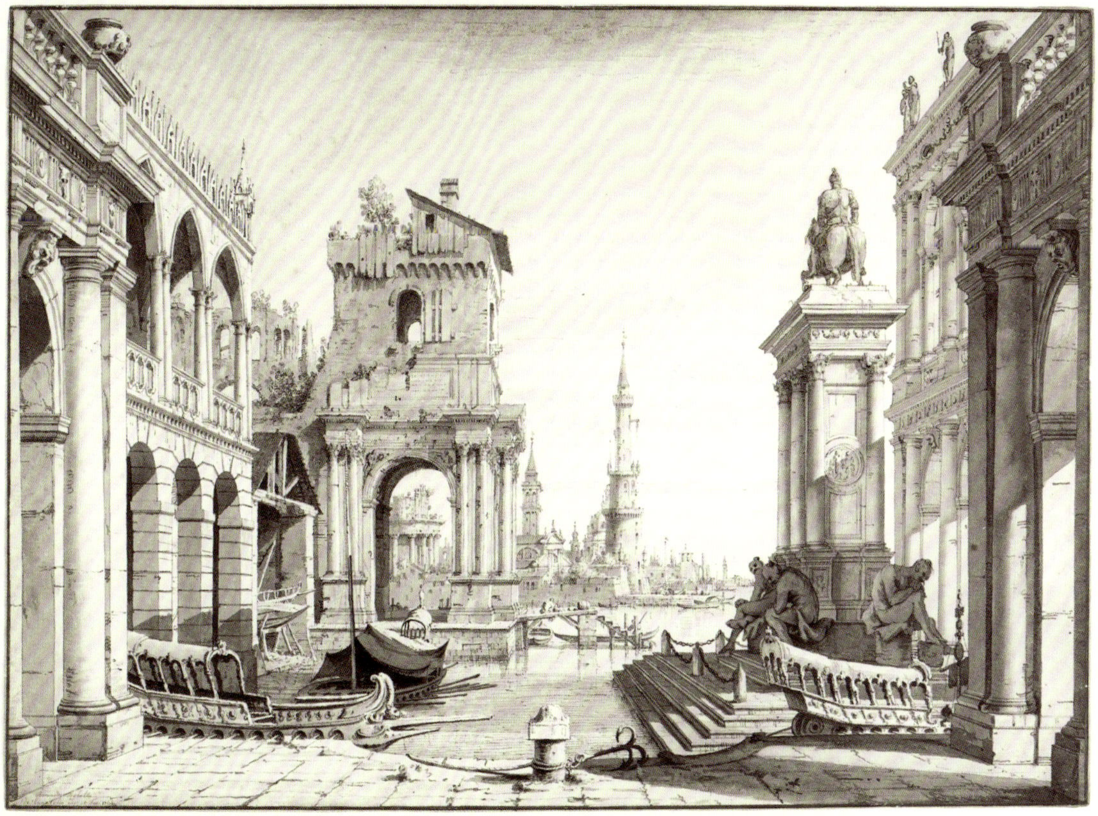

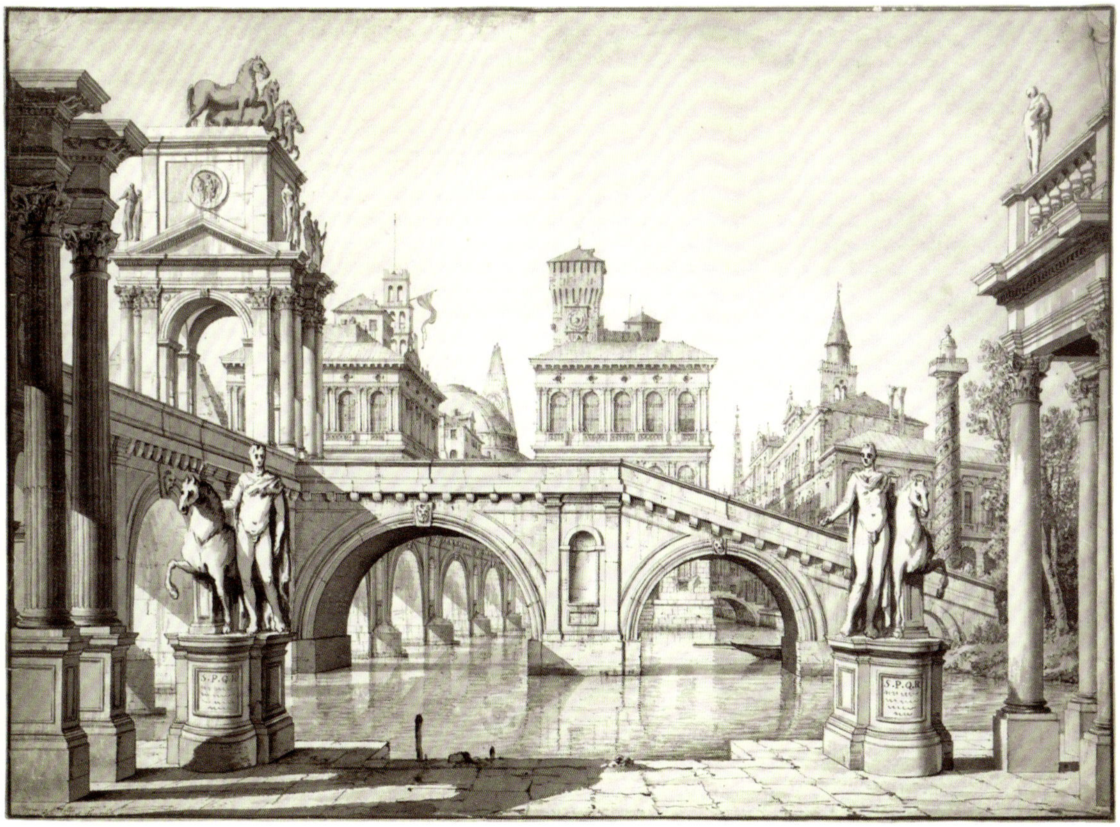
S.P.Q.R.
S.P.Q.R.

89

BERNARDO BELLOTTO

(Venice 1722 – Warsaw 1780)

Le Turc Généreux
1759

engraving on laid paper, I state of two; 472 x 626 cm (plate)
Warsaw, Muzeum Narodowe, Rys. Pol. 2075

Inscriptions: on lower margin, 'Le Turc Genereux. / Ballet Pantomine executé à Vienne sur le Teatre près de la Cour, le 26. Avril, 1.7.58. /Presenté à S. Ecc. Mons. Le Comte de Durazzo, Conseiller intime actuel de EE: M.M.I.I. et R.R. et Surintendant / General des Plaisirs et Spectacles &.&.&. / par Ber: Belotti dit Canatetto Peintre. de SM. Le Roi de Pol: Elec. de Saxe: &.&.&. 1759'.

This fresh impression of the only print showing a theatrical subject in Bellotto's repertoire, obtained from a richly inked plate that has not been perfectly cleaned, reveals a first state that is here noted for the first time: the message on the margin erroneously states Bellotto's nickname as 'Canatetto' (this was corrected in the second state, as was 'Pantomine' to 'Pantomime'); the date '1758' is interspersed with points, subsequently cancelled and integrated into the letters.
The precise, elegant work is dedicated to the Genoese Earl Giacomo Durazzo (1717–1794), general director of the theatre in the Habsburg capital. He was highly cultured and in his ideas for the reform of musical theatre, was supported by the chancellor, Wenzel Anton von Kaunitz-Rietberg (1711–1794), both of whom were committed to promoting the German composer Christoph Willilbald Gluck (1714–1787).
A lush but balanced stage – with an imaginative pavilion on the left, fountains on the right, and the sea in the distance seen through a well-cultivated garden – welcomes the finale of the first of the four *entrées* of the most famous French Baroque opera-ballet *Les Indes galantes*, by Jean-Philippe Rameau (1683–1764), with libretto by Louis Fuzelier. The theatre lodges and the orchestra pit frame the scene. The opera, staged for the first time on 26 April 1758 by choreographer Franz Hilverding, was chosen in honour of Rasmi Achmed Effendi, who had arrived in Vienna to announce the coronation of the new Sultan, Mustafa III. Bellotto chose the most dramatic moment, when the protagonist, Osman Pasha, 'Le Turc genereux', discovers the love between his slave Emilie and the shipwrecked Valère – the famous dancer-actor, Gasparo Angiolini – but overcomes his wrath (he holds a knife!) and bestows freedom on the two lovers. The Earl Durazzo watches from the loggia on the right.

The print offers the finest and most complete image of a theatre performance in the eighteenth century, and is considered proof of Bellotto's work as a set designer at the court of Vienna, or at least of his direct involvement in the theatrical life there. The fact that on his return to Dresden at the beginning of 1762 the artist immediately began to paint a series of *capricci* with a clear theatrical setting (cf. cat. 85, 86), bearing witness to a maturity already acquired in his draughtsmanship, is a strong point in favour of this hypothesis. He was also a passionate admirer of the theatre, reading the works of Molière and Corneille, and of the contemporary Carlo Goldoni, Pietro Metastasio and Giovanni Claudio Pasquini, all of whom present in his library.
Drawn into the fabulous world of theatre, Bellotto gives his figures on the stage an idealised harmony; he attenuates the stinging caricature of the sketch of two spectators in the gallery on the left and in the outline of the group of actors shows a particular attention to the costumes (Warsaw, Muzeum Narodowe, Rys. Pol. 2060 and 2059).
On the day of the premiere, Bellotto was in Saxony. He left a Dresden at war with a passport to Bayreuth granted on 5 December 1758. Bayreuth had become the cultural capital with Wilhelmina, sister of the King of Prussia and wife of Frederick of Brandenburg-Bayreuth – she died in October of that year – who had hired Giuseppe Galli Bibiena (1696–1757) in 1747 to design the court theatre. The artist was probably bound for Italy, and in his traveling trunk there was a large folder of Italian drawings, ready to be used again. But between the end of 1758 or in January 1759 he was in Vienna, where he began a frantic activity. His first clients were Prince Joseph Wenzel Liechtenstein and Chancellor Kaunitz, who were probably the individuals who had promoted his arrival in the city and contact with the theatre.
On the *verso*, the print has the bookplate of Earl Stanisław Wronowski (1733–1839), an exceptional patron of the arts, leading collector and lover of theatre, who used to stage Polish performances in his palace at Lviv in the early nineteenth century.

Bożena Anna Kowalczyk

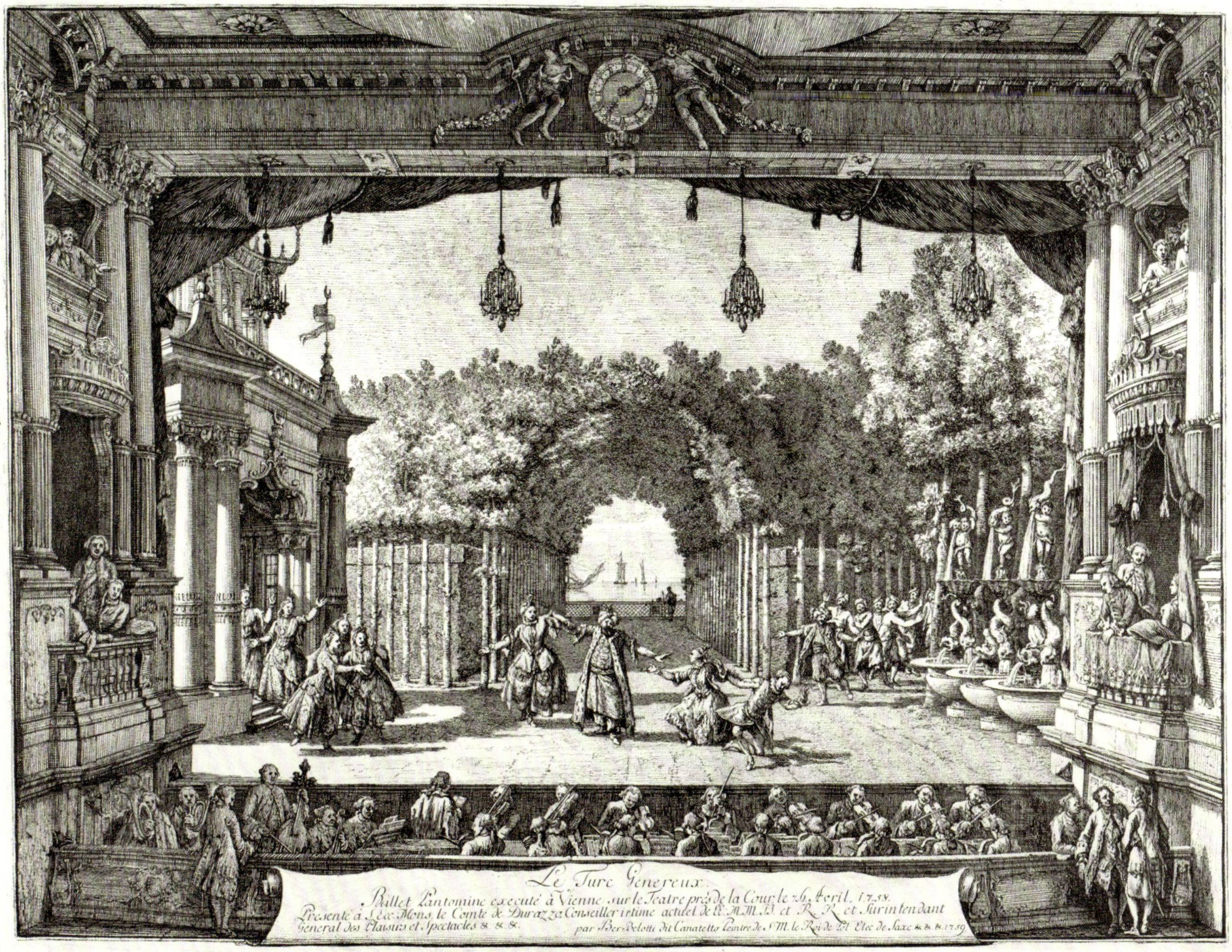
Le Turc Genereux.
Ballet Pantomine executé à Vienne sur le Teatre prés de la Cour le 26. Avril. 1758.
Presenté à S.Ex. Mons. le Comte de Durazzo Conseiller intime actuel de LL. MM. II. et R. R. et Surintendant
General des Plaisirs et Spectacles &. &. &.
par Ber. Belotti dit Canaletto Peintre de S.M. le Roi de Pol. Elec. de Saxe. &. &. &. 1759.

90

CANALETTO

(Venice 1697-1768)

Theatral Set Design
ca. 1753-1754

oil on canvas; 64.7 x 47.4 cm
Rome, Accademia di San Luca, 316

Canaletto began his career as a painter of stage sets; the passage by his first biographer, Anton Maria Zanetti di Alessandro, who explains the break with the theatre as a set designer, is famous: 'lasciato poi il teatro, annoiato dalla indiscretezza dei poeti drammatici; passò giovinetto a Roma, e tutto si diede a dipingere vedute dal naturale' (then he left the theatre, bored by the indiscretion of the dramatic poets; he travelled to Rome as a young man, and dedicated himself to painting views from the life) (Zanetti 1771, p. 463).
The link with the world of theatre took different forms: his first important Venetian commissions came from Owen McSwiny (1676–1754), a failed theatre impresario of Irish origin, who was in Venice in 1721 as a guest of Joseph Smith. McSwiny hired Canaletto in 1722 to paint the architectural parts of two large *capricci* – *The Tomb of Lord Somers* and *The Tomb of Archbishop Tillotson* – part of a series commemorating great Whig figures in English history, intended to decorate the dining room of the Goodwood residence of Charles Lennox, Lord March, later Duke of Richmond, for whom he was the agent (C/L 516 and 517). Along with Smith and Zanetti, at the end of the 1720s McSwiny was the promoter of Canaletto in England; and upon the artist's arrival in London in 1746, it was he who introduced him to the Duke of Richmond.
This painting is the only one to bear eloquent witness to a link with the theatre, albeit in England, although not supported by documentary data. The composition is a delightful set design project executed in light and bright colours, enhanced by the recent cleaning (2013). A richly decorated baroque loggia, glittering with gold, frames the high stairway, topped with an equestrian statue beneath a triumphal arch; the buildings on the left and at the bottom, behind the statue, are invented but combine the motifs of Banqueting House by Inigo Jones, with decorations in bas-relief garlands in the first, with the division of the facade into columns in the second, and with the balustrade at the top in both. The link with Banqueting House suggests that the statue is that of King Charles I, a bronze by Hubert Le Sueur, which Canaletto presents in its real place in the drawing and painting of *Northumberland House, London* (cat. 67) and shows in a *capriccio* in the painting of *Banqueting House and Holbein Gate, London*, painted for Thomas Hollis in 1754–55 (C/L 472). The tower on the right is reminiscent of the York aqueduct over the river Thames, made of wood and 21 metres high, built in the last decade of the seventeenth century and operational until 1829, which was depicted by Canaletto on several occasions in his paintings and drawings (for example, C/L 427 and 747). The statues in bas-relief, formed with fluid brushstrokes to resemble white marble, are inspired by those of the Thames and Isis, planned to adorn the balustrade of Westminster bridge but never put in place. Canaletto shows them at the centre above the balustrade in one of the first paintings done on arrival in London in May 1746, *Westminster Bridge from the North with the Lord Mayor's Procession, October 29, 1746*, which depicts the new bridge, still unfinished, with a series of other elements of fantasy (New Haven, Yale Center for British Art, Paul Mellon Collection, C/L 435). In the three *capricci* painted in 1752–1755 for Edward Howard, the ninth Duke of Norfolk, today at Arundel Castle, Norfolk, we come across some of these motifs once more: a loggia with a decorated vault, a triumphal arch with female statues on top, a stairway, the decorative garlands, suggesting a date close to this *capriccio*, around 1753–54; the style and light are also similar (C/L 505–507).
This is one of Canaletto's paintings whose attribution has been most unjustly the subject of discussion, together with improbable dating and recognition of the subject. Its provenance from the collection of Domenico Pellegrini (1759–1840), an itinerant Venetian painter and friend of the famous engraver, Francesco Bartolozzi (1727–1815), suggests a purchase made during the twenty years spent in London, between 1792 and 1812.

Bożena Anna Kowalczyk

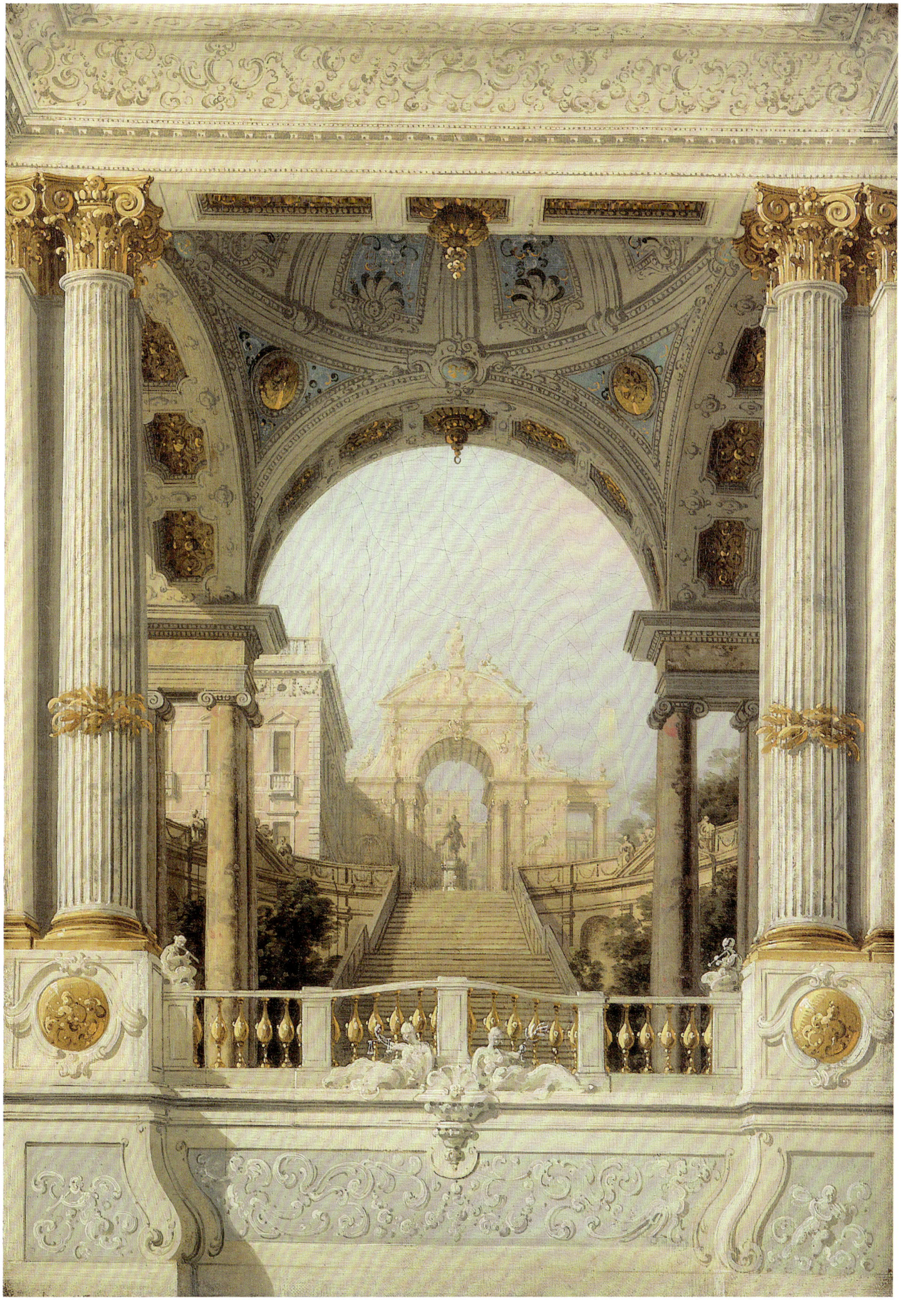

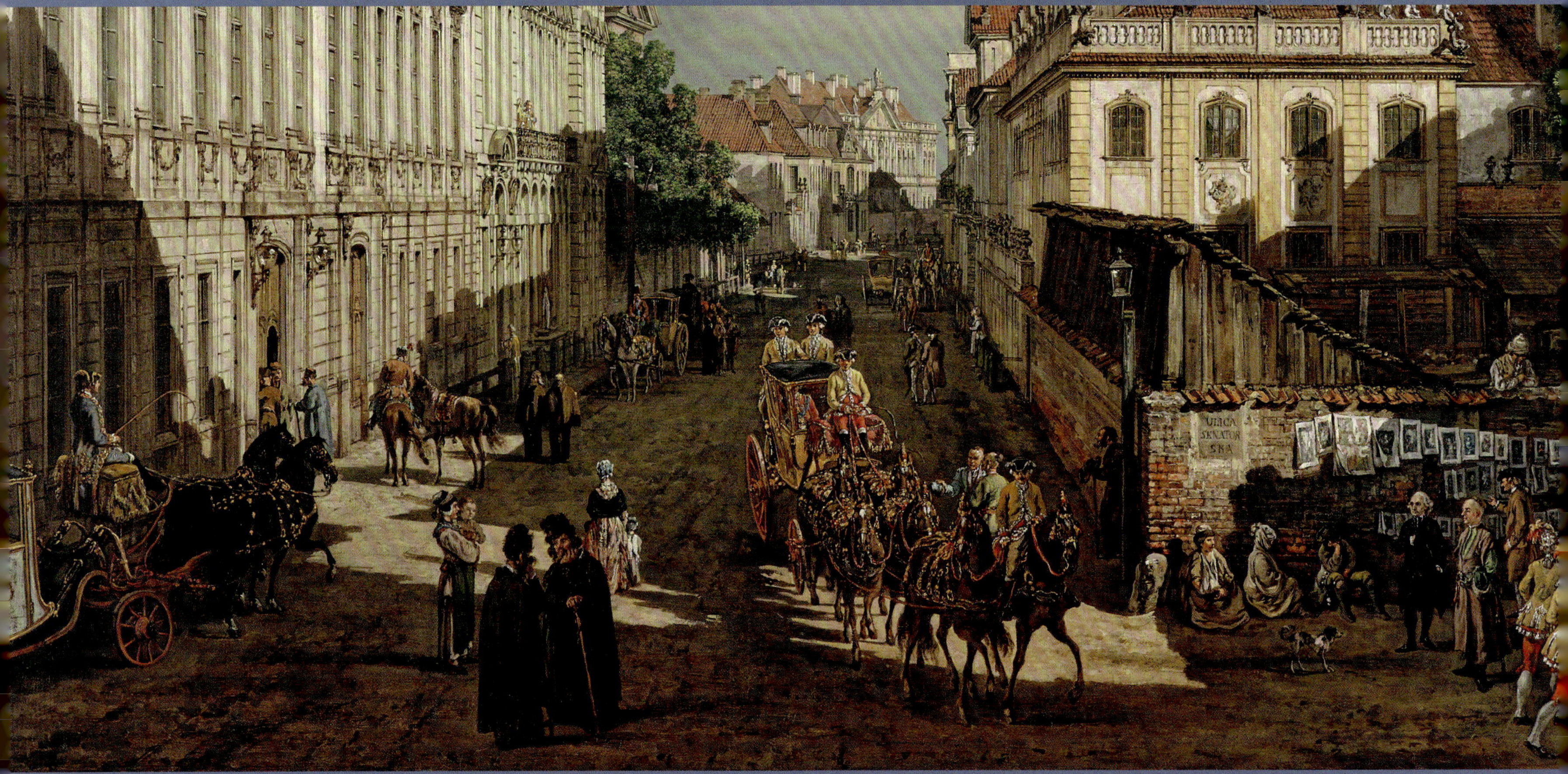
ULICA
SENATOR
SKA

10.
AN AVANT-GARDE CHRONICLER

Bellotto was not a photographer but a meticulous, passionate and sensitive chronicler of European civilisation. His attention to realism intensified in his final years, during which he produced images with immense historical value: in Dresden, a city gravely tested by the Seven Years' War, and in the Warsaw of the last king of Poland, Stanisław II August Poniatowski, marked by profound social conflict, where extreme wealth and desperate poverty coexisted, the capital of a country in serious political decline but pulsing with life.

The reassuring image presented in the print of *The Königstein Fortress with the Lilienstein* (cat. 91) came nearly ten years after the dramatic, icily lit painting commissioned by August III and produced shortly after the invasion of Saxony by the troops of Frederick II of Prussia. It was there, in that impenetrable fortress, that August III brought his art collections to keep them safe. Other works offer a raw vision of the city's suffering during those years of war (*The Ruins of the Kreuzkirche, Dresden*, cat. 93, and *The Ruins of the Suburb Pirna, Dresden*, cat. 92). We do not know whether these images were the result of specific commissions or, as is more probable and we prefer to think, the fruit of the choices of an enlightened artist, serving for the first time as a chronicler and shocked witness of the disasters brought by war.

The images of Warsaw in the excitement of the new Baroque buildings, depicting ornate magnates' palazzos and votive churches, lively markets and bustling street life, are even more striking when one thinks of the future destruction wrought by World War II, which seems to have been sadly prefigured in the views of the ruins of Dresden.

Bellotto did not shun new interests and brought the ones he had cultivated from the beginning to their full expression, interests surprisingly in line with the latest trends in English painting: the study of horses and equestrian portraits, and landscape. *The Prince Józef Poniatowski Receiving a Horse-Riding Lesson from the Colonel Königsfels* (cat. 98) is an extraordinarily innovative painting, as with the others in the same series. Delivered to the court of the King of Poland in 1773, they were to decorate an annex of the Belvedere Palace, the apartment of 'Madame Byszewska', where they were recorded in 1795. Of the two stunning landscapes, *View of Wilanów Meadows, Warsaw* (cat. 97) and *View of the Castle of Ujazdów, Warsaw* with nobles and peasants, depicted in the foreground next to thatched-roof houses and livestock, clearly alluding to the uniqueness of Polish society, only the former satisfied the patron, whereas the latter was immediately given to an unknown individual.

91

BERNARDO BELLOTTO

(Venice 1722 – Warsaw 1780)

The Königstein Fortress with the Lilienstein
1765

etching, II state of two; 420 x 631 mm (plate)
Dresden, Staatliche Kunstsammlungen, Kupferstich-Kabinett, A 85870

Inscriptions: in the margin, 'Vue du Roc, et Forteresse de Koenig -- stein du coté de l'Occident, et de la / Montée, aïant de l'autre coté le Lilienstein, au de-la de -- l'Elbe, et en distance, les Montagnes de la Lusace. / La Vue a eté prise du Cabaret nommé la Neueschenke. Se trouvent chez l'Auteur a Dresde, -- et chez Pierre Fouquet a Amsterdam. Peint et gravé par Ber: Belotto de Canaletto Peintre Elec. / N:o'.

Marks: (cat. 79) letters FAR [Fridericus Augustus Rex], on the top the crown; shared by the old Property but not present in Lugt.

In the spring of 1756, Augustus III (1696–1763) commissioned Bellotto to paint five *vedute* of the fortress of Königstein – perched on a steep hill above the Elbe Valley, 35 kilometres to the south-east of Dresden – three of its exterior elevations, from west, south-west and north-west, and two internal views. Following the invasion of Saxony by Frederick the Great of Prussia on 29 August 1756 and the outbreak of the Seven Years' War, Augustus III and Prime Minister Earl Brühl sought refuge in the Königstein. However, after the defeat of the Saxon troops on 16 October at the Lilienstein – a rock formation typical of the area that balances the fortress here on the left – they fled to Warsaw. Bellotto, equipped with a laissez-passer issued on 30 March 1756, finished his work before leaving for Vienna in December 1758, when Dresden was occupied by the Prussian army. It is not known where the pictures were during the bombing of Dresden in 1760; the paintings in the Gemäldegalerie Alte Meister, including Bellotto's views of Dresden and Pirna, were stored in the impregnable fortress. 'Quattro vedute di Königstein' are listed in the *Catalogo de Danni* but these must have been smaller copies (p. 16*r*). The king could not have seen the works before his return on 30 April 1763 but he died a few months later, on 5 October, and the painter was looking for another purchaser before leaving Dresden once and for all in January 1767. On 11 February 1765, he gave the Kupferstich-Kabinett a freshly engraved print depicting the *Vue de la Fortresse de Koenigstein*, probably this one, without requesting payment, and returned on 28 March with another 100, for which he was paid 100 thalers (see G. Metze, in Dresden 2011). The second known print of the bastion, *The Fortress of Königstein from the West*, which also bears the emblem of the elector of Saxony, must have been engraved in 1764 when the union with Poland came to an end on the death of Augustus III; at that time, the related paintings must have still been in Dresden.
In the painting, now at the National Gallery of Art, Washington (E.P. Bowron, in Venice-Houston 2001, p. 200), Bellotto uses all the pictorial means at his disposal to depict the power of the bastion and the drama of the war. The centuries-old fortress, perfectly integrated with the rock, is described lucidly and analytically, while the surrounding landscape is given the same grandeur with crisp forms that are well-defined by the light; it is an ideal integration of architecture with nature. The dead trunk in the foreground of the painting, a symbol of the danger of war, is replaced in the print by a thriving tree, shifting the accent onto the Arcadian aspect of the image. As in the painting, the landscape in the print is meticulously described, from the foreground occupied by a dense row of trees, partially in shadow and partially in the light, followed by tall fir trees and other types of well-defined trees, as far as the mountains of Saxon Switzerland. Evidence of the artist's mastery and sensitivity in measuring the intensity of the engraving – delicate and parallel when describing the rock in full light, brief and crossed here and there for the trees in shadow, and minute in the distance – this print is one of those that does not deserve the reproach given by Pierre-Jean Mariette in his discussion of Bellotto's Dresden etchings: 'on y trouve de même à redire trop d'égalité dans la touche et des dégradations de lumières pas assez sensibles' (*Abecedario*, vol. 1, p. 115).
The addition of 'N:o' beneath the right margin points to the fact that this sheet is the second state.

Bożena Anna Kowalczyk

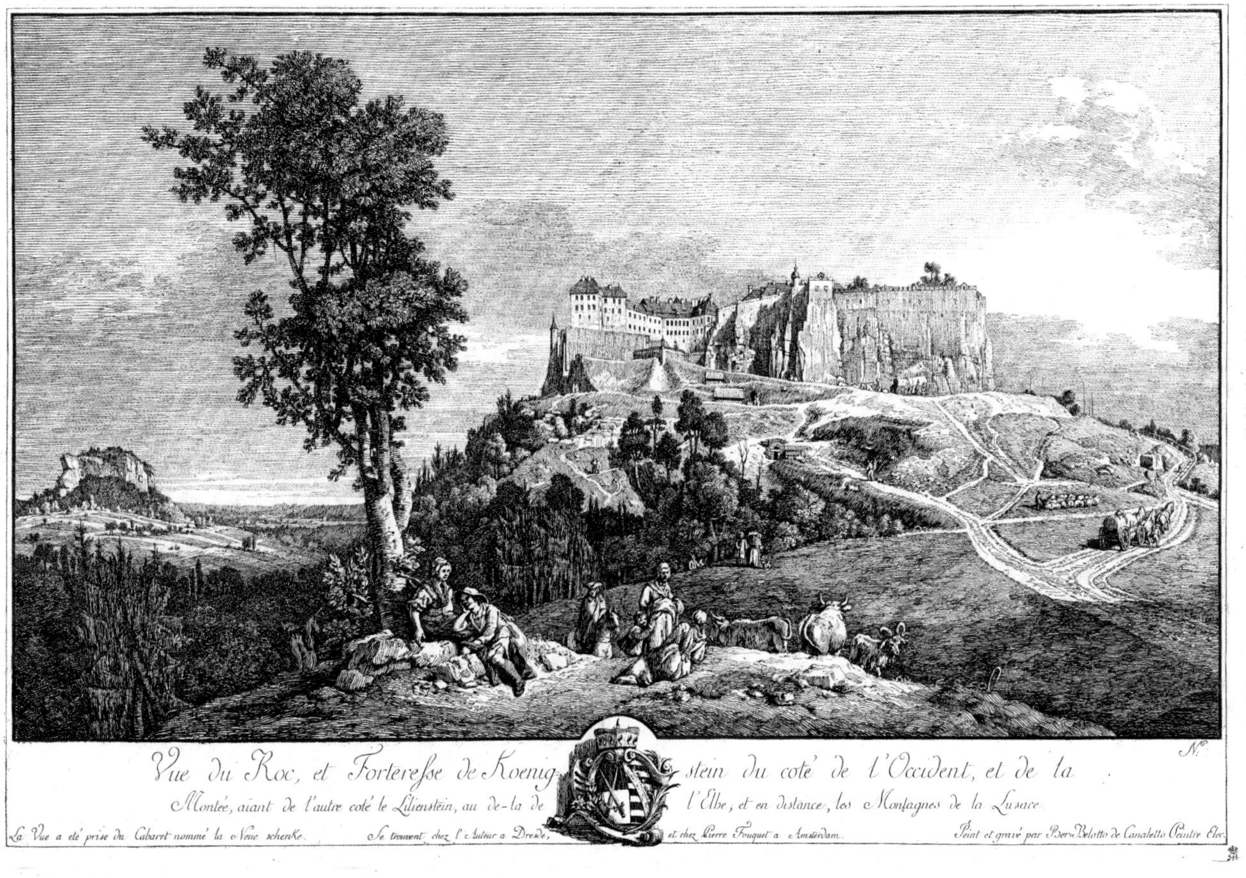
Vue du Roc, et Forteresse de Koenig-stein du coté de l'Occident, et de la
Montée, aïant de l'autre coté le Lilienstein, au de-la de l'Elbe, et en distance, les Montagnes de la Lusace
N.°
La Vue a eté prise du Cabaret nommé la Neue schenke.
Se trouvent chez l'Auteur a Drede, et chez Pierre Fouquet a Amsterdam.
Peint et gravé par Bern. Belotto de Canaletto Peintre Elec.

BERNARDO BELLOTTO

(Venice 1722 – Warsaw 1780)

The Ruins of the Suburb Pirna, Dresden
1762–63 (image and emblem); 1766 (script)

etching, only state; 530 x 648 mm (plate)
Geneve, Musées d'art et d'histoire de la Ville de Genève, Cabinet de Dessins et d'Estampes, E 2011-271009

Inscriptions: 'Vuë des ruines des Fauxbourgs de la Ville de Dresde -- entre aûtres, de la maison de Fürstenhof, près du fossé, / attenant au fauxbourg de Pirna, On découvre dans le lointain le -- rempart de la Ville neuve, la Vigne de Neuman, et les collines des environs. / Dédié a Son Altesse Royale Monseigneu le -- Prince Xavier Administrateur de Saxe &cc. &cc. &cc. / D'après le Tableau haut 2 pieds $10^1/_2$ p: Large n:p: que Son Altesse Royale possede. Peint et gravé -- par son très soumis Serviteur Bern: Belotto de Canaletto Mem:bre de l'Acca:mie Elec:le des Arts. 1766'.

Saxony was one of the main theatres of the violent Seven Years' War – the third for possession of Silesia – waged by Prussia against Austria and its ally France. In July 1760, Frederick the Great led his troops in the siege of Dresden, which had already been occupied in 1756 but was retaken by the Austrian army in 1759. After bombarding the city for days inside the walls around the Kreuzkirche and the Frauenkirche, and destroying the suburbs of Pirna with cannons brought from across the Elbe, the king of Prussia withdrew to face the Austrian troops at the Battle of Torgau.
Until Bellotto's house in Dresden was firmly identified on the Neumarkt, at the corner with Salzgasse (Liebsch 2006), it was believed that he had lived here, in the suburb of Pirna, one of the most badly damaged. This belief lent this representation, the print and the painting from which it is taken, at the Musée des Beaux-Arts in Troyes (Rosenverg 1974), a particularly emotional charge. We do not know why Bellotto should have chosen this particular part of the city for his portrayal of the disasters of the war and not the centre, where his house had been destroyed; nor do we know whether this was a specific commission or a choice made by the artist. The emblem of the union of Saxony and Poland in the margin of the print would point to a creation, of both print and painting, prior to the death of Augustus III on 5 October 1763, as previously supported by Fritzsche; the dedicatory inscription to the Prince Elector Francis Xavier (1730–1806), grandson of August III and ruler of Saxony with his sister-in-law Maria Antonia of Bavaria, was therefore added later, in 1766.
On his return to Dresden in February 1762, Bellotto found the ruins of Pirna already covered in wild vegetation. S. Kozakiewicz has identified the viewpoint as being between Amalienstrasse, Drehgasse and Äussere Rampische Gasse. The scene is dominated by the only recognisable building, the baroque house of Johann Georg Maximilian von Fürstenhoff (1683–1753) – architect and engineer of the fortifications of Dresden – that had already been damaged in the fire of 1758. In the distance, the Elbe is on the left and the Loschwitz mountains on the right. Instead of the carriage on the street facing the Fürstenhoff building in the painting, with dramatic reddish hues, a platoon of soldiers appears, heading in the opposite direction, in agreement with the few other figures.
A dramatic and particularly elaborate sky dominates the composition; as H.A. Fritzsche remembers, in the late eighteenth century, this lent a romantic value to the work, as if it were a landscape of classical ruins.
The delivery of one hundred of these prints is recorded in the *Journal beym Churfürstlichen Kupferstich-Cabinet pro Anno 1767*, p. 26r, kept by Christian Friedrich Wenzel, dated 17 January 1767 (G. Metze, in Dresden 2001).

Bożena Anna Kowalczyk

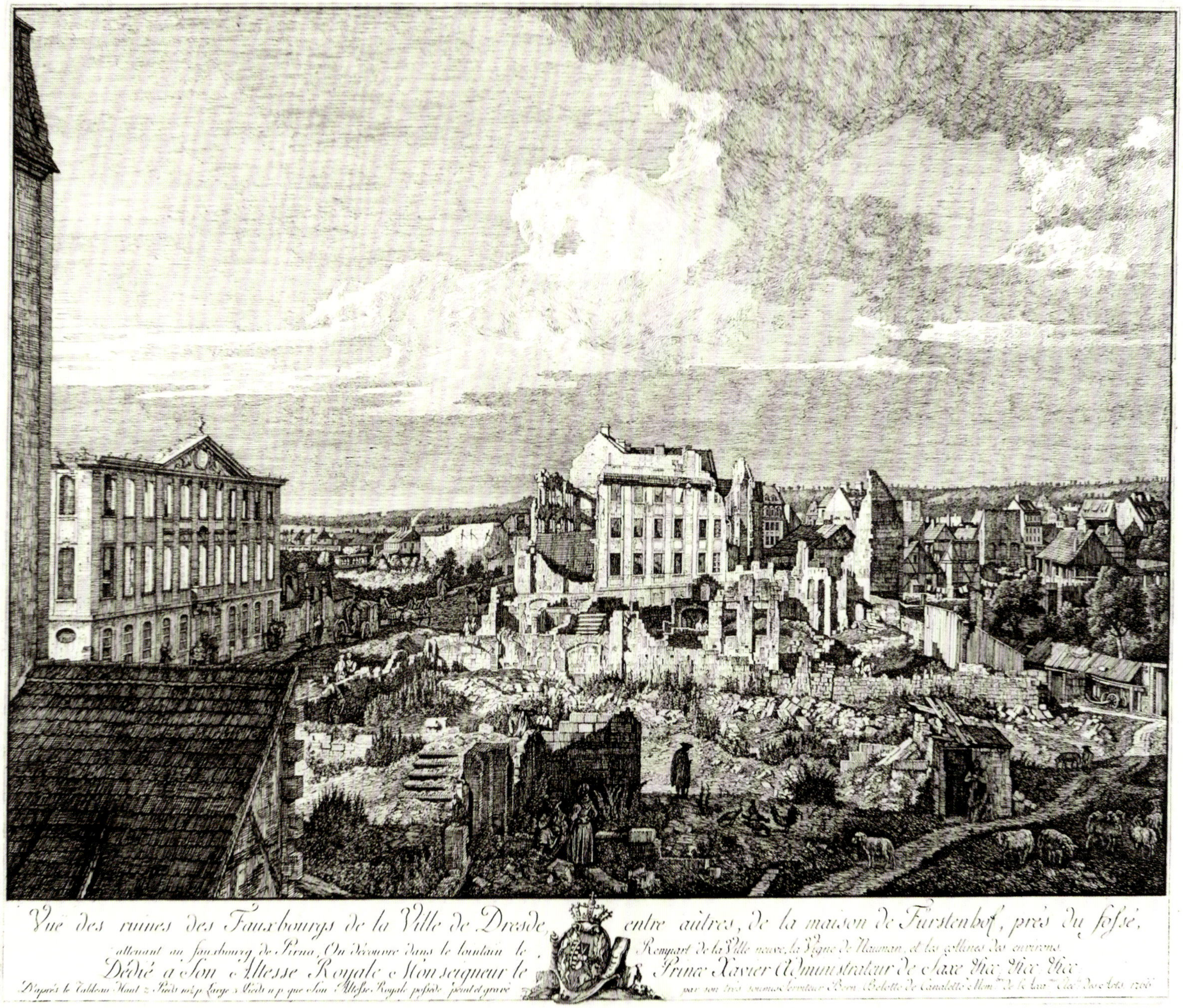
Vue des ruines des Fauxbourgs de la Ville de Dresde, entre autres, de la maison de Furstenhof, près du fossé,
attenant au fauxbourg de Pirna, On découvre dans le lointain le Rempart de la Ville neuve, la Vigne de Nauman, et les collines des environs.
Dédié à Son Altesse Royale Monseigneur le Prince Xavier Administrateur de Saxe &c. &c. &c.

BERNARDO BELLOTTO

(Venice 1722 – Warsaw 1780)

The Ruins of the Kreuzkirche, Dresden
1765

etching, II state of three; 553 x 640 mm (plate)
Dresden, Staatliche Kunstsammlungen, Kupferstich-Kabinett A 85871

Inscription: in the lower margin, 'Vue de Débris, de la Tour de S:te Croix, qui s'écroulà le 22.me -- de Juin 1765, dans le tems qu'on commencoit à relever l'E/glise, laquelle avoit péri par le Bombardement de la Ville de Dresde, en 1760. --10 au:nes de Dresde, selon le pan de Mur qui demeurà surpied, haut de 120 au:nes / Dedié à Son Altesse Royale, Madame– l'Electrice Douairiere de Saxe /La vue a eté prise, du Cabinet de M:r le Surintendant Ecclésiastique Docteuram Ende. -- par Son très Soumis Serviteur Bern: Belotto de Canaletto. Mem:bre de l'Acca:mie Elec:le des Arts 1765'.

Marks: (cat. 79) letters FAR [Fridericus Augustus Rex], on the top the crown; shared by the old Property but not present in Lugt.

As explained in the margin, on 22 June 1765 the tower of the Kreuzkirche collapsed unexpectedly; it had been damaged by bombing in 1760 but was already under reconstruction. Positioning himself at the window of the office of the Ecclesiastical Superintendent, Am Ende, Bellotto drew the ruins of the interior of the church from a point directly opposite that of the *Westwerk* from the 1750s (cat. 77). Before it was given to be printed in the *Catalogue des Tableaux de la Galerie Electorale à Dresde*, published in 1765, Bellotto managed to finish the painting *La Tour de l'Eglise de Ste. Croix à Dresde, tombée en ruine & les maisons à l'entour*, included in the appendix, from which this etching is taken.
Work on dismantling the dilapidated ruin is in full swing amid the piles of stones and planks, but what attracts the attention of the noblemen in the foreground and other spectators at the windows is the carpenters climbing to the top of the tower up a 'strange ladder' made of posts fixed together to demolish it stone by stone. A. Walther (in Venice 1986, p. 88) mentions that Bellotto himself also attempted to climb up on 5 July in order to record the truth of the scene authentically.
Bellotto's image, one of detached and visionary realism, has become the emblem for the destruction of war, of those gone by as well as those yet to come. Bellotto repeated it in a second picture belonging to the gallery of King Stanisław II August Poniatowski of Poland, now at the Kunsthaus in Zurich.
Fifty copies of this etching were delivered by Bellotto to the Kupferstich-Kabinett on 2 June 1766, followed by another 50 on 17 January 1767, just before he left Dresden for Saint Petersburg, stopping in Warsaw (G. Metze, in Dresden 2011).
In 1765, the Kupferstich-Kabinett in Dresden – one of the largest collections of prints in the world, greatly enhanced in the period of Augustus II and Augustus III (Lugt 1645–1648) – owned 814 'Views by Canaletto', collected to be used as gifts or prestigious objects for exchange (G. Metze, in Dresden 2011, p. 40).

Bożena Anna Kowalczyk

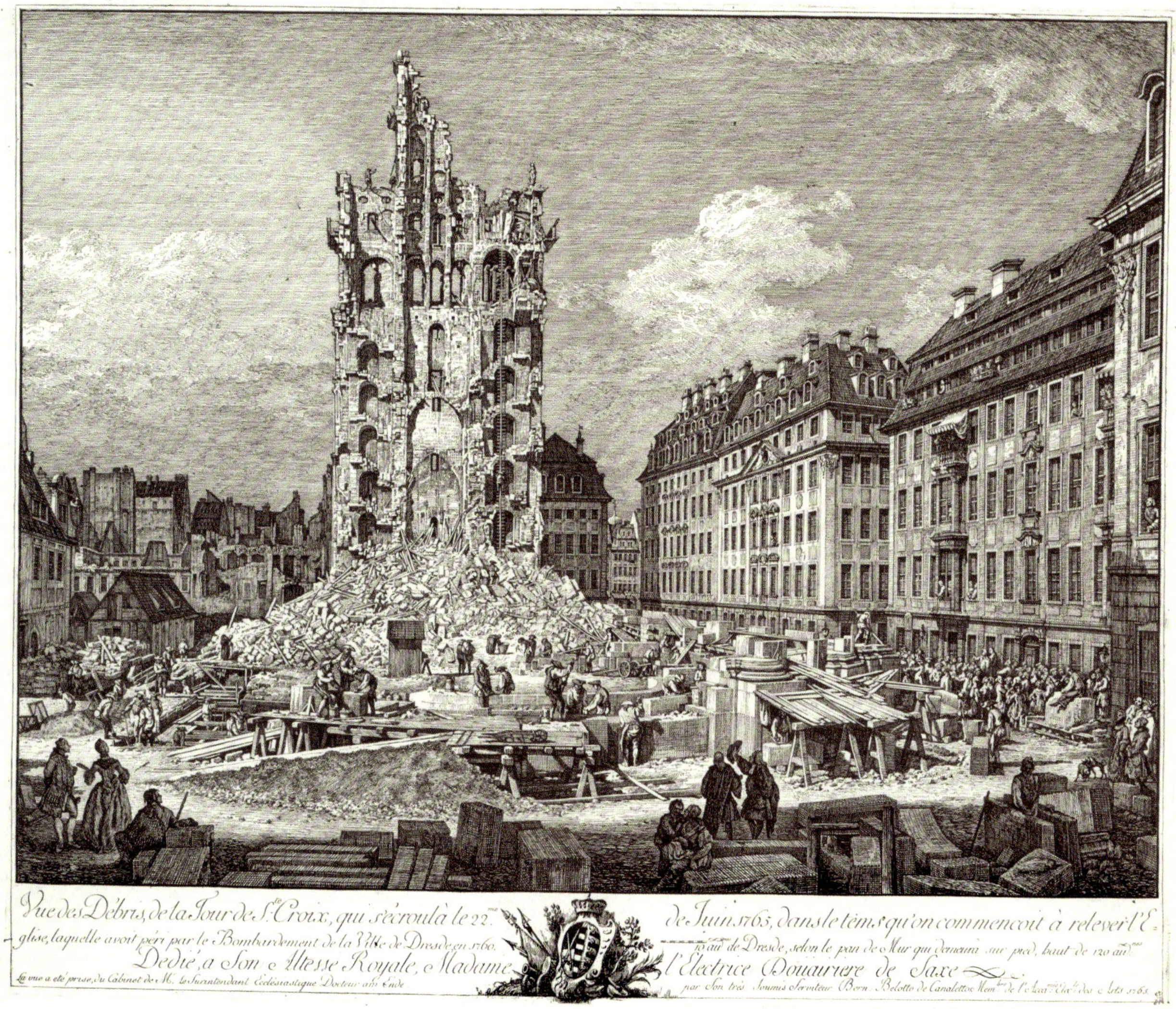
Vue des Débris, de la Tour de S.te Croix, qui s'écroula le 22 de Juin 1765, dans le têms qu'on commencoit à relever l'E=
glise, laquelle avoit péri par le Bombardement de la Ville de Dresde en 1760. 10 au. de Dresde, selon le pan de Mur qui demeura sur pied, haut de 120
Dedié, a Son Altesse Royale, Madame l'Electrice Douairiere de Saxe
La vue a eté prise, du Cabinet de M. le Surintendant Ecclésiastique Docteur am Ende
par Son très soumis Serviteur Bern. Belotto de Canaletto Mem.bre de l'Acad.mie Elec.le des Arts 1765.

94

BERNARDO BELLOTTO

(Venice 1722 – Warsaw 1780)

The Miodowa Street, Warsaw
1777

oil on canvas; 84 x 107.5 cm
Warsaw, Royal Castle, Museum, ZKW/443

The cycle of twenty-six large, medium and small views of Warsaw, executed between 1768 and 1780, of which twenty-three were placed from the end of 1777 in the Senate Antechamber ('Canaletto Room') in Warsaw's Royal Castle, is part of the history of the city, described with genuine participation. Since the second half of the seventeenth century, the Polish capital underwent a radical transformation, especially thanks to the great aristocratic families who, to build their residences in the city, employed a number of leading Polish and foreign architects. Miodowa Street that crosses the 'ulica' Senatorska, here indicated by the plaque on the wall, is a procession of late-baroque, rococo and neoclassical palaces, built shortly before the arrival of Bellotto. It was called Capuchin street from the church that stands with its tympanum behind the trees on the left, and this is how it is mentioned in the catalogue of the royal gallery drafted in 1795 (Mańkowski 1932). It was in the basement of this church, designed by Tylman van Gameren, that Bellotto would be buried.
The extended shade and oblique in the foreground, perhaps partly justified by the buildings of Senatorska street, which at that point was only opened at the end of the nineteenth century, involves the facade of the Palace of the Krakòw bishops, members of the Senate of Poland. Built in 1760–1762 in the late-baroque style by Jakub Fontana, and destroyed in the Warsaw uprising of 1944, it was rebuilt in line with this description but with two floors. This is followed by the building with the facade and two towers of a banker, Piotr Tepper, an original neoclassical design by the Polish architect, Efraim Schröger; at the end, where the grey clouds amass, there is the Krasinski Palace or Palace of the Republic, the subject of another painting in the 'Canaletto Room' (cat. 95). Bellotto accurately described the Branicki Palace on the right as well, down to the sculptures at the top. This was one of the richest aristocratic residences in the city, designed in the 1740s for Jan Klemens Branicki, Hetman of the Crown, by the Saxon architect Jan Zygmunt Deybel von Hammerau, and built by Fontana in collaboration with the sculptor Jan Chrysostom Redler. Along this side of the street, at the end, behind the other palaces, we can glimpse the roofs of the monastery of Piarist fathers, founders of the Collegium Nobilium. In this context, Bellotto does not fail to record the pictorial interest of the wooden hut which partially conceals the Branicki Palace and of the uneven wall plastered with prints belonging to a small merchant.
With the acute perspective imposed by the palaces and the improbable play of alternating light and shadow, Bellotto emphasises the vitality and the role of this road, a busy communication link between the Royal Castle and the Palace of the Republic. Citizens, aristocrats in Polish and foreign costume, riders, Capuchin monks, Jews, an abbot, servants, women with children: all of Polish society parades on Miodowa street. Dotted with colour, the reds and yellows stand out to draw the eye to the end. In the foreground, the coach with six horses is carrying a member from the order of the White Eagle to the castle, with the medal hanging on a blue ribbon (Rottermund).
The surveys conducted at the Royal Castle during the recent restoration (2000–2003) shows that Bellotto continued to use the same construction methods as in his youth, with a preparatory drawing in brush and brown wash, a ruler for the main constructive lines, incisions in the fresh paint with a sharp point, to give relief to the architectural parts. And it is colour that becomes softer and full-bodied, a rich impasto in the masterful final touches to define the details, especially those in the light.
The pendant of *Długa Street, Warsaw*, which also leads to Krasinski Square, with the Collegium Nobilium at the bottom left (Kozakiewicz 1972a, no. 414), it was intended to be placed in the third row of paintings between the prepared stucco cornices, but the painting reveals a strip of canvas measuring approximately 2–2.4 cm, added below when the picture was not yet finished or soon after, to adapt the height of the horizon to this disposition (P. Sadlej in Warsaw 2003–2004).

Bożena Anna Kowalczyk

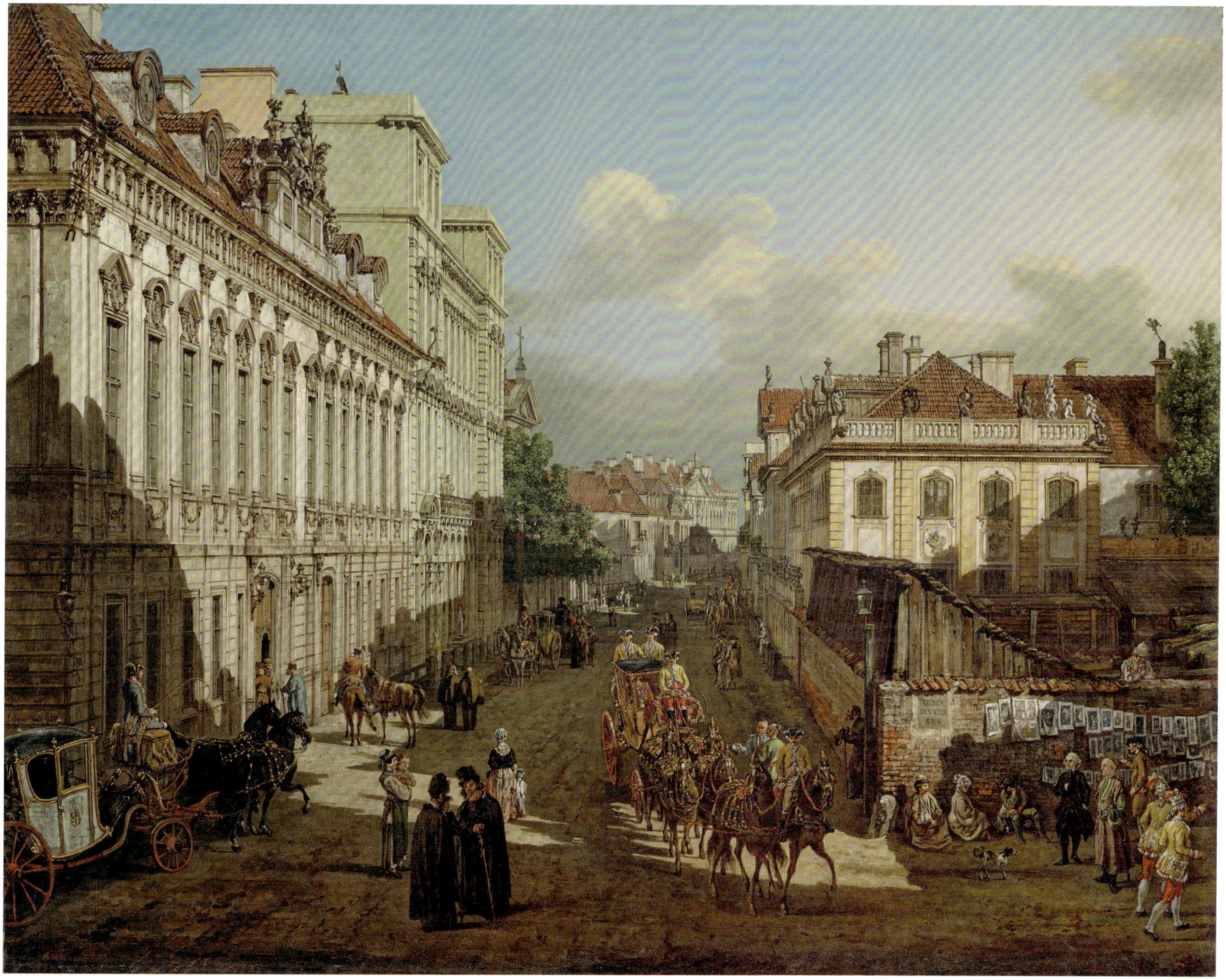

95

BERNARDO BELLOTTO

(Venice 1722 – Warsaw 1780)

Palace of the Republic of Poland, Warsaw
1778

oil on canvas; 116 x 164 cm
Warsaw, Royal Castle, Museum, ZKW/454

In the catalogue of the gallery of King Stanisław II August Poniatowski of 1795, this exceptional image is referred to as 'Vüe du Palais de la Commission' (Mańkowski 1932). The palace was bought by the Republic of Poland in 1765, a year after the election of the king, and housed various glorious institutions, including the Commission of the Treasury of the Crown and the National Education Commission, the most innovative Ministry of Education in Europe, founded in 1773 by a group of enlightened and noble Polish intellectuals, through the initiative of father Hugo Kołłątaj and with the collaboration, among others, of writer Julian Ursyn Niemcewicz. The grandeur of the building adapted perfectly to the role and its presentation in the 'Canaletto Room' was of great importance for the king and for the image of his kingdom. The palace was built between 1677 and 1695 for one of the most prominent figures of the time, the voivode of Potock, Jan Dobrogost Krasiński (1639–1717), a soldier, cultured patron and philanthropist. He was also a passionate collector and was close to the king, Jan III Sobieski, with whom he participated in the defence of Vienna in 1683. The Dutch architect Tylman van Gameren (1632–1706) designed one of his best projects for him, and Andreas Schlüter, the famous sculptor from Gdańsk, executed the bas-relief on the tympanum depicting the struggle between his legendary ancestor, Marcus Valerius Corvus with the Gauls, alluding to the Roman origin of his family; statues of Athens and Mars stand on either side. Destroyed in the uprising in Warsaw in 1944 and rebuilt, today it houses the holdings of antique collections and manuscripts from the National Library.
Bellotto shows a precise moment, the second Sunday in May, when the venerated statue of Our Lady of Grace, the patron saint of Warsaw, was carried in procession, emphasising the patriotic and symbolic value of its representation. The statue was preserved in the Piarist church in Długa street, pictured at the left margin with its baroque facade designed by Jakub Fontana. This is the starting point for the procession, which passes through a door to enter the space in front of the palace, moving diagonally across an open and untidy area, with heaps of stones and planks of wood, surrounded by modest buildings: an abandoned building site. In Warsaw, Bellotto saw the contrast between immense wealth and terrible poverty; this space in front of a splendid palace was well suited to his poetic. To the side of the majestic procession of nobles and religious bearing long lighted candles, observed by other aristocrats in carriages and elegant ladies, we cannot fail to notice the barefoot beggars and poor. All the authors writing on the painting note that on this site there used to be a little house, demolished only in 1959, from which Bellotto made his drawings.
The painting is one of the overdoors from the 'Canaletto Room'. By placing the horizon low and adapting every element of the composition to a vision from below – the perspective of the building, the view of the figures, the movement of the clouds – Bellotto shows that he knew where it was to be placed. It also had to be seen from a distance but the artist did not neglect any detail of the city on the horizon, from the facade of the Collegium Nobilium in Długa street, a school of university level founded by the Piarist fathers, the palaces of Miodowa Street with the Capuchin church, a row of rooftops described tile by tile, with chimneys, dormers and eaves, of the Radziwill, Potocki, Załuski and Brühl mansions, and on to the two towers of the Holy Cross church in Krakowskie Przedmieście in the distance.
Among the paintings of the 'Canaletto Room' which underwent various additions of canvas during the course of their history, other than that added by the artist himself, to adapt the perspective of already executed paintings to their position in the room – this one is very unusual, because it is made from six sewn pieces of different textures, as shown by the X-ray pictures taken during the restoration of 2000–2003 (P. Sadlej, Warsaw 2003–2004).

Bożena Anna Kowalczyk

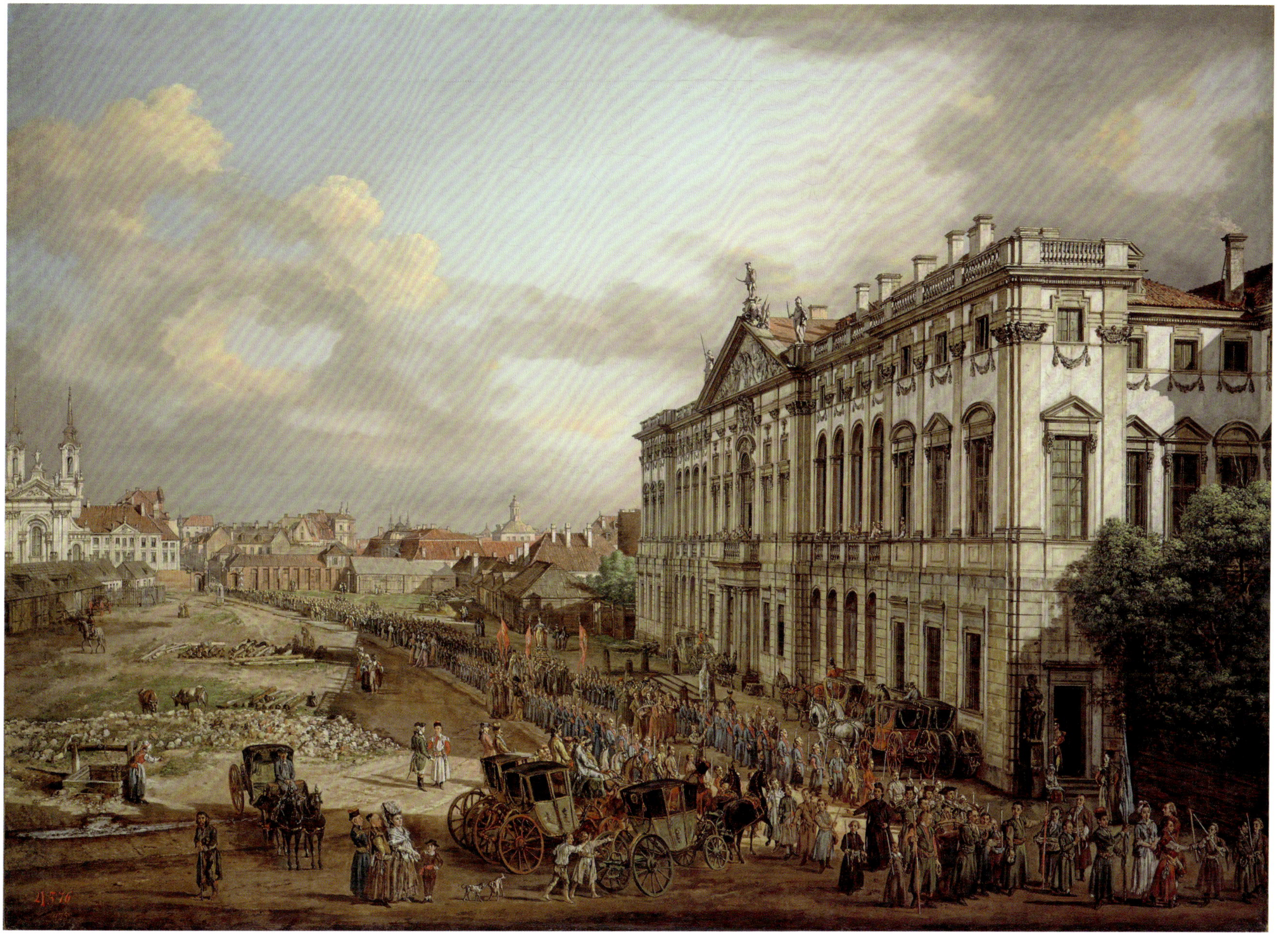

96

BERNARDO BELLOTTO

(Venice 1722 – Warsaw 1780)

The Church of the Holy Sacrament in the New Town, Warsaw
1778

oil on canvas; 84 x 106 cm
Warsaw, Royal Castle, Museum, ZKW/445

Warsaw's New Town has been known as such since the early fifteenth century, when the city expanded outside its fortifications, near the centuries-old gate, which was later replaced by the Barbican. In 1688, the Queen Marie Casimire (1641 ca.–1716) purchased land near the Market Square on which to build a church dedicated to Saint Casimir and the convent of the Sacramentine Sisters (more correctly the Benedictine Sisters of the Perpetual Adoration of the Most Holy Sacrament), invited by her from France to give thanks for the victory of her husband John III Sobieski over the Turks in Vienna. The project was entrusted to the architect Tylman van Gameren, who built his masterpiece, an elegant centrally-planned Greek cross church topped with a dome on an octagonal drum. Despite various alterations and a fire started by a lightning bolt in 1855, it survived as it was depicted by Bellotto until the Second World War. It was rebuilt in 1949–1955, as was the convent to its left and the houses in the painting, with the exception of Kotowski Palace behind the church, with its high tympanum and chimneys.
Bellotto turned the image of this site into a masterpiece. He chose cattle market day and treated it to one of his most virtuoso and engaging portrayals, in the architecture and the scenes observed in incredible detail and richness that follow a perspectival order and cadence of light; from the foreground in shadow to the street in the distance, it is a never-ending play of light. The carefully studied shapes and colours of the clouds heighten the sensation of movement.
The scene is viewed from a window in a house on the south side and converges exceptionally with real perspective. Bellotto portrays Warsaw's New Town with a sensitive understanding of the place. His description of the modest houses in the square and bourgeois palaces in the background provides valuable documentation of shapes and colours, alternating the white plaster with the red walls and thick-tiled roofs. The painting is weighty; it is not as sharp as Bellotto's scenes of Vienna or his first paintings of Warsaw but more pictorial in the almost sketched scenes of the market, goods, animals and figures that approach caricature at times. The technique remains the same: the delicate incisions that outline the windows of the houses and allow the light to slide over the church pilasters; the walls formed with layers of colour, which achieve a Corot-like effect in the painting of the dome.
Bellotto lived in the New Town, probably on Ulica Freta, the area's main artery; his rent was paid for by the king, as was his fire wood. The painter's death was registered at the church of the Visitation of the Most Blessed Virgin Mary, of which part of the nave and the Gothic bell tower can be seen to the right of Saint Casimir: '17 November Bernardus Canallety annos … maritus Elisabetha morte subitanea extinctus sepultus apud Pres Capucinos de consensu' (*Register of Deaths*, 1771–1788, p. 299). Despite being destroyed in the fire at the church in 1744, the record of his dea4h was transcribed in 1922 by T. Sawicki (in Warsaw 1944, p. 25).
The artistic value of this painting and the beauty, vitality and completeness of the description can be compared to the similar *The Miodowa Street, Warsaw* (cat. 96); both paintings are masterpieces of eighteenth-century painting. It too was enhanced at the bottom with a strip of linen cloth measuring 3.4–4 cm to raise the horizon, and was located beneath the other in the second order of the south wall in the 'Canaletto Room'. The pendant, *The Church of the Holy Cross*, depicts another convent church, of the Missionaries, with a market scene in Ulica Krakowskie Przedmieście (Kozakiewicz 1972a, n. 409).

Bożena Anna Kowalczyk

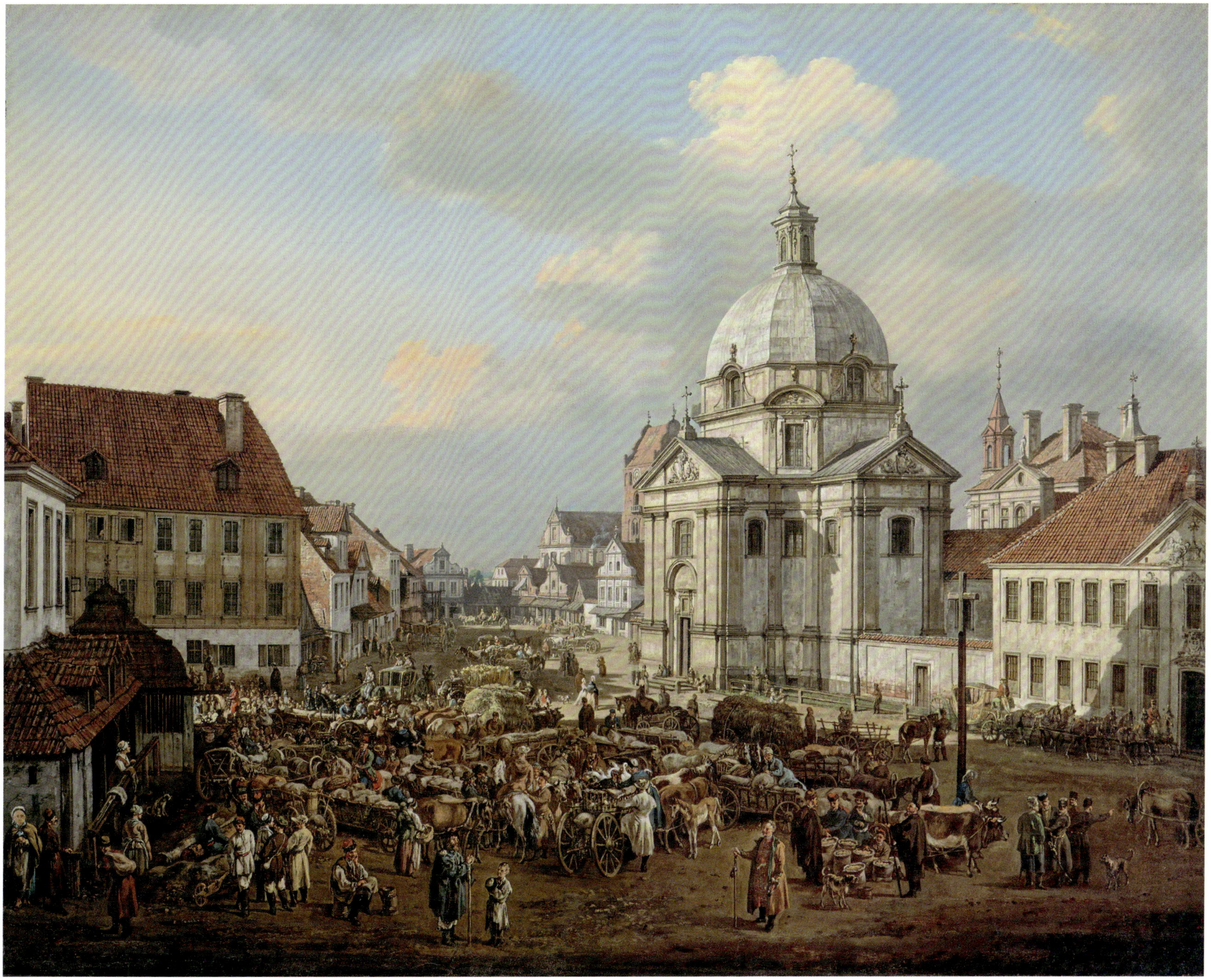

97

BERNARDO BELLOTTO

(Venice 1722 – Warsaw 1780)

View of Wilanów Meadows, Warsaw
1775

oil on canvas; 173 x 246 cm
Warsaw, The Royal Castle - Museum, ZKW/454

In the census of works produced for the Warsaw court between 1771 and 1780, personally prepared by Bernardo Bellotto, for the year 1775 (*Notta di Lavori fornitti alla Cortte*) the painting was described together with the work '*Due Quadri Grandi Fatti a Bel Veder*', for which the painter received 300 ducats (Central Archives of Ancient Documents Warsaw, Archive of Prince Józef Poniatowski 363 [A/254], p. 12-14; Rizzi 1990, p. 151). There is no doubt that these were the *View of the Wilanów Meadows* and the *View of Ujazdow and Łazienki*, both preserved at the Muzeum Narodowe of Warsaw (7717).
From the above-mentioned census, we can also infer that both of the works were to be hung in the seventeenth-century Belvedere Palace, located on a hill near the future royal residence in Łazienki Park. We know that King Stanisław August wanted to rebuild the Belvedere 'as an aristocratic residence'. The architects held, however, that 'it would be impossible' to transform it thus, and that it would be better to raze it to the ground and rebuild it from scratch (Tatarkiewicz 1957, p. 124). Following their advice, he ordered the preparation of plans between 1774 and 1779 for a new building to replace the old one (Kwiatkowski, pp. 121–124). Unfortunately, the king's vision was never realised, and the pictures painted by Bellotto in 1773 were never hung in the Belvedere. Instead, four years later the king hung the *View of the Wilanów Meadows* on the wooden panelling of the north wall of the Senate Antechamber (the 'Canaletto Room') in the Royal Castle of Warsaw.
The painting was listed in the inventory of the king's picture gallery as a '*Vüe de Willanow prise de Belvedere*' (Mańkowski 1932, p. 261, pos. 424). The exact spot from which Bellotto had painted the picture was therefore named, the Belvedere hill, the highest point of which is about 100 metres south of the current Belvedere Palace, which was built between 1819 and 1822.
During the restoration work carried out between 2000 and 2003, it was established that in 1776 the measurements of the painting were adapted to the wood panelling in the room (later called the Canaletto Room), where the king decided to display twenty-two paintings by Bellotto. The painting was enlarged, with the addition of a 22-cm wide strip of canvas to the top and a 5.5-6-cm strip to the right. The painting's original dimensions were 151 x 240.5 cm (P. Sadlej, in Warsaw 2003, pp. 31–32, 54). They were therefore very similar to the *View of Ujazdow and Łazienki*, 146 x 243 cm, which was never part of the royal collection (Kozakiewicz 1972a, no. 422).
Bellotto painted the works as an almost inseparable pair and this is why one can only fully appreciate their compositional value when viewing them side by side. The *View of the Wilanów Meadows* includes the environs south-east of Warsaw, while the *View of Ujazdow and Łazienki* includes the north-east zone. Together, they form a 270° panoramic view. They not only have the same horizon line, but the twisted path of the Vistula river matches up perfectly in both.

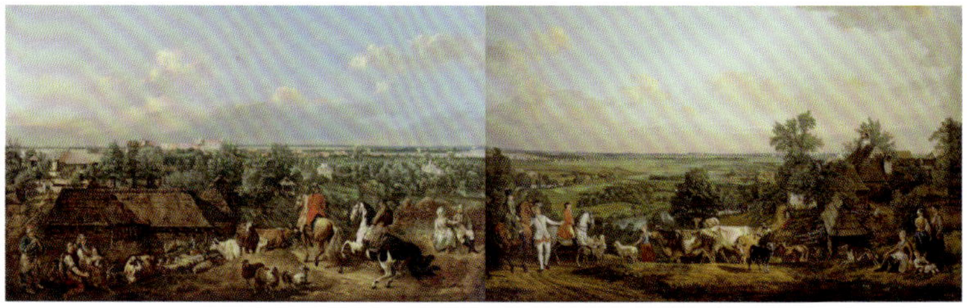

a. Side by side pendants

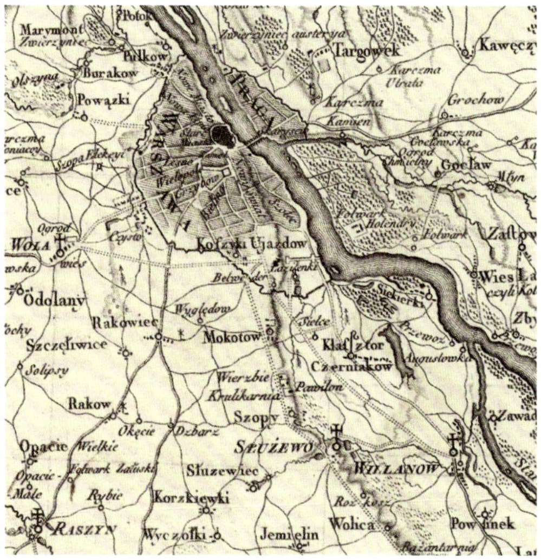

b. Warsaw and suburbs map

The fact that the *View of the Wilanów Meadows*, and not the *View of Ujazdow and Łazienki*, was adapted to the castle room was probably ideologically motivated. The king wanted to emphasise the power and wealth of the Czartoryski family (the family of the king's mother, Konstancja) by displaying their property in Wilanów. A broad view to the south and to the east shows an area that in large part belonged to the Czartoryski family, and on the horizon one can glimpse the village of Wilanów, with its church and palace. One of the most important

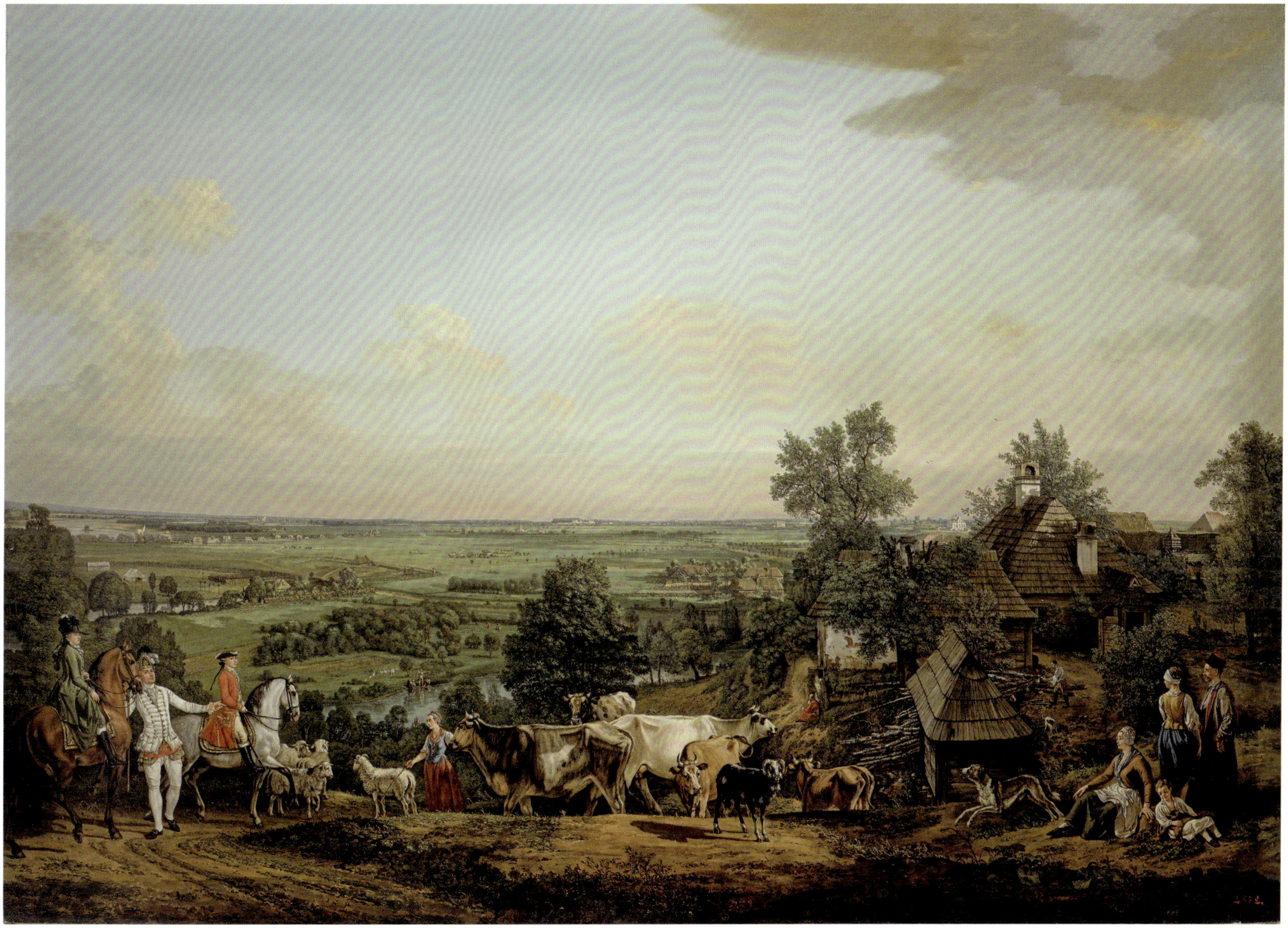

groupings is the village of Siekierki to the left. Shifting the gaze to the right, one can see the church of the Bernardines, dedicated to Saint Anthony, in the village of Czerniaków, and on the right side of the painting one glimpses the north facade of the church of Saint Catherine in Służew. Closer in, one sees the recently built villa (1772–1774) of Princess Izabela Czartoryska Lubomirska, called 'Mon Coteau'. In the foreground, Bellotto painted two people riding horseback. The Venetian art historian Alberto Rizzi has identified them as King Stanisław August's niece and nephew, Maria Teresa Poniatowski Tyszkiewiczowa and Józef Poniatowski (Rizzi 2006, p. 80, no. 23).

The base of the composition is the same horizon line for both paintings, where the artist painted individual buildings and groupings. This made it possible to obtain the spatial transparency of the vast territory surrounding Warsaw to the north, east and south. Of course Bellotto would not have been able to see all of the elements he painted from a single place. In order to create the image, he needed to use sketches made from different vantage points and draw on a range of visual sources. For example, for the villa Lubomirska in Mokotów, he needed the plans of the court architect, Efraim Schröger, realised in 1772 (Lorentz 1986, pp. 174–178) in order to show us the north facade of the villa (the only one with a mezzanine level), impossible to see from the Belvedere hill.

To fully assess the two panoramas, it is also necessary to consider the time and circumstances in which the artist found himself working for the Warsaw court.

Between the 1760s and 70s, the Polish-Lithuanian Commonwealth was mired in a tragic political situation (those were the years of the First Partition between Russia, Prussia and Austria), the consequences of which included severe economic difficulties for the royal court. This led in turn to the need to reduce spending on building projects and art. The renovation of the royal residence Ujazdów Castle was abandoned (a project that Bellotto had been working on), and the even bigger investments in the Royal Castle, the king's official residence, the summer residence Łazienki Palace and the above-mentioned Belvedere Palace were suspended.

During this period, Bellotto devoted himself to genre painting, with the four equestrian portraits commissioned by the royal court in 1773 (see cat. 98).

These are thematically linked to life at the Warsaw court, as well as the *View of Warsaw from the Terrace of the Royal Castle* and the painting in question here with its pendant, painted two years later.

The values of these paintings are determined primarily by Bellotto's characteristic way of understanding reality, which manifests itself in the capriccio setting of the genre scenes with elements familiar to him (paintings with an equestrian theme), or in the classical layout of the veduta.

Andrzej Rottermund

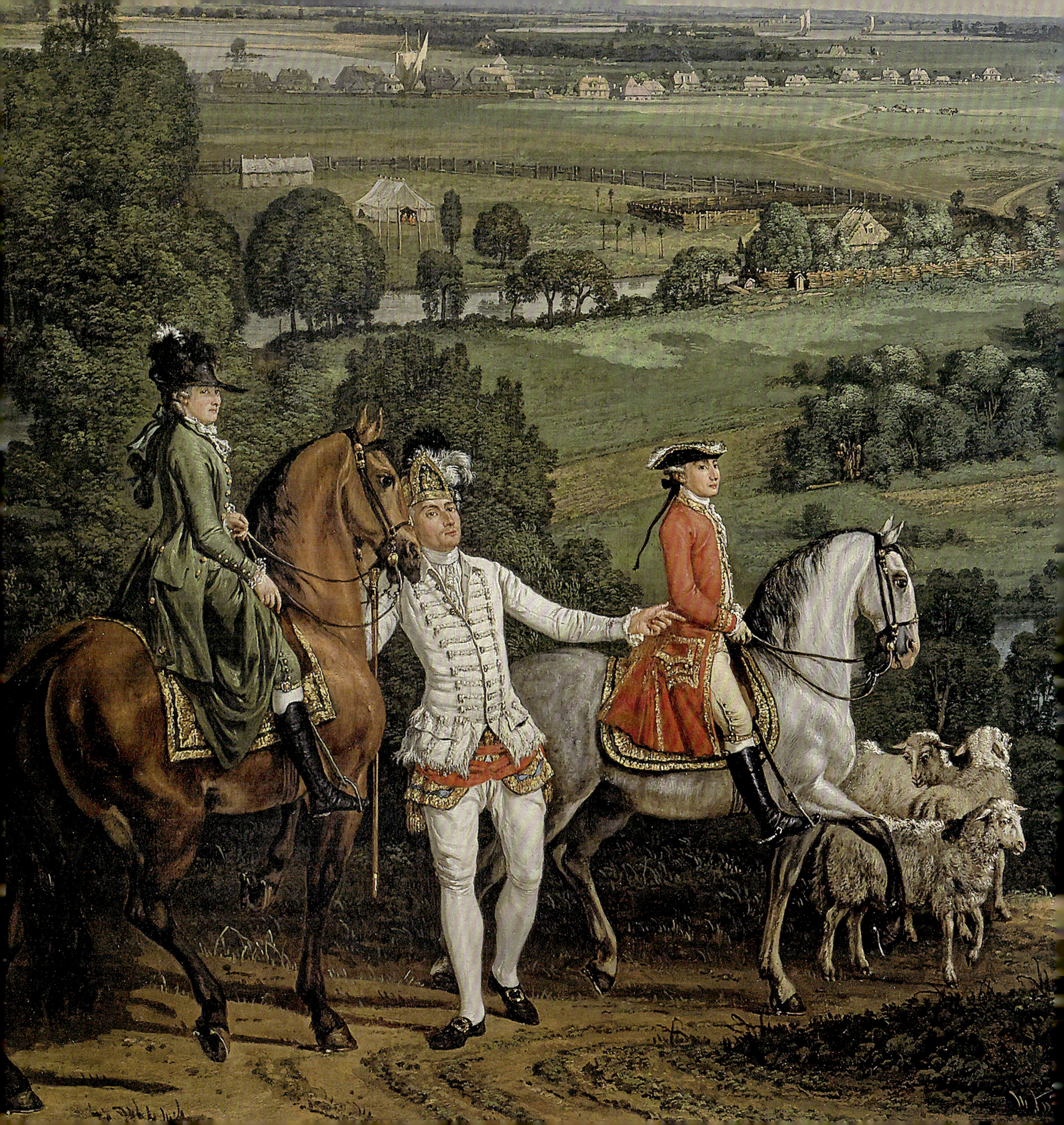

98

BERNARDO BELLOTTO

(Venice 1722 – Warsaw 1780)

The Prince Józef Poniatowski Receiving a Horse-Riding Lesson from the Colonel Königsfels
1773

oil on canvas, 73 x 81.5 cm
Warsaw, Muzeum Narodowe (MP 4283), on deposit in Warsaw, Royal Castle – Museum (ZKW/1883/ab/Dep)

The young Prince Józef Poniatowski (1763–1813), nephew of the king and future national hero, depicted on a white horse of a valuable breed of Oriental descent, goes from a walking gait to parade gait at the sign of the rod held by Colonel Königsfels. The riding lesson takes place in an imaginary setting that links this painting to the architectural *capricci* of the second Dresden period, although the equestrian portrait is a new departure in Bellotto's painting.
This painting was commissioned by King Stanisław II August Poniatowski (1732–1798), part of a series of 'four small invented pictures of horses taken from life with figures', as Bellotto himself wrote in the 'Notta di lavori forniti alla corte' (Work notes provided to the court), an accurate register of the paintings carried out for the King of Poland, with an indication of dates and fees (Kròl-Kaczorowska 1966; republished by Rizzi, with Italian corrections, 1991, p. 151). There are two pairs of pendants, linked by measurements and format, described in the 1795 catalogue of the gallery of the Royal Castle, Warsaw. The original title with which the painted was quoted is retained: '*Le colonel Koenigsfels donnat une leçon de manège au Pce Joseph Poniatowski, neveu du Roi* (n. 457)'. The accompanying picture with which it shared its history depicts a *Groom with a Horse* (*Palfrenier conduisant un cheval au manege* (n. 456), in an imaginary loggia). S. Kozakiewicz (1967) reconstructed the second pair, the same height but not as wide, '*Homme à cheval suivi d'un husar*' (n. 458), purchased by the Kunsthistorisches Museum from a private collection in Vienna in 1955, and '*Le page Gintowt à cheval, suivi d'un palfrenier à livrée du Roi*' (n. 459), known only to scholars from a photograph taken when it was in the Henry Kent collection in Florence in 1911, but found during the work for this exhibition in the collection of Baron Weidinger in Vienna (fig. a). The Polish scholar observed that the series of four *capricci* in Parma (cf. cat. 45, 46) is similarly composed, with two horizontal and two vertical paintings.
This painting is the first portrait of the prince, who also appears in the distance in *Warsaw from the terrace of the Royal Castle,* painted in the same year (Muzeum Narodowe, Warsaw). Józef Poniatowski wrote himself into Polish history as a brave patriot, commander of the Polish army against the Russians in 1792 and then again in 1809 against the Austrians. He allied himself with Napoleon, seeing him as the liberator of Poland, fought his wars and was appointed Marshal of the empire. He died a hero at the Battle of Leipzig on 19 October 1813.
S. Kozakiewicz (1967) identified the print by Johann Elias Ridinger (1698–1767) entitled *Die Parade im Schrittlinks* – from the series *Neue Reit Schulvorstellen deinen vollkommenen Reuter in allen Lectionen*, published in 1734 – from which Bellotto took and reversed the pose of the rider; that of the groom is more vaguely inspired by another engraving in the series. The majestic figure of Colonel Königsfels is one of Bellotto's most incisive portraits. The scene takes place beneath a classical portico, open onto a courtyard of high fences, overlooked by an imaginary three-arched building and the tympanum bearing the royal coat of arms of the Poniatowski family.

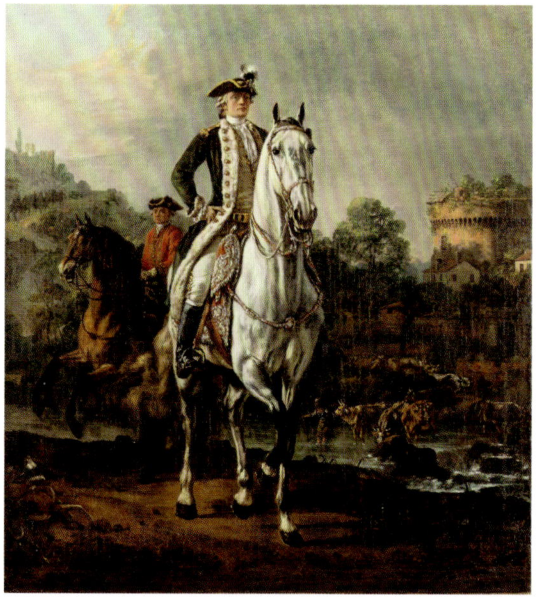

a. Bernardo Bellotto, *Equestrian Portrait of Page Gintowt*, oil on canvas, 73,5 x 65,5. Vienna, Collection Baron Weidinger

The king was known for the suggestions he made to artists but we would like to think that the series of four equestrian portraits was an expression of the interests of the painter and his study of horses, as he confirms, 'from nature', and the prints of contemporary English paintings, those of George Stubbs (1724–1806) in particular. Horses first make an appearance in his work in *Capriccio, with the Capitol* at the Galleria Nazionale in Parma (cat. 45), before continuing to appear in his European *vedute*, with riders or carriages and in carefully studied poses. The full modernity of the spirit of English painting in which horses appear in natural settings can be found in 1775 with the two pendants *View of Wilanow Meadows, Warsaw* and *View of Ujazdòw and Lazienki, Warsaw*; Prince Jòzef appears again in the first, with his sister Maria Teresa Tyszkiewicz, while in the second two riders on stunning horses are about to descend into the landscape (cf. cat. 97).

Bożena Anna Kowalczyk

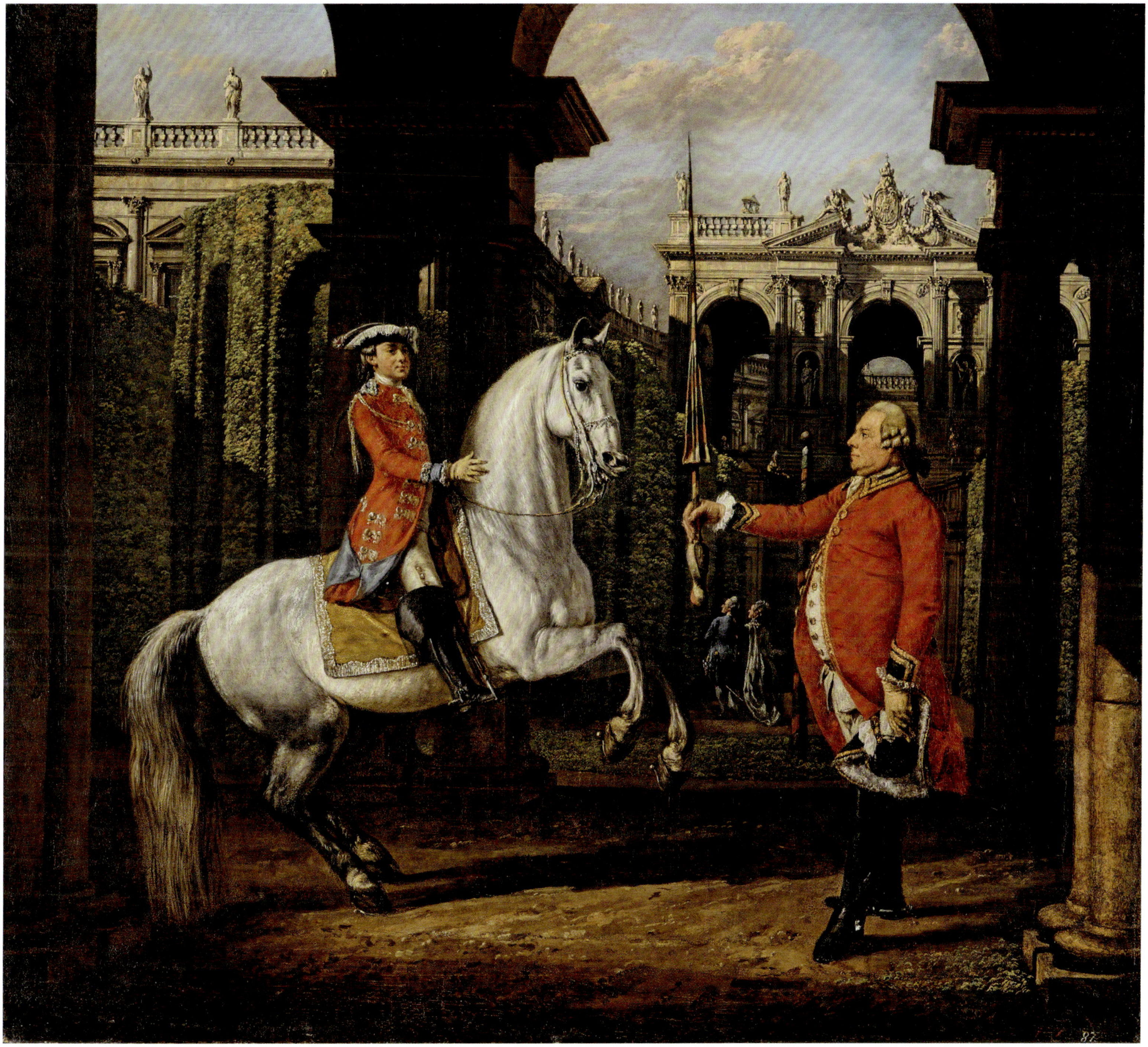

LIST OF WORKS

1.CANALETTO, BELLOTTO'S MASTER

CANALETTO
(Venice 1697-1768)

1 *The Campo Santi Giovanni e Paolo, Venice*
ca. 1738-39
oil on canvas; 46 x 78.4 cm
The Royal Collection / HM Queen Elizabeth II,
RCIN 400715

Provenance: commissioned from the artist by Joseph Smith (1674 ca.-1770); Palazzo Balbi (now Mangilli-Valmarana), Venice; sold with the collection by Smith to King George III in 1762.

Selected Bibliography: Constable 1962, vol. I, pl. 58; vol. II, p. 320, no. 308; Puppi 1968, no. 193 A; Vivian 1971, p. 178; O. Millar, in London 1980-1981, no. 21; O. Millar, in Venice 1982, no. 96; Corboz 1985, vol. I, pp. 219, 224; vol. II, no. P 308; D. Succi, in Venice 1986-1987, pp. 33-45, 248; Constable, Links 1989, vol. I, pl. 58; vol. II, pp. 341-342, no. 308; K. Baetjer, J.G. Links, in New York 1989-1990, no. 45; Levey 1991, no. 402, pl. 48; B.A. Kowalczyk, in Paris 2012-2013, pp. 112-113, no. 22.

CANALETTO
(Venice 1697-1768)

2 *The Piazzetta towards the Libreria, Venice*
ca. 1739
oil on canvas; 47 x 78.2 cm
Private Collection

Provenance: commissioned by Thomas Brand (1717 ca.-1770), The Hoo, Kimpton, Hertfordshire, 1738-1739; by descent to his son, Thomas Brand (1749-1794); grandson, Thomas, 20th Baron Dacre (1774-1851) and his younger brother, General Henry Otway Brand Trevor, 21st Baron Dacre (1777-1853); by descent to his son, Thomas Crosbie William Trevor, 22nd Baron Dacre (1808-1860), at The Hoo until circa 1938; subsequently, Millcourt, Alton, Hampshire; Christie's, London, 2 December 2008, lot 45.

Selected Bibliography: Constable 1962, vol. I, pl. 23; vol. II, p. 212, no. 69; Puppi 1968, p. 100, no. 111; Corboz 1985, vol. II, p. 631, no. P 222; Constable, Links 1989, vol. I, pl. 23; vol. II, p. 219, no. 69; B.A. Kowalczyk, in Venice-Houston 2001, p. 54; C. Beddington, in Treviso 2008-2009, pp. 280-281.

BERNARDO BELLOTTO
(Venice 1722 - Warsaw 1780)

3 The Campo Santa Maria Formosa, Venice (recto);
Figures Studies (verso)
1738-39
pen and brown ink, over free and ruled pencil
and pinpointing (*recto*); pencil (*verso*);
255 x 382 mm
Darmstadt, Hessisches Landesmuseum, AE 2210

Inscriptions: in the centre of the sky written with pen, 'Sta Maria Formosa'; up in to the right corner with red pencil, '20'; different writings and scrawls (*verso*).

Provenance: Bernardo Bellotto to Warsaw and to the artist's heirs in Warsaw 1798, then Vilnius, where it was purchased between 1804 and 1826 by Ludwig Heinrich Bojanus (1776-1827), in a group of about eighty drawings, of which three by Canaletto; Darmstadt, 1826; by descent, probably his sister Luise (or Louise?) (1689-1880), wife of Carl Christian Eigenbrodt (1769-1839); his son, Reinhart Eigenbrodt, lawyer to the grand-ducal court, sold the entire collection in 1829 to Ludwig I (1753-1830), Grand-Duke of Hessen-Darmstadt (for a negligible price: 140 florins and 7 kreuzen); Grand-Ducal Museum, Darmstadt (from 1918 Hessisches Landesmuseum).

Selected Bibliography: Hadeln 1929, p. 22; Fritzsche 1936, pp. 131-132, no. VZ 30; Parker 1948, p. 37; Constable 1962, vol. II, pp. 471-472; Kozakiewicz 1972a, vol. I, p. 20, vol. II, pp. 19-20, no. 22; M. Bleyl, in Darmstadt 1981, p. 25, no. 15; Kowalczyk 1987-1988, vol. II, pp. 122-128, no. 24; Constable, Links 1989, vol. II, pp. 515-516; Parker, Crowley 1990, pp. 37, 169; Kowalczyk 1996, pp. 83-84, fig. 18; B.A. Kowalczyk, in Venice-Houston 2001, pp. 46, 48; M. Clayton, in London-Edinburgh 2005-2007, pp. 129, 132 ; B.A. Kowalczyk, in Turin 2008, pp. 72, 76.

CANALETTO
(Venice 1697-1768)

4 *The Campo Santa Maria Formosa, Venice*
1738-1740
pen and brown ink, over free and ruled pencil
and pinpointing; 270 x 376 mm
The Royal Collection / HM Queen Elizabeth II,
RCIN 907478

Provenance: commissioned from the artist by Joseph Smith (1674 ca.-1770); Palazzo Balbi (now Mangilli-Valmarana), Venice; sold by Smith to King George III in 1762, with the *Experimenta et Schedae (Volume di Dissegni di Antonio Canale*...) album.

Selected Bibliography: Hadeln 1929, p. 22; Parker 1948, p. 37, no. 38; Constable 1962, vol. II, p. 471, no. 604; Kozakiewicz 1972a, vol. II, p. 20; Corboz 1985, vol. II, p. 688, no. D49; Constable, Links 1989, vol. II, pp. 327-328, 515, no. 604; Parker, Crawley 1990, pp. 37, 169, no. 38; B.A. Kowalczyk, in Venice-Houston 2001, pp. 46, 48; M. Clayton, in London-Edinburgh 2005-2007, pp. 128-129, 132, no. 36; B.A. Kowalczyk, in Turin 2008, pp. 72-73, no. 9.

CANALETTO
(Venice 1697-1768)

5 *The Rialto Bridge from the South, Venice*
ca. 1740
oil on canvas; 45 x 76 cm
Paris, Musée Jacquemart-André, MJAP-P-577-1

Provenance: Joseph Smith (ca. 1674-1770), Venice; purchased with the pendant by Édouard André for 18,500 francs from Charles Pillet at the hôtel Drouot, 21 April 1865; Mme Nélie Jacquemart who donated it to the Institut de France in 1912.

Selected Bibliography: Constable 1962, vol. II, pp. 278-279, no. 228-a; Puppi 1968, no. 242C; Links 1981, p. 22; Corboz 1985, vol. II, p. 657, no. P 339; Constable, Links 1989, vol. I, pl. 199; vol. II, p. 296, no. 228-a; Kowalczyk 1996, p. 87; C. Beddington, in London-Washington 2010-2011, no. 23; B.A. Kowalczyk, in Paris 2012-2013, pp. 100, 102-103, no. 17; B.A. Kowalczyk, in Budapest 2013-2014, p. 408.

BERNARDO BELLOTTO
(Venice 1722 - Warsaw 1780)

6 *The Rialto Bridge from the South, from the Palazzo Dolfin-Manin, Venice*
1739-40
pen and two shades of brown ink over free and ruled pencil and pinpointing; 217 x 385 mm
Private Collection
work not on display

Provenance: G.A.F. Cavendish-Bentinck (1821-1891); his sale, Christie's, London, 11 July 1891, lot 666 ('Canaletto'); purchased by Colnaghi; Miss Alexander; Sotheby's, London, 21 October 1963, lot 51 ('Canaletto'); P. & No. de Boer,, Amsterdam; sale, Christie's, London, 4 July 1995, lot 69.

Selected Bibliography: Constable, Links 1989, vol. II, p. 509, no. 591*; Kowalczyk 1996, pp. 87-88; B.A. Kowalczyk, in Turin 2008, pp. 64-65, 68 e 70, no. 5; B.A. Kowalczyk, in Paris 2012-2013, pp. 100 e 103.

BERNARDO BELLOTTO
(Venice 1722 - Warsaw 1780)

7 *The Grand Canal looking South from the Palazzi Foscari and Moro Lin to Santa Maria della Carità, Venice*
1738-39
oil on canvas; 59.7 x 89.5 cm
Private Collection, courtesy Fabrizio Moretti Ltd., London

Provenance: commissioned in Venice by Henry Howard (1694-1758), 4th Earl of Carlisle during his stay in the city in 1738-1739 through the agency of Antonio Maria Zanetti; sent to Castle Howard probably before June 1740; by descent, in Castle Howard, collection of the Earls of Carlisle, until sold at auction, Sotheby's, London, 8 July 2015, lot 21.

Selected Bibliography: H. Brigstocke, in York 1994, p. 72; D. Succi, in Padua 1994, pp. 54 and 266 no. 85; Links 1998, p. 33; D. Succi, in Mirano 1999, p. 52 *et passim*; B.A. Kowalczyk, in Venice-Houston 2001, p. 14, note 36 and p. 50; B.A. Kowalczyk, in Turin 2008, p. 62; Kowalczyk 2012, p. 31.

CANALETTO
(Venice 1697-1768)

8 *The Molo looking West, the Column of Saint Theodore on the Right, Venice*
ca. 1738
oil on canvas; 110.5 x 185.5 cm
Milan, Raccolte d'Arte Antica, Pinacoteca del Castello Sforzesco, 1474

Provenance: Commissioned by Thomas Osborne, 4th Duke of Leeds (1713-789), Hornby Castle, Bendale, Yorkshire; by descent, Dukes of Leeds, Hornby Castle, until its sale at Christie's, London on 11 June 1920, lot 2; purchased by A.H. Buttery, London; Senator Luigi Albertini, Milan, 1924; purchased by the Comune di Milano, 1995.

Selected Bibliography: Constable 1962, vol. I, pl. 27; vol. II, pp. 221-222, no. 95; Puppi 1968, p. 103, no. 144A; Corboz 1985, vol. II, p. 637, no. P 252; Constable, Links 1989, vol. I, pl. 27; vol. II, pp. 230-231, no. 95; B.A. Kowalczyk, in Rome 2005, pp. 130, 136, no. 28; E. Lucchese, in Treviso 2008-2009, pp. 262-263, no. 35; E. Lucchese, in Brescia 2016, p. 92, no. 5.

BERNARDO BELLOTTO
(Venice 1722 - Warsaw 1780)

9 *The Molo looking West, the Column of Saint Theodore on the Right, Venice*
ca. 1739
oil on canvas; 62.2 x 94 cm
Madrid, Abelló Collection

Provenance: Edmund Higginson (1802-1871), Saltmarshe Castle, Herefordshire; The Hon. Edward Gordon-Douglas-Pennant (1800-1886), subsequently Baron Penrhyn of Llandegai, Penrhyn Castle, Gwynedd; by descent, until the sale at Sotheby's, 3 December 1924, lot 59 ('Canaletto'); Thomas Agnew & Sons, London; Alvan Fuller, Boston, MA; Mr and Mrs RL Henderson, Boston, MA; private European collection, 1977; purchased by the present owner in October 2016.

Selected Bibliography: Constable 1962, vol. II, p. 222, no. 95-b ('doubtfully by Canaletto'); Kozakiewicz 1972a, vol. II, p. 405, A 50 no. Z 50 ('atelier of Canaletto'); Camesasca 1974, p. 120, no. 291 ('attributed to Bellotto'); Constable, Links 1989, vol. II, p. 232, no. 95-b; D. Succi, in Mirano 1999, pp. 39-40, fig. 20 ('Bellotto'); C. Beddington, in Venice-Houston 2001, p. 78; D. Succi, in Madrid 2001, pp. 70-71, fig. 10.

BERNARDO BELLOTTO
(Venice 1722 - Warsaw 1780)

10 *Six Figures around Bird-Coops*
1742-43
pen and brown ink over free and ruled pencil and pinpointing, on white paper;
210-208 x 293 mm
New York, The Metropolitan Museum of Art, Anonymous Gift, 1997.454

Inscriptions: numbered at top centre, with the same pen and ink as the drawing: '42'.

Watermark: difficult to make out, letters in a *cartouche*.

Provenance: private collection, Bergamo; Agnew's, London, 1970; private collection, London; Christie's, London, 6 July 1982, lot 72; Katrin Bellinger - W.M. Brady&Co., New York, 1995; anonymous donation to Metropolitan Museum, New York, 1997.

Selected Bibliography: Pignatti 1973, p. 183; Constable, Links 1976, vol. II, p. 615, no. 840** ('attributed to Canaletto'); A. Bettagno, in Venice 1982, p. 44 ('Canaletto'); Corboz 1985, vol. I, p. 136, note 82; vol. II, p. 766, no. P 217; Pantazzi 1987, p. 53; Constable, Links 1989, vol. I, pp. LXXXIV-LXXXV; vol. II, pp. 615-616, no. 840**; B.A. Kowalczyk, in Venice-Houston 2001, pp. 12, 74, 76 ('Bellotto'); Beddington 2004, p. 670; B.A. Kowalczyk, in Rome 2005, pp. 204-205, no. 51; B.A. Kowalczyk, in Munich 2014-2015, p. 162.

CANALETTO
(Venice 1697-1768)

11 *Camera Optica*
Venice, eighteenth century
wood, glass and mirror; 38 x 24.2 x 22.5 cm
Venice, Museo Correr, Cl. XXIX, s.n. 30

Inscriptions: engraved on the flap, 'A. CANAL'.

Selected Bibliography: Pignatti 1958, p. 21; Gioseffi 1959, p. 22; Puppi 1968, p. 87, fig. p. 86; Nepi Sciré 1997, p. 15; F. Camerota, in Florence 2001-2002, pp. 227-240; Camerota 2008, pp. 65-66; D. Maran, in Venice 2012, pp. 46, 49; B.A. Kowalczyk, in Aix-en-Provence 2015, no. 32.

2. BELLOTTO, CANALETTO'S ALTER EGO

BERNARDO BELLOTTO
(Venice 1722 - Warsaw 1780)

12 *Santa Maria dei Miracoli and the Apse of Santa Maria Nova, Venice*
ca. 1741
oil on canvas; 41.6 x 66 cm
Hanover, Niedersächsisches Landesmuseum, Landesgalerie, L 29
(on permanent loan from The Fritz Behrens Foundation)

Provenance: Gregory Stroganov (1829-1910), Rome; Camillo Castiglioni, Vienna; F. Muller sale, Amsterdam, 17-20 November 1925, lot 28 (unsold); Ball and Graupe sale, Berlin, 28-29 November, 1930, no. 30; Sotheby's, New York, 9 June 1983, lot 155; bought by Richard Green; P & D. Colnaghi, London.

Selected Bibliography: Muñoz 1911, vol. II, p. 46 ('Bellotto'); Constable 1962, vol. II, p. 409, no. 464 ('attributed to Canaletto'); Kozakiewicz 1972a, vol. I, pp. 25-26; vol. II, pp. 80, 83, no. 105; ('Bellotto'); Camesasca 1974, p. 89, no. 14; Grohn 1995, p. 32, no. 11; Constable, Links 1989, vol. II, p. 441, no. 464; B.A. Kowalczyk, in Venice-Houston 2001, p. 58, no. 6; J. Toma, in Munich 2014-2015, p. 170, no. 10.

BERNARDO BELLOTTO
(Venice 1722 - Warsaw 1780)

13 *The Grand Canal looking East, from the Palazzo Loredan Cini in Campo San Vio, Venice*
ca. 1742
oil on canvas; 61 x 97.5 cm
London, Private Collection

Provenance: Isidor Ostrer (1889-1975), Berkshire, UK; his daughter, Pamela Mason (1916-1996), Beverly Hills, California; Christie's New York, 18 June 1982, lot 87 ('Canaletto'); private collection, USA; Sotheby's, London, 11 December 1985, lot 24 ('attributed to Canaletto'); purchased by Alfred Taubman (1924-2015); Sotheby's, New York, 27 January 2016, lot 50 ('Bellotto'), Richard Green Ltd., from whom purchased by the present owner.

Selected Bibliography: Constable, Links 1989, vol. II, p. 731, no. 187-b ('Canaletto'); Levey 1991, p. 27; Manzelli 1991, p. 86, no. A.36.1 ('Francesco Albotto'); Links 1998, p. 72 ('Canaletto'); Manzelli 2002, p. 127, no. A.36.1 ('Francesco Albotto').

BERNARDO BELLOTTO
(Venice 1722 - Warsaw 1780)

14 *The Grand Canal with Santa Maria della Salute from the Campo Santa Maria del Giglio, Venice*
ca. 1743
oil on canvas; 135.5 x 232.5 cm
Los Angeles, The J. Paul Getty Museum, 91.PA.73

Provenance: William, 2nd Earl of Craven (1809-1866), Combe Abbey, Warwickshire (exhibited Birmingham 1831, no.); by descent to William George Robert, 4th Earl of Craven (1883-1921); Cornelia, Duchess of Craven (1921-1961), Hamstead Marshall, Berkshire; Sotheby's sale, London, 29 November 1961, lot 41, purchased by Julius Weitzner; Robert Lehman, New York, 1991; Newhouse Galleries, New York, 1991; acquired by The J. Paul Getty Museum, 1991, in exchange for a painting by Canaletto (Links 1998, no. 160*).

Selected Bibliography: Constable 1962, vol. I, pl. 38; vol. II, p. 259, no. 180 ('Canaletto, early thirties'); Puppi 1968, p. 102, no. 134 A; Kozakiewicz 1972a, vol. II, pp. 13 and 419 ('Canaletto'); Corboz 1985, vol. II, p. 634, no. P 234; Kowalczyk 1996, pp. 83, 89 ('Bellotto and atelier'); Constable, Links 1989, vol. I, pl. 38; vol. II, p. 273, no. 180 ('Canaletto, a period when Bellotto was active in the studio'); B.A. Kowalczyk, in Venice-Houston 2001, pp. 64-69, no. 8 ('Bellotto'); C. Beddington, in London-Washington 2010-2011, p. 53, note 44 ('Bellotto responsible… at last predominantly'); E.P. Bowron, in Rimini 2012, p. 45 ('Bellotto').

BERNARDO BELLOTTO
(Venice 1722 - Warsaw 1780)

15 *The Piazza San Marco looking South-West, Venice*
1742-43
oil on canvas; 136.2 x 232.5 cm
Cleveland, The Cleveland Museum of Art, Leonard C. Hanna, Jr. Fund, 1962.169

Provenance: William, 2nd Earl of Cravey (1809-1866), Combe Abbey, Warwickshire (exhibited *Birmingham 1833,* no. 126); by inheritance, William George Robert, 4th Earl of Craven (1883-1921); Cornelia, Duchess of Craven (1921-1961), Hamstead Marshall, Berkshire; Sotheby's sale, London, 29 November 1961, lot 42 ('Canaletto'), purchased by Faroni; M.H. Drey, London; acquired by The Cleveland Museum of Art, 1962.

Selected Bibliography: Waagen 1854, p. 219; Constable 1962, vol. II, p. 204, no. 53 ('Canaletto, early thirties'); Puppi 1968, p. 102, no. 133 A ('Canaletto, 1732-1733'); Pignatti 1981 ('Bellotto'); Corboz 1985, vol. II, p. 634, no. P 233; Constable, Links 1989, vol. I, pl. 20, pp. 208-209, no. 53 ('Canaletto'); Kowalczyk 1996, pp. 83 e 89 (Bellotto); Links 1998, p. 8, no. 53; B.A. Kowalczyk, in Venice-Houston 2001, pp. 64-69; M. Clayton Clayton, in London-Edinburgh 2005-2007, p. 202 ('Canaletto'); B.A. Kowalczyk, in Paris 2012-2013, p. 89.

CANALETTO
(Venice 1697-1768)

16 *The Ducal Palace: the Scala dei Giganti, Venice*
ca. 1743
oil on canvas; 175.2 x 139.5 cm
Alnwick Castle, The Duke of Northumberland Collection, 03341

Provenance: commissioned by Sir Hugh Smithson (1712-1786), who succeeded to the Earldom of Northumberland in 1750 and was created the 1st Duke of Northumberland in 1766; Stanwick Hall, Yorkshire, 1818; Alnwick Castle, Northumberland, 1922.

Selected Bibliography: Constable 1962, vol. II, p. 215, no. 80; Puppi 1968, p. 118, no. 323 B; Corboz 1985, vol. II, p. 729, no. P 447; Constable, Links 1989, vol. I, pl. 189 e pp. LXIV-LXV; vol. II, pp. 223, 743, no. 80; Links 1998, p. 50; B.A. Kowalczyk, in Rome 2005, pp. 216, 218, no. 56; C. Beddington, in London-Washington 2010-2011, p. 70.

CANALETTO
(Venice 1697-1768)

17 *The Piazza San Marco looking West, Venice*
ca. 1743
oil on canvas; 175.2 x 139.5 cm
Alnwick Castle, The Duke of Northumberland Collection, 03327

Provenance: commissioned by Sir Hugh Smithson (1712-1786), who succeeded to the Earldom of Northumberland in 1750 and was created the 1st Duke of Northumberland in 1766; Stanwick Hall, Yorkshire, 1818; Alnwick Castle, Northumberland, 1922.

Selected Bibliography: Constable 1962, vol. I, pl. 18; vol. II, p. 197, no. 36; Puppi 1968, p. 116, no. 295; Corboz 1985, vol. II, p. 722, no. P 424; Constable, Links 1989, vol. I, pl. 18 and pp. LXIV-LXV; vol. II, pp. 200-201, no. 36; B.A. Kowalczyk, in Rome 2005, p. 220, no. 57; C. Beddington, in London-Washington 2010-2011, p. 70.

3. BELLOTTO: FAR FROM VENICE

GIUSEPPE ZOCCHI
(Florence 1717-1767)

18 *Anton Maria Zanetti di Girolamo and Andrea Gerini*
1740-1744
oil on copper; 37 x 28 cm
Venice, Ca' Rezzonico, Museo del Settecento Veneziano, Cl. I no. 144

Inscriptions: on the letter, 'ILL.MO SIG. A.M. ZANETTI Q. JER.VENEZIA.'.

Provenance: Gianmaria Sasso (1803); his sale, 1803, no. 381; Teodoro Correr (1750-1830); bequeathed to the City on 10 January 1830.

Selected Bibliography: Pignatti 1960, pp. 298-299, no. 144; Haskell 1960, pp. 32-37; Morassi 1962, pp. 3 and 5; Mattioli Rossi 1980, p. 84; Tosi 1997, pp. 54-55, 57; Kowalczyk 2012, p. 27; C. Lenzi Iacomelli, in Florence 2009, p. 242, no. 86; Ingendaay 2013, pp. 113-114.

BERNARDO BELLOTTO
(Venice 1722 - Warsaw 1780)

19 *The Piazza della Signoria looking East, Florence*
1740
oil on canvas; 61 x 90 cm
Budapest, Szépművészeti Múzeum, 645

Provenance: commissioned by Marquis Vincenzo Riccardi (1704-1752), Florence (mentioned for the first time in the inventory of his private collection, 1741); Prince Miklos Esterházy (1756-1833), Vienna, 1820 and then Paul Esterházy, Budapest, 1865; National Gallery of Paintings, Budapest, 1871.

Selected Bibliography: Kozakiewicz 1972a, vol. I, p. 33-34; vol. II, pp. 41-42, no. 57; B.A. Kowalczyk, in Venice-Houston 2001, pp. 86-87, no. 13; G. Gruber, in Vienna 2005, pp. 74,77, no. 3; D. Rodríguez, in Madrid 2011-2012, pp. 278-279, no. 80; Kowalczyk 2012, pp. 24-31; B.A. Kowalczyk, in Budapest 2013-2014, p. 414, no. 136; B.A. Kowalczyk, in Munich 2014-2015, p. 182, no. 16.

BERNARDO BELLOTTO
(Venice 1722 - Warsaw 1780)

20 *Landscape with Motifs of Rota, near Tolfa (recto)*
Basilica di San Marco, Venice. Studies of the South Front (verso)
1743-44
pen and brown link over over free and ruled pencil and pinpointing; 278 x 305 mm
Venice, Museo Correr, Gabinetto dei Disegni e delle Stampe, C1. III n. 8633

Watermark: three crescent moons.

Marks: below on the *recto* a brown oval with an intertwined F and C, not present in Lugt.

Provenance: Cesare Frigerio, Milan (d. 1976); Antonio Morassi, before 1960; gift to the museum, 1960.

Selected Bibliography: T. Pignatti, in Venice 1964, no. 73; Kozakiewicz 1972a, vol. II, p. 80, no. 104; Kowalczyk 1987-1988, pp. II, 327-330, no. 67; B.A. Kowalczyk, in Venice 1995, pp. 445-446, no. 165; B.A. Kowalczyk, in Munich 2014-2015, p. 74; Kowalczyk 2015.

GIUSEPPE ZOCCHI
(Firenze 1717-1767)

21 *Landscape with Motifs of Rota, near Tolfa*
1746-1750
oil on canvas; 83 x 53.5 cm
Private Collection, courtesy Jean-Luc Baroni Ltd., London

22 *Landscape with Motifs of Rota with the Brick-Kiln, near Tolfa*
1746-1750
oil on canvas; 83 x 53.5 cm
Private Collection, courtesy Jean-Luc Baroni Ltd., London

Provenance: Marquis Andrea Gerini (1691-1766), Florence (mentioned for the first time in the *Catalogo 1825*, nos. 67-68); Jean-Luc Baroni Ltd., London and New York, 2003.

Selected Bibliography: D. Garstang, in New York 2003, nos. 14a e 14b; Kowalczyk 2015.

FABIO BERARDI
(Siena 1736 - Venice 1788)

23 *Landscape with Motifs of Rota, near Tolfa*
1765-1770
etching and engraving, II state of two; 343 x 496 mm
Private Collection

Inscriptions: in the margin, 'Zocchi dipinse Fabio Berardi Scol. app.o Wagner Venice C.P.E.S. / Anco in mezzo a dirupi in valle oscura / Trovan conforto de' mortali i cuori, / I passeggi, le caccie, ed i lavori / Sono dell'uom trattenimento e cura'; fragment of number lower left '[N° 60.2]'.

Provenance: antiquarian bookshop Linea d'Acqua, Venice, 2010.

Selected Bibliography: Tosi 1997, p. 118; D. Garstang, in New York 2003, nos. 14a and 14b; Dri 2004-2005, pp. 174-176, fig. 2; Ingendaay 2013, vol. I, p. 94; Kowalczyk 2015, pp. 76-77.

FABIO BERARDI
(Siena 1736 - Venice 1788)

24 *Landscape with Motifs of Rota with the Brick-Kiln, near Tolfa*
1765-1770
etching and engraving, single state; 328 x 452 mm
Venice, Fondazione Querini Stampalia, cart. XVI, no. 1

Inscriptions: on the margin, 'Zocchi dipinse Fabio Berardi Scol. appo Wagner Venice C.P.E.S: / Quando il sole è all'occaso ha per costume / Che della greggia è alla custodia intento / Guidar dal pasco il satolato armento / A qualche fonte, ad un ruscello, a un fiume'; lower left, 'N°60.1'.

Provenance: unknown.

Selected Bibliography: D. Succi, in Venice-Gorizia 1983, p. 78, no. 48; Tosi 1997, p. 118; D. Garstang, in New York 2003, no. 14a e 14b; Dri 2004-2005, pp. 174-176, fig. 1; Ingendaay 2013, p. 94; Kowalczyk 2015, pp. 76-77.

BERNARDO BELLOTTO
(Venice 1722 - Warsaw 1780)

25 *The Watermill on a River, probably Mignone; Study of the Torre dell'Orologio, Venice (recto)*
The Basilica di San Marco, Venice: the Upper Part of the South Front; the West Facade in Perspective (verso)
1743-44

pen and brown ink over a lightly sketched pencil, only free and ruled pencil with pinpointing (*recto*); pencil (*verso*); 323 x 290 mm
Private Collection, courtesy Jean-Luc Baroni Ltd., London

Watermark: three crescent moons.

Provenance: Emile Calando (1850-1900) (Lugt 837; see also, for Emile Calando fils (d. 1953), Lugt *Suppl.* 426b); P.& D. Colnaghi & Co. Ltd., London, 1952; Peter Wick, Boston, 1953; Sotheby's sale, London, 5 July 2000, lot 67; Thierry De Maigret sale, Paris, 13 June 2007, lot 4; Jean-Luc Baroni Ltd., from whom purchased by the current owner.

Selected Bibliography: Constable 1962, vol. II, p. 512., no. 712 ("Canaletto?'); Kozakiewicz 1972a, vol. II, p. 458, no. A 307 ("attributed to Bellotto'); Kowalczyk 1987-1988, p. II-329-330 ('Bellotto'); Constable, Links 1989, vol. II, no. 712; B.A. Kowalczyk, in Venice 1995, p. 446; B.A. Kowalczyk, in Turin 2008, p. 174; B.A. Kowalczyk in Munich 2014-2015, p. 74 ; Kowalczyk 2015.

FABIO BERARDI
(Siena 1736 - Venice 1788)

26 *The Watermill on a River, probably Mignone*
1765-1770
etching and engraving, I state of two; 345 x 504 mm, Milan, Civica Raccolta delle Stampe 'Achille Bertarelli', Art. g 2-17

Inscriptions: on lower margin, 'Zocchi dipinse Fabio Berardi incise / L'Originale è appresso -- L'Eminentissimo Signore / Cardinale Pozzobonelli -- Arcivescovo di Milano'.

Provenance: Musei Artistici Milanesi.

Selected Bibliography: Tosi 1997, p. 58; Dri 2004-2005, pp. 174-176, fig. 5; Ingendaay 2013, pp. 110-111; Kowalczyk 2015, p. 77.

BERNARDO BELLOTTO
(Venice 1722 - Warsaw 1780)

27 *The Ducal Palace: the Porta della Carta, Venice*
1740-1743
pen and brown ink over traces of pencil; 432 x 192 mm
Leipzig, Museum für Bildende Künste, I2198/c

Inscriptions: '60 parte della metà della porta dela Carta con il rimanente del folio 61'; a horizontal line drawn in pencil with a ruler.

Provenance: acquired by the Museum from an unknown collector, 1913.

Selected Bibliography: Binion 1980 ('Canaletto, early 1730'); Constable, Links 1989, vol. I, p. LXXXIII, pl. 238; vol. II. p. 742, no. 541*; Links 1998, p. 49, no. 541*; B.A. Kowalczyk, in Rome 2005, p. 204 ('Bellotto').

BERNARDO BELLOTTO
(Venice 1722 - Warsaw 1780)

28 *Capriccio with a Bridge on a River*
1745
oil on canvas; 48.5 x 73 cm
Madrid, Museo Thyssen Bornemisza, 40, 1934.2

Provenance: Camillo Castiglioni (Trieste 1879-Rome 1967), Vienna; sale of his collection, F. Muller & Co., Amsterdam, 17-20 November 1925; T. Agnew & Sons, London, 1926; Thyssen-Bornemisza Collection, Lugano, 1934, 1934.2

Selected Bibliography: Kozakiewicz 1972a, vol. I, p. 43; vol. II, pp. 84, 93, 488, no. 109; Camesasca 1974, p. 88, no. 13; G. Marini, in Verona 1990, p. 92, no. 20; Pita Andrade, Del Mar Borobia Guerriero 1992, pp. 395, 663; E.P. Bowron, in London-Washington 1994-1995, p. 362; G. Marini, in London-Washington 1994-1995, p. 428, no. 253; Kowalczyk 1993-1996, no. 31; Del Mar Borobia Guerriero 1992, pp. 395, 663, no. 40*; Contini 2002, pp. 244-248, no. 52; D. Delgado, in Madrid 2011-2012, pp. 358-359, no. 119; B.A. Kowalczyk, in Munich 2014-2015, p. 220.

4. THE CAPRICCIO

BERNARDO BELLOTTO
(Venice 1722 - Warsaw 1780)

29 *Capriccio with a Ruined Triumphal Arch on the Shores of the Lagoon*
1743
oil on canvas; 40.5 x 49 cm.
Asolo (Treviso), Museo Civico, 470

Provenance: bequest of Canon Giacomo Bertoldi (1846-1910), Asolo, 1910.

Selected Bibliography: R. Pallucchini, in Venice 1946, pp. 188-189, no. 307; Parker 1948, p. 56, no. 133; Constable 1962, vol. I, pl. 89; vol. II, p. 416, no. 482; P. Zampetti, in Venice 1967, no. 86; Puppi 1968, no. 363; Kozakiewicz 1972a, vol. I, p. 45; vol. II, no. 116; Camesasca 1974, no. 16; Constable, Links 1989, vol. I, pl. 89; vol. II, p. 451, no. 483; G. Marini, in Verona 1990, no. 27; B.A. Kowalczyk, in Venice-Houston 2001, no. 27; B.A. Kowalczyk, in Turin 2008, p. 148, no. 51; B.A. Kowalczyk in Paris 2012-2013, p. 177, no. 46; B.A. Kowalczyk, in Munich 2014-2015, p. 180, no. 15.

CANALETTO
(Venice 1697-1768)

30 *Capriccio with a Ruined Triumphal Arch on the Shores of the Lagoon*
1742-43
pen and brown ink with blue-grey wash over pinpricked pencil drawn freehand, with a ruler and pinpointing; the arches and medallion are pinpricked; the drawing appears within a ruled ink line; 198 x 278 mm
The Royal Collection / HM Queen Elizabeth II, RCIN 907533

Provenance: commissioned from the artist by Joseph Smith (1674 ca.-1770); Palazzo Balbi (currently Mangilli-Valmarana), Venice; sold by Smith to King George III in 1762, as part of the *Experimenta et Schedae (Volume di Dissegni di Antonio Canale*…) album.

Selected Bibliography: Parker 1948, no. 133; Constable 1962, vol. I, pl. 149; vol. II, p. 547, no. 789; Kozakiewicz 1972a, vol. I, pp. 23 e 25; vol. II, p. 88; Corboz 1985, vol. II, no. D 206; Constable, Links 1989, vol. I, pl. 149; vol. II, p. 596, no. 789; M. Clayton, in London-Edinburgh 2005-2007, pp. 207, 220, no. 80; B.A. Kowalczyk, in Paris 2012-2013, p. 177.

BERNARDO BELLOTTO
(Venice 1722 - Warsaw 1780)

31 *Capriccio with the Ruins of a Roman Temple on the Shores of the Lagoon*
1743
oil on canvas; 40.5 x 49 cm
Asolo (Treviso), Museo Civico, 471

Provenance: bequest of Canon Giacomo Bertoldi (1846-1910), Asolo, 1910.

Selected Bibliography: R. Pallucchini, in Venice 1946, pp. 188-189, no. 306; Parker 1948, p. 51, no. 106; Constable

1962, vol. I, pl. 89; vol. II, pp. 416-417, no. 483; P. Zampetti, in Venice 1967, no. 86; Puppi 1968, no. 364; Kozakiewicz 1972a, vol. I, p. 45; vol. II, p. 93, no. 118; Camesasca 1974, p. 89, no. 15; Constable, Links 1989, vol. I, pl. 89; vol. II, p. 451, no. 483; G. Marini, in Verona 1990, no. 28; B.A. Kowalczyk, in Venice-Houston 2001, no. 28; B.A. Kowalczyk, in Turin 2008, p. 148, no. 51; B.A. Kowalczyk, in Paris 2012-2013, p. 177.

BERNARDO BELLOTTO
(Venice 1722 - Warsaw 1780)

32 *Capriccio with a Ruined Roman Temple and a Isolated Column*
1742-43
pen in brown ink, over freehand and ruled pencil and pinpointing; traces of contour line at top and bottom; 259 x 377 mm
Darmstadt, Hessisches Landesmuseum, AE 2185

Inscriptions: numbered at top in pen, '19'; above, a '15' in red pencil; inscribed on the verso in pencil, 'A.C.'.

Provenance: Provenance: Bernardo Bellotto in Warsaw and the artist's heirs in Warsaw until 1798, then Vilnius, where it was bought between 1804 and 1826 by Ludwig Heinrich Bojanus (1776-1827), as part of a group of about eighty sheets, among which three by Canaletto; Darmstadt, 1826; by descent, probably to his sister Luise (or Louise?) (1689-1880), wife of Carl Christian Eigenbrodt (1769-1839); the son, Reinhart Eigenbrodt, lawyer to the grand-ducal court, sold the entire collection in 1829 to Ludwig I (1753-1830), Grand-Duke of Hessen-Darmstadt (the price was derisory: 140 florins and 7 kreuzen); Grand-ducal Museum, Darmstadt (the Hessisches Landesmuseum since 1918).

Selected Bibliography: Fritzsche 1936, p. 130, no. VZ 11; Constable 1962, vol. II, pp. 544-545, no. 784; Kozakiewicz 1972a, vol. II, p. 93, no. 121; M. Bleyl, in Darmstadt 1981, no. 27; Constable, Links 1989, vol. II, p. 594 (no. 784); Kowalczyk 1987-1988, no. 50; G. Marini, in Verona 1990, p. 106.

CANALETTO
(Venice 1697-1768)

33a *The Portico with a Lantern*
ca. 1742-43
etching, proof; 300 x 434 mm (plate), 303 x 439 mm (sheet)
Rome, Istituto Centrale per la Grafica, on deposit at the Accademia Nazionale dei Lincei, F.C. 37701

Inscriptions: beneath the image, in the centre, 'A. Canal. f. V.'

Provenance: Fondo Corsini.

Selected Bibliography: De Vesme 1906, no. 10; Bromberg 1974, no. 32-I; Constable, Links 1989, vol. II, *Etchings*, p. 655, no. 11; Montecuccoli degli Erri 2002, no. 10 ('proof').

CANALETTO
(Venice 1697-1768)

33b *The Cart on the Bridge*
1742-43 ca.
etching, proof; 141 x 129 mm (plate), 143 x 129 mm (sheet)
Roma, Istituto Centrale per la Grafica F.C. 37714

Inscriptions: beneath the image, on the right, 'A. Canal. f.'

Provenance: Fondo Corsini.

Selected Bibliography: De Vesme 1906, no. 31; Bromberg 1974, no. 10-I; Constable, Links 1989, vol. II, *Etchings*, p. 660, no. 29a; Montecuccoli degli Erri 2002, no. 31 ('proof').

BERNARDO BELLOTTO
(Venice 1722 - Warsaw 1780)

34 *Capriccio with a Classical Gate and Reminiscences of Padua and Verona*
1746
pen in brown ink with brown wash and heightening in body-colour, over freehand and ruled pencil and pinpointing; 270 x 379 mm
The Royal Collection / HM Queen Elisabeth II, RCIN 907508

Provenance: commissioned from the artist by Joseph Smith (1674 ca.-1770); Palazzo Balbi (now Mangilli-Valmarana), Venice; purchased from Smith by King George III in 1762, in the album of drawings of Antonio Visentini (1688-1782).

Selected Bibliography: Hadeln 1929, p. 25 ('Canaletto'); Parker 1948, pp. 54-55, no. 123; Constable 1962, vol. I, pl. 147, vol. II, p. 543, no. 780 ('Canaletto'); Kozakiewicz 1972a, vol. II, p. 95; Miller 1983, p. 5 ('Canaletto?'); Corboz 1985, vol. I, pp. 115-116, 139, note 217 ('Bellotto?'); Kowalczyk 1987-1988, vol. I, p. 43; vol. II, p. 202; Constable, Links 1989, vol. I, pl. 147; vol. II, p. 592, no. 780; G. Marini, in Verona 1990, pp. 140, 142, no. 41 ('Bellotto'); Parker, Crawley 1990, pp. 54-55, no. 123 e p. 173; B.A. Kowalczyk, in Turin 2008, p. 194, no. 77.

BERNARDO BELLOTTO
(Venice 1722 - Warsaw 1780)

35 *Capriccio with a Paduan Villa*
1760
oil on canvas; 48 x 79 cm
Private Collection, courtesy Fabrizio Moretti Ltd., London

Provenance: Olivier Lathan; his sale, Christie's, London, 13 April 1850, lot 27; purchased by Hoare for 16 guineas with the pendant (*La Breite Gasse, Pirna*); William Lygon, 7th Earl of Beauchamp (1872-1938), London; Arthur Tooth & Sons, who on 1 April 1939 sold it to Karl Haberstock, Berlin (the pair of pendants is mentioned in the inventories of the Haberstock collection in Augsburg in 1939 and 1940, and in storage in bank of Dresden at Tegersee in 1941); returned by the Allies to Haberstock in 1946; sold to Julius Boehler, Munich, in 1951 (who sold the pendant to the Art Institute, Chicago in 1961); anonymous sale, London, Christie's, Manson&Woods, 29 November 1974, lot 99; purchased by the family of the current owner.

Selected Bibliography: Kozakiewicz 1972a, vol. II, pp. 189-190, no. 246; Camesasca 1974, p. 95, no. 73; Corboz 1985, vol. I, p. 127; Rizzi 1996, p. 99, no. 83; B.A. Kowalczyk, in Aix-en-Provence 2015, p. 171.

5. TOWARDS ROME

BERNARDO BELLOTTO
(Venice 1722 - Warsaw 1780)

36 *The Arno towards Ponte Vecchio, Florence*
1744
oil on canvas; 73.3 x 105.7 cm
Cambridge, The Fitzwilliam Museum, 192

Provenance: A.A. Vansittart (1824-1882) (Lugt *Suppl* 2449); donated to the museum in 1876.

Selected Bibliography: Fritzsche 1936, pp. 27, 105, no. VG 17; Levey 1964, pp. 55, 66, no. 418; Goodison, Robertson 1967, p. 15, no. 192; Kozakiewicz 1972a, vol. I, pp. 38, 41, no. 54; M. Chiarini, in Florence 1994, p. 156, no. 90; Villis 2000, p. 81; E.P. Bowron, in Venice-Houston 2001, pp. 90-92, no. 15; B.A. Kowalczyk, in Turin 2008, pp. 112, 114, no. 30; Kowalczyk 2012, pp. 24, 30; B.A. Kowalczyk, in Munich 2014-2015, p. 186, no. 18.

BERNARDO BELLOTTO
(Venice 1722 - Warsaw 1780)

37 *The Arno towards Ponte alla Carraia, Florence*
1744
oil on canvas; 73.7 x 105.4 cm
Cambridge, Fitzwilliam Museum, 195

Provenance: A.A. Vansittart (1824-1882) (Lugt *Suppl* 2449); donated to the Museum in 1876.

Selected Bibliography: Fritzsche 1936, pp. 27, 105, no. VG 16; Goodison, Robertson 1967, p. 15, no. 192; Kozakiewicz 1972a, vol. I, p. 34; vol. II, p. 41, no. 55; M. Chiarini, in Florence 1994, p. 156; Villis 2000, p. 81; E.P. Bowron, in Venice-Houston 2001, pp. 90, 92, no. 16; B.A. Kowalczyk, in Turin 2008, pp. 112, 114, no. 31; Kowalczyk 2012, pp. 24, 30; B.A. Kowalczyk, in Munich 2014-2015, p. 186.

CANALETTO
(Venice 1697-1768)

38 *The Roman Forum towards the Capitol with the Temple of Castor and Pollux, Rome*
ca. 1742
oil on canvas; 61.9 x 95.3 cm
The Royal Collection / HM Queen Elisabeth II,
RCIN 409047

Provenance: Collection of James Du Pre Alexander, 3rd Earl of Caledon (1812-1855), 5, Carlton House Terrace, London, 1854; with Agnew, London; James Henly Batty (1868-1946), London, 1946; his bequest to H.M. King George VI (1895-1952), 1946.

Selected Bibliography: Ashby, Constable 1925, pp. 208, 213; Watson 1954, p. 20; Constable 1962, vol. I, pl. 70; vol. II, pp. 359-360, no. 379; Levey 1964, p. 66, no. 418 and p. 55, no. 372 ('Studio of Canaletto'); Puppi 1968, no. 201A; Kozakiewicz 1972a, vol. II, p. 459, no. A 317 e p. 51; Corboz 1985, vol. II, no. P 313; Constable, Links 1989, vol. I, pl. 70; vol. II, p. 386, no. 379; Levey 1991, pp. 48-49, no. 418 ('Canaletto and Studio'); Links 1998, p. 38, no. 379; C. Beddington, in Venice-Houston 2001, pp. 96 and 98; B.A. Kowalczyk, in Turin 2008, pp. 124, 126.

CANALETTO
(Venice 1697-1768)

39 *The Temple of Antoninus and Faustina in the Roman Forum, Rome*
ca. 1742
oil on canvas; 61 x 95.3 cm
The Royal Collection / HM Queen Elisabeth II,
RCIN 409046

Inscriptions: on the temple architrave, 'DIVO. ANTONINO. ET. / DIVAE. FAUSTINAE. EX. S.C.'.

Provenance: collection of James Du Pre Alexander, 3rd Earl of Caledon (1812-1855), 5, Carlton House Terrace, London, 1854; with Agnew, London; James Henry Batty (1868-1946), London, 1946; his bequest to H.M. King George VI (1895-1952), 1946.

Selected Bibliography: Ashby, Constable 1925, pp. 208, 213; Watson 1954, p. 20; Constable 1962, vol. I, pl. 70; vol. II, p. 361, no. 381; Levey 1964, p. 66, no. 417 ('Studio of Canaletto'); Puppi 1968, no. 202 A; Kozakiewicz 1972a, vol. II, pp. 52, 460, no. A 322; Corboz 1985, vol. II, no. P 314; Constable, Links 1989, vol. I, pl. 70; vol. II, p. 388, no. 381; Levey 1991, p. 48, no. 417 ('Canaletto and Studio'); Links 1998, p. 38, no. 381; C. Beddington, in Venice-Houston 2001, pp. 96 and 98; B.A. Kowalczyk, in Turin 2008, pp. 124, 126, 128, illustrated in colour, p. 126, fig. 37.2.

BERNARDO BELLOTTO
(Venice 1722 - Warsaw 1780)

40 *The Roman Forum towards the Capitol with the Temple of Castor and Pollux, Rome*
1743
oil on canvas; 87 x 148 cm
Melbourne, National Gallery of Victoria, Felton Bequest, 964-3

Provenance: collection of Frederick Ponsonby, 6th Earl of Bessborough (1815-1895); his sale, Christie's, 14 March 1891, lot 149; purchased by Agnew, £126 and 10 shillings; Francis Pelham Clinton Hope, 8th Duke of Newcastle-under-Lyme (1866-1941); then sold at Christie's, 20 July 1917, lot 76, as 'B. Canaletto'; purchased by Pawsy and Paine, £210; A.H. Buttery, London; purchased by Robert Ross, advisor to the Felton Bequest, Melbourne, as 'a very brilliant example' of Canaletto, 1918; National Gallery of Victoria, Melbourne, 1948 ('Canaletto').

Selected Bibliography: Ashby, Constable 1925, p. 208; Constable 1962, vol. II, p. 360, no. 379-a; Levey 1964, p. 66; Puppi 1968, p. 107, no. 201B; Kozakiewicz 1972a, vol. II, pp. 51 (no. 69) and 460, no. A 318; Corboz 1985, vol. II, p. 652, no. P 315; Constable, Links 1989, vol. II, pp. 386-387, no. 379-a; Bowron 1994; Hoff 1995, p. 12; Links 1998, p. 38, no. 379-a; Villis 2000; C. Beddington, in Venice-Houston 2001, p. 96; B.A. Kowalczyk, in Venice-Houston 2001, pp. 118, 120, 136; B.A. Kowalczyk, in Rome 2005, pp. 188-189, no. 46; B.A. Kowalczyk, in Turin 2008, p. 130, no. 39; Villis 2008, pp. 23-35.

BERNARDO BELLOTTO
(Venice 1722 - Warsaw 1780)

41 *The Porta Santo Spirito looking North-West, Rome*
1743-44
oil on canvas; 98.5 x 75 cm
Private Collection, courtesy Pym's Gallery, London

Provenance: commissioned or purchased by a member of the King family, probably Thomas (1712-1779, 5th Lord King, Baron of Ockham, and by descent at Ockham Hall, Surrey, to William, 7th Lord King, raised in 1828 to Earl of Lovelace; Peter Malcolm, 4th Earl of Lovelace (1905-1964); Sotheby's, 13 July 1937, lot 82 ('Bellotto'); Manon, Countess of Lovelace; Christie's, London 10 December 1993, lot 60.

Selected Bibliography: Watson 1954, p. 17; Constable 1962, vol. II, p. 363; Kozakiewicz 1972a, vol. I, p. 40; vol. II, p. 52, no. 74; Camesasca 1974, p. 90, no. 30; Constable, Links 1989, vol. II, p. 392; Marini 1993, p. 131; Bowron 1994, p. 31; Links 1998, p. 38, no. 386-a; E.P. Bowron, in Venice-Houston 2001, pp. 104-105, no. 22; B.A. Kowalczyk, in Turin 2008, p. 144, no. 49.

BERNARDO BELLOTTO
(Venice 1722 - Warsaw 1780)

42 *The Arch of Titus, Rome*
1743-44
oil on canvas; 98.5 x 75 cm
Private Collection, courtesy Pym's Gallery, London

Inscriptions: on the pediment, 'SENATUS. / POPULUSQUE. ROMANUS. / DIVO. TITO. DIVI. VESPASIANI. F.[ILIO] / VESPASIANO. AUGUSTO.'.

Provenance: commissioned or purchased by a member of the King family, probably Thomas (1712-1779), 5th Lord King, Baron of Ockham, and by descent at Ockham Hall, Surrey, to William, VIII Lord King, raised in 1838 to Earl of Lovelace; Peter Malcolm King, 4th Earl of Lovelace (1905-1964); Sotheby's, 13 July 1937, lot 82 ('Bellotto'); Manon, Countess of Lovelace; Christie's, London, 10 December 1993, lot 60.

Selected Bibliography: Watson 1954, p. 17; Constable 1962, vol. II, p. 363, no. 386-a; Kozakiewicz 1972a, I, p. 40; II,

p. 52, no. 72; Camesasca 1974, p. 90, no. 27; Marini 1993, p. 131; Constable, Links 1989, vol. II, p. 392, no. 386-a; Levey 1991, p. 14; Bowron 1994, p. 31; Links 1998, p. 38, no. 386-a; E.P. Bowron, in Venice-Houston 2001, pp. 106-107, no. 23; B.A. Kowalczyk, in Turin 2008, p. 142, no. 48.

BERNARDO BELLOTTO
(Venice 1722 - Warsaw 1780)

43 *The Arch of Titus, Rome*
ca. 1744
oil on canvas; 38 x 28 cm
Bergamo, Accademia Carrara, 240, 58AC00149

Inscriptions: on the pediment, 'SENATUS POPULUSQUE ROMA[...] / DIVO TITO DIVI VESPASIANI F. / VESPASIANO AUGUSTO'.

Provenance: lawyer Giacomo Bettame de' Bazini, Bergamo; by inheritance to his son, Antonio Bettame (d. 1784); Earl Giacomo Carrara (1714-1796), 1784; Carrara bequest, 1796.

Selected Bibliography: Constable 1962, vol. II, p. 363, no. 386-b; Kozakiewicz 1972a, vol. II, p. 52, no. 73; Camesasca 1974, p. 90, no. 29; Constable, Links 1989, vol. II, p. 392, no. 386-b; Rossi 1989, p. 21, no. 78; G. Marini, in Verona 1990, p. 70, no. 10; Bowron 1994, p. 31; Kowalczyk 1993-1996, no. 50; E.P. Bowron, in Venice-Houston 2001, p. 106; D. Succi, in Conegliano 2011, pp. 33-34, 224, no. 3.

BERNARDO BELLOTTO
(Venice 1722 - Warsaw 1780)

44 *Santa Maria d'Aracoeli and the Capitol, Rome*
1742-43
pencil freehand and ruled with pinpointing; the central part finished in pen in dark-brown ink, applied freehand
310 x 538 mm
Warsaw, Muzeum Narodowe, Rys. Pol. 2040

Inscriptions: words 'più chiaro' (lighter) added repeatedly over the facade of Santa Maria d'Aracoeli; numbers and text in pencil on the stairs leading to the church ('quinte di 8', 'da 8 quindeci'; 'da 4..'...).

Watermark: a fragment, 'IV'.

Provenance: Bernardo Bellotto in Warsaw and heirs in Warsaw until 1798, then in Vilnius, where, probably between 1822 and 1828, it is purchased by Earl Konstanty Tyszkiewicz (1806-1868), Łohojsk, Belarus, with a group of artist's drawings; the Tyszkiewicz family donates the collection to the Association for the Protection of Monuments of Warsaw, before 1914; purchased by Muzeum Narodowe, 1930.

Selected Bibliography: Starzyński 1933-1934, p. 103-104; Fritzsche 1936, p. 136, no. VZ 102; Kozakiewicz 1972a, vol. II, pp. 55-56, no. 78; Kowalczyk 1987-1988, pp. II-292-296, no. 60; Constable, Links 1989, vol. II, p. 399; Marini 1991, p. 150; E.P. Bowron, in Venice-Houston 2001, p. 100; B.A. Kowalczyk, in Venice-Houston 2001, p. 136; K. Załęski, in Vienna 2005, p. 218, no. 54; B.A. Kowalczyk, in Munich 2014-2015, p. 198, no. 24.

BERNARDO BELLOTTO
(Venice 1722 - Warsaw 1780)

45 *Capriccio with the Capitol*
1746
oil on canvas, 117 x 132 cm
Parma, Galleria Nazionale, 237

Provenance: Earl Stefano II Sanvitale (1764-1838); purchased by the Gallery in 1835.

Selected Bibliography: Kozakiewicz 1972a, vol. I, pp. 38-39; vol. II, pp. 56 and 94-96, no. 129; Camesasca 1974, p. 94, no. 60; G. Marini, in Verona 1990, pp. 138-140; B.A. Kowalczyk, in Venice 1995, pp. 301, 308; R. Cattani, in *Galleria Nazionale di Parma* 2000, pp. 60-62, no. 671; B.A. Kowalczyk, in Venice-Houston 2001, pp. 136, 138; B.A. Kowalczyk, in Turin 2008, pp. 144, 146; B.A. Kowalczyk, in Munich 2014-2015, p. 198.

BERNARDO BELLOTTO
(Venice 1722 - Warsaw 1780)

46 *Capriccio with the Coliseum*
1746
oil on canvas; 134 x 119 cm
Parma, Galleria Nazionale, 238

Provenance: Earl Stefano II Sanvitale (1764-1838); acquired by the Gallery in 1835.

Selected Bibliography: Kozakiewicz 1972a, vol. I, p. 38, 45; vol. II, pp. 94-96, no. 126; Camesasca 1974, p. 94, no. 58; G. Marini, in Verona 1990, pp. 138, 140; B.A. Kowalczyk, in Venice 1995, pp. 301, 308; R. Cattani, in *Galleria Nazionale di Parma* 2000, pp. 66-67, no. 672; B.A. Kowalczyk, in Venice-Houston 2001, pp. 136, 138, no. 35; D. Rodríguez, in Madrid 2011-2012, pp. 359-360, no. 120; A. Gottdang, in Munich 2014-2015, p. 224, no. 37.

BERNARDO BELLOTTO
(Venice 1722 - Warsaw 1780)

47 *The Piazza San Giovanni in Laterano, Rome*
1743-44
oil on canvas; 63.5 x 98.5 cm
Private Collection, courtesy Robilant+Voena, London

Provenance: purchased by a member of the King family, Ockham Park near Guildford, Surrey, in the eighteen century; by descent, to William, 8th Lord King, raised in 1838 to Earl of Lovelace; Peter Malcolm King, 4th Earl of Lovelace (1905-1964); his sale, Sotheby's, 13 July 1937, lot 128 ('Canaletto'); purchased by Dudley Tooth; Arthur Tooth & Sons Ltd., London, from whom purchased in July 1942 by Mr (later Sir) Clifford Curzon, London; his sale, Christie's London, 10 December 1982, lot 81; Richard Green, from whom purchased by a European collector; sale, Sotheby's London, 7 July 2005, lot 51; Voena+Robilant /Fabrizio Moretti, from whom purchased by the current owner.

Selected Bibliography: Parker 1948, pp. 51-52 ('Canaletto'); Watson 1950, p. 292, note 11; Watson 1955, p. 262 ('Bellotto'); Constable 1962, vol. I, pl. 73; vol. II, pp. 371, 515 and 522, no. 400 ('Canaletto'); Puppi 1968, p. 109, no. 211 ('Canaletto'), ill. p. 108 ('Canaletto'); Kozakiewicz 1972a, vol. II, p. 470, no. A 347 ('Canaletto'); Links 1981, no. 181; Corboz 1985, vol. II, p. 653, no. P 319; Constable 1989, vol. I, pl. 73; vol. II, pp. 400-401, 562 e 568, no. 400; Kowalczyk 1993-1996, no. 56 ('Bellotto'); Links 1998, p. 39, no. 400 ('Canaletto)"; C. Beddington, in Venice 2001, p. 23; H. Chapman, in Venice 2001, p. 60; no. 12 ('Bellotto'); C. Beddington, in Venice-Houston 2001, pp. 112-115, no. 26; B.A. Kowalczyk, Venice-Houston 2001, p. 136; Beddington 2004, pp. 665 e 673; B.A. Kowalczyk, in Turin 2008, p. 136.

BERNARDO BELLOTTO
(Venice 1722 - Warsaw 1780)

48 *The Piazza San Giovanni in Laterano, Rome*
1743
pen and dark grey ink with grey wash over pencil, free and ruled pencil and pinpointing; first outlined in pencil and ruler, then reinforced in pen;
199 x 284 mm
The Royal Collection / HM Queen Elizabeth II, RCIN 907517

Provenance: commissioned from the artist by Joseph Smith (ca. 1674-1770); Palazzo Balbi (now Mangilli-Valmarana), Venice; purchased from Smith by King George III in 1762, in the *Experimenta et Schedae (Volume di Dissegni di Antonio Canale…)* album.

Selected Bibliography: Ashby, Constable 1925, p. 293; Hadeln 1929, p. 26; Parker 1948, pp. 51-52, no. 109; Constable 1962, vol. II, p. 568, no. 727; Constable, Links 1989, vol. I, pl. 134, vol. II, no. 727; C. Beddington, in Venice 2001, p. 47; H. Chapman, in Venice 2001, p. 60; C. Beddi ngton, in Venice-Houston 2001, p. 112; B.A. Kowalczyk, in Turin 2008, pp. 136-137, no. 42.

BERNARDO BELLOTTO
(Venice 1722 - Warsaw 1780)

49 *The Piazza Navona looking North, Rome*
1743
oil on canvas; 88 x 149 cm
Private Collection

Provenance: Jules Porgès (1839-1921), Avenue Montaigne, Paris; Brown, Boveri & Cie, Baden, Baden, 1955; Sotheby's, London, 2 July 1986, lot 123; purchased by the current owner from Christie's, Munich, 22 June 1991, lot 140.

Selected Bibliography: Constable 1962, II, p. 372, no. 401-d; Kozakiewicz 1972a, vol. I, p. 38; vol. II, p. 56, no. 79; Camesasca 1974, p. 90, no. 31; M. Natale, in Pfäffikon-Ginevra 1978, no. 166; Constable, Links 1989, vol. II, p. 401, no. 401-d; Bowron 1994, p. 30.

6. BELLOTTO: BOLD PERSPECTIVES

BERNARDO BELLOTTO
(Venice 1722 - Warsaw 1780)

50 *San Paolo Converso and Sant'Eufemia, Milan*
1744
oil on canvas; 61 x 97 cm
Private Collection

Provenance: Archibishop of Milan, Giuseppe Pozzobonelli (1696-1783); Palazzo Arcivescovile, Milan, 1802; Christie's, 30 November 1971, lot 100; 1.

Provenance: Archbishop of Milan, Giuseppe Pozzobonelli (1696-1783); Palazzo Arcivescovile, Milan, 1802; Christie's, 30 November 1971, lot 100; Pietro Barilla collection, Parma; Marco Voena, Milan, late nineties of the twentieth century; from whom it was sold to the current owner, 2002.

Selected Bibliography: M. Natale, in Pfäffikon-Ginevra 1978, p. 187, no. 167; M. Olivari, in Verona 1990, p. 84; Bona Castellotti 1991, p. 103, note 53; Marinelli 1993, p. 84; M. Olivari, in Milan 1999-2000, p. 217, no. 1; A. Morandotti, in Milan 1999-2000, pp. 40-41; B.A. Kowalczyk, in Turin 2008, p. 158, no. 57.

BERNARDO BELLOTTO
(Venice 1722 - Warsaw 1780)

51 *The Castello Sforzesco, Milan*
1744
oil on canvas; 61 x 97.5 cm
Castle Náměšť nad Oslavou (Czech Republic), The National Heritage Institute,
Regional Historic Sites Management in České Budějovice

Provenance: collection of the Counts Haugwitz, Plaveč Castle, Slovakia.

Selected Bibliography: Kozakiewicz 1972a, vol. II, pp. 56, 59, no. 82; Camesasca 1974, p. 93, no. 47; M. Natale, in Pfäffikon-Geneva 1978, p. 167; S. Marinelli, in Verona 1990, pp. 41-42; M. Olivari, in Verona 1990, p. 84, no. 16; *The Art Newspaper*, September 1996, p. 1; A. Morandotti, in Milan 1999-2000, pp. 40-41; M. Olivari, in Milan 1999-2000, pp. 218-219, no. 4; B.A. Kowalczyk, in Turin 2008, p. 156, no. 56.

BERNARDO BELLOTTO
(Venice 1722 - Warsaw 1780)

52 *The Palazzo dei Giureconsulti and the Broletto Nuovo, Milan*
1744
oil on canvas; 71 x 56 cm
Milan, Raccolte d'Arte Antica, Pinacoteca del Castello Sforzesco, 1506

Provenance: Thomas Hollis (1720-1774), Corscombe, Dorset; by whom donated with all his property to his friend Thomas Brand (1719-1804), The Hyde, near Ingatestone, Essex; by whom donated with all his property to Reverend John Disney (1756-1816), The Hyde, near Ingatestone, Essex; where it remained, by descent, to his son John Disney (1779-1857) and grand-son, Edgar Disney (d. 1881); sale, Christie's, London, 3 May 1884, lot 134; purchased by Mervyn Edward Wingfield, Viscount Powerscourt (1836-1904), Powerscourt Estate, Enniskerry, County Wicklow, sale, Christie's, London, 23 April 1887; purchased by Martin Colnaghi (1821-1908), who sold it to Sir Stephenson Clarke; by descendants, Clarke Estate; Matthiesen Fine Art Ltd., 1991; purchased by the Museum in 1998.

Selected Bibliography: Succi 1991, pp. 50-57; Marinelli 1993, p. 84; D. Succi, in Padua 1994, p. 58, no. 88; Kowalczyk 1993-1996, no. 64; M. Olivari, in Milano 1999-2000, p. 219, no. 5; F. Magani, in *Castello Sforzesco. Pinacoteca* 2000, pp. 44-47; B.A. Kowalczyk, in Turin 2008, p. 160, no. 58.

BERNARDO BELLOTTO
(Venice 1722 - Warsaw 1780)

53 *The Old Bridge over the Po River, Turin*
1745
oil on canvas; 128.5 x 173 cm
Turin, Galleria Sabauda, 469

Provenance: commissioned with its pendant by Charles Emmanuel III, King of Sardinia (1701-1773) (a payment of 975 liras is noted in the accounts of the Real Cassa with the date of 21 June 1745); mentioned for the first time in the catalogue of *La Galleria di S.M. il re di Sardegna* (1822), with its pendant (nos. 26-27).

Selected Bibliography: De Vesme 1906, pp. 161-162; Fritzsche 1936, pp. 27, 106, no. VG 25; Kozakiewicz 1972a, vol. I, pp. 43-44; vol. II, pp. 66, 73, 475, no. 93; Camesasca 1974, no. 56; C. Mossetti, G. Romano, in Verona 1990, pp. 98-101, no. 23; B.A. Kowalczyk Trupiano, in Venice 1995, p. 312, no. 77; E.P. Bowron, in Venice-Houston 2001, pp. 132, 134, no. 34; D. Magnetti, in Turin 2008, pp. 45-53; C. Mossetti, G. Romano, in Turin 2008, p. 172, no. 64.

BERNARDO BELLOTTO
(Venice 1722 - Warsaw 1780)

54 *Castelvecchio and the Ponte Scaligero, Verona*
1745
oil on canvas; 84.5 x 137.5 cm
Verona, Fondazione Cassa di Risparmio di Verona Vicenza Belluno e Ancona, Collezione della Fondazione Cariverona

Provenance: Prince Alexis Orloff; his posthumous sale, Galerie Georges Petit, Paris, 29 April 1920, lot 7; purchased by Margossian; bought by a private French collector shortly afterwards; sold by his children, Christie's, London, 7 July 2000, lot 84; purchased by the current owner.

Selected Bibliography: Kozakiewicz 1972a, vol. I, p. 44; vol. II, pp. 73-74, no. 94; Camesasca 1974, p. 95, no. 64; M. Bleyl, in Darmstadt 1981, p. 61, no. 49; P. Brownell, in Verona 1990, pp. 116-118, no. 32; P. Marini, C. Beddington, in Venice-Houston 2001, p. 140, no. 36; B.A. Kowalczyk, in Verona-Vicenza 2013-2014, p. 415, no. 32.

7. LANDSCAPE

BERNARDO BELLOTTO
(Venice 1722 - Warsaw 1780)

55 *Vaprio and Canonica on the Adda, looking North-West, Lombardy*
1744
oil on canvas; 4.1 x 99.7 cm
New York, The Metropolitan Museum, Joseph Pulitzer Bequest, 1939, 39.142

Provenance: Commissioned by conte Antonio Simonetta (d. 1759), Milan, 1744; by descent to his wife Teresa Castelbarco (d. 1786); and to his daughter Francesca Simonetta (1731-1796) who in 1749 married Cesare Ercole Castelbarco (1730-1755); Castelbarco family, Milan; the Quintavalle family, Milan, until the early decades of the twentieth century (according to Giulio Melzi d'Eril's claim in a letter to the Museum dated 17 April 1973); Marquis Guiscardo Zaccaria, son of Carolina Melzi d'Eril and of Giuseppe Zaccaria (who sold it to Heimann); Jacob M. Heimann, New York, around 1935-1939.

Selected Bibliography: P. Zampetti, in Venice 1967, pp. 198-199; Kozakiewicz 1972a, vol. I, p. 42; vol. II, pp. 59-60, no. 83 (with erroneous provenance); M. Olivari, in Verona 1990, pp. 76, 78, no. 13; Marinelli 1993, p. 84; B.A. Kowalczyk Trupiano, in Venice 1995, pp. 301 e 310, no. 76; M. Olivari, in Milan 1999-2000, p. 50, pp. 217-218, no. 2; B.A. Kowalczyk, in Turin 2008, pp. 156, 162-163, 166, 168, no. 59; Marciari 2015, p. 189, note 1.

BERNARDO BELLOTTO
(Venice 1722 - Warsaw 1780)

56 *Vaprio and Canonica on the Adda, looking South, Lombardy*
1744
Oil on canvas; 64 x 99 cm
Naples, Museo di Capodimonte, Q 1829

Provenance: commissioned by Earl Antonio Simonetta (d. 1759), Monasterolo and Milan, 1744; by descent to his wife, Teresa Castelbarco (d. 1786); and to his daughter Francesca Simonetta (1731-1796) who in 1749 married Cesare Ercole Castelbarco (1730-1755); L. Bloch, Vienna; his sale, F. Muller & Cie, Amsterdam, 14 November 1905, lot 6; Mario Crespi, Milan; Bianca de Feo Leonardi and Antonino Leonardi, Rome; donated to the Museum, 2004.

Selected Bibliography: Kozakiewicz 1972a, vol. I, p. 42; vol. II, pp. 60, 65, no. 86; Camesasca 1974, p. 93, no. 49; M. Olivari, in Verona 1990, pp. 78, 80, 82; M. Olivari, in Milan 1999-2000, p. 218, no. 3; B.A. Kowalczyk, in Turin 2008, p. 162; B.A. Kowalczyk, in Munich 2014-2015, p. 208.

BERNARDO BELLOTTO
(Venice 1722 - Warsaw 1780)

57 *Vaprio and Canonica on the Adda, looking North-West, Lombardy*
ca. 1744
oil on canvas; 47 x 71 cm
Private Collection

Provenance: Dukes of Abercorn, Baron's Court, Northern Ireland; Christie's auction, London, 13 December 1991, lot 100; Richard Green, London, from whom by the current owner.

Selected Bibliography: Kozakiewicz 1972a, vol. I, p. 42, II, p. 60, no. 85; Camesasca 1974, no. 50; Martini 1982, p. 539, note 292; A. Bettagno, in Verona 1990, p. 16; M. Olivari, in Verona 1990, pp. 78, 80 and 82; B.A. Kowalczyk, in Venice 1995, p. 310; Pallucchini 1996, p. 502; Briganti 1996, p. 253; M. Olivari, in Milan 1999-2000, pp. 220-221, no. 7a; C. Beddington, in Venice-Houston 2001, pp. 124, 126, no. 30; B.A. Kowalczyk, in Turin 2008, pp. 166 and 168, no. 61; B.A. Kowalczyk, in Munich 2014-2015, pp. 202, 204 and 206, n. 26.

BERNARDO BELLOTTO
(Venice 1722 - Warsaw 1780)

58 *Vaprio and Canonica on the Adda, looking North-West, Lombardy*
1744
pen and brown ink over pencil line, free and ruled pencil, marked with a compass, thick white paper; the drawing is outlined in pen with a ruler;
the horizon line is marked at 12.3 cm from the outline; divided into four equal parts with four thin vertical lines in pencil and with a ruler; 337 x 502 mm
Warsaw, Muzeum Narodowe, Rys. Pol. 2039

Inscriptions: written between the outline and the edge of the sheet, to the left, in pencil, 'quadro si trova a Dresda'; in the centre, in pen and ink, 'Copia dela Vista di Vaver Fatta dal S. (?) Bernardo Bellotto de:o il Canaletto'; on the facade of the building on the left, in pen and brown ink: 'depento'; in the background on the right, at the foot of the mountains, in pen with the same ink: 'bergamo'.

Watermark: trefoil dominating a sphere containing three balls.

Provenance: Bernardo Bellotto in Warsaw and the artist's heirs in Warsaw until 1798, then Vilnius, where it was acquired by Count Konstanty Tyszkiewicz (1806-1868), Łohojsk, Belarus, probably between 1822 and 1828; the Tyszkiewicz family, until the early twentieth century; collection of the architect Andrea Boni (1894-1962), Warsaw; acquired by the National Museum in Warsaw, 1939.

Selected Bibliography: Kozakiewicz 1972a, II, p. 60, no. 86; M. Bleyl, in Darmstadt 1981, p. 60; Martini 1982, p. 539; Kowalczyk 1987-1988, pp. II-315-316, no. 65; B.A. Kowalczyk Trupiano, in Venice 1995, p. 310; M. Olivari, in Milan 1999-2000, p. 220; C. Beddington, in Venice-Houston 2001, p. 124; K. Załęski, in Vienna 2005, pp. 218-219, no. 55; D. Folga, in Turin 2008, pp. 40-41; B.A. Kowalczyk, in Turin 2008, no. 60; B.A. Kowalczyk, in Munich 2014-2015, pp. 202, 206-207, no. 28.

BERNARDO BELLOTTO
(Venice 1722 - Warsaw 1780)

59 *Vaprio and Canonica on the Adda, looking South, Lombardy*
1744
oil on canvas; 47 x 71 cm
Private Collection

Provenance: Dukes of Abercorn, Baron's Court, Northern Ireland; Christie's auction, London, 13 December 1991, lot 100; Richard Green, London, from whom acquired by the current owner.

Selected Bibliography: Kozakiewicz 1972a, I, p. 42; vol. II, p. 65, no. 88; Camesasca 1974, p. 93, no. 50; Martini 1982, p. 539, note 292; A. Bettagno, in Verona 1990, p. 16; M. Olivari, in Verona 1990, pp. 76, 78, 80 and 82; B.A. Kowalczyk, in Venice 1995, p. 310; Briganti 1996, p. 253; Pallucchini 1996, p. 502; M. Olivari, in Milan 1999-2000, pp. 220-201, no. 7b; C. Beddington, in Venice-Houston 2001, p. 124, no. 29; B.A. Kowalczyk, in Turin 2008, pp. 164, 166, 168, no. 62; B.A. Kowalczyk, in Munich 2014-2015, pp. 202, 204-205, 206, no. 27.

BERNARDO BELLOTTO
(Venice 1722 - Warsaw 1780)

60 *Villa Perabò, Gazzada, Lombardy*
1744
oil on canvas; 65 x 100 cm
Milan, Pinacoteca di Brera, 235

Provenance: acquired from the antiquarian and painter Alessandro Brison, for 1,000 Austrian on 11 March 1831.

Selected Bibliography: Fritzsche 1936, pp. 27, 106, no. VG 20; Kozakiewicz 1972a, vol. I, pp. 42-43; vol. II, pp. 65-66, no. 91; Camesasca 1974, p. 93, no. 52; M. Olivari, in *Pinacoteca di Brera* 1990, pp. 63-65, no. 27; M. Olivari, in Verona 1990, pp. 86-89, no. 18; Kowalczyk 1999, pp. 196-198; M. Olivari, in Milan 1999-2000, pp. 219-220, no. 6a; E.P. Bowron, in Venice-Houston 2001, pp. 128; G. Gruber, in Vienna 2005, p. 77, no. 5; B.A. Kowalczyk, in Turin 2008, p. 170, no. 63; T. Wagener, in Munich 2014-2015, p. 200, no. 25.

BERNARDO BELLOTTO
(Venice 1722 - Warsaw 1780)

61 *The Village of Gazzada, Lombardy*
1744
oil on canvas; 65 x 100 cm
Milan, Pinacoteca di Brera, 236

Provenance: acquired from the antiquarian and painter Alessandro Brison, for 1,000 Austrian on 11 March 1831.

Selected Bibliography: Fritzsche 1936, pp. 27, 106, no. VG 20; Kozakiewicz 1972a, vol. I, pp. 42-43; vol. II, pp. 65-66, no. 90; Camesasca 1974, p. 93, no. 53; M. Olivari, in *Pinacoteca di Brera* 1990, pp. 65-67, no. 28; M. Olivari, in Verona 1990, pp. 86-89, no. 17; Kowalczyk 1999, pp. 196-198; M. Olivari, in Milan 1999-2000, pp. 219-220, no. 6b; E.P. Bowron, in Venice-Houston 2001, p. 128, no. 31; B.A. Kowalczyk, in Turin 2008, p. 170.

BERNARDO BELLOTTO
(Venice 1722 - Warsaw 1780)

62 *Pirna from the Boatmen's Village*
1753-1755
oil on canvas; 36 x 237 cm
Dresden, Staatliche Kunstsammlungen, Gemäldegalerie Alte Meister, 626

Provenance: commissioned by Augustus III, King of Poland and Elector of Saxony with the name of Frederick Augustus II (1696-1763); probably completed by the artist before 1756; catalogued for the first time by Matthäi in 1834, no. 55.

Selected Bibliography: Fritzsche 1936, pp. 54, 112, 173, no. VG 82; Kozakiewicz 1972a, vol. I, pp. 84, 100-102; vol. II, p. 173, no. 217; Camesasca 1974, p. 103, no. 135; A. Walther, in Venice 1986, p. 91, no. 19; Rizzi 1996, p. 76, no. 54; Schmidt 2000, pp. 86-93; G.J.M. Weber, in Venice-Houston 2001, p. 186, no. 58.

BERNARDO BELLOTTO
(Venice 1722 - Warsaw 1780)

63 *Pirna from the Sonnenstein Fortress*
1753-1755
oil on canvas; 133 x 234 cm
Dresden, Staatliche Kunstsammlungen, Gemäldegalerie Alte Meister, 625

Provenance: Commissioned by Augustus III, King of Poland, Elector of Saxony with the name of Frederick Augustus II (1696-1763); probably completed by the artist before 1756; catalogued for the first time by Matthäi in 1834, no. 52.

Selected Bibliography: Fritzsche 1936, pp. 54, 112, no. VG 83; Kozakiewicz 1972a, vol. I, pp. 84, 100-102; vol. II, p. 179, no. 225; Camesasca 1974, p. 103, no. 130; A. Walther, in Venice 1982, pp. 95-96, no. 24; Rizzi 1996, p. 82, no. 65; Schmidt 2000, pp. 134-141; G.J.M. Weber, in Venice-Houston 2001, p. 190, no. 60; A. Schumacher, in Munich 2014-2015, p. 240, no. 46.

BERNARDO BELLOTTO
(Venice 1722 - Warsaw 1780)

64 *Pirna from the Right Bank of the Elbe near Kopitz 1753-1755*
oil on canvas; 133 x 237.5 cm
San Petersburg, The State Hermitage Museum, GE 208

Provenance: commissioned by Heinrich, Earl von Brühl (1700-1763); purchased from his heirs by Catherine the Great (1729-1796), 1768; exhibited at the new Hermitage (mentioned for the first time in 1773 in the *Handwritten Inventory* of the Museum, inv. no. 515); transferred by Tsar Alexander I (1777-1825) to the Tauride Palace in Saint Petersburg, 1820-1825; moved again, this time by Tsar Alexander II (1818-1881) to the Gatchina Palace, near the capital, 1858-1859; returned to the Hermitage, 1923.

Selected Bibliography: Stählin, *Notes* 1990, vol. I, p. 374; vol. II, p. 111; Muňich 1773-1783, pp. 163-164, no. 515; Kozakiewicz 1972a, vol. I, pp. 85, 100-102; vol. II, p. 161, no. 197; Camesasca 1974, p. 101, no. 116; Rizzi 1996, p. 68, no. 42.

BERNARDO BELLOTTO
(Venice 1722 - Warsaw 1780)

65 *Wilanòw Palace from the Garden, Warsaw*
1777
oil on canvas; 117 x 164 cm
Warsaw, Royal Castle, Museum, ZKW / 460

Provenance: commissioned by King Stanisław II August Poniatowski (1732-1798) for his private collection in Warsaw; installed in 1777 in the antechamber of the Senate of the Royal Castle in Warsaw ('Canaletto room'), where it remained until 1807; by descent, the king's nephew, Prince Józef Poniatowski, 1798; sold with the majority of Bellotto's pictures from the 'Canaletto room', to Frederick Augustus, King of Saxonia and Grand Prince of Warsaw; sent by Tsar Nicholas I to Russia, as retaliation for the insurrection of Warsaw of 1830-1831 and placed in the Tauride Palace, Saint Petersburg (together with fifteen views of Dresden and Pirna, purchased by the Tsarina Catherine II from the heirs of Earl Brühl); moved by Alexander II to the Gatchina Palace, close to the capital, 1858-1859; preserved in the Hermitage, Saint Petersburg, during the First World War; returned to the Royal Castle with the Peace of Riga, 1922; transferred to the Muzeum Narodowe in September 1939; confiscated by the German government and sent to Germany, 1939-1945; returned in 1945 and preserved in the Muzeum Narodowe until 1984, when it was returned to the rebuilt Royal Castle.

Selected Bibliography: Mańkowski 1932, p. 262, no. 433; Fritzsche 1936, pp. 89, 119-120, VG 153; Kozakiewicz 1972a, vol. I, pp. 170-171; vol. II, p. 373-374, no. 427; Camesasca 1974, p. 115, no. 238; Rizzi 1990, p. 80, no. 25; B.A. Kowalczyk, in Munich 2014-2015, p. 93; T. Wagner, in Munich 2014-2015, p. 280.

CANALETTO
(Venice 1697-1768)

66 *Eton College*
ca. 1754
oil on canvas; 61.6 x 107.7 cm
London, The National Gallery, Wynn Ellis Bequest, NG 942

Provenance: Sir John Tobin; Griffiths sale, Liverpool, 22 March 1860, lot 33; Wynn Ellis (1790-1875), of Ponsbourne Park, near Hatfield, Hertfordshire, Tankerton Castle, Whitstable, Kent, and 30 Cadogan Place, London; bequeathed to the National Gallery, together with another 93 paintings, 1876.

Selected Bibliography: Finberg 1921, pp. 29 e 56, pl. XIV (b); Constable 1962, vol. I, pp. 36 e 145, pl. 84; vol. II, pp. 400-401, no. 450; Puppi 1968, p. 117, no. 313; Corboz 1985, vol. I, pp. 74-75, 127, 267 e 294, fig. 59 (particolare); vol. II, p. 725, no. P 435; Constable, Links 1989, vol. I, pp. LXIV, 36 e 145, pl. 84; vol. II, pp. 431-432, no. 450; Levey 1991, pp. 27-29, no. 942; Links 1998, p. 211, pl. 187; C. Beddington, in New Haven-London 2006-2007, pp. 136-137, no. 40.

8. CANALETTO IN LONDON, BELLOTTO IN DRESDEN

CANALETTO
(Venice 1697-1768)

67 *Northumberland House, London*
1752-53
oil on canvas; 84 × 137 cm
Alnwick Castle, The Duke of Northumberland Collection, 03327

Provenance: commissioned in 1752 by Sir Hugh Smithson (1714-1786), Earl of Northumberland, then 1st Duke of Northumberland, and kept in the family collection.

Selected Bibliography: Finberg 1921, pp. 40 and 59-60; Constable 1962, vol. I, pl. 76; vol. II, pp. 382-383, no. 419; Puppi 1968, p. 116, no. 297; Corboz 1985, vol. II, p. 723, no. P 427; Constable, Links 1989, vol. I, pl. 76; vol. II, pp. 411-412, no. 419; K. Baetjer, J.G. Links, in New York 1989-1990, p. 258, no. 70; C. Beddington, in New Haven-London 2006-2007, p. 79.

BERNARDO BELLOTTO
(Venice 1722 - Warsaw 1780)

68 *The Neumarkt from the Jüdenhof, Dresden*
1749-1752
oil on canvas; 134.5 x 236.5 cm
San Petersburg, The State Hermitage Museum, GE 203

Provenance: commissioned by Heinrich, Earl von Brühl (1700-1763); purchased from his heirs by Catherine the Great (1729-1796), 1768; exhibited at the new Hermitage (mentioned for the first time in 1773 in the *Handwritten Inventory* of the Museum, inv. no. 462); transferred by Tsar Alexander I (1777-1825) to the Tauride Palace in Saint Petersburg, 1820-1825; moved again, this time by Tsar Alexander II (1818-1881) to the Gatchina Palace, near the capital, 1858-1859; returned to the Hermitage, 1923.

Selected Bibliography: Stählin, *Notes* 1990, vol. I, p. 374; vol. II, p. 111; Muňich 1773-1783, no. 462; Kozakiewicz 1972a, vol. I, pp. 85, 100-110; vol. II, , p. 132, no. 168; Walther 1995, pp. 42-43, Rizzi 1996, p. 50, no. 23; I. Artemieva, in Venice-Houston 2001, p. 164, no. 47; J.G.M. Weber, in Venice-Houston 2001, p. 162; A. Henning, in Dresden 2011, p. 110, no. 7; A. Schumacher, in Munich 2014-2015, pp. 232, 234, no. 41.

BERNARDO BELLOTTO
(Venice 1722 - Warsaw 1780)

69 *Dresden from the Left Bank of the Elbe, below the Fortifications*
1748
oil on canvas; 133 x 235 cm
signed at the bottom, slightly to the left 'BERNARD.° BELOTO DETTO / CANALETO. F. AN.° 1748'
Dresden, Staatliche Kunstsammlungen, Gemäldegalerie Alte Meister, 608

Provenance: supplied by the artist, it is assumed in 1748, to the court of the Prince Elector Frederick Augustus II of Saxony. Between 1748 and 1749 it was included (no. 4007) in the so-called 'lost inventory of the year 1747 and following' of the Royal Gallery in Dresden. From 1754 in the inventory of the Royal Gallery in Dresden (no. 535).

Selected Bibliography: Kozakiewicz 1972b, vol. II, p. 121 seg., no. 151; Camesasca 1974, p. 97, no. 81; Löffler 1985, pp. 16 ss., figs. 16-20; Walther 1995, pp. 48 ss., no. 13; Rizzi 1996, p. 38 s., no. 11; G.J.M. Weber, in Venice-Houston 2001, p. 154 s., no. 42; Weber 2003, p. 60, fig. 7; A. Henning, in Versailles 2006, p. 146, no. 5; S. Oesinghaus, in Dresden 2011, p. 106, no. 3.

BERNARDO BELLOTTO
(Venice 1722 - Warsaw 1780)

70 *Dresden from the left Bank of the Elbe, the Palace on the left, the Hofkirche Straight Ahead*
1748
etching; I state of two; 544 x 837 mm
signed on the bottom left, inside the image, 'CANALETO. F.'
Milan, Civica Raccolta delle Stampe 'Achille Bertarelli', vol. FF 25, pl. 3.

Inscriptions: on lower margin, 'Perspective de la Façade de la Roïale -- Eglise Catolique, avec une part du Palais / de S.M. et des Environs de Neudorff sur l'Elbe, tirée -- du Jardin de S.E.ce Mgr. Le Comte de Brühl Le Pre.r Ministre. / Ce Tableau fait par ordre de S.M. le Roy de Pologne et Elec. De Sax. &.&.&. -- Peint, dessiné, et gravé par Bernard Belloto dit Canaletto. 1748'.

Provenance: acquired by the Comune di Milano as part of the collection of Prince Luigi Alberico Trivulzio (1868-1938), 1935.

Selected Bibliography: Stübel 1911, no. 11; Fritzsche 1936, p. 144, no. VR 11; Kozakiewicz 1972a, vol. II, p. 122, no. 153; Rizzi 1996, p. 199, n. I-3; D. Succi, in Conegliano 2001, p. 229, no. 40; G. Metze, in Dresden 2001, p. 121, no. 19.

BERNARDO BELLOTTO
(Venice 1722 - Warsaw 1780)

71 *Dresden from the Left Bank of the Elbe, the Palace on the Left, the Catholic Hofkirche Streight Ahead*
1748
oil on canvas; 134 x 231 cm
signed lower left, 'BERNARDO BELOTTO DE.o / CANALETO F A.o 1748'
Pinacoteca Giovanni e Marella Agnelli, Turin

Provenance: commissioned by Earl Heinrich Brühl (1700-1763), prime minister of Saxony and Poland; probably placed in his gallery in Dresden until circa 1748; Brühl bequest, Dresden, 1763; Charles Henry Mills, 1st Baron Hillingdon (1830-1898), Hillingdon Court, Uxbridge, England, around 1894; Arthur Robert Mills, 3rd Baron Hillingdon (1891-1952); his sale, Christie's, London, 3 May 1946, lot 42; purchased by Agnew, London; Sir Alexander Korda (1893-1956), London, 1953-1954; Gianni and Marella Agnelli collection, Turin and New York, 1955; Pinacoteca Agnelli, Turin, 2001.

Selected Bibliography: Kozakiewicz 1972a, vol. I, pp. 85-86, 91, 102, 107; vol. II, p. 122, no. 152; Camesasca 1974, p. 98, no. 82; Rizzi 1996, p. 38, no. 12; G.J.M. Weber, in Venice-Houston 2001, p. 154; Pedrocco 2002, p. 48.

BERNARDO BELLOTTO
(Venice 1722 - Warsaw 1780)

72 *Dresden from the Left Bank of the Elbe, below the Fortifications*
1748
oil on canvas; 133 x 234 cm
signed lower left on the stone block, 'Bernardo Bellotto detto Canaletto F.An.° 1748'
Dresden, Staatliche Kunstsammlungen, Gemäldegalerie Alte Meister, 607

Provenance: commissioned by Augustus III, King of Poland and Prince Elector of Saxony with the name of Frederick Augustus II (1696-1763); put in 1748-49 as no. 4006 of the so-called 'lost inventory year 1747 and following' the Royal Picture Gallery; since 1754 in the inventory of Royal Picture Gallery of Dresden, mentioned as 'Prospect of the new town of Dresden, taken from the reserve. 4.8.8.4' (Oesterreich 1754).

Selected Bibliography: Fritzsche 1936, pp. 53, 109, no. VG 54; Kozakiewicz 1972a, vol. I, pp. 84, 86, 100-102; vol. II, pp. 122, 127, no. 154; Camesasca 1974, p. 97, no. 79; A. Walther, in Venice 1986, pp. 71-72, no. 2; Rizzi 1996, p. 40, no. 13; G.J.M. Weber, in Bilbao 1998, p. 40, no. 2; G.J.M. Weber, in Venice-Houston 2001, p. 156, no. 43; G.J.M. Weber, in Udine 2004, pp. 86-100; S. Oesinghaus, in Dresden 2011, p. 107, no. 4; A. Schumacher, in Munich 2014-2015, p. 230, no. 40.

BERNARDO BELLOTTO
(Venice 1722 - Warsaw 1780)

73 *Dresden from the Left Bank of the Elbe, below the Fortifications*
1747
etching, III state of five; 538 x 850 mm (plate)
Milan, Civica Raccolta delle Stampe 'Achille Bertarelli', vol. FF 25, pl. 1

Inscriptions: on lower margin, 'Perspective de La ville neuve, et du Palais -- de S.M. dit d'hollande et des Environs de / la Campagne de Loschùwitz, avec une partie de La -- Roïale Eglise Catolique et des Bastions de la ville de / Dresde, prise de la prairie Joignante aux Ecuries Roïales et à L'orangerie -- Ce tableau fait par ordre de Sa Majeste Le Roy de Pologne et Ele~c: de Sax. &.&.&. / Peint, dessiné et grave par Ber: Bellotto dit Canaletto Pein:R.le/1747'.

Provenance: acquired by the Comune di Milano as part of the collection of Prince Luigi Alberico Trivulzio (1868-1938), 1935.

Selected Bibliography: Stübel 1911, pp. 494-495, no. 9; Fritzsche 1936, p. 143, no. VR 9; Kozakiewicz 1972a, vol. II, p. 127, no. 156; Rizzi 1996, p. 200, no. I-4; D. Succi, in Conegliano 2001, p. 229, no. 42; G. Metze, in Dresden 2011, p. 121, no. 20.

BERNARDO BELLOTTO
(Venice 1722 - Warsaw 1780)

74 *The Courtyard of the Zwinger, Dresden*
1751-52
oil on canvas; 134 x 237 cm
Dresden, Staatliche Kunstsammlungen, Gemäldegalerie Alte Meister, 629

Provenance: supplied by the artist, probably in 1752, to the court of the Prince Elector Frederick Augustus II in Dresden, as in that year it was included (no. 4312) in the so-called 'lost inventory of the year 1747 and following' of the Royal Picture Gallery in Dresden. From 1754 in the inventory of the Royal Picture Gallery in Dresden (Oesterreich 1754, p. 42, n. 532).

Selected Bibliography: Kozakiewicz 1972b, vol. II, p. 131, no. 164; Camesasca 1974, p. 99., no. 101; Löffler 1985, pp. 34 ss., figs. 34-37; Walther 1995, pp. 32-35, no. 6; Rizzi 1996, pp. 48-49, no. 20; G.J.M. Weber, in Venice-Houston 2001, pp. 176-177, no. 53; Weber 2003, p. 64, fig. 18; A. Henning, in Dresden 2011, p. 117, no. 14.

BERNARDO BELLOTTO
(Venice 1722 - Warsaw 1780)

75 *The Old Fortifications of Dresden South of the Zwinger (the Saturn Bastion)*
1749-1752
oil on canvas; 130 x 236.5 cm
San Petersburg, The State Hermitage Museum, GE 207

Provenance: commissioned by Heinrich, Earl von Brühl (1700-1763); purchased from his heirs by Catherine the Great (1729-1796); exhibited at the new Hermitage (mentioned for the first time in 1773 in the *Handwritten Inventory* of the Museum, inv. no. 462); transferred by Tsar Alexander I (1777-1825) to the Tauride Palace in Saint Petersburg, 1820-1825; moved again, this time by Tsar Alexander II (1818-1881) to the Gatchina Palace, near the capital, 1858-1859; returned to the Hermitage, 1923.

Selected Bibliography: Stählin, *Notes* 1990, vol. I, p. 374; vol. II, p. 111; Munich 1773-1783, no. 462; Fritzsche 1936, p. 110, no. VG 59; Kozakiewicz 1972a, vol. I, pp. 85, 100-102; vol. II, p. 131, no. 162; Walther 1995, pp. 42-43; Rizzi 1996, no. 19; I. Artemieva, in Venice-Houston 2001, p. 160, no. 45.

BERNARDO BELLOTTO
(Venice 1722 - Warsaw 1780)

76 *The Old Fortifications of Dresden South of the Zwinger (the Saturn Bastion)*
1750
etching; 544 x 841 mm (plate); 522 x 820 (sheet)
II state of two
Milan, Civica Raccolta delle Stampe 'Achille Bertarelli', vol. FF 25, pl. 8

Inscriptions: lower margin, 'Vue exterieure de la Porte d[te] Wilsche Thor -- Rempars de la Ville de Dresden et de / partie des magnifiques Pavillons où sont actuelle -- ment la Biblioteque Roïale et le Théatre de l'Opera / Peint et gravé par Ber: Bellotto, dit Canaletto, Peintre Du: Roi. 1750'.

Provenance: acquired by the Comune di Milano as part of the collection of Prince Luigi Alberico Trivulzio (1868-1938), 1935.

Selected Bibliography: Fritzsche 1936, pp. 144-145, no. VR 16; Kozakiewicz 1972a, vol. II, p. 131, no. 163; Rizzi 1996, p. 204, no. I-6; G. Metzu, in Dresden 2001, p. 122, no. 22; D. Succi, in Conegliano 2011, pp. 136-137, 230, no. 51.

BERNARDO BELLOTTO
(Venice 1722 - Warsaw 1780)

77 *The Kreuzkirche, Dresden*
ca. 1753
oil on canvas; 197 x 187 cm
San Petersburg, The State Hermitage Museum, GE 203

Provenance: collection of Heinrich, Earl of Brühl (1700-1763), Dresden; purchased by Catherine II, 1768; purchased from his heirs by Catherine the Great (1729-1796); exhibited at the new Hermitage (mentioned for the first time in 1773 in the *Handwritten Inventory* of the Museum, inv. no. 462); transferred by Tsar Alexander I (1777-1825) to the Tauride Palace in Saint Petersburg, 1820-1825; moved again, this time by Tsar Alexander II (1818-1881) to the Gatchina Palace, near the capital, 1858-1859; returned to the Hermitage, 1923.

Selected Bibliography: Stählin, *Notes*, 1990, vol. I, p. 374; vol. II, p. 111; Muňich 1773-1783, vol. I, p. 160, no.

505; Fritzsche 1936, p. 68; Kozakiewicz 1972a, vol. I, pp. 84-85, 100-102; vol. II, no. 182; Camesasca 1974, p. 99, no. 100; A. Walther, in Venice 1986, pp. 80-81, no. 9; Fomichova 1992, p. 80, no. 46; Rizzi 1996, p. 60, no. 32; I. Artemieva, in Venice-Houston 2001, p. 170, n. 50; A. Schumacher, in Munich 2014-2015, pp. 236-239, no. 43.

BERNARDO BELLOTTO
(Venice 1722 - Warsaw 1780)

78 *The Kreuzkirche, Dresden*
ca. 1756
pen and grayish ink over pencil free and ruled, some red pencil lines
and pinpointing; 586 x 480 mm
Warsaw, Muzeum Narodowe, Rys. Pol. 2042

Provenance: Bernardo Bellotto in Warsaw and heirs in Warsaw until 1789, then Vilnius; subsequently purchased, probably between 1822 and 1828, together with a group of the artist's drawings by Earl Konstanty Tyszkiewicz (1806-1868), Łohojsk, Belarus; the Tyszkiewicz family donated the entire holding to the Association for the Protection of Warsaw's Monuments, before 1914; acquired by the Muzeum Narodowe in 1930.

Selected Bibliography: Fritzsche 1936, p. 136, no. VZ 104; Kozakiewicz 1972a, vol. I, p. 85; vol. II, p. 148, no. 183; Rizzi 1996, p. 167, no. D1; K. Załeski, in Vienna 2005, pp. 220-221, no. 57; R. Groh, in Dresden 2011, pp. 54-55; A. Schumacher, in Munich 2014-2015, pp. 236-239.

BERNARDO BELLOTTO
(Venice 1722 - Warsaw 1780)

79 *The Kreuzkirche, Dresden*
1757
engraving, only state; 770 x 620 mm (plate)
Dresden, Staatliche Kunstsammlungen,
Kupferstich-Kabinett, A 85868

Inscriptions: on the margin, 'Vuë, de l'Eglise et de la -- Rue de Sainte Croix, / ainsi que d'une partie de l'Hôtel de S: E: -- Mons.gr le Comte Rutowski, Feld Marechal General / Peint et gravé par Ber:d Bellotto dit Canaletto Pein.r - R 1757'.

Marks: letters FAR [Fridericus Augustus Rex], on the top the crown; shared by the old Property but not present in Lugt.

Provenance: collection of Augustus III (1696-1763), King of Poland and Elector of Saxony (as Frederick Augustus II).

Selected Bibliography: Fritzsche 1936, no. VR 20; Kozakiewicz 1972a, vol. II, p. 148, no. 184; D. Succi, in Mirano 1999, p. 98, no. 20; G. Metze, in Dresden 2011, pp. 41, 125, no. 28; A. Schumacher, in Munich 2014-2015, p. 239, n. 45.

BERNARDO BELLOTTO
(Venice 1722 - Warsaw 1780)

80 *The Market Square, Pirna*
1753-54
oil on canvas; 134 x 238 cm
Dresden, Gemäldegalerie Alte Meister, Staatliche Kunstsammlungen, 623

Provenance: mentioned for the first time in the inventory of the Royal Picture Gallery as 'Prospect of Pirna, the Market Square, on canvas, 4.8.8.4' (Oesterreich 1754, p. 43, n. 546).

Selected Bibliography: Fritzsche 1936, pp. 54, 103, 113, 157, no. VG 85; Kozakiewicz 1972a, vol. I, pp. 100-102, 108; vol. II, p. 166, no. 211; Camesasca 1974, pp. 9, 100, no. 107; Walther 1995, pp. 73-75, no. 25; Rizzi 1996, p. 78, no. 56; Schmidt 2000, pp. 48, 50, 104-113; G.J.M. Gregor, in Venice-Houston 2001, p. 182, n. 56.

BERNARDO BELLOTTO
(Venice 1722 - Warsaw 1780)

81 *The Market Square, Pirna (recto)*
Study for a View of the Kreuzkirche, Dresden
ca. 1756
pen and gray ink; 377 x 650 mm
Warsaw, Muzeum Narodowe, no. Rys.Pol. 2044

Provenance: Bernardo Bellotto in Warsaw and heirs in Warsaw until 1798, then Vilnius; subsequently purchased, probably between 1822 and 1828, together with a group of the artist's drawings by Earl Konstanty Tyszkiewicz (1806-1868), Łohojsk, Belarus; the Tyszkiewicz family donated the entire holding to the Association for the Protection of Warsaw's Monuments, before 1914; acquired by the Muzeum Narodowe in 1930.

Selected Bibliography: Fritzsche 1936, p. 136, no. VZ 108; Kozakiewicz 1972a, vol. I, p. 85; vol. II, pp. 166, 173, no. 216; Walther 1995, p. 74; Rizzi 1996, p. 168, no. D 3; G.J.M. Gregor, in Venice-Houston 2001, p. 182.

9. PRIVATE PASSIONS

BERNARDO BELLOTTO
(Venice 1722 - Warsaw 1780)

82 *Architectural Capriccio with Self-Portrait*
1764-65
oil on canvas; 156.2 x 112.4 cm

Provenance: Earl Alessandro Augusto. Contini-Bonacossi (1899-1994), Florence; Christie's London, 7 July 1972, lot 85; acquired by Eugene Thaw and Stanley Moss who sell it to Walter Percy Chrysler Jr, 1976; Chrysler Museum, Norfolk, Virginia; Chrysler sale, Sotheby's, New York, 1 June 1989, lot 84; acquired by Rudolf Flick, London, who sells it to Alfred Bader, 2010; Otto Naumann Ltd., New York, from whom it was acquired by the present owner, October 2016.

Selected Bibliography: Kozakiewicz 1972a, vol. I, pp. 139-140; vol. II, p. 265, no. 334a; Camesasca 1974, p. 110, no. 194; G. Marini, in Verona 1990, p. 166; G. Marini, in London-Washington 1994-1995, p. 430; Rizzi 1996, p. 158, no. 134; E.P. Bowron, in Venice-Houston 2001, p. 246; S. Oesinghaus, in Dresden 2001, pp. 23-27; Manikowska 2014, pp. 161-222; A. Gottdang, in Munich 2014-2015, p. 272, no. 60.

BERNARDO BELLOTTO
(Venice 1722 - Warsaw 1780)

83 *Catalogo de Danni*
ch'ho' avuto, io, Bernardo Belotto de Canaletto:
L'Anno. 1760.
(Nel Bombardamento, che fece il Re di Prussia) nel mio
Alogio
Nella Salz:Gassen, in Casa del Sig.re Caesar. del. Valore:
Di Talleri Cinquanta Mille. dicco……… T: 50000.

July 1760-February 1762
manuscript; 33.5 x 20.3 cm

Vilnius, The Wróblewski Library of the Lithuanian Academy of Sciences,
The Manuscript Department, inv. F 22-26

Watermark: not identified.

Provenance: Bernardo Bellotto in Warsaw and then the artist's heirs in Warsaw until 1798, then Vilnius, where it was probably acquired between 1823 and 1828, with a group of the artist's drawings, by Earl Konstanty

Tyszkiewicz (1806-1868), Łohojsk, Belarus; by inheritance, the family in Łohojsk, where it was still located in 1911; from World War I, the Lenin State Library in Moscow; brought with the manuscripts from the Public Library of Vilnius to the Lithuanian Academy of Sciences (in 2009, named the Wróblewski Library of the Lithuanian Academy of Sciences), with protocol 16 March 1946, Wróblewski Library, coll. F 75-347, p. 3.

Selected Bibliography: Stübel 1911, p. 477; Fritzsche 1936, pp. 72, 211, note 99; Kozakiewicz 1972a, vol. I, p. 131; Manikowska 2012; Manikowska 2014.

BERNARDO BELLOTTO
(Venice 1722 - Warsaw 1780)

84 *Snippet of a Letter (verso)*
Statue of Saint John Evangelist in a Niche (recto)
1762
pen and brown ink; 145 x 80 mm
Warsaw, Muzeum Narodowe, Rys. Pol. 2064

Provenance: Bernardo Bellotto in Warsaw and the artist's heirs in Warsaw until 1798, then Vilnius, where it was acquired by Earlt Konstanty Tyszkiewicz (1806-1868), Łohojsk, Belarus, probably between 1822 and 1828; the Tyszkiewicz family donated the entire holding to the Association for the Protection of Warsaw's Monuments, before 1914; acquired by the Muzeum Narodowe in 1930.

Selected Bibliography: Fritzsche 1936, p. 135, no. VZ 89; Kozakiewicz 1972a, vol. II, pp. 277, 278, no. 351; Rizzi 1996, pp. 160, 187, no. D 52.

BERNARDO BELLOTTO
(Venice 1722 - Warsaw 1780)

85 *Two Polish Hussars*

1762
pen and brown ink over pencil;
561-562 x 322-320 mm
Warsaw, Muzeum Narodowe, Rys. Pol. 2082

Inscriptions: on the left-hand figure, 'Pele, Ple, mani/ca Pio; Roso, R so'; on the right-hand figure, 'Pele, Zolobin, Zolo no, Zb no'.

Watermark: right-hand profile of a galloping unicorn with a monogram of 'L' in its body, not identified.

Provenance: Bernardo Bellotto in Warsaw and the artist's heirs in Warsaw until 1798, then Vilnius, where it was acquired by Earlt Konstanty Tyszkiewicz (1806-1868), Łohojsk, Belarus, probably between 1822 and 1828; the Tyszkiewicz family donated the entire holding to the Association for the Protection of Warsaw's Monuments, before 1914; acquired by the Muzeum Narodowe in 1930.

Selected Bibliography: Starzyński 1933-1934, pp. 102, 107, XIX; Fritzsche 1936, p. 136, no. VZ 95; Kozakiewicz 1972a, vol. II, pp. 258-259, no. 325; Rizzi 1996, p. 180, no. D 31; K. Załęski, in Vienna 2005, p. 232, no. 68; B.A. Kowalczyk, in Turin 2008, pp. 230-231, no. 93; B.A. Kowalczyk, in Munich 2014-2015, p. 270.

BERNARDO BELLOTTO
(Venice 1722 - Warsaw 1780)

86 *Two Balkan Hajduks and a Man with Cocked Hat*
1762
pen and brown ink over pencil; 560 x 320 mm
Warsaw, Muzeum Narodowe, Rys. Pol. 2075

Inscriptions: in pen, over the cape of the left-hand figures, 'roso sporcho' (dirty pink); above the central one: on the hat, 'Gialato' (yellowish), on the garments: 'Rso', and repeatedly, 'B' and 'R'; above the cape of the man with cocked hat: 'lacheta (?) sporcha'.

Watermark: right-hand profile of a galloping uncorn with a monogram of 'L' in its body, not identified.

Selected Bibliography: Starzyński 1933-1934, pp. 102, 106-107; Fritzsche 1936, pp. 125 e 136, no. VZ 97; Kozakiewicz 1972a, I, p. 141; vol. II, pp. 254, 257, no. 320; Rizzi 1996, p. 178, no. D 27; G.J.M. Weber, in Udine 2004, p. 130; B.A. Kowalczyk, in Munich 2014-2015, p. 270.

BERNARDO BELLOTTO
(Venice 1722 - Warsaw 1780)

87 *Architectural Capriccio with an Equestrian Monument*
1764
pen and grey-black and brown ink, grey wash, over free and ruled pencil with pinpointing; the design is outlined in pen and ruler; 443 x 619 mm
signed at lower left in brown ink, 'Bernardo Belotto/ de' Canaletto inv: et Fec. 1764'.
London, Victoria and Albert Museum, E. 30-1939

88 *Architectural Capriccio with an Equestrian Monument*
1764
pen and grey-black and brown ink, grey wash, over free and ruled pencil with pinpointing; the design is outlined in pen and ruler; 443 x 619 mm
signed at lower left in brown ink, 'Bernardo Belotto/ de' Canaletto inv: et Fec. 1764'.
London, Victoria and Albert Museum, E. 31.1939

Provenance: George A. Simonson collection, before 1927; gift to the Museum of his sister, Mrs. A. Simonson, dedicated to his memory, 1939.

Selected Bibliography: (both) Hadeln 1929, p. 8; Kozakiewicz 1972a, vol. II, p. 520, nos. A 521 and A 522; Ward-Jackson 1980, pp. 116-117, nos. 927 and 926; E.P. Bowron, in London-Washington 1994-1995, pp. 371-372; G. Marini, in London-Washington 1994-1995, p. 430, nos. 258 e 259; Rizzi 1996, pp. 174-175, no. D 20; B.A. Kowalczyk, in Turin 2008, pp. 224-227, nos. 90 e 91.

BERNARDO BELLOTTO
(Venice 1722 - Warsaw 1780)

89 *Le Turc Généreux*
1759
engraving on laid paper, I state of two;
472 x 626 cm (plate)
Warsaw, Muzeum Narodowe, Rys. Pol. 2075

Inscriptions: on lower margin, 'Le Turc Genereux. / Ballet Pantomine executé à Vienne sur le Teatre près de la Cour, le 26. Avril, 1.7.58. / Presenté à S. Ecc. Mons. Le Comte de Durazzo, Conseiller intime actuel de EE: M.M.I.I. et R.R. et Surintendant / General des Plaisirs et Spectacles &.&.&. / par Ber: Belotti dit Canatetto Peintre. de SM. Le Roi de Pol: Elec. de Saxe: &.&.&. 1759'.

Ex-libris: in *verso*, within the woodcut frame, with the letters S W D R in the corners, the Topór-Starża, Starza crest, also in woodcut, and penned ink writing: Ex Bibliotheca Illusm. D / Stanislai to Wronow / Starza Wronowski CR / Tribus first Justi. Leo / polis Consilis.

Provenance: Earl Stanisław Wronowski (1733-1839), Leopoli .

Selected Bibliography: Michel 1945; Kozakiewicz 1972a, vol. II, p. 227, no. 287; no. 287; A. Grochala and K. Schütze, in Vienna 2005, p. 235, no. 69.

CANALETTO
(Venice 1697-1768)

90 *Theatral Set Design*
ca. 1753-1754
oil on canvas; 64.7 x 47.4 cm
Rome, Accademia di San Luca, 316

Provenance: Domenico Pellegrini (1759-1840) collection; bequest to the Accademia di San Luca, 1840.

Selected Bibliography: Constable 1962, vol. I, pl. 93; vol. II, p. 429, no. 510; Puppi 1968, p. 118, no. 317; Constable, Links 1989, vol. I, pl. 93; vol. II, p. 467, no. 510.

10. AN AVANT-GARDE CHRONICLER

BERNARDO BELLOTTO
(Venice 1722 - Warsaw 1780)

91 *The Königstein Fortress with the Lilienstein*
1765
etching, II state of two; 420 x 631 mm (plate)
Dresden, Staatliche Kunstsammlungen,
Kupferstich-Kabinett, A 85870

Inscriptions: in the margin, 'Vue du Roc, et Forteresse de Koenig -- stein du coté de l'Occident, et de la / Montée, aïant de l'autre coté le Lilienstein, au dela de -- l'Elbe, et en distance, les Montagnes de la Lusace. / La Vue a eté prise du Cabaret nommé la Neueschenke. Se trouvent chez l'Auteur a Dresde, -- et chez Pierre Fouquet a Amsterdam. Peint et gravé par Ber: Belotto de Canaletto Peintre Elec. / N:o'.

Marks: letters FAR [Fridericus Augustus Rex], on the top the crown; shared by the old Property but not present in Lugt.

Provenance: given by the artist to the Kupferstich-Kabinett of Dresden, 28 March 1765 or 17 January 1767.

Selected Bibliography: Fritzsche 1936, pp. 146-147, no. VR 30; Kozakiewicz 1972a, vol. II, p. 183, no. 232; A. Walther, in Venice 1986, pp. 97-98, no. 26; Rizzi 1996, p. 216, no. I-21; D. Succi, in Conegliano 2011, p. 232, no. 61; G. Metze, in Dresden 2011, pp. 40-41, note 11.

BERNARDO BELLOTTO
(Venice 1722 - Warsaw 1780)

92 *The Ruins of the Suburb Pirna, Dresden*
1762-63 (image and emblem); 1766 (script)
etching, only state; 530 x 648 mm (plate)
Geneve, Musées d'art et d'histoire de la Ville de Genève, Cabinet de Dessins et d'Estampes, E 2011-271009

Inscriptions: 'Vuë des ruines des Fauxbourgs de la Ville de Dresde -- entre aûtres, de la maison de Fürstenhof, près du fossé, / attenant au fauxbourg de Pirna, On découvre dans le lointain le -- rempart de la Ville neuve, la Vigne de Neuman, et les collines des environs. / Dédié a Son Altesse Royale Monseigneur le - Prince Xavier Administrateur de Saxe &cc. &cc. &cc. / D'après le Tableau haut 2 pieds $10^1/_2$ p: Large n:p: que Son Altesse Royale possede. Peint et gravé -- par son très soumis Serviteur Bern: Belotto de Canaletto Mem:bre de l'Acca:mie Elec:le des Arts. 1766'.

Provenance: Ancient Fund (part of the Museum collection before 1920).

Selected Bibliography: Fritzsche 1936, p. 147, VR 33; Kozakiewicz 1972a, vol. II, p. 242, no. 302; Rosenberg 1974, pp. 286-287; A. Walther, in Venice 1986, pp. 85-86, no. 14; Rizzi 1996, pp. 224-225, no. I-26; G. Metze, in Dresden 2001, pp. 40-41, note 13 e p. 126, no. 30.

BERNARDO BELLOTTO
(Venice 1722 - Warsaw 1780)

93 *The Ruins of the Kreuzkirche, Dresden*
1765
etching, II state of three; 553 x 640 mm (plate)
Dresden, Staatliche Kunstsammlungen, Kupferstich-Kabinett A 85871

Inscriptions: in the lower margin, 'Vue de Débris, de la Tour de S:te Croix, qui s'écroulà le 22.me -- de Juin 1765, dans le tems qu'on commencoit à relever l'E/glise, laquelle avoit péri par le Bombardement de la Ville de Dresde, en 1760. ---10 au:nes de Dresde, selon le pan de Mur qui demeurà surpied, haut de 120 au:nes / Dedié à Son Altesse Royale, Madame– l'Electrice Douairiere de Saxe /La vue a eté prise, du Cabinet de M:r le Surintendant Ecclésiastique Docteur am Ende. -- par Son très Soumis Serviteur Bern: Belotto de Canaletto. Mem:bre de l'Acca:mie Elec:le des Arts 1765'.

Marks: letters FAR [Fridericus Augustus Rex], on the top the crown; shared by the old Property but not present in Lugt.

Provenance: given by the artist to the Kupferstich-Kabinett of Dresden, 2 June 1766 or 17 January 1967.

Selected Bibliography: Fritzsche 1936, p. VR 32; Kozakiewicz 1972a, vol. II, p. 241, no. 300; G. Metze, in Dresden 2001, pp. 40-41, note 13 e p. 127, no. 31; J. Toma, in Munich 2014-2015, pp. 262, 264, no. 56.

BERNARDO BELLOTTO
(Venice 1722 - Warsaw 1780)

94 *The Miodowa Street, Warsaw*
1777
oil on canvas; 84 x 107.5 cm
Warsaw, Royal Castle, Museum, ZKW/443

Provenance: commissioned by King Stanisław II August Poniatowski (1732-1798) for his private collection in Warsaw; installed in 1777 in the antechamber of the Senate of the Royal Castle in Warsaw ('Canaletto room'), where it remained until 1807; by descent, the king's nephew, Prince Józef Poniatowski, 1798; sold with the majority of Bellotto's pictures from the 'Canaletto room', to Frederick Augustus, King of Saxonia and Grand Prince of Warsaw; sent by Tsar Nicholas I to Russia, as retaliation for the insurrection of Warsaw of 1830-1831 and placed in the Tauride Palace, Saint Petersburg (together with fifteen views of Dresden and Pirna, purchased by the Tsarina Catherine II from the heirs of Earl Brühl); moved by Alexander II to the Gatchina Palace, close to the capital, 1858-1859; preserved in the Hermitage, Saint Petersburg, during the World War I; returned to the Royal Castle with the Peace of Riga, 1922; transferred to Muzeum Narodowe in September 1939; confiscated by the German government and sent to Germany, 1939-1945; returned in 1945 and preserved in Muzeum Narodowe until 1984, when it was returned to the rebuilt Royal Castle.

Selected Bibliography: Mańkowski, 1932, p. 263, no. 439; Kozakiewicz 1972a, pp. 349-350, no. 412; Camesasca 1974, p. 115, no. 239; Rizzi 1990, pp. 84-87, no. 27; A. Rottermund, in Venice-Houston 2011, p. 260, no. 90; A. Rottermund, in Warsaw 2003-2004, pp. 19-20; P. Sadlej, in Warsaw 2003-2004, pp. 32, 44.

BERNARDO BELLOTTO
(Venice 1722 - Warsaw 1780)

95 *Palace of the Republic of Poland, Warsaw*
1778
oil on canvas; 116 x 164 cm
Warsaw, Royal Castle, Museum, ZKW/454

Provenance: commissioned by King Stanisław II August Poniatowski (1732-1798) for his private collection in

Warsaw; installed in 1777 in the antechamber of the Senate of the Royal Castle in Warsaw ('Canaletto room'), where it remained until 1807; by descent, the king's nephew, Prince Józef Poniatowski, 1798; sold with the majority of Bellotto's pictures from the 'Canaletto room', to Frederick Augustus, King of Saxonia and Grand Prince of Warsaw; sent by Tsar Nicholas I to Russia, as retaliation for the insurrection of Warsaw of 1830-1831 and placed in the Tauride Palace, Saint Petersburg (together with fifteen views of Dresden and Pirna, purchased by the Tsarina Catherine II from the heirs of Earl Brühl); moved by Alexander II to the Gatchina Palace, close to the capital, 1858-1859; preserved in the Hermitage, Saint Petersburg, during the World War I; returned to the Royal Castle with the Peace of Riga, 1922; transferred to Muzeum Narodowe in September 1939; confiscated by the German government and sent to Germany, 1939-1945; returned in 1945 and preserved in Muzeum Narodowe until 1984, when it was returned to the rebuilt Royal Castle.

Selected Bibliography: Mańkowski 1932, p. 261, no. 425; Kozakiewicz 1972a, p. 350, no. 413; Camesasca 1974, p. 116, no. 242; Rizzi 1990, pp. 90, 92, no. 29; A. Rottermund , in Venice-Houston 2001, pp. 33-39, 262, no. 91; P. Sadlej, in Varsavia 2003-2004, pp. 35, 50.

BERNARDO BELLOTTO
(Venice 1722 - Warsaw 1780)

96 *The Church of the Holy Sacrament in the New Town, Warsaw*
1778
oil on canvas; 84 x 106 cm
Warsaw, Royal Castle, Museum, ZKW/445

Provenance: commissioned by King Stanisław II August Poniatowski (1732-1798) for his private collection in Warsaw; installed in 1777 in the antechamber of the Senate of the Royal Castle in Warsaw ('Canaletto room'), where it remained until 1807; by descent, the king's grandson, Prince Józef Poniatowski, 1798; sold with the majority of Bellotto's pictures from the 'Canaletto room', to Frederick Augustus, King of Saxonia and Grand Prince of Warsaw; sent by Tsar Nicholas I to Russia, as retaliation for the insurrection of Warsaw of 1830-1831 and placed in the Tauride Palace, Saint Petersburg (together with fifteen views of Dresden and Pirna, purchased by the Tsarina Catherine II from the heirs of Earl Brühl); moved by Alexander II to the Gatchina Palace, close to the capital, 1858-1859; preserved in the Hermitage, Saint Petersburg, during the World War I; returned to the Royal Castle with the Peace of Riga, 1922; transferred to Muzeum Narodowe in September 1939; confiscated by the German government and sent to Germany, 1939-1945; returned in 1945 and preserved in Muzeum Narodowe until 1984, when it was returned to the rebuilt Royal Castle.

Selected Bibliography: Mańkowski 1932, p. 262, no. 438; Kozakiewicz 1972a, pp. 363-364, no. 421; Camesasca 1974, p. 116, no. 244; Rizzi 1990, p. 96, no. 31; A. Rottermund, in Venice-Houston 2001, p. 264, no. 92; A. Rottermund, in Vienna 2005, pp. 194, 197, no. 44

BERNARDO BELLOTTO
(Venice 1722 - Warsaw 1780)

97 *View of Wilanów Meadows, Warsaw*
1775
oil on canvas; 173 x 246 cm
Warsaw, The Royal Castle - Museum, ZKW/454

Provenance: commissioned by King Stanisław II August Poniatowski (1732-1798) for the royal collection, to be hung in the Belvedere Palace in the hills near the royal residence in Łazienki Park; in 1777, hung on the wooden panelling of the Senate Antechamber ('Canaletto Room') in the Royal Castle of Warsaw; brought to Russia by order of Tsar Nicholas I in 1832. Returned to the castle in 1922. Transfered to Muzeum Narodowe in September 1939. Taken to Germany in 1940. Reclaimed in 1945 and transfered to Muzeum Narodowe. After the renovation of the Royal Castle of Warsaw in 1984, it was brought back to the castle and hung on the wooden panelling of the Senate Antechamber ('Canaletto Room').

Selected Bibliography: Mańkowski 1932, p. 261, no. 424; Fritzsche 1936, VG 154, pp. 90, 95. 120, ill. 111; Tatarkiewicz 1957, pp. 123-124; Kozakiewicz 1972a, vol. II, pp. 364, 369, no. 423; Rizzi, 1991, pp. 72-73; A. Rottermund, in Turin 2008, p. 246, no. 101; A. Rottermund, in Conegliano 2011, pp. 202-204.

BERNARDO BELLOTTO
(Venice 1722 - Warsaw 1780)

98 *The Prince Józef Poniatowski Receiving a Horse-Riding Lesson from the Colonel Königsfels*
1773
oil on canvas, 73 x 81.5 cm
Warsaw, Muzeum Narodowe (MP 4283), on deposit in Warsaw, Royal Castle - Museum (ZKW/1883/ab/Dep)

Provenance: commissioned by the King Stanisław II August Poniatowski (1732-1798), 1773; initially kept at the gallery of the Royal Castle in Warsaw, 'au cabinet de l'atelier en bas', then at the Belweder Palace, Warsaw, 'à la première chambre [de l'officine] ou logeoit M.de Byszewska' (Katarzyna Agnieszka Byszewski (1749-1797), wife of Arnold Anastazy Byszewski); it was bequeathed to the king's nephew, Józef Poniatowski (1763-1813), 1798 (in 1809 it was located in his residence, Pod Blachą Palace, Warsaw); his sister, Maria Teresa Tyszkiewicz (1760-1834), Warsaw, from 1813 at least until 1819, later in Russia; A.A. Kozen, Saint Petersburg, 1914; Krosnowski collection, Saint Petersburg and Russia; Royal Castle Warsaw, 1929; Muzeum Narodowe, 1939; currently on display at the Pod Blachą Palace in Warsaw.

Selected Bibliography: Mańkowski 1932, p. 265, no. 457; Fritzsche 1936, p. 119, no. VG 147; Król-Kaczorowska 1966, p. 68, no. 3; Kozakiewicz 1967; Kozakiewicz 1972a, vol. I, pp. 164, 166, 173; vol. II, pp. 386-387, no. 431 (with the wrong number of the Royal Gallery); Camesasca 1974, p. 116, no. 251; Rizzi 1990, pp. 126-127, no. 42.

BIOGRAPHY
BERNARDO BELLOTTO

1718
Marriage of Lorenzo Antonio Bellotto, administrator of the assets of Marc'Antonio Giustinian, procurator of San Marco, and Fiorenza Domenica Canal, Canaletto's sister.

1722
20 May, Bernardo Francesco Paolo Ernesto Bellotto was born in Venice, in the parish of Santa Margherita.

1726
Death of Michiel Angelo Bellotto, Bernardo's grandfather and chancellor in Vodnjan, Istria.

1736
Became a student in Canaletto's atelier.
Before June, made the drawing *The Grand Canal at the Fondamenta di Santa Chiara to the Church of Santa Croce* (Darmstadt, Hessisches Landesmuseum, AE 2208) and wrote a letter to his father on the back.

1738–1740
With Anton Maria Zanetti di Girolamo acting as mediator, painted fifteen views of Venice for Henry Howard, 4th Earl of Carlisle, three of which are still preserved at Castle Howard (Yorkshire).

1740
Painted *The Grand Canal from the Palazzo Foscari and Moro Lin towards the Carità* (Stockholm, The National Museum of Fine Arts), commissioned to commemorate the visit to Venice of Frederick Christian, son of the Elector of Saxony and King of Poland August III, who was a guest at the palazzo Foscari from December 1739 to June 1740.
22 April, received an advance from Anton Maria Zanetti di Girolamo, on behalf of the marchese Andrea Gerini, for his trip to Florence.
30 September, was paid by the marchese Gerini for four views of Florence.
20 November, the secretary of Field Marshal von der Schulenburg was reimbursed 9 zecchini for the purchase of four views of Venice by 'Canaletto's nephew'.
8 December, signed the drawing *The Campo Santi Giovanni e Paolo* (Darmstadt, Hessisches Landesmuseum, AE 2218).

1741
Two views of Florence, *The Piazza della Signoria* and *The River Arno looking towards the Ponte alla Carraia* (Budapest, Museum of Fine Arts), are cited in the inventory of the personal collection of the Marquis Vincenzo Riccardi in Florence.
5 October, marriage contract between the painter and his future father-in-law Giambattista Pizzorno, concluded on 2 November.
5 November, marriage to Elisabetta Pizzorno, daughter of Giambattista quondam Zorzi, celebrated in the church of the Redentore, witnessed by Earl Bonomo Algarotti.
Investment of part of his wife's dowry (850 ducats) in the Scuola Grande della Misericordia; his mother Fiorenza wrote a document stating that the family had been abandoned by her husband Lorenzo and that her sole possessions would go to Bernardo, who was supporting her and his brother Pietro, hosting them in his own home.
His brother Pietro Bellotto (view painter in Toulouse and Nantes) affirmed before the same notary that Bernardo had taught him to paint; in order to continue living with his brother and perfect his professional training, he committed to pay him 120 ducats annually.

1742
Spring, the period during which it is supposed that he travelled to Rome.
25 July, Bernardo was in Venice, where his contract with Pietro was terminated.
2 August, his mother Fiorenza's will, naming Bernardo her heir and asking him to take care of his sister, a tertiary at San Francesco della Vigna.
15 October, the birth of Bernardo's first son, Lorenzo Francesco, in the parish of Santa Marina.

1743
16 August, displayed two views at the exhibition of San Rocco, one of the Campidoglio (Petworth House, The National Trust) and the other of the *Chiovere di San Giovanni Evangelista* (lost).

1744
Trip to Milan and Lombardy; painted two pictures for the Archbishop Giuseppe Pozzobonelli. In Vaprio, painted for the Earl Antonio Simonetta (New York, The Metropolitan Museum of Art and Private Collection), as stated in a note on the preparatory drawings (Darmastadt, Hessisches Landesmuseum, AE 2215 and 2216). In Gazzada, painted the village and the villa of the Perabò brothers (Milan, Pinacoteca di Brera).
July, the birth of his daughter Fiorenza.

1745
Bernardo was documented as a resident of the parish of Santa Marina, on the Fondamenta Nuove, where he rented a flat for his family (his mother, wife and two children) for 60 ducats.
Painted two views of Turin (Turin, Galleria Sabauda), for which he was paid in the summer.
12 August, death of his daughter Fiorenza in Venice.
29 November, birth of his daughter Francesca Elisabetta (godfather: Pietro Guarienti).

1746
2 December, birth of his son Giambattista Francesco (godfather: Giuseppe Camerata).

Probable date of the two large views of Verona (Powis Castle, The National Trust; Edinburgh, The National Gallery of Scotland, anonymous loan).

1747
5 April, letter of attorney in the name of his father-in-law Giambattista Pizzorno for management of his wife's dowry.
Shortly after, he departed for Dresden.
8 May, death in Venice of his son Giambattista Francesco.
Signed a few paintings and etchings in Dresden.

1748
Frederick August II, Prince Elector of Saxony and King of Poland under the name August III, appointed Bellotto court painter with an annual salary of 1,750 thalers, and gave him a diamond-studded gold snuffbox filled with 300 louis d'or.

During his eleven years in Dresden, before the outbreak of the Seven Year's War, the artist painted fourteen views of Dresden and eleven of Pirna, in large format, for the Royal Gallery, and made copies of the same subjects in thirteen views of Dresden and eight of Pirna for the prime minister, Earl Heinrich Brühl, for which he was never paid.
Made etchings of his paintings.
July, was listed among those 'che abitano in Sta Marina e possono pagar tansa per li Ferali' (who live in Sta Marina and can pay the lamp tax), even though he was already in Dresden.
24 September, the baptism of his daughter Maria Anna (godparents: Earl Brühl and his wife).

1750
4 March, the death of his daughter Maria Anna Henrica Isabella.
4 August the baptism of his daughter Maria Josepha Friedrica.

1752
26 August, the baptism of his daughter Christiana Xaveria.
27 November, the death of his daughter Antonia Friederica.

1753
26 April, received the decree from August II addressed to the bailiff Crusius in Pirna, to facilitate his work in that city.

1754
16 November, his father, Lorenzo Bellotto, who found himself in Dresden, sent a letter to Earl Brühl complaining about his son Bernardo's character and behaviour.

1756
March, the Prince Elector of Saxony issued a decree to facilitate the painter's depictions of the Fortress of Königstein. Between 1756 and 1758, painted five large views of the fortress.

1757
2 November, the baptism of his daughter Theresia Francisca.

1758
5 December, the painter was issued a passport for Bayreuth.

1759
January, the artist arrived in Vienna with his son Lorenzo between the end of 1758 and January 1759, where he remained for two years, painting a series of panoramic views of the city and a few medium-sized city views commissioned by Empress Maria Theresa; for Chancellor Wenzel Kaunitz and Prince Joseph Wenzel Liechtenstein, painted views of their gardens and castles.

1760
July, during a Prussian bombardment, the painter's home in Dresden, in the Salzgasse, near Neumarkt, was destroyed, and he valued his losses, including his library, collection, furnishings, artworks and engraving plates, at 50,000 thalers, which he detailed in an itemized inventory (*Catalogo de Danni*).

1761
4 January, Empress Maria Theresa wrote a letter recommending the painter to Princess Marie Antoinette, who was in Munich at the court of her brother, Maximilian III Joseph, together with her husband Frederick Christian.
14 January, Bellotto arrived in Munich with six other painters working for the Saxon court – his son Lorenzo probably among them – taking lodging at the most famous hotel in the city, the Black Eagle in Kauffingergasse. After less than one year in the city, he painted a view of the city and two of Nymphenburg for Maximilian III Joseph of Bavaria.

1762
13 January Earl Brühl sent a letter from Warsaw addressed to the painter in Dresden.
February, Bellotto returned to Dresden with his son Lorenzo; he painted two *Allegories* of the political situation in Saxony at the end of the Seven Year's War and two overdoor capriccios (Dresden, Gemäldegalerie).

1763
October, Bellotto's two patrons died: King August III and Earl Brühl.

1764
The founding the Fine Arts Academy of Dresden, headed by Christian Ludwig Hagedorn (1712–1780) and guided by neoclassical ideas. The painter, initially kept on the sidelines, was appointed 'membro aggregato per la prospettiva' (perspective instructor) with an annual salary of 600 thalers, a post obtained solely through the support of the court.
Brought a case in vain against the heirs of Earl Brühl, claiming payment for the paintings he had commissioned, the agreed upon price for which was 200 thalers each. Was called upon to take responsibility for his son Lorenzo's debts.

1765
March, he exhibited at the Academy of Fine Arts shows two pairs of pendant, *Architectural Capriccio with Self-Portrait* (cat. 82) and *Expulsion of the Money Changers from the Temple*; *Temple of Love* and *Temple of Venus*, now lost. Painted his admission piece for the Academy, *The old town of Dresden from the left bank of the river Elba with the August bridge* (Karlsruhe, Staatliche Kunsthalle), with which he participated in the Academy's second exhibition, in 1766.

1766
20 December, asked Hagedorn for permission to go to Saint Petersburg for nine months.

1767
26 January, in a letter sent from Dresden to his colleague Marcello Bacciarelli, the head artist of the Polish court, the painter Giuseppe Rosa announced the imminent arrival of Bellotto in Warsaw.
Bacciarelli presented Bellotto to the king of Poland, Stanisław II August Poniatowski.
May, the painter and his son were commissioned to fresco the castle of Ujazdów.
27 August, sent a request to the Dresden Academy to extend his permission, which was granted up to 31 January 1768.
He then decided to remain in Poland, sending for his family.

1768
The king of Poland named Bellotto court painter, with an annual salary of 400 ducats, as well as 150 for lodging, 120 for his carriage, 40 for firewood and 120 for the theatre.
In Warsaw, the artist was primarily busy with a series of twenty-six views of the city and of Wilanów commissioned for the 'Canaletto Room' in the Royal Castle.
20 April, in Venice, Bernardo and his brothers Michiel and Pietro were named in documents relative to matters of inheritance following the death of Canaletto.
1 March, in a letter to Bacciarelli, the painter Giuseppe Rosa described Bernardo's temperamental character.

1769
Together with his son, signed two paintings from the series of Roman views after Piranesi's prints, commissioned for the Castle of Ujazdów.
His eldest daughter Maria Josepha Friederica married the court geographer Hermann Karl Perthées, originally from Dresden.

1770
In the view of Warsaw from the Prague suburb (Warsaw, Zamek Kròlewski) he depicted himself alongside his son and father-in-law, awaiting the arrival of the king.
20 October, the death of his son Lorenzo; the funeral was paid for by the king, and he was buried in Warsaw, in the church of the Reformed.

1779
For Earl Jòzef Ossolinński, he painted *The Entry into Rome of the Polish ambassador Jòzef Ossoliński* (Wrocław, Salesian Museum), the only documented painting from the Polish period that was not commissioned by either the crown and Earl Brühl.

1780
Wrote a list (*Notta*) of the works he had produced between 1771 and 1780, indicating the prices and date of execution.
17 November, died in Warsaw; his death was announced on the same day by his son-in-law Perthées and he was buried the next day in the church of the Capuchins on Miodowa Street; his tomb has been lost for many years. His death certificate, prepared by the priest of the church the Visitation of the Holy Virgin Mary of the New City where he lived, was destroyed during World War II in a fire at the church.

BIOGRAPHY
CANALETTO (GIOVANNI ANTONIO CANAL)

1697
Born in Venice on 18 October in the parish of San Lio, to Bernardo Canal, a theatrical scene painter, and Artemisia Barbieri.

1716–1718
Worked with his father and his older brother Cristoforo on sets for the Sant'Angelo and San Cassiano theatres in Venice.

1718
11 November, his father Bernardo Canal signed a letter of attorney in the name of his brother Cristoforo, entrusting him with seeing to the family's business.
He left for Rome shortly after, accompanied by Antonio and possibly also his older son Cristoforo.

1719–1720
Worked with his father on scenes for Alessandro Scarlatti's *Tito Sempronio Greco* and *Turno Aricino*, which were performed at the Teatro Capranica in Rome during Carnival in 1720.

1720
August, made the drawing *The Arch of Constantine, Rome* which is part of the series of twenty-three small sheets with views of Roman monuments now at the British Museum in London and the Hessisches Landesmuseum in Darmstadt.
This was the year in which he joined the painters' guild in Venice.

1722
Owen McSwiny, an Irish theatre impresario and the agent of Charles Lennox, who later became the Duke of Richmond, commissioned the young Canaletto to paint the architecture in commemorative paintings of Lord Sommers and the Archbishop Tillotson, in a series planned for the nobleman's dining room at Goodwood House, Chichester, West Sussex, in collaboration with figure and landscape painters. Canaletto completed his work on the project before 17 December 1723.

1723
Signed one of the two *Architectural Capriccios* in private collections, listed in the inventory of the assets of the Giovannelli brothers in Noventa Padovana.

1725
Painted *The Stonemasons' Yard*, now at the National Gallery, London.
2 August, received 10 zecchini as an advance for the two early views for Stefano Conti.
16 August, displayed the *Campo Santi Giovanni e Paolo*, now at the Gemäldegalerie in Dresden, at the Festa di San Rocco; purchased by Earl Giambattista Colloredo, imperial ambassador, who later commissioned another painting.
10 November, was working on two paintings for the French ambassador, Earl Languet de Gergy.
25 November, stated that he had painted two views for Stefano Conti and that he had received 30 zecchini.
22 December, received a deposit of 10 zecchini for two additional views for Stefano Conti.

1726
8 March, Owen McSwiny wrote to the Duke of Richmond in Goodwood about the series of canvases celebrating illustrious English figures; two works in the series, *The Tomb of Lord Somers* and *The Tomb of Archbishop Tillotson*, on which Canaletto, Cimaroli, Pittoni and Piazzetta collaborated, were complete.
15 June, received a 'gift' of 10 zecchini from Stefano Conti, following his payment of 80 zecchini for four paintings.
15 June, stated that he had painted another two views for Stefano Conti.
Painted *The Bacino di San Marco*, at Upton House, which depicts Earl Giambattista Colloredo entering the Ducal Palace on 3 April.
Commission for *The Reception of the French Ambassador Jacques-Vincent Languet, Comte de Gergy, at the Doge's Palace* (Saint Petersburg, The State Museum Hermitage), which took place on 5 November 1726.

1727–1729
The correspondence between Owen Swiny and the Duke of Richmond continued, with the mention of a few works on copper that Canaletto had made for the noble Englishman.

1728
Painted the *Grand Canal from the Palazzo Balbi to the Rialto Bridge*, now at the Uffizi, for Francesco Niccolò Gabburri of Florence.

1729
March, dated the drawing of *The Riva degli Schiavoni from the Bacino di San Marco* at the Hessisches Landesmuseum in Darmstadt.

1730
Painted two pendants for Samuell Hill of Tatton Park (*Riva degli Schiavoni looking East* and *Molo looking West*).
22 August, the two paintings for Hugh Howard, later the Earl of Wicklow, were documented in England: *The Grand Canal from the Rialto Bridge to the Palazzo Foscari* and the *Entrance to the Canal Grande with the Dogana and Santa Maria della Salute*.

1732
Began the series of twenty-four views of Venice for the Duke of Bedford, which he completed in 1736.
July, made the drawing of *The Piazzetta looking North* at the Hessisches Landesmuseum in Darmstadt.

1735
The first edition of the *Prospectus Magni Canalis Venetiarum* (published by Giambattista Pasquali) with fourteen etchings by Antonio Visentini of paintings by Canaletto in the collection of Joseph Smith.
A 'view by Canaletto' (*The Fonteghetto della Farina*) was mentioned in the inventory of the collection of Giambattista Recanati in Venice.

1736
16 June, letter from Gustav Tessin to Carl Horleman in which Canaletto appeared 'committed to work for four years exclusively for an English patron by the name of Smitt'.
23 February, the field marshal Matthias von der Schulenburg paid 120 zecchini for the *Riva degli Schiavoni looking West*, currently at the Sir John Soane's Museum in London.

1737
Two views of Venice by Canaletto were cited in the

inventory of the Wallenstein Collection in the Castle of Dux in Bohemia.

1738
23 November, a ‘Quadro veduta del sito della Carità del Canaletto’ is cited in the inventory of the palazzo Sagredo on Campo Santa Sofia in Venice.
The Schulenburg inventory lists ‘Prima maniera Canaletto – Quadri due compagni Rappresentano Prospettive con Architetture e figurine, alti 7, lar. 9, Costo [36] zecchini, Stima 100 [zecchini]’.

1738–1739
Henry Howard, 4th Earl of Carlisle, visited Venice and commissioned *The Bacino di San Marco* now at the Museum of Fine Arts, Boston.

1739
7 October, Canaletto was proclaimed independent from his father Bernardo (A.S.V., Notarile Atti, notary Francesco Domestici, b. 5102, cc. 364–365).

1740
23 August, the declaration, from which we learn that he owned (together with his sisters and his cousins, the sons of Cristoforo Canal, Antonio, Giovanni Battista and their sisters) a house in San Lio for his personal use and another that was rented to Domenico Coronato.

1741
Date of the engraving of the *Imaginary View of Venice*, part of the series of thirty-one etchings *Vedute Altre prese da i luoghi altre ideate*, dedicated to Joseph Smith after his appointment to the post of British Consul in Venice in 1744.

1742
Signed five paintings with Roman subjects for Joseph Smith, now at Winsor Castle.
Second edition of the *Prospectus* published by Pasquali, completed with twenty-four new engravings by Visentini of views by Canaletto.

1743
24 October, signed and dated *The Piazzetta looking North, towards the Torre dell'Orologio* and the *Molo with the Palazzo Ducale*, now at Windsor Castle; signed a few capriccios from the series of thirteen overdoors commissioned by Smith.

1744
12 March, his father Bernardo died.

1745
23 April, signed and dated the drawing of the *The Campanile of San Marco Damaged by Lightning* (London, The Royal Library).

1746
May, left for England; arrived in London at the end of the month, as noted by Vertue.
20 May, letter from Thomas Hill to the Duke of Richmond mentioning a view of the Thames at Richmond House.

1747
11 June, completed a view of Windsor Castle for Algernon Seymour, Earl of Hertford, later 7th Duke of Somerset and the 1st Duke of Northumberland (1684-1750).

1748
28 July, receipt for the payment of ten guineas by Lord Brook's bailiff for a small view of *Warwick Castle*; this was followed by other receipts recorded in the archive of Hoare's Bank in London.

1749
19 July, received a payment from the Duke of Somerset of thirty-two guineas for the painting of *Syon House*.
25 July, published an announcement in the *Daily Advertiser*, inviting people to visit his studio on Silver Street, to dispel the rumours that he was not the famous Canaletto.

1750
Returned to Venice for a few months.

1751
8 March, pledged the sum of 2,150 ducats to the Scuola dei Luganegheri in the parish of San Basilio in Venice.
30 July, published a second announcement in the *Daily Advertiser*.

1753
28 July, Pietro Gradenigo noted ‘Antonio Canaletto Veneziano Celebre Pittore da Vedute ritorna da Inghilterra in Patria’ (Antonio Canaletto, the famous Venetian view painter, returns home from England).

1754
Wrote on the reverse of the five views painted for Thomas Hollis: ‘Made in the year 1754 in London ... requested by Sir Hollis...’.
Signed and dated the *Capriccio of a Ruined Gothic Chapel by a Sluice Gate* (Boston, Museum of Fine Arts).

1755
Returned to Venice before 12 December 1755, when he visited the office of the notary Vettor Todeschini to invest the sum of 2,200 ducats, earned in England, in the Pio Ospedale degli Incurabili.

1759
28 September, letter from Francesco Algarotti in Riolo to Prospero Pesci in Bologna, mentioning the *Capriccio with Palladian buildings* (Parma, Galleria Nazionale) and defining the capriccio genre.

1762
Sale of Joseph Smith's collection to King George III of England.

1763
16 January, the Academy of Painting and Sculpture in Venice turned down Canaletto's candidacy for professor of perspective.
11 September, Admitted to the Academy of Painting and Sculpture.

1765
Delivered his admission piece to the Academy of Painting and Sculpture, *Capriccio with Colonnade and*

Courtyard, which is still today at the Accademia in Venice.

1766
Signed the drawing of the *Singers in Basilica di San Marco*, made 'in ettà de Anni 68 cenzza Ochiali' (at 68 years of age without glasses).

1767
23 August, attended his last meeting at the Accademia.

1768
20 April, died in his home in Corte Perina, at seven o'clock in the evening, and was buried in the church of San Lio, where all traces of his tomb have long been lost.
14 May, the inventory was drawn up that lists 'quadretti mezzanelli e piccoli n. 28' ('28 small and medium pictures'). His assets, totalling 2,588 ducats, were divided between his three sisters along with some furniture and a few pieces of jewellery.

BIBLIOGRAPHY

Abbreviations

C/L: W.G. Constable, *Canaletto. Giovanni Antonio Canal, 1697-1768*, second edition. Revised by J.G. Links. Reprinted with supplement, Oxford 1989.

Churchill: W.A. Churchill, *Watermarks in paper in Holland, England, France, etc., in the XVII and XVIII centuries and their Interconnection*, Amsterdam 1935.

Lugt: F. Lugt, *Les marques de collections de dessins & d'estampes*, La Haye 1956.

Lugt *Suppl.*: F. Lugt, *Les marques de collections de dessins & d'estampes. Supplément*, La Haye 1956.

P [C]: K.T. Parker, *The Drawings of Antonio Canaletto in the Collection of His Majesty the King at Windsor Castle* [Oxford 1948], edition with appendix by C. Crawley, Bologna 1990.

Volumes and Articles

Abecedario 1851-1853
Abecedario de P. J. Mariette et autres notes inédites de cet amateur sur les arts et les artistes. Ouvrage publié d'après les manuscrits autographes, conservés au cabinet des estampes de la Bibliothèque Impériale, et annoté par MM. Ph. De Chennevières et A. de Montaiglon, Paris, J.-B. Dumoulin, 1851-1853.

Ashby 1915
T. Ashby, *Le diverse edizioni dei* 'Vestigi dell'Antichità di Roma', Florenxce 1915.

Ashby 1916
T. Ashby, *Topographical study in Rome in 1581. Description of Rome by Etienne du Pérac*, London 1916.

Ashby, Constable 1925
T. Ashby, W.G. Constable, 'Canaletto and Bellotto in Rome', in *The Burlington Magazine*, XLVI, 266, May 1925, pp. 207-214 (1st part); XLVI, 267, June 1925, pp. 288-299 (2nd part).

Athenaeum 1878
The Athenaeum and Literary Chronicle, 1878, September 14, n. 2655, p. 348.

Beddington 2004
C. Beddington, 'Bernardo Bellotto and His Circle in Italy. Part I: not Canaletto but Bellotto', in *The Burlington Magazine*, CXLVI, 1219, October 2004, pp. 665-674.

Bettagno 1983
A. Bettagno, 'In margine a una mostra', in *Notizie da Palazzo Albani*, XII, 1-2, 1983, pp. 222-228.

Bettagno 1998
A. Bettagno, *Una data per i Capricci?*, in *Giambattista Tiepolo nel terzo centenario della nascita*, ed. by L. Puppi, Proceedings of International Congress, Venice 1998, vol. I, pp. 39-41.

Binion 1980
A. Binion, 'Three drawings by Canaletto', in *Master Drawings*, vol. 18, no. 4, Winter 1980, pp. 373-375.

Binion 1990
A. Binion, *La galleria scomparsa del maresciallo von der Schulenburg. Un mecenate nella Venezia del Settecento*, Milan 1990.

Bona Castellotti 1991
M. Bona Castellotti, *Collezionisti a Milano nel '700. Giovanni Battista Visconti, Gian Matteo Pertusati, Giuseppe Pozzobonelli*, Florence 1991.

Borroni Salvatori 1974
F. Borroni Salvatori, 'Le esposizioni d'arte a Firenze dal 1674 al 1767', in *Mitteilungen des Kunsthistorischen Institutes in Florenz*, 18, 1974.

Bowron 1994
E.P. Bowron, 'A Venetian abroad. Bellotto and 'the most beautiful views' of Rome', in *Apollo*, CXL, 391, September 1994, pp. 26-32.

Bowron 1995
E.P. Bowron, 'Un nuevo descubrimiento: un capriccio arquitectónico de Bernardo Bellotto', in *Anuario/Urtekaria*, 1995, Museo de Bellas Artes de Bilbao, pp. 13-19.

Bowron 1998
E.P. Bowron, review: Alberto Rizzi, 'Bernardo Bellotto: Dresden, Vienna, Munich (1747-1766)', Venice, Canal & Stamperia Ed., 1996 , in *The Burlington Magazine*, 140, October 1998, pp. 47-48.

Briganti 1996
G. Briganti, *Gaspar Van Wittel*, new edition by L. Laureati et L. Trezzani, Milan 1996.

Bromberg 1974
R. Bromberg, *Canaletto's Etchings*, London & New York 1974.

Camerota 2008
F. Camerota, 'Gli strumenti scientifici delle collezioni dei Musei Civici Veneziani', in *Bollettino dei Musei Civici Veneziani*, 3, Venice 2008.

Camesasca 1974
E. Camesasca, *L'opera completa del Bellotto*, Milan 1974.

Castello Sforzesco. Pinacoteca 2000
Museo d'Arte Antica del Castello Sforzesco. Pinacoteca, vol. IV, Milan 2000.

Catalogo de' quadri [1803]
Catalogo de' quadri del q. Gianmaria Sasso, che si mettono all'incanto nella sua casa al ponte di Canal Regio [n.d.; Venice 1803].

Catalogue 1825
Catalogo e Stima dei Quadri e Bronzi esistenti nella Galleria del Sig. Marchese Giovanni Gerini a Firenze, Florence 1825.

Catalogue 1902
Historical and Descriptive Catalogue of Pictures belonging to His Grace the Duke of Leeds, London 1902.

Ceschi Lavagetto, Talignani
P. Ceschi Lavagetto, A. Talignani, *Palazzo Sanvitale a Parma. Storia architettura e arte*, Turin 2006.

Comachio 1979
L. Comachio, *Storia di Asolo. Il Museo Civico dal 1463 al 1952*, vol. XV, Asolo 1979.

Constable 1962
W.G. Constable, *Canaletto: Giovanni Antonio Canal 1697-1768*, London 1962.

Constable, Links 1976
W.G. Constable, *Canaletto: Giovanni Antonio Canal 1697-1768*, 2nd edition by J.G. Links, Oxford 1976.

Constable, Links 1989
W.G. Constable, *Canaletto: Giovanni Antonio Canal 1697-1768*, 2nd edition by J.G. Links with additional and new plates, Oxford 1989.

Contini 2002
R. Contini, *The Thyssen-Bornemisza Collection. Seventeenth and Eighteenth Century Italian Painting*, London 2002.

Corboz 1985
A. Corboz, *Canaletto. Una Venezia immaginaria*, Milan 1985.

De Juliis 1981
G. De Juliis, 'Appunti su una quadreria fiorentina. La collezione dei marchesi Riccardi', in *Paragone*, 375, 1981, p. 57-92.

De Vesme 1906
A. De Vesme, *Le Peintre-Graveur Italien*, Milan 1906.

Dri 2004-2005
A. Dri, *Fabio Berardi incisore 1736-1788*, University of Trieste, Faculty Literature and Philosophy, thesis in History of Modern Art, a.y. 2004-2005.

Encyclopédie 1753
Encyclopédie, ou dictionnaire raisonné des sciences, des arts et des métiers, ed. by D. Diderot and J.-B. d'Alembert, vol. III, Paris 1753.

Finberg 1921
H.F. Finberg, '*Canaletto in England*', in *The Walpole Society*, IX, 1921, pp. 1-78.

Fomichova 1992
T.D. Fomichova, *The Hermitage. Catalogue of Western European Painting. Venetian Painting. Fourtheenth to Eighteenth Centuries*, Moscow-Florence 1992.

Fritzsche 1936
H.A. Fritzsche, *Bernardo Belotto genannt Canaletto*, Burg bei Magdeburg 1936.

Galleria Nazionale di Parma 2000
Galleria Nazionale di Parma. Catalogo delle opere. Il Settecento, ed. by and with an essay by Lucia Fornari Schianchi, Milan 2000.

Gioseffi 1959
D. Gioseffi, *Canaletto – Il quaderno delle Gallerie veneziane e l'impiego della camera oscura*, Trieste 1959.

Goodison, Robertson 1967
J.W. Goodison, G.H. Robertson, *Fitzwilliam Museum Cambridge. Catalogue of paintings*, II, *Italian Schools*, Cambridge 1967.

Grohn 1995
H.W. Grohn, *Niedersächsichen Landesmuseum Hannover. Die italienischen Gemälde. Kritischer Katalog mit Abbildungen aller Werke*, ed. by H. W. Grohn, Hannover 1995

Hadeln 1929
D. von Hadeln, *The Drawings of Antonio Canal called Canaletto*, translation by C. Dodgson, London 1929.

Haskell 1960
F. Haskell, 'A Note on Artistic Contacts between Florence and Venice in the 18th Century', in *Bollettino dei Musei Civici Veneziani*, 1960, no. 3-4, pp. 32-36.

Heawood 1957
E. Heawood, *Watermarks: mainly of the 17th and 18th centuries*, Hilversum (Holland) 1957.

Hoff 1995
U. Hoff, *European Painting and Sculpture before 1800 in the National Gallery of Victoria*, Melbourne 1995.

Ingamells 1997
J. Ingamells, *A Dictionary of British and Irish Travellers in Italy 1701-1800, compiled from the Brinsley Ford Archive*, New Haven and London 1997.

Ingendaay 2009
M. Ingendaay, 'Pompeo Batoni: le lettere, l'autoritratto e il rapporto con tre committenti toscani (Conti, Riccardi, Gerini)', in *Intorno a Batoni*, conference proceedings (Rome, Palazzo delle Esposizioni, 3-4 Marche 2009), ed. by L. Barroero and F. Mazzocca, Lucca 2009, p. 137.

Ingendaay 2013
M. Ingendaay, '*I migliori pennelli*'. *I marchesi Gerini mecenati e collezionisti nella Firenze barocca. Il palazzo e la galleria 1600-1825*, Milan 2013.

An Inventory 1865
An Inventory and Valuation of the Household Furniture, Pictures...[ecc.] *of Stanwick Park, Yorkshire. Taken for purpose of probate by Farebrothers Lye & Wheeler*, April 1865, Syon MSS. H.IX.1.0, Duke of Northumberland Archive.

Kowalczyk 1987-1988
B.A. Kowalczyk, *I disegni veneziani del Bellotto*, thesis, Univeristy of Venice, a.y. 1987-1988.

Kowalczyk 1993-1996
B.A. Kowalczyk, *Il Bellotto italiano*, PhD thesis, University of Venice, VIII course, Venice 1993-1996.

Kowalczyk 1995
B.A. Kowalczyk, 'Il Bellotto veneziano nei documenti', in *Arte Veneta*, 47, 1995, pp. 68-77.

Kowalczyk 1996
B.A. Kowalczyk, 'Il Bellotto veneziano: "grande intendimento ricercasi"', in *Arte Veneta*, 48, 1996, pp. 70-89.

Kowalczyk 1998
B.A. Kowalczyk, 'I Canaletto della National Gallery di Londra', in *Arte Veneta*, 53, 1998, pp. 73-99.

Kowalczyk 1999
B.A. Kowalczyk, 'I primi sostenitori veneziani di Bernardo Bellotto', in *Saggi e Memorie di Storia dell'Arte*, 23, 1999, pp. 198-218.

Kowalczyk 2012
B.A. Kowalczyk, 'Bellotto and Zanetti in Florence', in *The Burlington Magazine*, CLIV, 1306, January 2012, pp. 24-31.

Kowalczyk 2015
B.A. Kowalczyk, 'Bellotto e Zocchi tra Venezia, Firenze e Roma', in *Venezia Settecento. Studi in memoria di Alessandro Bettagno*, Cinisello Balsamo 2016, pp. 75-83.

Kozakiewicz 1967
S. Kozakiewicz, 'Ricostruzione di un gruppo di dipinti bellottiani del periodo polacco', in *Bulletin du Musée National de Varsovie*, VIII, 1967, n. 1-2, pp. 32-45.

Kozakiewicz 1972a
S. Kozakiewicz, *Bernardo Bellotto*, 2 vols., Milan, 1972.

Kozakiewicz 1972b
S. Kozakiewicz, *Bernardo Bellotto genannt Canaletto*, 2 vols., Recklinghausen 1972.

Król-Kaczorowska 1966
B. Król-Kaczorowska, 'Svolta dei lavori forniti alla corte di Varsavia ed altri documenti bellottiani', *Bulletin du Musée National de Varsovie*, VII, 1966, pp. 68-75.

Kwiatkowski 1983
M. Kwiatkowski, *Stanisław August. Król-Architekt*, Wrocław 1983.

Kwiatkowski 1989
M. Kwiatkowski, *Architektura mieszkaniowa Warszawy*, Wrocław 1989.

Levey 1964
M. Levey, *The Later Italian Pictures in the Collection of Her Majesty the Queen*, London 1964.

Levey 1991
M. Levey, *The Later Italian Pictures in the Collection of Her Majesty the Queen*, Cambridge 1991 (2nd edition).

Levinson-Lessing 1985
V. Levinson-Lessing, *Istoria Kartinnoi galerei Ermitazha (1764-1917)*, Leningrad 1985.

Liebsch 2006
T. Liebsch, 'Anmerkungen zu Bernardo Bellottos "Der Neumarkt zu Dresden vom Jüdenhof" und ein neuer Hinweis auf die Dresdener Wohnadresse des Malers', in *Dresdener Kunstblätter*, 2006, 50, no. 3, pp. 163-168.

Links 1981
J.G. Links, *Canaletto. The Complete Paintings*, St. Albans 1981.

Links 1998
J.G. Links, *A Supplement to W.G. Constable's Canaletto: Giovanni Antonio Canal 1697-1768,* London 1998.

F. Löffler, *Bernardo Bellotto genannt Canaletto. Dresden im 18. Jahrhundert*, Leipzig 1985.

Lorentz 1986
S. Lorentz, *Efraim Szreger. Architekt polski XVIII wieku*, Wrocław 1986.

Manikowska 2012
E. Manikowska, 'The rediscovery of Bernardo Bellotto's inventory', in *The Burlington Magazine*, CLIV, 1306, gennaio 2012, pp. 32-36.

Manikowska 2014
E. Manikowska, *Bernardo Bellotto i jego drezdeński apartament. O tożsamości społecznej i artystycznej weneckiego wedutysty*, Warszawa 2014.

Mańkowski 1932
T. Mańkowski, *Galeria Stanisława Augusta*, part II, Lwów 1932

Manzelli 1991
M. Manzelli, *Michele Marieschi e il suo alter-ego Francesco Albotto*, Venice 1991.

Manzelli 2002
M. Manzelli, *Michele Marieschi e il suo alter-ego Francesco Albotto*, 2nd edition, Venice 2002.

Marciari 2015
J. Marciari, *Italian, Spanish, and French Paintings Before 1850 in the San Diego Museum of Art*, San Diego 2015.

Marinelli 1993
S. Marinelli, 'Aggiornamenti su Bellotto', in *Arte Veneta*, 1993, 44, pp. 83-86.

Marini 1991
G. Marini, *Il fiume e il castello. Precisazioni sul viaggio romano del Bellotto*, in "Artibus et Historiae", 24, 1991, pp. 147-163.

Martini 1982
E. Martini, *La pittura del Settecento veneto*, Udine 1982.

Matthäi 1834
F. Matthäi, *Beschreibung der neuerrichteten Sammlung vaterländischer Prospekte von Alexander Thiele und Canaletto*, Dresden 1834.

Mattioli Rossi 1980
L. Mattioli Rossi, 'Collezionismo e mercato dei vedutisti nella Venezia del Settecento', in *Ricerche di Storia dell'Arte*, 11, 1980, pp. 79-82.

Michel 1945
A. Michel, 'Two Great XVIII Century Ballet Masters, Jean-Baptiste de Hesse and Franz Hilverding: La Guinguette and Le Turc généreux Seen by G. de Saint-Aubin and Canaletto', in *Gazette de Beaux-Arts*, XXVII, 1945, pp. 271-286.

Miller 1983
C. Miller, *Fifty Drawings by Canaletto from the Royal Library, Windsor Castle*, London and New York 1983.

Montecuccoli degli Erri 2002
F. Montecuccoli degli Erri, *Canaletto incisore*, Venice 2002.

Morassi 1962
A. Morassi, 'Circa alcune opere sconosciute di Giuseppe Zocchi', in *Bollettino dei Musei Civici Veneziani*, 1962, no. 1, pp. 3-10.

Moschini 1954
V. Moschini, *Canaletto*, Milan 1954.

Muňich 1773–1783
E. Muňich, *Catalogue raisonné des Tableaux qui se trouvent dans les Galeries, Sallons et Cabinets du Palais Impérial de St. Petersbourg, commencé en 1773. et continué jusqu'en 1783*, ms., St. Petersburg, Ermitage State Archive, f. 1, inv. VI-A, n. 85., 2 vols., 1773-1783.

Muñoz 1911
A. Muñoz, 'Moyen-âge, renaissance, époque moderne', in A. Muñoz, L. Pollak, *Pièces de choix de la collection du comte Grégoire Stroganoff à Rome*, II, Rome 1911.

Murray 1882
J. Murray, *Handbook for Travellers in Yorkshire, and for Residents in the County. Third edition, thoroughly revised. With Map and Plans*, London 1882.

Nepi Sciré 1997
G. Nepi Sciré, *Il quaderno di Canaletto*, Venezia 1997.

Oesterreich 1754
M. Oesterreich, *Inventarium von der Königlichen Bilder Galerie zu Dresden*, ms, 1754, Dresden, Gemäldegalerie, FF.41 v bis 42v, nos. 528-549.

Orlandi, Guarienti 1753
P. Orlandi, *Abecedario pittorico del M.R.P. Pellegrino Antonio Orlandi… corretto e notabilmente accresciuto da Pietro Guarienti*, Venice 1753.

Pallucchini 1996
R. Pallucchini, '*Bernardo Bellotto*', in *La pittura nel Veneto. Il Settecento*, II, 1995, Milan 1996, pp. 493-523.

Pantazzi 1987
M. Pantazzi, in M. Laskin jr and M. Pantazzi, *Catalogue of the National Gallery of Canada. European and American Painting, Sculpture and Decorative Arts*, vol. I, 1300-1800, Ottawa 1987, pp. 19-24, 48-55.

Parker 1948
K.T. Parker, *The Drawings of Antonio Canaletto in the Collection of His Majesty the King at Windsor Castle*, Oxford 1948.

Parker, Crawley 1990
K.T. Parker, *The Drawings of Antonio Canaletto in the Collection of His Majesty the Queen at Windsor Castle* [Oxford 1948], edition with appendix by C. Crawley, Bologna 1990.

Pedrocco 2002
F. Pedrocco, *Bernardo Bellotto*, in *Pinacoteca Giovanni e Marella Agnelli al Lingotto*, Geneva-Milan 2002, pp. 47-55.

Pignatti 1958
T. Pignatti, *Il Quaderno dei disegni del Canaletto alle Gallerie di Venezia*, Venice 1958.

Pignatti 1960
T. Pignatti, *Il Museo Correr di Venezia. Dipinti del XVII e XVIII secolo* (Cataloghi di raccolte d'arte 6), Venice 1960.

Pignatti 1970
T. Pignatti, *Canaletto. Selected Drawings*, Philadelphia 1970.

Pignatti 1973
T. Pignatti, *Venetian* 'Drawings of the Eighteenth Century', in *Master Drawings*, 11, 1973, pp. 181-182.

Pignatti 1981
T. Pignatti, 'Le prospettive impossibili del Canaletto e del Bellotto', in *Ars Auro Prior Studia Joanni Bialostocki sexagenario dicata*, Warszawa 1981, pp. 543-549.

Pinacoteca di Brera, Scuola Veneta, Milan 1990.

Pita Andrade, Del Mar Borobia Guerrero 1992
J.M. Pita Andrade, M. Del Mar Borobia Guerrero, *Maestros Antiguos del Museo Thyssen-Bornemisza*, Madrid 1992 (3rd edition 1994).

Puppi 1968
L. Puppi, *L'Opera completa del Canaletto*, Milan 1968.

Rizzi 1990
A. Rizzi, *La Varsavia di Bellotto*, Milan 1990.

Rizzi 1996
A. Rizzi, *Bernardo Bellotto. Dresda, Vienna, Monaco 1747-1766*, Venice 1996.

Rizzi 2006
A. Rizzi, *Canaletto w Warszawie*, Warszawa 2006.

Rosenberg 1974
P. Rosenberg, 'Un chef-d'oeuvre de Bellotto à Troyes', in *Arte Veneta*, XXVIII, 1974, pp. 285-287.

Rossi 1989
F. Rossi, *Accademia Carrara di Belle Arti di Bergamo. Catalogo dei dipinti sec. XVII-XVIII*, Cinisello Balsamo 1989.

Sale Catalogues 1760
All catalogues…. of the Principal Collection of Pictures (One Hundred & Seventy One in Number) Sold by Auction in England within the years 1711-1759, The greater part of them with the Prices and Names of Purchasers; M.r Kents sale of Signor Borris Pictures, 29-30 Mars 1759, vol. II, pp. 173-178; ms., 1760 ca., London, Victoria and Albert Museum, The National Art Library.

Sani 2007
B. Sani, *Rosalba Carriera 1673-1757. Maestra del pastello nell'Europa ancien régime*, Turin 2007.

Scarsbrick 1987
D. Scarsbrick, 'Connoisseurship in Gems - the 4th Earl of Carlisle's Correspondence with Francesco de Ficoroni and Antonio Maria Zanetti', in *The Burlington Magazine*, CXXIX, 1007, February 1987, pp. 90-104.

Schmidt 2000
W. Schmidt, *Bernardo Bellotto genannt Canaletto in Pirna und auf der Festung Köningstein*, Pirna 2000.

Simonson 1904
G.A. Simonson, *Francesco Guardi 1712-1793*, London-Methuen 1904.

Stählin, *Notes* 1990
K.V. Malinowski, *Notes by Jakob Staehlin (1709-1785) on Fine Arts in Russia* [in Russian], 2 vols., Moskow 1990.

Starzyński 1933-1934
J. Starzyński, 'Rysunki Canaletta w Warszawskiem Muzeum Narodowem', in *Biuletyn Historji Sztuki i Kultury*, II, 1933-1934, pp. 99-111.

Stübel 1911
M. von Stübel, 'Der jüngere Canaletto und seine Radierunge', in *Monatshefte für Kunstwissenschaft*, IV, 1911, pp. 471-501.

Succi 1991
D. Succi, '*Bernardo Bellotto, Il Palazzo dei Giureconsulti e il Broletto Nuovo, Milano*,' in *Inverno '91*, exhibition catalogue (Milan, Solamon Gallery), Milan 1991, pp. 50-57.

Tatarkiewicz 1957
W. Tatarkiewicz, *Łazienki Warszawskie*, Wrocław 1957.

Tosi 1997
A. Tosi, *Inventare la realtà. Giuseppe Zocchi e la Toscana del Settecento*, Florence 1997.

Vasari 1943
G. Vasari, *Le vite dei più eccellenti pittori, scultori e architetti* [1568], ed. by C.L. Ragghianti, vol. II, Milan-Rome 1943.

Venturi 1900
A. Venturi, 'I quadri di scuola italiana nella Galleria Nazionale di Budapest', in *L'Arte*, III, 1900, 185-240.

Villis 2000
C. Villis, 'Bernardo Bellotto's seven large views of Rome, c. 1743', in *The Burlington Magazine*, CXLII, 1163, February 2000, pp. 76-81.

Villis 2008
C. Villis, 'Materiali, tecnica e procedimento esecutivo nell'opera del giovane Bernardo Bellotto', in *Canaletto e Bellotto: l'arte della veduta*, exhibition catalogue by B.A. Kowalczyk (Turin, Palazzo Bricherasio), Cinisello Balsamo 2008, pp. 23-35.

Vivian 1971
F. Vivian, *Il Console Smith, Mercante e Collezionista*, Vicenza 1971.

Waagen 1854
G.F. Waagen, *Treasures of Art in Great Britain: being an AcEarl of the Chief Collections of Paintings, Drawings, Sculptures, illuminated Mss., &c. &c. Three Volumes*, London 1854.

Waagen 1857
G.F. Waagen, *Galleries and Cabinets of Art in Great Britain: being an AcEarl of more than Forty Collections of Paintings, Drawings, Sculptures, Mss., &c. &c. visited in 1854 and 1856, and now for the First Time Described. Supplemental Volume to the Treasures of Art in Great Britain, Three Volumes*, London 1857.

Walther 1995
A. Walther, *Bernardo Bellotto genannt Canaletto. Ein Venezianer malte Dresden, Pirna und den Königstein*, Dresden 1995.

Ward-Jackson 1980
P. Ward-Jackson, *Italian Drawings. Volume Two. 17th-18th century*, London 1980.

Watson 1950
F.J.B. Watson, 'Notes on Canaletto and his Engravers - I', in *The Burlington Magazine*, XVII, 571, October 1950, pp. 291-293

Watson 1954
F.J.B. Watson, *Canaletto*, London 1954.

Watson 1955
F.J.B. Watson, '*Venetian Paintings at the Royal Academy 1954-1955*', in *Arte Veneta*, IX, 1955, pp. 253-264.

Weber 1998
G.J.M. Weber, 'Bernardo Bellotto, Nicolaes Berchem und das pastorale Pirna', in *Dresdener Kunstblätter*, 42, 2, 1998, pp. 46-53.

Weber 2003
G.J.M. Weber, *Die Veduten Dresdens von Bernardo Bellotto. Anmerkungen zu ihrer frühen Geschichte und Konzeption*, in Cologne 2003, pp. 59-71.

Zanetti 1771
A.M. Zanetti, *Della pittura veneziana e delle opere pubbliche de' veneziani maestri*, Venice 1771.

Zecchini 2008
M. Zecchini, 'La vita di Francesco Antonio Simonini nelle carte di Muzio Piccolomini', in 'Paragone Arte', LIX, III s., 79 (699), May 2008, pp. 15-58.

Exhibition Catalogues

Aix-en-Provence 2015
Canaletto. Rome, Londres, Venise. Le triomphe de la lumière, exhibition catalogue by B.A. Kowalczyk (Aix-en-Provence, Hôtel de Caumont), Bruxelles 2015.

Atlanta, Seattle e Minneapolis 1995-1996
Treasures of Venice: Paintings from the Museum of Fine Arts, Budapest, exhibition catalogue by G. Keyes, I. Barkóczi, J. Satkowski, (Atlanta, High Museum of Art; Seattle Art Museum; The Minneapolis Museum of Art), Minneapolis, 1995.

Berlin 1985
Vedute, architektonisches Capriccio und Lanschaft in der venezianischen Graphik des 18. Jahrhunderts, exhibition catalogue by P. Dreyer (Berlino, Kupferstich-Kabinett, Staatliche Museen Preussischer Kulturbesitz), Berlin 1985.

Bilbao 1998
Bernardo Bellotto en Dresde, exhibition catalogue (Bilbao, Museo de Bellas Artes), Bilbao 1998.

Birmingham 1831
Birmingham, Society of Arts, 1831.

Birmingham 1833
Catalogue of Pictures, Chiefly by the Old Masters of the Italian, Flemish, and Spanish Schools (Birmingham, Society of Arts), Birmingham 1833.

Brescia 2016
Lo splendore di Venezia. Canaletto, Bellotto, Guardi e i vedutisti dell'Ottocento, exhibition catalogue by D. Dotti (Brescia, Palazzo Martinengo Cesaresco), Cinisello Balsamo 2016.

Bruxelles 1983
Dessins vénitiens du dix-huitième siècle, catalogo della mostra, texts by A. Bettagno, A. Mariuz, T. Pignatti, L. Puppi and U. Ruggeri (Bruxelles, Palais des Beaux-Arts), Bruxelles 1983.

Budapest 2013-2014
Caravaggio to Canaletto. The Glory of Italian Baroque and Rococo Painting, exhibition catalogue by Z. Dobos, with D. Salay and A. Varga (Budapest, Szépművészeti Múzeum), Budapest 2013.

Compiègne 2007
Nicolas Esterházy 1765-1833: Un prince hongrois collectionneur, exhibition catalogue by E. Starcky (Compiègne, Musée National), Compiègne 2007 .

Cologne 2003
Kunst für Könige. Malerei in Dresden im 18. Jahrhundert, exhibition catalogue by D. Gedlich (Cologne, Wallraf-Richartz-Museum - Fondation Corboud), Cologne 2003.

Conegliano 2011
Bernardo Bellotto. Il Canaletto delle corti europee, exhibition catalogue by D. Succi (Conegliano, Palazzo Sarcinelli), Venice 2011.

Darmstadt 1981
Bernardo Bellotto genannt Canaletto. Zeichnungen aus dem Hessischen Landesmuseum Darmstadt, exhibition catalogue by M. Bleyl (Darmstadt, Hessisches Landesmuseum), Darmstadt 1981.

Dresden 2011
Bernardo Bellotto. Der Canaletto-Blick, exhibition catalogue by A. Henning, S. Oesinghaus e S. Benfeldt (Dresden, Gemäldegalerie Alte Meister), Dresden 2011.

Florence 1994
Firenze e la sua immagine. Cinque secoli di vedutismo, exhibition catalogue by S. Petrolio (Firenze, Forte del Belvedere), Venezia 1994.

Florence 2001-2002
Nel segno di Masaccio. L'invenzione della prospettiva, exhibition catalogue by F. Camerota (Firenze, Galleria degli Uffizi), Firenze 2001.

Florence 2009
Il fasto e la ragione. Arte del Settecento a Firenze, exhibition catalogue by C. Sisi and R. Spinelli (Florence, Galleria degli Uffizi), Florence 2009.

Gorizia 1988
Capricci veneziani del Settecento, exhibition catalogue by D. Succi (Gorizia, Castello), Torino 1988.

Hanover-Düsseldorf 1991
Venedigs Ruhm im Norden. Die grossen venezianischen Maler des 18. Jahrhunderts, ihre Auftraggeber und Sammler, exhibition catalogue by M. Trudzinski and B. Schälicke (Hannover, Niedersächsisches Landesmuseum; Düsseldorf, Kunstmuseum), Hanover 1991.

London 1957
Bernardo Bellotto 1720-1780. Paintings and Drawings from the National Museum of Warsaw, exhibition catalogue by S. Lorentz (paintings) and S. Kozakiewicz (drawings) (London, Whitechapel Art Gallery), London 1957.

London 1980-1981
Canaletto. Paintings and Drawings, exhibition catalogue by O. Millar (paintings) and C. Miller (paintings) (London, Queen's Gallery, Buckingham Palace), London 1980.

London 2010
Treasure from Budapest. European Masterpieces from Leonardo to Schiele, exhibition catalogue by D. Ekserdjian (London, The Royal Academy of Arts), London 2007.

London-Edinburgh 2005-2007
Canaletto in Venice, exhibition catalogue by M. Clayton (London, The Queen's Gallery, Buckingham Palace; Edinburgh, The Queen's Gallery, Palace of Holyroodhouse), London 2005.

London-Washington 1994-1995
The Glory of Venice: Art in the Eighteenth Century, exhibition catalogue by J. Martineau e A. Robison (London, Royal Academy of Arts; Washington, National Gallery of Art), New Haven & London (Yale University Press), Italian edition Milan 1994.

London-Washington 2010-2011
Venice: Canaletto and his Rivals, exhibition catalogue by C. Beddington, with the contribution of A. Bradley (London, The National Gallery; Washington, National Gallery of Art), London 2010.

Madrid 2001
Una Venecia imaginaria, exhibition catalogue by D. Succi, A. Delneri (Madrid, Museo Thyssen-Bornemisza), Madrid 2001.

Madrid 2011-2012
Arquitecturas pintadas del Renacimiento al siglo XVIII, exhibition catalogue by D. Rodríguez and M. Borobia (Madrid, Museo Thyssen-Bornemisza; Fundación Caja), Madrid 2011.

Milan 1999-2000
La Milano del Giovin Signore. Le arti nel Settecento di Parini, exhibition catalogue by F. Mazzocca and A. Morandotti (Milan, Palazzo Morando Attendolo Bolognini), Milan 1999.

Mira 1996
Immagini della Brenta. Ville venete e scene di vita sulla riviera nel '700 veneziano, exhibition catalogue (Mira, Villa Principe Pio), Milan 1996.

Mirano 1999
Bernardo Bellotto detto il Canaletto, exhibition catalogue by D. Succi (Mirano, Barchessa di Villa Morosini), Venice 1999.

Munich 2014-2015
Canaletto. Bernardo Bellotto Paints Europe, exhibition catalogue by A. Schumacher, with texts by A. Gottdang, E. Götz, B.A. Kowalczyk, P.O. Krückmann, C. Quaeitzsch, A. Schumacher, B. Schwabe, J. Thoma, T. Wagener, W. Wiedemann, W. Zech (Munich, Alte Pinakothek), Munich 2014.

New Haven-London 2006-2007
Canaletto in England. A Venetian Artist Abroad, 1746-1755, exhibition catalogue by C. Beddington (New Haven, CT, Yale Center for British Art; London, Dulwich Picture Gallery), New Haven-London 2006.

New York 1989-1990
Canaletto, ed. by K.B. Baetjer, J.G. Links (New York, Metropolitan Museum of Art), New York 1989.

New York 2003
Master Paintings and Sculpture, exhibition catalogue by D. Garstang (New York, Adam Williams Fine Art Ltd.), New York 2003.

Padua 1994
Luca Carlevarijs e la veduta veneziana del Settecento, exhibition catalogue by D. Succi (Padua, Palazzo della Ragione), Milan 1994.

Paris 1971
Venise au XVIIIe siècle, ed. by P. Rosenberg (Paris, Orangerie des Tuileries), Paris 1971.

Paris 2012-2013
Canaletto et Guardi. Les deux maitres de Venise, exhibition catalogue by B.A. Kowalczyk (Paris, Musée Jacquemart-André), Bruxelles 2012.

Pfäffikon-Geneva 1978
Art Vénitien en Suisse et au Liechtenstein, exhibition catalogue by M. Natale (Pfäffikon SZ, Seedamm-Kulturzentrum; Ginevra, Musée d'art et d'histoire), Milano 1978.

Rimini 2012
Da Vermeer a Kandinsky: capolavori dai musei del mondo a Rimini, exhibition catalogue by M. Goldin, V. Tonon *et al.* (Rimini, Castel Sismondo), Crocetta del Montello 2012.

Rome 2005
Canaletto: il trionfo della veduta, exhibition catalogue by B.A. Kowalczyk (Roma, Palazzo Giustiniani), Cinisello Balsamo 2005.

Treviso 2008-2009
Canaletto. Venezia e i suoi splendori, exhibition catalogue by G. Pavanello and A. Craievich (Treviso, Casa dei Carraresi), Venezia 2008.

Turin 2008
Canaletto e Bellotto: l'arte della veduta, exhibition catalogue by B.A. Kowalczyk (Turin, Palazzo Bricherasio), Cinisello Balsamo 2008.

York 1994
Masterpieces from Yorkshire Houses, Yorkshire Families at Home and Abroad 1700-1850, exhibition catalogue by H. Brigstocke (York, City Art Gallery), York 1994.

Udine 2004
Arte per i Re. Capolavori del '700 dalla Galleria Statale di Dresda, exhibition catalogue by H. Marx (Castello di Udine), Udine 2004.

Warsaw 2003-2004
Bernardo Bellotto. Sekrety jego malarstwa / I segreti della sua pittura. Prace konserwatorskie przy obrazach Bellotta / I lavori di restauro sui dipinti del Bellotto (2000-2003), exhibition catalogue by P. Sadlej (Warsaw, Castello Reale), Warsaw 2003.

Venice 1946
Capolavori dei Musei veneti, exhibition catalogue by R. Pallucchini (Venice, Museo Correr), Venice 1946.

Venice 1955
Mostra di Bernardo Bellotto 1720-1780 Alessandro Gierymski 1850-1901. Opere provenienti dalla Polonia, exhibition catalogue by S. Kozakiewicz e S. Lorentz (Venice, Palazzo Grassi), Venice-Milan 1955.

Venice 1964
Disegni veneti del Settecento nel Museo Correr di Venezia, exhibition catalogue by T. Pignatti (Venice, Fondazione Giorgio Cini), Venice 1964.

Venice 1967
I vedutisti veneziani del Settecento, exhibition catalogue by P. Zampetti (Venice , Palazzo Ducale) Milan 1967.

Venice 1982
Canaletto. Disegni-dipinti-incisioni, exhibition catalogue by A. Bettagno (Venice, Fondazione Giorgio Cini), Vicenza 1982.

Venice, Gorizia 1983
Da Carlevarijs a Tiepolo. Incisori veneti e friulani del Settecento, exhibition catalogue by D. Succi (Venice, Museo Correr; Gorizia, Palazzo Attems), Venice 1983.

Venice 1985
Varsavia 1764-1830. Da Bellotto a Chopin, exhibition catalogue by S. Konarski, M. Kwiatkowski, A. Rizzi (Venice, Museo del Settecento Veneziano Ca' Rezzonico), Venice 1985.

Venice 1986
Le vedute di Dresda di Bernardo Bellotto, exhibition catalogue by A. Bettagno (Venice, Fondazione Giorgio Cini), Vicenza 1986.

Venice 1986-1987
Canaletto & Visentini. Venezia & Londra, exhibition catalogue by D. Succi (Venice, Museo d'Arte Moderna Ca' Pesaro), Cittadella (Padua) 1986.

Venice 1990
I rami di Visentini per le vedute di Venezia del Canaletto, exhibition catalogue by G. Lari (Venice, Museo Correr), Bergamo 1990.

Venice 1995
Splendori del Settecento veneziano, ed. by G. Nepi Sciré and G. Romanelli (Venice, Museo del Settecento Veneziano Ca' Rezzonico; Gallerie dell'Accademia; Palazzo Mocenigo), Milan 1995.

Venice 2001
Canaletto prima maniera, exhibition curated by A. Bettagno and B.A. Kowalczyk, catalogue by B.A. Kowalczyk, with C. Ceschi and S. Guerriero (Venice, Fondazione Giorgio Cini), Milan 2001.

Venice 2012
Canaletto. Il Quaderno veneziano, exhibition catalogue by A. Perissa Torrini (Venice, Palazzo Grimani), Venice 2012.

Venice-Houston 2001
Bernardo Bellotto 1722-1780, exhibition catalogue by B.A. Kowalczyk and M. Da Cortà Fumei (Venice, Museo Correr), Milan 2001; English edition *Bernardo Bellotto and the Capitals of Europe*, ed. by E. P. Bowron (Houston, Museum of Fine Arts), New Haven & London 2001.

Verona 1990
Bernardo Bellotto. Verona e le città europee, exhibition catalogue by S. Marinelli (Verona, Museo del Castelvecchio), Milano 1990.

Verona-Vicenza 2013-2014
Verso Monet. Storia del paesaggio dal Seicento al Novecento, exhibition catalogue by M. Goldin (Verona, Palazzo della Gran Guardia; Vicenza, Basilica Palladiana), Crocetta del Montello 2013.

Versailles 2006
Splendeurs de la cour de Saxe. Dresde à Versailles, exhibition catalogue by B. Saule, D. Syndram *et al.* (Versailles, Musée National de Châteux de Versailles et de Trianon), Paris 2006.

Vienna 2005
Bernardo Bellotto genannt Canaletto. Europäische Veduten, exhibition catalogue by W. Seipel (Vienna, Kunsthistorisches Museum), Vienna 2005.

Photo Credits

Cover
Bernardo Bellotto, *The Piazza San Marco looking South-West, Venice*
detail, 1742–43
oil on canvas; 136.2 x 232.5 cm
The Cleveland Museum of Art, Leonard C. Hanna, Jr Fund, 1962.169

Silvana Editoriale

Direction
Dario Cimorelli

Art Director
Giacomo Merli

Editorial Coordinator
Sergio Di Stefano

Copy Editor
Sara Tedesco

Translations
Contextus S.r.l., Pavia (Laura Bennett, Lucian Henry Comoy,
Sarah Elizabeth Cree, Daniela Innocenti)

Layout
Donatella Ascorti

Production Coordinator
Antonio Micelli

Editorial Assistant
Ondina Granato

Photo Editor
Alessandra Olivari, Silvia Sala

Press Office
Lidia Masolini, press@silvanaeditoriale.it

ISBN 9788836635566

Available through ARTBOOK | D.A.P.
155 Sixth Avenue, 2nd Floor, New York, N.Y. 10013
Tel: (212) 627-1999 Fax: (212) 627-9484

Silvana Editoriale S.p.A.
via dei Lavoratori, 78
20092 Cinisello Balsamo, Milano
tel. 02 453 951 01
fax 02 453 951 51
www.silvanaeditoriale.it

Reproductions, printing and binding
in Italy
Printed by Grafiche Aurora S.r.l., Verona
December 2016